T0364965

Ford Escort & Orion diesel
Service and Repair Manual

R M Jex

(4081 - 256 - 8AK1)

Models covered

Ford Escort Hatchback, Saloon, Estate and Van, and Orion Saloon models, including special/limited editions
1753 cc (1.8 litre) diesel engine, including Endura-DE and turbocharged variants

For information on petrol models, see manual number 1737

© J H Haynes & Co. Ltd. 2007

A book in the **Haynes Service and Repair Manual Series**

ISBN **978 1 78521 457 8**

British Library Cataloguing in Publication Data
A catalogue record for this book is available from the British Library.

**J H Haynes & Co. Ltd.
Haynes North America, Inc**

www.haynes.com

Contents

LIVING WITH YOUR FORD ESCORT DIESEL

Roadside repairs

Weekly checks

Lubricants and fluids

Tyre pressures

MAINTENANCE

Routine maintenance and servicing

Contents

REPAIRS & OVERHAUL

Engine and associated systems

Transmission

Brakes and suspension

Body equipment

Wiring diagrams

REFERENCE

Index

Advanced driving

Many people see the words 'advanced driving' and believe that it won't interest them or that it is a style of driving beyond their own abilities. Nothing could be further from the truth. Advanced driving is straightforward safe, sensible driving - the sort of driving we should all do every time we get behind the wheel.

An average of 10 people are killed every day on UK roads and 870 more are injured, some seriously. Lives are ruined daily, usually because somebody did something stupid. Something like 95% of all accidents are due to human error, mostly driver failure. Sometimes we make genuine mistakes - everyone does. Sometimes we have lapses of concentration. Sometimes we deliberately take risks.

For many people, the process of 'learning to drive' doesn't go much further than learning how to pass the driving test because of a common belief that good drivers are made by 'experience'.

Learning to drive by 'experience' teaches three driving skills:

☐ Quick reactions. (Whoops, that was close!)
☐ Good handling skills. (Horn, swerve, brake, horn).
☐ Reliance on vehicle technology. (Great stuff this ABS, stop in no distance even in the wet...)

Drivers whose skills are 'experience based' generally have a lot of near misses and the odd accident. The results can be seen every day in our courts and our hospital casualty departments.

Advanced drivers have learnt to control the risks by controlling the position and speed of their vehicle. They avoid accidents and near misses, even if the drivers around them make mistakes.

The key skills of advanced driving are **concentration,** effective all-round **observation, anticipation** and **planning.** When **good vehicle handling** is added to

these skills, all driving situations can be approached and negotiated in a safe, methodical way, leaving nothing to chance.

Concentration means applying your mind to safe driving, completely excluding anything that's not relevant. Driving is usually the most dangerous activity that most of us undertake in our daily routines. It deserves our full attention.

Observation means not just looking, but seeing and seeking out the information found in the driving environment.

Anticipation means asking yourself what is happening, what you can reasonably expect to happen and what could happen unexpectedly. (One of the commonest words used in compiling accident reports is 'suddenly'.)

Planning is the link between seeing something and taking the appropriate action. For many drivers, planning is the missing link.

If you want to become a safer and more skilful driver and you want to enjoy your driving more, contact the Institute of Advanced Motorists at www.iam.org.uk, phone 0208 996 9600, or write to IAM House, 510 Chiswick High Road, London W4 5RG for an information pack.

Working on your car can be dangerous. This page shows just some of the potential risks and hazards, with the aim of creating a safety-conscious attitude.

General hazards

Scalding

• Don't remove the radiator or expansion tank cap while the engine is hot.
• Engine oil, automatic transmission fluid or power steering fluid may also be dangerously hot if the engine has recently been running.

Burning

• Beware of burns from the exhaust system and from any part of the engine. Brake discs and drums can also be extremely hot immediately after use.

Crushing

• When working under or near a raised vehicle, always supplement the jack with axle stands, or use drive-on ramps. *Never venture under a car which is only supported by a jack.*

• Take care if loosening or tightening high-torque nuts when the vehicle is on stands. Initial loosening and final tightening should be done with the wheels on the ground.

Fire

• Fuel is highly flammable; fuel vapour is explosive.
• Don't let fuel spill onto a hot engine.
• Do not smoke or allow naked lights (including pilot lights) anywhere near a vehicle being worked on. Also beware of creating sparks
(electrically or by use of tools).
• Fuel vapour is heavier than air, so don't work on the fuel system with the vehicle over an inspection pit.
• Another cause of fire is an electrical overload or short-circuit. Take care when repairing or modifying the vehicle wiring.
• Keep a fire extinguisher handy, of a type suitable for use on fuel and electrical fires.

Electric shock

• Ignition HT voltage can be dangerous, especially to people with heart problems or a pacemaker. Don't work on or near the ignition system with the engine running or the ignition switched on.

• Mains voltage is also dangerous. Make sure that any mains-operated equipment is correctly earthed. Mains power points should be protected by a residual current device (RCD) circuit breaker.

Fume or gas intoxication

• Exhaust fumes are poisonous; they often contain carbon monoxide, which is rapidly fatal if inhaled. Never run the engine in a confined space such as a garage with the doors shut.
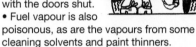
• Fuel vapour is also poisonous, as are the vapours from some cleaning solvents and paint thinners.

Poisonous or irritant substances

• Avoid skin contact with battery acid and with any fuel, fluid or lubricant, especially antifreeze, brake hydraulic fluid and Diesel fuel. Don't syphon them by mouth. If such a substance is swallowed or gets into the eyes, seek medical advice.
• Prolonged contact with used engine oil can cause skin cancer. Wear gloves or use a barrier cream if necessary. Change out of oil-soaked clothes and do not keep oily rags in your pocket.
• Air conditioning refrigerant forms a poisonous gas if exposed to a naked flame (including a cigarette). It can also cause skin burns on contact.

Asbestos

• Asbestos dust can cause cancer if inhaled or swallowed. Asbestos may be found in gaskets and in brake and clutch linings. When dealing with such components it is safest to assume that they contain asbestos.

Special hazards

Hydrofluoric acid

• This extremely corrosive acid is formed when certain types of synthetic rubber, found in some O-rings, oil seals, fuel hoses etc, are exposed to temperatures above 400°C. The rubber changes into a charred or sticky substance containing the acid. *Once formed, the acid remains dangerous for years. If it gets onto the skin, it may be necessary to amputate the limb concerned.*
• When dealing with a vehicle which has suffered a fire, or with components salvaged from such a vehicle, wear protective gloves and discard them after use.

The battery

• Batteries contain sulphuric acid, which attacks clothing, eyes and skin. Take care when topping-up or carrying the battery.
• The hydrogen gas given off by the battery is highly explosive. Never cause a spark or allow a naked light nearby. Be careful when connecting and disconnecting battery chargers or jump leads.

Air bags

• Air bags can cause injury if they go off accidentally. Take care when removing the steering wheel and/or facia. Special storage instructions may apply.

Diesel injection equipment

• Diesel injection pumps supply fuel at very high pressure. Take care when working on the fuel injectors and fuel pipes.

⚠ *Warning: Never expose the hands, face or any other part of the body to injector spray; the fuel can penetrate the skin with potentially fatal results.*

Remember...

DO

• Do use eye protection when using power tools, and when working under the vehicle.

• Do wear gloves or use barrier cream to protect your hands when necessary.

• Do get someone to check periodically that all is well when working alone on the vehicle.

• Do keep loose clothing and long hair well out of the way of moving mechanical parts.

• Do remove rings, wristwatch etc, before working on the vehicle – especially the electrical system.

• Do ensure that any lifting or jacking equipment has a safe working load rating adequate for the job.

DON'T

• Don't attempt to lift a heavy component which may be beyond your capability – get assistance.

• Don't rush to finish a job, or take unverified short cuts.

• Don't use ill-fitting tools which may slip and cause injury.

• Don't leave tools or parts lying around where someone can trip over them. Mop up oil and fuel spills at once.

• Don't allow children or pets to play in or near a vehicle being worked on.

1996 Escort 5-door Hatchback

The latest versions of the Ford Escort and Orion model range were introduced in September 1990. As with their predecessors, the line-up was extensive, including Escort three- and five-door Hatchback, five-door Estate and Van versions, with the traditional four-door Orion Saloon featuring a conventional rear boot. For the 1994 model year, in keeping with Ford's policy of enhanced product identity, the Orion badge was deleted and the Escort name was applied to all models in the range.

Initially, the only diesel engine available was the normally-aspirated 1.8 litre unit, first seen in the previous Escort in 1988. July 1993 saw the introduction of the first turbo-diesel Escort, using essentially the same engine as before, but with a turbocharger and intercooler added, boosting power by over 50%. By 1996, a new Euro emissions standard forced the introduction of a low-pressure turbo engine without an intercooler – this new engine ran alongside the existing intercooled unit.

All models have a five-speed manual transmission with an integral differential unit to transfer drive directly to the front roadwheels.

The Escort range has received plenty of improvements during its life, with two major facelifts (in September 1992 and January 1995) to keep up with the competition. Improved crash safety and suspension revisions have also been made at each facelift. Disc front brakes and drum rear brakes are fitted to all models covered by this manual, with an anti-lock braking system (ABS) available as an option.

As with earlier variants of the range, all models are designed with the emphasis on economical motoring, ease of maintenance and good performance.

Your Escort diesel manual

The aim of this manual is to help you get the best value from your vehicle. It can do so in several ways. It can help you decide what work must be done (even should you choose to get it done by a garage). It will also provide information on routine maintenance and servicing, and give a logical course of action and diagnosis when random faults occur. However, it is hoped that you will use the manual by tackling the work yourself. On simpler jobs it may even be quicker than booking the car into a garage and going there twice, to leave and collect it. Perhaps most important, a lot of money can be saved by avoiding the costs a garage must charge to cover its labour and overheads.

The manual has drawings and descriptions to show the function of the various components so that their layout can be understood. Tasks are described and photographed in a clear step-by-step sequence. The illustrations are numbered by the Section number and paragraph number to which they relate – if there is more than one illustration per paragraph, the sequence is denoted alphabetically.

References to the 'left' or 'right' of the vehicle are in the sense of a person in the driver's seat, facing forwards.

Acknowledgements

Certain illustrations are the copyright of the Ford Motor Company, and are used with their permission. Thanks are due to Draper Tools Limited, who provided some of the workshop tools, and to all those people at Sparkford who helped in the production of this manual.

We take great pride in the accuracy of information given in this manual, but vehicle manufacturers make alterations and design changes during the production run of a particular vehicle of which they do not inform us. No liability can be accepted by the authors or publishers for loss, damage or injury caused by any errors in, or omissions from, the information given.

1994 Escort 4-door Saloon (formerly Orion)

The following pages are intended to help in dealing with common roadside emergencies and breakdowns. You will find more detailed fault finding information at the back of the manual, and repair information in the main chapters.

If your car won't start and the starter motor doesn't turn

☐ Open the bonnet and make sure that the battery terminals are clean and tight (unclip the battery cover for access).
☐ Switch on the headlights and try to start the engine. If the headlights go very dim when you're trying to start, the battery is probably flat. Get out of trouble by jump starting (see next page) using a friend's car.

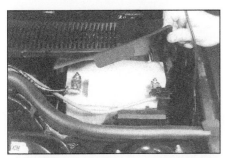

A Check the security and condition of the battery connections – unclip and remove the battery cover for access.

B Check the connector plugs and wiring connections around the injection pump, or on the air mass meter, as applicable.

C Check that none of the engine compartment fuses have blown.

If your car won't start even though the starter motor turns as normal

☐ Is there fuel in the tank?
☐ Has the engine immobiliser been deactivated? This should happen automatically, on inserting the ignition key. However, if a replacement key has been obtained (other than from a Ford dealer), it may not contain the transponder chip necessary to deactivate the system. Even 'proper' replacement keys have to be 'coded' to work properly – a procedure for this is outlined in the vehicle handbook.
☐ Is there moisture on electrical components under the bonnet? Diesel engines are less prone to damp-related starting problems, but they're not immune. Switch off the ignition, then wipe off any obvious dampness with a dry cloth. Spray a water-repellent aerosol product (WD-40 or equivalent) on electrical connectors.

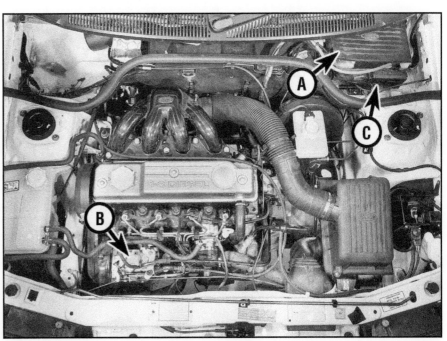

Check that all electrical connections are secure (with the ignition switched off). Spray the connector plugs with a water-dispersant spray like WD-40 if you suspect a problem due to damp. Diesel models do not usually suffer from damp starting problems, but check all visible connector plugs just in case.

When jump-starting a car using a booster battery, observe the following precautions:

✔ Before connecting the booster battery, make sure that the ignition is switched off.

✔ Ensure that all electrical equipment (lights, heater, wipers, etc) is switched off.

✔ Take note of any special precautions printed on the battery case.

Jump starting

✔ Make sure that the booster battery is the same voltage as the discharged one in the vehicle.

✔ If the battery is being jump-started from the battery in another vehicle, the two vehicles MUST NOT TOUCH each other.

✔ Make sure that the transmission is in neutral (or PARK, in the case of automatic transmission).

1 Connect one end of the red jump lead to the positive (+) terminal of the flat battery

2 Connect the other end of the red lead to the positive (+) terminal of the booster battery.

3 Connect one end of the black jump lead to the negative (-) terminal of the booster battery

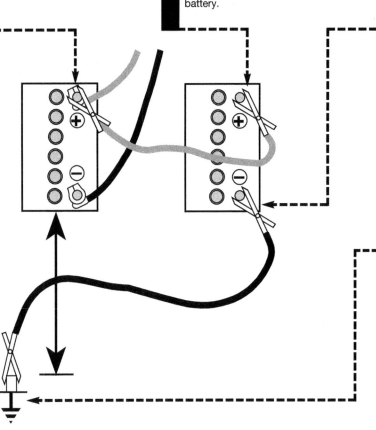

4 Connect the other end of the black jump lead to a bolt or bracket on the engine block, well away from the battery, on the vehicle to be started.

5 Make sure that the jump leads will not come into contact with the fan, drive-belts or other moving parts of the engine.

6 Start the engine using the booster battery and run it at idle speed. Switch on the lights, rear window demister and heater blower motor, then disconnect the jump leads in the reverse order of connection. Turn off the lights etc.

Wheel changing

 Warning: Do not change a wheel in a situation where you risk being hit by another vehicle. On busy roads, try to stop in a lay-by or a gateway. Be wary of passing traffic while changing the wheel - it is easy to become distracted by the job in hand.

Preparation

☐ When a puncture occurs, stop as soon as it is safe to do so.
☐ Park on firm level ground, if possible, and well out of the way of other traffic.
☐ Use hazard warning lights if necessary.

☐ If you have one, use a warning triangle to alert other drivers of your presence.
☐ Apply the handbrake and engage first or reverse gear.
☐ Chock the wheel diagonally opposite the

one being removed – a couple of large stones will do for this.
☐ If the ground is soft, use a flat piece of wood to spread the load under the foot of the jack.

Changing the wheel

1 Lift up the luggage compartment trim (where necessary) and remove the spare wheel, tools and jack from their location.

2 Remove the wheel centre trim, either by pulling it straight off (plastic trim) or by prising off the centre trim.

3 Slacken each wheel nut by half a turn using the wheel brace in the tool kit.

4 Position the jack head under the reinforced jacking point on the sill nearest the wheel to be removed. With the base of the jack on firm ground, turn the jack handle clockwise until the wheel is raised clear of the ground. Unscrew the wheel nuts and remove the wheel.

5 Fit the spare wheel, and screw in the nuts. Lightly tighten the nuts with the wheelbrace then lower the vehicle to the ground.

6 Securely tighten the wheel nuts in the sequence shown then refit the wheel trim. Stow the punctured wheel and tools back in the luggage compartment and secure them in position. The wheel nuts should be slackened and then retightened to the specified torque at the earliest opportunity.

Finally...

☐ Remove the wheel chocks.
☐ Check the tyre pressure on the tyre just fitted. If it is low, or if you don't have a pressure gauge with you, drive slowly to the next garage and inflate the tyre to the correct pressure. Particularly in the case of the narrow 'space-saver' spare wheel, this pressure is much higher than for a normal tyre.
☐ Have the damaged tyre or wheel repaired as soon as possible, or another puncture will leave you stranded.

Identifying leaks

Puddles on the garage floor or drive, or obvious wetness under the bonnet or underneath the car, suggest a leak that needs investigating. It can sometimes be difficult to decide where the leak is coming from, especially if the engine bay is very dirty already. Leaking oil or fluid can also be blown rearwards by the passage of air under the car, giving a false impression of where the problem lies.

 Warning: Most automotive oils and fluids are poisonous. Wash them off skin, and change out of contaminated clothing, without delay.

 The smell of a fluid leaking from the car may provide a clue to what's leaking. Some fluids are distinctively coloured. It may help to clean the car carefully and to park it over some clean paper overnight as an aid to locating the source of the leak.
Remember that some leaks may only occur while the engine is running.

Sump oil

Engine oil may leak from the drain plug...

Oil from filter

...or from the base of the oil filter.

Gearbox oil

Gearbox oil can leak from the seals at the inboard ends of the driveshafts.

Antifreeze

Leaking antifreeze often leaves a crystalline deposit like this.

Brake fluid

A leak occurring at a wheel is almost certainly brake fluid.

Power steering fluid

Power steering fluid may leak from the pipe connectors on the steering rack.

Towing

When all else fails, you may find yourself having to get a tow home – or of course you may be helping somebody else. Long-distance recovery should only be done by a garage or breakdown service. For shorter distances, DIY towing using another car is easy enough, but observe the following points:
☐ Use a proper tow-rope – they are not expensive. The vehicle being towed must display an ON TOW sign in its rear window.
☐ Always turn the ignition key to the 'on' position when the vehicle is being towed, so that the steering lock is released, and that the direction indicator and brake lights will work.
☐ The towing eye is located below the right-hand headlight – do not attach a tow rope to any other part of the vehicle.
☐ Before being towed, release the handbrake and make sure the transmission is in neutral.
☐ Note that greater-than-usual pedal pressure will be required to operate the brakes, since the vacuum servo unit is only operational with the engine running.
☐ The driver of the car being towed must keep the tow-rope taut at all times to avoid snatching.
☐ Make sure that both drivers know the route before setting off.
☐ Only drive at moderate speeds and keep the distance towed to a minimum. Drive smoothly and allow plenty of time for slowing down at junctions.

Introduction

There are some very simple checks which need only take a few minutes to carry out, but which could save you a lot of inconvenience and expense.

These *Weekly checks* require no great skill or special tools, and the small amount of time they take to perform could prove to be very well spent, for example;

☐ Keeping an eye on tyre condition and pressures, will not only help to stop them wearing out prematurely, but could also save your life.

☐ Many breakdowns are caused by electrical problems. Battery-related faults are particularly common, and a quick check on a regular basis will often prevent the majority of these.

☐ If your car develops a brake fluid leak, the first time you might know about it is when your brakes don't work properly. Checking the level regularly will give advance warning of this kind of problem.

☐ If the oil or coolant levels run low, the cost of repairing any engine damage will be far greater than fixing the leak, for example.

Underbonnet check points

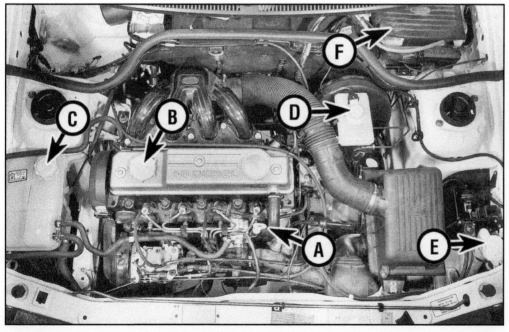

◀ 1.8 litre

A *Engine oil level dipstick*

B *Engine oil filler cap*

C *Coolant expansion tank*

D *Brake fluid reservoir*

E *Screen washer fluid reservoir*

F *Battery*

Engine oil level

Before you start

✔ Make sure that your car is on level ground.
✔ Check the oil level before the car is driven, or at least 5 minutes after the engine has been switched off.

 HAYNES HINT *If the oil is checked immediately after driving the vehicle, some of the oil will remain in the upper engine components, resulting in an inaccurate reading on the dipstick.*

The correct oil

Modern engines place great demands on their oil. It is very important that the correct oil for your car is used (See *Lubricants and fluids*).

Car Care

● If you have to add oil frequently, you should check whether you have any oil leaks. Place some clean paper under the car overnight, and check for stains in the morning. If there are no leaks, the engine may be burning oil (see *Fault Finding*), or the oil may only be leaking when the engine is running.

● Always maintain the level between the upper and lower dipstick marks. If the level is too low severe engine damage may occur. Oil seal failure may result if the engine is overfilled by adding too much oil.

1 The dipstick top is yellow for easy identification (see *Underbonnet check points* for exact location). Withdraw the dipstick.

3 Oil is added through the filler cap. Unscrew the cap . . .

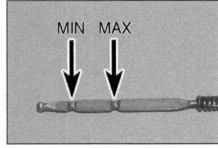

2 Using a clean rag or paper towel, remove all oil from the dipstick. Insert the dipstick into the tube as far as it will go, then withdraw it again. Note the oil level on the end of the dipstick, which should be between the MAX and MIN marks. If the oil level is only just above, or below, the MIN mark, topping-up is required.

4 . . . and top-up the level; a funnel may be useful in reducing spillage. Add the oil slowly, checking the level on the dipstick often, and allowing time for the oil to fall to the sump. Add oil until the level is just up to the MAX mark on the dipstick – don't overfill (see *Car care*).

Coolant level

 Warning:
DO NOT attempt to remove the expansion tank pressure cap when the engine is hot, as there is a very great risk of scalding. Do not leave open containers of coolant about, as it is poisonous.

Car Care

● With a sealed-type cooling system, adding coolant should not be necessary on a regular basis. If frequent topping-up is required, it is likely there is a leak. Check the radiator, all hoses and joint faces for signs of staining or wetness, and rectify as necessary.

● It is important that antifreeze is used in the cooling system all year round, not just during the winter months. Don't top-up with water alone, as the antifreeze will become too diluted.

1 The coolant level varies with the temperature of the engine, and is visible through the expansion tank. When the engine is cold, the coolant level should be between the MAX and MIN marks on the side of the reservoir. When the engine is hot, the level may rise slightly above the MAX mark.

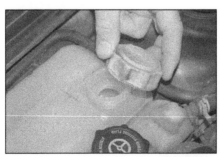

2 If topping up is necessary, **wait until the engine is cold**. Slowly unscrew the expansion tank cap, to release any pressure present in the cooling system, and remove it.

3 Add a mixture of water and antifreeze to the expansion tank until the coolant level is halfway between the level marks. Use only the specified antifreeze – if using Ford antifreeze, make sure it is the same type and colour as that already in the system. Refit the cap and tighten it securely.

Brake fluid level

Warning:
● Brake fluid can harm your eyes and damage painted surfaces, so use extreme caution when handling and pouring it.
● Do not use fluid that has been standing open for some time, as it absorbs moisture from the air, which can cause a dangerous loss of braking effectiveness.

HAYNES HINT *The fluid level in the reservoir will drop slightly as the brake pads wear down, but the fluid level must never be allowed to drop below the MIN mark.*

Before you start
✔ Make sure that your car is on level ground.

Safety First!
● If the reservoir requires repeated topping-up this is an indication of a fluid leak somewhere in the system, which should be investigated immediately.

● If a leak is suspected, the car should not be driven until the braking system has been checked. Never take any risks where brakes are concerned.

1 The brake fluid reservoir is located on the left-hand side of the engine compartment.

2 The MAX and MIN marks are indicated on the side of the reservoir. The fluid level must be kept between the marks at all times.

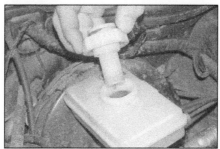

3 If topping-up is necessary, first wipe clean the area around the filler cap to prevent dirt entering the hydraulic system. Unscrew the reservoir cap and carefully lift it out of position, holding the wiring connector plug and taking care not to damage the level sender float. Inspect the reservoir; if the fluid is dirty, the hydraulic system should be drained and refilled (see Chapter 1).

4 Carefully add fluid, taking care not to spill it onto the surrounding components. Use only the specified fluid; mixing different types can cause damage to the system. After topping-up to the correct level, securely refit the cap and wipe off any spilt fluid.

Power steering fluid level

Before you start
✔ Park the vehicle on level ground.
✔ Set the steering wheel straight-ahead.
✔ The engine should be cold and turned off.

HAYNES HINT *For the check to be accurate, the steering must not be turned once the engine has been stopped.*

Safety First!
● The need for frequent topping-up indicates a leak, which should be investigated immediately.

1 The reservoir is mounted at the side of the engine compartment, next to the coolant expansion tank.

2 The fluid level can be viewed through the reservoir body, and should be between the MIN and MAX marks when the engine is cold. If the level is checked when the engine is running or hot, the level may rise slightly above the MAX mark.

3 If topping-up is necessary, use the specified type of fluid – do not overfill the reservoir. Take care not to introduce dirt into the system when topping-up. When the level is correct, securely refit the cap.

Tyre condition and pressure

It is very important that tyres are in good condition, and at the correct pressure - having a tyre failure at any speed is highly dangerous. Tyre wear is influenced by driving style - harsh braking and acceleration, or fast cornering, will all produce more rapid tyre wear. As a general rule, the front tyres wear out faster than the rears. Interchanging the tyres from front to rear ("rotating" the tyres) may result in more even wear. However, if this is completely effective, you may have the expense of replacing all four tyres at once!

Remove any nails or stones embedded in the tread before they penetrate the tyre to cause deflation. If removal of a nail does reveal that

the tyre has been punctured, refit the nail so that its point of penetration is marked. Then immediately change the wheel, and have the tyre repaired by a tyre dealer.

Regularly check the tyres for damage in the form of cuts or bulges, especially in the sidewalls. Periodically remove the wheels, and clean any dirt or mud from the inside and outside surfaces. Examine the wheel rims for signs of rusting, corrosion or other damage. Light alloy wheels are easily damaged by "kerbing" whilst parking; steel wheels may also become dented or buckled. A new wheel is very often the only way to overcome severe damage.

New tyres should be balanced when they are fitted, but it may become necessary to re-balance them as they wear, or if the balance weights fitted to the wheel rim should fall off. Unbalanced tyres will wear more quickly, as will the steering and suspension components. Wheel imbalance is normally signified by vibration, particularly at a certain speed (typically around 50 mph). If this vibration is felt only through the steering, then it is likely that just the front wheels need balancing. If, however, the vibration is felt through the whole car, the rear wheels could be out of balance. Wheel balancing should be carried out by a tyre dealer or garage.

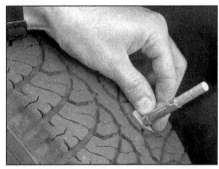

1 Tread Depth - visual check
The original tyres have tread wear safety bands (B), which will appear when the tread depth reaches approximately 1.6 mm. The band positions are indicated by a triangular mark on the tyre sidewall (A).

2 Tread Depth - manual check
Alternatively, tread wear can be monitored with a simple, inexpensive device known as a tread depth indicator gauge.

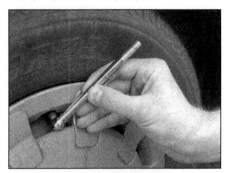

3 Tyre Pressure Check
Check the tyre pressures regularly with the tyres cold. Do not adjust the tyre pressures immediately after the vehicle has been used, or an inaccurate setting will result.

Tyre tread wear patterns

Shoulder Wear

Underinflation (wear on both sides)
Under-inflation will cause overheating of the tyre, because the tyre will flex too much, and the tread will not sit correctly on the road surface. This will cause a loss of grip and excessive wear, not to mention the danger of sudden tyre failure due to heat build-up.
Check and adjust pressures
Incorrect wheel camber (wear on one side)
Repair or renew suspension parts
Hard cornering
Reduce speed!

Centre Wear

Overinflation
Over-inflation will cause rapid wear of the centre part of the tyre tread, coupled with reduced grip, harsher ride, and the danger of shock damage occurring in the tyre casing.
Check and adjust pressures

If you sometimes have to inflate your car's tyres to the higher pressures specified for maximum load or sustained high speed, don't forget to reduce the pressures to normal afterwards.

Uneven Wear

Front tyres may wear unevenly as a result of wheel misalignment. Most tyre dealers and garages can check and adjust the wheel alignment (or "tracking") for a modest charge.
Incorrect camber or castor
Repair or renew suspension parts
Malfunctioning suspension
Repair or renew suspension parts
Unbalanced wheel
Balance tyres
Incorrect toe setting
Adjust front wheel alignment
Note: *The feathered edge of the tread which typifies toe wear is best checked by feel.*

Washer fluid level

● The windscreen washer reservoir also supplies the tailgate washer jet, where applicable. On models so equipped, the same reservoir also serves the headlight washers.

● Screenwash additives not only keep the windscreen clean during foul weather, they also prevent the washer system freezing in cold weather - which is when you are likely to need it most. Don't top up using plain water as the screenwash will become too diluted, and will freeze during cold weather. *On no account use coolant antifreeze in the washer system - this could discolour or damage paintwork.*

1 The washer fluid reservoir is located at the front left-hand side of the engine compartment.

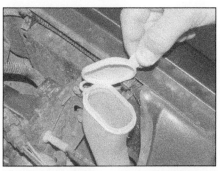

2 On early models, you can check the level by covering the hole on the filler cap with your finger and removing the cap and dipstick/tube. View the fluid level in the tube which will indicate the fluid quantity in the reservoir. Otherwise, just remove the cap for topping-up.

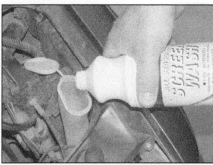

3 When topping-up the reservoir, a screen-wash additive should be added in the quantities recommended on the bottle.

Wiper blades

● Only fit good-quality replacement blades.
● When removing an old wiper blade, note how it is fitted. Fitting new blades can be a fiddly exercise, and noting how the old blade came off can save time.
● While the wiper blade is removed, take care not to knock the wiper arm from its locked position, or it could strike the glass.
● Offer the new blade into position the same way round as the old one. Ensure that it clicks home securely, otherwise it may come off in use, damaging the glass.
Note: *Fitting details for wiper blades vary according to model, and according to whether genuine Ford wiper blades have been fitted. Use the procedures and illustrations shown as a guide for your car.*

HAYNES HiNT *If smearing is still a problem despite fitting new wiper blades, try cleaning the glass with neat screenwash additive or methylated spirit.*

1 Check the condition of the wiper blades; if they are cracked or show any signs of deterioration, or if the glass swept area is smeared, renew them. Wiper blades should be renewed annually, regardless of their apparent condition.

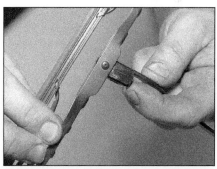

2 To remove a windscreen wiper blade, pull the arm fully away from the glass until it locks. Swivel the blade through 90°, press the locking tab with your fingers and slide the blade out of the arm's hooked end. Don't forget to check the tailgate wiper blade as well (where applicable). Remove the blade using a similar technique to the windscreen wiper blades.

Battery

Caution: Before carrying out any work on the vehicle battery, read the precautions given in 'Safety first' at the start of this manual.

✔ Make sure that the battery tray is in good condition, and that the clamp is tight. Corrosion on the tray, retaining clamp and the battery itself can be removed with a solution of water and baking soda. Thoroughly rinse all cleaned areas with water. Any metal parts damaged by corrosion should be covered with a zinc-based primer, then painted.

✔ Periodically check the charge condition of the battery. On the original-equipment battery, the state of charge is shown by an indicator 'eye' in the top of the battery, which should be green – if the indicator is clear, or red, the battery may need charging or even renewal (see Chapter 5A).

✔ If the battery is flat, and you need to jump start your vehicle, see *Roadside Repairs*.

HAYNES HINT

Battery corrosion can be kept to a minimum by applying a layer of petroleum jelly to the clamps and terminals after they are reconnected.

1 The battery is located in the left-hand rear corner of the engine compartment – unclip and remove the battery cover to gain access. The exterior of the battery should be inspected periodically for damage such as a cracked case or cover.

2 Check the tightness of battery clamps to ensure good electrical connections. You should not be able to move them. Also check each cable for cracks and frayed conductors.

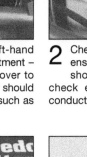

3 If corrosion (white, fluffy deposits) is evident, remove the cables from the battery terminals, clean them with a small wire brush, then refit them. Automotive stores sell a tool for cleaning the battery post . . .

4 . . . as well as the battery cable clamps

Bulbs and fuses

✔ Check all external lights and the horn. Refer to the appropriate Sections of Chapter 12 for details if any of the circuits are found to be inoperative.

✔ Visually check all accessible wiring connectors, harnesses and retaining clips for security, and for signs of chafing or damage.

HAYNES HINT

If you need to check your brake lights and indicators unaided, back up to a wall or garage door and operate the lights. The reflected light should show if they are working properly.

1 If a single indicator light, stop-light or headlight has failed, it is likely that a bulb has blown and will need to be replaced. Refer to Chapter 12 for details. If both stop-lights have failed, it is possible that the switch has failed (see Chapter 9).

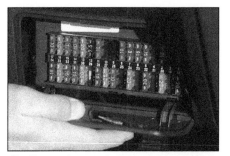

2 If more than one indicator light or tail light has failed, it is likely that either a fuse has blown or that there is a fault in the circuit (see Chapter 12). The main fusebox is located below the facia panel on the passenger's side, and is accessed by opening and removing the glovebox (press in the sides of the glovebox, and lower it completely). The auxiliary fusebox is located next to the brake fluid reservoir – unclip and remove the cover for access.

3 To replace a blown fuse, simply pull it out and fit a new fuse of the correct rating (see Chapter 12). Spare fuses, and a fuse removal tool, are provided in the auxiliary fusebox. If the fuse blows again, it is important that you find out why – a complete checking procedure is given in Chapter 12.

Lubricants and fluids

Engine	Multigrade engine oil, viscosity SAE 10W/40, to ACEA A3-96 or B3-96
Cooling system	Motorcraft Super Plus 4 antifreeze (blue/green) to Ford specification ESD-M97 B49-A, or Motorcraft Super Plus 2000 antifreeze (orange) to Ford specification WSS-M97 B44-D*
Manual transmission	SAE 75W/90 gear oil, to Ford specification WSD-M2C 200-C
Brake hydraulic system	Hydraulic fluid to Ford specification ESD-M6C 57-A, Super DOT 4, paraffin-free
Power steering	Automatic transmission fluid to Ford specification ESP-M2C 166-H

Do not mix the two types of coolant listed with each other, nor top-up with any other type of coolant. Alternative types of coolant may only be used once the system has been drained and completely flushed, as described in Chapter 1.

Choosing your engine oil

Engines need oil, not only to lubricate moving parts and minimise wear, but also to maximise power output and to improve fuel economy.

HOW ENGINE OIL WORKS

• Beating friction

Without oil, the moving surfaces inside your engine will rub together, heat up and melt, quickly causing the engine to seize. Engine oil creates a film which separates these moving parts, preventing wear and heat build-up.

• Cooling hot-spots

Temperatures inside the engine can exceed 1000° C. The engine oil circulates and acts as a coolant, transferring heat from the hot-spots to the sump.

• Cleaning the engine internally

Good quality engine oils clean the inside of your engine, collecting and dispersing combustion deposits and controlling them until they are trapped by the oil filter or flushed out at oil change.

OIL CARE - FOLLOW THE CODE

To handle and dispose of used engine oil safely, always:

- **Avoid skin contact with used engine oil. Repeated or prolonged contact can be harmful.**
- **Dispose of used oil and empty packs in a responsible manner in an authorised disposal site. Call 0800 663366 to find the one nearest to you. Never tip oil down drains or onto the ground.**

Tyre pressures (cold)

1991 to 1993 model year vehicles	Front	Rear
Saloon, Hatchback and Estate models:		
Normally-laden *	2.0 bars (29 psi)	1.8 bars (26 psi)
Fully-laden *	2.3 bars (33 psi)	2.8 bars (41 psi)
Van "40" models:		
Normally-laden *	2.0 bars (29 psi)	1.8 bars (26 psi)
Fully-laden *	2.3 bars (33 psi)	3.0 bars (44 psi)
Van "60" models:		
Normally-laden *	2.0 bars (29 psi)	1.8 bars (26 psi)
Fully-laden *	2.3 bars (33 psi)	3.5 bars (51 psi)

1995 model year vehicles	Front	Rear
Saloon, Hatchback and Estate models:		
Partial load *	2.3 bars (33 psi)	2.0 bars (29 psi)
Full load *	2.5 bars (36 psi)	2.8 bars (41 psi)
Van "55" models:		
Partial load *	2.0 bars (29 psi)	1.8 bars (26 psi)
Full load *	2.4 bars (35 psi)	3.0 bars (44 psi)
Van "75" models:		
Partial load *	2.4 bars (35 psi)	2.4 bars (35 psi)
Full load *	2.6 bars (38 psi)	3.5 bars (51 psi)

1998 and 1999 model year vehicles	Front	Rear
Saloon, Hatchback and Estate models:		
Normally-laden *	2.3 bars (33 psi)	2.0 bars (29 psi)
Fully-laden *	2.5 bars (36 psi)	3.1 bars (45 psi)
Van "55" models:		
Normally-laden *	2.1 bars (30 psi)	1.8 bars (26 psi)
Fully-laden *	2.4 bars (35 psi)	3.0 bars (44 psi)
Van "75" models:		
Normally-laden *	2.4 bars (35 psi)	2.4 bars (35 psi)
Fully-laden *	2.6 bars (38 psi)	3.5 bars (51 psi)

Note: *Normally-laden or partial load means up to 3 persons or the driver and 375 lbs (170 kg) of luggage; fully-laden or full load means anything more than that, up to the maximum permissible payload. For sustained high speeds above 100 mph (160 km/h), increased pressures are necessary; consult the driver's handbook supplied with the vehicle. Tyre pressures should be checked when the tyres are cold (before a journey); do not forget to check the spare. Pressures apply only to original-equipment tyres, and may vary if other makes or types are fitted; check with the tyre manufacturer or supplier for correct pressures if necessary.*

Chapter 1
Routine maintenance and servicing

Contents

Degrees of difficulty

Easy, suitable for novice with little experience | **Fairly easy,** suitable for beginner with some experience | **Fairly difficult,** suitable for competent DIY mechanic | **Difficult,** suitable for experienced DIY mechanic | **Very difficult,** suitable for expert DIY or professional

Lubricants and fluids

Refer to *Weekly checks*

Capacities

Engine oil (including filter) .... 4.5 litres
Cooling system (approximate) .... 9.3 litres
Transmission:
    B5 type .... 3.1 litres
    iB5 type .... 2.8 litres

Engine

Valve clearances (cold):
    Inlet .... 0.35 ± 0.05 mm
    Exhaust .... 0.50 ± 0.05 mm
    Tappet shim thicknesses available .... 3.00 to 4.75 mm in increments of 0.05 mm

Cooling system

Coolant protection at standard 50% antifreeze/water mixture ratio:
    Slush point .... −25°C (−13°F)
    Solidifying point .... −30°C (−22°F)
Coolant specific gravity at standard 50% antifreeze/water mixture ratio
    and 15°C/59°F – with no other additives in coolant 1.061
Note: *Refer to antifreeze manufacturer for latest recommendations.*

Clutch

Pedal free play:
    Pre-1996 models .... Automatic adjustment
    1996 models on .... 150 ± 5 mm (RHD)
    145± 5 mm (LHD)

Brakes

Friction material minimum thickness
    Front brake pads .... 1.5 mm
    Rear brake shoes .... 1.0 mm

Tyres

Tyre pressures .... See *Weekly checks*

Torque wrench settings	Nm	lbf ft
Auxiliary drivebelt cover fasteners	8	6
Auxiliary drivebelt adjustment:		
Adjusting bolt (sliding arm)	22	16
Central (clamp) nut/bolt	22	16
Pinion (adjuster) nut	12	9
Alternator mounting bolts	25	18
Engine oil drain plug	25	18
Handbrake cable adjuster nut (1996-on models)	4	3
Roadwheel nuts	85	63
Seat belt mounting bolts	38	28
Transmission filler/level plug	20	15

The maintenance intervals in this manual are provided with the assumption that you, not the dealer, will be carrying out the work. These are the minimum maintenance intervals recommended by us for vehicles driven daily. If you wish to keep your vehicle in peak condition at all times, you may wish to perform some of these procedures more often. We encourage frequent maintenance, because it enhances the efficiency, performance and resale value of your vehicle.

If the vehicle is driven in dusty areas, used to tow a trailer, or driven frequently at slow speeds (idling in traffic) or on short journeys, more frequent maintenance intervals are recommended.

When the vehicle is new, it should be serviced by a factory-authorised dealer service department, in order to preserve the factory warranty.

Every 250 miles (400 km) or weekly
☐ Refer to *Weekly checks*.

Every 5000 miles or 6 months, whichever comes first
☐ Renew the engine oil and filter (Section 3)
Note: *Ford recommend that the engine oil and filter are changed every 10 000 miles or 12 months. However, oil and filter changes are good for the engine, and we recommend that the oil and filter are renewed more frequently, especially if the vehicle is used on a lot of short journeys.*

Every 10 000 miles or 12 months, whichever comes first
☐ Drain water from the fuel filter (Section 4)
☐ Check the condition and tension of the auxiliary drivebelt(s) (Section 5)
☐ Check all components, pipes and hoses for fluid leaks (Section 6)
☐ Check the condition of all engine compartment wiring (Section 7)
☐ Check the condition of all air conditioning system components, where applicable (Section 8)
☐ Check and if necessary adjust the clutch pedal free play – 1996 models onwards (Section 9)
☐ Check the transmission oil level (Section 10)
☐ Check the front brake pads and discs for wear (Section 11)
☐ Check the rear brake shoes and drums for wear (Section 12)
☐ Check the steering and suspension components for condition and security (Section 13)
☐ Check the exhaust system (Section 14)
☐ Check the underbody, and all fuel/brake lines (Section 15)
☐ Check the condition of the driveshaft gaiters (Section 16)
☐ Check the doors, boot, tailgate and bonnet, and lubricate their hinges and locks (Section 17)
☐ Check the roadwheel nuts are tightened to the specified torque (Section 18)
☐ Check the seat belts (Section 19)
☐ Check the condition of the bodywork, paint and exterior trim (Section 20)
☐ Carry out a road test (Section 21)

Every 20 000 miles
☐ Renew the fuel filter (Section 22)

Every 30 000 miles
☐ Check and, if necessary, adjust the valve clearances (Section 23)
☐ Renew the air filter (Section 24)
☐ Check the emission control system (Section 25)
☐ Check the handbrake adjustment (Section 26)

Every 40 000 miles
☐ Renew the timing belt and injection pump belt (Section 27)

Every 3 years, regardless of mileage
☐ Renew the brake fluid (Section 28)

Every 4 years, regardless of mileage
☐ Renew the coolant and check the condition of the expansion tank pressure cap (Section 29)

Engine compartment – non-turbo engine

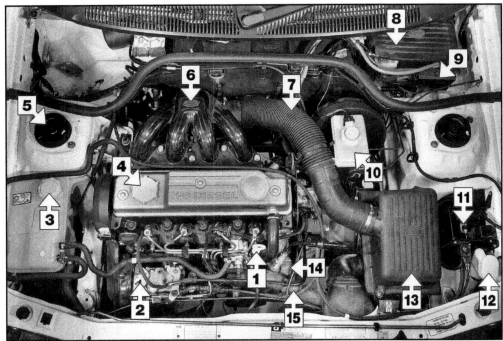

1 Engine oil dipstick
2 Fuel injection pump
3 Coolant expansion tank
4 Engine oil filler cap
5 Suspension upper mounting
6 Inlet manifold plastic section
7 Air intake duct
8 Battery
9 Engine compartment fuses
10 Brake fluid reservoir
11 Idle-up control unit
12 Washer fluid reservoir
13 Air cleaner
14 Brake vacuum pump
15 Cooling system bleed screw

Engine compartment – turbocharged intercooled engine

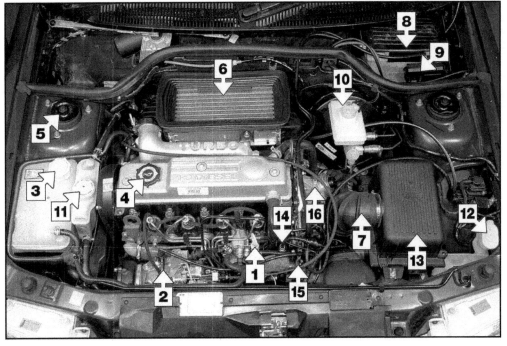

1 Engine oil dipstick
2 Fuel injection pump
3 Coolant expansion tank
4 Engine oil filler cap
5 Suspension upper mounting
6 Intercooler
7 Air intake duct (to turbo)
8 Battery
9 Engine compartment fuses
10 Brake fluid reservoir
11 Power steering fluid reservoir
12 Washer fluid reservoir
13 Air cleaner
14 Brake vacuum pump
15 Cooling system bleed screw
16 Fuel filter housing

Front underbody view

1 Engine oil filter
2 Engine oil drain plug
3 Engine sump (cast aluminium
   type shown)
4 Horn
5 Alternator
6 Starter motor
7 Radiator cooling fan
8 Transmission
9 Engine/transmission mounting
10 Driveshaft
11 Front brake caliper
12 Suspension arm
13 Track rod
14 Gearchange linkage
15 Exhaust system

Rear underbody view (petrol model shown, diesel similar)

1 Fuel filler pipe
2 Handbrake cable adjuster
3 Fuel tank
4 Suspension mounting
5 Rear axle beam
6 Exhaust rear silencer
7 Exhaust system
   support/insulator

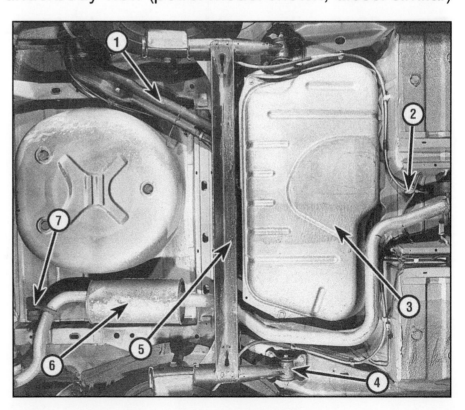

1 General information

1 This Chapter is designed to help the home mechanic maintain his/her vehicle for safety, economy, long life and peak performance.
2 The Chapter contains a master maintenance schedule, followed by Sections dealing specifically with each task in the schedule. Visual checks, adjustments, component renewal and other helpful items are included. Refer to the accompanying illustrations of the engine compartment and the underside of the vehicle for the locations of the various components.
3 Servicing your vehicle in accordance with the mileage/time maintenance schedule and the following Sections will provide a planned maintenance programme, which should result in a long and reliable service life. This is a comprehensive plan, so maintaining some items but not others at the specified service intervals, will not produce the same results.
4 As you service your vehicle, you will discover that many of the procedures can – and should – be grouped together, because of the particular procedure being performed, or because of the proximity of two otherwise-unrelated components to one another. For example, if the vehicle is raised for any reason, the exhaust can be inspected at the same time as the suspension and steering components.

5 The first step in this maintenance programme is to prepare yourself before the actual work begins. Read through all the Sections relevant to the work to be carried out, then make a list and gather all the parts and tools required. If a problem is encountered, seek advice from a parts specialist, or a dealer service department.

2 Regular maintenance

1 If, from the time the vehicle is new, the routine maintenance schedule is followed closely, and frequent checks are made of fluid levels and high-wear items, as suggested throughout this manual, the engine will be kept in relatively good running condition, and the need for additional work will be minimised.
2 It is possible that there will be times when the engine is running poorly due to the lack of regular maintenance. This is even more likely if a used vehicle, which has not received regular and frequent maintenance checks, is purchased. In such cases, additional work may need to be carried out, outside of the regular maintenance intervals.
3 If engine wear is suspected, a compression test or leakdown test (refer to Chapter 2A) will provide valuable information regarding the overall performance of the main internal components. Such a test can be used as a basis to decide on the extent of the work to be carried out. If, for example, a compression

or leakdown test indicates serious internal engine wear, conventional maintenance as described in this Chapter will not greatly improve the performance of the engine, and may prove a waste of time and money, unless extensive overhaul work is carried out first.
4 The following series of operations are those most often required to improve the performance of a generally poor-running engine:

Primary operations

a) Clean, inspect and test the battery (refer to 'Weekly checks').
b) Check all the engine-related fluids (refer to 'Weekly checks').
c) Check the condition and tension of the auxiliary drivebelt (Section 5).
d) Check the condition of the air filter, and renew if necessary (Section 24).
e) Renew the fuel filter (Section 22).
f) Check the condition of all hoses, and check for fluid leaks (Section 6).

5 If the above operations do not prove fully effective, carry out the following secondary operations:

Secondary operations

All items listed under *Primary operations*, plus the following:
a) Check the charging system (refer to Chapter 5A).
b) Check the pre-heating system (refer to Chapter 5B).
c) Check the fuel system (refer to Chapter 4A).

Every 5000 miles or 6 months, whichever comes first

3 Engine oil and filter renewal

1 Frequent oil and filter changes are the most important preventative maintenance procedures which can be undertaken by the DIY owner. As engine oil ages, it becomes diluted and contaminated, which leads to premature engine wear.

2 Before starting this procedure, gather together all the necessary tools and materials. Also make sure that you have plenty of clean rags and newspapers handy, to mop up any spills. Ideally, the engine oil should be warm, as it will drain more easily, and more built-up sludge will be removed with it. Take care not to touch the exhaust or any other hot parts of the engine when working under the vehicle. To avoid any possibility of scalding, and to protect yourself from possible skin irritants and other harmful contaminants in used

engine oils, it is advisable to wear gloves when carrying out this work.
3 Firmly apply the handbrake then jack up the front of the vehicle and support it on axle stands (see *Jacking and vehicle support*).
4 Remove the oil filler cap.
5 Using a spanner, or preferably a suitable socket and bar, slacken the drain plug about half a turn **(see illustration)**. Position the draining container under the drain plug, then remove the plug completely.
6 Allow some time for the oil to drain, noting that it may be necessary to reposition the container as the oil flow slows to a trickle.
7 After all the oil has drained, wipe the drain plug and the sealing washer with a clean rag. Examine the condition of the sealing washer, and renew it if it shows signs of scoring or other damage which may prevent an oil-tight seal. Clean the area around the drain plug opening, and refit the plug complete with the washer and tighten it securely.
8 Move the container into position under the oil filter which is located on the rear of the cylinder block **(see illustration)**.
9 Use an oil filter removal tool to slacken the filter initially, then unscrew it by hand the rest

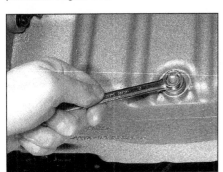

3.5 Engine oil drain plug on the sump

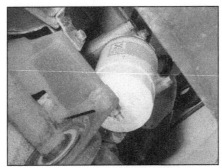

3.8 View of the oil filter from under the rear of the engine

of the way. Empty the oil from the old filter into the container.

10 Use a clean rag to remove all oil, dirt and sludge from the filter sealing area on the engine.

11 Apply a light coating of clean engine oil to the sealing ring on the new filter, then screw the filter into position on the engine. Tighten the filter firmly by hand only – **do not** use any tools.

12 Remove the old oil and all tools from under the vehicle then lower the vehicle to the ground.

13 Fill the engine through the filler hole, using the correct grade and type of oil (refer to *Weekly checks* for details of topping-up). Pour in half the specified quantity of oil first, then wait a few minutes for the oil to drain into the sump. Continue to add oil, a small quantity at a time, until the level is up to the lower mark on the dipstick. Adding approximately a further 1.0 litre will bring the level up to the upper mark on the dipstick.

14 Start the engine and run it for a few minutes, while checking for leaks around the oil filter seal and the sump drain plug. Note

that there may be a delay of a few seconds before the low oil pressure warning light goes out when the engine is first started, as the oil circulates through the new oil filter and the engine oil galleries before the pressure builds up.

15 Stop the engine, and wait a few minutes for the oil to settle in the sump once more. With the new oil circulated and the filter now completely full, recheck the level on the dipstick, and add more oil as necessary.

16 Dispose of the used engine oil safely with reference to *General repair procedures*.

Every 10 000 miles or 12 months, whichever comes first

4 Fuel filter water draining

Caution: Before starting any work on the fuel filter, wipe clean the filter assembly and the area around it; it is essential that no dirt or other foreign matter is allowed into the system. Obtain a suitable container into which the filter can be drained and place rags or similar material under the filter assembly to catch any spillages. Do not allow diesel fuel to leak into the clutch bellhousing, or it will contaminate the clutch driven plate friction material – this will cause severe clutch slip, which can be cured only by the renewal of the clutch plate and the degreasing of all fouled surfaces. Similarly, diesel fuel should never be allowed to contaminate components such as the alternator and starter motor, the coolant hoses and engine mountings, and any wiring.

1 Access to the fuel filter will be considerably improved by loosening/releasing the hose clip(s) and disconnecting the air inlet duct from the air cleaner. On later turbo engines, disconnect the wiring plug from the air mass meter. Move the duct to one side.

2 In addition to taking the precautions noted above to catch any fuel spillages, connect a tube to the drain spigot on the base of the fuel filter. Place the other end of the tube in a clean jar or can.

3 Open the drain cock by unscrewing the knurled wheel.

4 Allow the filter to drain until clean fuel, free of dirt or water, emerges from the tube (approximately 100 cc is usually sufficient). Close the drain cock and remove the tube, containers and rag, mopping up any spilt fuel.

5 If, as often happens, no fuel emerges on opening the drain cock, slacken the vent screw on the filter head to allow sufficient air into the filter for fuel to flow. If this does not work, remove the filter cartridge and check it carefully until the reason for the lack of flow can be identified and is cured. It is unwise simply to probe the drain cock with a piece of wire in an attempt to clear the obstruction;

the small seals in the drain cock may be damaged or dislodged. Note that the system may require bleeding if the vent screw is disturbed or the filter unscrewed (refer to Chapter 4A).

6 On completion, dispose safely of the drained. Check carefully all disturbed components to ensure that there are no leaks (of air or fuel) when the engine is restarted.

5 Auxiliary drivebelt check and renewal

Checking

1 The auxiliary drivebelt is fitted at the right-hand side of the engine, and drives the alternator, air conditioning compressor and power steering pump (as applicable) from the crankshaft pulley. Later models with air conditioning and power steering have a separate ribbed belt for the power steering pump, driven off the injection pump sprocket.

2 Due to their function and material makeup, drivebelts are prone to failure after a long period of time, and should therefore be inspected regularly.

3 The alternator drivebelt is located very close to the right-hand side of the engine compartment, and better access can be gained from below. Apply the handbrake, and loosen the right-hand front roadwheel nuts. Raise the front of the vehicle and support it on

axle stands (see *Jacking and vehicle support*). On later models, first remove the engine undershield, which is held on by five bolts. Remove the right-hand front wheel. Where fitted, remove the plastic belt guard **(see illustration)**.

4 The separate power steering drivebelt fitted to later models can be worked on from above – unbolt and remove the plastic belt guard fitted above the belt for access, noting that one of the bolts may also be used to secure a power steering hose bracket **(see illustration)**.

5 With the engine stopped, inspect the full length of the drivebelt for cracks and separation of the belt plies (slight cracking in the belt ribs is normal). It will be necessary to turn the engine (using a spanner or socket and bar on the crankshaft pulley bolt) in order to move the belt away from the pulleys so that the belt can be inspected thoroughly. Twist the belt between the pulleys so that both sides can be viewed. Also check for fraying, and glazing which gives the belt a shiny appearance. Check the pulleys for nicks, cracks, distortion and corrosion.

Renewal

6 To remove the alternator drivebelt, if not already done, raise the front of the vehicle as described in paragraph 3. The separate power steering drivebelt fitted to later models can be worked on from above – unbolt and remove the plastic belt guard fitted above the belt for access.

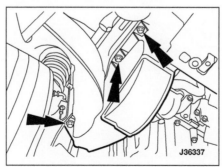

5.3 Auxiliary drivebelt plastic guard bolts (arrowed)

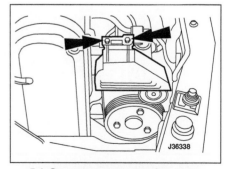

5.4 Separate power steering pump drivebelt plastic guard bolts (arrowed)

5.7 Early models may be fitted with a slotted-link adjuster

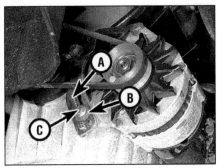

5.12a Drivebelt adjuster link (A) pinion nut (B) and clamp bolt (C) – model without air conditioning

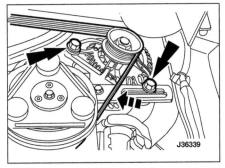

5.12b Removing the drivebelt on a model with air conditioning – alternator pivot and adjuster clamp bolts arrowed

5.12c Removing the main drivebelt

5.14 Using a crowfoot adapter to apply torque to the pinion nut, while the clamp bolt is tightened

5.16 Loosen the clamping nut on the tensioner pulley

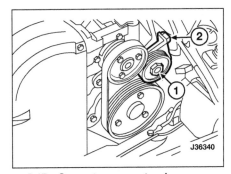

5.17a Separate power steering pump drivebelt clamping nut (1) and adjustment bolt (2)

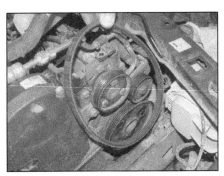

5.17b Removing the power steering pump drivebelt

Early models

7 On models fitted with a slotted link type adjuster strap, loosen both the adjuster bolt and the link pivot bolt at the top **(see illustration)**.

8 Loosen off the alternator mounting bolts, pivot the alternator inwards towards the engine to slacken the tension of the drivebelt, then disengage the drivebelt from the pulleys and remove it.

9 Locate the new drivebelt on the pulleys, making sure it is correctly seated.

10 Carefully lever the alternator away from the engine to tension the belt – do not lever on any part of the engine or alternator which could be damaged (excessive force should not be required in any case). As a rough guide, the belt tension is correct when there is approximately 4 mm of total belt deflection between the pulleys.

11 Hold the alternator in this position while tightening the adjuster, link pivot bolt and alternator mountings securely.

Later models – main drivebelt

12 Loosen the alternator pivot and adjustment clamp bolts, and turn the large pinion nut behind the clamp bolt to move the alternator and release the drivebelt tension. Release the drivebelt from the alternator, crankshaft and air conditioning compressor pulleys, as applicable **(see illustrations)**.

13 Fit the new belt to the pulleys, and turn the pinion nut until the slack is removed from the belt.

14 Ford's procedure for tensioning the new belt is to apply and hold a torque to the pinion nut, while tightening the adjuster clamp bolt in front of it **(see illustration)**. For most DIY mechanics, this will not be possible, so alternatively use a spanner on the pinion nut to set and hold the belt tension so that there is roughly a 4 mm deflection in the belt, midway between the pulleys, and tighten the clamp and alternator pivot bolts firmly.

15 Refit the plastic belt guards and other removed components, and lower the vehicle to the ground.

Later models – power steering pump drivebelt

16 Loosen only (do not remove) the adjustment clamping nut located in the centre of the tensioner pulley **(see illustration)**.

17 Back off the adjustment bolt to release the tension on the belt, then release it from the pulleys and remove it **(see illustrations)**. On our car, a size 7 Torx socket was needed for the adjustment bolt, and access was not easy.

18 Locate the new drivebelt on the pulley and around the tensioner. Make sure that the drivebelt is correctly seated in all of the pulley grooves.

19 Tighten the adjustment bolt until it is possible to deflect the drivebelt midway between the pulleys on the longest run approximately 3 mm under firm thumb pressure.

20 Refit the plastic belt guard on completion.

6 Hose and fluid leak check

1 Visually inspect the engine joint faces, gaskets and seals for any signs of water or oil leaks. Pay particular attention to the areas around the cylinder head cover, cylinder head, oil filter and sump joint faces. Bear in mind that, over a period of time, some very slight seepage from these areas is to be expected – what you are really looking for is any indication of a serious leak. Should a leak be found, renew the offending gasket or oil seal by referring to the appropriate Chapters in this manual.

2 Also check the security and condition of all the engine-related pipes and hoses, and all braking system pipes and hoses. Ensure that all cable-ties or securing clips are in place, and in good condition. Clips which are broken or missing can lead to chafing of the hoses, pipes or wiring, which could cause more serious problems in the future.

3 Carefully check the radiator hoses and heater hoses along their entire length. Renew any hose which is cracked, swollen or deteriorated. Cracks will show up better if the hose is squeezed. Pay close attention to the hose clips that secure the hoses to the cooling system components. Hose clips can pinch and puncture hoses, resulting in cooling system leaks. If the crimped-type hose clips are used, it may be a good idea to replace them with standard worm-drive clips.

4 Inspect all the cooling system components (hoses, joint faces, etc) for leaks.

5 Where any problems are found on system components, renew the component or gasket with reference to Chapter 3.

6 With the vehicle raised, inspect the fuel tank and filler neck for punctures, cracks and other damage. The connection between the filler neck and tank is especially critical. Sometimes a rubber filler neck or connecting hose will leak due to loose retaining clamps or deteriorated rubber.

7 Carefully check all rubber hoses and metal fuel lines leading away from the fuel tank. Check for loose connections, deteriorated hoses, crimped lines, and other damage. Pay particular attention to the vent pipes and hoses, which often loop up around the filler neck and can become blocked or crimped. Follow the lines to the front of the vehicle, carefully inspecting them all the way. Renew damaged sections as necessary. Similarly, whilst the vehicle is raised, take the opportunity to inspect all underbody brake fluid pipes and hoses.

8 From within the engine compartment, check the security of all fuel, vacuum and brake hose attachments and pipe unions, and inspect all hoses for kinks, chafing and deterioration.

9 Where applicable, check the condition of the power steering fluid pipes and hoses.

HAYNES HINT

A leak in the cooling system will usually show up as white- or rust-coloured deposits on the area adjoining the leak.

7 Engine compartment wiring check

1 With the vehicle parked on level ground, apply the handbrake firmly and open the bonnet. Using an inspection light or a small electric torch, check all visible wiring within and beneath the engine compartment.

2 What you are looking for is wiring that is obviously damaged by chafing against sharp edges, or against moving suspension/transmission components and/or the auxiliary drivebelt, by being trapped or crushed between carelessly-refitted components, or melted by being forced into contact with the hot engine castings, coolant pipes, etc. In almost all cases, damage of this sort is caused in the first instance by incorrect routing on reassembly, after previous work has been carried out.

3 Depending on the extent of the problem, damaged wiring may be repaired by rejoining the break or splicing-in a new length of wire, using solder to ensure a good connection, and remaking the insulation with adhesive insulating tape or heat-shrink tubing, as appropriate. If the damage is extensive, given the implications for the vehicle's future reliability, the best long-term answer may well be to renew that entire section of the loom, however expensive this may appear.

4 When the actual damage has been repaired, ensure that the wiring loom is re-routed correctly, so that it is clear of other components, and not stretched or kinked, and is secured out of harm's way using the plastic clips, guides and ties provided.

5 Check all electrical connectors, ensuring that they are clean, securely fastened, and that each is locked by its plastic tabs or wire clip, as appropriate. If any connector shows external signs of corrosion (accumulations of white or green deposits, or streaks of 'rust'), or if any is thought to be dirty, it must be unplugged and cleaned using electrical contact cleaner. If the connector pins are severely corroded, the connector must be

renewed; note that this may mean the renewal of that entire section of the loom – see your local Ford dealer for details.

6 If the cleaner completely removes the corrosion to leave the connector in a satisfactory condition, it would be wise to pack the connector with a suitable material which will exclude dirt and moisture, preventing the corrosion from occurring again; a Ford dealer may be able to recommend a suitable product.

7 Check the condition of the battery connections – remake the connections or renew the leads if a fault is found. Use the same techniques to ensure that all earth points in the engine compartment provide good electrical contact through clean, metal-to-metal joints, and that all are securely fastened. (In addition to the earth connection at the engine lifting eye, and that from the transmission to the body/battery, there are others in various places, so check carefully).

8 Air conditioning system check

⚠️ *Warning: The air conditioning system is under high pressure. Do not loosen any fittings or remove any components until after the system has been discharged. Air conditioning refrigerant must be properly discharged into an approved container, at a dealer service department or an automotive air conditioning repair facility capable of handling the refrigerant safely. Always wear eye protection when disconnecting air conditioning system fittings.*

1 The following maintenance checks should be performed on a regular basis, to ensure that the air conditioner continues to operate at peak efficiency:

a) Check the auxiliary drivebelt. If it is worn or deteriorated, renew it (see Section 5).

b) Check the system hoses. Look for cracks, bubbles, hard spots and deterioration. Inspect the hoses and all fittings for oil bubbles and seepage. If there's any evidence of wear, damage or leaks, renew the hose(s).

c) Inspect the condenser fins for leaves, insects and other debris. Use a 'fin comb' or compressed air to clean the condenser.

d) Check that the drain tube from the front of the evaporator is clear – note that it is normal to have clear fluid (water) dripping from this while the system is in operation, to the extent that quite a large puddle can be left under the vehicle when it is parked.

⚠️ *Warning: Wear eye protection when using compressed air.*

2 It's a good idea to operate the system for about 30 minutes at least once a month, particularly during the Winter. Long term

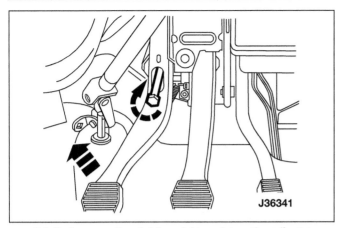

9.5 To increase the clutch pedal travel, turn the adjuster clockwise

10.2 Unscrewing the transmission oil filler/level plug (using an Allen bit)

non-use can cause hardening, and subsequent failure, of the seals.

3 Because of the complexity of the air conditioning system and the special equipment necessary to service it, in-depth fault diagnosis and repairs are not included in this manual. For more complete information on the air conditioning system, refer to the Haynes *Automotive Heating and Air Conditioning Manual*.

4 The most common cause of poor cooling is simply a low system refrigerant charge. If a noticeable drop in cool-air output occurs, the following quick check will help you determine if the refrigerant level is low.

5 Warm up the engine to operating temperature.

6 Place the air conditioning temperature selector at the coldest setting, and put the blower at the highest setting. Open the doors – to make sure the air conditioning system doesn't cycle off as soon as it cools the passenger compartment.

7 With the compressor engaged – the clutch will make an audible click, and the centre of the clutch will rotate – feel the inlet and outlet pipes at the compressor. One side should be cold, and one hot. If there's no perceptible difference between the two pipes, there's something wrong with the compressor or the system. It might be a low charge – it might be something else. Take the vehicle to a dealer service department or an automotive air conditioning specialist.

9 Clutch pedal free play adjustment (1996 models onwards)

Note: *This adjustment is only applicable to 1996 models onwards with manual clutch adjustment, and earlier models which have been converted from automatic to manual adjustment retrospectively.*

1 The clutch pedal free play is checked by measuring the clutch pedal travel. Before doing this, settle the cable by depressing and

releasing the pedal a few times (at least ten times if new clutch components or cable have been fitted).

2 Ensure that there are no obstructions beneath the clutch pedal then measure the distance from the third groove of the clutch pedal rubber to the floor with the pedal in the at-rest position. Depress the clutch pedal fully, and again measure the distance from the third groove of the pedal rubber to the floor.

3 Subtract the second measurement from the first to obtain the clutch pedal travel. If this is not within the range given in the Specifications, adjust the clutch as follows.

4 Locate the cable adjuster which is a bolt which protrudes through an opening near the top of the clutch pedal.

5 To increase the pedal travel, turn the adjuster clockwise; to decrease the travel, turn the adjuster anti-clockwise **(see illustration)**.

6 Recheck the pedal travel and make any further adjustments as necessary until the correct setting is obtained.

10 Transmission oil level check

1 Position the vehicle over an inspection pit, on vehicle ramps, or jack it up, but make sure that it is level.

10.3 Topping-up the transmission oil level

2 Remove all traces of dirt then unscrew the filler/level plug from the lower front face of the transmission. Typically, a large Allen key will be required – and the plug will probably be very tight (take care to avoid injury) **(see illustration)**.

3 The level must be up to the bottom edge of the filler/level plug hole – feel inside with the end of your finger (if no oil came out when the plug was removed, which is what usually happens). If necessary, top up the level with the specified grade of oil (see *Weekly checks*) **(see illustration)**.

4 When the level is correct, clean and refit the filler level plug and tighten it firmly.

5 Lower the car to the ground.

11 Front brake pad and disc wear check

1 Apply the handbrake, loosen the front wheel nuts, then jack up the front of the car and support it securely on axle stands (see *Jacking and vehicle support*). Remove the front roadwheels.

2 For a comprehensive check, the brake pads should be removed and cleaned. The

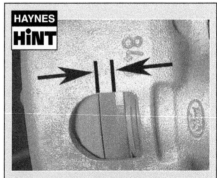

For a quick check, the thickness of friction material remaining on each brake pad can be measured through the aperture in the caliper body.

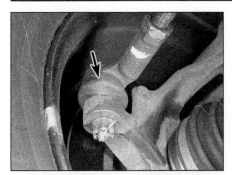

13.2a Check the condition of the track rod end balljoint dust cover (arrowed)

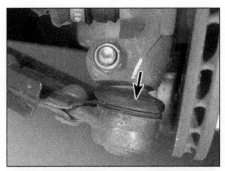

13.2b Check the condition of the lower arm balljoint dust cover (arrowed) . . .

13.2c . . . and check the condition of the steering rack gaiters

operation of the caliper can then also be checked, and the condition of the brake disc itself can be fully examined on both sides. Refer to Chapter 9 for further information.

3 On completion refit the roadwheels and lower the car to the ground.

12 Rear brake shoe and drum wear check

Remove the rear brake drums, and check the brake shoes for signs of wear or contamination. At the same time, also inspect the wheel cylinders for signs of leakage, and the brake drum for signs of wear. Refer to the relevant Sections of Chapter 9 for further information.

13 Steering and suspension check

Front suspension and steering

1 Raise the front of the vehicle, and securely support it on axle stands (see *Jacking and vehicle support*).

2 Visually inspect the balljoint dust covers and the steering rack-and-pinion gaiters for splits, chafing or deterioration **(see illustrations)**. Any wear of these components will cause loss of lubricant, together with dirt and water entry, resulting in rapid deterioration of the balljoints or steering gear.

3 On vehicles with power steering, check the fluid hoses for chafing or deterioration, and the pipe and hose unions for fluid leaks. Also check for signs of fluid leakage under pressure from the steering gear rubber gaiters, which would indicate failed fluid seals within the steering gear.

4 Grasp the roadwheel at the 12 o'clock and 6 o'clock positions, and try to rock it **(see illustration)**. Very slight free play may be felt, but if the movement is appreciable, further investigation is necessary to determine the source. Continue rocking the wheel while an assistant depresses the footbrake. If the movement is now eliminated or significantly

reduced, it is likely that the hub bearings are at fault. If the free play is still evident with the footbrake depressed, then there is wear in the suspension joints or mountings.

5 Now grasp the wheel at the 9 o'clock and 3 o'clock positions, and try to rock it as before. Any movement felt now may again be caused by wear in the hub bearings or the steering track-rod balljoints. If the outer balljoint is worn, the visual movement will be obvious. If the inner joint is suspect, it can be felt by placing a hand over the rack-and-pinion rubber gaiter and gripping the track-rod. If the wheel is now rocked, movement will be felt at the inner joint if wear has taken place.

6 Using a large screwdriver or flat bar, check for wear in the suspension mounting bushes by levering between the relevant suspension component and its attachment point. Some movement is to be expected, as the mountings are made of rubber, but excessive wear should be obvious. Also check the condition of any visible rubber bushes, looking for splits, cracks or contamination of the rubber.

7 With the car standing on its wheels, have an assistant turn the steering wheel back and forth, about an eighth of a turn each way. There should be very little, if any, lost movement between the steering wheel and roadwheels. If this is not the case, closely observe the joints and mountings previously described. In addition, check the steering column universal joints for wear, and also check the rack-and-pinion steering gear itself.

Rear suspension

8 Chock the front wheels, then jack up the rear of the vehicle and support securely on axle stands (see *Jacking and vehicle support*).

9 Working as described previously for the front suspension, check the rear hub bearings, the suspension bushes and the strut or shock absorber mountings (as applicable) for wear.

Shock absorbers

10 Check for any signs of fluid leakage around the shock absorber body, or from the rubber gaiter around the piston rod. Should any fluid be noticed, the shock absorber is defective internally, and should be renewed.

Note: *Shock absorbers should always be renewed in pairs on the same axle.*

11 The efficiency of the shock absorber may be checked by bouncing the vehicle at each corner. Generally speaking, the body will return to its normal position and stop after being depressed. If it rises and returns on a rebound, the shock absorber is probably suspect. Also examine the shock absorber upper and lower mountings for any signs of wear.

14 Exhaust system check

1 With the engine cold (at least three hours after the vehicle has been driven), check the complete exhaust system, from its starting point at the engine to the end of the tailpipe. Ideally, this should be done on a hoist, where unrestricted access is available; if a hoist is not available, raise and support the vehicle on axle stands (see *Jacking and vehicle support*).

2 Check the pipes and connections for evidence of leaks, severe corrosion, or damage. Make sure that all brackets and rubber mountings are in good condition, and tight; if any of the mountings are to be renewed, ensure that the replacements are of the correct type **(see illustration)**. Leakage at any of the joints or in other parts of the system will usually show up as a black sooty stain in the vicinity of the leak. **Note:** *Exhaust sealants should not be used on any part of the exhaust system upstream of the catalytic converter – even if the sealant does*

13.4 Check for wear in the hub bearings by grasping the wheel and trying to rock it

14.2 If any of the exhaust system rubber mountings are to be renewed, ensure that the replacements are of the correct type – their colour is a good guide. Those nearest to the catalytic converter are more heat-resistant than the others

16.1 Check the condition of the driveshaft gaiters

not contain additives harmful to the converter, pieces of it may break off and foul the element, causing local overheating.

3 At the same time, inspect the underside of the body for holes, corrosion, open seams, etc, which may allow exhaust gases to enter the passenger compartment. Seal all body openings with silicone or body putty.

4 Rattles and other noises can often be traced to the exhaust system, especially the rubber mountings. Try to move the system, silencer(s) and catalytic converter. If any components can touch the body or suspension parts, secure the exhaust system with new mountings.

15 Underbody and fuel/brake line check

1 With the vehicle raised and supported on axle stands or over an inspection pit, thoroughly inspect the underbody and wheel arches for signs of damage and corrosion. In particular, examine the bottom of the side sills, and any concealed areas where mud can collect. Where corrosion and rust is evident, press and tap firmly on the panel with a screwdriver, and check for any serious corrosion which would necessitate repairs. If the panel is not seriously corroded, clean away the rust, and apply a new coating of underseal. Refer to Chapter 11 for more details of body repairs.

2 At the same time, inspect the PVC-coated lower body panels for stone damage and general condition.

3 Inspect all of the fuel and brake lines on the underbody for damage, rust, corrosion and leakage. Also make sure that they are correctly supported in their clips. Where applicable, check the PVC coating on the lines for damage.

16 Driveshaft gaiter check

1 With the vehicle raised and securely supported on stands, turn the steering onto full lock then slowly rotate the roadwheel. Inspect the condition of the outer constant velocity (CV) joint rubber gaiters while squeezing the gaiters to open out the folds **(see illustration)**. Check for signs of cracking, splits or deterioration of the rubber which may allow the grease to escape and lead to water and grit entry into the joint. Also check the security and condition of the retaining clips. Repeat these checks on the inner CV joints. If any damage or deterioration is found, the gaiters should be renewed as described in Chapter 8.

2 At the same time check the general condition of the CV joints themselves by first holding the driveshaft and attempting to rotate the wheel. Repeat this check by holding the inner joint and attempting to rotate the driveshaft. Any appreciable movement indicates wear in the joints, wear in the drive-shaft splines or loose driveshaft retaining nut.

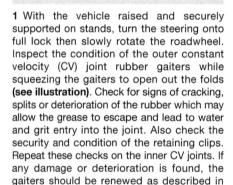

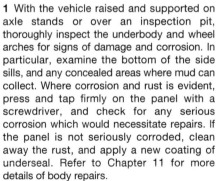

17.2 Lubricate the bonnet lock with grease

17 Hinge and lock lubrication

1 Work around the vehicle and lubricate the hinges of the bonnet, doors and tailgate with a light machine oil.

2 Lightly lubricate the bonnet release mechanism and exposed section of inner cable with a smear of grease **(see illustration)**.

3 Check carefully the security and operation of all hinges, latches and locks, adjusting them where required. Check the operation of the central locking system (if fitted).

4 Check the condition and operation of the tailgate struts, renewing them if either is leaking or no longer able to support the tailgate securely when raised.

18 Roadwheel nut tightness check

1 Where applicable, remove the wheel trims, and slacken the roadwheel nuts slightly.

2 Tighten the nuts to the specified torque, using a torque wrench.

19 Seat belt check

1 Check the seat belts for satisfactory operation and condition. Inspect the webbing for fraying and cuts. Check that they retract smoothly and without binding into their reels.

2 Check that the seat belt mounting bolts are tight, and if necessary tighten them to the specified torque wrench setting.

20 Bodywork, paint and exterior trim check

1 The best time to carry out this check is after the car has been washed, so that any surface blemish or scratch will be clearly evident and not hidden by a film of dirt.
2 Starting at one front corner check the paintwork all around the car, looking for minor scratches or more serious dents. Check all the trim and make sure that it is securely attached over its entire length.
3 Check the security of all door locks, door mirrors, badges, bumpers, front grille and wheel trim. Anything found loose, or in need of further attention should be done with reference to the relevant Chapters of this manual.
4 Rectify any problems noticed with the paintwork or body panels as described in Chapter 11.

21 Road test

Instruments and electrical equipment

1 Check the operation of all instruments and electrical equipment.

2 Make sure that all instruments read correctly, and switch on all electrical equipment in turn, to check that it functions properly.

Steering and suspension

3 Check for any abnormalities in the steering, suspension, handling or road 'feel'.
4 Drive the vehicle, and check that there are no unusual vibrations or noises.
5 Check that the steering feels positive, with no excessive 'sloppiness', or roughness, and check for any suspension noises when cornering and driving over bumps.

Drivetrain

6 Check the performance of the engine, clutch, transmission and driveshafts.
7 Listen for any unusual noises from the engine, clutch and transmission.
8 Make sure that the engine runs smoothly when idling, and that there is no hesitation when accelerating.
9 Check that the clutch action is smooth and progressive, that the drive is taken up smoothly, and that the pedal travel is not excessive. Also listen for any noises when the clutch pedal is depressed.
10 Check that all gears can be engaged smoothly without noise, and that the gear lever action is smooth and not abnormally vague or 'notchy'.

11 Listen for a metallic clicking sound from the front of the vehicle, as the vehicle is driven slowly in a circle with the steering on full-lock. Carry out this check in both directions. If a clicking noise is heard, this indicates wear in a driveshaft joint (see Chapter 8).

Braking system

12 Make sure that the vehicle does not pull to one side when braking, and that the wheels do not lock prematurely when braking hard.
13 Check that there is no vibration through the steering when braking.
14 Check that the handbrake operates correctly, without excessive movement of the lever, and that it holds the vehicle stationary on a slope.
15 Test the operation of the brake servo unit as follows. Depress the footbrake four or five times to exhaust the vacuum, then start the engine. As the engine starts, there should be a noticeable 'give' in the brake pedal as vacuum builds up. Allow the engine to run for at least two minutes, and then switch it off. If the brake pedal is now depressed again, it should be possible to detect a hiss from the servo as the pedal is depressed. After about four or five applications, no further hissing should be heard, and the pedal should feel considerably harder.

Every 20 000 miles

22 Fuel filter renewal

Note: Before starting work, refer to the caution regarding fuel spillage at the start of Section 4.
1 The fuel filter is located on a bracket on the left-hand end of the cylinder head (see illustration).
2 Drain the fuel filter with reference to Section 4.
3 Loosen the clamp bolt retaining the filter to the mounting bracket.
4 Note the location of the fuel lines, then squeeze the tabs and disconnect the quick-release fittings from the inlet and outlet stubs on the filter. The inlet fuel line is the line from the fuel heater, and the outlet fuel line is the line leading to the injection pump.

5 Remove the filter from the retaining bracket and withdraw from the engine compartment. Note the fitted positions of all seals, and use the new ones provided when fitting the new filter.
6 Fit the new filter using a reversal of the removal procedure. Use the new seals provided with the new filter, and tighten the clamp bolt securely. Push the fuel inlet pipe fully onto the stub (the direction of fuel flow is indicated on the top of the filter by arrows), but leave the outlet pipe disconnected for the moment.
7 Prime the fuel filter by depressing the plunger several times, until fuel flows from the filter outlet stub. Reconnect the outlet pipe, ensuring it is pushed fully onto the stub.
8 Refit the air inlet duct. On completion, start the engine (this may take a little longer than usual), and let it idle for about five minutes to

ensure all the air has been bled from the system. While the engine is idling, check carefully for any signs of fuel leakage.

22.1 The fuel filter is located on a bracket at the left-hand end of the cylinder head

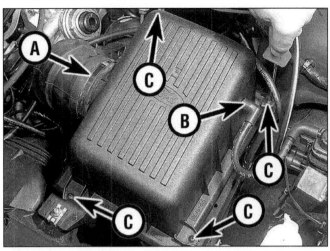

24.1a Loosen the hose clip (A), detach the air inlet duct, unplug the vent pipe (B) and remove the cover retaining screws (C)

24.1b On later models, the air inlet duct may be secured by two wire clips (arrowed)

Every 30 000 miles

23 Valve clearance check and adjustment

This procedure is described in Chapter 2A.

24 Air filter element renewal

1 The air cleaner is located in the left-hand front corner of the engine compartment. First unscrew the screws securing the cover to the air cleaner housing (early models may have spring clips instead). Disconnect the air inlet duct from the cover – depending on model, this will either be a screw-type hose clip, or two over-centre wire clips. Finally, where applicable, pull off the small vent hose from the air cleaner cover (see illustrations).
2 Lift the cover and remove the filter element from the base (see illustration). Note which way round it is fitted. Due to the position of the battery, the element is best removed from the rear of the base.

24.2 Removing the element from the base of the air cleaner

3 Wipe clean the interior surfaces of the cover and base.
4 Insert the new element, noting any direction-of-fitting markings, and making sure that it is seated correctly in the base.
5 Refit the cover and secure with the retaining screws. Reconnect the air inlet duct.

25 Emission control system check

General

1 Of the emission control systems that may be fitted, only the crankcase ventilation system requires regular checking, and even then, the components should require minimal attention.
2 Should it be felt that the other systems are not functioning correctly, the advice of a dealer should be sought.

Crankcase ventilation system

3 The function of the crankcase ventilation system is to reduce the emission of unburned hydrocarbons from the crankcase, and to minimise the formation of oil sludge. By ensuring that a depression is created in the crankcase under most operating conditions, particularly at idle, and by positively inducing fresh air into the system, the oil vapours and 'blow-by' gases collected in the crankcase are drawn from the crankcase, through the air cleaner or oil separator, into the inlet tract, to be burned by the engine during normal combustion.
4 Check that all components of the system are securely fastened, correctly routed (with no kinks or sharp bends to restrict flow) and in sound condition; renew any worn or damaged components.
5 Disconnect the hoses at the rocker cover, and clean if necessary by blowing through with light pressure from an air line. Remove

the hose for thorough cleaning if it is badly congested.
6 If oil leakage is noted, disconnect the various hoses and pipes, and check that all are clear and unblocked. Remove the air cleaner assembly cover, and check that the hose from the cylinder head cover to the air cleaner housing is clear and undamaged.

26 Handbrake adjustment

Pre-1996 drum brake models

1 Chock the front wheels, then jack up the rear of the car and support it on axle stands (see Jacking and vehicle support). Fully release the handbrake.
2 Check that the handbrake cables are correctly routed and secured by the retaining clips at the appropriate points under the vehicle.
3 The handbrake is checked for adjustment by measuring the amount of movement possible in the handbrake adjuster plungers. These are located on the inside face of each rear brake backplate (see illustration). The

26.3a Handbrake adjustment plunger on drum brake models

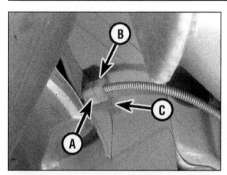

26.3b Handbrake cable adjuster sleeve (A) locknut (B) and lockpin (C)

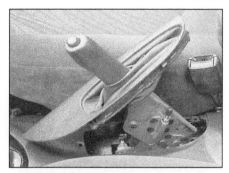

26.10 Unclip the handbrake lever gaiter and . . .

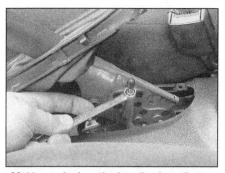

26.11 . . . slacken the handbrake adjuster nut

total movement of the two plungers combined should be between 0.5 and 2.0 mm. If the movement measured is outside of this tolerance, the handbrake is in need of adjustment. Adjustment is made altering the position of the in-line cable adjuster sleeve **(see illustration)**.

4 When adjustment to the handbrake is necessary, a new adjustment sleeve locking pin will be required, and this must therefore be obtained before making the adjustment.

5 To adjust the handbrake, first ensure that it is fully released, then firmly apply the footbrake a few times to ensure that the rear brake adjustment is taken up by the automatic adjusters. Extract the locking pin from the adjuster sleeve, then turn the sleeve to set the combined movement of the plungers within the tolerance range specified (0.5 to 2.0 mm). Turn the locking nut by hand as tight as is possible (two clicks) against the adjustment sleeve. Now grip the locknut with a suitable wrench, and turn it a further two clicks (maximum).

6 Secure the adjustment by inserting the new lock pin.

7 Check that the operation of the handbrake is satisfactory, then lower the vehicle to the ground, apply the handbrake and remove the chocks from the front wheels.

1996-on drum brake models

Caution: If the handbrake is incorrectly adjusted, the rear brake automatic adjustment mechanism will not be able to function correctly. This will lead to the brake shoe-to-drum clearance becoming excessive as the shoe linings wear, resulting in excessive brake pedal travel.

8 Chock the front wheels.

9 Fully release the handbrake then apply the footbrake firmly several times to ensure that the self-adjust mechanism is fully adjusted.

10 Unclip the handbrake lever gaiter to gain access to the adjuster nut on the side of the lever **(see illustration)**.

11 From the fully-released position, pull the handbrake lever up, noting the number of clicks from the ratchet. The handbrake should be fully applied between three and six clicks. If adjustment is necessary, turn the adjusting nut as required until the correct setting is achieved **(see illustration)**. On completion, clip the gaiter back into position. If after adjustment, the handbrake operation is still unsatisfactory, the rear brakes may need to be stripped, cleaned and adjusted (see Chapter 9).

Disc brake models

12 Chock the front wheels, then jack up the

rear of the car and support it on axle stands (see *Jacking and vehicle support*). Fully release the handbrake.

13 Check that the handbrake cables are correctly routed and secured by the retaining clips at the appropriate points under the vehicle.

14 Remove the blanking plug from the rear of the brake carrier plate, just below and to the rear of the brake caliper.

15 With the handbrake released, insert a screwdriver through the blanking plug hole and engage the end of the screwdriver in the teeth of the adjuster wheel. Move the screwdriver up and down to turn the adjuster wheel as necessary, until the wheel is just locked.

16 Now back off the adjuster wheel until the wheel can be turned freely without binding.

17 Repeat this procedure on the other brake assembly, then check the operation of the handbrake. Ensure that both wheels are locked when the handbrake lever is applied, and that both are released, with no trace of binding when the lever is fully released.

18 When all is satisfactory, refit the blanking plugs, and lower the vehicle to the ground. Reapply the handbrake and remove the chocks from the front wheels.

Every 40 000 miles

27 Timing belt and injection pump belt renewal

The procedure is described in Chapter 2A.

Every 3 years, regardless of mileage

28 Brake fluid renewal

⚠ *Warning: Brake hydraulic fluid can harm your eyes and damage painted surfaces, so use extreme caution when handling and pouring it. Do not use fluid that has been*

standing open for some time, as it absorbs moisture from the air. Excess moisture can cause a dangerous loss of braking effectiveness.

1 The procedure is similar to that for the bleeding of the hydraulic system as described in Chapter 9 except that, on models with a conventional braking system, the brake fluid reservoir should be emptied by syphoning, using a clean poultry baster or

similar before starting, and allowance should be made for the old fluid to be expelled when bleeding a section of the circuit. On models fitted with ABS, reduce the fluid level in the reservoir (by syphoning or using a poultry baster), but do not allow the fluid level to drop far enough to allow air into the system – if air enters the ABS hydraulic unit, the unit must be bled using special Ford test equipment (see Chapter 9).

2 Working as described in Chapter 9, open the first bleed screw in the sequence, and pump the brake pedal gently until nearly all the old fluid has been emptied from the master cylinder reservoir. Top-up to the MAX level with new fluid, and continue pumping until only the new fluid remains in the reservoir, and new fluid can be seen emerging from the bleed screw. Tighten the screw, and top the reservoir level up to the MAX level line.

 HAYNES HiNT *Old hydraulic fluid is invariably much darker in colour than the new, making it easy to distinguish the two.*

3 Work through all the remaining bleed screws in the sequence until new fluid can be seen at all of them. Be careful to keep the master cylinder reservoir topped-up to above the MIN level at all times, or air may enter the system and greatly increase the length of the task.

4 When the operation is complete, check that all bleed screws are securely tightened, and that their dust caps are refitted. Wash off all traces of spilt fluid, and recheck the master cylinder reservoir fluid level.

5 Check the operation of the brakes before taking the car on the road.

Every 4 years, regardless of mileage

29 Coolant renewal and pressure cap check

Cooling system draining

⚠️ **Warning: Wait until the engine is cold before starting this procedure. Do not allow antifreeze to come in contact with your skin, or with the painted surfaces of the vehicle. Rinse off spills immediately with plenty of water. Never leave antifreeze lying around in an open container, or in a puddle in the driveway or on the garage floor. Children and pets are attracted by its sweet smell, but antifreeze can be fatal if ingested.**

1 With the engine completely cold, remove the expansion tank filler cap. Turn the cap anti-clockwise, wait until any pressure remaining in the system is released, then unscrew it and lift it off.

2 Where applicable, remove the engine undershield, then position a suitable container beneath the radiator drain screw, at the bottom left-hand corner of the radiator.

3 Slacken the drain screw (a coin is ideal for this – the screw shouldn't be too tight), and allow the coolant to drain into the container **(see illustration)**.

4 When the flow of coolant stops, tighten the radiator drain screw.

5 To drain the entire system, move the container under the cylinder block drain plug (located on the front of the block, next to the dipstick tube) **(see illustration)**. Remove the

plug, and allow the rest of the coolant to drain. On completion, refit and tighten the plug.

6 If the coolant has been drained for a reason other than renewal, then provided it is clean and less than two years old, it can be re-used, though this is not recommended.

Cooling system flushing

7 If coolant renewal has been neglected, or if the antifreeze mixture has become diluted, then in time, the cooling system may gradually lose efficiency, as the coolant passages become restricted due to rust, scale deposits, and other sediment. The cooling system efficiency can be restored by flushing the system clean.

8 The radiator should be flushed independently of the engine, to avoid unnecessary contamination.

Radiator flushing

9 Disconnect the top and bottom hoses and any other relevant hoses from the radiator, with reference to Chapter 3.

10 Insert a garden hose into the radiator top inlet. Direct a flow of clean water through the radiator, and continue flushing until clean water emerges from the radiator bottom outlet.

11 If after a reasonable period, the water still does not run clear, the radiator can be flushed with a good proprietary cleaning agent. It is important that their manufacturer's instructions are followed carefully. If the contamination is particularly bad, insert the hose in the radiator bottom outlet, and reverse-flush the radiator.

Engine flushing

12 Remove the thermostat as described in Chapter 3 then, if the radiator top hose has been disconnected from the engine, temporarily reconnect the hose.

13 With the top and bottom hoses disconnected from the radiator, insert a garden hose into the radiator top hose. Direct a clean flow of water through the engine, and continue flushing until clean water emerges from the radiator bottom hose.

14 On completion of flushing, refit the thermostat and reconnect the hoses with reference to Chapter 3.

Antifreeze mixture

15 When new, the cooling system in the Focus will have been filled with Super Plus 4 antifreeze (which is blue/green), to specification ESD-M97B-49-A. On models from approximately 1998 onwards, the system will have Super Plus 2000 antifreeze (which is orange) to specification WSS-M97 B44-D. The two types of coolant must not be mixed with each other, and should also not be mixed with any other type of coolant.

16 If the vehicle's history (and therefore the quality of the antifreeze in it) is unknown, owners are advised to drain and thoroughly reverse-flush the system, before refilling with fresh coolant mixture. If the Ford antifreeze is used, the coolant can then be left for 6 years (Super Plus 4, blue/green coolant type) or 10 years (Super Plus 2000, orange coolant type).

17 If any antifreeze other than Ford's is to be used, the coolant must be renewed at regular intervals to provide an equivalent degree of protection; the conventional recommendation is to renew the coolant every four years.

18 If the antifreeze used is to Ford's specification, the levels of protection it affords are indicated in the Specifications Section of this Chapter. To give the recommended *standard* mixture ratio for antifreeze, 50% (by volume) of antifreeze must be mixed with 50% of clean, soft water; if you are using any other type of antifreeze, follow its manufacturer's instructions to achieve the correct ratio.

19 It is best to make up slightly more than the system's specified capacity, so that a supply is available for subsequent topping-up. However, note that you are unlikely to fully drain the system at any one time (unless the engine is being completely stripped), and the

29.3 Use a coin to unscrew the radiator drain screw

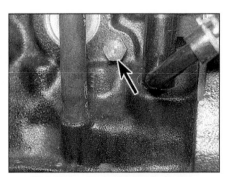
29.5 The cylinder block drain plug (arrowed) is next to the dipstick tube

capacities quoted are therefore slightly academic for routine coolant renewal. As a guide, only two-thirds of the system's total capacity is likely to be needed for coolant renewal.

20 Before adding antifreeze, the cooling system should be completely drained, preferably flushed, and all hoses checked for condition and security. As noted earlier, fresh antifreeze will rapidly find any weaknesses in the system.

21 After filling with antifreeze, a label should be attached to the expansion tank, stating the type and concentration of antifreeze used, and the date installed. Any subsequent topping-up should be made with the same type and concentration of antifreeze.

22 Do not use engine antifreeze in the windscreen/tailgate washer system, as it will damage the vehicle's paintwork. A screen wash additive should be added to the washer system in its maker's recommended quantities.

Cooling system filling

23 Before attempting to fill the cooling system, make sure that all hoses and clips are in good condition, and that the clips are tight. Note that an antifreeze mixture must be used all year round, to prevent corrosion of the engine components. Also check that the cylinder block drain plug is in place and tight.

24 Check whether there is a bleed screw fitted into the radiator top hose – if one is fitted, loosen it now **(see illustration)**.

25 Remove the expansion tank filler cap, and slowly fill the system until the coolant level reaches the MAX mark on the side of the

expansion tank (refer to *Weekly checks*). Refit and tighten the expansion tank filler cap. When coolant emerges from the bleed screw, tighten the screw securely.

26 Start the engine, and allow it to run until it reaches normal operating temperature (until the cooling fan cuts in and out).

27 Stop the engine, and allow it to cool, then re-check the coolant level with reference to *Weekly checks*. Top-up the level if necessary and refit the expansion tank filler cap. Where applicable, refit the engine undershield.

Airlocks

28 If, after draining and refilling the system, symptoms of overheating are found which did not occur previously, then the fault is almost certainly due to trapped air at some point in the system, causing an airlock and restricting the flow of coolant; usually, the air is trapped because the system was refilled too quickly.

29 If an airlock is suspected, first try gently squeezing all visible coolant hoses. A coolant hose which is full of air feels quite different to one full of coolant, when squeezed. After refilling the system, most airlocks will clear once the system has cooled, and been topped up.

30 While the engine is running at operating temperature, switch on the heater and heater fan, and check for heat output. Provided there is sufficient coolant in the system, lack of heat output could be due to an airlock in the system.

31 Airlocks can have more serious effects than simply reducing heater output – a severe airlock could reduce coolant flow around the

29.24 Bleed screw (arrowed) in the radiator top hose

engine. Check that the radiator top hose is hot when the engine is at operating temperature – a top hose which stays cold could be the result of an airlock (or a non-opening thermostat).

32 If the problem persists, stop the engine and allow it to cool down **completely**, before unscrewing the expansion tank filler cap or loosening the hose clips and squeezing the hoses to bleed out the trapped air. In the worst case, the system will have to be at least partially drained (this time, the coolant can be saved for re-use) and flushed to clear the problem.

Pressure (expansion tank) cap check

33 Clean the pressure cap, and inspect the seal inside the cap for damage or deterioration. If there is any sign of damage or deterioration to the seal, fit a new pressure cap.

Notes

Chapter 2 Part A:
Engine in-car repair procedures

Contents

Degrees of difficulty

Easy, suitable for novice with little experience	**Fairly easy,** suitable for beginner with some experience	**Fairly difficult,** suitable for competent DIY mechanic	**Difficult,** suitable for experienced DIY mechanic	**Very difficult,** suitable for expert DIY or professional

Specifications

General

Engine code (type): *

Non-turbo (44 kW), without cat	RTE or RTF
Non-turbo (44 kW), with cat	RTH
Turbo, no intercooler (51 kW), with cat	RVA (TC)
Turbo, intercooler (66 kW), without cat	RFD (TCI)
Turbo, intercooler (66 kW), with cat	RFK (TCI)
Turbo, intercooler (66 kW), with cat, one-piece turbo/manifold	RFS (TCI)

* *Stamped in box 8 ('Motor/Engine') of VIN plate and on left-hand end of cylinder head or of cylinder block/crankcase – refer to 'Vehicle Identification'.*

Capacity	1 753 cc
Bore	82.5 mm
Stroke	82 mm
Compression ratio	21.5:1
Compression pressure (at starter motor cranking speed)	28 to 34 bar
Firing order	1-3-4-2 (No 1 cylinder at timing belt end)
Direction of crankshaft rotation	Clockwise (seen from right-hand side of vehicle)

Maximum power (DIN):

Non-turbo	44 kW (60 PS) @ 4800 rpm
Turbo without intercooler	51 kW (70 PS) @ 4500 rpm
Turbo with intercooler	66 kW (90 PS) @ 4500 rpm

Maximum torque (DIN):

Non-turbo	110 Nm (82 lbf ft) @ 2500 rpm
Turbo without intercooler	135 Nm (101 lbf ft) @ 2500 rpm
Turbo with intercooler	180 Nm (134 lbf ft) @ 2000 rpm

Cylinder block

Cylinder bore diameter:

Class A	82.500 to 82.515 mm
Class B	82.515 to 82.530 mm
Class C	82.660 to 82.675 mm
Class D	82.675 to 82.690 mm
Class E (first rebore)	83.000 to 83.015 mm
Class F (second rebore)	83.500 to 83.515 mm

Crankshaft

Main bearing journal diameter:
- Standard . . . . 53.970 to 53.990 mm
- Undersize (0.25 mm) . . . . 53.720 to 53.740 mm
- Undersize (0.50 mm) . . . . 53.470 to 53.490 mm

Main bearing running clearance . . . . 0.025 to 0.085 mm

Big-end bearing journal diameter:
- Standard . . . . 48.970 to 48.990 mm
- Undersize (0.25 mm) . . . . 48.720 to 48.740 mm
- Undersize (0.50 mm) . . . . 48.470 to 48.490 mm

Big-end bearing running clearance:
- Non-turbo models . . . . 0.016 to 0.074 mm
- Turbo models . . . . 0.025 to 0.085 mm

Crankshaft endfloat:
- Non-turbo models . . . . 0.09 to 0.37 mm
- Turbo models . . . . 0.14 to 0.37 mm

Connecting rod to crank web axial clearance . . . . 0.125 to 0.325 mm

Torque to rotate fitted crankshaft (without connecting rods or pistons) 10 Nm (7 lbf ft) max

Connecting rods

Big-end bore diameter . . . . 52.000 to 52.020 mm
Small-end bore diameter (with bush) . . . . 26.012 to 26.020 mm

Pistons

Diameter (measured at 90° to gudgeon pin bore):
- Class A . . . . 82.461 to 82.479 mm
- Class B . . . . 82.476 to 82.494 mm
- Class C . . . . 82.621 to 82.639 mm
- Class D . . . . 82.636 to 82.654 mm
- Class E (first rebore) . . . . 82.961 to 82.979 mm
- Class F (second rebore) . . . . 83.461 to 83.479 mm

Clearance in bore (new) . . . . 0.021 to 0.054 mm
Piston protrusion at TDC . . . . 0.500 to 0.840 mm
Gudgeon pin diameter . . . . 25.96 to 26.00 mm

Piston rings

Clearance in groove:
- Except TC engine:
  - Top compression . . . . 0.090 to 0.122 mm
  - Second compression . . . . 0.050 to 0.082 mm
  - Oil control . . . . 0.030 to 0.062 mm
- TC engine:
  - Top compression . . . . 0.000 to 0.040 mm
  - Second compression . . . . 0.070 to 0.102 mm
  - Oil control . . . . 0.050 to 0.080 mm

End gap (fitted):
- Top compression . . . . 0.30 to 0.50 mm
- Second compression . . . . 0.30 to 0.50 mm
- Oil control . . . . 0.250 to 0.580 mm

Camshaft

Endfloat . . . . 0.100 to 0.240 mm
Bearing journal diameter . . . . 27.960 to 27.980 mm
Bearing running clearance . . . . 0.020 to 0.079 mm

Valve timing

Inlet opens . . . . 6° BTDC
Inlet closes . . . . 32° ABDC
Exhaust opens . . . . 57° BTDC
Exhaust closes . . . . 7° ATDC

Valve clearances (cold)

Inlet . . . . 0.35 ± 0.05 mm
Exhaust . . . . 0.50 ± 0.05 mm
Tappet shim thicknesses available . . . . 3.00 to 4.75 mm in increments of 0.05 mm

Cylinder head gasket
Selection according to piston protrusion:
0.500 to 0.680 mm	1.36 mm thick (2 tooth marks)
0.681 to 0.740 mm	1.42 mm thick (3 tooth marks)
0.741 to 0.840 mm	1.52 mm thick (4 tooth marks)

Cylinder head
Distortion limit	0.08 mm overall (skimming not permitted)
Swirl chamber projection	0.000 to 0.061 mm

Valve tappet bore diameter:
Standard	35.000 to 35.030 mm
Oversize	35.500 to 35.530 mm

Valve guide bore diameter:
Standard	8.000 to 8.025 mm
First oversize	8.263 to 8.288 mm
Second oversize	8.463 to 8.488 mm
Valve spring free length	43 mm approx.

Lubrication system
Oil pressure – @ oil temperature of 80 °C:	Idle speed	2000 rpm
Oil pressure switch with black cover – engines up to 7/1998	0.75 bar	1.5 bar
Oil pressure switch with green cover – engines from 8/1998	0.5 bar	1.3 bar
Oil pressure relief valve setting	2 to 4 bars	
Oil pump inner-to-outer rotor maximum clearance	0.174 mm	

Torque wrench settings
	Nm	lbf ft
Alternator mounting bracket-to-cylinder block bolts	42	31
Auxiliary shaft toothed pulley bolt	45	33
Auxiliary shaft oil seal housing	23	17
Auxiliary shaft thrustplate bolts	9	7
Big-end bearing cap bolts:		
Stage 1	25	18
Stage 2 (tighten bolt through angle of)	60°	60°
Stage 3 (**further tighten** bolt through angle of)	20°	20°
Camshaft bearing cap nuts	20 to 23	15 to 17
Camshaft toothed pulley fasteners – up to 1996 model year:		
Pulley-to-hub bolts	9	7
Pulley hub-to-camshaft centre bolt	30	22
Camshaft toothed pulley-to-camshaft bolt – 1997 model year onwards:		
8 mm bolt – engines up to 7/1998	35	26
10 mm bolt – engines 7/1998 onwards	48	35
Coolant pipe-to-sump bolts	25	18
Coolant pipe bracket nut	27	20
Crankshaft left-hand oil seal carrier bolts	20	15
Crankshaft pulley-to-toothed pulley flange bolts	35	26
Crankshaft speed/position sensor bracket bolt	21	16
Crankshaft toothed pulleys' centre bolt:		
Stage 1	150	111
Stage 2 (**slacken** bolt through angle of)	90°	90°
Stage 3 (**tighten** bolt to)	120	88
Stage 4 (**further tighten** bolt through angle of)	60°	60°
Cylinder block oilway blanking plugs	22	16
Cylinder head bolts:		
Stage 1	10	7
Stage 2	100	74
Stage 3 (after waiting 3 minutes):		
a) **Slacken** No 1 bolt through angle of	180°	
b) **Tighten** No 1 bolt to	70	52
c) **Further tighten** No 1 bolt through angle of	120°	
Repeat Stage 3 with each of the remaining bolts in sequence		
Cylinder head cover bolts	5	4
Driveshaft intermediate bearing bracket-to-cylinder block bolts	48	35
Driveshaft intermediate bearing flange nuts	26	19
Earth lead-to-cylinder block retaining bolt	40	30
Engine front plate/timing belt inner shield bolt	24	18
Engine lifting eye-to-engine mounting/power steering pump bracket bolts	23	17
Engine mounting/power steering pump bracket-to-cylinder block bolts	47	34
Engine oil drain plug	See Chapter 1	

Torque wrench settings (continued)

	Nm	lbf ft
Engine mountings:		
Brace to transmission front bracket	50	37
Front right-hand brace nuts/bolts	69	51
Front right-hand mounting nuts to inner wing	84	62
Left-hand mounting to side member	69	51
Mounting-to-block bolts	69	51
Mounting-to-front crossmember bolts	84	62
Rear bracket-to-transmission bolts	50	37
Right-hand rear mounting:		
Large nut/bolts	83	61
Three smaller nuts	69	51
Roll restrictor link bolts	120	89
Exhaust Gas Recirculation (EGR) pipe bolts	23	17
Exhaust downpipe/catalytic converter to manifold/turbocharger	40	30
Flywheel:		
Stage 1	18	13
Stage 2 (**tighten** bolt through angle of)	45°	45°
Stage 3 (**further tighten** bolt through angle of)	45°	45°
Fuel injection pump drivebelt tensioner centre bolt	45	33
Fuel injection pump toothed pulley-to-hub bolts	23	17
Fuel injection pump toothed pulley hub-to-pump shaft nut	Not available	
Gearshift stabiliser bar bolt	55	41
Inlet and exhaust manifold studs-to-cylinder head	10 maximum	7 maximum
Inlet and exhaust manifold nuts and bolts	24	18
Main bearing cap bolts:		
Stage 1	27	20
Stage 2 (**tighten** bolt through angle of)	75°	75°
Oil baffle plate mounting nuts	20	15
Oil cooler mounting bolt	70	51.5
Oil cooler mounting bracket bolts	23 to 25	17 to 18
Oil dipstick tube bracket mounting bolt	10	7
Oil pressure warning light switch	20	15
Oil pump:		
Except TCI engine	18	13
TCI engine	24	18
Oil pump pick-up pipe bracket bolts	22	16
Power steering line-to-body bracket bolts	10	7
Retaining plate for fuel filter and fuel heater	20	15
Sump bolts	11	8
Timing belt automatic tensioner centre bolt	50	37
Timing belt cover bolts	8	6
Timing belt idler pulley bolt:		
Up to 1996 model year	45	33
1997 model year onwards – eccentric idler pulley bolt	20	15
Timing belt inner shield/engine front plate bolt	24	18
Timing belt tensioner backplate bolts	9	7
Timing belt/drivebelt housing fasteners	24	18
Timing pin blanking plug	24	18
Transmission-to-engine mounting bolts	40	30
Turbocharger:		
Turbocharger-to-exhaust manifold mounting nuts – early models	38	28
Turbocharger mounting bracket-to-turbocharger bolts	23	17
Turbocharger mounting bracket-to-cylinder block bolt	47	34
Oil return hose clamp	5	4
Oil feed line banjo union bolts	18	13
Oil feed line mounting bracket bolt	23	17

1 General information

How to use this Chapter

This Part of Chapter 2 is devoted to repair procedures possible while the engine is still installed in the vehicle, and includes only the Specifications relevant to those procedures. Since these procedures are based on the assumption that the engine is installed in the vehicle, if the engine has been removed from the vehicle and mounted on a stand, some of the preliminary dismantling steps outlined will not apply.

Information concerning engine/trans- mission removal and refitting and engine overhaul, can be found in Part B of this Chapter, which also includes the Specifications relevant to those procedures.

General description

While various different diesel engines have been fitted to the Escort, most differences lie essentially in whether the engine is turbocharged or normally-aspirated, and in the emission control systems, updated to keep pace with the introduction of ever-stricter anti-pollution legislation.

When the Mk 5 Escort was launched in September 1990, the only diesel engine available was the non-turbo unit. In 1993, the first turbo-diesel Escort appeared, badged the TD, fitted with an intercooler, this ran alongside the non-turbo model. In March 1996, a new turbo-diesel unit without an intercooler was introduced – this now became the TD model, with the original turbo-diesel engine (with an intercooler) re-badged the TDi (Turbo-diesel intercooler). By now, the non-turbo model was about to be phased out of the Escort passenger car range – the remaining two turbo-diesel units were further re-badged as Endura-DE at this time. Ford's system of engine naming refers to the two turbo-diesels as the Endura-DE (TC) and Endura-DE (TCI), with the I signifying the presence of an intercooler. Since the Escort model designation TD could apply to an engine with or without an intercooler, throughout this manual, we will refer to the turbo engines as follows:

a) Turbocharged engine with an intercooler – TCI engine
b) Turbocharged engine without intercooler – TC engine

The new Endura-DE designation indicates only minor mechanical changes, with modified timing belt tensioner components and manifolds – the exhaust manifold incorporates the (previously separate) turbocharger, while the intake manifold incorporates the (previously separate) Exhaust Gas Recirculation (EGR) valve.

Configuration

The engine is of four-cylinder, in-line type, mounted transversely at the front of the vehicle, with the (clutch and) transmission on its left-hand end. It is a four-stroke compression-ignition (diesel) unit, with conventional indirect injection using pintle-type injectors spraying fuel into separate swirl chambers fitted into the cylinder head. On turbo models, its power output is boosted by the fitment of a turbocharger, and further boosted with an intercooler on many models. Both the cylinder block and the cylinder head are of cast iron, while (on all except the earliest models) the sump is of cast aluminium alloy.

Two toothed drivebelts are fitted – the inboard one to drive the fuel injection pump, and the outboard one (the timing belt) to drive the single overhead camshaft, the (oil pump) auxiliary shaft and the water pump. The valves are operated by bucket tappets. Valve clearance adjustment is by means of a shim located in a recess in the top of each tappet. The cam lobes bear directly on the shims and tappets, which in turn bear directly on the valves. The inlet and exhaust valves are each closed by coil springs; they operate in guides which are shrink-fitted into the cylinder head, as are the valve seat inserts. The camshaft runs in five renewable shell bearings and drives the braking system vacuum pump via a pushrod operated by an eccentric on the camshaft's left-hand end.

The crankshaft runs in five main bearings, the centre main bearing's upper half incorporating thrustwashers to control crankshaft endfloat. The connecting rods rotate on horizontally-split bearing shells at their big-ends. The pistons are attached to the connecting rods by gudgeon pins which are fully floating in the connecting rod small-end eyes and are retained by circlips. The aluminium alloy pistons are fitted with three piston rings: two compression rings and an oil control ring. Pistons, gudgeon pins and connecting rods are carefully selected to be of matching weight. The connecting rods are also graded by length. After manufacture, the cylinder bores and piston skirts are measured and classified into four grades, which must be carefully matched together to ensure the correct piston/cylinder clearance; two oversizes are available to permit reboring.

The water pump is bolted to the right-hand end of the cylinder block, inboard of the timing belt and is driven with the (oil pump) auxiliary shaft and camshaft by the timing belt.

The crankshaft toothed pulley incorporates a flange for the crankshaft pulley which drives the alternator, power steering pump and air conditioning compressor (where fitted), via an auxiliary drivebelt.

When working on this engine, note that Torx-type (both male and female heads) and hexagon socket (Allen head) fasteners are widely used; a good selection of bits, with the necessary adapters, will be required, so that these can be unscrewed without damage and, on reassembly, tightened to the torque wrench settings specified.

Lubrication system

The oil pump is mounted externally, at the rear of the engine, and is driven by the auxiliary shaft. The pump is an eccentric-rotor trochoidal type which draws oil through a strainer located in the sump and forces it through an externally-mounted full-flow cartridge-type filter – an oil cooler is fitted to the oil filter mounting, so that clean oil entering the engine's galleries is cooled by the main engine cooling system. From the filter, the oil is pumped into a main gallery in the cylinder block/crankcase, from where it is distributed to the crankshaft (main bearings) and cylinder head. A separate supply serves the turbocharger through an external line.

The big-end bearings are supplied with oil via internal drillings in the crankshaft. Each piston crown is cooled by a spray of oil directed at its underside by a jet. These jets are fed by passages off the crankshaft oil supply galleries.

While the crankshaft and camshaft bearings and the tappets receive a pressurised supply, the camshaft lobes and valves are lubricated by splash, as are all other engine components.

Valve clearances – general

It is necessary for a clearance to exist between the tip of each valve stem and the valve operating mechanism, to allow for the expansion of the various components as the engine reaches normal operating temperature. These engines are fitted with conventional tappets and shims. These require that the clearances be checked at regular intervals (see Chapter 1) and may need the shims to be changed to compensate for wear, as described in Section 15 of this Chapter.

2 Repair operations possible with the engine in the vehicle

The following major repair operations can be accomplished without removing the engine from the vehicle. However, owners should note that any operation involving the removal of the sump requires careful forethought, depending on the level of skill and the tools and facilities available; refer to the relevant text for details.

a) Compression pressure – testing
b) Cylinder head cover – removal and refitting
c) Timing belt covers – removal and refitting
d) Timing belt and injection pump drivebelt – renewal
e) Timing belt/drivebelt tensioners and toothed pulleys – removal and refitting
f) Camshaft oil seal – renewal
g) Camshaft and tappets – removal and refitting
h) Auxiliary shaft oil seal – renewal
i) Cylinder head – removal, overhaul and refitting
j) Cylinder head and pistons – decarbonising
k) Sump – removal and refitting
l) Crankshaft oil seals – renewal
m) Oil pump – removal and refitting
n) Piston/connecting rod assemblies – removal and refitting (but see note below)
o) Flywheel – removal and refitting
p) Engine/transmission mountings – removal and refitting

Clean the engine compartment and the exterior of the engine with some type of degreaser before any work is done. It will make the job easier and will help to keep dirt out of the internal areas of the engine.

Depending on the components involved, it may be helpful to remove the bonnet, to improve access to the engine as repairs are performed (refer to Chapter 11 if necessary). Cover the wings to prevent damage to the paint; special covers are available, but an old bedspread or blanket will also work.

If vacuum, exhaust, oil or coolant leaks develop, indicating a need for component/gasket or seal replacement, the repairs can generally be made with the engine in the vehicle. The intake and exhaust manifold gaskets, sump gasket, crankshaft oil seals and cylinder head gasket are all accessible with the engine in place.

Exterior components such as the intake and exhaust manifolds, the sump, the oil pump, the water pump, the starter motor, the alternator and the fuel system components can be removed for repair with the engine in place.

Since the cylinder head can be removed without lifting out the engine, camshaft and valve component servicing can also be accomplished with the engine in the vehicle, as can renewal of the timing belt and toothed pulleys.

In extreme cases caused by a lack of necessary equipment, repair or renewal of piston rings, pistons, connecting rods and big-end bearings is possible with the engine in the vehicle. However, this practice is not recommended, because of the cleaning and preparation work that must be done to the components involved and because of the amount of preliminary dismantling work required – these operations are therefore covered in Part B of this Chapter.

3 Compression and leakdown tests – description and interpretation

Compression test

Note: *A compression tester specifically designed for diesel engines must be used for this test.*

1 When engine performance is down, or if misfiring occurs which cannot be attributed to a fault in the fuel system, a compression test can provide diagnostic clues as to the engine's condition. If the test is performed regularly it can give warning of trouble before any other symptoms become apparent.

2 A compression tester specifically intended for diesel engines must be used, because of the higher pressures involved. The tester is connected to an adapter which screws into the glow plug or injector hole. It is unlikely to be worthwhile buying such a tester for occasional use, but it may be possible to borrow or hire one – if not, have the test performed by a garage.

3 Unless specific instructions to the contrary are supplied with the tester, observe the following points:

a) *The battery must be in a good state of charge, the air filter must be clean and the engine should be at normal operating temperature.*

b) *All the injectors or glow plugs should be*

removed before starting the test. If removing the injectors, also remove the fire seal washers (which must be renewed when the injectors are refitted – see Chapter 4A), otherwise they may be blown out.

c) *It is advisable to disconnect the stop solenoid on the pump, to reduce the amount of fuel discharged as the engine is cranked.*

4 There is no need to hold the accelerator pedal down during the test, because a diesel engine's air inlet is not throttled.

5 The actual compression pressures measured are not as important as the balance between cylinders. All cylinders should produce very similar pressures; any difference greater than 10% indicates the existence of a fault.

6 The cause of poor compression is less easy to establish on a diesel engine than on a petrol one. The effect of introducing oil into the cylinders ('wet' testing) is not conclusive, because there is a risk that the oil will sit in the swirl chamber or in the recess on the piston crown instead of passing to the rings. However, the following can be used as a rough guide to diagnosis:

7 The compression should build up quickly in a healthy engine; low compression on the first stroke, followed by gradually increasing pressure on successive strokes, indicates worn piston rings. A low compression reading on the first stroke, which does not build up during successive strokes, indicates leaking valves or a blown head gasket (a cracked head could also be the cause). Deposits on the undersides of the valve heads can also cause low compression.

8 A low reading from two adjacent cylinders is almost certainly due to the head gasket having blown between them; the presence of coolant in the engine oil will confirm this.

9 If one cylinder is about 20 percent lower than the others and the engine has a slightly rough idle, a worn camshaft lobe could be the cause.

10 If the compression is unusually high, the combustion chambers are probably coated with carbon deposits. If this is the case, the cylinder head should be removed and decarbonised.

Leakdown test

11 A leakdown test measures the rate at which compressed air is lost that has been fed into the cylinder. It is an alternative to a compression test and in many ways it is better, since the escaping air provides easy identification of where pressure loss is occurring (piston rings, valves or head gasket).

12 The equipment needed for leakdown testing is unlikely to be available to the home mechanic. If poor compression is suspected, have the test performed by a suitably-equipped garage.

4 Top Dead Centre (TDC) for No 1 piston – locating

General

1 It is useful for several servicing procedures to be able to position the engine at Top Dead Centre (TDC). The TDC position is the highest point in its travel up-and-down its cylinder bore that each piston reaches as the crankshaft rotates. While each piston reaches TDC both at the top of the compression stroke and again at the top of the exhaust stroke, for the purpose of timing the engine, TDC refers to the No 1 piston position at the top of its compression stroke. No 1 piston and cylinder are at the right-hand (timing belt) end of the engine (right-and left-hand are always quoted as seen from the driver's seat). Note that the crankshaft rotates clockwise when viewed from the right-hand side of the vehicle. Proceed as follows.

Locating TDC

Note: *A timing pin and, on engines with a timing belt automatic tensioner, a camshaft aligning tool will be required for this procedure (see text).*

2 Disconnect the battery negative (earth) lead (refer to Chapter 5A) unless the starter motor is to be used to turn the engine.

3 Apply the handbrake, then jack up the front of the vehicle and support it on axle stands (see *Jacking and vehicle support*). If the engine is to be turned using the right-hand front roadwheel with top gear engaged, it is only necessary to raise the right-hand front roadwheel off the ground.

4 Where necessary, remove the engine undershield for access to the crankshaft pulley and bolt.

5 It is best to rotate the crankshaft using a spanner applied to the crankshaft pulley bolt; however, it is possible also to use the starter motor (switched on either by an assistant using the ignition key, or by using a remote starter switch) to bring the engine close to TDC, then finish with a spanner. If the starter is used, be sure to disconnect the battery leads immediately it is no longer required. Alternatively, remove the glow plugs as described in Chapter 5B – this will enable the engine to be turned easily with a spanner.

Up to March 1996

Timing belt mechanical tensioner

Note: *Engines fitted to early models can be identified by removing the timing belt outer cover (see Section 9) – the camshaft toothed pulley is secured to its hub by four small bolts; the hub being secured to the camshaft itself by a large centre bolt – as shown in illustration 10.29. The timing belt mechanical tensioner itself is fitted with an external coil spring.*

6 Remove the timing belt outer covers as described in Section 9.

4.8 Disconnect the breather hoses . . .

4.9 . . . then unbolt and remove the cylinder head cover

4.10 Offset slot (arrowed) in camshaft left-hand end – note larger segment uppermost

7 The piston of No 1 cylinder must now be positioned just before top dead centre (TDC). To do this, have an assistant turn the crankshaft until the timing hole in the camshaft toothed pulley is aligned with the corresponding hole in the cylinder head and the slot in the injection pump toothed pulley is in the 11 o'clock position. Turn the crankshaft slightly anti-clockwise from this position (viewed from the right-hand end of the engine).

March 1996 onwards

Timing belt automatic tensioner

Note: *In addition to the points noted in Section 1 of this Chapter, engines fitted to later models can be identified by removing the timing belt outer cover (see Section 9) – the camshaft toothed pulley has five spokes and is secured to the camshaft by a single bolt – as shown in illustration 10.41. The timing belt automatic tensioner no longer has an external coil spring.*

8 Disconnect the crankcase breather hoses from the cylinder head cover **(see illustration)**. Plug the rear hose's opening with clean rag to prevent dirt or other objects falling into the turbocharger, where applicable.

9 Unbolt the cylinder head cover and retrieve the gasket **(see illustration)**.

10 The piston of No 1 cylinder must now be positioned just before top dead centre (TDC). To do this, have an assistant turn the crankshaft until the slot in the left-hand end of the camshaft is parallel with the upper surface of the cylinder head. Note that the slot is slightly offset, so make sure that the larger semi-circular segment is uppermost. Turn the crankshaft slightly anti-clockwise from this position (viewed from the right-hand end of the engine) **(see illustration)**.

All engines

11 Unscrew the blanking plug from the right-hand side front of the engine cylinder block **(see illustration)**. Especially on later models with air conditioning, access is greatly improved by removing the alternator as described in Chapter 5A. Take care not to drop the blanking plug as it is unscrewed – it tends to wedge itself in the alternator bracket otherwise.

12 A timing pin (Ford service tool 21-104 – now 303-193), obtainable from Ford dealers or a tool supplier) must now be inserted and tightened into the hole. If necessary, a home-made pin can be made from an M10 bolt cut to a length of 47.5 mm from beneath its head to the tip; however it will be necessary to grind and slot the head to allow it to be inserted. If difficulty is experienced in using this modified bolt as a timing pin when inserted, it will be necessary to grind the first 36 mm of the threaded length down to a diameter of 6 mm **(see illustrations)**.

13 With the timing pin in position, turn the crankshaft slowly clockwise until the specially machined surface on the crank web just touches the timing pin. No 1 piston is now at TDC on its compression stroke.

14 On engines with a mechanical tensioner, it should now be possible to insert a timing pin

(Ford service tool 23-019 – now 310-018) through the camshaft toothed pulley timing hole and into the cylinder head hole. If the Ford special tool is not available, a 6 mm drill bit will serve as an adequate substitute. **Note:** *The camshaft aligning tool described below is equally applicable to these earlier engines, but will of course require the removal of the cylinder head cover to establish TDC.*

15 On engines with an automatic tensioner, obtain Ford service tool 21-162B (now 303-376), or fabricate a substitute from a strip of metal 5 mm thick (while the strip's thickness is critical, its length and width are not, but should be approximately 180 to 230 mm by 20 to 30 mm). The tool should slip snugly into the slot while resting on the cylinder head mating surface **(see illustration)**.

16 On all engines, remove the timing belt covers (see Section 9) and insert Ford timing

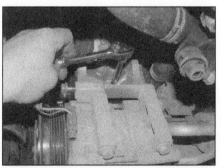

4.11 Unscrewing the timing pin blanking plug

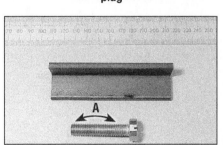

4.12b Home-made tools for setting the valve timing

A Head of bolt and area indicated will need grinding to allow the timing pin to be inserted

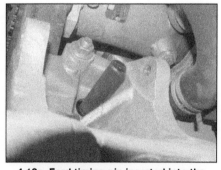

4.12a Ford timing pin inserted into the timing hole (seen from below)

4.15 Home-made camshaft aligning tool inserted in the offset slot

4.16 Timing 'pin' inserted through the injection pump toothed pulley

pin 23-019/310-018 (or 6 mm drill bit) through the injection pump toothed pulley timing hole, down the slot in the pulley hub and into the hole in the pump body **(see illustration)**.

17 If any of the timing pins cannot be fitted, reset the valve timing as described in Section 10.

18 Once work is complete, remove the timing pins and (where applicable) the camshaft aligning tool, then refit the blanking plug, tightening it to its specified torque wrench setting. Refit all removed components referring to the relevant Chapters.

Caution: NEVER use a timing pin (or the camshaft aligning tool) as a means of locking the crankshaft (or camshaft) – they are not strong enough for this and will shear off. Always ensure that all timing pins are removed before the crankshaft pulley bolt (or similar fasteners) is slackened or tightened.

5.2 Removing the cylinder head cover

6.2a Inlet manifold plastic upper section and mounting bolts

5 Cylinder head cover – removal and refitting

Removal

1 Disconnect the two crankcase breather hoses from the left-hand end of the cylinder head cover. Plug the rear hose's opening with clean rag to prevent dirt or other objects falling into the turbocharger (where applicable). On models with air conditioning, one of the power steering hoses runs across the cylinder head cover, and will need to be moved aside.

2 Unscrew the mounting bolts and withdraw the cylinder head cover **(see illustration)**. Check the gasket and renew it if necessary.

3 Check that the sealing faces are undamaged, and that the rubber seal at each retaining bolt is serviceable; renew any worn or damaged seals.

Refitting

4 On refitting, clean the cover and cylinder head gasket faces carefully, then fit the gasket to the cover, ensuring that it locates correctly in the cover grooves **(see illustration)**.

5 Refit the cover to the cylinder head, then insert the rubber seal at each bolt location – apply a thin smear of engine oil to each seal and to the gasket to help it seat. Start all bolts finger-tight, ensuring that the gasket remains seated in its groove.

5.4 Check that the cover gasket is correctly located

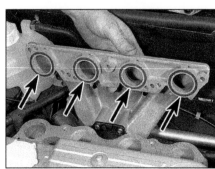

6.2b Removing the upper section of the inlet manifold – note O-ring seals (arrowed)

6 Tighten the cover bolts evenly to the specified torque wrench setting.

7 Reconnect the crankcase breather hoses.

6 Inlet manifold – removal and refitting

Removal

1 On TCI engines, remove the intercooler (see Chapter 4A) – unbolt and remove completely the intercooler mounting brackets and the intercooler/inlet manifold ducting. Pack the turbocharger opening with clean rag to prevent dirt or other objects falling in.

2 On non-turbo engines, loosen the clip and disconnect the air inlet duct from the inlet manifold. Undo the retaining bolts, lift the plastic upper section clear of the inlet manifold and collect the four O-ring seals from the grooves in the mating face **(see illustrations)**. If required, the inlet duct connector can be detached from the upper section by unscrewing the four retaining bolts.

3 Disconnect the Exhaust Gas Recirculation (EGR) pipe to separate the inlet manifold from the exhaust manifold. On early models, either unscrew the two bolts securing the pipe to the valve and withdraw the pipe with the inlet manifold, or unscrew the three bolts to separate the pipe from the inlet manifold. On later models, disconnect the vacuum hose from the EGR valve, then unscrew the two bolts securing the pipe to the exhaust manifold, and withdraw the pipe with the inlet manifold.

4 Unscrew the nuts and bolts securing the manifold to the cylinder head and withdraw it. Take care not to damage vulnerable components such as the EGR pipe and valve as the manifold assembly is manoeuvred out of the engine compartment.

Refitting

5 Refitting is the reverse of the removal procedure, noting the following points:

a) When using a scraper and solvent to remove all traces of old gasket material and sealant from the manifold and cylinder head, be careful not to scratch or damage the material of either; while the cylinder head is of cast iron, the manifold is of aluminium alloy and requires care. If the gasket was leaking, have the mating surfaces checked for warpage at an automotive machine shop. While it may be possible to have the cylinder head manifold surface skimmed if necessary, to remove any distortion, the manifold must be renewed if it is found to be warped, cracked (check with special care around the mounting points for components such as the EGR pipe) or otherwise faulty.

b) Provided the relevant mating surfaces are clean and flat, a new gasket will be sufficient to ensure the joint is gas-tight.

Do not *use any kind of silicone-based sealant on any part of the fuel system or inlet manifold.*
c) *Fit a new gasket, then locate the manifold on the head and install the nuts and bolts.*
d) *Tighten the nuts/bolts in three or four equal steps to the torque listed in this Chapter's Specifications. Work from the centre outwards, to avoid warping the manifold.*
e) *On non-turbo models, locate new ring seals into the grooves in the plastic upper section prior to fitting it into position and tightening the bolts.*

7 Exhaust manifold –
removal, inspection and refitting

> ⚠ **Warning: The engine must be completely cool before beginning this procedure.**

Note: *For all turbo engines, this procedure incorporates the removal and refitting of the turbocharger. On early models (up to March 1996), the turbocharger can be separated from the manifold once the assembly has been removed from the engine. On later models (March 1996 onwards), the turbo-charger is an integral part of the manifold.*

Note: *In addition to the new gaskets and any other parts, tools or facilities needed to carry out this operation, a new plastic guide sleeve will be required on reassembly.*

Manifold without turbocharger and non-turbo models

Removal

1 On turbo models, remove the intercooler (see Chapter 4A) – unbolt and remove completely the intercooler mounting brackets and the intercooler/inlet manifold ducting. Pack the turbocharger opening with clean rag to prevent dirt or other objects falling in.
2 Disconnect the crankcase breather hose from the rear left-hand end of the cylinder head cover. Plug the hose opening with clean rag to prevent dirt or other objects falling into the turbocharger, where applicable.
3 Disconnect the vacuum hose from the Exhaust Gas Recirculation (EGR) valve.
4 Disconnect the EGR pipe to separate the exhaust manifold from the inlet manifold. Either unscrew the three bolts securing the pipe to the inlet manifold and withdraw the pipe (and valve) with the exhaust manifold, or unbolt the pipe and valve as an assembly from both manifolds.
5 On turbo models, disconnect the battery negative (earth) lead – see Chapter 5A, Section 1. Release the hose clips securing the rubber inlet duct to the turbocharger and air cleaner/air mass meter, and remove the inlet duct **(see illustration)**. Pack the turbocharger opening with clean rag to prevent dirt or other objects falling in.

7.5 Removing the rubber inlet duct

6 On turbo models, unscrew the banjo bolt securing the oil feed line to the turbocharger. Collect the copper washer on each side of the union – these must be renewed as a matter of course whenever they are disturbed **(see illustration)**.
7 On turbo models, slacken the hose clip securing the oil return hose and disconnect the hose from the return pipe on the turbocharger. Disconnect also the vacuum line to the turbocharger wastegate.
8 On turbo models, unscrew the bolt(s) securing the turbocharger mounting bracket to the turbocharger or to the cylinder block/crankcase.
On all models,
9 On all models, unscrew the nuts to disconnect the exhaust system front downpipe.
10 On all models, unscrew the nuts and bolts securing the exhaust manifold to the cylinder head and withdraw it. Take care not to

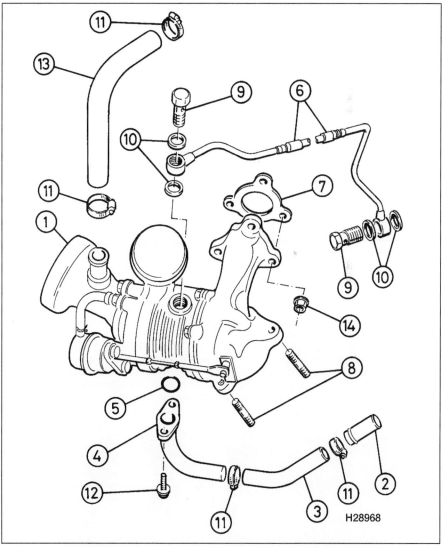

7.6 Turbocharger and associated components – separate unit

1 Turbocharger	5 O-ring	8 Stud	11 Hose clamp
2 Oil drain pipe	6 Oil feed	9 Union bolt	12 Screw
3 Oil return hose	pipe	10 Copper	13 Vent hose
4 Oil drain	7 Inlet gasket	washer	14 Nut

damage vulnerable components such as the EGR pipe and valve as the manifold/ turbocharger assembly is manoeuvred out of the engine compartment.

11 On turbo models, the turbocharger can be separated from the manifold after removing the three mounting nuts. Discard the gasket – this must be renewed on reassembly.

Inspection

Note: *Due to the Positive Crankcase Ventilation system's being routed through the turbocharger, it is quite normal to see small deposits of oil in the compressor. The turbocharger oil seals will normally only fail if the turbocharger bearings are badly worn.*

12 Use a scraper to remove all traces of old gasket material and carbon deposits from the manifold and cylinder head mating surfaces. If the gasket was leaking, have the manifold checked for warpage at an automotive machine shop, and have it resurfaced if necessary.

13 Provided both mating surfaces are clean and flat, a new gasket will be sufficient to ensure the joint is gas-tight. Do not use any kind of exhaust sealant upstream of the catalytic converter.

14 On early models, note that the downpipe is secured to the manifold by two bolts, with a coil spring, spring seat and self-locking nut on each. On refitting, tighten the nuts until they stop on the bolt shoulders; the pressure of the springs will then suffice to make a leakproof joint.

15 Do not overtighten the nuts to cure a leak – the bolts will shear; renew the gasket and the springs if a leak is found. The bolts themselves are secured by spring clips to the manifold and can be renewed easily if damaged.

Refitting

16 Refitting is the reverse of the removal procedure, noting the following points:
a) *Fit a new gasket to the exhaust manifold. Where removed, refit the turbocharger, tightening its mounting nuts to the specified torque wrench setting.*
b) *Position a new gasket over the manifold studs, and fit a new plastic guide sleeve to the stud nearest to the timing belt, so that the manifold will be correctly located.*

Do not refit the manifold without this sleeve.
c) *Refit the manifold and finger-tighten the mounting nuts and bolts.*
d) *Working from the centre out and in three or four equal steps, tighten the nuts and bolts to the specified torque wrench setting.*
e) *Refit the remaining parts in the reverse order of removal. Tighten all fasteners to the specified torque wrench settings.*
f) *Fit new copper washers to the turbocharger oil feed line banjo union, and tighten the bolt to the specified torque wrench setting.*
g) *Run the engine and check for exhaust leaks.*

Manifold with integral turbocharger

Removal

17 Remove the intercooler (see Chapter 4A) – unbolt and remove completely the intercooler mounting brackets and the intercooler/inlet manifold ducting. Pack the turbocharger opening with clean rag to prevent dirt or other objects falling in.

18 Disconnect the crankcase breather hose from the rear left-hand end of the cylinder head cover. Plug the hose opening with clean rag to prevent dirt or other objects falling into the turbocharger.

19 Disconnect the vacuum hose from the Exhaust Gas Recirculation (EGR) valve.

20 Unbolt the EGR pipe from the exhaust manifold and from the inlet manifold.

21 Disconnect the battery negative (earth) lead – see Chapter 5A, Section 1. Slacken the hose clip securing the rubber inlet duct to the turbocharger. Unplugging the electrical connector and releasing the two clips at the air cleaner assembly, remove the air mass meter and the rubber inlet duct. Pack the turbocharger opening with clean rag to prevent dirt or other objects falling in.

22 Unscrew the banjo bolt securing the oil feed line to the turbocharger. Collect the copper washer on each side of the union – these must be renewed as a matter of course whenever they are disturbed.

23 Slacken the hose clip securing the oil return hose, and disconnect the hose from the

return pipe on the turbocharger. Disconnect also the vacuum line to the turbocharger wastegate.

24 Unscrew the nuts to disconnect the catalytic converter from the turbocharger.

25 Unscrew the nuts and bolts securing the exhaust manifold to the cylinder head, and withdraw it. Take care not to damage vulnerable components as the manifold/ turbocharger assembly is manoeuvred out of the engine compartment.

Inspection

26 Refer to paragraphs 12 to 13 (and Note) above.

Refitting

27 Refitting is the reverse of the removal procedure, noting the following points:
a) *Position a new gasket over the manifold studs, and fit a new plastic guide sleeve to the stud nearest to the timing belt, so that the manifold will be correctly located. Do not refit the manifold without this sleeve.*
b) *Refit the manifold and finger-tighten the mounting nuts and bolts.*
c) *Working from the centre out and in three or four equal steps, tighten the nuts and bolts to the specified torque wrench setting.*
d) *Refit the remaining parts in the reverse order of removal. Tighten all fasteners to the specified torque wrench settings.*
e) *Fit new copper washers to the turbocharger oil feed line banjo union, and tighten the bolt to the specified torque wrench setting*
f) *Run the engine and check for exhaust leaks*

8 Crankshaft pulley – removal and refitting

Removal

1 Apply the handbrake, and loosen the right-hand front roadwheel nuts. Jack up the front of the vehicle and support it on axle stands (see *Jacking and vehicle support*). Remove the right-hand front roadwheel.

2 Remove the auxiliary drivebelt as described in Chapter 1.

3 Unscrew the four bolts and remove the crankshaft pulley from the crankshaft toothed pulleys **(see illustrations)**. Providing the glow plugs have not yet been removed, the bolts should come undone quite easily. If the pulley turns, have an assistant engage top gear and depress the footbrake pedal, or alternatively remove the starter motor and have an assistant insert a wide-bladed screwdriver in the teeth of the starter ring gear.

Refitting

4 Refitting is a reversal of removal, but tighten all bolts to the specified torque.

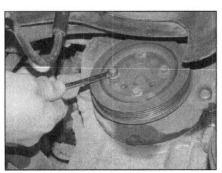

8.3a Unscrew the four bolts . . .

8.3b . . . and remove the crankshaft pulley

9 Timing belt covers – removal and refitting

Removal

1 Apply the handbrake, then jack up the front of the vehicle and support it on axle stands (see *Jacking and vehicle support*).

2 Referring to Chapter 1 if required, slacken and remove the auxiliary drivebelt(s). On later models, it may be necessary to completely remove the alternator, if not already done (see Chapter 5A).

3 Working under the vehicle, unscrew the front and rear retaining bolts, then withdraw the drivebelt lower cover from the crankshaft pulley/vibration damper **(see illustrations)**.

4 Where fitted, detach the plastic fuel deflector from the alternator mounting bracket.

5 Improved access to the upper cover may be gained by unbolting the coolant expansion tank and lifting out the power-assisted steering fluid reservoir (where applicable) **(see illustrations)**. These can be moved aside (without disconnecting them) as required.

6 Release the timing belt upper cover retaining clip(s) and unscrew the retaining bolt(s), then manoeuvre the cover upwards and withdraw it **(see illustrations)**.

7 Remove the crankshaft pulley (see Section 8).

8 The timing belt lower cover is secured by five bolts, while the small cover around the injection pump toothed pulley has three bolts **(see illustrations)**. The various bolts holding

9.3a Removing the early type timing belt lower cover

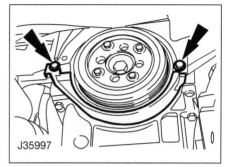

9.3b Later type timing belt lower cover – retaining bolts arrowed

9.5a The power steering fluid reservoir lifts off its mountings on the expansion tank . . .

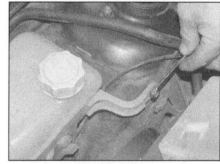

9.5b . . . while the expansion tank is secured by two bolts to the inner wing

the lower covers are of different lengths, so note their locations.

9 If required, the timing belt inner shield can be unbolted from the cylinder head once the

timing belt and injection pump drivebelt have been removed and their associated tensioner components, idler pulleys, etc, have been unbolted (see Sections 10 and 11).

9.6a On early engines, release the three camshaft drivebelt cover retaining clips . . .

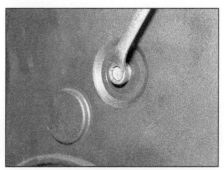

9.6b . . . unscrew the single (central) cover retaining bolt . . .

9.6c . . . then manoeuvre the cover upwards and withdraw it . . .

9.6d . . . to provide access to the drivebelts

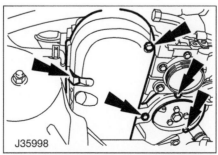

9.6e Timing belt upper cover retaining clip and bolt – also shown are the injection pump cover bolts (arrowed)

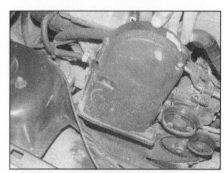

9.6f Removing the timing belt upper cover

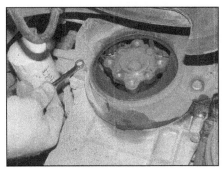

9.8a Remove the bolts . . .

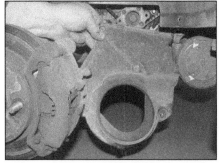

9.8b . . . and take off the timing belt lower cover

9.8c Removing the injection pump drivebelt cover

Refitting

10 Refitting is a reversal of removal, but tighten all fasteners to their specified torque wrench settings.

10 Timing belt and injection pump drivebelt – removal, refitting and adjustment

⚠️ *Warning: Never re-use or re-tension a timing belt/injection pump drivebelt. This could lead to the belt becoming over-tensioned, leading to its failure and resulting in serious engine damage.*

Note: *Ford have changed both the type of tensioner used, and the various idler pulleys, during the life of the Escort diesel. Before going to obtain any new parts, it would be wise*

to remove the timing belt covers (as far as possible), and finding out exactly what's fitted to your engine. Engines from March 1996 onwards cannot use the tensioner and idler components from previous engines. Having the vehicle identification number (VIN) to hand may also prove useful when ordering parts, especially from a Ford dealer.

Removal

1 Disconnect the battery negative (earth) lead (see Chapter 5A).
2 Apply the handbrake, and loosen the right-hand front roadwheel nuts. Jack up the front of the vehicle and support it on axle stands (see *Jacking and vehicle support*). On later models, remove the engine undershield, which is secured by a total of five bolts. Remove the right-hand front roadwheel.
3 On later models, detach the radiator upper cover, which is secured by four screws and

nine clips (removed by tapping through their centre pins) around its edge **(see illustrations)**.
4 Using long cable-ties, tie up the radiator (and air conditioning condenser, where applicable) to the front crossmember ('slam panel') **(see illustration)**. Working under the car, unbolt the radiator support crossmember from the car and from the radiator/condenser – the crossmember is held by four bolts, with two nuts securing it to the radiator, and three further nuts to the dehydrator/accumulator.
5 On models with a separate ribbed drivebelt for the power steering pump, unbolt and remove the drivebelt pulley (three bolts) from the injection pump sprocket – loosening the three bolts is best done prior to removing the drivebelt **(see illustrations)**.
6 Remove the timing belt covers as described in Section 9. Set piston No 1 to TDC on its compression stroke as described in Section 4 **(see illustration)**. This includes, on later

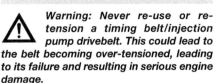

10.3a The radiator upper cover is secured by four bolts along the front edge . . .

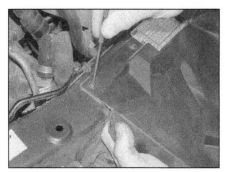

10.3b . . . and by nine clips with push-through centre pins further back

10.3c Removing the radiator upper cover

10.5a Loosen the power steering pump drivebelt pulley bolts with the belt still on, if possible . . .

10.5b . . . then remove the belt and take off the pulley

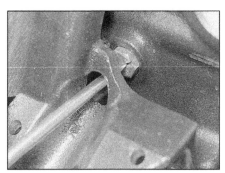

10.6 Screwing in the crankshaft timing pin

10.7 Drill bit used as a timing pin inserted through the camshaft toothed pulley – early models

models, the removal of the cylinder head cover to enable the use of the camshaft aligning tool.

Up to March 1996 (mechanical tensioner)

7 With piston No 1 at TDC on its compression stroke (crankshaft web firmly in contact with the timing pin), insert a timing pin (see Section 4) through the camshaft toothed pulley and into the special hole in the cylinder head **(see illustration)**.

8 Loosen the bolts securing the camshaft toothed pulley to its hub.

9 Loosen the tensioner centre bolt, then use a pair of water pump pliers or similar to compress the tensioner spring; retighten the tensioner bolt to release the tension from the belt, and to hold the tensioner away from the belt **(see illustration)**.

10 Remove the timing belt from the crankshaft and camshaft toothed pulleys, and from the tensioner and idler pulley.

10.11b ... and turn the eccentric round to the 6 o'clock position to release the belt tension

10.15 Use a screwdriver blade and a drift to release the camshaft pulley from its taper

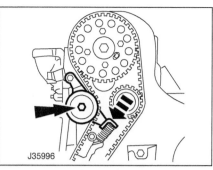

10.9 Loosen the tensioner centre bolt (arrowed), and compress the spring to relieve the belt tension

March 1996 onwards (automatic tensioner)

11 With piston No 1 at TDC on its compression stroke (crankshaft web firmly in contact with the timing pin), slacken the eccentric idler pulley's bolt, then turn the eccentric's teardrop anti-clockwise to the 6 o'clock position – i.e., the narrow end of the plate should be facing vertically downwards – to release the belt tension **(see illustrations)**.

12 Remove the timing belt from the camshaft toothed pulley, tensioner and idler pulley, and finally from the crankshaft toothed pulley **(see illustration)**.

13 Check that the camshaft aligning tool is still fitted into its slot.

14 Hold the camshaft toothed pulley stationary using a tool which engages the pulley holes, then loosen the retaining bolt two or three turns – there's no need to remove the bolt **(see illustration)**.

10.12 Removing the timing belt

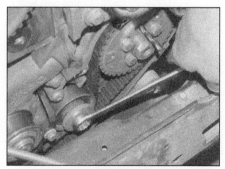

10.16a Loosen the injection pump drivebelt tensioner bolt . . .

10.11a Loosen the eccentric idler bolt . . .

15 Insert a screwdriver between the timing belt inner shield and the camshaft toothed pulley, and apply light pressure to the pulley. Insert a soft metal drift through the hole in the inner shield, and tap lightly on the pulley to release it from the camshaft taper **(see illustration)**. The camshaft pulley can remain in position for now – it has to be loose to accurately set the belt tension (just make sure that the camshaft aligning tool remains engaged in its slot).

All engines

16 To remove the injection pump drivebelt, loosen the tensioner bolt, then use a pair of water pump pliers or similar to compress the tensioner spring; retighten the tensioner bolt to release the tension from the belt, and to hold the tensioner away from the belt. Remove the belt from the crankshaft and injection pump toothed pulleys, and from the tensioner **(see illustrations)**.

10.14 Use a sprocket-holding tool and loosen the camshaft pulley bolt

10.16b ... then compress the tensioner spring with pliers and re-tighten the bolt

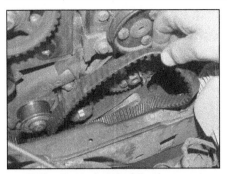

10.16c Removing the injection pump drivebelt

10.19 When fitting a new drivebelt, look for direction-of-rotation arrows

10.20 With the new drivebelt in place, slacken the injection pump pulley bolts

Inspection

Note: *On early models, do not interchange the timing belt and injection pump drivebelt tensioner springs. Note their installed direction before removing either spring, and ensure that each is refitted the same way round.*

17 Clean the toothed pulleys, idler pulley and tensioner pulleys and wipe them dry. **Do not** apply excessive amounts of solvent to the idler pulley and tensioner pulleys, otherwise the bearing lubricant may be contaminated. Also clean the timing belt covers and inner shield, the timing belt/drivebelt housing, and the surfaces of the cylinder head and block. If signs of oil or coolant contamination are found, trace the source of the leak and rectify it, then wash down the engine timing belt area and related components, to remove all traces of oil or coolant.

18 Examine carefully the timing belt/drivebelt for any signs of oil or coolant – the presence of either would indicate a leak, which must be cured before fitting the new belts. A new timing belt and injection pump drivebelt **must** be fitted once the old ones have been removed – **never** refit a used drivebelt of this type. Similarly, check each tensioner spring (where fitted), renewing it if there is any doubt about its condition. Check also the toothed pulleys for signs of wear or damage and

ensure that the tensioner and idler pulleys rotate smoothly on their bearings; renew any worn or damaged components. **Note:** *It is considered good practice by many professional mechanics to renew tensioner and idler pulley assemblies as a matter of course, whenever the timing belt/drivebelt is renewed. Ford dealers are nowadays reluctant to sell just the drivebelts, and offer kits containing the belts, tensioner and idler pulleys – see the Note at the start of this Section.*

Refitting

Caution: The engine must be cold, having been switched off for at least 4 hours.

All engines

19 With piston No 1 at TDC on its compression stroke (crankshaft web firmly in contact with the timing pin), locate the new injection pump drivebelt on the crankshaft and injection pump toothed pulleys so that it is taut between the two pulleys, with all slack on the tensioner side and the directional arrows correct for normal crankshaft rotation **(see illustration)**. Ensure that the drivebelt is fully pushed onto the centre of the pulleys.

20 Slacken through half a turn the injection pump toothed pulley bolts **(see illustration)** and the tensioner bolt – allow the tensioner pulley to snap against the belt. Retighten all

the slackened bolts, and make sure that the injection pump toothed pulley bolts are centralised in their elongated holes.

Up to March 1996 (mechanical tensioner)

21 With piston No 1 at TDC on its compression stroke (crankshaft web firmly in contact with the timing pin), locate the new timing belt on the pulleys so that it is taut between the pulleys, with all slack on the tensioner side and the directional arrows correct for normal crankshaft rotation. Fit it first on the crankshaft toothed pulley, then over the auxiliary shaft toothed pulley and water pump pulley, over the camshaft toothed pulley and idler pulley, then onto the tensioner. Ensure that the timing belt is fully pushed onto the centre of all pulleys.

22 The bolts securing the camshaft toothed pulley to its hub should still be slack, with each in the middle of its elongated hole. Slacken through half a turn the tensioner centre bolt – allow the tensioner to snap against the belt.

23 Retighten all slackened bolts, and make sure that the toothed pulley bolts are centralised in the elongated holes. Remove all the timing pins and turn the crankshaft through two revolutions in the normal direction of rotation until the slot in the injection pump toothed pulley is at the 12 o'clock position.

24 Turn the injection pump pulley back until the slot is again at the 11 o'clock position.

25 Screw in the crankshaft timing pin as described in Section 4, then slowly turn the crankshaft clockwise until the crankshaft web contacts the timing pin.

26 Insert the timing pins in the camshaft and the injection pump toothed pulleys.

27 Slacken the bolts (through half a turn) that secure the camshaft and injection pump toothed pulleys.

28 Slacken the bolts (through one-quarter of a turn) that secure the belt tensioners.

29 If all timing pins fit perfectly and the pulley-to-hub bolts are centralised in their elongated holes, retighten all slackened bolts to their specified torque wrench settings. The valve timing is now set correctly **(see illustration)**.

10.29 Timing belt and injection pump drivebelt components – early models

1 Camshaft toothed pulley
2 Idler pulley
3 Injection pump toothed pulley
4 Injection pump drivebelt tensioner
5 Crankshaft pulley
6 Auxiliary shaft toothed pulley
7 Coolant pump pulley
8 Timing belt tensioner

10.31 Apply oil to the camshaft pulley bolt head

10.33 Setting the initial belt tension – turn eccentric with an Allen key, and lock in place with the bolt

10.34 With the belt tension set, tighten the camshaft pulley bolt

March 1996 onwards (automatic tensioner)

30 Make sure that the crankshaft is positioned at TDC with the crankshaft web in contact with the timing pin and the camshaft aligning tool fitted into the camshaft slot.

31 Apply engine oil to the head contact face of the camshaft toothed pulley bolt **(see illustration)**. Refit the pulley, screw in the bolt finger-tight then undo it a quarter-turn. Make sure that the pulley is free to turn on the camshaft.

32 Locate the new timing belt on the pulleys so that it is taut between the pulleys, with all slack on the eccentric idler pulley's side and the directional arrows correct for normal crankshaft rotation. Fit it first on the crankshaft toothed pulley, then over the auxiliary shaft toothed pulley and water pump pulley, over the tensioner pulley and camshaft toothed pulley, then on the idler. Ensure that the timing belt is fully pushed onto the centre of all pulleys.

33 Unscrew the eccentric idler pulley's bolt and apply engine oil to the head contact face. Screw in the bolt finger-tight, then turn the eccentric idler's teardrop clockwise to the 9 o'clock position (with an Allen key) to tension the timing belt, and tighten the bolt to lock the idler pulley **(see illustration)**.

34 Hold the camshaft toothed pulley stationary using a tool which engages the pulley holes, then tighten the retaining bolt **(see illustration)**. This bolt has to be loosened again later to reset the belt tension.

35 Remove all timing pins and the camshaft aligning tool, then turn the crankshaft through six revolutions in the normal direction of rotation until the camshaft aligning tool can be refitted into the camshaft slot. Turn the engine back slightly (anti-clockwise) from this point.

36 Screw in the timing pin as far as it will go.

37 Slowly turn the crankshaft clockwise until the crankshaft web contacts the timing pin.

38 Slacken (through half a turn) the eccentric idler pulley's bolt, then if necessary, turn the camshaft using water pump pliers (avoiding the cam lobes) until the camshaft aligning tool will fit exactly into the camshaft slot.

39 Hold the camshaft toothed pulley stationary using a tool which engages the pulley holes, then loosen the retaining bolt through three turns.

40 Insert a screwdriver between the timing belt inner shield and the camshaft toothed pulley, and apply light pressure to the pulley. Insert a soft metal drift through the hole in the inner shield and tap lightly on the pulley to release it from the camshaft taper. Tighten the pulley retaining bolt finger-tight, then undo it half a turn. Make sure that the pulley is free to turn on the camshaft.

41 Using an Allen key engaged in the socket on the eccentric's teardrop, turn the teardrop in a clockwise direction to tension the timing belt until the arrow on the tensioner aligns with the right-hand edge of the setting window, then tighten the eccentric idler pulley's bolt to the specified torque wrench setting **(see illustration)**. **Note:** *Turn the eccentric smoothly, and make sure that it is finally set between the 6 o'clock (MIN) and 12 o'clock (MAX) positions. It may be necessary to use a mirror to view the tensioner arrow and setting window – an assistant will be useful here.*

42 If the tensioner setting is correct – the arrow on the tensioner aligns with the fixed arrow (at least within the limits of the

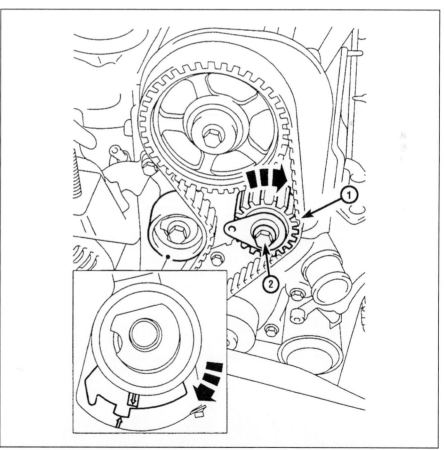

10.41 Turn the eccentric idler pulley's teardrop (1) until the arrow on the tensioner (inset) is aligned with the right-hand edge of the adjustment range, then tighten the pulley's bolt (2)

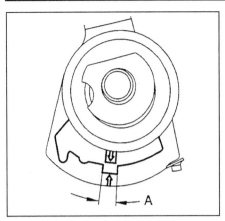

10.42 The timing belt tension is correct when the arrows align – or are at least within the limits shown by the range A

adjustment range A) – proceed with the next step **(see illustration)**. If the tensioner setting is not correct, repeat the procedure given in paragraph 41.

43 Hold the camshaft toothed pulley stationary using a tool which engages the pulley holes, then tighten the retaining bolt to its specified torque wrench setting.

44 Remove all timing pins and the camshaft aligning tool, then turn the crankshaft through six revolutions in the normal direction of rotation until the camshaft aligning tool can be refitted into the camshaft slot. Turn the engine back slightly (anti-clockwise) from this point.

45 Screw in the timing pin as far as it will go.

46 Slowly turn the crankshaft clockwise until the crankshaft web contacts the timing pin.

47 Recheck the tensioner setting. If it is correct, proceed with the next step. If the tensioner setting is not correct, repeat the procedure from paragraph 38 onwards.

48 Check that the camshaft aligning tool will fit exactly into the camshaft slot. If it is not possible to fit the aligning tool, repeat the procedure from paragraph 38 onwards.

49 Remove the timing pin and camshaft aligning tool, then refit the cylinder head cover with a new gasket and tighten the bolts.

50 Reconnect the crankcase breather hoses.

All engines

51 Refit and tighten the timing pin blanking plug **(see illustration)**.

11.3 Removing the crankshaft outboard (timing belt) toothed pulley

10.51 Refitting the timing pin blanking plug

52 Refit the timing belt covers with reference to Section 9. Refit and tension the auxiliary drivebelt(s) as described in Chapter 1.

53 Refit the coolant expansion tank and power steering reservoir.

54 On later models, refit the radiator support crossmember and the radiator upper cover.

55 Refit the wheel arch liner and the engine undershield (where applicable).

56 Refit the roadwheel and lower the vehicle to the ground.

57 Reconnect the battery negative (earth) lead (see Chapter 5A).

---

11 Timing belt/drivebelt tensioners and toothed pulleys – removal and refitting

Note: *A new timing belt and injection pump drivebelt must always be fitted whenever either of them is disturbed.*

Crankshaft toothed pulleys

Note: *On early engines – up to October 1995 – the inboard toothed pulley is located on the crankshaft by a roll pin fitted in the crankshaft end, while a V-shaped lug on the outboard toothed pulley engages with a notch on the inboard pulley, positively to lock the two pulleys together. On later engines, the roll pin is fitted to the inboard toothed pulley which engages in holes in both the crankshaft end and in the outboard toothed pulley. Ford state that this revised assembly relies entirely for security and for correct location on the clamping pressure of the crankshaft toothed pulleys' centre bolt.*

11.4a Removing the crankshaft inboard (injection pump drivebelt) toothed pulley

Removal

1 Remove the timing belt and injection pump drivebelt as described in Section 10. This procedure includes removal of the crankshaft pulley.

2 Hold the crankshaft stationary using a length of metal bar bolted to the outboard toothed pulley flange, then unscrew the centre bolt. **Note:** *The bolt is very tight. Discard the bolt – a new one must be obtained for refitting.*

Caution: NEVER use a timing pin (or the camshaft aligning tool) as a means of locking the crankshaft (or camshaft) – they are not strong enough for this and will shear off. Always ensure that all timing pins are removed before the crankshaft pulleys' bolt (or similar fasteners) is slackened or tightened

3 Remove the outboard toothed pulley, using a suitable puller if necessary **(see illustration)**.

4 Remove the inboard toothed pulley and recover the O-ring from the pulley **(see illustrations)**. To remove the pulley, use the Ford special tool (No 21-200 – now 303-497) which uses an expanding collet to engage the inside diameter of the pulley or a similar tool (if no such tool is available, the timing belt/drivebelt housing must be removed completely so that an ordinary legged puller can be used). Check that the roll pin is a tight fit in the crankshaft or inboard toothed pulley (as applicable) – if necessary to avoid its loss, remove the roll pin and store it with the toothed pulleys. Discard the inboard toothed pulley's O-ring – this must be renewed as a matter of course.

Inspection

5 Examine the pulleys for wear and damage, and renew them if necessary. Wipe clean the inboard toothed pulley oil seal surface, and check for grooves or raised areas which might damage the seal lips and cause oil leakage.

6 If there is any sign of oil leakage from the crankshaft right-hand oil seal, renew it with reference to Section 21. Note that the support ring on the new oil seal must remain in position until just before the inboard toothed pulley is fitted.

11.4b Crankshaft inboard toothed pulley, showing O-ring seal (arrowed)

Refitting

7 On early engines, make sure that the roll pin is fitted into the crankshaft. Check that the crankshaft spigot and the bore of the inboard toothed pulley are completely clean and free from traces of oil.

8 Fit a new O-ring to the inboard toothed pulley groove, and lubricate the O-ring with a thin smear of clean engine oil. Remove the oil seal support ring, then slide on the toothed pulley – on early engines, ensure that the roll pin passes through the hole; on later engines, ensure that the roll pin engages the hole in the crankshaft. Press the toothed pulley fully onto the crankshaft.

9 Fit the outboard toothed pulley onto the inboard toothed pulley, making sure that the vee in the outboard pulley engages with the cut-out in the inboard pulley (early engines only) and that the outboard pulley engages correctly with the roll pin. Lubricate the head of a new bolt with oil (but keep the threads dry), then insert it and tighten it while holding the toothed pulley stationary. Observe the four stages specified and use an angle gauge where required.

10 Fit the new timing belt and injection pump drivebelt as described in Section 10.

Camshaft toothed pulley

Removal

11 Remove the timing belt as described in Section 10 – there is no need to remove the injection pump drivebelt.

12 On engines with a timing belt mechanical tensioner, hold the toothed pulley stationary using a tool engaged with the holes in the pulley, then loosen the hub centre bolt and the four pulley-to-hub retaining bolts **(see illustration)**. Remove the toothed pulley from the hub, then extract the hub from the end of the camshaft using a suitable puller. Remove the Woodruff key from the groove in the camshaft.

13 On engines with a timing belt automatic tensioner, hold the toothed pulley stationary using a tool engaged with the holes in the pulley, then loosen through two or three turns the retaining bolt. Insert a screwdriver between the timing belt inner shield and the camshaft toothed pulley, and apply light pressure to the pulley. Insert a soft metal drift through the hole in the inner shield and tap lightly on the pulley to release it from the camshaft taper. Fully unscrew the bolt and remove the pulley.

Inspection

14 Inspect the toothed pulley for wear and damage and renew it if necessary.

Refitting

15 Refit the toothed pulley to the camshaft using a reversal of the removal procedure. On engines with a timing belt automatic tensioner, leave the bolt finger-tight. On engines with a timing belt mechanical tensioner, fully tighten the hub centre bolt, but leave the pulley-to-hub retaining bolts finger-tight and centralised in their elongated holes.

11.12 Unscrewing the camshaft toothed pulley-to-hub retaining bolts – early models

16 Fit the new timing belt with reference to Section 10.

Auxiliary shaft toothed pulley

Removal

17 Remove the timing belt as described in Section 10 – there is no need to remove the injection pump drivebelt.

18 Unscrew the timing belt side cover retaining bolt immediately above the auxiliary shaft toothed pulley. The pulley must now be held stationary while the bolt is loosened. To do this, wrap the old timing belt around the pulley and clamp it with a pair of water pump pliers, self-locking pliers or similar.

19 Unscrew the bolt and remove the toothed pulley – note the presence of the locating dowel pin in the end of the auxiliary shaft; if necessary to avoid its loss, remove the dowel pin and store it with the toothed pulley **(see illustration)**.

Inspection

20 Inspect the toothed pulley for wear and damage and renew it if necessary.

Refitting

21 Refitting is a reversal of removal, but tighten all nuts and bolts to the specified torque – do not forget the timing belt side cover retaining bolt. Fit the new timing belt as described in Section 10.

Injection pump toothed pulley

Removal

22 Remove the timing belt (camshaft drivebelt) as described in Section 10 – do not

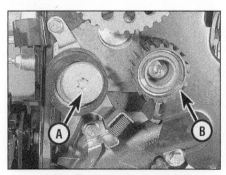

11.29a Timing belt mechanical tensioner (A) and idler pulley (B)

11.19 Removing the auxiliary shaft toothed pulley

immediately remove the injection pump drivebelt.

23 Hold the toothed pulley stationary using a suitable tool engaged with the pulley holes. Alternatively, if the injection pump drivebelt is still fitted and the timing pin is still in place, the pulley will be locked in position anyway. Take care that the timing pin does not bend if holding the pulley this way.

24 Unscrew the three pulley-to-hub bolts and remove the toothed pulley from its hub.

Inspection

25 Inspect the toothed pulley for wear and damage and renew it if necessary.

Refitting

26 Locate the toothed pulley on its hub ensuring that each of the pulley-to-hub bolts is in the centre of its slotted hole in the pulley. Leave the pulley-to-hub retaining bolts finger-tight.

27 Fit the new timing belt/injection pump drivebelt as described in Section 10.

Mechanical tensioner (timing belt and injection pump drivebelt)

Note: *Do not interchange the timing belt and injection pump drivebelt tensioner springs. Note their installed direction before removing either spring, and ensure that each is refitted the same way round.*

Removal

28 Remove the timing belt/injection pump drivebelt as described in Section 10.

29 Unscrew the bolts and remove the tensioner and tension spring **(see illustrations)**.

11.29b Injection pump drivebelt tensioner and spring removed

11.32 Injection pump drivebelt tensioner backplate locating peg (arrowed)

Inspection

Note: *It is considered good practice by many professional mechanics to renew tensioner assemblies as a matter of course, whenever the timing belt/injection pump drivebelt is renewed.*
30 Spin the tensioner pulley by hand and check for roughness and resistance. If evident, renew the tensioner. Similarly, check the tensioner spring, renewing it if there is any doubt about its condition. Check the tensioner components for wear and damage, and renew as necessary if there is the slightest doubt about their condition.

Refitting

31 Clean the tensioner pulley and wipe it dry. **Do not** apply excessive amounts of solvent to the pulley, otherwise the bearing lubricant may be contaminated. Also clean the timing belt covers and inner shield, the timing belt/drivebelt housing, and the surfaces of the cylinder head and block.
32 Refit the tensioner and spring, and tighten the mounting bolt to the specified torque. The tensioner backplate locates over a peg on the side of the engine, while the spring ends fit over tabs on the engine and the tensioner body **(see illustration)**.
33 Fit the new timing belt/injection pump drivebelt as described in Section 10.

Automatic tensioner (timing belt)

Removal

34 Remove the timing belt as described in Section 10 – there is no need to remove the injection pump drivebelt.

12.3 Auxiliary shaft oil seal housing on the timing belt/drivebelt housing

---

35 Unscrew the tensioner centre bolt to release the tensioner.
36 Unscrew the backplate bolt and remove the tensioner assembly **(see illustration)**.

Inspection

Note: *It is considered good practice by many professional mechanics to renew tensioner assemblies as a matter of course, whenever the timing belt/injection pump drivebelt is renewed.*
37 Spin the tensioner pulley by hand and check for noisy bearings, roughness and resistance. Check the tensioner components for wear and damage, and renew as necessary if there is the slightest doubt about their condition.

Refitting

38 Clean the tensioner pulley and wipe it dry. **Do not** apply excessive amounts of solvent to the pulley, otherwise the bearing lubricant may be contaminated. Also clean the timing belt covers and inner shield, the timing belt/drivebelt housing, and the surfaces of the cylinder head and block.
39 Refit the tensioner and tighten the bolts to the specified torque wrench settings.
40 Fit the new timing belt as described in Section 10.

Idler pulley

Removal

41 Remove the timing belt as described in Section 10 – there is no need to remove the injection pump drivebelt.
42 Unbolt and remove the idler **(see illustration)**.

12.6a Auxiliary shaft oil seal retainer with plastic fitting ring

---

11.36 Timing belt automatic tensioner and centre bolt

11.42 Removing the idler pulley

Inspection

Note: *It is considered good practice by many professional mechanics to renew idler pulley assemblies as a matter of course, whenever the timing belt/injection pump drivebelt is renewed.*
43 Spin the idler pulley by hand and check for noise, roughness and resistance in the bearings. Check also the pulley teeth for signs of wear or damage such as cracks or chips; if a plastic idler is fitted, place a straight-edge across its teeth and check that there is no more than 0.5 mm gap (ie, wear) between the straight-edge and the teeth at any point. If any wear at all is evident, renew the pulley.

Refitting

44 Refit the idler pulley and tighten the mounting bolt to the specified torque. On engines with a timing belt automatic tensioner, turn the eccentric's teardrop anti-clockwise to the 6 o'clock position – i.e., the narrow end of the plate should be facing vertically downwards – to minimise the belt tension.
45 Fit the new timing belt as described in Section 10.

---

12 Auxiliary shaft oil seal – renewal

1 Remove the auxiliary shaft toothed pulley as described in Section 11.
2 Unbolt and remove the timing belt side cover.
3 Unscrew the bolts and remove the oil seal housing **(see illustration)**. The oil seal is integral with the housing.
4 Clean the timing belt/drivebelt housing, the cylinder block and the auxiliary shaft end.
5 Smear fresh engine oil on the auxiliary shaft and on the sealing lips of the new oil seal. Before fitting the new seal, locate the special fitting ring inside the sealing lips.
6 Locate the new oil seal over the end of the auxiliary shaft, then insert the bolts and tighten **(see illustrations)**.
7 Carefully remove the special ring and make sure that the seal lips are located on the shaft correctly.

12.6b Tightening the auxiliary shaft oil seal housing bolts

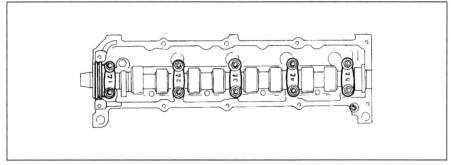

14.5 Camshaft bearing caps – note numbers and arrows

8 Refit the timing belt side cover and tighten the bolts.

9 Refit the auxiliary shaft toothed pulley as described in Section 11.

13 Camshaft oil seal – renewal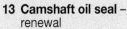

1 Remove the camshaft toothed pulley as described in Section 11.

2 Note the fitted depth of the oil seal before removing it, as a guide to fitting the new one.

3 Using a screwdriver or suitable hooked instrument, pull the oil seal from the cylinder head. If the seal is tight, drill two or three small holes in its outer face, then screw in self-tapping screws. Pull on the screws with a pair of pliers to remove the oil seal.

4 Wipe clean the seating and end of the camshaft.

5 Dip the new seal in oil, then locate it over the camshaft and initially press it in by hand making sure that it enters the cylinder head squarely.

6 Using a piece of metal tubing or a socket, carefully drive the oil seal into the cylinder head to the previously-noted depth.

7 Wipe any excess oil from the oil seal and surrounding area.

8 Refit the camshaft toothed pulley and fit a new timing belt with reference to Section 11.

14 Camshaft and tappets – removal, inspection and refitting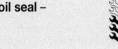

Removal

1 Remove the camshaft toothed pulley (and hub, on early engines) as described in Section 11.

2 Disconnect the crankcase breather hose from the left-hand rear of the cylinder head cover. Plug the hose opening with clean rag to prevent dirt or other objects falling into the turbocharger, where applicable.

3 Disconnect the crankcase breather hose from the left-hand front of the cylinder head

cover, then unscrew the bolts and remove the cover.

4 Unscrew the nuts and remove the baffle plate.

5 Undo the nuts of bearing caps Nos. 2 and 4. Remove these caps and their shells. Keep the shells with their caps if they are to be re-used. Note that the caps are numbered and carry an arrow pointing to the pulley end of the engine **(see illustration)**.

6 Slacken the nuts of bearing caps Nos. 1, 3 and 5 one turn at a time, working from end to end so that the camshaft is released gradually. Remove the bearing caps and shells, again keeping the shells with their caps if necessary.

7 Lift out the camshaft with its oil seal. Recover the lower half bearing shells, keeping them in order if necessary.

8 If purchasing new bearing shells, note that either standard or oversize shells may have been fitted in production. Oversize shells are identified by a green mark.

9 Obtain eight small, clean containers, and number them 1 to 8 from the timing end. Lift the tappets one by one from the cylinder head keeping the shims with their respective tappets.

Inspection

10 With the camshaft and tappets removed, check for signs of obvious wear (scoring, pitting etc) and for ovality, and renew if necessary.

11 If possible, use a micrometer to measure the outside diameter of each tappet – take

14.17 Fitting a camshaft lower bearing shell

measurements at the top and bottom of each tappet, then a second set at right-angles to the first; if any measurement is significantly different from the others, the tappet is tapered or oval (as applicable) and must be renewed. If the tappets or the cylinder head bores are excessively worn, new tappets and/or a new cylinder head will be required.

12 Visually examine the camshaft lobes for score marks, pitting, and evidence of overheating (blue, discoloured areas). Look for flaking away of the hardened surface layer of each lobe. If any such signs are evident, renew the component concerned.

13 Examine the camshaft bearing journals and the bearing shells for signs of obvious wear or pitting. If any such signs are evident, renew the camshaft and/or obtain a set of bearing shells.

14 To check camshaft endfloat, remove the tappets, clean the bearing surfaces carefully, and refit the camshaft and bearing caps with shells. Tighten the bearing cap nuts to the specified torque wrench setting, then measure the endfloat using a dial gauge mounted on the cylinder head so that its tip bears on the camshaft end.

15 Tap the camshaft fully towards the gauge, zero the gauge, then tap the camshaft fully away from the gauge, and note the gauge reading. If the endfloat measured is found to be more than the value given in the Specifications, fit a new camshaft and repeat the check; if the clearance is still excessive, the cylinder head must be renewed.

Refitting

16 Commence reassembly by lubricating the cylinder head tappet bores and the tappets with engine oil. Carefully refit the tappets (together with their respective shims – lettering facing downwards) to the cylinder head, ensuring that each tappet is refitted to its original bore. Some care will be required to enter the tappets squarely into their bores.

17 Place the lower half bearing shells (the ones with the oil holes) in position **(see illustration)**. Lubricate the shells.

18 Make sure that all tappets, shims and the vacuum pump pushrod are in place. Remove the old oil seal, if not already done, and place

14.18 Fitting the camshaft

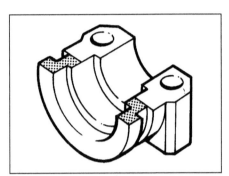

**14.19b Camshaft No 1 bearing cap –
coat shaded area with sealant**

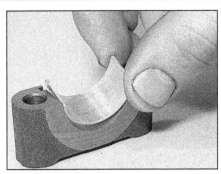

**14.19a Fitting a camshaft upper bearing
shell to its cap**

**14.22 Tightening the camshaft bearing cap
nuts**

15 Valve clearances –
checking and adjustment

Note: *For DIY purposes, note that while checking the valve clearances is a relatively easy operation, changing the shims requires the use of Ford special tools – owners may prefer to have this work carried out by a Ford dealer.*

Checking

1 Remove the cylinder head cover as described in Section 5.

2 Unscrew the nuts and remove the oil baffle plate from the camshaft bearing caps **(see illustration)**. Temporarily refit and tighten the removed nuts to their specified torque – this must be done, in order to fully locate the camshaft in position.

3 During the following procedure, the crankshaft must be turned to position the camshaft lobes away from the valves. To do this, either turn the crankshaft on the pulley bolt or alternatively raise the front right-hand corner of the vehicle, engage top gear and turn the front roadwheel. Access to the pulley bolt is gained by jacking up the front of the vehicle and supporting on axle stands, then removing the pulley lower cover.

4 If desired, to enable the crankshaft to be turned more easily, remove the glow plugs (Chapter 5B) or the fuel injectors (Chapter 4A).

5 Draw the valve positions on a piece of paper, numbering them 1 to 8 from the timing end of the engine. Identify them as inlet or exhaust (i.e. 1I, 2E, 3I, 4E, 5I, 6E, 7I, 8E).

6 Turn the crankshaft until the valves of No 4 cylinder (flywheel end) are 'rocking'. The exhaust valve will be closing and the inlet valve will be opening. The piston of No 1 cylinder will be at the top of its compression stroke, with both valves fully closed. The clearances for both valves of No 1 cylinder may be checked at the same time.

7 Insert a feeler blade of the correct thickness (see Specifications) between the cam lobe and the shim on the top of the tappet bucket, and check that it is a firm sliding fit **(see illustration)**. If it is not, use the feeler blades to ascertain the exact clearance, and record this for use when calculating the new shim thickness required. Note that the inlet and exhaust valve clearances are different, so it is important that you know which valve clearance you are checking.

8 With No 1 cylinder valve clearances checked, turn the engine through half a turn so that No 2 valves are 'rocking', then check the valve clearances of No 3 cylinder in the same way. Similarly check the valve clearances of No 4 cylinder with No 1 valves 'rocking' and No 2 cylinder with No 3 valves 'rocking'.

Adjustment

9 If adjustment is required, turn the engine in the normal direction of rotation through

the camshaft on the lower half bearings **(see illustration)**. Position the camshaft so that the slot in its left-hand end is parallel with the cylinder head mating surface and the larger semi-circular segment is uppermost (see Section 4).

19 Clean any old sealant from No. 1 bearing cap. Fit the upper bearing shells to their caps and lubricate them. Coat the mating surfaces of No. 1 cap with sealant (to Ford specification SPM-4G-9112-F/G) in the areas shown **(see illustrations)**.

20 Fit bearing caps and shells Nos. 1, 3 and 5, making sure that they are the right way round (the arrows point to the timing belt end). Tighten the cap nuts, half a turn at a time, in the sequence 1-3-5. Carry on until the caps are seated.

21 Fit caps and shells Nos. 2 and 4, tapping them down with a mallet if necessary to seat them. Fit their nuts.

22 Tighten all the bearing cap nuts to the specified torque wrench setting **(see illustration)**.

23 Insert the camshaft aligning tool into the slot in the camshaft left-hand end – check that it is a snug fit.

24 Fit a new oil seal to the camshaft right-hand end as described in Section 13. Apply a thin smear of sealant to the joint between No. 1 bearing cap and the cylinder head.

25 Lubricate the cam lobes liberally with engine oil, or with special cam lubricant if supplied with a new camshaft.

26 Refit the baffle plate and tighten the nuts.

27 Refit the cylinder head cover together with a new gasket and tighten the bolts to the specified torque.

28 Reconnect the crankcase breather hoses, then refit the camshaft toothed pulley (and hub) as described in Section 11. Remember that a new timing belt must be fitted.

**15.2 Unscrew the four nuts (arrowed) and
remove the oil baffle plate**

**15.7 Measuring a valve clearance with a
feeler blade**

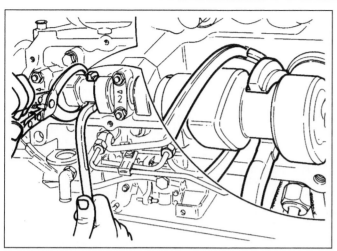

15.9a Maker's tools for tappet depression and shim extraction

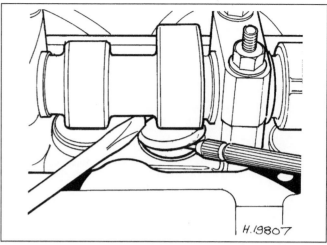

15.9b Depressing a tappet with a screwdriver and removing a shim

approximately 90°, to bring the pistons to mid-stroke. If this is not done, the pistons at TDC will prevent the tappets being depressed, and damage may result. Depress the tappets, then either shim can be withdrawn if the peak of the cam does not prevent access. The Ford service tools for this operation are tappet depressor No 21-106 (now 303-195), and shim pliers No 21-107 (now 303-196), but with care and patience a C-spanner or screwdriver can be used to depress the tappet and the shim can be flicked out with a small screwdriver (see illustrations).

10 If the valve clearance was too small, a thinner shim must be fitted. If the clearance was too large, a thicker shim must be fitted. The thickness of the shim (in mm) is engraved on the side facing away from the camshaft (see illustration). If the marking is missing or illegible, a micrometer will be needed to establish shim thickness.

11 When the shim thickness and the valve clearance are known, the required thickness of the new shim can be calculated as follows:

Sample calculation – clearance too small

Desired clearance (A)   = 0.50 mm
Measured clearance (B)   = 0.35 mm
Shim thickness found (C)   = 3.95 mm
Shim thickness required (D) = C + B − A = 3.80 mm

Sample calculation – clearance too large

Desired clearance (A)   = 0.35 mm
Measured clearance (B)   = 0.40 mm
Shim thickness found (C)   = 4.05 mm
Shim thickness required (D) = C + B − A = 4.10 mm

12 With the correct shim fitted, release the tappet depressing tool. Turn the engine back so that the cam lobes are again pointing upwards and check that the clearance is now correct.

13 Repeat the process for the remaining

valves, turning the engine each time to bring a pair of cam lobes upwards.

14 It will be helpful for future adjustment if a record is kept of the thickness of shim fitted at each position. The shims required can be purchased in advance once the clearances and the existing shim thicknesses are known.

15 It is permissible to interchange shims between tappets to achieve the correct clearances. but do not turn the camshaft with any of the shims removed, since there is a risk that the cam lobe will jam in the empty tappet.

16 When all the clearances are correct, refit the fuel injectors or glow plugs (Chapter 4A or 5B), then refit the oil baffle plate and tighten the nuts to the specified torque. Refit the cylinder head cover with the gasket, and tighten the bolts to the specified torque.

17 Reconnect the crankcase breather hoses to the cylinder head cover.

16 Cylinder head – removal and refitting

Removal

1 Disconnect the battery negative (earth) lead (see Chapter 5A).

2 Apply the handbrake, then jack up the front of the vehicle and support it on axle stands (see Jacking and vehicle support). Where fitted, remove the engine undershield. Remove the right-hand front roadwheel, then undo the retaining screws and remove the wheel arch liner.

3 Drain the cooling system as described in Chapter 1. Refit the coolant drain plug and tighten it to the specified torque wrench setting.

4 Unplugging the electrical connector and disconnecting the vacuum hose (where fitted), remove the air cleaner assembly with the air mass meter and the resonator (where fitted) as described in Chapter 4A.

5 On TCI engines, remove the intercooler (Chapter 4A) – unbolt and remove completely the intercooler mounting brackets and the intercooler/inlet manifold ducting. Pack the turbocharger opening with clean rag to prevent dirt or other objects falling in.

6 Remove the timing belt as described in Section 10. There is no need to remove the injection pump drivebelt.

7 If a support bar was used to take the weight of the engine, locate a trolley jack and block of wood beneath the sump, then remove the support bar.

8 Remove the camshaft toothed pulley (early engines) and timing belt tensioner with reference to Section 11.

9 On early engines only, disconnect the crankcase breather hoses from the left-hand of the cylinder head cover. Plug the rear hose's opening with clean rag to prevent dirt or other objects falling into the turbocharger, where applicable.

10 Unplugging their electrical connectors, disconnect the coolant temperature gauge sender unit, the engine coolant temperature sensor and the needle lift sensor (later engines only). Unscrew the nut to disconnect the glow plug wiring.

11 Disconnect the hose from the coolant expansion tank.

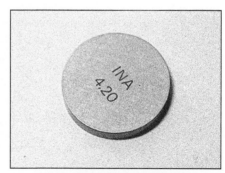

15.10 Shim thickness marking

16.27 Removing the cylinder head

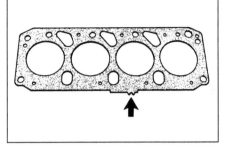

16.28 Cylinder head gasket thickness is indicated by the number of teeth or holes at point arrowed

12 Disconnect the fuel return pipe from the fuel injection pump union.

13 Disconnect the wiring from the oil pressure switch and from the fuel heater.

14 Unplugging the two electrical connectors located next to the fuel filter, disconnect the engine wiring loom.

15 Disconnect the fuel pipes from the top of the filter.

16 Unscrew the union nut and disconnect the vacuum line from the top of the vacuum pump (see Chapter 9). Release the retaining clip and disconnect the oil return hose from the base of the pump.

17 Unbolt the glow plug wiring bracket, then unbolt the oil dipstick tube. Discard the seal.

18 Unbolt the thermostat housing and withdraw it from the cylinder head. Discard the gasket.

19 Disconnect the fuel leak-off pipes from the injectors.

20 Unscrew the union nuts and remove the injection pipes from the injectors and injection pump. Be prepared for some loss of fuel and cover the pump, injection pipe and injector openings (see Chapter 4A) to prevent the entry of dirt.

21 Unbolt the fuel filter assembly and withdraw it from the cylinder head.

22 Unclip the coolant hoses from the cylinder head and secure them out of the way. Disconnect the vacuum hose from the Exhaust Gas Recirculation (EGR) valve.

23 Unscrew the nuts securing the exhaust system front downpipe/catalytic converter.

24 On turbo models, slacken the hose clip securing the oil return hose and disconnect the hose from the return pipe on the turbo-

charger. On models where the turbocharger is separate to the exhaust manifold, it may be necessary to completely remove the turbo, as described in Section 7.

25 Remove the injectors and fire seal washers as described in Chapter 4A.

26 Unscrew the cylinder head bolts **in the reverse** of the sequence shown in illustration 16.37. As new bolts will be required when refitting the cylinder head, note that the new bolts have an M12 thread and a Torx TX70 head.

27 With the help of an assistant, lift the cylinder head, with the manifolds and the timing belt inner shield, from the block **(see illustration)**.

28 Remove the cylinder head gasket, but retain it for comparison with the new gasket. Three possible thicknesses of gasket are available according to the piston protrusion, the details of which are given in the Specifications at the start of this Chapter **(see illustration)**.

Inspection

29 The mating faces of the cylinder head and block must be perfectly clean before refitting the head. Use a scraper to remove all traces of gasket and carbon, and also clean the tops of the pistons. Take particular care with the aluminium cylinder head, as the soft metal is damaged easily. Also, make sure that debris is not allowed to enter the oil and water channels – this is particularly important for the oil circuit, as carbon could block the oil supply to the camshaft or crankshaft bearings. Using adhesive tape and paper, seal the water, oil and bolt holes in the cylinder block. Clean the piston crowns in the same way.

30 Check the block and head for nicks, deep scratches and other damage. If slight, they may be removed carefully with a file. More serious damage may be repaired by machining, but this is a specialist job.

31 If warpage of the cylinder head is suspected, use a straight-edge to check it for distortion. Refer to Chapter 2B if necessary.

32 Clean out the bolt holes in the block using a pipe cleaner, or a rag and screwdriver. Make sure that all oil is removed, otherwise there is a possibility of the block being cracked by hydraulic pressure when the bolts are tightened.

33 Examine the bolt threads and the threads in the cylinder block for damage. If necessary, use the correct-size tap to chase out the threads in the block.

34 If necessary, the valve clearances may be checked and adjusted with the cylinder head on the bench. Refer to Section 15.

Refitting

35 Before fitting the cylinder head, ensure that the slot in the camshaft left-hand end is parallel with the cylinder head mating surface, with the larger semi-circular segment uppermost, and that the crankshaft is at TDC (see Section 4).

36 Fit the new selected gasket and use new cylinder head bolts. Make sure that the centralising dowel sleeves are located at bolt holes 8 and 10, and the word TOP/OBEN is visible.

37 Fit the cylinder head, ensuring that the timing belt inner shield locates correctly and is not damaged, screw in new bolts (**do not** oil the threads), and tighten in the stages indicated in the Specifications and in the sequence shown **(see illustration)**.

38 Refit the injectors and fire seal washers as described in Chapter 4A.

39 Fit and tension a new timing belt with reference to Section 10.

40 With the valve clearances checked and correct (see Section 15), refit the oil baffle plate and tighten the nuts to the specified torque wrench setting. Refit the cylinder head cover with a new gasket, and tighten the bolts to the specified torque wrench setting.

41 Reconnect the crankcase breather hoses to the cylinder head cover.

42 Refit the timing belt covers with reference to Section 9. Refit and tension the auxiliary drivebelt(s) as described in Chapter 1.

43 On turbo models, connect the oil return hose to the turbocharger return pipe and tighten the securing hose clip.

44 Reconnect the radiator bottom hose to the water pump union.

45 Refit the engine right-hand mounting and bracket. Remove the trolley jack and block of wood from beneath the sump.

46 Refit the coolant expansion tank, then clip the coolant expansion tank hoses to the cylinder head and the fuel return pipe into its brackets. Reconnect the vacuum hose to the Exhaust Gas Recirculation (EGR) valve.

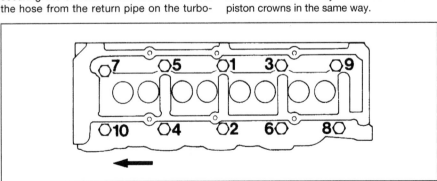

16.37 Cylinder head bolt tightening sequence. Arrow points to timing end of engine

47 Refit the exhaust system front downpipe/catalytic converter (using a new gasket if required), then tighten the retaining nuts to the specified torque wrench setting.

48 Refit the fuel filter assembly.

49 Refit the injection pipes and tighten the union nuts. Reconnect the leak-off pipes.

50 Refit the thermostat housing, using a new gasket.

51 Refit the glow plug wiring bracket and, using a new seal, the oil dipstick tube.

52 Reconnect the vacuum line and the oil return hose to the vacuum pump (see Chapter 9).

53 Reconnect the fuel pipes to the filter, then reconnect the wiring to the oil pressure switch, fuel heater and engine wiring loom.

54 Reconnect the hose to the coolant expansion tank and the fuel return pipe to the fuel injection pump.

55 Reconnect the wiring to the coolant temperature gauge sender, the engine coolant temperature sensor, the needle lift sensor (later engines only), and the glow plugs.

56 Refit the intercooler (where removed) and the air cleaner assembly with the air mass meter and the resonator (where fitted) – see Chapter 4A.

57 Refill the cooling system as described in Chapter 1.

58 Lower the vehicle to the ground, then reconnect the battery earth lead (see Chapter 5A).

59 The fuel system can now be primed, with reference to Chapter 4A, Section 3.

60 Start the engine and run it to normal operating temperature. Check for leaks of oil and coolant.

17 Sump – removal and refitting

Removal

Note 1: *The crankshaft left-hand oil seal carrier is bolted directly onto the sump and cylinder block, making it necessary to remove the flywheel (and therefore the clutch and transmission) and the housing before the sump can be unbolted.*

Note 2: *The full procedure outlined below must be followed so that the mating surfaces can be cleaned and prepared to achieve an oil-tight joint on reassembly and so that the sump can be aligned correctly; depending on your skill and experience and the tools and facilities available, it may be that this task can be carried out only with the engine removed from the vehicle.*

1 Apply the handbrake, then jack up the front of the vehicle and support it on axle stands (see *Jacking and vehicle support*).

2 Drain the engine oil, then check the sealing washer and renew if necessary. Clean and refit the engine oil drain plug together with the washer, and tighten it to the specified torque

wrench setting. Although not strictly necessary as part of the dismantling procedure, owners are advised to remove and discard the oil filter, so that it can be renewed with the oil (see Chapter 1).

3 Remove the transmission as described in Chapter 7. Make sure the engine is adequately and safely supported.

4 Remove the flywheel as described in Section 22.

5 Unbolt the crankshaft left-hand oil seal carrier and withdraw it from the crankshaft (refer to Section 21).

6 If necessary, remove the crankshaft position sensor and unbolt its bracket from the sump (make alignment markings if necessary, to ensure that the fitted position of the sensor is preserved). Unbolt the coolant pipe bracket from the sump and unscrew the nut securing the coolant pipe's remaining bracket. Secure the coolant pipe clear of the sump.

7 Progressively unscrew the sump retaining bolts, then lower the sump from the crankcase and withdraw it from under the vehicle.

8 Recover and discard the sump gasket **(see illustration)**.

9 While the sump is removed, take the opportunity to remove the oil pump pick-up/strainer pipe and clean it with reference to Section 18.

Refitting

Note: *The sump gasket must be renewed whenever it is disturbed.*

10 Thoroughly clean the contact surfaces of the sump and crankcase. If necessary, use a cloth rag to clean the interior of the sump and crankcase. If the oil pump pick-up/strainer pipe was removed, fit a new O-ring and refit the pipe with reference to Section 18.

11 Apply suitable sealant (Ford recommend SPM-4G-9112-F/G) to the joint (on each side) between the timing belt/drivebelt housing and cylinder block/crankcase **(see illustration)**. Once the sealant has been applied, the sump must be refitted within 20 minutes.

12 Locate the gasket on the sump, then offer the sump onto the cylinder block/crankcase and insert the retaining bolts finger-tight.

13 Before tightening the bolts, the sump must be accurately aligned with the end face of the cylinder block using a straight-edge.

14 Fit the crankshaft left-hand oil seal carrier and tighten the bolts to the specified torque (refer to Section 21). It is advisable to fit a new oil seal as part of this procedure.

15 Once the sump is correctly aligned and the oil seal carrier is installed, progressively tighten the sump-to-crankcase bolts to the specified torque wrench setting.

16 If removed, refit the crankshaft position sensor and bracket – it is essential that the sensor is aligned correctly, to ensure that the fuel injection timing is retained. Refit the coolant pipe to the sump and tighten the mounting bolt and nut to their specified torque wrench settings.

17.8 Removing the sump gasket from the crankcase

17 Refit the flywheel with reference to Section 22.

18 Refit the transmission as described in Chapter 7.

19 Lower the vehicle to the ground, then fit a new oil filter (if necessary) and refill the engine with oil with reference to Chapter 1.

20 Finally start the engine and check for signs of oil or coolant leaks.

18 Oil pump – removal, inspection and refitting

Note: *Engines built after August 1998 were fitted with a new oil pump, and these can be identified by the colour of the oil pressure warning light switch fitted (the switch is on the left-hand end of the cylinder head, near the fuel filter). Engines with the later pump have a switch with a green cover, while earlier engines have a black switch. The two oil pumps should not be interchanged.*

Removal

1 On TCI engines, remove the intercooler (see Chapter 4A) – unbolt and remove completely the intercooler mounting brackets and the intercooler/inlet manifold ducting. Pack the turbocharger opening with clean rag to prevent dirt or other objects falling in.

2 Drain the engine oil and unscrew the oil filter with reference to Chapter 1.

3 Unbolt the coolant pipe bracket from the

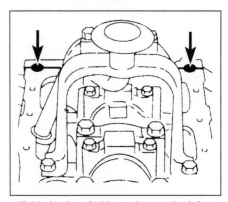

17.11 Apply suitable sealant to the joints arrowed

18.8a Unscrew the mounting bolts . . .

18.8b . . . remove the oil pump from the cylinder block . . .

18.8c . . . and recover the gasket

sump and unscrew the nut securing the coolant pipe's remaining bracket. Secure the coolant pipe clear of the sump.

4 Unscrew the nuts to disconnect the exhaust system front downpipe from the manifold or turbocharger. If the additional working clearance is required, unbolt the downpipe/catalytic converter completely.

5 Unscrew the oil cooler's retaining bolt and separate the cooler from its adapter – collect and discard the gasket.

6 Unscrew the two bolts and single nut securing the oil cooler mounting bracket to the cylinder block/crankcase.

7 On turbo models, unscrew the banjo bolt securing the turbocharger oil feed line to the oil pump. Collect the copper washer on each side of the union – these must be renewed as a matter of course whenever they are disturbed. Unbolt the oil feed line bracket from the cylinder block/crankcase.

8 Unscrew the mounting bolts and move the oil pump so that the oil cooler mounting bracket can be withdrawn, then withdraw the pump itself. Recover and discard the gasket **(see illustrations)**.

Inspection

9 Unscrew the special bolt and separate the oil cooler/oil filter adapter from the oil pump, then undo the crosshead screws and remove the cover plate from the pump.

10 Clean all parts and inspect them for wear or damage. Using a feeler gauge, measure the inner-to-outer rotor clearance. If the clearance exceeds that specified, then the pump must be renewed as pump components are not

available individually. It is wise to renew the pump on a precautionary basis at time of major overhaul, especially if there is evidence of oil starvation elsewhere.

11 If there are any signs of metallic debris inside the oil pump, it is recommended that the sump be removed and the pick-up pipe and strainer cleaned thoroughly. Renew the pick-up tube O-ring and the sump gasket on refitting and tighten the bolts to the specified torque **(see illustrations)**.

Refitting

12 Before refitting the oil pump, pour approximately 10 cc of engine oil into the pump to prime it, and oil the pump drive gear and driven gear. Refit the cover plate using a new gasket and tighten the crosshead screws securely and evenly.

13 Clean the mating faces of the pump and cylinder block, then refit the oil pump (with the oil cooler mounting bracket) using a new gasket. Tighten by hand the oil pump mounting bolts; tighten the mounting bracket's bolts to the specified torque wrench setting.

14 Tighten the oil pump mounting bolts to the specified torque wrench setting.

15 Fit new copper washers to the turbocharger oil feed line banjo union, and tighten the bolt to the specified torque wrench setting. Bolt the oil feed line bracket on to the cylinder block/crankcase.

16 Refit the oil cooler to its adapter, using a new gasket, and tighten the cooler's retaining bolt to the specified torque wrench setting.

17 Refit the coolant pipe to the sump and

tighten the mounting bolt and nut to their specified torque wrench settings.

18 Refit the exhaust system front downpipe/catalytic converter, and the intercooler (where applicable).

19 Fit a new oil filter and fill the engine with fresh oil as described in Chapter 1.

20 Lower the vehicle to the ground.

19 Oil cooler – removal and refitting

Note: *While the following procedure does not necessitate the removal of the oil filter, it is strongly recommended that the filter be renewed and that the engine oil should be changed whenever the oil cooler is disturbed.*

Removal

1 Drain the engine oil and unscrew the oil filter, then drain the coolant with reference to Chapter 1.

2 Disconnect the coolant hose from the oil cooler.

3 Unscrew the retaining bolt and withdraw the oil cooler; note how its unions are aligned and be prepared for oil loss from the cooler. Note also the arrangement of washers, sealing rings and O-rings underneath the bolt and the gasket sealing the oil cooler/adapter joint – all seals must be renewed as a matter of course whenever they are disturbed.

Refitting

4 Refitting is the reverse of the removal procedure, noting the following points:

a) Renew all O-rings and seals disturbed on removal.

b) Align the cooler's unions as noted on removal and tighten securely the retaining bolt.

c) Refill the cooling system (see Chapter 1).

d) Refit the oil filter, then check the engine oil level and top-up as necessary (see 'Weekly checks').

e) Check for signs of oil or coolant leaks once the engine has been restarted and warmed-up to normal operating temperature.

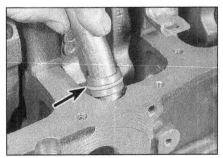

18.11a Removing the oil pump pick-up tube from the crankcase – note the O-ring which must be renewed

18.11b Tightening the oil pump pick-up tube mounting bolts

20 Oil pressure warning light switch – removal and refitting

Note: *Two different types of switch have been fitted – engines built up to July 1998 were fitted with a switch with a black cover, while engines built from August 1998 onwards were fitted with a switch with a green cover – the switch must only be replaced by a switch with a cover of the same colour. The change in switch is associated with the fitment of a revised oil pump from the same date, and the two switches should not be interchanged.*

Removal

1 The switch is screwed into the left-hand end of the cylinder head, next to the fuel filter.
2 With the vehicle parked on firm level ground, open the bonnet and disconnect the battery negative (earth) lead – see Chapter 5A, Section 1.
3 Unplug the wiring from the switch and unscrew it; be prepared for some oil loss.

Refitting

4 Refitting is the reverse of the removal procedure; apply a thin smear of suitable sealant to the switch threads, and tighten it to the specified torque wrench setting. Check the engine oil level and top-up as necessary (see *Weekly checks*). Check for signs of oil leaks once the engine has been restarted and warmed-up to normal operating temperature.

21 Crankshaft oil seals – renewal

Right-hand (timing belt end) seal

1 Remove the crankshaft toothed pulleys as described in Section 11.
2 Note the fitted depth of the oil seal in the timing belt/drivebelt housing.
3 Using a screwdriver or other suitable instrument, prise the oil seal from the timing belt/drivebelt housing. An alternative method is to drill two small holes in the oil seal, then screw in self-tapping screws and use grips to pull out the oil seal. If this method is used, make sure that all swarf is removed.
4 Inspect the seal rubbing surface on the crankshaft inboard toothed pulley and if necessary renew the pulley.
5 Wipe clean the oil seal seating in the timing belt/drivebelt housing.
6 Note that the new oil seal is supplied with a support ring, which **must** remain in position until just before the crankshaft inboard toothed pulley is fitted. The oil seal must be fitted dry.
7 Using a length of metal tube or a socket, drive the new oil seal into the timing belt/drivebelt housing to the previously-noted depth. Leave the support ring in place at this stage.

8 Refit the crankshaft toothed pulleys and timing belt with reference to Section 11.

Left-hand (flywheel end) seal

9 Remove the flywheel as described in Section 22.
10 Unbolt the left-hand oil seal carrier from the sump and cylinder block and withdraw it over the end of the crankshaft. Note that the carrier incorporates an integral oil seal and a vulcanised gasket.
11 Wipe clean the mating faces of the sump and cylinder block. Also wipe all oil from the crankshaft end. Note that the oil seal must be fitted dry.
12 Make sure that the support ring is located inside the oil seal, then locate the carrier over the crankshaft. Screw in the retaining bolts finger-tight.
13 Make sure that the oil seal is centred on the end of the crankshaft, then progressively tighten the carrier mounting bolts to the specified torque **(see illustration)**.
14 Carefully remove the support ring so that the lips of the oil seal rest on the crankshaft. If the ring is tight, it is likely that the left-hand faces of the sump and cylinder block/crankcase are not accurately aligned with each other. To rectify this situation, loosen all the sump bolts, reposition the sump and retighten the bolts to the specified torque.
15 With the carrier bolts tightened, refit the flywheel and transmission with reference to Section 22.

22 Flywheel – removal, inspection and refitting

Removal

1 Remove the transmission as described in Chapter 7.
2 Remove the clutch components with reference to Chapter 6.
3 Make alignment marks on the flywheel and crankshaft to ensure correct refitting.
4 Hold the flywheel stationary using a locking tool engaged with the starter ring gear. A suitable home-made tool bolted to one of the transmission mounting bolt holes and engaged with the ring gear can be fabricated out of metal bar.
5 Unscrew the mounting bolts and lift the flywheel from the rear of the crankshaft. Take care not to drop the flywheel, as it is very heavy. Discard the bolts and obtain new ones for the refitting procedure.

Inspection

6 Examine the clutch mating surface of the flywheel for scoring or cracks. Light grooving or scoring may be ignored. Surface cracks or deep grooving can sometimes be removed by specialist machining, provided not too much metal is taken off; otherwise the flywheel must be renewed.

21.13 Tightening the left-hand oil seal carrier mounting bolts

7 Inspect the starter ring gear for damaged or missing teeth. A damaged ring gear can be renewed separately. The average DIY mechanic may prefer to leave the job to a Ford dealer or other competent workshop; for the enthusiast the procedure is as follows.
8 Drill two adjacent holes, 7 or 8 mm in diameter, through the ring gear. Take care not to drill into the flywheel.
9 Knock the ring gear off the flywheel with a hammer. Use light blows, evenly spaced around the ring.
10 Heat the new ring gear evenly to between 260° and 280°C (500° and 536°F). This is just about within the capability of most domestic ovens. Take care not to overheat the ring gear or its temper will be lost.
11 Using tongs or asbestos gloves, place the ring gear on the flywheel and tap it into place. Allow it to cool naturally. If the teeth have a bevelled lead-in for the starter motor pinion, make sure this is facing outwards (ie towards the clutch face).
12 If renewing the flywheel, transfer the clutch locating dowels to the new unit.

Refitting

13 Commence refitting by placing the flywheel on the end of the crankshaft. Observe the alignment marks if refitting the original unit.
14 Insert the new bolts, and tighten them to the torque and angles given in the Specifications **(see illustration)**.
15 Refit the clutch components with reference to Chapter 6.
16 Refit the transmission with reference to Chapter 7.

22.14 Angle-tightening the flywheel bolts

23 Engine/transmission mountings –
inspection and renewal

Inspection

1 The engine/transmission mountings seldom require attention, but broken or deteriorated mountings should be renewed immediately, or the added strain placed on the driveline components may cause damage or wear.

2 During the check, the engine/transmission must be raised slightly, to remove its weight from the mountings.

3 Apply the handbrake, then jack up the front of the vehicle and support it on axle stands (see *Jacking and vehicle support*). Position a jack under the sump, with a large block of wood between the jack head and the sump, then carefully raise the engine/transmission just enough to take the weight off the mountings.

4 Check the mountings to see if the rubber is cracked, hardened or separated from the metal components. Sometimes, the rubber will split right down the centre.

5 Check for relative movement between each mounting's brackets and the engine/transmission or body (use a large screwdriver or lever to attempt to move the mountings). If movement is noted, lower the engine and check the mounting nuts and bolts for tightness.

Renewal

6 The engine mountings can be removed if the weight of the engine/transmission is supported by one of the following alternative methods. Remember that 'left' and 'right' are as seen from the driver's seat.

7 Either support the weight of the assembly from underneath using a jack and a suitable piece of wood between the jack and the sump (to prevent damage), or from above by attaching a hoist to the engine. A third method is to use a suitable support bar with end pieces which will engage in the water channel each side of the bonnet lid aperture. Using an adjustable hook and chain connected to the engine, the weight of the engine and transmission can then be taken from the mountings.

8 Once the weight of the engine and transmission is suitably supported, any of the mountings can be unbolted and removed.

9 To remove the right-hand mounting, first unbolt the reinforcement bracket then unscrew the nuts and remove the upper bracket. Unscrew the bolts and remove the lower bracket from the cylinder head. Unbolt the insulator from the right-hand side of the engine compartment.

10 To remove the left-hand mounting, loosen the clips and remove the air inlet duct from between the air mass air flow sensor on the air cleaner and the throttle housing (on some models, it may be best to remove the air cleaner completely). Unscrew the mounting nuts from the left-hand engine mounting, then unscrew the bolts and remove the upper bracket. Unscrew the bolts and remove the insulator from the left-hand side of the engine compartment.

11 To remove the engine rear mounting/link, apply the handbrake, then jack up the front of the vehicle and support it on axle stands (see *Jacking and vehicle support*). Unscrew the through-bolts and remove the engine rear mounting link from the bracket on the transmission and from the bracket on the underbody. Hold the engine stationary while the bolts are being removed since the link will be under tension.

12 Refitting of all mountings is a reversal of the removal procedure. Do not fully tighten the mounting nuts/bolts until all of the mountings are in position. Check that the mounting rubbers do not twist or distort as the mounting bolts and nuts are tightened to their specified torques.

Chapter 2 Part B:
Engine removal and overhaul procedures

Contents

Degrees of difficulty

| Easy, suitable for novice with little experience | | Fairly easy, suitable for beginner with some experience | | Fairly difficult, suitable for competent DIY mechanic | 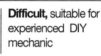 | Difficult, suitable for experienced DIY mechanic | 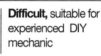 | Very difficult, suitable for expert DIY or professional | |

Specifications

Refer to Chapter 2A Specifications

1 General information and precautions

How to use this Chapter

This Part of Chapter 2 is devoted to engine/transmission removal and refitting, to those repair procedures requiring the removal of the engine/transmission from the vehicle, and to the overhaul of engine components. Refer to Part A for Specifications and torque wrench settings.

General information

The information ranges from advice concerning preparation for an overhaul and the purchase of replacement parts, to detailed step-by-step procedures covering removal and installation of internal engine components and the inspection of parts.

The following Sections have been written based on the assumption that the engine has been removed from the vehicle. For information concerning in-vehicle engine repair, as well as removal and installation of the external components necessary for the overhaul, see Part A of this Chapter.

When overhauling the engine, it is essential to establish first exactly what replacement parts are available. At the time of writing, very few under- or oversized components are available for engine reconditioning. In many

cases, it would appear that the easiest and most economically-sensible course of action is to replace a worn or damaged engine with an exchange unit.

2 Engine overhaul – general information

It's not always easy to determine when, or if, an engine should be completely overhauled, as a number of factors must be considered.

High mileage is not necessarily an indication that an overhaul is needed, while low mileage doesn't preclude the need for an overhaul. Frequency of servicing is probably the most important consideration. An engine that's had regular and frequent oil and filter changes, as well as other required maintenance, will most likely give many thousands of miles of reliable service. Conversely, a neglected engine may require an overhaul very early in its life.

Excessive oil consumption is an indication that piston rings, valve seals and/or valve guides are in need of attention. Make sure that oil leaks aren't responsible before deciding that the rings and/or guides are worn. Perform a cylinder compression check (Part A of this Chapter) to determine the extent of the work required.

Loss of power, rough running, knocking or

metallic engine noises, excessive valve train noise and high fuel consumption rates may also point to the need for an overhaul, especially if they're all present at the same time. If a full service doesn't remedy the situation, major mechanical work is the only solution.

An engine overhaul involves restoring all internal parts to the specification of a new engine. **Note:** *Always check first what replacement parts are available before planning any overhaul operation; refer to Section 1 of this Part. Ford dealers, or a good engine reconditioning specialist/automotive parts supplier may be able to suggest alternatives which will enable you to overcome the lack of replacement parts.*

During an overhaul, it is usual to renew the piston rings, and to rebore and/or hone the cylinder bores; where the rebore is done by an automotive machine shop, new oversize pistons and rings will also be installed – all these operations, of course, assume the availability of suitable replacement parts. The main and big-end bearings are generally renewed and, if necessary, the crankshaft may be reground to restore the journals.

Generally, the valves are serviced as well during an overhaul, since they're usually in less-than-perfect condition at this point. While the engine is being overhauled, other components, such as the starter and alternator, can be renewed as well, or rebuilt, if the necessary parts can be found. The end result should be an as-new engine that will give many trouble-free miles. **Note:** *Critical cooling system components such as the hoses, drivebelt, thermostat and water pump MUST be replaced with new parts when an engine is overhauled. The radiator should be checked carefully, to ensure that it isn't clogged or leaking (see Chapter 3). Also, as a general rule, the oil pump should be renewed when an engine is rebuilt.*

Before beginning the engine overhaul, read through the entire procedure to familiarise yourself with the scope and requirements of the job. Overhauling an engine isn't difficult, but it is time-consuming. Plan on the vehicle being off the road for a minimum of two weeks, especially if parts must be taken to an automotive machine shop for repair or reconditioning. Check on availability of parts, and make sure that any necessary special tools and equipment are obtained in advance. Most work can be done with typical hand tools, although a number of precision measuring tools are required, for inspecting parts to determine if they must be replaced. Often, an automotive machine shop will handle the inspection of parts, and will offer advice concerning reconditioning and replacement. **Note:** *Always wait until the engine has been completely dismantled, and all components, especially the cylinder block/crankcase, have been inspected, before deciding what service and repair operations must be performed by an automotive machine shop. Since the block's condition will be the major factor to consider when determining whether to overhaul the original engine or buy a rebuilt one, never purchase parts or have machine work done on other components until the cylinder block/crankcase has been thoroughly inspected.* As a general rule, time is the primary cost of an overhaul, so it doesn't pay to install worn or sub-standard parts.

As a final note, to ensure maximum life and minimum trouble from a rebuilt engine, everything must be assembled with care, in a spotlessly-clean environment.

3 Engine/transmission removal – methods and precautions

If you've decided that an engine must be removed for overhaul or major repair work, several preliminary steps should be taken.

Locating a suitable place to work is extremely important. Adequate work space, along with storage space for the vehicle, will be needed. If a workshop or garage isn't available, at the very least, a flat, level, clean work surface made of concrete or asphalt is required.

Cleaning the engine compartment and engine/transmission before beginning the removal procedure will help keep tools clean and organised.

The engine can only be withdrawn by removing it complete with the transmission; the vehicle's body must be raised and supported securely, sufficiently high that the engine/transmission can be unbolted as a single unit and lowered to the ground; the engine/transmission unit can then be withdrawn from under the vehicle and separated. An engine hoist or A-frame will therefore be necessary. Make sure the equipment is rated in excess of the combined weight of the engine and transmission. Safety is of primary importance, considering the potential hazards involved in removing the engine/transmission from the vehicle.

If this is the first time you have removed an engine, a helper should ideally be available. Advice and aid from someone more experienced would also be helpful. There are many instances when one person cannot simultaneously perform all of the operations required when removing the engine/transmission from the vehicle.

Plan the operation ahead of time. Arrange for, or obtain, all of the tools and equipment you'll need prior to beginning the job. Some of the equipment necessary to perform engine/transmission removal and installation safely and with relative ease, and which may have to be hired or borrowed, includes (in addition to the engine hoist) a heavy-duty trolley jack, a strong pair of axle stands, some wooden blocks, and an engine dolly (a low, wheeled platform capable of taking the weight of the engine/transmission, so that it can be moved easily when on the ground). A complete set of spanners and sockets (as described in the front of this manual) will obviously be needed, together with plenty of rags and cleaning solvent for mopping-up spilled oil, coolant and fuel. If the hoist is to be hired, make sure that you arrange for it in advance, and perform all of the operations possible without it beforehand. This will save you money and time.

Plan for the vehicle to be out of use for quite a while. A machine shop will be required to perform some of the work which the do-it-yourselfer can't accomplish without special equipment. These establishments often have a busy schedule, so it would be a good idea to consult them before removing the engine,

4.7 Oil pressure switch (arrowed)

to accurately estimate the amount of time required to rebuild or repair components that may need work.

Always be extremely careful when removing and installing the engine/transmission. Serious injury can result from careless actions. By planning ahead and taking your time, the job (although a major task) can be accomplished successfully.

4 Engine/transmission – removal, separation and refitting

Note: *Read through the entire Section, as well as reading the advice in the preceding Section, before beginning this procedure. The engine and transmission are removed as a unit, lowered to the ground and removed from underneath, then separated outside the vehicle.*

Note: *The engine/transmission assembly is lowered from the engine compartment, then separated on the bench.*

Removal

1 Apply the handbrake, then jack up the front of the vehicle and support it on axle stands (see *Jacking and vehicle support*). Where applicable, remove the engine undershield and the plastic panels at the front of the wheel arches.

2 Drain the cooling system as described in Chapter 1. Although not essential for engine removal, if the engine is to be overhauled, it makes sense to also drain the engine oil.

3 Lower the car to the ground. Disconnect the battery negative (earth) lead (see Chapter 5A).

4 Remove the air cleaner and intercooler as described in Chapter 4A.

5 On later models, remove the radiator upper shroud, which is secured by a total of four bolts and nine clips – the clips are removed by tapping out their centre pins.

6 Loosen the hose clips and disconnect the vent hose from the expansion tank, and the radiator hoses from the engine. Identify the heater hoses on the bulkhead, then loosen the clips and disconnect them. Trace the coolant supply hose to the oil cooler, and disconnect this also.

7 Disconnect the following wiring, as applicable:
a) *Injection pump wiring loom.*
b) *Glow plug wiring.*
c) *Temperature gauge sender unit.*
d) *Engine coolant temperature sensor.*
e) *Radiator cooling fan.*
f) *Oil pressure switch on the left-hand side of the cylinder head* **(see illustration).**
g) *Diesel fuel heater on the left-hand side of the cylinder head.*
h) *Multi-function switch wiring plug on the left-hand inner wing (left as seen from the driver's seat).*
i) *Exhaust gas recirculation valve.*

4.11 Disconnecting the brake servo vacuum hose from the vacuum pump

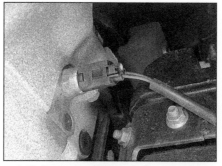

4.12 Reversing light switch and wiring plug

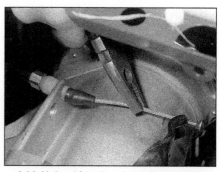

4.14 Unhooking the clutch inner cable

8 Pull out the clip and disconnect the outer accelerator cable from the bracket on the injection pump. Disconnect the inner cable from the lever.

9 Disconnect the fuel return line from the injection pump, and the fuel feed line from the filter.

10 On models with air conditioning, unhook and release the idle adjuster cable from the bracket on top of the injection pump.

11 Unscrew the brake servo vacuum pipe union from the vacuum pump **(see illustration)**.

12 Unbolt and remove the earth lead from the transmission, then disconnect the reversing light switch and detach the wiring harness from the top of the transmission **(see illustration)**.

13 Pull off the vacuum hose from the EGR valve.

14 Disconnect the clutch cable from the operating lever on the top of the transmission – unhook the inner cable, and release the outer cable from the bracket **(see illustration)**.

15 On models with air conditioning, the power steering hoses must be disconnected. Anticipate fluid spillage when the return hose to the reservoir is removed; the other hose runs across the cylinder head cover, and has a screw connection.

16 Loosen the front wheel nuts, then jack up the front of the vehicle and support it on axle stands (see *Jacking and vehicle support*). The vehicle should be raised to a sufficient height to allow the engine/transmission to be withdrawn underneath.

17 Disconnect the exhaust front downpipe from the manifold. On models with the TC (non-intercooler) engine, Ford recommend separating the exhaust ahead of the flexible section – care should be taken not to over-flex the exhaust flexible section during separation.

18 Disconnect the wiring from the starter motor and alternator – note the location of the wiring carefully, as it can be confusing when refitting **(see illustrations)**.

19 On models with air conditioning:

a) *Detach the refrigerant pipework and associated wiring from the radiator support crossmember.*

b) *Remove the three nuts securing the*

dehydrator/accumulator from the crossmember.

c) *Unbolt the condenser from the crossmember, and tie it up to the front 'slam panel' using cable-ties.*

d) *Remove the alternator as described in Chapter 5A.*

e) *Disconnect the wiring plug from the air conditioning compressor.*

f) *Remove the four compressor mounting bolts visible from below, then tie the compressor up to a convenient point at the front, clear of the engine.*

 Warning: Do not disconnect the refrigerant hoses.

20 Refer to Chapter 3 and remove the radiator. This is essential on models with air conditioning, but is advisable on all models, given the risk of damage occurring to it during engine removal and refitting.

4.18a Starter motor wiring

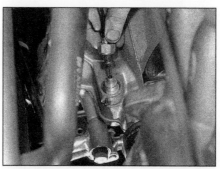

4.21 Disconnecting the speedometer drive cable

21 Unscrew the nut securing the speedometer cable to the transmission **(see illustration)**. On later models where a vehicle speed sensor is fitted, two spanners may be needed for this operation (also disconnect the sensor wiring plug).

22 Remove the two large bolts securing the engine roll restrictor. On later models, also disconnect the wiring plug from the crankshaft position sensor which is located nearby **(see illustration)**.

23 Remove the bolt securing the gearshift stabiliser bar, and also disconnect the gearchange linkage from the transmission **(see illustrations)**.

24 Where a transmission oil drain plug is fitted, drain the oil now, or be prepared for oil spillage when the driveshafts are disconnected later.

25 Remove the bolt from the engine right-hand rear mounting **(see illustration)**.

4.18b Typically, the alternator main wiring plug is secured using a spring clip (arrowed) – push aside to release it

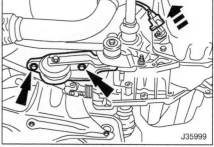

4.22 Engine roll restrictor bolts (arrowed) and disconnecting the crankshaft position sensor wiring plug

4.23a Gearchange stabiliser rod – note location of the plain washer (arrowed)

4.23b Gearchange linkage joint and clamp

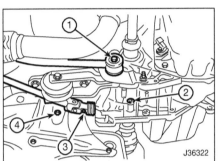

4.25 Engine removal details

1 *Gearshift stabiliser bolt*
2 *Transmission oil drain plug*
3 *Gearchange linkage bolt*
4 *Engine right-hand rear mounting bolt*

26 Remove the driveshafts as described in Chapter 8.

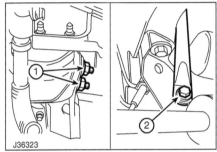

4.28 Engine front right-hand mounting brace-to-engine mounting nuts (1) and bolt to front crossmember (2)

27 Take the weight of the engine/transmission unit, using the lifting eyes provided on the cylinder head.
28 Remove the nuts and bolt securing the engine front right-hand mounting brace from the engine front mounting and front cross-member **(see illustration)**.
29 Remove the nut and bolt from the engine rear right-hand mounting **(see illustration)**.
30 Remove the three nuts from the engine rear right-hand mounting **(see illustration)**.
31 Remove the two nuts from the engine front right-hand mounting **(see illustration)**.
32 Finally, remove the two bolts securing the rear left-hand mounting from the side member **(see illustration)**.
33 Do a final check around the engine/transmission, to ensure that there is nothing to prevent the engine/transmission from being lowered out of the vehicle.
34 With the help of an assistant, carefully lower the assembly from the engine compartment, making sure that it clears the surrounding components and bodywork **(see illustrations)**.
35 If the engine is to be overhauled, remove the wiring loom from the engine, noting its location and routing.

Separation

36 To separate the transmission from the engine, first remove the starter motor with reference to Chapter 5A.
37 Unscrew and remove the bolts securing the transmission to the engine.
38 With the help of an assistant, withdraw the transmission directly from the engine, making sure that its weight is not allowed to bear on the clutch friction disc. Remove the adapter plate from the dowels on the cylinder block.

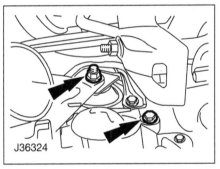

4.29 Engine rear right-hand mounting nut and bolt (arrowed)

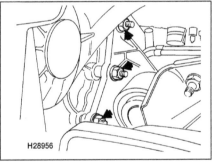

4.30 Remove the three nuts (arrowed) from the engine rear right-hand mounting

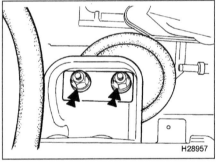

4.31 Engine front right-hand mounting nuts (arrowed)

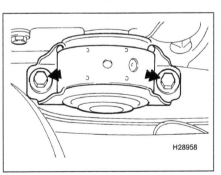

4.32 Engine rear left-hand mounting bolts (arrowed)

4.34a Lowering out the engine/transmission

4.34b If the engine/transmission unit is lowered onto a board, this makes moving the assembly easier

Refitting

39 Refitting is a reversal of removal, noting the following additional points:

a) Make sure that all mating faces are clean.

b) Apply a smear of high-melting-point grease to the splines of the transmission input shaft. Do not apply too much, otherwise there is the possibility of the grease contaminating the clutch friction disc.

c) Make sure that the clutch release bearing is correctly located inside the transmission bellhousing.

d) Ensure that the engine adapter plate is correctly seated on the locating dowels on the engine **(see illustration)**.

e) Fit new circlips to the grooves in the inner end of each driveshaft CV joint, and ensure that they fully engage as they are fitted into the transmission.

f) Refit the engine mountings as described in Chapter 2A.

g) Check and if necessary adjust the gearchange linkage as described in Chapter 7.

h) Replenish the transmission oil, and check the level with reference to Chapter 1.

i) Check the clutch adjustment as described in Chapter 1.

j) Refill the engine with oil and refill the cooling system as described in Chapter 1.

k) Tighten all nuts and bolts to the specified torque setting.

5 Engine overhaul – dismantling sequence

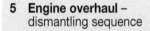

1 It is much easier to disassemble and work on the engine if it is mounted on a portable engine stand. These stands can often be hired from a tool hire shop. Before the engine is mounted on a stand, the flywheel should be removed from the engine, so that the engine stand bolts can be tightened into the end of the cylinder block.

2 If a stand is not available, it is possible to disassemble the engine with it blocked up on a sturdy workbench or on the floor. Be extra-careful not to tip or drop the engine when working without a stand.

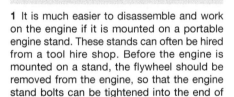

6.2a Removing the vacuum pump operating plunger . . .

4.39 Engine adapter plate (arrowed)

3 If you are going to obtain a reconditioned engine, all external components must be removed first, to be transferred to the replacement engine (just as they will if you are doing a complete engine overhaul yourself). **Note:** When removing the external components from the engine, pay close attention to details that may be helpful or important during refitting. Note the fitted position of gaskets, seals, spacers, pins, washers, bolts and other small items. These external components include the following:

a) Alternator mounting bracket.

b) Fuel injection pump and mounting bracket, and fuel injectors and glow plugs.

c) Thermostat and cover.

d) Inlet and exhaust manifolds.

e) Oil cooler.

f) Engine lifting brackets, hose brackets and wiring brackets.

g) Ancillary (power steering pump, air conditioning compressor) brackets.

h) Oil pressure warning light switch.

i) Coolant temperature sensors.

j) Wiring harnesses and brackets.

k) Coolant pipes and hoses.

l) Oil filler tube and dipstick.

m) Clutch.

n) Flywheel.

4 If you are obtaining a 'short' motor (which, when available, consists of the engine cylinder block, crankshaft, pistons and connecting rods all assembled), then the cylinder head, sump, oil pump, and timing belt (where applicable) will have to be removed also.

6.2b . . . and the oil pressure switch

5 If you are planning a complete overhaul, the engine can be disassembled and the internal components removed in the following order:

a) Engine external components (including inlet and exhaust manifolds).

b) Timing sprockets and belts.

c) Cylinder head.

d) Flywheel.

e) Sump.

f) Oil pump.

g) Pistons and connecting rods.

h) Crankshaft and main bearings.

6 Before beginning the disassembly and overhaul procedures, make sure that you have all of the correct tools necessary. Refer to the reference section at the end of this manual for further information.

6 Cylinder head – dismantling

Note: New and reconditioned cylinder heads are available from the manufacturers, and from engine overhaul specialists. Due to the fact that some specialist tools are required for the dismantling and inspection procedures, and new components may not be readily available (refer to Section 1), it may be more practical and economical for the home mechanic to purchase a reconditioned head, rather than to dismantle, inspect and recondition the original head.

1 Remove the camshaft and tappets (Part A of this Chapter).

2 If not already done, remove all the external cylinder head components, such as the engine lifting eyes, oil pressure switch and vacuum pump **(see illustrations)**.

3 Using a valve spring compressor, depress one valve spring retainer to gain access to the collets. The valves are deeply recessed, so the end of the compressor may need to be extended with a tube or box section with a 'window' for access. Remove the collets and release the compressor. Recover the valve, spring and retainer **(see illustrations)**. Pull out the valve stem oil seals using thin-nosed pliers.

4 If, when the valve spring compressor is screwed down, the spring upper seat refuses

6.3a Valve spring compressor in use – note extension tube (arrowed)

6.3b Removing a valve spring and retainer

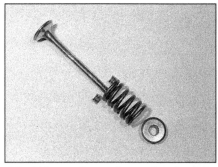

6.3c Valve, spring, spring seat and collets

6.5 Use a clearly-labelled bag to store and identify the valve components

6.6 Cylinder head oil-retaining valve (arrowed)

7.5 Measuring swirl chamber projection

to free and expose the split collets, gently tap the top of the tool, directly over the upper seat, with a light hammer. This will free the seat.

5 It is essential that the valves are kept together with their collets, spring seats and springs, and in their correct sequence (unless they are so badly worn that they are to be renewed). If they are going to be kept and used again, place them in a labelled polythene bag or similar small container **(see illustration)**. Note that No 1 valve is nearest to the timing belt end of the engine.

6 If the oil-retaining valve is to be removed (to flush out the cylinder head oil galleries thoroughly), seek the advice of a Ford dealer as to how it can be extracted; it may be that the only course of action involves destroying the valve as follows. Screw a self-tapping screw into its ventilation hole, and use the screw to provide purchase with which the

valve can be drawn out; a new valve must be purchased and pressed into place on reassembly **(see illustration)**.

7 Cylinder head and valve components – cleaning and inspection

1 Thorough cleaning of the cylinder head and valve components, followed by a detailed inspection, will enable you to decide how much valve service work must be carried out during the engine overhaul. **Note:** *If the engine has been severely overheated, it is best to assume that the cylinder head is warped, and to check carefully for signs of this.*

Cleaning

2 Scrape away all traces of old gasket material and sealing compound from the cylinder head.

3 Scrape away the carbon from the combustion chambers and ports, then wash the cylinder head thoroughly with paraffin or a suitable solvent.

4 Scrape off any heavy carbon deposits that may have formed on the valves, then use a power-operated wire brush to remove deposits from the valve heads and stems.

5 The swirl chambers may be removed from their locations using a soft metal drift inserted through the injector holes (if this is done, mark the swirl chambers so that they can be refitted in their original locations). Before removing the swirl chambers use feeler blades and a straight-edge to measure their projection, and

compare with the information given in the Specifications (see Part A of this Chapter) **(see illustration)**. Alternatively, use a dial test indicator to make the check. Zero the dial test indicator on the gasket surface of the cylinder head, then measure the protrusion of the swirl chamber.

6 If the head is extremely dirty, it should be steam cleaned. On completion, make sure that all oil holes and oil galleries are cleaned.

Inspection

Note: *Be sure to perform all the following inspection procedures before concluding that the services of a machine shop or engine overhaul specialist are required. Make a list of all items that require attention.*

Cylinder head

7 Inspect the head very carefully for cracks, evidence of coolant leakage, and other damage. If cracks are found, a new cylinder head should be obtained.

8 Use a straight-edge and feeler blade to check that the cylinder head surface is not distorted. Do not position the straight-edge over the swirl chambers, as these may be proud of the cylinder head face. If the specified distortion limit is exceeded, machining of the gasket face is not recommended by the manufacturers, so the only course of action is to renew the cylinder head.

9 Examine the valve seats in each of the combustion chambers. If they are severely pitted, cracked or burned, then they will need to be renewed or re-cut by an engine overhaul specialist. If they are only slightly pitted, this can be removed by grinding-in the valve heads and seats with fine valve-grinding compound, as described below.

10 If the valve guides are worn, indicated by a side-to-side motion of the valve in the guide, new guides must be fitted. If necessary, insert a new valve in the guides to determine if the wear is on the guide or valve. If new guides are to be fitted, the valves must be renewed as a matter of course. Valve guides may be renewed using a press and a suitable mandrel, however, the work is best carried out by an engine overhaul specialist, since if it is not done skillfully, there is a risk of damaging the cylinder head.

11 The renewal of valve guides is best carried out by an engine overhaul specialist.

12 If the valve seats are to be re-cut, this must be done only after the guides have been renewed.

13 Inspect the swirl chambers for burning or cracks, and renew the chambers if necessary.

Valves

14 Examine the head of each valve for pitting, burning, cracks and general wear, and check the valve stem for scoring and wear ridges. Rotate the valve, and check for any obvious indication that it is bent. Look for pits and excessive wear on the end of each valve stem. If the valve appears satisfactory at this

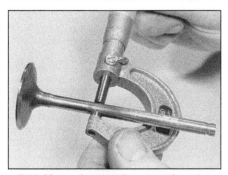

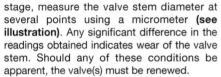

7.14 Measuring the diameter of a valve stem

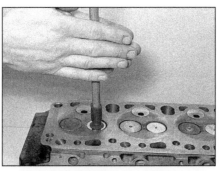

7.17 Grinding in a valve

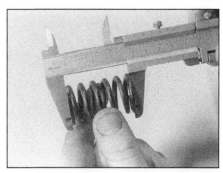

7.20 Checking the valve spring free length

stage, measure the valve stem diameter at several points using a micrometer **(see illustration)**. Any significant difference in the readings obtained indicates wear of the valve stem. Should any of these conditions be apparent, the valve(s) must be renewed.

15 If the valves are in satisfactory condition, they should be ground (lapped) into their respective seats, to ensure a smooth gas-tight seal. If the seat is only lightly pitted, or if it has been re-cut, fine grinding compound only should be used to produce the required finish. Coarse valve-grinding compound should not be used unless a seat is badly burned or deeply pitted; if this is the case, the cylinder head and valves should be inspected by an expert, to decide whether seat re-cutting, or even the renewal of the valve or seat insert, is required.

16 Valve grinding is carried out as follows. Place the cylinder head upside-down on a bench, with a block of wood at each end to give clearance for the valve stems.

17 Smear a trace of (the appropriate grade of) valve-grinding compound on the seat face, and press a suction grinding tool onto the valve head. With a semi-rotary action, grind the valve head to its seat, lifting the valve occasionally to redistribute the grinding compound **(see illustration)**. A light spring placed under the valve head will greatly ease this operation.

18 If coarse grinding compound is being used, work only until a dull, matt even surface is produced on both the valve seat and the valve, then wipe off the used compound, and repeat the process with fine compound. When a smooth unbroken ring of light grey matt finish is produced on both the valve and seat, the grinding operation is complete. Do not grind in the valves any further than absolutely necessary, or the seat will be prematurely sunk into the cylinder head.

19 When all the valves have been ground-in, carefully wash off all traces of grinding compound, using paraffin or a suitable solvent, before reassembly of the cylinder head.

Valve components

20 Examine the valve springs for signs of damage and discolouration, and also measure their free length (or compare each of the existing springs with a new component) **(see illustration)**.

21 Stand each spring on a flat surface, and check it for squareness. If any of the springs are damaged, distorted, or have lost their tension, obtain a complete set of new springs.

22 Check the spring seats and collets for obvious wear and cracks. Any questionable parts should be renewed, as extensive damage will occur if they fail during engine operation. Any damaged or excessively-worn parts must be renewed; the valve stem oil seals must be renewed as a matter of course whenever they are disturbed.

23 Check the tappets as described in Part A of this Chapter.

8 Cylinder head – reassembly

1 Regardless of whether or not the head was sent away for repair work of any sort, make sure that it is clean before beginning reassembly. Be sure to remove any metal particles and abrasive grit that may still be present from operations such as valve grinding. Use compressed air, if available, to blow out all the oil holes and passages.

2 If the swirl chambers have been removed, refit them to their original locations. Check the protrusion of the swirl chambers as described in Section 7.

3 Beginning at one end of the head, lubricate and install the first valve. Apply molybdenum disulphide-based grease or clean engine oil to

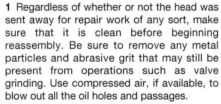

8.4 Fitting a valve stem oil seal. The end of the stem is covered with plastic film

the valve stem, and refit the valve. Where the original valves are being re-used, ensure that each is refitted in its original guide. If new valves are being fitted, insert them into the locations to which they have been ground.

4 Fit the plastic protector supplied with new valve stem oil seals to the end of the valve stem – if no sleeves are provided, cover the collet grooves at the top of each valve by wrapping round a little adhesive tape. Lubricate the oil seal with clean engine oil, and put the seal squarely on top of the valve stem **(see illustration)**. Fit the seals by pushing into position using a suitable deep socket. Ensure that the seals are fully engaged with the valve guide. Note that new inlet and exhaust seals are usually different colours – green for the inlet valves, red for the exhaust valves.

5 Refit the valve spring and spring seat, keeping the components in their original fitted positions, as applicable.

6 Compress the spring with a valve spring compressor, and carefully install the collets in the stem grooves. Apply a small dab of grease to each collet to hold it in place if necessary **(see illustration)**. Slowly release the compressor, and make sure the collets seat properly.

7 When the valve is installed, place the cylinder head flat on the bench and, using a hammer and interposed block of wood, tap the end of the valve stem gently, to settle the components.

8 Repeat the procedure for the remaining valves.

9 Refit the tappets as described in Part A of this Chapter.

8.6 Apply a little grease to the collets before installation, to hold them in place

9.5a Withdraw the auxiliary shaft a little, then remove the thrust plate

9 Auxiliary shaft – removal, inspection and refitting

Note: *A new auxiliary shaft oil seal/housing and oil pump gasket will be required on refitting.*

Removal

1 Remove the auxiliary shaft toothed pulley and the oil pump as described in Chapter 2A.
2 Unbolt the timing belt inner shield.
3 Unscrew the bolts and remove the oil seal housing from the cylinder block. The oil seal is integral with the housing.
4 Unscrew the bolts securing the thrustplate to the cylinder block, then carefully withdraw the auxiliary shaft, taking care not to allow the oil pump gear to snag on the shaft bearing.
5 Remove the thrustplate from the shaft, noting that the oilways are facing outwards **(see illustrations)**.

Inspection

6 Examine the auxiliary shaft and oil pump drivegear for pitting, scoring or wear ridges on the bearing journals, and for chipping or wear of the gear teeth. Renew as necessary. Check the auxiliary shaft bearings in the cylinder block for wear and, if worn, have these renewed by your Ford dealer or suitably-equipped engineering works. Wipe them clean if they are still serviceable.
7 Temporarily fit the thrustplate to its position on the auxiliary shaft, and check for excessive

10.2 Each connecting rod and big-end bearing cap will have a flat-machined surface, with the cylinder number etched in it

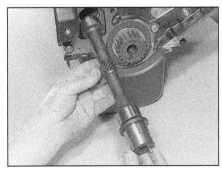

9.5b Removing the auxiliary shaft

wear. If possible, compare the shaft and thrustplate with new components to indicate the amount of wear, and renew them if necessary.

Refitting

8 Lubricate the bearing journals of the auxiliary shaft and the bearings in the cylinder block with fresh engine oil.
9 Lubricate the thrustplate, then locate it on the shaft with the oilways facing outwards (i.e. towards the toothed pulley). Insert the shaft and thrustplate into the cylinder block, then refit the bolts and tighten to the specified torque.
10 Clean the timing belt/drivebelt housing, the cylinder block and the auxiliary shaft end.
11 Smear fresh engine oil on the auxiliary shaft, and on the sealing lips of the new oil seal. Before fitting the new seal, locate the special fitting ring inside the sealing lips.
12 Locate the new oil seal housing over the end of the auxiliary shaft, then insert the bolts and tighten.
13 Carefully remove the special ring and make sure that the seal lips are located on the shaft correctly.
14 Refit the timing belt side cover and tighten the bolts.
15 Refit the auxiliary shaft toothed pulley and the oil pump as described in Chapter 2A.

10 Piston/connecting rod assemblies – removal

1 Remove the cylinder head, sump, oil pump pick-up tube and baffle plate with reference to Chapter 2A.
2 Rotate the crankshaft so that No 1 big-end cap (timing end of the engine) is at the lowest point of its travel. If the big-end cap and rod are not already numbered, mark them with a marker pen **(see illustration)**. Mark both cap and rod to identify the cylinder they operate in.
3 Unscrew and remove the big-end bearing cap bolts, and withdraw the cap complete with shell bearing from the connecting rod. Make sure that the shell remains in the cap, and if necessary identify it for position.

4 If only the bearing shells are being attended to, push the connecting rod up and off the crankpin, and remove the upper bearing shell. Keep the bearing shells and cap together in their correct sequence if they are to be refitted.
5 If the piston is being removed, push the connecting rod up and remove the piston and rod from the top of the bore. Note that if there is a pronounced wear ridge at the top of the bore, there is a risk of damaging the piston as the rings foul the ridge. However, it is reasonable to assume that a rebore and new pistons will be required in any case if the ridge is so pronounced.
6 Repeat the procedure for the remaining piston/connecting rod assemblies. Ensure that the caps and rods are marked before removal, as described previously, and keep all components in order.

11 Crankshaft – removal

1 Remove the timing belts, crankshaft sprocket, timing belt inner shield, sump, oil pick-up tube, flywheel and left-hand/flywheel end oil seal housing. The pistons/connecting rods must be free of the crankshaft journals, however it is not essential to remove them completely from the cylinder block.
2 Before the crankshaft is removed, check the endfloat. Mount a dial gauge with the probe in line with the crankshaft and just touching the crankshaft **(see illustration)**.
3 Push the crankshaft fully away from the gauge, and zero it. Next, lever the crankshaft towards the gauge as far as possible, and check the reading obtained. The distance that the crankshaft moved is its endfloat; if it is greater than specified, new thrustwashers will be required (see Chapter 2A Specifications).
4 If no dial gauge is available, feeler blades can be used. Gently lever or push the crankshaft in one direction, then insert feeler blades between the crankshaft web and the main bearing to determine the clearance.
5 Check that the main bearing caps have marks to indicate their respective fitted

11.2 Checking crankshaft endfloat with a dial gauge

positions in the block. They also have arrow marks pointing towards the timing end of the engine to indicate correct orientation (see illustration).

6 Unscrew the retaining bolts, and remove the main bearing caps. If the caps are reluctant to separate from the block face, lightly tap them free using a plastic- or copper-faced hammer. If the bearing shells are likely to be used again, keep them with their bearing caps for safekeeping. However, unless the engine is known to be of low mileage, it is recommended that they be renewed.

7 Lift the crankshaft out from the crankcase, then extract the upper bearing shells and side thrustwashers (see illustration). Keep them with their respective caps for correct repositioning if they are to be used again.

12 Cylinder block/crankcase – cleaning and inspection

Cleaning

1 For complete cleaning, the core plugs should be removed. Drill a small hole in them, then insert a self-tapping screw and pull out the plugs using a pair of grips or a slide-hammer (see illustration). Also remove all external components and senders (if not already done), noting their locations. Remove the oil jets from the bottom of each bore.

2 Scrape all traces of gasket or sealant from the cylinder block, taking care not to damage the head and sump mating faces.

3 If the block is extremely dirty, it should be steam-cleaned.

4 After the block has been steam-cleaned, clean all oil holes and oil galleries one more time. Flush all internal passages with warm water until the water runs clear, dry the block thoroughly and wipe all machined surfaces with a light rust-preventative oil. If you have access to compressed air, use it to speed up the drying process and to blow out all the oil holes and galleries.

 Warning: Wear eye protection when using compressed air.

5 If the block is not very dirty, you can do an adequate cleaning job with hot soapy water and a stiff brush. Take plenty of time, and do a thorough job. Regardless of the cleaning method used, be sure to clean all oil holes and galleries very thoroughly, dry the block completely and coat all machined surfaces with light oil.

6 The threaded holes in the block must be clean to ensure accurate torque wrench readings during reassembly. Run the proper-size tap into each of the holes to remove rust, corrosion, thread sealant or sludge, and to restore damaged threads (see illustration). If possible, use compressed air to clear the holes of debris produced by this operation.

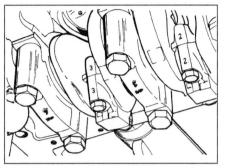
11.5 Big-end and main bearing cap markings

Now is a good time to clean the threads on the head bolts and the main bearing cap bolts as well.

7 Where applicable, refit the main bearing caps, and tighten the bolts finger-tight.

8 After coating the mating surfaces of the new core plugs with suitable sealant, refit them in the cylinder block. Make sure that they are driven in straight and seated properly, or leakage could result. Special tools are available for this purpose, but a large socket, with an outside diameter that will just slip into the core plug, will work just as well (see illustration).

9 Make sure that the oil jets are cleaned thoroughly. After cleaning the cylinder block, refit the jets (see illustration).

10 If the engine is not going to be re-

12.1 The core plugs should be removed with a puller – if they're driven into the block, they may be impossible to retrieve

12.8 A large socket on an extension can be used to drive the new core plugs into their bores

11.7 Felt marker pens can be used as shown to identify bearing shells without damaging them

assembled right away, cover it with a large plastic bag to keep it clean and prevent it rusting.

Inspection

11 Visually check the block for cracks, rust and corrosion. Look for stripped threads in the threaded holes. If there has been any history of internal water leakage, it may be worthwhile having an engine overhaul specialist check the block with special equipment. If defects are found, have the block repaired, if possible, or renewed.

12 Check the cylinder bores for scuffing and scoring. Normally, bore wear will be evident in the form of a wear ridge at the top of the bore. This ridge marks the limit of piston travel.

13 Measure the diameter of each cylinder at

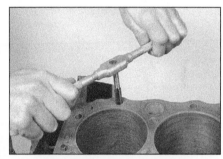
12.6 All bolt holes in the block – particularly the main bearing cap and head bolt holes – should be cleaned and restored with a tap

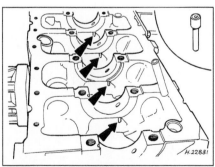
12.9 Piston-cooling oil jet locations (arrowed)

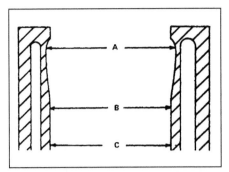

12.13 Measure the diameter of each cylinder just under the wear ridge (A), at the centre (B) and at the bottom (C)

12.19a A 'bottle-brush' hone will produce better results if you have never honed cylinders before

the top (just under the ridge area), centre and bottom of the cylinder bore, parallel to the crankshaft axis **(see illustration)**.

14 Next measure each cylinder's diameter at the same three locations across the crankshaft axis. If the difference between any of the measurements is greater than 0.20 mm, indicating that the cylinder is excessively out-of-round or tapered, then remedial action must be considered.

15 Repeat this procedure for the remaining cylinders, then measure the diameter of each piston at right-angles to the gudgeon pin axis, and compare the result with the information given in the Specifications **(see illustration)**. By comparing the piston diameters with the bore diameters, an idea can be obtained of the clearances.

16 If the cylinder walls are badly scuffed or

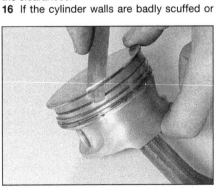

13.2 Using feeler blades to remove piston rings

12.15 Measure the piston skirt diameter at right-angles to the gudgeon pin axis, just above the base of the skirt

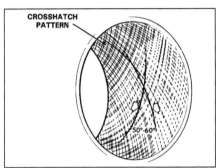

12.19b The cylinder hone should leave a smooth, cross-hatch pattern with the lines intersecting at approximately a 60° angle

scored, or if they are excessively out-of-round or tapered, have the cylinder block rebored (where possible) by an engine overhaul specialist. New pistons (oversize in the case of a rebore) will also be required.

17 If the cylinders are in reasonably good condition, then it may only be necessary to renew the piston rings.

18 If this is the case, the bores should be honed in order to allow the new rings to bed in correctly and provide the best possible seal. The conventional type of hone has spring-loaded stones, and is used with a power drill. You will also need some paraffin or honing oil and rags.

19 The hone should be moved up and down the cylinder to produce a crosshatch pattern, and plenty of honing oil should be used. Ideally, the crosshatch lines should intersect

13.4 Piston ring grooves can be cleaned using a piece of an old ring

at approximately a 60° angle **(see illustrations)**. Do not take off more material than is necessary to produce the required finish. If new pistons are being fitted, the piston manufacturers may specify a finish with a different angle, so their instructions should be followed.

20 Do not withdraw the hone from the cylinder while it is still being turned, but stop it first (keep the hone moving up-and-down the bore while it slows down). After honing a cylinder, wipe out all traces of the honing oil. If equipment of this type is not available, or if you are not sure whether you are competent to undertake the task yourself, an engine overhaul specialist will carry out the work at a moderate cost.

21 Refit all external components and senders in their correct locations, as noted before removal.

13 Piston/connecting rod assemblies – inspection and reassembly

Inspection

1 Before the inspection process can begin, the piston/connecting rod assemblies must be cleaned, and the original piston rings removed from the pistons.

2 Carefully expand the old rings over the top of the pistons. The use of two or three old feeler blades will be helpful in preventing the rings dropping into empty grooves **(see illustration)**. Note that the oil control scraper ring is in two sections.

3 Scrape away all traces of carbon from the top of the piston. A hand-held wire brush or a piece of fine emery cloth can be used once the majority of the deposits have been scraped away.

4 Remove the carbon from the ring grooves in the piston by cleaning them using an old ring **(see illustration)**. Break the ring in half to do this. Be very careful to remove only the carbon deposits; do not remove any metal, or scratch the sides of the ring grooves. Protect your fingers – piston rings are sharp.

5 Once the deposits have been removed, clean the piston/connecting rod assembly with paraffin or a suitable solvent, and dry thoroughly. Make sure the oil return holes in the ring grooves are clear.

6 If the pistons and cylinder bores are not damaged or worn excessively, and if the cylinder block does not need to be rebored, the original pistons can be re-used. Normal piston wear appears as even vertical wear on the piston thrust surfaces, and slight looseness of the top ring in its groove. New piston rings, however, should always be used when the engine is reassembled.

7 Carefully inspect each piston for cracks around the skirt, at the gudgeon pin bosses, and at the piston ring lands (between the piston ring grooves).

8 Look for scoring and scuffing on the sides of the skirt, holes in the piston crown, and burned areas at the edge of the crown. If the skirt is scored or scuffed, the engine may have been suffering from overheating and/or abnormal combustion, which caused excessively-high operating temperatures. The cooling and lubricating systems should be checked thoroughly. Scorch marks on the sides of the pistons show that blow-by has occurred and the rings are not sealing correctly. A hole in the piston crown is an indication that abnormal combustion has been occurring. If any of the above problems exist, the causes must be corrected, or the damage will occur again – incorrect injection pump timing or a faulty injector may be the cause.

9 Corrosion of the piston, in the form of small pits, indicates that coolant is leaking into the combustion chamber and/or the crankcase. Again, the cause must be corrected, or the problem may persist in the rebuilt engine.

10 If new rings are being fitted to old pistons, measure the piston ring-to-groove clearance by placing a new piston ring in each ring groove and measuring the clearance with a feeler blade. Check the clearance at three or four places around each groove (see illustration). Where no values are specified, if the measured clearance is excessive – say greater than 0.10 mm – new pistons will be required. If the new ring is excessively tight, the most likely cause is dirt remaining in the groove.

11 Check the piston-to-bore clearance by measuring the cylinder bore (see Section 16) and the piston diameter. Measure the piston across the skirt, at a 90° angle to the gudgeon pin, approximately half-way down the skirt. Subtract the piston diameter from the bore diameter to obtain the clearance. If this is greater than the figures given in the Specifications, the block will have to be rebored and new pistons and rings fitted.

12 Check the fit of the gudgeon pin by twisting the piston and connecting rod in opposite directions. Any noticeable play indicates excessive wear, which must be corrected. The gudgeon pins are secured by circlips, so the pistons and connecting rods can be separated without difficulty (see illustration). Note the position of the piston relative to the rod before dismantling, and use new circlips on reassembly.

13 Before refitting the rings to the pistons, check their end gaps by inserting each of them in their cylinder bores. Use the piston to make sure that they are square. Using feeler blades, check that the gaps are within the tolerances given in the Specifications (see illustration). Genuine rings are supplied pre-gapped; no attempt should be made to adjust the gaps by filing.

Reassembly

14 Install the new rings by fitting them over the top of the piston, starting with the oil

13.10 Checking the ring-to-groove clearance

13.13 Measuring a piston ring end gap

control scraper ring sections. Use feeler blades in the same way as when removing the old rings. New rings generally have their top surfaces identified, and must be fitted the correct way round (see illustrations). Note that the first and second compression rings have different sections. Be careful when handling the compression rings; they will break if they are handled roughly or expanded too far. With all the rings in position, space the ring gaps at 120° to each other. The oil control scraper ring expander must also be positioned opposite to the actual ring.

14 Crankshaft – inspection

1 Clean the crankshaft and dry it with compressed air if available. Be sure to clean the oil holes with a pipe cleaner or similar probe.

 Warning: Wear eye protection when using compressed air.

2 Check the main and big-end bearing journals for uneven wear, scoring, pitting and cracking.

3 If the crankshaft has been reground, check for burrs around the crankshaft oil holes (the holes are usually chamfered, so burrs should not be a problem unless regrinding has been carried out carelessly). Remove any burrs with a fine file or scraper, and thoroughly clean the oil holes as described previously.

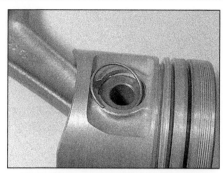
13.12 Removing a gudgeon pin circlip

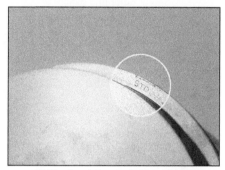
13.14a Look for etched markings identifying the piston ring top surface

4 Using a micrometer, measure the diameter of the main bearing and connecting rod journals, and compare the results with the

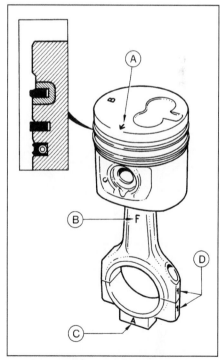
13.14b Piston and connecting rod. Inset shows ring profiles

A Arrow
B Front mark
C Length class mark
D Cylinder number

14.4 Measure the diameter of each crankshaft journal at several points, to detect taper and ovality

Specifications **(see illustration)**. By measuring the diameter at a number of points around each journal's circumference, you will be able to determine whether or not the journal is out-of-round. Take the measurement at each end of the journal, near the webs, to determine if the journal is tapered. If any of the measurements vary by more than 0.025 mm, the crankshaft will have to be reground, and undersize bearings fitted.
5 Check the oil seal contact surfaces at each end of the crankshaft for wear and damage. If an excessive groove is evident in the surface of the crankshaft, consult an engine overhaul specialist who will be able to advise whether a repair is possible or if a new crankshaft is necessary.

15 Main and big-end bearings – inspection

1 Even though the main and big-end bearings should be renewed during the engine overhaul, the old bearings should be retained for close

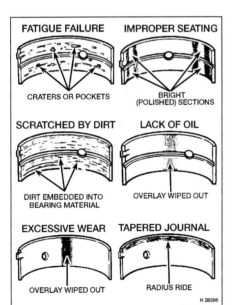

15.2 Typical bearing shell failures

examination, as they may reveal valuable information about the condition of the engine. The size of the bearing shells is stamped on the back metal, and this information should be given to the supplier of the new shells.
2 Bearing failure occurs because of lack of lubrication, the presence of dirt or other foreign particles, overloading the engine, and corrosion. Regardless of the cause of bearing failure, it must be corrected before the engine is reassembled, to prevent it from happening again **(see illustration)**.
3 When examining the bearings, remove them from the engine block, the main bearing caps, the connecting rods and the rod caps, and lay them out on a clean surface in the same general position as their location in the engine. This will enable you to match any bearing problems with the corresponding crankshaft journal.
4 Dirt and other foreign particles get into the engine in a variety of ways. Dirt may be left in the engine during assembly, or it may pass through filters or the crankcase ventilation system. It may get into the oil, and from there into the bearings. Metal chips from machining operations and normal engine wear are often present. Abrasives are sometimes left in engine components after reconditioning, especially when parts are not thoroughly cleaned using the proper cleaning methods. Whatever the source, these foreign objects often end up embedded in the soft bearing material, and are easily recognised. Large particles will not embed in the bearing, and will score or gouge the bearing and journal. The best prevention for this cause of bearing failure is to clean all parts thoroughly, and keep everything spotlessly-clean during engine assembly. Frequent and regular engine oil and filter changes are also recommended.
5 Lack of lubrication (or lubrication breakdown) has a number of interrelated causes. Excessive heat (which thins the oil), overloading (which squeezes the oil from the bearing face) and oil leakage (from excessive bearing clearances, worn oil pump or high engine speeds) all contribute to lubrication breakdown. Blocked oil passages, which usually are the result of misaligned oil holes in a bearing shell, will also oil-starve a bearing and destroy it. When lack of lubrication is the cause of bearing failure, the bearing material is wiped or extruded from the steel backing of the bearing. Temperatures may increase to the point where the steel backing turns blue from overheating.
6 Driving habits can have a definite effect on bearing life. Full-throttle, low-speed operation (labouring the engine) puts very high loads on bearings, which tends to squeeze out the oil film. These loads cause the bearings to flex, which produces fine cracks in the bearing face (fatigue failure). Eventually, the bearing material will loosen in pieces and tear away from the steel backing. Short-trip driving leads to corrosion of bearings, because insufficient engine heat is produced to drive

off the condensed water and corrosive gases. These products collect in the engine oil, forming acid and sludge. As the oil is carried to the engine bearings, the acid attacks and corrodes the bearing material.
7 Incorrect bearing installation during engine assembly will lead to bearing failure as well. Tight-fitting bearings leave insufficient bearing oil clearance, and will result in oil starvation. Dirt or foreign particles trapped behind a bearing shell result in high spots on the bearing which lead to failure.
8 If new bearings are to be fitted, the bearing running clearances should be measured before the engine is finally reassembled, to ensure that the correct bearing shells have been obtained (see Sections 17 and 18). If the crankshaft has been reground, the engineering works which carried out the work will advise on the correct size bearing shells to suit the work carried out.

16 Engine overhaul – reassembly sequence

1 Before reassembly begins, ensure that all new parts have been obtained and that all necessary tools are available. Read through the entire procedure to familiarise yourself with the work involved, and to ensure that all items necessary for reassembly of the engine are at hand. In addition to all normal tools and materials, jointing and thread locking compound will be needed during engine reassembly. Do not use any kind of silicone-based sealant on any part of the fuel system or inlet manifold, and never use exhaust sealants upstream (on the engine side) of the catalytic converter.
2 In order to save time and avoid problems, engine reassembly can be carried out in the following order:
a) Crankshaft and main bearings.
b) Pistons and connecting rods.
c) Oil pump.
d) Sump.
e) Flywheel.
f) Cylinder head.
g) Timing sprockets and belts.
h) Engine external components (including inlet and exhaust manifolds).
3 Ensure that everything is clean prior to reassembly. As mentioned previously, dirt and metal particles can quickly destroy bearings and result in major engine damage. Use clean engine oil to lubricate during reassembly.

17 Crankshaft – main bearing clearance check and refitting

1 It is assumed at this point that the cylinder block/crankcase and crankshaft have been cleaned and repaired or reconditioned as necessary. Position the engine upside-down.

2 Remove the main bearing cap bolts, and lift out the caps. Lay the caps out in the proper order, to ensure correct installation.

3 If they're still in place, remove the old bearing shells from the block and the main bearing caps. Wipe the bearing recesses of the block and caps with a clean, lint-free cloth. They must be kept spotlessly-clean.

Main bearing clearance check

4 Wipe clean the main bearing shell seats in the crankcase, and clean the backs of the bearing shells. Insert the respective upper shells (dry) into position in the crankcase. Note that the upper shells have grooves in them (the lower shells are plain, and have a wider location lug). Note also that the No 1 lower shell has a groove. Where the old main bearings are being refitted, ensure that they are located in their original positions. Make sure that the tab on each bearing shell fits into the notch in the block or cap **(see illustrations)**. No lubrication should be used at this time.

Caution: Don't hammer the shells into place, and don't damage the bearing faces.

5 Before the crankshaft can be permanently installed, the main bearing running clearance should be checked; this can be done in either of two ways. One method is to fit the main bearing caps to the cylinder block, with the bearing shells in place. With the cap retaining bolts tightened to the specified torque, measure the internal diameter of each assembled pair of bearing shells using a vernier dial indicator or internal micrometer. If the diameter of each corresponding crankshaft journal is measured and then subtracted from the bearing internal diameter, the result will be the main bearing running clearance. The second (and more accurate) method is to use a product known as Plastigauge. This consists of a fine thread of perfectly-round plastic which is compressed between the bearing cap and the journal. When the cap is removed, the deformation of the plastic thread is measured with a special card gauge supplied with the kit. The running clearance is determined from this gauge. The procedure for using Plastigauge is as follows.

6 Place the crankshaft thrustwashers into position in the crankcase, so that their oil grooves are facing outwards (away from the central web) **(see illustration)**. Hold them in position with a little grease. Clean the bearing surfaces of the shells in the block, and the crankshaft main bearing journals with a clean, lint-free cloth.

7 With the crankshaft clean, carefully lay it in position in the main bearings **(see illustration)**. Do not use any lubricant; the crankshaft journals and bearing shells must be perfectly clean and dry.

8 Cut several pieces of the appropriate-size Plastigauge (they should be slightly shorter than the width of the main bearings), and place one piece on each crankshaft journal axis **(see illustration)**.

17.4a Fit the main bearing shells to their locations in the crankcase

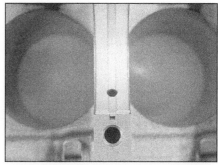

17.4b Each bearing shell's tab engages the notch in the block or cap – shell oil holes must align with block oilways

9 With the bearing shells in position in the caps, fit the caps to their numbered or previously-noted locations. Take care not to disturb the Plastigauge.

10 Starting with the centre main bearing and working outward, tighten the main bearing cap bolts progressively to their specified torque setting. Don't rotate the crankshaft at any time during this operation.

11 Remove the bolts and carefully lift off the main bearing caps, keeping them in order. Don't disturb the Plastigauge or rotate the crankshaft. If any of the bearing caps are difficult to remove, tap them from side-to-side with a soft-faced mallet.

12 Compare the width of the crushed Plastigauge on each journal to the scale printed on the gauge to obtain the main bearing running clearance **(see illustration)**. Always take the measurement at the widest point of the Plastigauge.

13 If the clearance is not as specified, the bearing shells may be the wrong size (or excessively-worn if the original shells are being re-used). Before deciding that different size shells are needed, make sure that no dirt or oil was trapped between the bearing shells and the caps or block when the clearance was measured. If the Plastigauge was wider at one end than at the other, the journal may be tapered.

14 Carefully scrape away all traces of the Plastigauge material from the crankshaft and bearing shells, using a fingernail or something similar which is unlikely to score the shells.

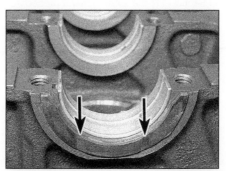

17.6 Place the crankshaft thrustwashers into position with their oil grooves facing outwards

17.7 Lowering the crankshaft onto the main bearings

17.8 Lay the Plastigauge strips (arrowed) on the main bearing journals, parallel to the crankshaft centre-line

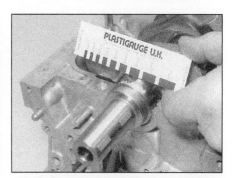

17.12 Compare the width of the crushed Plastigauge to the scale on the envelope to determine the main bearing clearance

18.2 The tab on each big-end bearing shell must engage with notch in connecting rod or cap

18.4a The arrow on the piston crown must point to the timing end of the engine

18.4b The piston can be driven gently into the cylinder bore with the end of a wooden or plastic hammer handle

Final crankshaft refitting

15 Carefully lift the crankshaft out of the engine. Clean the bearing surfaces of the shells in the block, then apply a thin layer of clean engine oil to each shell. Coat the thrustwasher bearing surfaces as well.

16 Make sure the crankshaft journals are clean, then lay the crankshaft back in place in the block. Clean the bearing surfaces of the shells in the caps, then lubricate them with oil. Install the caps in their respective positions, with the arrows pointing to the timing belt/chain end of the engine.

17 Working on one cap at a time, from the centre main bearing outwards (and ensuring that each cap is tightened down squarely and evenly onto the block), tighten the main bearing cap bolts to the specified torque wrench setting. When all the bolts have been tightened to the Stage 1 torque, angle-tighten the bolts further in the same sequence using an angle-tightening adapter on a socket.

18 Rotate the crankshaft a number of times by hand, to check for any obvious binding.

19 Check the crankshaft endfloat (refer to Section 11).

20 Refit the crankshaft left-hand/flywheel end oil seal housing and a new seal, as described in Chapter 2A.

21 Refit the components removed in Section 11.

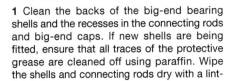

18 Piston/connecting rod assemblies – big-end bearing clearance check and refitting

1 Clean the backs of the big-end bearing shells and the recesses in the connecting rods and big-end caps. If new shells are being fitted, ensure that all traces of the protective grease are cleaned off using paraffin. Wipe the shells and connecting rods dry with a lint-free cloth.

2 Press the big-end bearing shells into the connecting rods and caps in their correct positions. Make sure that the location tabs are

engaged with the cut-outs in the connecting rods **(see illustration)**.

Big-end bearing clearance check

3 Lubricate No 1 piston and piston rings, and check that the ring gaps are spaced at 120° intervals to each other.

4 Fit a ring compressor to No 1 piston, then insert the piston and connecting rod into No 1 cylinder. Make sure that the arrow on the piston crown is facing the timing end of the engine. With No 1 crankpin at its lowest point, drive the piston carefully into the cylinder with the wooden handle of a hammer, at the same time guiding the connecting rod onto the crankpin **(see illustrations)**.

5 To measure the big-end bearing running clearance, refer to the information contained in Section 17; the same general procedures apply. If the Plastigauge method is being used, ensure that the crankpin journal and the big-end bearing shells are clean and dry, then engage the connecting rod with the crankpin. Place the Plastigauge strip on the crankpin, fit the bearing cap in its previously-noted position, then tighten the bolts to the specified torque. Do not rotate the crankshaft during this operation. Remove the cap and check the running clearance by measuring the Plastigauge as previously described.

6 Repeat the above procedures on the remaining piston/connecting rod assemblies.

Final refitting

7 Having checked the running clearance of all the crankpin journals and taken any corrective action necessary, clean off all traces of Plastigauge from the bearing shells and crankpin.

8 Liberally lubricate the crankpin journals and big-end bearing shells. Refit the bearing caps once more, ensuring correct positioning as previously described. Tighten the bearing cap bolts to the specified torque and angles, and turn the crankshaft each time to make sure that it is free before moving on to the next assembly.

9 On completion, refit the sump and cylinder head as described in Chapter 2A.

19 Engine – initial start-up after overhaul

1 With the engine refitted in the vehicle, double-check the engine oil and coolant levels (see *Weekly checks*). Make a final check that everything has been reconnected, and that there are no tools or rags left in the engine compartment.

2 Prime the fuel system as described in Chapter 4A, Section 3.

3 Turn the ignition key and wait for the pre-heating warning light to go out.

4 Start the engine. Additional cranking may be necessary to completely bleed the fuel system before the engine starts.

5 Once started, keep the engine running at fast tickover. Check that the oil pressure light goes out, then check that there are no leaks of oil, fuel and coolant. Where applicable, check the power steering pipe/hose unions for leakage. Do not be alarmed if there are some odd smells and smoke from parts getting hot and burning off oil deposits.

6 Keep the engine idling until hot coolant is felt circulating through the radiator top hose, indicating that the engine is at normal operating temperature, then stop the engine and allow it to cool.

7 Recheck the oil and coolant levels and top up if necessary (see *Weekly checks*).

8 Check the idle speed as described in Chapter 4A.

9 If new pistons, rings or bearings have been fitted, the engine must be run-in at reduced speeds and loads for the first 500 miles (800 km) or so. Do not operate the engine at full throttle, or allow it to labour in any gear during this period. It is recommended that the engine oil and filter be changed at the end of this period.

Chapter 3
Cooling, heating and air conditioning systems

Contents

Degrees of difficulty

Easy, suitable for novice with little experience	Fairly easy, suitable for beginner with some experience	Fairly difficult, suitable for competent DIY mechanic	Difficult, suitable for experienced DIY mechanic	Very difficult, suitable for expert DIY or professional
				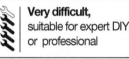

Specifications

Coolant
Mixture type . . . . See Chapter 1
Cooling system capacity . . . . See Chapter 1

System pressure
Pressure test . . . . 1.2 bars – should hold this pressure for at least 10 seconds

Expansion tank filler cap
Pressure rating . . . . 1.2 bars approximately – see cap for actual value

Thermostat
Starts to open . . . . 85°C to 89°C

Coolant temperature sensor
Resistance (typical):
    At 0°C . . . . 89 to 102 kilohms
    At 20°C . . . . 35 to 40 kilohms
    At 100°C . . . . 1.9 to 2.5 kilohms
    At 120°C . . . . 1.0 to 1.4 kilohms

Air conditioning system
Refrigerant . . . . R12 or R134a

Torque wrench settings	Nm	lbf ft
Air conditioning compressor mountings	24	18
Coolant temperature sensor	12	9
Thermostat housing securing bolts	18	13
Water pump securing bolts	20	15

1 General information and precautions

General information

Engine cooling system

The cooling system is of the pressurised type consisting of a timing belt-driven pump, aluminium crossflow radiator, expansion tank, electric cooling fan and a thermostat. The system functions as follows. Cold coolant in the bottom of the radiator passes through the bottom hose to the water pump, where it is pumped around the cylinder block and head passages. After cooling the cylinder bores, combustion surfaces and valve seats, the coolant reaches the underside of the thermostat, which is initially closed. The coolant passes through the heater and inlet manifold and is returned to the water pump.

When the engine is cold, the coolant circulates through the cylinder block, cylinder head, heater and inlet manifold. When the coolant reaches a predetermined temperature, the thermostat opens, and the coolant then passes through the top hose to the radiator. As the coolant circulates through the radiator, it is cooled by the inrush of air when the car is in forward motion. Airflow is supplemented by the action of the electric cooling fan when necessary. Upon reaching the bottom of the radiator, the coolant is now cooled, and the cycle is repeated.

When the engine is at normal operating temperature, the coolant expands, and some of it is displaced into the expansion tank. This coolant collects in the tank, and is returned to the radiator when the system cools.

The electric cooling fan, mounted behind the radiator, is controlled by a thermostatic switch. At a predetermined coolant temperature, the switch contacts close, thus actuating the fan. On later models, the radiator fan may also be operated by the engine management system main module.

Heating system

The heating system consists of a blower fan and heater matrix (radiator) located in the heater unit, with hoses connecting the heater matrix to the engine cooling system. Hot engine coolant is circulated through the heater matrix. When the heater temperature control on the facia is operated, a flap door opens to expose the heater matrix to the passenger compartment. Air entering the vehicle passes over the matrix and is thus heated – the supply of air can be supplemented by operating the blower fan as required.

Air conditioning system

See Section 11.

Precautions

 Warning: DO NOT attempt to remove the expansion tank filler cap, or to disturb any part of the cooling system, while it or the engine is hot, as there is a very great risk of scalding. If the expansion tank filler cap must be removed before the engine and radiator have fully cooled down (even though this is not recommended) the pressure in the cooling system must first be released. Cover the cap with a thick layer of cloth, to avoid scalding, and slowly unscrew the filler cap until a hissing sound can be heard. When the hissing has stopped, showing that pressure is released, slowly unscrew the filler cap further until it can be removed; if more hissing sounds are heard, wait until they have stopped before unscrewing the cap completely. At all times, keep well away from the filler opening.

 Warning: Do not allow antifreeze to come in contact with your skin, or with the painted surfaces of the vehicle. Rinse off spills immediately with plenty of water. Never leave antifreeze lying around in an open container, or in a puddle in the driveway or on the garage floor. Children and pets are attracted by its sweet smell, but antifreeze can be fatal if ingested.

Warning: If the engine is hot, the electric cooling fan may start rotating even if the engine is not running, so be careful to keep hands, hair and loose clothing well clear when working in the engine compartment.

Warning: Refer to Section 13 for precautions to be observed when working on vehicles equipped with air conditioning.

2 Antifreeze – general information

Note: *Refer to the warnings given in Section 1 of this Chapter before proceeding.*

The cooling system should be filled with a water/ethylene glycol-based antifreeze solution, of a strength which will prevent freezing down to at least -25°C, or lower if the local climate requires it. Antifreeze also provides protection against corrosion, and increases the coolant boiling point.

The cooling system should be maintained according to the schedule described in Chapter 1. If antifreeze is used that is not to Ford's specification, old or contaminated coolant mixtures are likely to cause damage, and encourage the formation of corrosion and scale in the system. Use distilled water with the antifreeze, if available – if not, be sure to use only soft water. Clean rainwater is suitable.

Before adding antifreeze, check all hoses and hose connections, because antifreeze tends to leak through very small openings. Engines don't normally consume coolant, so if the level falls regularly, find the cause and correct it.

The exact mixture of antifreeze-to-water which you should use depends on the relative weather conditions. The mixture should contain at least 40% antifreeze, but not more than 70%. Consult the mixture ratio chart on the antifreeze container before adding coolant. Hydrometers are available at most automotive accessory shops to test the coolant. Use only good-quality ethylene-glycol-based antifreeze which meets the vehicle manufacturer's specifications.

3 Cooling system hoses – disconnection and renewal

Note: *Refer to the warnings given in Section 1 of this Chapter before starting work.*

1 If the checks described in Chapter 1 reveal a faulty hose, it must be renewed as follows.

2 First drain the cooling system (refer to Chapter 1); if the antifreeze is not due for renewal, the drained coolant may be re-used, if it is collected in a clean container.

3 To disconnect any hose, use a pair of pliers to release the spring clamps (or a screwdriver to slacken screw-type clamps), then move them along the hose clear of the union. Carefully work the hose off its stubs. The hoses can be removed with relative ease when new – on an older car, they may have stuck.

4 If a hose proves stubborn, try to release it by rotating it on its unions before attempting to work it off. Gently prise the end of the hose with a blunt instrument (such as a flat-bladed screwdriver), but do not apply too much force, and take care not to damage the pipe stubs or hoses. Note in particular that the radiator hose unions are fragile; do not use excessive force when attempting to remove the hoses.

 HAYNES HiNT *If all else fails, cut the hose with a sharp knife, then slit it so that it can be peeled off in two pieces. Although this may prove expensive if the hose is otherwise undamaged, it is preferable to buying a new radiator.*

5 When refitting a hose, first slide the clamps onto the hose, then work the hose onto its unions. If the hose is stiff, use a little soapy water as a lubricant, or soften the hose by soaking it in hot water. Do not use oil or grease, which may attack the rubber.

6 Work each hose end fully onto its union, then check that the hose is settled correctly and is properly routed. Slide each clip along the hose until it is behind the union flared end, before tightening it securely.

7 Refill the system with coolant (see Chapter 1).

8 Check for leaks as soon as possible after disturbing any part of the cooling system.

4 Thermostat –
removal, testing and refitting

Note: *Refer to the warnings given in Section 1 of this Chapter before starting work. A new thermostat sealing ring will be required on refitting.*

Removal

1 Disconnect the battery negative (earth) lead (refer to Chapter 5A, Section 1).
2 Drain the cooling system (see Chapter 1).
3 Unscrew the securing bolts, and lift off the thermostat cover **(see illustration)**.
4 Lift out the thermostat and recover the sealing ring.

Testing

5 Before assuming the thermostat is to blame for a cooling system problem, check the coolant level and temperature gauge operation.
6 If the engine seems to be taking a long time to warm up (based on heater output or temperature gauge operation), the thermostat is probably stuck open. Renew the thermostat.
7 If the engine runs hot, use your hand to check the temperature of the radiator top hose. If the hose isn't hot, but the engine is, the thermostat is probably stuck closed, preventing the coolant inside the engine from escaping to the radiator – renew the thermostat.
Caution: Don't drive the vehicle without a thermostat. The lack of a thermostat will slow warm-up time. On later models, the engine management system will stay in its warm-up mode for longer than necessary, causing emissions and fuel economy to suffer.
8 If the radiator top hose is hot, it means that the coolant is flowing and the thermostat is open. Consult *Fault finding* in the *Reference Section* at the end of this manual to assist in tracing possible cooling system faults.
9 If the thermostat remains in the open position at room temperature, it is faulty, and must be renewed as a matter of course.
10 To test it fully, suspend the (closed)

4.3 Thermostat cover (arrowed)

thermostat on a length of string in a container of cold water, with a thermometer beside it; ensure that neither touches the side of the container **(see illustration)**.
11 Heat the water, and check the temperature at which the thermostat begins to open; compare this value with that specified. It's not possible to check the fully-open temperature, because this occurs above the boiling point of water at normal atmospheric pressure. If the temperature at which the thermostat began to open was as specified, then it is most likely that the thermostat is all right. Remove the thermostat, and allow it to cool down; check that it closes fully.
12 If the thermostat does not open and close as described, if it sticks in either position, or if it does not open at the specified temperature, it must be renewed.

Refitting

13 Refitting is a reversal of removal, bearing in mind the following points:
a) *Thoroughly clean the mating faces of the thermostat housing and cover.*
b) *Refit the thermostat using a new sealing ring.*
c) *Refill the cooling system as described in Chapter 1.*

5 Radiator electric
cooling fan assembly –
testing, removal and refitting

Note: *Refer to the warnings given in Section 1 of this Chapter before starting work.*

4.10 Testing the thermostat

Testing

1 If it is suspected that the cooling fan is not operating when high engine temperature would normally require it to do so, first check the relevant fuses and relays (see Chapter 12).
2 Detach the wiring multi-plug from the thermostatic switch, which is located in the base of the thermostat housing (later models may have the switch in the side of the housing, or screwed into the underside of the radiator top hose). Using a suitable piece of wire, bridge the two connections within the plug. Switch the ignition on and check if the cooling fan operates. If the fan now operates, the thermostatic switch is at fault, and should be renewed as described in Section 6. Remove the bridging wire from the plug, and reconnect the wiring connector to complete the test.
3 If the fan failed to operate in the previous test, either the fan motor is at fault, or there is a fault in the wiring loom (see Chapter 12 for testing details).

Removal

4 Disconnect the battery negative (earth) lead (refer to Chapter 5A, Section 1).
5 Detach the wiring multi-plug from the fan motor, and the additional in-line wiring connector on the side of the shroud on later models. Unclip and remove the wiring from the retaining clips on the shroud **(see illustrations)**. Also where applicable, disconnect the coolant heater hose from the location clips on the cooling fan shroud, or unscrew the metal coolant pipe retaining bolts.

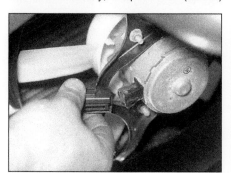

5.5a Detach the cooling fan motor wiring connector . . .

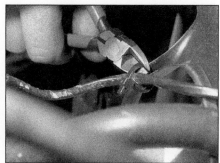

5.5b . . . and release the wiring from the shroud/motor support arm . . .

5.5c . . . and from the locating clip

5.7 Withdrawing the cooling fan shroud and motor from under the vehicle

5.8 Fan motor-to-shroud nuts (arrowed)

6 Unscrew the two nuts (one each side) securing the cooling fan shroud to the radiator.

7 Lift the fan unit complete with its shroud so that the shroud is clear of the radiator attachments, then lower and remove the assembly from underneath the vehicle **(see illustration)**. Take care not to damage the core of the radiator as the fan assembly is withdrawn.

8 If required, the fan motor can be detached from the shroud by unscrewing the three retaining nuts **(see illustration)**.

Refitting

9 Refitting is a reversal of the removal procedure. Tighten the shroud-to-radiator nuts and the fan-to-shroud nuts securely. Ensure that the wiring connection is cleanly and securely made, and locate the loom in the retaining clips.

---

6 Cooling system electrical switches and sensors – testing, removal and refitting

Note: *Refer to the warnings given in Section 1 of this Chapter before starting work.*

Coolant temperature sender

Testing

1 If the coolant temperature gauge is inoperative, check the fuses first (refer to Chapter 12).

2 If the gauge indicates overheating at any time, consult the *Fault finding* in the *Reference Section* at the end of this manual, to assist in tracing possible cooling system faults.

3 If the gauge indicates overheating shortly after the engine is started from cold, unplug the coolant temperature sender's electrical connector. The sender is located in the thermostat housing at the front of the engine. Later models with an engine management

system may have two sensors, both fitted to the thermostat housing – one for the gauge, one for fuel system **(see illustrations)**.

4 If the gauge reading drops when the sender is unplugged, renew the sender. If the reading remains high, the wire to the gauge may be shorted to earth, or the gauge is faulty.

5 If the gauge fails to indicate after the engine has been warmed up (approximately 10 minutes) and the fuses are known to be sound, switch off the engine. Unplug the sender's electrical connector, and use a jumper wire to ground the connector to a clean earth point (bare metal) on the engine. Switch on the ignition without starting the engine. If the gauge now indicates Hot, renew the sender.

6 If the gauge still does not work, the circuit may be open, or the gauge may be faulty. See Chapter 12 for additional information.

Removal

7 Disconnect the battery negative lead with reference to Chapter 5A.

8 Drain the cooling system as described in Chapter 1. Alternatively, be prepared for some loss of coolant when the sender is removed.

9 Disconnect the wiring plug from the coolant temperature sensor.

10 Unscrew the sensor from the thermostat housing.

Refitting

11 Refitting is a reversal of removal. Refill (or top-up) the cooling system as described in Chapter 1.

Radiator fan switch

Testing

12 Refer to the procedures contained in Section 5.

Removal

13 Disconnect the battery negative (earth) lead (refer to Chapter 5A, Section 1).

14 Drain the cooling system as described in Chapter 1. Alternatively, be prepared for some loss of coolant when the switch is removed.

15 On early models, the switch is located in the base of the thermostat housing; later models may have the switch in the side of the housing, or screwed into the underside of the radiator top hose.

16 Disconnect the wiring multi-plug from the switch.

17 Where the switch is fitted to the top hose, the hose should be removed as described in Section 3.

18 Unscrew the switch from its location, and recover the sealing washer **(see illustration)**.

6.3a Coolant temperature sensor – early models

6.3b Coolant temperature sensor (arrowed) – later models

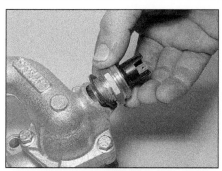

6.18 Unscrewing the radiator fan switch from the thermostat housing (housing removed)

Refitting

19 Refitting is a reversal of removal, but fit a new sealing washer and tighten the switch securely. Refill (or top-up) the cooling system as described in Chapter 1, then reconnect the battery.

7 Radiator and expansion tank – removal, inspection and refitting

Note: *Refer to the warnings given in Section 1 of this Chapter before starting work.*

Radiator

Removal

HAYNES HiNT

If leakage is the reason for removing the radiator, bear in mind that minor leaks can often be cured using a radiator sealant without removing the radiator.

1 Disconnect the battery negative (earth) lead (refer to Chapter 5A, Section 1).
2 On later models, remove the radiator upper shroud, which is secured by a total of four bolts and nine clips – the clips are removed by tapping through their centre pins.
3 On models with air conditioning, tie the condenser up to the front crossmember ('slam panel') with cable-ties. Release the air cleaner

intake duct from the front panel to allow access to the radiator hoses.
4 Drain the cooling system (see Chapter 1).
5 Remove the cooling fan assembly as described in Section 5.
6 Chock the rear wheels, then jack up the front of the car and support it on axle stands (see *Jacking and vehicle support*).
7 Loosen off their retaining clips, and detach the top, bottom and expansion tank hoses from the radiator.
8 On later models, remove the wheel arch liner extensions each side, if fitted.
9 If air conditioning is fitted, carry out the following operations as necessary:
  a) *Remove the alternator drivebelt as described in Chapter 1, disconnect the air conditioning compressor wiring plug, remove the four bolts securing the compressor, and lower it as far as the pipes will allow. Support the compressor under the car using cable-ties.*
  b) *Remove the starter motor as described in Chapter 5A.*
  c) *Disconnect the alternator wiring plug, and unclip the alternator wiring from the front of the vehicle, noting how it is routed.*
  d) *Remove the splash shield (see paragraph 10), then undo the three retaining nuts and detach the air conditioning condenser from the side of the radiator side deflector.*
10 Unscrew the two retaining bolts on each side of the radiator (underneath the radiator) – on models with air conditioning, there is an additional nut each side to remove. Lower the radiator clear of the mounting studs at the top, and carefully withdraw it from underneath the front end of the vehicle **(see illustration)**.
11 Detach the rubber mounts, the side deflectors and the bottom mounting from the radiator. If required, the splash shield can be removed from the radiator by undoing the six retaining screws or drilling out the pop-rivets and extracting the retaining clips (according to type) **(see illustrations)**.
12 With the radiator removed, it can be inspected for leaks and damage. If it needs repair, have a radiator specialist or dealer service department perform the work, as special techniques are required.
13 Insects and dirt can be removed from the

radiator with a garden hose or a soft brush. Don't bend the cooling fins as this is done.

Refitting

14 Refitting is a reversal of removal, but check the mounting bushes, and if necessary renew them. If the splash shield was detached from the base of the radiator, refit it using new pop-rivets and retaining clips or screws, according to type. Refill the cooling system with reference to Chapter 1.

Expansion tank

Removal

15 Partially drain the cooling system, so that the coolant level drops below the expansion tank. Refer to Chapter 1 for details.
16 Where fitted, withdraw the power steering fluid reservoir from the side of the expansion tank, and move it aside as far as the hoses will permit.
17 Before disconnecting the coolant hoses from the expansion tank, it is advisable to clamp them just short of their connections to the expansion tank, to prevent spillage of coolant and the ingress of air when they are detached.
18 Loosen off the coolant hose clips at the expansion tank, and detach the hoses from it. If they are not clamped, secure them so that their ends are raised, to minimise coolant spillage.
19 Unscrew the two retaining screws, and remove the expansion tank from the inner wing panel.

Refitting

20 Refit in the reverse order of removal. Top-up the cooling system as described in *Weekly checks*.

8 Water pump – removal and refitting

Removal

1 Disconnect the battery negative lead with reference to Chapter 5A.
2 Drain the cooling system as described in Chapter 1.

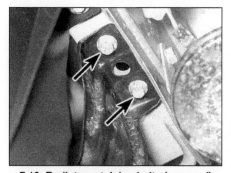
7.10 Radiator retaining bolts (arrowed)

7.11a Radiator mounting rubber

7.11b Drilling out a radiator-to-splash shield rivet

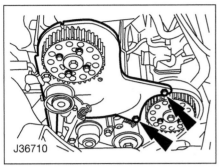

8.5 Timing belt inner shield securing bolts (arrowed)

8.8 Coolant pump securing bolts (arrowed)

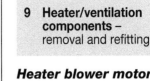

3 Remove the timing belt and injection pump drivebelt as described in Chapter 2A.
4 Remove the timing belt idler pulley as described in Chapter 2A.
5 Remove the timing belt inner shield, which is secured by two bolts **(see illustration)**.
6 Remove the timing belt tensioner pulley as described in Chapter 2A.
7 Loosen the hose clip, and disconnect the coolant hose from the elbow on the water pump.
8 Unscrew the remaining water pump securing bolts, then raise the engine until the

water pump can be manipulated out from the engine compartment **(see illustration)**. Recover the gasket.

Refitting

9 Refitting is a reversal of removal, bearing in mind the following points:
 a) Tighten all fixings to the specified torque.
 b) Fit a new timing belt and fuel injection pump drivebelt as described in Chapter 2A.
 c) On completion, refill the cooling system as described in Chapter 1.

9 Heater/ventilation components – removal and refitting

Heater blower motor

Removal

1 Disconnect the battery negative (earth) lead (refer to Chapter 5A, Section 1).
2 For improved access, refer to Chapter 4A, and remove the intercooler (where applicable).
3 Peel back the seal strip from the top edge of the bulkhead.
4 Cut the ties and detach the hose and wiring loom from the bulkhead.
5 Undo the six retaining bolts, and remove the cover from the air chamber **(see illustration)**.
6 Release the heater blower cover from its guides, and remove it.
7 Disconnect the wires from the blower motor, then undo the two retaining nuts and withdraw the blower motor from the air chamber **(see illustration)**.
8 To remove the motor from its housing, prise free the locking clips and release the securing lugs using a pin punch **(see illustration)**. Detach the connector from the blower resistor unit, bend the retaining tabs up, and then separate the motor (with resistor) from the retainer. Remove the motor from the housing.

Refitting

9 Refitting is a reversal of the removal procedure. When reassembling the blower motor housing covers, ensure that the locating lugs are fully engaged.

Heater blower motor resistor

Removal

10 On models without air conditioning, carry out the operations described in paragraphs 1 to 5 above. On models with air conditioning, Remove the cover of the resistor by releasing the retaining clips.
11 Detach the wiring connector and the multi-plug from the resistor unit. Bend up the securing tabs, or unscrew the two retaining bolts (as applicable) and remove the resistor from its location.

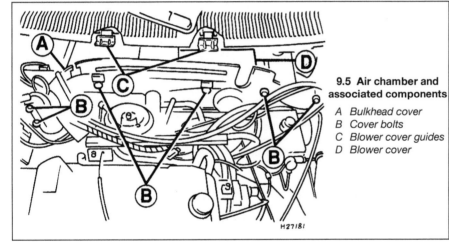

9.5 Air chamber and associated components

A Bulkhead cover
B Cover bolts
C Blower cover guides
D Blower cover

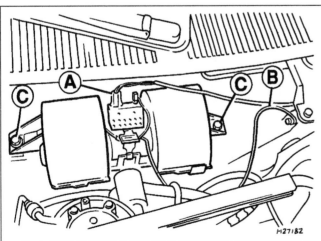

9.7 Heater blower motor unit

A Resistor multi-plug
B Earth lead
C Blower unit securing nuts

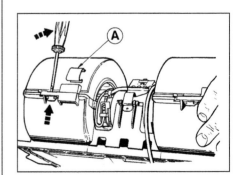

9.8 Heater blower unit locking clip (A) removal

Refitting

12 Refit in the reverse order of removal.

Heater unit and matrix

Removal

13 Disconnect the battery negative (earth) lead (refer to Chapter 5A, Section 1).
14 Drain the cooling system (see Chapter 1).
15 Undo the retaining clips, and detach the heater coolant supply and return hoses at their bulkhead connections (see illustration).
16 A small amount of coolant (about half a litre), will have remained in the heater matrix after draining. In order to prevent the possibility of the coolant spilling onto the carpets during the removal of the heater, it is advisable to blow through one of the connections to eject the remaining coolant out through the other open connection.
17 Undo the two retaining screws, and detach the heater matrix cover plate and gasket from the bulkhead.
18 Undo the two retaining screws, and remove the upper steering column shroud.
19 Similarly, undo the four screws and remove the lower steering column shroud.
20 Refer to Chapter 10 and remove the steering wheel.
21 Undo the single retaining screw, and withdraw the multi-function switch from the steering column. Disconnect the wiring multi-plugs.
22 On 1996 models onward, pull off the three operating knobs from the heater controls.
23 Undo the two retaining screws from the underside top edge of the instrument panel bezel and withdraw the bezel, releasing it from the location clips each side and underneath (refer to Chapter 12 for details). On later models, disconnect the bezel wiring multi-plugs.
24 Refer to Chapter 12 for details, and remove the radio/cassette unit from the facia.
25 Undo the two retaining screws, and remove the stowage unit from under the radio/cassette aperture.
26 Peel back the front door weatherstrip (seal) from the A-pillar adjacent to the facia. Undo the retaining screw, and remove the A-pillar trim. Repeat the procedure on the opposite side.
27 Referring to Chapter 11, undo the facia retaining screws as necessary.
28 Refer to Chapter 11 for details, and remove the centre console.
29 Pull free the covers from the right- and left-hand heater control levers, then unclip and disconnect the cables from their connections on the heater unit each side.
30 Prise free the cover from each of the three facia securing bolt apertures on the top face of the facia, also the cover from the radio/cassette recess.
31 Unscrew and remove the Torx-type retaining bolts, and pull the facia rearwards to partially withdraw it, taking care not to stretch the wiring harnesses under the facia (see Chapter 11).

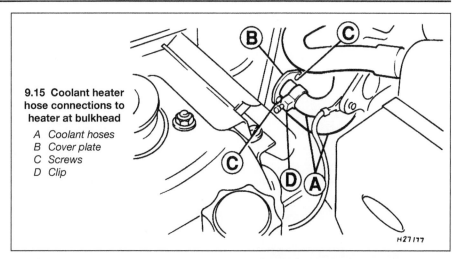

9.15 Coolant heater hose connections to heater at bulkhead

A Coolant hoses
B Cover plate
C Screws
D Clip

32 Where fitted, unbolt the two heater unit support struts.
33 Pull free the footwell air vent from the heater housing connection.
34 Pull free the air ducts from the heater housing connections (two each side, and two in the centre).
35 Undo the two retaining nuts, and disconnect the heater housing from the cowl panel by withdrawing it downwards and removing it from the side (see illustration).
36 To remove the heater matrix (radiator) from the heater unit, undo the two retaining screws and carefully withdraw it (see illustration).

Refitting

37 Refitting is a reversal of the removal procedure. When fitting the heater unit into position, engage the lugs of its flange with the support bracket on the cowl panel, and guide the matrix into position through the opening in the bulkhead.
38 Check that all wiring, coolant hose and air duct connections are securely made. Tighten the housing retaining nuts to the specified torque.
39 On completion, refill the cooling system as described in Chapter 1, then reconnect the battery.

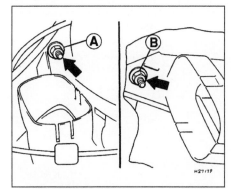

9.35 Left-hand (A) and right-hand (B) heater housing securing nuts (arrowed)

Face-level air vent (right-hand)

Removal (pre-1996 models)

40 Disconnect the battery negative (earth) lead (refer to Chapter 5A, Section 1).
41 Undo the two retaining screws from its upper edge, and withdraw the instrument panel surround.
42 Undo the two retaining screws, and withdraw the face-level vent from the facia. Where applicable, detach the wiring connectors from the switches in the panel.

Removal (1996 models onward)

43 Disconnect the battery negative (earth) lead (refer to Chapter 5A, Section 1).
44 Undo the two retaining screws, and remove the upper steering column shroud.
45 Similarly, undo the four retaining screws and remove the lower steering column shroud.
46 Refer to Chapter 10 and remove the steering wheel.
47 Carefully prise free the three heater/fresh air and blower/air conditioning switch control knobs.
48 Undo the two retaining screws from the underside top edge of the instrument panel bezel. Release the bezel from the retaining clips (two at the top, four along the bottom,

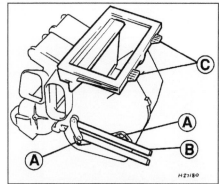

9.36 Heater unit showing matrix retaining screws (A), matrix (B) and unit locating lugs (C)

9.52 Prising free the left-hand side vent

9.56b ... undo the retaining screws ...

9.56a Prise free the control knobs ...

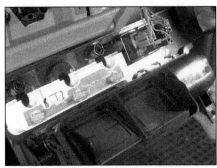

9.56c ... and partially withdraw the air vent unit

Removal (1996 models onward)

58 Disconnect the battery negative (earth) lead (refer to Chapter 5A, Section 1).

59 Undo the two retaining screws, and remove the upper steering column shroud.

60 Similarly, undo the four screws and remove the lower steering column shroud.

61 Refer to Chapter 10 and remove the steering wheel.

62 Carefully prise free the three heater/fresh air and blower/air conditioning switch control knobs.

63 Undo the two retaining screws from the underside top edge of the instrument panel bezel and withdraw the bezel. Disconnect the wiring multi-plugs and remove the bezel.

64 Release the retaining clips and remove the vent from the facia.

Refitting

65 Refitting is the reversal of removal.

---

10 Heater/air conditioning controls – removal and refitting

---

and one at the side furthest away from the steering wheel). Use a screwdriver with protective pad or cloth to prevent damage to the bezel and facia when releasing the clips. Withdraw the bezel and disconnect the wiring multi-plugs

49 Release the retaining clips and remove the vent from the facia.

Refitting

50 Refitting is the reversal of removal.

Face-level air vent (left-hand)

Removal

51 Disconnect the battery negative (earth) lead (refer to Chapter 5A, Section 1).

52 Open the glovebox lid, then unscrew the vent retaining screw from the underside of the box roof (directly under the vent). Carefully prise free and remove the vent **(see illustration)**.

Refitting

53 Refitting is the reversal of removal.

Face-level air vent (centre)

Removal (pre-1996 models)

54 Disconnect the battery negative (earth) lead (refer to Chapter 5A, Section 1).

55 Undo the two retaining screws from its upper edge, and withdraw the instrument panel surround.

56 Carefully prise free the three heater/fresh air and blower/air conditioning switch control knobs. Loosen off the centre air vent retaining screws, and partially withdraw the air vent unit just enough to allow access to the wiring connectors on the inside face of the unit **(see illustrations)**.

57 Where applicable, disconnect the wiring multi-plugs from the heated rear window and rear foglight or heated windscreen switches, then remove the centre air vent unit.

Heater/air conditioning controls

Removal

1 Remove the centre face-level air vent as described in the previous Section.

2 Pull free the covers, then disconnect the control cables from each side of the heater unit. The right-hand side cable operates the temperature control valve, and the left-hand cable operates the air distribution valve **(see illustration)**.

3 Undo the two screws securing the heater control panel to the facia. Withdraw the panel from the facia just enough to allow the heater blower/air conditioning switch wiring plug to be detached, then fully withdraw the control panel, and feed the control cables through the facia aperture **(see illustrations)**.

Refitting

4 Refit in the reverse order of removal. Ensure that the control cables are correctly re-routed (with no tight bends). Check that the cables and the wiring connectors are securely refitted.

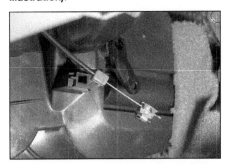

10.2 Heater temperature control cable connection on the right-hand side of the heater unit

10.3a Control panel retaining screws (arrowed)

10.3b Control panel removal

Heater/air conditioning cables

Removal

5 Remove the control panel as previously described.

6 Bend the retaining tabs straight, and then detach the cover from the baseplate to open the heater control unit **(see illustration)**.

7 Cut the cable retaining clips free, then release the cables from the toothed guide strips to remove them. Note that the retaining clips will need to be renewed during reassembly.

Refitting

8 Refitting is a reversal of the removal procedure.

11 Air conditioning system –
general information
and precautions

General information

The air conditioning system consists of a

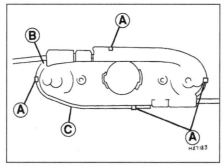

10.6 Heater control unit retaining tabs (A), cover (B) and baseplate (C)

condenser mounted in front of the radiator, an evaporator mounted adjacent to the heater matrix, a compressor mounted on the engine, a dehydrator, and the plumbing connecting all of the above components **(see illustration)**.

A blower fan forces the warmer air of the passenger compartment through the evaporator core (rather like a radiator in reverse), transferring the heat from the air to the refrigerant. The liquid refrigerant boils off

into low-pressure vapour, taking the heat with it when it leaves the evaporator.

Precautions

⚠ *Warning: The air conditioning system is under high pressure. Do not loosen any fittings or remove any components until after the system has been discharged. Air conditioning refrigerant should be properly discharged into an approved type of container, at a dealer service department or an automotive air conditioning repair facility capable of handling the refrigerant safely. Always wear eye protection when disconnecting air conditioning system fittings.*

When an air conditioning system is fitted, it is necessary to observe the following special precautions whenever dealing with any part of the system, its associated components, and any items which necessitate disconnection of the system:

a) *While the refrigerant used on later models – R134a – is less harmful to the environment than the previously-used R12, both are very dangerous substances.*

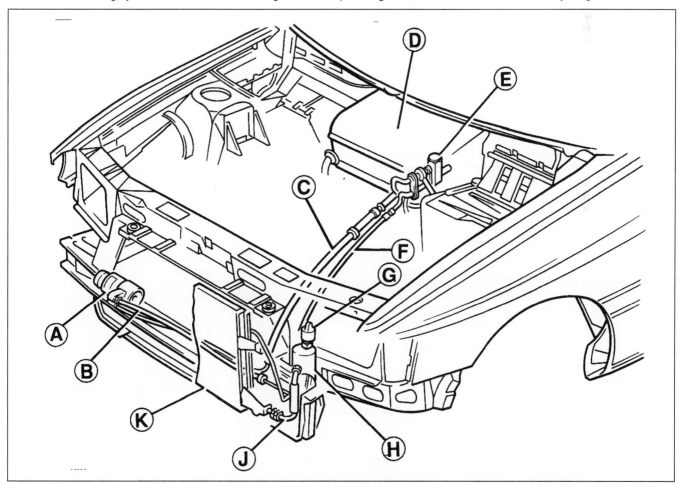

11.1 Air conditioning system layout

A *Compressor*
B *Compressor-to-condenser pipe*

C *Compressor-to-expansion valve*
D *Evaporator and blower*
E *Expansion valve*

F *Expansion valve-to-dehydrator pipe*
G *High-pressure switch*

H *Dehydrator*
J *Dehydrator-to-condenser pipe*
K *Condenser*

They must not come into contact with the skin or eyes, or there is a risk of frostbite. They must also not be discharged in an enclosed space, as there is a risk of suffocation. The refrigerant is heavier than air, and so must never be discharged over a pit.

b) *The refrigerant must not be allowed to come in contact with a naked flame, otherwise a poisonous gas will be created – under certain circumstances, this can form an explosive mixture with air. For similar reasons, smoking in the presence of refrigerant is highly dangerous, particularly if the vapour is inhaled through a lighted cigarette.*

c) *Never discharge the system to the atmosphere – R134a is not an ozone-depleting ChloroFluoroCarbon (CFC) as is R12, but is instead a hydrofluorocarbon, which causes environmental damage by contributing to the 'greenhouse effect' if released into the atmosphere.*

d) *R134a refrigerant must not be mixed with R12; the system uses different seals (now green-coloured, previously black) and has different fittings requiring different tools, so that there is no chance of the two types of refrigerant becoming mixed accidentally.*

e) *If for any reason the system must be disconnected, entrust this task to your Ford dealer or a refrigeration engineer.*

f) *It is essential that the system be professionally discharged prior to using any form of heat – welding, soldering, brazing, etc – in the vicinity of the system, before having the vehicle oven-dried at a temperature exceeding 70°C after repainting, and before disconnecting any part of the system.*

12 Air conditioning system components – removal and refitting

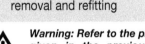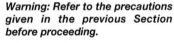

⚠ **Warning: Refer to the precautions given in the previous Section before proceeding.**

Note: *This Section refers to the components of the air conditioning system itself – refer to Sections 9 and 10 for details of components common to the heating/ventilation system.*

Condenser

1 Have the refrigerant discharged at a dealer service department or an automotive air conditioning repair facility.

2 Disconnect the battery negative (earth) lead (see Chapter 5A, Section 1).

3 Secure the radiator to the front body panel using string or wire to prevent it dropping when the mounting bracket is removed in a subsequent operation.

4 Chock the rear wheels then jack up the front of the car and support it on axle stands (see *Jacking and vehicle support*).

5 Undo the six plastic screws, and remove the cover from under the condenser/radiator mounting bracket.

6 Using the Ford service tool 34-001, disconnect the refrigerant lines from the condenser. Immediately cap the open fittings, to prevent the entry of dirt and moisture.

7 Undo the two bolts and one nut securing the dehydrator to the condenser/radiator mounting bracket, and move the dehydrator to one side.

8 Undo the two bolts each side securing the condenser/radiator mounting bracket to the body side members.

9 Detach the condenser and mounting bracket from the right-hand then the left-hand upper radiator mountings, and withdraw the assembly from under the car.

10 Release the clips and remove the air deflector from the condenser, then undo the two nuts and remove the mounting bracket. If required, unscrew the two mountings.

11 Refitting is the reversal of removal.

12 Have the system evacuated, charged and leak-tested by the specialist who discharged it.

Evaporator and blower motor

13 Have the refrigerant discharged at a dealer service department or an automotive air conditioning repair facility.

14 Disconnect the battery negative (earth) lead (refer to Chapter 5A, Section 1), followed by the positive lead, then remove the battery from its location.

15 For improved access, refer to Chapter 4A, and remove the intercooler (where applicable).

16 Peel back the seal strip from the top edge of the bulkhead.

17 Cut the ties and detach the hose and wiring loom from the bulkhead.

18 Undo the three bolts, and detach the air conditioning pipe gasket retaining plate complete with gasket, from the bulkhead.

19 Undo the six retaining bolts, and remove the cover from the air chamber.

20 Release the evaporator housing cover from its guides and remove it.

21 Undo the retaining bolt, and disconnect the compressor low-pressure pipe and the dehydrator liquid pipe from the front of the expansion valve.

22 Disconnect the blower motor resistor multi-plug, and disconnect the blower motor earth lead at the connection on the body.

23 At the vacuum reservoir, disconnect the multi-plugs for the vacuum motor switch and de-ice switch, and detach the two vacuum hoses. Undo the screw and remove the vacuum reservoir assembly from the evaporator housing.

24 Disconnect the two condensation hoses from the front of the evaporator housing.

25 Undo the two bolts and two nuts, and remove the evaporator housing from the car.

26 From the side of the evaporator housing, release the vacuum motor linkage clamp screw, then undo the two nuts and remove

the vacuum motor. Undo the two screws securing the de-ice switch, and withdraw the switch sensor.

27 Disconnect the blower motor resistor wiring plug, then undo the three screws and withdraw the evaporator housing cover.

28 Undo the two screws, release all the retaining clips securing the upper and lower halves of the evaporator housing, and lift off the upper half.

29 Undo the two screws, and detach the expansion valve from the side of the evaporator. Recover the valve seals.

30 Lift the evaporator out of the lower half of the housing.

31 To remove the blower motor, undo the securing bolt from the motor retaining strap, and lift out the motor.

32 Refitting is a reversal of the removal procedure, but use new seals where applicable, and tighten all fastenings to the specified torque wrench settings (where given).

33 Have the system evacuated, charged and leak-tested by the specialist who discharged it.

Compressor

34 Have the refrigerant discharged at a dealer service department or an automotive air conditioning repair facility.

35 Disconnect the battery negative (earth) lead (see Chapter 5A, Section 1).

36 Chock the rear wheels, then jack up the front of the car and support it on axle stands (see *Jacking and vehicle support*).

37 Remove the auxiliary drivebelt (see Chapter 1).

38 Undo the six plastic screws, and remove the cover from under the condenser/radiator mounting bracket.

39 Disconnect the compressor clutch wiring multi-plug, then undo the retaining bolt to detach the compressor high- and low-pressure pipes.

40 Undo the four bolts, and remove the compressor from its mounting bracket. **Note:** *Keep the compressor level during handling and storage. If the compressor has seized, or if you find metal particles in the refrigerant lines, the system must be flushed out by an air conditioning technician, and the dehydrator must be renewed.*

41 Refit the compressor in the reverse order of removal; renew all seals disturbed.

42 Have the system evacuated, charged and leak-tested by the specialist that discharged it.

Dehydrator

43 Have the refrigerant discharged at a dealer service department or an automotive air conditioning repair facility.

44 Disconnect the battery negative (earth) lead (see Chapter 5A, Section 1).

45 Unscrew the pipe to the expansion valve and the compressor connecting pipe at the dehydrator.

46 Disconnect the high-pressure switch multi-plug, then remove the high-pressure switch.

47 Chock the rear wheels then jack up the front of the car and support it on axle stands (see *Jacking and vehicle support*).

48 Undo the six plastic screws, and remove the cover from under the condenser/radiator mounting bracket.

49 Undo the two bolts and one nut securing the dehydrator to the condenser/radiator mounting bracket, and remove the dehydrator from under the vehicle.

50 Refit the dehydrator in the reverse order of removal; renew all seals disturbed.

51 Have the system evacuated, charged and leak-tested by the specialist that discharged it.

Electric cooling fan motor

52 Disconnect the battery negative (earth) lead (refer to Chapter 5A, Section 1).

53 Detach the wiring multi-plugs from the air conditioning fan motor and the motor resistor. Cut free the cable-ties securing the wires to the bracket.

54 Working from above, unscrew the left-hand retaining nut from the fan motor support frame. Apply the handbrake, then raise and support the vehicle, then working from underneath, unscrew and remove the right-hand retaining nut from the support frame.

55 Undo the four retaining bolts, and detach the transmission brace (where fitted) from the bearer and transmission flange.

56 Remove the starter motor (Chapter 5A).

57 Detach and remove the exhaust downpipe.

58 Lift the support frame and fan motor from the mounting each side, and withdraw it from underneath the vehicle. If required, undo the three retaining nuts and detach the fan unit from the support frame.

59 Refit in the reverse order of removal. Tighten all fastenings to their specified torque wrench settings (where given). Ensure that all wiring connections are securely made and, where applicable, relocate the wiring using new cable-ties.

De-ice switch

60 Disconnect the battery negative (earth) lead (refer to Chapter 5A, Section 1), followed by the positive lead, then remove the battery from its location.

61 For improved access, refer to Chapter 4A and remove the intercooler (where applicable).

62 Peel back the seal strip from the top edge of the bulkhead.

63 Cut the ties and detach the hose and wiring loom from the bulkhead.

64 Undo the three bolts, and detach the air conditioning pipe gasket retaining plate complete with gasket, from the bulkhead.

65 Undo the six retaining bolts, and remove the cover from the air chamber.

66 Release the evaporator housing cover from its guides and remove it.

67 At the vacuum reservoir, disconnect the multi-plugs for the vacuum motor switch and de-ice switch, and detach the two vacuum hoses. Undo the screw, and remove the vacuum reservoir assembly from the evaporator housing.

68 Undo the two bolts and two nuts, and remove the evaporator housing from the vehicle.

69 Undo the two screws securing the de-ice switch, and withdraw the switch from the housing.

70 Refitting is a reversal of the removal procedure.

Air conditioning control switch

71 The switch is located in the main heating and ventilation control panel. Remove the control panel from the facia as described in Section 10, then unclip the air conditioning/blower motor switch from the control unit.

72 Disconnect the wiring multi-plug and the light lead from the switch.

73 Refit in the reverse order of removal.

Vacuum motor switch

74 Disconnect the battery negative (earth) lead (refer to Chapter 5A, Section 1), followed by the positive lead, then remove the battery from its location.

75 Detach the wiring multi-plug from the vacuum motor switch, then undo the two retaining screws and remove the switch from the vacuum reservoir.

76 Refit in the reverse order of removal, but ensure that the seal is seated correctly.

Vacuum motor

77 Disconnect the battery negative (earth) lead (refer to Chapter 5A, Section 1), followed by the positive lead, then remove the battery from its location.

78 For improved access, refer to Chapter 4A and remove the intercooler (where applicable).

79 Peel back the seal strip from the top edge of the bulkhead.

80 Cut the ties and detach the hose and wiring loom from the bulkhead.

81 Undo the three bolts, and detach the air conditioning pipe gasket retaining plate complete with gasket, from the bulkhead.

82 Undo the six retaining bolts and remove the cover from the air chamber.

83 Release the evaporator housing cover from its guides and remove it.

84 From the side of the evaporator housing, release the vacuum motor linkage clamp screw, then undo the two nuts and remove the vacuum motor. As it is withdrawn, detach the vacuum hose.

85 Refit in the reverse order of the removal. Ensure that the vacuum hose and wiring connections are securely made. Renew the cable-ties to relocate the wiring to the bulkhead cover.

Vacuum reservoir

86 Proceed as described in paragraphs 77 to 83 inclusive above, then continue as follows.

87 Detach the two vacuum hoses from the vacuum reservoir. Detach the wiring multi-plug from the vacuum motor switch, then undo the retaining screw and remove the vacuum reservoir from the evaporator housing.

88 Undo the two screws and remove the vacuum motor switch from the reservoir.

89 Refit in the reverse order of the removal. Ensure that the vacuum hose and wiring connections are securely made. Renew the cable-ties to relocate the wiring to the bulkhead cover.

Notes

Chapter 4 Part A:
Fuel and exhaust systems

Contents

Degrees of difficulty

| Easy, suitable for novice with little experience | | Fairly easy, suitable for beginner with some experience | | Fairly difficult, suitable for competent DIY mechanic | | Difficult, suitable for experienced DIY mechanic | | Very difficult, suitable for expert DIY or professional | |

Specifications

General

System type	Rear-mounted fuel tank, combined lift and injection pump, indirect injection
Firing order	1 – 3 – 4 – 2 (No. 1 at timing belt end)

Fuel

Fuel type	Commercial diesel fuel for road vehicles (DERV)

Injection pump

Make and type:	
Non-turbo engines	Bosch VE
Turbo engines	CAV RotoDiesel
Rotation (viewed from crankshaft pulley end)	Clockwise
Drive	By toothed belt from crankshaft

Injectors

Type	Pintle
Needle seat leakage/Injector dribble	Holds 125 bar (1813 psi) for 10 seconds

Adjustment data

Idle speed	800 to 900 rpm
Injection pump timing	By timing pegs, at TDC
Maximum no-load speed:	
Continuous:	
Non-turbo models	4800 rpm
Turbo models	4500 rpm
Intermittent	5250 ± 50 rpm
Injection pump timing	By timing pins, at TDC
Deceleration time (no load at idle)	5 seconds maximum

Torque wrench settings

	Nm	lbf ft
Catalytic converter to exhaust manifold	40	30
Fuel injector delivery pipe unions	20	15
Fuel injectors	95	70
Glow plugs	28	21
Injection pump toothed pulley	23	17
Injection pump mounting bolts	24	18
Injection pump rear support bracket	22	16

1 General information and precautions

General information

The fuel system comprises a rear-mounted fuel tank, a fuel filter, fuel injection pump, injectors and associated components.

Fuel is drawn from the tank by the transfer pump incorporated in the injection pump. En route it passes through the fuel filter, located in the engine bay, where foreign matter and water are removed. The injection pump is driven by a toothed belt from the crankshaft and supplies fuel under very high pressure to each injector in turn as it is needed. The amount of fuel delivered is determined by the pump governor, which reacts to throttle position and to engine speed. Injection timing is varied automatically to suit the prevailing speed and load.

Rigid pipes connect the pump and injectors. There are four injectors, situated where spark plugs would be found on a petrol engine. Each injector sprays fuel into a pre-combustion or 'swirl' chamber as its piston approaches TDC on the compression stroke. This system is known as indirect injection. The injectors only open under very high pressure. Lubrication is provided by allowing a small quantity of fuel to leak back past the injector internal components. The leaked-back fuel is returned to the pump and then to the fuel tank.

Two systems, both automatic, assist cold starting. A cold start advance device on the injection pump alters the injection timing and causes fuel delivery to be increased during cold starts. It contains a heating element which is energised when the engine is running. Preheater or 'glow' plugs are fitted to each swirl chamber: they are electrically heated before, during and immediately after a cold start. A warning light illuminates when the ignition is switched on, showing that the glow plugs are in operation. When the light goes out, preheating is complete and the engine can be started. The glow plugs are controlled by a special relay which incorporates a temperature sensor.

To stop the engine, a solenoid valve ('stop solenoid') at the rear of the fuel pump is used. The valve is of the 'fail safe' type, so it must be energised to allow the engine to run. When power is removed from the valve, its plunger moves under spring pressure and interrupts fuel delivery. The solenoid is also used as part of the vehicle alarm/immobiliser system, preventing the engine from being started until the anti-theft system has been deactivated by the driver.

The fuel system on diesel engines is normally very reliable. Provided that clean fuel is used and the specified maintenance is conscientiously carried out, no problems should be experienced. The injection pump and injectors may require overhaul after a high mileage has been covered, but this cannot be done on a DIY basis.

The components of the CAV RotoDiesel and Bosch systems are not interchangeable. Of the two pump types fitted, the CAV RotoDiesel fuel injection pump can be identified by the two large octagonal plugs on the side of the pump body.

Precautions

Fuel

Many of the procedures given in this Chapter involve the disconnection of fuel pipes and system components which may result in some fuel spillage. Before carrying out any operation on the fuel system, refer to the precautions given in the *Safety first!* Section at the beginning of this Manual and follow them implicitly.

Tamperproof adjustment screws

Certain adjustment points in the fuel system are protected by 'tamperproof' caps, plugs or seals. The purpose of such tamperproofing is to discourage adjustment by unqualified operators. In some EEC countries (though not yet in the UK) it is an offence to drive a vehicle with missing or broken tamperproof seals. Before disturbing a tamperproof seal, satisfy yourself that you will not be breaking local or national anti-pollution regulations by doing so. Fit a new seal when adjustment is complete when this is required by law. Do not break tamperproof seals on a vehicle which is still under warranty.

Working procedures

When working on fuel system components, scrupulous cleanliness must be observed, and care must be taken not to introduce any foreign matter into fuel lines or components. Care should be taken not to disturb any components unnecessarily. Before attempting work, ensure that the relevant spares are available. If persistent problems are encountered, it is recommended that the advice of a Ford dealer or a diesel specialist is sought.

2 Air filter housing – removal and refitting

Note: *It is not necessary to remove the air filter cover to facilitate removal of the cleaner casing.*

1 Loosen the hose retaining clip and remove the air inlet duct from the air filter cover (or from the air mass meter, on later models) – also unplug the vent pipe from the casing cover **(see illustration)**.

2 On later models, disconnect the multi-plug from the air mass meter. The air mass meter may be removed from the air filter if wished, after releasing the two retaining clips **(see illustration)**.

3 The air filter housing is secured by a number of mounting nuts, two of which are located underneath the housing. Make sure all the nuts have been removed before pulling the housing free of the mounting studs and the front panel air inlet duct – the duct can be removed from the front panel later if required **(see illustrations)**.

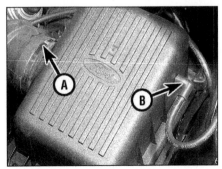

2.1 Release the hose retaining clip (A) and vent pipe (B) . . .

2.2 Disconnecting the air mass meter multi-plug – retaining clips arrowed

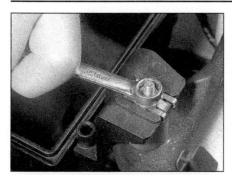

2.3a Remove the mounting nuts . . .

2.3b . . . and pull the housing free of the mounting studs (arrowed) and front inlet duct

2.3c The air inlet duct can be pulled free from the front panel if required

4 Refit in the reverse order of removal. Tighten the hose retaining clip(s) securely, to prevent air leaks.

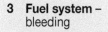

3 Fuel system – bleeding

Non-turbo models

1 As this system is intended to be 'self-bleeding', no hand-priming pump or separate bleed screws/nipples are fitted.

2 When any part of the system has been disturbed therefore, air must be purged from the system by cranking the engine on the starter motor until it starts. When it has started, keep the engine running for approximately 5 minutes to ensure that all air has been removed from the system. To minimise the strain on the battery and starter motor when trying to start the engine, crank it in 10-second bursts, pausing for 30 seconds each time, until the engine starts.

3 Depending on the work that has been carried out, it may be possible partially to prime the system so as to spare the battery by reducing as much as possible the amount of cranking time required to start the engine. To spare the battery, fill the filter with clean fuel via its vent screw opening but it is essential that no dirt is introduced into the system and that no diesel fuel is poured over vulnerable components when doing this.

4 If a hand-operated vacuum pump is available, this can be connected to the pump's fuel return union and used to suck fuel through the supply lines and filter. This will obviously save the battery a good deal of work. If a long length of clear plastic tubing is used to connect the vacuum pump to the injection pump union, it will be easier to see when fuel emerges free from air bubbles. Do not forget to energise the fuel shut-off solenoid by switching on the ignition, to position II so that fuel can pass through the pump.

Turbo models

5 This system is fitted with a hand-priming pump, operated by depressing repeatedly the black button on the top of the filter assembly. If air has entered the system always purge it from the filter bleed nipple first, then (if required) from the pump union and the injector pipes. Ensure that rags are placed underneath the bleeding point to catch the spilt fuel. Diesel fuel must not be allowed to contaminate vulnerable components, especially the clutch, alternator and starter motor.

6 To bleed air from the system as far as the fuel filter, slacken the bleed nipple on the filter outlet union and operate the hand-priming pump until fuel emerges free from air bubbles. Tighten securely the bleed nipple, mop up any spilt fuel and operate the hand-priming pump until increased resistance is felt.

7 If air has reached the fuel injection pump, energise the fuel shut-off solenoid by switching on the ignition to position II, slacken the pump's fuel return union and operate the hand-priming pump until fuel emerges free from air bubbles. Tighten securely the union banjo bolt, mop up any spilt fuel and operate the hand-priming pump until increased resistance is felt. Switch off the ignition.

8 Finally, start the engine and keep it running for approximately 5 minutes to ensure that all air is removed from the system.

All models

9 If air has entered the injector pipes, slacken each union at the injectors and crank the engine until fuel emerges, then tighten securely all unions and mop up the spilt fuel. Start the engine and keep it running for a few minutes to ensure that all air has been expelled. **Note:** *The valve fitted between the filter and the pump on later engines is used at the factory only to fill and bleed the system on production. Check regularly that it is tightly closed*

4 Fuel system – contamination

1 If, at any time, sudden fuel filter blockage, poor starting or otherwise unsatisfactory engine performance should be traced to the appearance of black sludge or slime within the fuel system, this may be due to corrosion caused by the presence of various micro-organisms in the fuel. These can live in the fuel tank if water is allowed to remain there in significant quantities, their waste products causing corrosion of steel and other metallic components of the fuel system.

2 If the fuel system is thought to be contaminated in this way, immediately seek the advice of a Ford dealer or diesel specialist. Thorough treatment is required to cure the problem and to prevent it from occurring again.

3 If you are considering treating the vehicle on a DIY basis proceed as follows. Do not re-use contaminated fuel.

4 First drain and remove the fuel tank, flush it thoroughly with clean diesel fuel and inspect as much as possible of its interior. If the contamination is severe, the tank must be steam-cleaned internally and then flushed again with clean diesel fuel.

5 Disconnect the fuel feed and return hoses from the injection pump, remove the fuel filter element and flush through the system's feed and return lines with clean diesel fuel.

6 Renew the filter element, refit the fuel tank and reconnect the fuel lines, then fill the tank with clean diesel fuel and bleed the system as described above. Watch carefully for signs of the problem occurring again.

7 While it is unlikely that such contamination will be found beyond the fuel filter, if it is thought to have reached the injection pump, the pump may require cleaning. This is a task only for the local Bosch or CAV RotoDiesel agent. Do not attempt to disturb any part of the pump (other than the few adjustments detailed in this manual) or to clean it yourself.

8 The most common cause of excessive quantities of water being in the fuel is condensation from the water vapour in the air. Diesel tanks (whether underground storage tanks or that in the vehicle) are more susceptible to this problem than petrol tanks because of petrol's higher vapour pressure. Water formation in the vehicle's tank can be minimised by keeping the tank as full as possible at all times and by using the vehicle regularly.

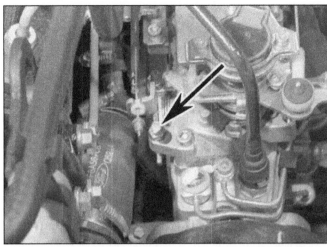

5.5a Idle speed adjustment screw and locknut (arrowed)

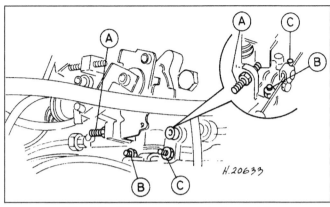

5.5b Adjusting screws – non-turbo models

A Idle speed
B Maximum no-load speed – do not alter
C Fast idle adjuster screw

9 Note that proprietary additives are available to inhibit the growth of micro-organisms in vehicle fuel tanks or storage tanks.

10 If you buy all your fuel from the same source and suspect that to be the source of the contamination, the owner or operator should be advised. Otherwise, the risk of taking on contaminated fuel can be minimised by using only reputable filling stations which have a good turnover.

5 Idle speed – checking and adjustment

1 The usual type of tachometer (rev counter), which works from ignition system pulses, cannot be used on diesel engines. If it is not felt that adjusting the idle speed 'by ear' is satisfactory, one of the following alternatives must be used:

a) Purchase or hire of an appropriate tachometer
b) Delegation of the job to a Ford dealer or other specialist
c) Timing light (strobe) operated by a petrol engine running at the desired speed. If the timing light is pointed at a chalk mark on the diesel engine crankshaft pulley, the mark will appear stationary when the two engines are running at the same speed (or multiples of that speed)
d) Calculating the mph/rpm relationship for a particular gear and running the engine, in that gear, with the front wheels free. The speedometer accuracy may not be adequate, especially at low speeds. Stringent safety precautions must be observed

2 The adjustment must be carried out with the engine at normal operating temperature. If necessary, take the vehicle on a short run.

3 On models with air conditioning, mark the position of the idle speed control cable in relation to the clip located on the injection pump, then release it from the clip.

Non-turbo models

4 Start the engine and allow it to idle, then check that the idle speed is as given in the Specifications. If adjustment is necessary, proceed as follows.

5 Loosen the idle speed adjustment screw locknut then turn the screw as necessary until the engine is idling at the specified speed. Tighten the locknut on completion (see illustrations).

6 Increase the engine speed by temporarily moving the idle lever on the injection pump. With the lever released, check that the engine returns to the specified idling speed.

5.7a Check for play in the cold start cable at the pump end . . .

5.9 Insert a 4.0 mm gauge between the residual fuel screw and throttle lever

Turbo models

Checking

7 Check that there is 2.0 mm of play on the cold start cable at the pump end. If necessary, use the cable adjuster to alter the amount of play (see illustrations).

8 Take a note of the idle speed.

9 Insert a 4.0 mm gauge (feeler blade, or twist drill), between the residual fuel screw and throttle lever (see illustration).

10 Rotate the stop lever in a clockwise direction and insert a 3.0 mm diameter pin, or twist drill, through the idle lever (see illustration). Take a note of the idle speed once more.

5.7b . . . and, if necessary, use the cable adjuster to alter the amount of play

5.10 Rotate the stop lever in a clockwise direction and insert a 3.0 mm diameter 'pin' through the idle lever

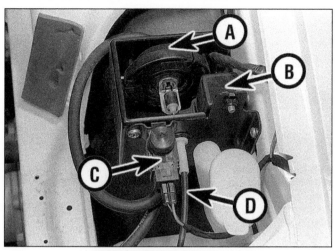

6.1 Idle-up control system components

A *Vacuum diaphragm*
B *Glow plug relay*
C *Reverse light switch circuit connector*
D *Idle-up operating cable*

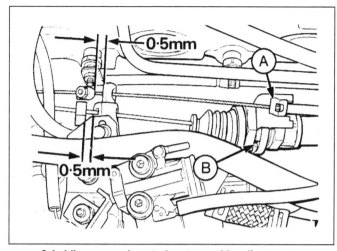

6.4a Idle up speed control system cable adjustment –
non-turbo models

A *Idle-up cable clip – on fast idle cold start device cable bracket*
B *Slot in bracket for cable removal and refitting*

11 If the idle speed is correct, check that the engine deceleration time from maximum no-load speed to idle is no more than 5 seconds, without stalling. If adjustment is required, proceed as follows:

Setting

12 Insert a 4.0 mm feeler blade between the residual fuel screw and throttle lever.
13 Rotate the stop lever in a clockwise direction and insert a 3.0 mm diameter pin through the idle lever.
14 Adjust the residual fuel screw to give an engine speed of 900 ± 100 rpm.
15 Remove the feeler blade and pin.
16 Turning the idle speed adjuster screw, set the idle speed to 850 ± 50 rpm.
17 Now check that the engine deceleration time from maximum no-load speed to idle is no more than 5 seconds without stalling.
18 If the engine stalls, turn the residual fuel screw anti-clockwise (viewed from the rear of the pump) one quarter-turn.
19 Recheck all operations from paragraph 12.
20 If the deceleration time exceeds 5 seconds, turn the residual fuel screw clockwise (viewed from the rear of the pump) one quarter-turn.

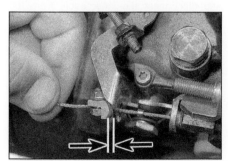

6.4b Adjust the idle-up operating cable to
give the required clearance between
clamp and lever (see text)

21 Recheck all operations from paragraph 12.

All models

22 On models with air conditioning, refit the idle speed control cable and adjust it as described in Section 13.
23 Disconnect the tachometer (if applicable).

---

6 Idle-up control system – checking, adjustment and renewal

Checking

1 An idle-up device may be fitted to automatically raise the engine speed and prevent stalling when reverse gear is selected. The unit is attached to a bracket on the left-hand inner wing panel in the engine compartment. The glow plug relay has been moved from its original position and is now secured to the idle-up unit bracket **(see illustration)**.
2 The control unit operates in conjunction with the reversing light circuit and the brake vacuum system. It differs according to the fuel injection type.
3 To check the idle-up speed system for satisfactory operation, first check that the system wiring and vacuum hoses are in good condition and securely connected.

Adjustment

4 Check that the operating cable adjustment is as follows according to system:

Non-turbo models

Fully extend the cold start operating cable by switching on the ignition and leaving it in position II for a period of three minutes, then check that the clearance between the cable clamp and the idle lever is 0.5 mm **(see illustration)**.

Turbo models

Ensure that the idle operating cable is fully released and there is no vacuum in the servo, then check that there is a clearance of 0.5 to 1.0 mm between the idle-up speed operating cable clamp and the idle lever **(see illustration)**. If necessary, loosen off the adjuster clamp screw and move the clamp to set the clearance then retighten the screw.

All models

5 If adjustment is required on either system, loosen off the cable clamp screw and set the clamp as required.
6 Start the engine and allow it to idle for a period of 5 minutes, then engage reverse gear. The idle speed should rise and then level off within three seconds of reverse gear being engaged. Now disengage reverse gear and check that the idle speed drops and levels off within three seconds of disengagement.

Renewal

7 To remove the idle-up device, first disconnect the battery earth lead.
8 Unplug the electrical connector, and pull off the lower vacuum pipe from the device.
9 Disconnect the idle-up operating cable from the fuel injection pump.
10 Remove the retaining bolts and withdraw the idle-up device from the vehicle.
11 Refitting is the reverse of the removal procedure. Adjust the cable as described above.

---

7 Idle speed control system (air conditioned models) – adjustment, removal and refitting

Checking

1 With the engine at normal operating temperature, raise the engine speed to above

1400 rpm. Check that the idle speed control cable moves the idle lever against the high idle adjustment screw, then backs it off slightly. If this is not the case, adjustment is required.

Adjustment

Note: *Accurate adjustment requires the use of a tachometer and the FDS 2000 Ford Diagnostic Tester – this Section is included for the benefit of those who have access to these instruments. If necessary, have the work carried out by a Ford dealer.*

2 The idle speed control system is fitted to models with air conditioning only. The system consists of a control motor located beneath the battery tray with a cable connected to the idle lever on the injection pump.

3 Connect the Tester to the diagnostic socket in accordance with its manufacturer's instructions. The adjustment is carried out with the ignition switched off.

4 Release the idle speed control cable from the clip on the injection pump.

5 Using the Tester, extend the idle speed control motor plunger.

6 Move the outer cable away from the idle lever until the lever is touching the high idle adjustment screw, then secure the outer cable in this position by refitting the clip. **Note:** *Push the outer cable rather than pull it, as a precaution against stretching it.*

7 Disconnect the Tester then connect a tachometer to the engine.

8 Start the engine and allow it to idle.

9 Move the main speed control (throttle) lever to increase the engine speed above 1400 rpm. Check that the idle speed control cable moves the idle lever against the high idle adjustment screw, then backs it off slightly. If this is not the case, carry out the idle speed control cable adjustment again.

10 Switch off the engine and disconnect the tachometer.

Removal

11 Release the idle speed control cable from the clip on the injection pump.

12 Disconnect the inner cable from the idle lever.

13 Disconnect the inner cable from the control motor, and the outer cable from the support.

8.1 The cold start cable (arrowed) is located at the rear of the injection pump

Refitting

14 Refitting is a reversal of removal, but adjust the cable as described in paragraphs 2 to 10.

8 Cold start cable – adjustment, removal and refitting

Adjustment

1 The cold start cable is fitted to models without air conditioning only. It is located on the cylinder head side of the injection pump **(see illustration)**. The adjustment must be carried out with the engine cold.

2 Release the clip securing the cold start cable to the support bracket.

3 Hold the idle lever fully against its stop, then position the outer cable so that there is between 1.0 and 2.0 mm play in the inner cable. With the cable held in this position, refit the clip to the support bracket.

Removal

4 Drain the cooling system (see Chapter 1).

5 Release the clip securing the cold start cable to the support bracket.

6 Disconnect the inner cable from the idle lever on the injection pump.

7 Unscrew the cold start cable wax element from the thermostat housing and withdraw the cable from the engine compartment. Be prepared for some loss of coolant – place cloth rags beneath the thermostat housing.

Refitting

8 Refitting is a reversal of removal, but adjust the cable as described in paragraphs 1 to 3. Refill the cooling system as described in Chapter 1.

9 Maximum speed – checking and adjustment

Caution: The maximum speed adjustment screw is sealed by the manufacturers at the factory, using paint or a locking wire and a lead seal. There is no reason why it should require adjustment. Do not disturb the screw if the vehicle is still within the warranty period, otherwise the warranty will be invalidated.

1 The maximum no-load speed may be checked if wished, using one of the methods described in Section 5. Running the engine with the wheels free is not recommended, because of the risk of damage or injury if anything goes wrong.

2 The maximum speed adjusting screw is sealed in production. Adjustment should only be made by a Ford dealer or authorised fuel injection specialist. Unauthorised adjustment may invalidate the warranty.

3 When checking the maximum speed, do

not hold the engine at this speed for more than five seconds. Keep well clear of the water pump/alternator drivebelt and pulleys.

4 The engine speed should drop from maximum to idle within the specified time when the throttle is released. If not, check that the throttle linkage is not binding or obstructed. If this is in order, seek specialist advice.

10 Fuel injection pump timing – checking and adjustment

Injection pump timing is carried using the TDC setting method described in Chapter 2A, Section 4. Providing the setting tools can be fitted satisfactorily, the pump timing is sufficiently correct – routine adjustment should not be necessary. If the injection pump timing is suspected of being out, this may in fact be an indication that new timing and injection pump drivebelts are needed, or that the fuel injectors need servicing.

At the time of writing, no information was available in connection with the internal setting of the injection pump plunger using a dial test indicator. Where necessary, the injection pump should be checked and adjusted by a Ford dealer or diesel engine specialist.

11 Fuel injection pump – removal and refitting

Caution: Be careful not to allow dirt into the injection pump or injector pipes during this procedure. New sealing rings should be used on the fuel pipe banjo unions when refitting.

Removal

1 Disconnect the battery earth lead.

2 Refer to Chapter 2A and remove the timing belt (camshaft drivebelt) – do not remove the injection pump drivebelt at this stage.

3 Pull out the adjustment clip securing the accelerator cable ferrule to the support on the injection pump, then release the outer cable and disconnect the inner cable from the speed control (throttle) lever **(see illustration)**.

4 On models without air conditioning, release the clip securing the cold start cable to the support bracket, then disconnect the inner cable from the idle lever on the injection pump. Similarly, disconnect the idle-up cable from the injection pump.

5 On models with air conditioning, release the idle speed control cable from the clip on the injection pump, then disconnect the inner cable from the idle lever.

6 Release the wiring loom from the clip, then disconnect the injection pump multi-plug.

7 Note the location of the fuel leak-off pipe, then disconnect it at the fuel return union.

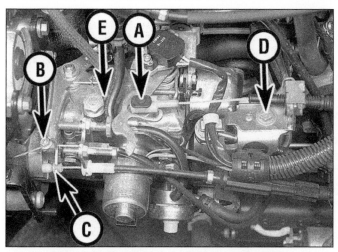

11.3 Fuel injection pump connections (typical)

A Throttle cable end fitting
B Idle up speed cable end clamp
C Cold start cable grommet
D Throttle cable bracket screw
E Fuel supply connection

11.10 Fuel pipe unions at the injection pump

8 Identify the fuel inlet and return pipes, then disconnect the quick-release fittings by squeezing the lugs together. Be prepared for some loss of fuel by placing cloth rags beneath the pipes.

9 Disconnect the fuel injector leak-off pipes from the injectors.

10 Release the fuel supply pipe from the support clips, then unscrew the union nuts at the injector pump and injectors and remove the delivery pipes as an assembly (see illustration).

11 Loosen the injection pump drivebelt tensioner bolt, then lever the tensioner away from the drivebelt and secure it by re-tightening the bolt. Take care not to damage the drivebelt.

12 With the timing pin (Chapter 2A, Section 4) inserted, loosen the injection pump toothed pulley bolts. Take care not to bend the timing pin.

13 Slip the drivebelt from the pulley teeth. Ford recommend that the drivebelt is renewed after removal.

14 Remove the timing pin, then unscrew the bolts and remove the drive gear from the injection pump.

Non-turbo models

15 Unscrew the four bolts from the injection pump rear support bracket (see illustration).

Turbo models

16 Remove the two injection pump support bracket bolts located below the four fuel delivery pipe unions (see illustration).

17 Remove the alternator as described in Chapter 5A.

18 On models with air conditioning, working from below, disconnect the compressor multi-plug, then remove the four compressor mounting bolts and carefully move the compressor to one side without disturbing the pipework. Tie the compressor up so that the pipes are not under strain.

All models

19 Support the weight of the injection pump. Unscrew and remove the three front mounting Torx bolts from within the drivebelt housing, and withdraw the injection pump from the engine (see illustrations).

20 If required, unbolt the rear support bracket from the injection pump.

Refitting

21 Refitting the pump is a reversal of the removal procedure, noting the following points:

a) Before fitting a new pump, remove the blanking plugs and prime it with clean fuel, poured in through the return port.
b) Ensure that the mounting surfaces are clean before bolting the pump into position.
c) Tighten the pump toothed pulley retaining bolts finger-tight only, until the drivebelt is tensioned.
d) Fit the new injection pump drivebelt and timing belt as described in Chapter 2A.
e) Tighten all fasteners to the specified torques.

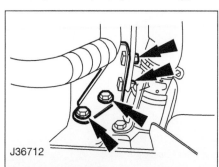

11.15 Injection pump rear support bracket bolts (arrowed) – non-turbo models

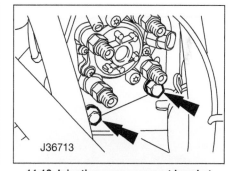

11.16 Injection pump support bracket bolts (arrowed) – turbo models

11.19a Unscrew the three Torx bolts inside the drivebelt housing . . .

11.19b . . . and remove the injection pump

f) Prime and bleed the fuel system as described in Section 3.

g) On completion, check the adjustment of all cables, and for signs of fuel leakage.

12 Fuel injection pipes – removal and refitting

Caution: Be careful not to allow dirt into the injection system during this procedure.

Removal

1 The injection pipes should be removed as a set. Individual pipes may then be renewed if necessary after releasing the anti-rattle clips.

2 Disconnect the battery negative (earth) lead (see Chapter 5A). Clean around the pipe unions at the injectors and at the pump.

3 Protect the alternator against fuel spillage, then disconnect the fuel leak-off pipes from the injectors.

4 Release the fuel supply pipe from the clips on numbers 2 and 4 injectors.

5 Counterhold the pump adapters and unscrew the pipe union nuts.

6 Similarly unscrew the injector union nuts, counterholding the injector bodies as the nuts are slackened.

7 Remove the pipe assembly. Plug or cap open unions to keep fuel in and dirt out.

Refitting

8 When refitting, make sure that all the anti-rattle clips are in place. Do not bend or strain the pipes. Blow through the pipes with compressed air (from an air line or a foot pump) to expel any debris.

9 Refit the pipe assembly to both the injectors and injection pump, initially hand-tightening the union nuts. With the assembly in place, fully tighten the nuts to the specified torque.

10 Refit the fuel supply pipe to the clips and reconnect the fuel leak-off pipes to the injectors.

11 Reconnect the battery negative (earth) lead (see Chapter 5A).

12 Prime and bleed the fuel system as described in Section 3.

13 Run the engine and check the disturbed unions for leaks.

13 Fuel injectors – removal, testing and refitting
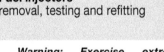

⚠️ *Warning: Exercise extreme caution when working on the fuel injectors. Never expose the hands or any part of the body to injector spray, as the high working pressure can cause the fuel to penetrate the skin, with possibly fatal results. You are strongly advised to have any work which involves testing the injectors under pressure carried out by a dealer or fuel injection specialist.*

Caution: Be careful not to allow dirt into the injection system during this procedure.

Removal

1 Disconnect the battery negative (earth) lead (see Chapter 5A). Clean around the injectors and the injection pipe unions.

2 Disconnect the fuel return hoses from the injectors **(see illustration)**.

3 Remove the injection pipes as described in Section 12.

4 Unscrew and remove the injectors. A 27 mm box spanner or deep socket will be required. On later models, disconnect the wiring plug for the injection pulse sensor which is fitted to No 3 injector **(see illustrations)**.

5 Retrieve the heat protection washers from the injector bores. Obtain new washers for reassembly **(see illustration)**.

6 Take care not to drop the injectors, nor allow the needles at their tips to become damaged.

Testing

7 Testing of injectors is quite simple, but requires a special high pressure pump and gauge. Should such equipment be available, use it in accordance with its maker's instructions, referring to the Specifications for the desired values. Do not expose the skin to spray from the injectors – the pressure is high enough to penetrate the skin.

8 Defective injectors should be renewed or professionally repaired. DIY repair is not a practical proposition.

Refitting

9 Commence refitting by inserting new heat protection washers, domed faces downwards, to the injector bores.

10 Insert the injectors and screw them in by hand, then tighten them to the specified torque. No outer sealing washer is used and the injectors are a taper fit in the head.

11 Refit the injection pipes with reference to Section 12.

14 Fuel shut-off ('stop') solenoid – removal and refitting

Caution: Be careful not to allow dirt into the injection system during this procedure.

1 If the fuel shut-off (or 'stop') solenoid is disconnected or defective, the engine will not run. The solenoid forms part of the vehicle anti-theft alarm/immobiliser system – if the

13.2 Disconnecting a fuel return hose from an injector

13.4a Disconnecting the injection pulse sensor wiring plug

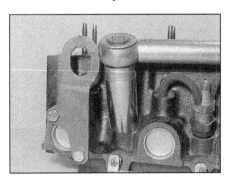

13.4b Removing an injector, using a deep socket

13.4c Withdrawing an injector . . .

13.5 . . . followed by a heat protection washer

system develops a fault, the solenoid will not function. If the plunger jams in the raised position, the engine will not stop (in an emergency, the engine can be stalled by engaging top gear, then gently letting the clutch out with the brakes firmly applied). A defective solenoid should be removed for inspection or renewal as follows.

2 Disconnect the battery earth lead.

3 Disconnect the electrical lead from the solenoid (see illustration).

4 Wipe clean around the solenoid, then unscrew it from the fuel injection pump using a deep socket or box spanner.

Caution: If the solenoid has recently been energised, it may be hot. Recover the spring and plunger.

5 A defective solenoid must be renewed. Renew the O-ring in any case (see illustration).

6 Refit the plunger, spring and solenoid to the pump. Tighten the solenoid body moderately.

7 Reconnect the solenoid lead and the battery earth lead. Run the engine to check for correct operation.

15 Throttle cable – removal and refitting

Removal

1 Disconnect the battery earth lead.

2 Free the cable inner from the pump by prising off the retaining clip (see illustration). If this is done carefully, the clip can be re-used. Otherwise, obtain a new clip for reassembly.

3 Free the cable outer from the pump bracket by pulling out the retaining clip (see illustration). If this proves difficult in situ, unbolt the bracket from the pump and remove it with the cable.

4 Trace the cable back to the bulkhead, noting its routing, and releasing it from any retaining clips.

5 Working inside the vehicle, remove the driver's side lower trim panel (unclip the fusebox cover, remove five/six screws) to improve access to the throttle pedal.

6 Disconnect the cable inner from the pedal by releasing the pedal collar and moving the cable inner through the slot in the pedal (see illustration).

7 Free the cable outer retainer from the bulkhead.

8 Withdraw the cable from the engine bay.

9 Transfer any hardware to the new cable, if applicable.

Refitting

10 Refitting is a reversal of removal. On completion, adjust the cable if necessary, so that with the pedal released there is a small amount of slack in the inner. Have an assistant operate the throttle pedal, and check that the throttle lever on the pump moves through its full range of travel (as

14.3 Fuel shut-off solenoid electrical connector

limited by the idle and maximum speed adjusting screws).

16 Throttle damper – removal and refitting

A revised throttle damper unit can be fitted to non-turbo models where the vehicle is regularly used under low speed and light throttle application, to help prevent vehicle shake and power 'on/off' effect at low engine speeds.

The damper is detached by prising free the top balljoint and moving the damper up so that the lower joint disconnects from the throttle end (see illustration). When refitting the damper, press it into position on the top and bottom end joints but ensure that the large diameter end joint is fitted to the top.

15.2 Removing the throttle cable inner retaining clip

15.6 Throttle cable-to-pedal attachment collar (arrowed)

14.5 Solenoid, spring and plunger (O-ring arrowed)

17 Turbocharger – removal and refitting

Refer to Chapter 2A, Section 7.

18 Intercooler – general information, removal and refitting

General information

1 An intercooler is fitted to most of the turbocharged models in the Escort range (refer to Chapter 2A, Section 1). The intercooler is effectively an 'air radiator', used to cool the pressurised inlet air before it enters the engine.

2 When the turbocharger compresses the

15.3 Releasing the throttle cable outer retaining clip

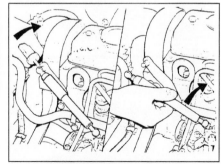

16.2 Throttle damper removal

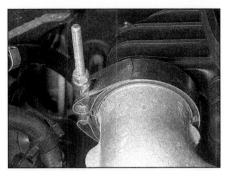

18.4 Loosen the right-hand (inlet manifold end) retaining clip . . .

18.5 . . . then remove the intercooler retaining nut and washers

18.6 Release the left-hand (turbocharger end) retaining clip, and slide it downwards

18.7a Lift out the intercooler assembly . . .

18.7b . . . noting the fitted position of the support washers

inlet air, one side-effect is that the air is heated, causing the air to expand. If the inlet air can be cooled, a greater effective volume of air will be inducted, and the engine will produce more power.
3 The compressed air from the turbocharger, which would normally be fed straight into the inlet manifold, is instead ducted upwards into the intercooler, mounted on top of the engine. The heated air entering the unit is cooled by the air flow over the intercooler fins, much as with the radiator – cool air is fed over the engine through a special duct incorporated in the underbonnet insulation panel. When it reaches the driver's side of the intercooler, the cooled air is then ducted downwards into the inlet manifold.

Removal

4 Loosen the hose clip to the right of the intercooler assembly (right as seen from the

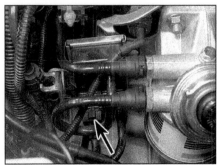

19.2 Fuel heater multi-plug (arrowed)

driver's seat) where the intercooler joins the inlet manifold **(see illustration)**.
5 Remove the air cooler retaining nut and the two support washers from the top of the engine **(see illustration)**.
6 Release the hose retaining clip to the left of the charge air cooler assembly, and slide the clip down the pipe towards the turbocharger **(see illustration)**.
7 Lift the cooler clear of the engine, noting the fitted position of the front support washers **(see illustrations)**.
8 Refitting is a reversal of removal. Check the inlet and outlet pipes for signs of damage, and make sure that the pipe clips are securely fitted/tightened, to prevent air leaks.

19 Fuel heater – removal and refitting

Removal

1 Obtain a container in which to catch any fuel spillage.
2 Disconnect the battery negative (earth) lead and then the multi-plug from the base of the fuel heater **(see illustration)**.
3 Separate the quick release connectors of the fuel inlet and outlet lines to the heater, catching any fuel spillage.
4 Remove the two retaining screws and detach the heater from the engine.

Refitting

5 Refitting is the reverse of the removal

procedure. On completion, prime and bleed the fuel system as described in Section 3, then check for leaks directly after the engine is first started.

20 Fuel tank – removal, inspection and refitting

Note: Refer to the warning note in Section 1 before proceeding.

Removal

1 Run the fuel level as low as possible prior to removing the tank.
2 Disconnect the battery negative (earth) lead (refer to Chapter 5A, Section 1).
3 Remove the fuel filler cap, then syphon or pump out the remaining fuel from the fuel tank (there is no drain plug). The fuel must be emptied into a suitable container for storage.
4 Chock the front wheels, then raise and support the vehicle on axle stands at the rear (see *Jacking and vehicle support*).

Hatchback, Saloon and Estate

5 Undo the two bolts securing the fuel filler pipe to the vehicle underbody.
6 Disconnect the handbrake cable locating strap from the vent hose pipe stub on the rear of the fuel tank **(see illustration)**. Undo the clip and disconnect the vent hose from the pipe stub.
7 Undo the screw securing the upper end of the fuel filler pipe to the body inside the filler

20.6 Handbrake cable locating strap on the fuel tank pipe connection

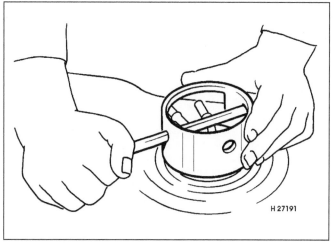

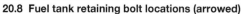

20.8 Fuel tank retaining bolt locations (arrowed)

21.2 Sender unit removal from the fuel tank using special tool No 23-014

flap opening. On models without a filler flap, release the filler pipe surround using a screwdriver, then rotate the retaining ring clockwise to release the filler pipe from the body.

8 Support the underside of the fuel tank to hold it in position, then remove the four tank retaining bolts **(see illustration)**.

9 Partially lower the fuel tank, and detach the roll-over valve tube from the tank top surface. Also disconnect the fuel gauge sender unit wiring multi-plug and the fuel hoses. Where quick-release couplings are used on the fuel hoses, release the protruding locking lugs on each union, by squeezing them together and carefully pulling the coupling apart. Note that the fuel supply hose couplings are identified by a white colour band and the return hose couplings by a yellow colour band.

10 Slowly lower the tank, complete with filler pipe, and remove it from under the vehicle. With the tank removed, detach the filler pipe, if required.

Van

11 Disconnect the fuel gauge sender unit wiring at the in-line connector.

12 Support the underside of the fuel tank to hold it in position, then remove the two tank retaining strap bolts.

13 Release the three clips and detach the vent pipe from the tank.

14 Undo the screw securing the upper end of the fuel filler pipe to the body inside the filler flap opening. On models without a filler flap, release the filler pipe surround using a screwdriver, then rotate the retaining ring clockwise to release the filler pipe from the body.

15 Undo the two front retaining bolts then partially lower the fuel tank.

16 Slacken the clip and disconnect the vent pipe from the tank.

17 Detach the roll-over valve tube from the tank top surface and disconnect the two fuel

hoses. Where quick-release couplings are used on the fuel hoses, release the protruding locking lugs on each union, by squeezing them together and carefully pulling the coupling apart. Note that the fuel supply hose couplings are identified by a white colour band and the return hose couplings by a yellow colour band.

18 Slowly lower the tank, complete with filler pipe, and remove it from under the vehicle. With the tank removed, detach the filler pipe, if required.

Inspection

19 Whilst removed, the fuel tank can be inspected for damage or deterioration. Removal of the sender unit (see Section 21) will allow a partial inspection of the interior. If the tank is contaminated with sediment or water, swill it out with clean fuel. Do not under any circumstances undertake any repairs on a leaking or damaged fuel tank; this work must be carried out by a professional who has experience in this critical and potentially-dangerous work.

20 Whilst the fuel tank is removed from the vehicle, it should not be placed in an area where sparks or open flames could ignite the fumes coming out of the tank. Be especially careful inside garages where a natural-gas type appliance is located, because the pilot light could cause an explosion.

21 Check the condition of the filler pipe seal in the fuel tank, and renew it if necessary.

Refitting

22 Refitting is a reversal of the removal procedure. Apply a light smear of grease to the filler pipe seal, to ease fitting. Ensure that all connections are securely fitted. Where quick-release fuel couplings are fitted, press them together until the locking lugs snap into their groove. If evidence of contamination was found, do not return any previously-drained fuel to the tank unless it is carefully filtered first.

21 Fuel gauge sender unit – removal and refitting

Note: *Ford specify the use of their service tool 23-014 or 23-026 (a large box spanner with projecting teeth to engage the fuel gauge sender unit retaining ring's slots) for this task. While alternatives are possible, in view of the difficulty experienced in removing and refitting the sender unit, owners are strongly advised to obtain the correct tool before starting work. The help of an assistant will be required. Refer to the warning note in Section 1 before proceeding.*

Removal

1 Remove the fuel tank as described in Section 20.

2 Engage the special tool into the sender unit, then carefully turn the sender unit and release it from the tank **(see illustration)**.

Refitting

3 Refit the sender unit in the reverse order of removal. Be sure to fit a new seal, and lubricate it with a smear of grease to prevent it from distorting when fitting the sender unit.

22 Roll-over valve – removal and refitting

Note: *Refer to the warning note in Section 1 before proceeding.*

Removal

1 Disconnect the battery negative (earth) lead (refer to Chapter 5A, Section 1).

2 Chock the front wheels, then jack up the rear of the car and support it on axle stands (see *Jacking and vehicle support*). Remove the rear wheel on the fuel filler cap side to improve the access under the wheel arch.

22.3 Roll-over valve location on fuel filler pipe

3 Undo the retaining screw, withdraw the roll-over valve from the filler pipe, detach the vent hoses and remove the valve (see illustration).

Refitting

4 Refit in the reverse order of removal.

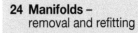

23 Fuel tank filler pipe – removal and refitting

Note: *Refer to the warning note in Section 1 before proceeding.*

Removal

1 Refer to Section 20 and remove the fuel tank.
2 Detach the roll-over valve clamp, undo the filler pipe securing screws, then lower the pipe from the vehicle.

Refitting

3 Refit in the reverse order of removal. Lubricate the filler pipe seal to ease assembly prior to fitting.
4 When the fuel tank is refitted, refill with fuel, and check for any signs of leaks from the filler pipe and associated connections.

24 Manifolds – removal and refitting

Refer to Chapter 2A.

25 Exhaust system – inspection and repair

Inspection

1 Inspect the system periodically for leaks, corrosion and other damage, and check the security and condition of the mountings. Small leaks are more easily detected if an assistant partly obstructs the tailpipe with a wad of cloth whilst the engine is idling.
2 Proprietary pastes and bandages are available for the repair of holes and splits. They work well in the short term (as will having the system welded up), but renewal of the section concerned will probably prove more satisfactory in the long run.
3 The rubber mountings will crack and split eventually, and should then be renewed. It is sound practice to renew the mountings when renewing other parts of the system.

Repair

⚠️ *Warning: Inspection and repair of exhaust system components should be done only after enough time has elapsed to allow the system to cool completely. This applies particularly to the catalytic converter (where fitted), which runs at very high temperatures. Also, when working under the vehicle, make sure it is securely supported on axle stands (see 'Jacking and vehicle support').*

4 If the exhaust system components are extremely corroded or rusted together, they will probably have to be cut from the exhaust system. The most convenient way of accomplishing this is to have a quick-fit exhaust repair specialist remove the corroded sections. Alternatively, you can simply cut off the old components with a hacksaw. If you do decide to tackle the job at home, be sure to wear eye protection, to protect your eyes from metal chips, and work gloves, to protect your hands. If the production-fit system is still fitted, it must be cut at the points shown (see illustrations) for

25.4a Exhaust system components

1 *Front downpipe*	5 *Rubber mounting*
2 *Front silencer*	5A *Rubber mounting*
section (or	6 *U-bolt*
catalytic	7 *Clamp*
converter)	8 *Spring*
2A *Centre section*	9 *Bolt*
3 *Rear silencer*	10 *Self-locking nut*
section	11 *Nut*
4 *Gasket*	12 *Rear silencer*
4A *Sealing ring*	*outlet trim*

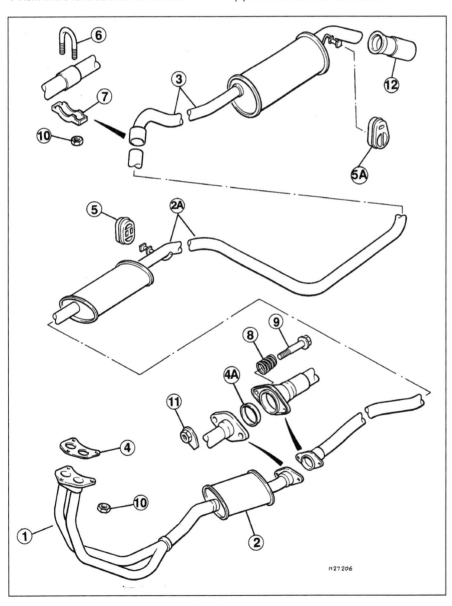

H27206

the service-replacement system sections to fit.

5 Here are some simple guidelines to apply when repairing the exhaust system:

a) *Work from the back to the front when removing exhaust system components.*

b) *Apply penetrating fluid to the exhaust system component fasteners, to make them easier to remove.*

c) *Use new gaskets, rubber mountings and clamps when installing exhaust system components.*

d) *Apply anti-seize compound to the threads of all exhaust system fasteners during reassembly.*

e) *Note that on some models, the downpipe is secured to the manifold by two bolts, with a coil spring, spring seat and self-locking nut on each. On refitting, tighten the nuts until they stop on the bolt shoulders; the pressure of the springs will then suffice to make a gas-tight joint. Do not overtighten the nuts to cure a leak – the bolts will shear. Renew the gasket and the springs if a leak is found.*

f) *Be sure to allow sufficient clearance between newly-installed parts and all points on the underbody, to avoid overheating the floorpan, and possibly damaging the interior carpet and insulation. Pay close attention to the catalytic converter and its heat shield.*

26 Engine management system – description and component renewal

General information

1 The engine management system fitted to most turbo models consists of the Ford EEC V control unit, known as the powertrain control module, and a number of sensors and actuators **(see illustration)**. The sensors supply the main module with input signals relating to the engine operating conditions. Once the module has processed all the information, it sends out signals to the actuators as necessary to control various engine functions.

Exhaust gas recirculation (EGR) system

2 The EGR system consists of the EGR valve and a vacuum regulator. The valve is linked to the inlet and exhaust manifolds by steel pipes. When the vacuum regulator fitted to the left-hand inner wing is activated, vacuum is applied to the valve, which opens the pipe joining the inlet and exhaust manifolds. Under the action of the main module, the EGR valve allows a proportion of exhaust gas back into the inlet air – this reduces combustion temperatures, and in turn reduces the amount of oxides of nitrogen emitted by the vehicle. Reducing combustion temperatures is particularly important on turbocharged engines.

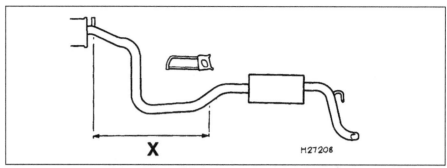

25.4b Cut at points indicated (according to model) when renewing the rear silencer

X = 720 mm (all models except Van)   *X = 914 mm (Van models)*

Engine coolant temperature sensor

3 Information from the coolant temperature sensor used to operate the temperature gauge is also used by the main module as a means of determining engine operating temperature. The coolant temperature sensor is screwed into the thermostat housing at the front of the engine – refer to Chapter 3, Section 6. for more details.

Idle speed compensation actuator

4 The system comprises an actuator and control cable attached to the injection pump idle lever. Under the action of the main module, the system provides for all aspects of idle speed control, including cold start, deceleration control and compensation for engine load when the alternator is charging or when the air conditioning is switched on.

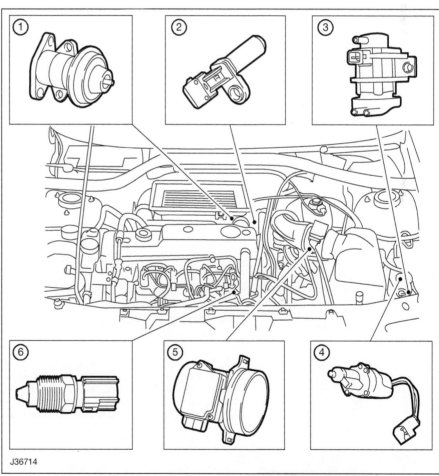

26.1 Engine management system components and locations

1 *EGR valve*
2 *Crankshaft position sensor*
3 *EGR system vacuum regulator*
4 *Idle speed compensation actuator*
5 *Air mass meter*
6 *Coolant temperature sensor*

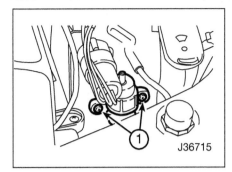

26.17a EGR vacuum regulator securing screws (1) – TC engine

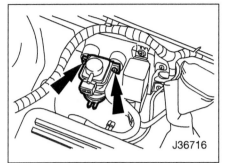

26.17b EGR vacuum regulator securing screws (arrowed) – TCI engine

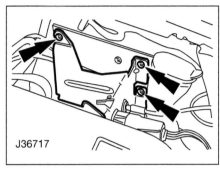

26.22 Idle speed compensation actuator mounting bracket screws (arrowed)

Crankshaft position sensor

5 The inductive head of the sensor runs just above the engine flywheel, and scans a series of 36 protrusions on the flywheel periphery. As the crankshaft rotates, the sensor transmits a pulse to the module every time a protrusion passes it. There is one missing protrusion in the flywheel periphery at a point corresponding to 90° BTDC. The module recognises the absence of a pulse from the crankshaft position sensor at this point to establish a reference mark for crankshaft position. Similarly, the time interval between absent pulses is used to determine engine speed.

Air mass meter

6 The air mass meter is based on a 'hot-wire' system, sending the module a constantly-varying (analogue) voltage signal corresponding to the mass of air passing into the engine. Since air mass varies with temperature (cold air being denser than warm), measuring air mass provides the module with a very accurate means of determining the correct amount of fuel required to achieve the ideal air/fuel mixture ratio.

Cold start system (waxstat)

7 All models except those with air conditioning are fitted with a separate cold start system. A wax element inside the thermostat housing is linked to a control cable attached to the idle lever on the injection pump. This system is intended to provide a stable idle under cold conditions.

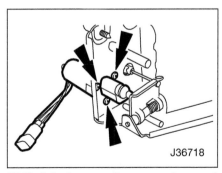

26.23 Actuator mounting screws (arrowed)

Injection pulse sensor

8 Models with an engine management system may have an injection pulse (needle lift) sensor fitted to No 3 injector. The sensor, which is not available separately, informs the main module of the exact moment when injection starts.

Removal and refitting

Powertrain control module

9 First, ensure that the ignition is switched off (take out the key) – the module will be damaged if the plug is disconnected while the ignition is on. The module is located behind the passenger side kick panel in the footwell. To remove the panel, use a screwdriver to twist and release the turnbuckle fastener at the front, then unhook the panel from the three clips at the back edge.

10 The module is released either by pulling it straight down, or by pressing the two retaining clips at the base sideways, then pushing the module up slightly.

11 The module wiring plug is either secured by a bolt (which is unscrewed), or by sliding the plug retaining clips sideways. When disconnecting the plug, do not pull on the wires – just the plug itself.

12 Refitting is a reversal of removal. Make sure that the wiring plug is securely connected, and that the module itself is also clipped properly into place.

EGR valve

13 Refer to Chapter 4B.

EGR vacuum regulator

14 The regulators fitted to Escorts differ according to whether an intercooler is fitted (TC or TCI engine), but removal and refitting details are the same. The regulator is fitted to the left-hand inner wing (left as seen from the driver's seat), next to the air filter housing.

15 Noting their fitted positions, detach the upper and lower vacuum/vent pipes from the regulator.

16 Disconnect the wiring multi-plug.

17 Remove the two securing screws, and take out the regulator (see illustrations).

18 Refitting is a reversal of removal. Ensure that the vacuum/vent pipes are free of any damage, and that they are reconnected in the correct positions.

Idle speed compensation actuator

19 The actuator is mounted on its own bracket, next to the EGR vacuum regulator on the left-hand inner wing. Remove the EGR vacuum regulator as described previously in this Section.

20 Disconnect the actuator wiring plug, then unclip the plug and relay from the actuator mounting bracket.

21 Unclip the actuator cable from the actuator lever by first pulling on the inner cable. The other end of the cable can similarly be disconnected from the idle lever on the injection pump if required.

22 Remove the three mounting screws and lift out the actuator and its mounting bracket (see illustration).

23 The actuator can be separated from its bracket after removing the three screws around the actuator body (see illustration).

24 Refitting is a reversal of removal.

Crankshaft position sensor

25 The crankshaft position sensor is located at the rear of the engine, just behind the left-hand driveshaft (left as seen from the driver's seat). While the sensor itself can be removed safely, the boss in which the sensor locates should not be disturbed, otherwise Ford special tools will be required to realign it.

26 On most models, access to the sensor is best gained from below. Jack up the front of the vehicle, and support it on axle stands (see *Jacking and vehicle support*).

27 Reach up behind the driveshaft, and disconnect the sensor wiring plug (see illustration).

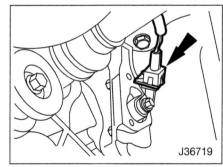

26.27 Crankshaft position sensor wiring plug (arrowed)

28 Unscrew the single bolt securing the sensor, and remove it from its mounting boss **(see illustration)**. The two bolts inboard of the sensor secure the mounting boss – these bolts should not be loosened, or the sensor alignment will be lost. If for any reason the boss must be removed, make clear alignment marks before touching the bolts, so that the boss can be refitted in the same position.

29 Refitting is a reversal of removal. Make sure that the sensor is clean, and tighten its mounting bolt securely.

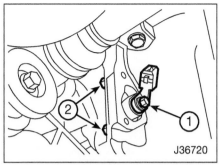

26.28 Remove the single bolt (1) securing the sensor – do not disturb the two boss mounting bolts (2)

Notes

Chapter 4 Part B:
Emission control systems

Contents

Degrees of difficulty

Easy, suitable for novice with little experience	Fairly easy, suitable for beginner with some experience	Fairly difficult, suitable for competent DIY mechanic	Difficult, suitable for experienced DIY mechanic 	Very difficult, suitable for expert DIY or professional

Specifications

Torque wrench setting	Nm	lbf ft
EGR valve mounting bolts	20	15

1 General information and precautions

1 All diesel engine models are designed to meet strict emission requirements, and are also equipped with a crankcase emission control system. In addition to this, all models from 1993 model year are fitted with a two-way 'oxidation' catalytic converter to reduce harmful exhaust emissions.

2 To further reduce emissions, an exhaust gas recirculation (EGR) system is fitted to most engines.

3 Stricter EEC legislation introduced in 1996 led to the Escort diesel range being further modified, with the introduction of the low-pressure turbo, non-intercooled engine (dubbed the TC engine), which featured the same engine management control as the existing turbo (TCI) models. The Ford EEC V engine management system is still quite a simple, low-maintenance affair, which electronically controls the operation of the existing EGR, cold start and advance systems which were already in place. With no user-serviceable components fitted, in the event of a suspected engine management problem, it is recommended that the advice of a Ford dealer is sought in the first instance.

4 The emission control systems function as follows.

Crankcase emission control

5 To reduce the emission of unburned hydrocarbons from the crankcase into the atmosphere, the engine is sealed and the blow-by gases and oil vapour are drawn from inside the crankcase, through a hose located on the rear of the engine, into the inlet manifold to be burned by the engine during normal combustion. A further hose from the cylinder head cover to the crankcase ensures the blow-by gases are circulated freely. Since the inlet manifold depression does not vary on a diesel engine, there is no regulating valve as fitted to petrol engines.

Exhaust emission control

6 To minimise the level of exhaust pollutants released into the atmosphere, a catalytic converter is fitted in the exhaust system of all models from 1993 model year.

7 The catalytic converter consists of a canister containing a fine mesh impregnated with a catalyst material, over which the hot exhaust gases pass. The catalyst speeds up the oxidation of harmful carbon monoxide, unburnt hydrocarbons and soot, effectively reducing the quantity of harmful products released into the atmosphere via the exhaust gases.

Exhaust gas recirculation

8 This system is designed to recirculate small quantities of exhaust gas into the inlet manifold, and therefore into the combustion process. This process reduces the level of oxides of nitrogen present in the final exhaust gas which is released into the atmosphere.

9 The volume of exhaust gas recirculated is controlled by a regulator supplied with vacuum from the brake servo vacuum pump. The regulator is controlled by the engine management module.

2 Emission control systems – testing and component renewal

Crankcase emission control

1 The components of this system require no attention other than to check that the hoses are clear and undamaged at regular intervals.

Exhaust emission control

Testing

2 The performance of the catalytic converter can be checked only by measuring the exhaust gases using a good-quality, carefully-calibrated exhaust gas analyser.

3 Before assuming that the catalytic converter is faulty, it is worth checking the problem is not due to a faulty injector. Refer to your Ford dealer for further information.

Catalytic converter renewal

4 The converter is an integral part of the front downpipe – for general information on exhaust system repair, refer to Chapter 4A.

Exhaust gas recirculation

Testing

5 Testing of the system should be entrusted to a Ford dealer.

Valve removal and refitting – TC engine

6 Loosen/release the clips and disconnect the air inlet duct from the air cleaner.

7 Disconnect the vacuum pipe from the valve body.

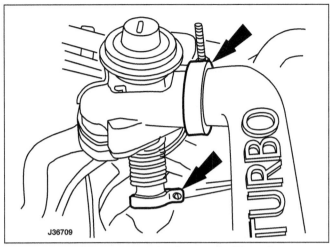

2.9 EGR valve pipe clips (arrowed) – TC engine

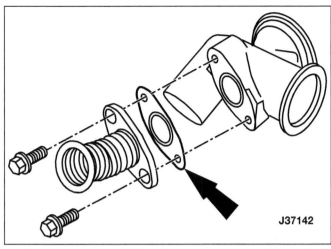

2.10 Exploded view of EGR valve – gasket arrowed (TC engine)

8 Loosen the upper hose clip securing the turbo boost pipe to the valve, and slide the clip down the pipe.

9 Loosen the EGR valve pipe clips at the exhaust and inlet manifolds **(see illustration)**, then lift the valve away.

10 If required, the transfer tube can be separated from the valve after removing the two flange bolts **(see illustration)**.

11 Refitting is a reversal of removal. Use new gaskets, and tighten the clamps securely **(see illustration)**.

Valve removal and refitting – TCI engine

12 Loosen/release the clips and disconnect the air inlet duct from the air cleaner. Although not essential, removing the intercooler (where applicable) as described in Chapter 4A will also improve access.

13 Disconnect the vacuum pipe from the valve body.

14 Unscrew the mounting bolts and remove the valve from the inlet manifold and transfer tube flange. Recover the gaskets.

15 Clean the mating faces of the valve and inlet manifold.

16 Refitting is a reversal of removal. Use new gaskets, and tighten the bolts to the specified torque **(see illustration)**.

3 Catalytic converter – general information and precautions

The catalytic converter is a reliable and simple device which needs no maintenance in itself, but there are some facts of which an owner should be aware if the converter is to function properly for its full service life.

a) Do not strike or drop the catalytic converter. The ceramic honeycomb which forms part of its internal structure may be damaged.

b) Always renew seals and gaskets upstream of the catalytic converter (between the engine and converter) whenever they are disturbed.

c) DO NOT use fuel or engine oil additives – these may contain substances harmful to the catalytic converter.

d) DO NOT continue to use the car if the engine burns oil to the extent of leaving a visible trail of blue smoke.

e) Remember that the catalytic converter operates at very high temperatures. DO NOT, therefore, park the car in dry undergrowth, over long grass or piles of dead leaves after a long run.

f) Remember that the catalytic converter is FRAGILE – do not strike it with tools during servicing work.

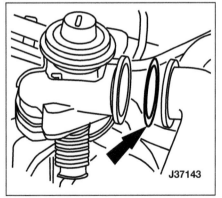

2.11 Renew the valve-to-inlet manifold gasket – TC engine

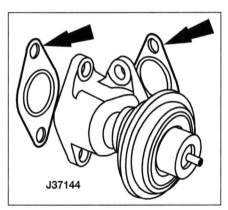

2.16 Use new gaskets (arrowed) when refitting the EGR valve – TCI engine

Chapter 5 Part A:
Starting and charging systems

Contents

Degrees of difficulty

Easy, suitable for novice with little experience	Fairly easy, suitable for beginner with some experience	Fairly difficult, suitable for competent DIY mechanic	Difficult, suitable for experienced DIY mechanic	Very difficult, suitable for expert DIY or professional

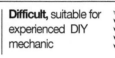

Specifications

General
System type . . . . 12-volt, negative-earth

Battery
Rating – Cold cranking/Reserve capacity . . . . 360 A/60 RC, 500 A/70 RC, 590 A/90 RC or 650 A/130 RC
Charge condition:
    Poor . . . . 12.5 volts
    Normal . . . . 12.6 volts
    Good . . . . 12.7 volts

Alternator
Make/type:
    Bosch . . . . K1-55A, K1-70A or NC 14V 60-90A
    Magneti-Marelli . . . . A127/55 or 127/70
    Mitsubishi . . . . A5T or A002T
Output (nominal at 13.5 volts with engine speed of 5000 rpm) . . . . 55, 70 or 90 amps
Regulating voltage at 3000 rpm engine speed and 3 to 7 amp load . . . 14.0 to 14.6 volts
Minimum brush length:
    Bosch and Magneti-Marelli . . . . 5.0 mm
    Mitsubishi . . . . 3.0 mm

Starter motor
Make/type:
    Bosch . . . . DM, DW or EV
    Magneti-Marelli . . . . M79 or M80R
    Nippondenso . . . . No type numbers given
Minimum brush length:
    Bosch and Magneti-Marelli . . . . 8.0 mm
    Nippondenso . . . . 10.0 mm

Torque wrench settings

	Nm	lbf ft
Alternator mounting bolts	25	18
Alternator adjustment bolts	22	16
Alternator pulley nut:		
With key	50	37
Without key	60	44
Starter motor mounting bolts	35	26
Starter motor support bracket bolt	25	18

1 General information and precautions

General information

The engine electrical system consists mainly of the charging and starting systems. Because of their engine-related functions, these components are covered separately from the body electrical devices such as the lights, instruments, etc (which are covered in Chapter 12). Information on the pre-heating system (glow plugs) is covered in Part B of this Chapter.

The electrical system is of the 12-volt negative-earth type.

The battery is of the low-maintenance or 'maintenance-free' (sealed for life) type and is charged by the alternator, which is belt-driven from the crankshaft pulley.

The starter motor is of the pre-engaged type, incorporating an integral solenoid. On starting, the solenoid moves the drive pinion into engagement with the flywheel ring gear before the starter motor is energised. Once the engine has started, a one-way clutch prevents the motor armature being driven by the engine until the pinion disengages from the flywheel.

Precautions

⚠ **Warning: It is necessary to take extra care when working on the electrical system to avoid damage to semi-conductor devices (diodes and transistors), and to avoid the risk of personal injury. In addition to the precautions given in 'Safety first!', observe the following when working on the system:**

• **Always remove rings, watches, etc before working on the electrical system.** Even with the battery disconnected, capacitive discharge could occur if a component's live terminal is earthed through a metal object. This could cause a shock or nasty burn.

• **Do not reverse the battery connections.** Components such as the alternator, electronic control units, or any other components having semi-conductor circuitry could be irreparably damaged.

• **Never disconnect the battery terminals, the alternator, any electrical wiring or any test instruments when the engine is running.**

• **Do not allow the engine to turn the alternator when the alternator is not connected.**

• **Never 'test' for alternator output by 'flashing' the output lead to earth.**

• **Always ensure that the battery negative lead is disconnected when working on the electrical system.**

• If the engine is being started using jump leads and a slave battery, connect the batteries **positive-to-positive** and **negative-to-negative** (see *Jump starting*). This also applies when connecting a battery charger.

• **Never** use an ohmmeter of the type incorporating a hand-cranked generator for circuit or continuity testing.

• Before using electric-arc welding equipment on the car, **disconnect the battery, alternator and components such as the electronic control units** (where applicable) to protect them from the risk of damage.

• The radio/cassette unit fitted as standard equipment by Ford is equipped with a built-in security code, to deter thieves. If the power source to the unit is cut, the anti-theft system will activate – see Disconnecting the battery in the Reference section for more information.

Battery disconnection

Refer to *Disconnecting the battery* in the Reference section for more information.

2 Electrical fault finding – general information

Refer to Chapter 12.

3 Battery – testing and charging

Testing

Standard and low-maintenance battery

1 If the vehicle covers a small annual mileage, it is worthwhile checking the specific gravity of the electrolyte every three months to determine the state of charge of the battery. Use a hydrometer to make the check and compare the results with the following table.

	Above 25°C	Below 25°C
Fully-charged	1.210 to 1.230	1.270 to 1.290
70% charged	1.170 to 1.190	1.230 to 1.250
Discharged	1.050 to 1.070	1.110 to 1.130

Note that the specific gravity readings assume an electrolyte temperature of 15°C (60°F); for every 10°C (18°F) below 15°C (60°F) subtract 0.007. For every 10°C (18°F) above 15°C (60°F) add 0.007.

2 If the battery condition is suspect, first check the specific gravity of electrolyte in each cell. A variation of 0.040 or more between any cells indicates loss of electrolyte or deterioration of the internal plates.

3 If the specific gravity variation is 0.040 or more, the battery should be renewed. If the cell variation is satisfactory but the battery is discharged, it should be charged as described later in this Section.

Maintenance-free battery

4 In cases where a 'sealed for life' maintenance-free battery is fitted, topping-up and testing of the electrolyte in each cell is not possible. The condition of the battery can therefore only be tested using a battery condition indicator or a voltmeter.

5 If testing the battery using a voltmeter, connect the voltmeter across the battery and compare the result with those given in the *Specifications* under 'charge condition'. The test is only accurate if the battery has not been subjected to any kind of charge for the previous six hours. If this is not the case, switch on the headlights for 30 seconds, then wait four to five minutes before testing the battery after switching off the headlights. All other electrical circuits must be switched off, so check that the doors and tailgate are fully shut when making the test.

6 If the voltage reading is less than 12.2 volts, then the battery is discharged, whilst a reading of 12.2 to 12.4 volts indicates a partially discharged condition.

7 If the battery is to be charged, remove it from the vehicle (Section 4) and charge it as described later in this Section.

Charging

Standard and low maintenance battery

Note: *The following is intended as a guide only. Always refer to the manufacturer's recommendations (often printed on a label attached to the battery) before charging a battery.*

8 Charge the battery at a rate of 3.5 to 4 amps and continue to charge the battery at this rate until no further rise in specific gravity is noted over a four-hour period.

9 Alternatively, a trickle charger charging at the rate of 1.5 amps can safely be used overnight.

10 Specially rapid 'boost' charges which are claimed to restore the power of the battery in 1 to 2 hours are not recommended, as they can cause serious damage to the battery plates through overheating.

11 While charging the battery, note that the temperature of the electrolyte should never exceed 37.8°C (100°F).

Maintenance-free battery

Note: *The following is intended as a guide only. Always refer to the manufacturer's recommendations (often printed on a label attached to the battery) before charging a battery.*

12 This battery type takes considerably longer to fully recharge than the standard type, the time taken being dependent on the extent of discharge, but it can take anything up to three days.

13 A constant voltage type charger is required, to be set, when connected, to 13.9 to 14.9 volts with a charger current below 25 amps. Using this method, the battery should be usable within three hours, giving a voltage reading of 12.5 volts, but this is for a partially discharged battery and, as mentioned, full charging can take considerably longer.

14 If the battery is to be charged from a fully discharged state (condition reading less than 12.2 volts), have it recharged by your Ford dealer or local automotive electrician, as the charge rate is higher and constant supervision during charging is necessary.

4 Battery – removal and refitting

Note: *Refer to the precautions in Section 1 before starting work.*

Removal

1 Undo the retaining nut, then detach the earth leads from the stud of the battery negative (earth) terminal post **(see illustration)**. This is the terminal to disconnect before working on, or disconnecting, any electrical component on the vehicle.
2 Pivot up the plastic cover from the positive terminal, then unscrew the positive lead retaining nut on the terminal. Detach the positive lead from the terminal.
3 Unscrew the two battery clamp bolts, and remove the clamp from the front of the battery.
4 Lift the battery from the tray, keeping it upright and taking care not to let it touch any clothing. Be careful – it's heavy.
5 Clean the battery terminal posts, clamps and the battery casing. If the bulkhead is rusted as a result of battery acid spilling onto it, clean it thoroughly and re-paint with reference to *Weekly checks*.
6 If you are renewing the battery, make sure that you get one that is identical, with the same dimensions, amperage rating, cold cranking rating, etc. Dispose of the old battery in a responsible fashion. Most local authorities have facilities for the collection and disposal of such items – batteries contain sulphuric acid and lead, and should not be simply thrown out with the household rubbish!

Refitting

7 Refitting is a reversal of removal. Smear the battery terminals with a petroleum-based jelly prior to reconnecting. Always connect the positive terminal clamp first and the negative terminal clamp last.

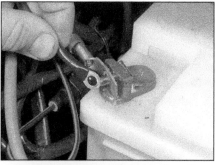

4.1 Detaching the earth leads from the stud of the battery negative (earth) terminal post

5 Charging system – testing
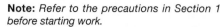

Note: *Refer to the precautions in Section 1 before starting work.*
1 If the no-charge warning light fails to illuminate when the ignition is switched on, first check the alternator wiring connections for security. If satisfactory, check that the warning light bulb has not blown, and that the bulbholder is secure in its location in the instrument panel. If the light still fails to illuminate, check the continuity of the warning light feed wire from the alternator to the bulbholder. If all is satisfactory, the alternator is at fault and should be renewed or taken to an auto-electrician for testing and repair.
2 If the no-charge warning light illuminates when the engine is running, stop the engine and check that the drivebelt is correctly tensioned (see Chapter 1) and that the alternator connections are secure. If all is so far satisfactory, have the alternator checked by an auto-electrician for testing and repair.
3 If the alternator output is suspect even though the warning light functions correctly, the regulated voltage may be checked as follows.
4 Connect a voltmeter across the battery terminals and start the engine.
5 Increase the engine speed until the voltmeter reading remains steady; the reading should be approximately 13.5 to 14.6 volts.

6 Switch on as many electrical accessories (eg, the headlights, heated rear window and heater blower) as possible, and check that the alternator maintains the regulated voltage at around 13 to 14 volts.
7 If the regulated voltage is not as stated, the fault may be due to worn brushes, weak brush springs, a faulty voltage regulator, a faulty diode, a severed phase winding or worn or damaged slip rings. The alternator should be renewed or taken to an auto-electrician for testing and repair.

6 Alternator – removal and refitting

Removal

1 Disconnect the battery negative (earth) lead (refer to Section 1).
2 Chock the rear wheels, then jack up the front of the car and support it on axle stands (see *Jacking and vehicle support*).
3 Remove the alternator drivebelt as described in Chapter 1.
4 Where applicable, detach and remove the alternator rear cover/heat shield **(see illustration)**.
5 Disconnect the wiring from the alternator, noting the location of each wire/plug **(see illustration)**. On some models, the main wiring plug is retained by a wire clip, which hinges to one side. Where a nut and washer arrangement is used, loosely refit the nut and washer once the wire has been disconnected, to avoid losing them.
6 Supporting the weight of the alternator from underneath, unscrew and remove the mounting bolts (two bolts plus the adjuster clamp bolt). Lower the alternator and it from the vehicle **(see illustration)**.

Refitting

7 Refit in the reverse order of removal. Refit the drivebelt, and ensure that it is correctly re-routed around the pulleys. Adjust the tension of the drivebelt (according to type) as described in Chapter 1.

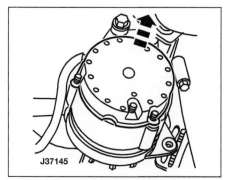

6.4 Unclip the alternator rear cover . . .

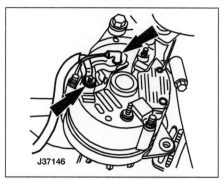

6.5 . . . then disconnect the wiring

6.6 Remove the alternator from below the vehicle

7.3a Undo the retaining screws and . . .

7.3b . . . withdraw the brush box/regulator unit (Bosch K1 alternator)

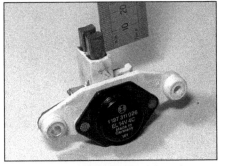

7.4 Measuring the brush lengths (Bosch K1 alternator)

7.7 Remove the three screws, and withdraw the plastic end cover (Bosch NC alternator)

7.9 Remove the regulator/brush holder from the end frame (Bosch NC alternator)

7 Alternator brushes and voltage regulator – renewal

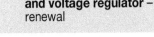

1 Disconnect the battery negative (earth) lead (refer to Section 1).
2 Remove the alternator from the vehicle as described in the previous Section.

Bosch K1-55A and K1-70A

3 Remove the two screws securing the combined brush box/regulator unit, and withdraw the assembly from the rear of the alternator (see illustrations).
4 Check the brush lengths (see illustration). If either is less than, or close to, the minimum specified length, renew them by unsoldering the brush wiring connectors and withdrawing the brushes and their springs.

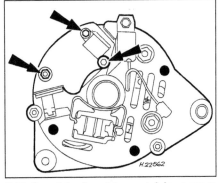

7.14 Regulator/brush box retaining screws on the Magneti-Marelli alternator

5 Clean the slip rings with a solvent-moistened cloth, then check for signs of scoring, burning or severe pitting. If evident, the slip rings should be attended to by an automobile electrician.
6 Refit in the reverse order of removal.

Bosch NC 14V 60-90A

7 Remove the three screws, and withdraw the plastic end cover (see illustration).
8 Remove the two voltage regulator/brush holder mounting screws.
9 Remove the regulator/brush holder from the end frame (see illustration).
10 Measure the exposed length of each brush, and compare it to the minimum length listed in the Specifications. If the length of either brush is less than the specified minimum, renew the assembly.

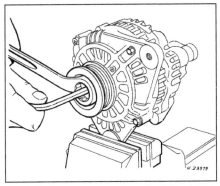

7.18 Pulley nut removal on the Mitsubishi alternator

11 Make sure that each brush moves smoothly in the brush holder.
12 Check that the slip rings – the ring of copper on which each brush bears – are clean. Wipe them with a solvent-moistened cloth; if either appears scored or blackened, take the alternator to a repair specialist for advice.
13 Refit in the reverse order of removal.

Magneti-Marelli

14 Remove the three screws securing the regulator/brush box unit on the rear face of the alternator, partially withdraw the assembly, detach the field connector, and remove the unit from the alternator (see illustration).
15 If the brushes are worn beyond the minimum allowable length specified, a new regulator and brush box unit must be fitted; the brushes are not available separately.
16 Clean the slip rings with a solvent-moistened cloth, then check for signs of scoring, burning or severe pitting. If evident, the slip rings should be attended to by an automobile electrician.
17 Refit in the reverse order of removal.

Mitsubishi

18 Hold the pulley nut stationary using an 8 mm Allen key, unscrew the pulley nut and remove the washer (see illustration).
19 Withdraw the pulley, cooling fan, spacer and dust shield from the rotor shaft.
20 Mark the relative fitted positions of the front housing, stator and rear housing (to ensure correct re-alignment when reassembling). Unscrew the through-bolts and remove the front housing from the rotor shaft, followed by the dust seal and the thin spacer (see illustrations).
21 Remove the rotor from the rear housing and the stator. If difficulty is experienced, heat the rear housing with a 200-watt soldering iron for three or four minutes (see illustration).
22 Unbolt the rectifier/brush box and stator assembly from the rear housing (see illustration).
23 Unsolder the stator and brush box from the rectifier, using the very minimum of heat. Use a pair of pliers as a heat sink to reduce the heat transference to the diodes (overheating may cause diode failure).

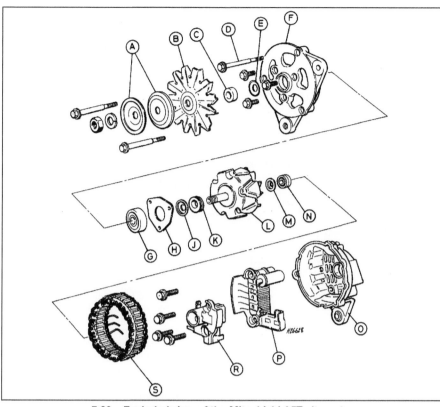

7.20a Exploded view of the Mitsubishi A5T alternator

A Pulley
B Fan
C Thick spacer
D Through-bolt
E Dust shield
F Drive end unit
G Bearing
H Bearing retainer
J Dust cap
K Thin spacer
L Rotor
M Seal
N Bearing
O Commutator end
P Diode pack
R Brush box
S Stator

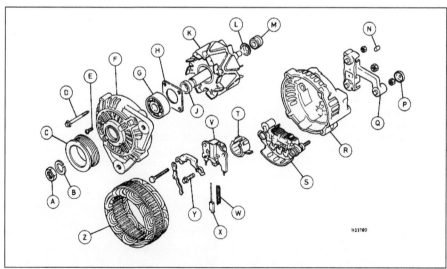

7.20b Exploded view of the A002T Mitsubishi alternator

A Pulley nut
B Spring washer
C Pulley
D Through-bolt
E Retainer plate screw
F Drive end housing
G Bearing
H Bearing retaining plate
J Spacer
K Rotor
L Spacer
M Slip ring end bearing
N Plug
P Cap
Q Terminal insulator
R Slip ring end housing
S Rectifier
T Dust cover
V Regulator
W Brush spring
X Brush
Y Regulator screw
Z Stator

24 Renew the brushes if they are worn down to, or beyond, the minimum specified length. Unsolder the brush wires at the points indicated **(see illustration)**, then solder the new brush leads so that the wear limit line projects 2 to 3 mm from the end of the holder **(see illustration)**.

25 Clean the slip rings with a solvent-moistened cloth, then check for signs of scoring, burning or severe pitting. If evident, the slip rings should be attended to by an automobile electrician.

26 Refit in the reverse order of removal.

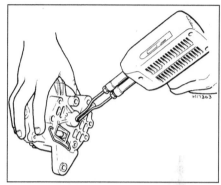

7.21 Using a soldering iron to heat the slip ring end housing for removal of the rotor from the rear housing on the Mitsubishi alternator

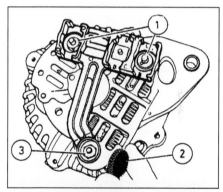

7.22 Rectifier/brush box (1) and regulator unit (3) retaining nuts on the Mitsubishi alternator. Note that cap (2) covers the regulator nut

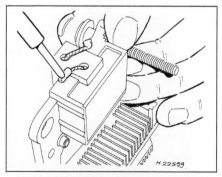

7.24a Unsoldering a brush wire on a Mitsubishi alternator

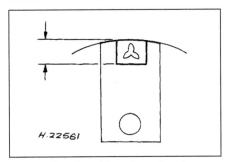

7.24b Fitted position of new brush on a Mitsubishi alternator

Insert a piece of wire through the access hole in the rear housing to hold the brushes in the retracted position as the rotor is refitted **(see illustration)**. Do not forget to release the brushes when assembled.

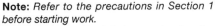

8 Starting system – testing

Note: *Refer to the precautions in Section 1 before starting work.*

1 If the starter motor fails to operate when the ignition key is turned to the correct position, the following possible causes may be to blame.
   a) *The battery is faulty.*
   b) *The electrical connections between the switch, solenoid, battery and starter motor are somewhere failing to pass the necessary current from the battery through the starter to earth.*
   c) *The solenoid is faulty.*
   d) *The starter motor is mechanically or electrically defective.*

2 To check the battery, switch on the headlights. If they dim after a few seconds, this indicates that the battery is discharged – recharge (see Section 3) or renew the battery. If the headlights glow brightly, operate the ignition switch and observe the lights. If they dim, then this indicates that current is reaching the starter motor, therefore the fault must lie in the starter motor. If the lights continue to glow brightly (and no clicking sound can be heard from the starter motor solenoid), this indicates that there is a fault in the circuit or solenoid – see following

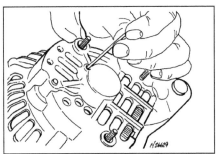

7.26 Use a length of wire rod to hold brushes in the retracted position when reassembling the rotor to the housing on the Mitsubishi alternator

paragraphs. If the starter motor turns slowly when operated, but the battery is in good condition, then this indicates that either the starter motor is faulty, or there is considerable resistance somewhere in the circuit.

3 If a fault in the circuit is suspected, disconnect the battery leads (including the earth connection to the body), the starter/solenoid wiring and the engine/transmission earth strap. Thoroughly clean the connections, and reconnect the leads and wiring, then use a voltmeter or test light to check that full battery voltage is available at the battery positive lead connection to the solenoid, and that the earth is sound. Smear petroleum jelly around the battery terminals to prevent corrosion – corroded connections are amongst the most frequent causes of electrical system faults.

4 If the battery and all connections are in good condition, check the circuit by disconnecting the wire from the solenoid blade terminal. Connect a voltmeter or test light between the wire end and a good earth (such as the battery negative terminal), and check that the wire is live when the ignition switch is turned to the 'start' position. If it is, then the circuit is sound – if not the circuit wiring can be checked as described in Chapter 12.

5 The solenoid contacts can be checked by connecting a voltmeter or test light between the battery positive feed connection on the starter side of the solenoid, and earth. When the ignition switch is turned to the 'start' position, there should be a reading or lighted bulb, as applicable. If there is no reading or lighted bulb, the solenoid is faulty and should be renewed.

6 If the circuit and solenoid are proved sound, the fault must lie in the starter motor. In this event, it may be possible to have the starter motor overhauled by a specialist, but check on the cost of spares before proceeding, as it may prove more economical to obtain a new or exchange motor.

9 Starter motor – removal and refitting

Removal

1 Disconnect the battery negative (earth) lead (refer to Section 1).
2 Chock the rear wheels then jack up the front of the car and support it on axle stands (see *Jacking and vehicle support*). Remove the front roadwheels.
3 Undo the two retaining nuts, and remove the starter motor heat shield (where fitted).
4 Prise free the cap, if fitted, then unscrew the nuts to disconnect the wiring from the starter/solenoid terminals **(see illustration)**.
5 Unscrew and remove the starter motor retaining bolts at the transmission/clutch housing and, where applicable, also unbolt and detach the support bracket. Withdraw the starter motor from its mounting, and remove it from the vehicle **(see illustrations)**.

Refitting

6 Refitting is a reversal of removal. Tighten the retaining bolts to the specified torque. Ensure that the wiring is securely reconnected to the starter motor (and solenoid).

10 Starter motor – testing and overhaul

If the starter motor is thought to be suspect, it should be removed from the vehicle and taken to an auto-electrician for testing. Most auto-electricians will be able to supply and fit brushes at a reasonable cost. However, check on the cost of repairs before proceeding as it may prove more economical to obtain a new or exchange motor.

9.4 Starter motor and wiring connections (typical)

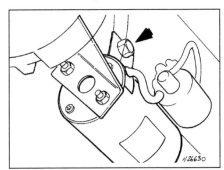

9.5a Starter motor support bracket bolt

9.5b Starter motor removal

Chapter 5 Part B:
Pre-heating system

Contents

Degrees of difficulty

Easy, suitable for novice with little experience	Fairly easy, suitable for beginner with some experience	Fairly difficult, suitable for competent DIY mechanic	Difficult, suitable for experienced DIY mechanic	Very difficult, suitable for expert DIY or professional

Specifications

Glow plugs

Type:
Models up to September 1995 . . . . Bosch 0 250 202 001
Models from September 1995 onwards . . . . Bosch 0 250 201 049

Torque wrench setting	Nm	lbf ft
Glow plugs	28	21

1 Pre-heating system –
description and testing

Description

1 Each swirl chamber has a heater plug (commonly called a glow plug) screwed into it. The plugs are electrically operated before, during, and a short time after start-up when the engine is cold. On early models, the glow plug system is controlled by a timer relay located on the left-hand inner wing (left as seen from the driver's seat). On later models, a simpler relay is used, and the timer function is performed by the engine management module. The glow plug fusible link appears on a fuse block attached to the battery **(see illustrations)**.
2 The glow plugs are energised when the ignition is switched on, and they remain on together with the indicator light for a period varying between 1 and 10 seconds, depending on the temperature of the engine coolant. After the indicator light is extinguished, the glow plugs remain energised for a period up to 3 seconds – however, if the engine is started in this period the glow plugs will remain on for a period up to 40 seconds depending on the engine coolant temperature. With the coolant at 80°C the period is 0 seconds and with the coolant at -40°C the period is 40 seconds.
3 A warning light in the instrument panel tells the driver that pre-heating is taking place. When the light goes out, the engine is ready to be started. If no attempt is made to start, the timer then cuts off the supply in order to avoid draining the battery and overheating of the glow plugs.

Testing

4 If the system malfunctions, testing is ultimately by substitution of known good units, but some preliminary checks may be made as follows.
5 Connect a voltmeter or 12-volt test light between the glow plug supply cable and earth (engine or vehicle metal). Make sure that the live connection is kept clear of the engine and bodywork.
6 Have an assistant switch on the ignition and check that voltage is applied to the glow plugs. Note the time for which the warning light is lit and the total time for which voltage is applied before the system cuts out. Switch off the ignition.
7 If the results of the check do not come within the periods indicated in paragraph 2, refer to Chapters 3, 4A or 12, and check the relevant temperature sensor and power supply.
8 If an ammeter of suitable range (0 to 50 amp approx) is available, connect it between the glow plug feed wire and the bus bar. During the preheating period the ammeter should show a current draw of approximately 8 amps per working plug, ie. 32 amps if all four plugs are working. If one or more plugs appear not to be drawing current, remove the bus bar and check each plug separately with a continuity tester or self-powered test light.
9 If there is no supply at all to the glow plugs, the associated wiring is at fault.
10 To locate a defective glow plug, disconnect the main supply cable and the interconnecting wire or strap from the top of the glow plugs. Be careful not to drop the nuts and washers.
11 Use a continuity tester, or a 12-volt test light connected to the battery positive

1.1a Glow plug relay (arrowed)

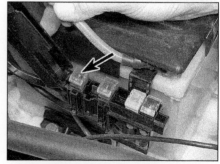
1.1b Glow plug fusible link (arrowed)

2.2 Glow plug feed wire connection

2.3 Unscrewing a glow plug terminal nut

2.4 Glow plug removed from cylinder head

terminal, to check for continuity between each glow plug terminal and earth. The resistance of a glow plug in good condition is very low (less than 1 ohm), so if the test light does not come on or the continuity tester shows a high resistance, the glow plug is certainly defective.

12 If an ammeter is available, the current draw of each glow plug can be checked. After an initial surge of around 15 to 20 amps, each plug should draw around 10 amps. Any plug which draws much more or less than this is probably defective.

13 As a final check the glow plugs can be removed and inspected as described in Section 2.

2 Glow plugs – removal, inspection and refitting

Removal

Caution: If the pre-heating system has just been energised, or if the engine has been running, the glow plugs may be very hot.

1 Disconnect the battery negative (earth) lead (see Chapter 5A).

2 Disconnect the feed wire from the bus bar **(see illustration)**.

3 Unscrew the terminal nut from each plug to be removed. Remove the nuts, washers and bus bar **(see illustration)**.

4 Clean around the glow plug seats then unscrew and remove them **(see illustration)**.

Inspection

5 Inspect the glow plugs for damage. Burnt or eroded glow plug tips can be caused by a bad injector spray pattern. Have the injectors checked if this sort of damage is found.

6 If the glow plugs are in good physical condition, check them electrically using a 12-volt test light or continuity tester as described in the previous Section.

7 The glow plugs can be energised by applying 12 volts to them to verify that they heat up evenly and in the required time. Observe the following precautions:

a) *Support the glow plug by clamping it carefully in a vice or self-locking pliers. Remember it will become red-hot.*

b) *Make sure that the power supply or test lead incorporates a fuse or overload trip to protect against damage from a short-circuit.*

c) *After testing, allow the glow plug to cool for several minutes before attempting to handle it.*

8 A glow plug in good condition will start to glow red at the tip after drawing current for 5 seconds or so. Any plug which takes much longer to start glowing, or which starts glowing in the middle instead of at the tip, is defective.

Refitting

9 When refitting, apply a little anti-seize compound to the glow plug threads. Screw the glow plugs into place and tighten them to the specified torque.

10 Refit the bus bar and washers and secure with the nuts. Make sure that the clamping areas are clean.

11 Reconnect the feed wire and the battery earth lead.

3 Fuel heater – general information, removal and refitting

General information

1 An electrically-operated fuel heater is fitted in the fuel line leading to the fuel filter housing, to prevent the fuel 'waxing' at low temperatures **(see illustration)**. The heater is controlled by an internal thermostat. When the fuel is below a predetermined temperature, current to the heater warms the fuel.

Removal

Caution: Be careful not to allow dirt into the fuel system during the following procedure.

2 Obtain a container to catch spilt fuel.

3 Disconnect the battery negative (earth) lead (see Chapter 5A).

4 Disconnect the multi-plug from the base of the fuel heater.

5 Depress the tabs on the quick-release connector and disconnect the fuel supply pipe from the heater inlet pipe.

6 Release the fuel filter inlet pipe from the support clip.

7 Depress the tabs on the quick-release connector and disconnect the inlet pipe from the fuel filter.

8 Unscrew the bolt and remove the fuel heater and bracket from the engine compartment.

9 Release the two clips and remove the heater from the bracket.

Refitting

10 Refitting is the reverse of the removal procedure. On completion, bleed and prime the fuel system with reference to Chapter 4A, then carry out leak checks directly after the engine is first started.

3.1 The fuel heater is located on the end of the cylinder head

Chapter 6
Clutch

Contents

Degrees of difficulty

| Easy, suitable for novice with little experience | | Fairly easy, suitable for beginner with some experience | | Fairly difficult, suitable for competent DIY mechanic | | Difficult, suitable for experienced DIY mechanic | | Very difficult, suitable for expert DIY or professional | |

Specifications

General

Type	Diaphragm spring, single dry plate, cable operation
Pedal free play:	
Pre-1996 models	Automatic adjustment
1996 models on	150 ± 5 mm (RHD)
	145 ± 5 mm (LHD)
Disc diameter	220 mm

Torque wrench settings

	Nm	lbf ft
Clutch cover (pressure plate) to flywheel	30	22
Clutch release lever to lever shaft	25	18

1 General information

All models are equipped with a cable-operated single dry plate diaphragm spring clutch assembly. The unit consists of a clutch disc (or driven plate), a steel cover (doweled and bolted to the rear face of the flywheel, it contains the pressure plate and diaphragm spring) and a release mechanism **(see illustration)**.

The clutch disc is free to slide along the splines of the transmission input shaft, and is held in position between the flywheel and the pressure plate by the pressure of the diaphragm spring. Friction lining material is riveted to the clutch disc, which has a spring cushioned hub to absorb transmission shocks and help ensure a smooth take-up of the drive.

The clutch is actuated by a cable, controlled by the clutch pedal. The clutch release mechanism consists of a release arm and bearing, which is in permanent contact with the fingers of the diaphragm spring. Depressing the clutch pedal actuates the release arm by means of the cable. The arm pushes the release bearing against the diaphragm fingers, so moving the centre of

1.1 Exploded view of the clutch and associated components

1 Clutch disc (driven plate)
2 Clutch cover and pressure plate unit
3 Dowel
4 Dowel
5 Bolt
6 Lockwasher
7 Clutch repair kit
8 Release lever
9 Bush
10 Seal
11 Clutch release shaft
12 Bolt
13 Nut
14 Clutch release bearing
15 Pin
16 Bolts
17 Clutch housing cover plate (lower)
18 Clutch housing intermediate plate (upper)
19 Bolt
20 Bolt

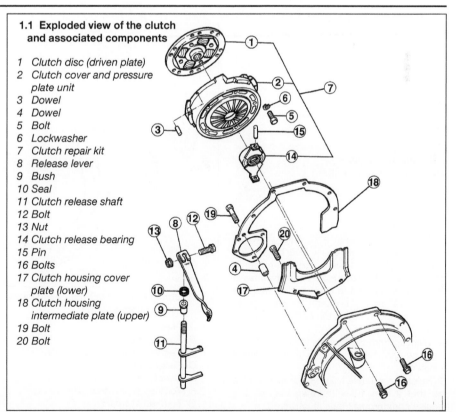

2.1a Disengage the clutch cable from the lever . . .

2.1b . . . and withdraw the cable through the locating lug

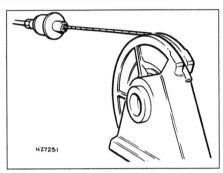

2.3 Clutch cable connection at the pedal end

the diaphragm spring inwards. As the centre of the spring is pushed in, the outside of the spring pivots out, so moving the pressure plate backwards and disengaging its grip on the clutch disc.

When the pedal is released, the diaphragm spring forces the pressure plate back into contact with the friction linings on the clutch disc. The disc is now firmly held between the pressure plate and the flywheel, thus transmitting engine power to the transmission.

On pre-1996 models, wear of the friction material on the clutch disc is automatically compensated for by a self-adjusting mechanism attached to the clutch pedal; this arrangement is replaced by a manual adjuster on later models. The self-adjusting mechanism consists of a toothed segment, a notched pawl and a tension spring. One end of the clutch cable is attached to the segment which is free to pivot on the pedal, but is kept in tension by the spring. As the pedal is depressed, the pawl contacts the segment, thus locking it and allowing the pedal to pull the cable and operate the clutch. As the pedal is released, the tension spring causes the segment to move free of the pawl and rotate slightly, thus taking up any free play that may exist in the cable.

2 Clutch cable – removal and refitting

Removal

1 At the transmission end, disengage the clutch cable from the release lever by gripping the inner cable with pliers, pulling it forwards to disengage the cable nipple from the release lever. Take care not to damage the cable if it is to be re-used. Disengage the outer cable from the support lug on top of the bellhousing **(see illustrations)**.

2 Working from the driver's footwell, unhook the segment tension spring from its pedal location.

3 Release the cable from the pedal segment so that it may be withdrawn through the engine compartment **(see illustration)**.

4 Pull the cable through the aperture in the bulkhead, and withdraw it from the engine compartment.

Refitting

5 To refit the cable, thread it through from the engine compartment and fit the inner cable over the segment, engaging the nipple to secure it. Reconnect the tension spring.

6 Reconnect the cable at the transmission end, passing it through the support lug on the top of the transmission and engaging it with the release lever.

7 On models with a self-adjusting clutch, operate the clutch and check it for satisfactory operation. On models with a manually-adjusted clutch, check and if

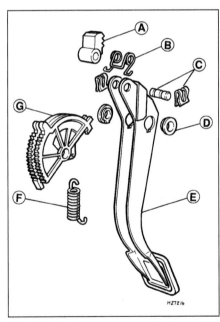

3.8a Clutch pedal and self-adjusting cable components

A *Pawl*
B *Pawl tension spring*
C *Pedal connecting rod and clip*
D *Pedal/shaft bushes*
E *Clutch pedal*
F *Toothed segment tension spring*
G *Toothed segment*

necessary adjust the clutch pedal free play as described in Chapter 1.

3 Clutch pedal – removal and refitting

Removal

1 Disconnect the battery negative (earth) lead (refer to Chapter 5A, Section 1).

2 Disconnect the clutch cable at the transmission end by slipping the cable nipple out of the release fork and disengaging the outer cable from the bracket on the bellhousing.

3 Referring to Chapter 12 for details, detach the fusebox and the relay multi-plugs, then position the fusebox unit out of the way to allow access to the clutch pedal.

4 Release the clutch cable from the pedal (see Section 2).

5 Release the brake stop-light switch in a clockwise direction, and extract it from the pedal bracket.

6 Release the clip securing the brake pedal connecting rod.

7 Release the retaining clip from the end of the pedal shaft, then slide the shaft through (away from the steering column) and remove the brake pedal, the spacer sleeves and the clutch pedal.

8 The pedal can now be dismantled as necessary by prising out the bushes, the tension spring or the adjustment mechanism as applicable **(see illustrations)**.

Refitting

9 Refitting is a reversal of the removal procedure. Apply a little grease to the pedal shaft and bushes, and ensure that the bushes are correctly located. On models with a self-adjusting clutch, do not refit the toothed segment tension spring into position until after the pedal is fitted onto the shaft. The pawl and its tension spring must be fitted so that the pawl is bearing on the toothed segment. Pull the spring into position using a suitable length of temporarily-attached wire **(see illustration)**.

10 On models with a self-adjusting clutch,

operate the clutch and check it for satisfactory operation. On models with a manually-adjusted clutch, check and if necessary adjust the clutch pedal free play as described in Chapter 1.

4 Clutch assembly –
removal, inspection and refitting

⚠️ *Warning: Dust created by clutch wear and deposited on the clutch components may contain asbestos, which is a health hazard. DO NOT blow it out with compressed air, or inhale any of it. DO NOT use petrol or petroleum-based solvents to clean off the dust. Brake system cleaner or methylated spirit should be used to flush the dust into a suitable receptacle. After the clutch components are wiped clean with rags, dispose of the contaminated rags and cleaner in a sealed, marked container.*

Removal

1 Access to the clutch may be gained in one of two ways. Either the engine or engine/transmission can be removed as described in Chapter 2B, and where applicable, the transmission separated from the engine, or the engine may be left in the car and the transmission removed independently, as described in Chapter 7. Unless the engine needs to be removed for any other reason, the preferred method is to remove the transmission.

2 Having separated the transmission from the engine, check if there are any marks identifying the relation of the clutch cover to the flywheel. If not, make your own marks using a dab of paint or a scriber. These marks will be used if the original cover is refitted, and will help to maintain the balance of the unit. A new cover may be fitted in any position allowed by the locating dowels.

3 Unscrew and remove the six clutch cover retaining bolts, working in a diagonal sequence and slackening the bolts only a few turns at a time. If necessary, the flywheel may be held stationary using a wide-bladed screwdriver, inserted in the teeth of the starter ring gear and resting against part of the cylinder block.

4 Ease the clutch cover off its locating dowels. Be prepared to catch the clutch disc, which will drop out as the cover is removed. Note which way round the disc is fitted **(see illustration)**.

Inspection

5 The most common problem which occurs in the clutch is wear of the clutch disc. However, all the clutch components should be inspected at this time, particularly if the vehicle has covered a high mileage.

6 Unless the clutch components are known to be virtually new, it is worth renewing them

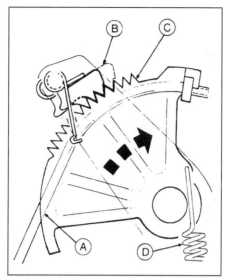

3.8b Clutch cable self-adjusting mechanism

A *Clutch cable*   C *Toothed segment*
B *Pawl*   D *Tension spring*

all as a set (disc, pressure plate and release bearing). Renewing a worn clutch disc by itself is not always satisfactory, especially if the old disc was slipping and causing the pressure plate to overheat.

7 Not renewing the release bearing is a false economy – it's bound to wear out eventually, and all the preliminary dismantling will have to be repeated if it's not renewed with the rest of the clutch.

8 Examine the linings of the clutch disc for wear and loose rivets, and the disc hub and rim for distortion, cracks, broken torsion springs, and worn splines. The surface of the friction linings may be highly glazed, but as long as the friction material pattern can be clearly seen, and the rivet heads are at least 1 mm below the lining surface, this is satisfactory.

9 If there is any sign of oil contamination, indicated by shiny black discoloration, the disc must be renewed, and the source of the contamination traced and rectified. This will be a leaking crankshaft oil seal or transmission input shaft oil seal. The renewal procedure for the former is given in Chapter 2A; renewal of

4.4 Removing the clutch cover and disc from the flywheel

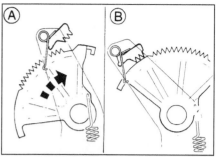

3.9 Positioning the clutch self-adjuster mechanism prior to refitting the pedal

A *Lift pawl and turn the segment*
B *Pawl bearing on smooth section of segment*

the transmission input shaft oil seal should be entrusted to a Ford dealer, as it involves major dismantling and the renewal of the clutch release bearing guide tube, using a press.

10 Check the machined faces of the flywheel and pressure plate. If either is grooved, or heavily scored, renewal is necessary. The pressure plate must also be renewed if any cracks are apparent, or if the diaphragm spring is damaged, or its pressure suspect. Pay particular attention to the tips of the spring fingers, where the release bearing acts upon them.

11 With the transmission removed, it is also advisable to check the condition of the release bearing, as described in Section 5. Having got this far, it is almost certainly worth renewing it.

Refitting

12 It is important that no oil or grease is allowed to come into contact with the friction material of the clutch disc or the pressure plate and flywheel faces. To ensure this, it is advisable to refit the clutch assembly with clean hands, and to wipe down the pressure plate and flywheel faces with a clean rag before assembly begins.

13 Begin reassembly by placing the clutch disc against the flywheel, ensuring that it is correctly orientated. It may be marked 'flywheel side' **(see illustration)**, but if not, position it with the word 'schwungradseite' stamped in the disc face towards the flywheel.

4.13 Clutch disc orientation markings

4.18 Centralising the clutch disc using a clutch aligning tool

14 Place the clutch cover over the dowels, refit the retaining bolts, and tighten them finger-tight so that the clutch disc is gripped, but can still be moved.

15 The clutch disc must now be centralised so that, when the engine and transmission are mated, the splines of the input shaft will pass through the splines in the centre of the clutch disc hub.

16 Centralisation can be carried out by inserting a round bar through the hole in the centre of the clutch disc, so that the end of the bar rests in the innermost hole in the rear end of the crankshaft. Move the bar sideways or up and down to move the clutch disc in whichever direction is necessary to achieve centralisation.

17 Centralisation can then be checked by removing the bar and viewing the clutch disc hub in relation to the diaphragm spring fingers. When the disc hub appears exactly in the centre of the circle created by the diaphragm spring fingers, the position is correct.

18 An alternative and more accurate method of centralisation is to use a commercially-available clutch-aligning tool, obtainable from most accessory shops **(see illustration)**.

19 Once the clutch is centralised, progressively tighten the cover bolts in a diagonal sequence to the torque setting given in the *Specifications*.

5.2 Withdrawing the clutch release bearing

20 Ensure that the input shaft splines, clutch disc splines and release bearing guide sleeve are clean. Apply a thin smear of high-melting-point grease to the input shaft splines and the release bearing guide sleeve. Only use a very small amount of grease, otherwise the excess will inevitably find its way onto the friction linings when the vehicle is in use.

21 The engine/transmission can now be refitted by referring to Chapter 2B.

5 Clutch release bearing – removal, inspection and refitting

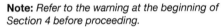

Note: *Refer to the warning at the beginning of Section 4 before proceeding.*

Removal

1 Separate the engine and transmission as described in the previous Section.

2 Withdraw the release bearing from its guide sleeve by turning the release arm **(see illustration)**.

Inspection

3 Check the bearing for smoothness of operation, and renew it if there is any sign of harshness or roughness as the bearing is spun. Do not attempt to dismantle, clean or lubricate the bearing.

4 As mentioned earlier, it is worth renewing the release bearing as a matter of course, unless it is known to be in perfect condition.

Refitting

5 Refitting of the clutch release bearing is a reversal of the removal procedure, making sure that it is correctly located on the release arm fork. It is helpful to slightly lift the release arm while locating the bearing on its guide sleeve. Keep the fork in contact with the plastic shoulders on the bearing (where fitted) as the bearing is being located.

6 Clutch release shaft and bush – removal and refitting

Removal

1 Remove the clutch release bearing as described in the previous Section.

2 Unscrew the clamp bolt securing the release arm to the shaft **(see illustration)**. Mark the relative position of the shaft to the arm, then withdraw the arm from the shaft. The shaft has a master spline, to ensure that the arm is fitted correctly.

3 Remove the protective cap from around the top of the release shaft splines to allow access to the bush.

4 Extract the bush by gently levering it from the housing using a pair of screwdrivers, then lift it out over the splines of the shaft.

5 With the bush removed, the release shaft can be withdrawn (if required) by lifting it from its lower bearing bore, manoeuvring it sideways and withdrawing it **(see illustration)**.

Refitting

6 Refit in the reverse order of removal. Slide the bush over the shaft, and locate it so that it is flush in the upper housing, then fit the protective cap.

7 Refit the release bearing as described in the previous Section.

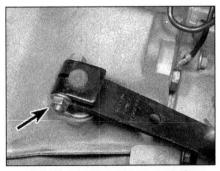

6.2 Clutch release lever-to-shaft connection with clamp bolt and nut (arrowed)

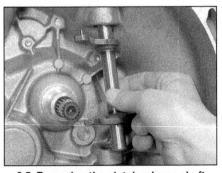

6.5 Removing the clutch release shaft

Chapter 7
Manual transmission

Contents

Degrees of difficulty

Easy, suitable for novice with little experience	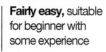	Fairly easy, suitable for beginner with some experience		Fairly difficult, suitable for competent DIY mechanic	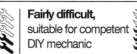	Difficult, suitable for experienced DIY mechanic		Very difficult, suitable for expert DIY or professional	

Specifications

Transmission type/application

All models . . . . B5 or iB5 type, 5-speed

Note: *It would appear that some late Diesel-engined models were fitted with the MTX-75 transmission used on DOHC petrol-engined Escorts and covered in manual No. 1737. In the absence of any information from the manufacturer to confirm this, the MTX-75 transmission is NOT covered in this manual.*

Gear ratios (typical)

1st	3.15:1
2nd	1.91:1
3rd	1.28:1
4th	0.95:1
5th	0.75:1
Reverse	3.62:1
Final drive	3.56:1

Torque wrench settings

	Nm	lbf ft
Clutch housing cover plate bolts	40	30
Engine-to-transmission bolts	40	30
Gearshift housing-to-floor	10	7
Gearshift linkage clamp bolt	16	12
Gearshift rod to transmission selector shaft	23	17
Gearshift stabiliser rod-to-housing	7	5
Gearshift stabiliser rod-to-transmission	55	41
Left-hand front mounting bracket brace	50	37
Left-hand front mounting bracket-to-mounting	68	50
Left-hand rear mounting bracket-to-mounting	68	50
Left-hand rear mounting bracket-to-transmission	50	37
Reversing light switch	18	13

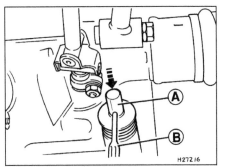

2.3a Loosen off the clamp bolt . . .

2.3b . . . and disengage the gearshift rod from the selector shaft

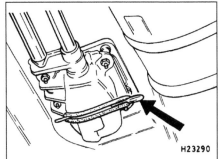

2.3c Gearchange linkage/mechanism adjustment

A Selector shaft   B Rod or punch

1 General information

All models are equipped with a 5-speed transmission mounted transversely in the engine bay, bolted directly to the engine. All types feature a compact, two-piece, light-weight aluminium alloy housing, containing both the transmission and the differential assemblies.

The transmission is lubricated inde-pendently of the engine, the capacity differing according to type (see Chapter 1). The transmission and differential both share the same lubricating oil. Torque from the transmission output shaft is transmitted to the crownwheel (which is bolted to the differential

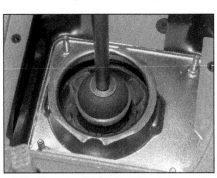

2.4 Gear lever locked in position by fabricated tool with elastic band to secure it

unit), and then from the differential gears to the driveshafts.

Gearshift is by means of a floor-mounted gear lever, connected by a remote control housing and gearshift rod to the transmission selector shaft.

2 Gearchange linkage – adjustment

1 Chock the rear wheels then jack up the front of the car and support it on axle stands (see *Jacking and vehicle support*).
2 Select 4th gear. It may be useful to have an assistant inside the vehicle, to hold the gear lever firmly in this position during adjustment.
3 Working from underneath the vehicle, loosen off the gearshift rod-to-gear selector

shaft clamp bolt, and disengage the shift rod from the transmission selector shaft (**see illustrations**). Slide the selector shaft back and forth to find its central position, then turn the selector shaft to the right and left to find the central position in the transverse plane. Hold the selector shaft in the centralised position, then insert a suitable rod (or punch) into the hole in the selector shaft in the transmission, and move it as far forwards as possible (**see illustration**).
4 Insert a fabricated 'lockpin' adjustment tool (from the left-hand side), and secure it in position with a sturdy elastic band or similar (**see illustration**).
5 Check that the selector shaft coupling surfaces are free of grease, then reconnect the gearshift rod onto the transmission selector shaft, and secure it by tightening the clamp bolt to the specified torque setting.
6 Extract the locking pin, then check for the satisfactory engagement of all gears, selecting each gear in turn to confirm that the mechanism has been correctly reset. Further minor adjustment may be required.
7 With the adjustment correctly made, lower the vehicle to complete.

3 Gearchange linkage and gear lever – removal and refitting

Removal

1 Working inside the car, first engage 4th gear – this will provide the correct re-engagement and adjustment for the gearchange mechanism during reassembly.
2 Unscrew and remove the gear lever knob.
3 Prise free and release the gear lever surround and gaiter from the centre console, and remove it upwards from the gear lever. If required, the gear lever-to-selector unit can be prised free and withdrawn to inspect the selector balljoint from above (**see illustrations**).
4 Loosen off the four gear lever retaining nuts (**see illustration**).
5 Chock the rear wheels, then jack up the front of the car and support it on axle stands (see *Jacking and vehicle support*).

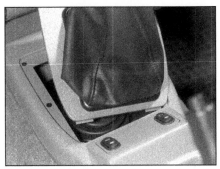

3.3a Disengage the gear lever-to-console boot for access to the unit retaining nuts

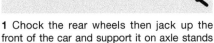

3.3b Remove the lever gaiter to inspect the gear lever balljoint from above

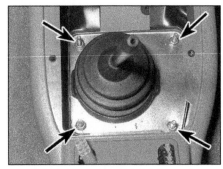

3.4 Four gear lever retaining nuts (arrowed)

6 Working beneath the vehicle, release the flexible exhaust pipe mountings, and disconnect the exhaust system from the downpipe. On catalytic converter models, also detach the heat shield from the underside of the floorpan to allow access to the underside of the gear lever for its removal **(see illustration)**.

7 Mark the relative fitted positions of the selector shaft and gearshift rod, then undo the clamp bolt and separate the shaft from the rod.

8 Unscrew and remove the gearshift rod stabiliser retaining bolt. Note the position of the washer as the bolt is withdrawn **(see illustration)**. Support the gear lever assembly from underneath, and have an assistant unscrew and remove the four gear lever retaining nuts within the vehicle, then lower and withdraw the gearchange mechanism from underneath the vehicle.

Refitting

9 Refitting is a reversal of removal, but lubricate the pivot points with grease. Before lowering the vehicle from the axle stands, check and if necessary adjust the gearchange linkage as described in Section 2. Tighten the fastenings to the specified torque setting, where given.

4 Speedometer drive pinion – removal and refitting

Removal

1 Disconnect the battery negative (earth) lead (refer to Chapter 5A, Section 1).

2 Undo the retaining nut, and withdraw the speedometer cable from the drive pinion or vehicle speed sensor in the top face of the transmission **(see illustration)**. If a vehicle speed sensor is fitted, use two spanners to loosen the nut – one to counterhold the sensor, and the other to unscrew the cable nut.

3 Where applicable, disconnect the wiring from the vehicle speed sensor, then unscrew the sensor from the top of the drive pinion.

4 Grip the drive pinion retaining pin with self-locking grips or pliers, and withdraw it from the drive pinion housing.

5 Pull the drive pinion and bearing out of the housing, but take care not to tilt it, because the pinion and bearing are not secured and can easily be separated if the pinion is snagged **(see illustration)**.

6 Using a small screwdriver, prise the O-ring from the groove in the bearing; obtain a new one for reassembly.

7 Wipe clean the drive pinion and bearing, also the seating bore in the transmission casing.

Refitting

8 Refitting is a reversal of the removal procedure, but lightly oil the new O-ring

3.6 Detach the exhaust system at the front joint (A) and the heat shield from the points indicated (B) on catalytic converter models

before inserting the assembly in the transmission casing. Drive in the retaining roll pin using a hammer **(see illustration)**.

5 Oil seals – renewal

1 Oil leaks frequently occur due to wear or deterioration of the differential side gear seals and/or the gearchange selector shaft oil seal and speedometer drive pinion O-ring. Renewal of these seals is relatively easy, since the repairs can be performed without removing the transmission from the vehicle.

Differential side gear seals

2 The differential side gear oil seals are located at the sides of the transmission,

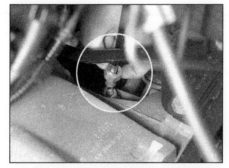

4.2 Disconnecting the speedometer cable from the pinion

4.8 Insert the speedometer drive pinion/bearing (A) and secure with a new retaining pin (B)

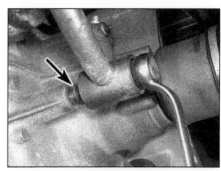

3.8 Unscrewing the stabiliser-to-transmission bolt. Note washer (arrowed)

where the driveshafts enter the transmission. If leakage at the seal is suspected, raise the vehicle and support it securely on axle stands (see *Jacking and vehicle support*). If the seal is leaking, oil will be found on the side of the transmission below the driveshaft.

3 Refer to Chapter 8 and remove the appropriate driveshaft.

4 Wipe clean the old oil seal and note its orientation and measure its fitted depth below the casing edge. This is necessary to determine the correct fitted position of the new oil seal.

5 Using a large screwdriver or lever, carefully prise the oil seal out of the transmission casing, taking care not to damage the casing **(see illustration)**. If the oil seal is reluctant to move, it is sometimes helpful to carefully drive it *into* the transmission a little way, applying the force at one point only. This will have the

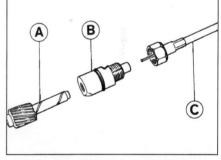

4.5 Speedometer drive pinion (A) pinion bearing (B) and drive cable (C)

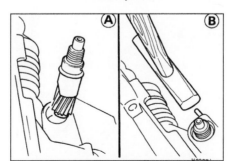

5.5 Levering out an old driveshaft oil seal

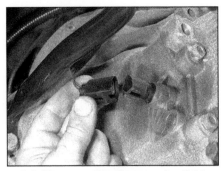

5.8 Driving a new driveshaft oil seal into position using a suitable socket

effect of swivelling the seal out of the casing, and it can then be pulled out. If the oil seal is particularly difficult to remove, an oil seal removal tool may be obtained from a garage or accessory shop.

6 Wipe clean the oil seal seating in the transmission casing.

7 Dip the new oil seal in clean oil, then press it a little way into the casing by hand, making sure that it is square to its seating.

8 Using suitable tubing or a large socket, carefully drive the oil seal fully into the casing up to its previously-noted fitted depth **(see illustration)**.

9 Refit the driveshaft with reference to Chapter 8.

Gear selector shaft seal

10 Apply the handbrake, then jack up the front of the vehicle and support it on axle stands.

11 Unscrew the bolt securing the gearchange linkage to the shaft on the rear of the transmission. Pull off the linkage and remove the rubber boot.

12 Using a suitable tool or grips, pull the oil seal out of the transmission casing. Ford technicians use a slide hammer, with an end fitting which locates over the oil seal extension. In the absence of this tool, if the oil seal is particularly tight, drill one or two small holes in the oil seal, and screw in self-tapping screws. The oil seal can then be removed from the casing by pulling on the screws.

13 Wipe clean the oil seal seating in the transmission.

14 Dip the new oil seal in clean oil, then press

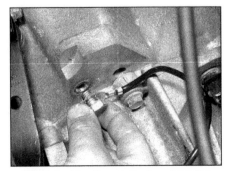

7.8 Detaching the earth strap from the transmission

6.2 Disconnecting the reversing light switch lead

it a little way into the casing by hand, making sure that it is square to its seating.

15 Using suitable tubing or a large socket, carefully drive the oil seal fully into the casing.

16 Locate the rubber boot over the selector shaft.

17 Refit the gearchange linkage to the shaft on the rear of the transmission, and tighten the bolt to the specified torque setting.

18 If necessary, adjust the gearchange linkage as described in Section 2 of this Chapter.

Speedometer pinion seal

19 The procedure is covered in Section 4 of this Chapter.

6 Reversing light switch – removal and refitting

Removal

1 Chock the rear wheels then jack up the front of the car and support it on axle stands (see *Jacking and vehicle support*).

2 Disconnect the wiring from the reversing light switch **(see illustration)**.

3 Unscrew the switch from the side of the transmission, and remove the washer.

Refitting

4 Clean the location in the transmission, and the threads of the switch.

5 Insert the switch together with a new washer, and tighten it to the specified torque wrench setting.

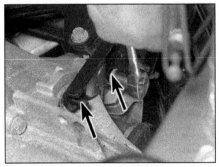

7.9 Unscrew the two engine/transmission mounting bracket nuts (arrowed)

6 Reconnect the wiring.

7 Check and top-up the transmission oil level if necessary, with reference to Chapter 1.

8 Lower the vehicle to the ground.

7 Manual transmission – removal and refitting

Note: *Read through this procedure before starting work to see what is involved, particularly in terms of lifting equipment. Depending on the facilities available, the home mechanic may prefer to remove the engine and transmission together, then separate them on the bench, as described in Chapter 2B.*

Removal

1 The manual transmission is removed downwards from the engine compartment, after disconnecting it from the engine. Due to the weight of the unit, it will be necessary to have a suitable method of supporting the transmission as it is lowered during removal and subsequently raised during its refitting. A trolley jack fitted with a suitable saddle to support the transmission as it is removed will be ideal, but failing this, an engine lift hoist and sling will suffice. The weight of the engine will also need to be supported whilst the transmission is detached from it – an engine support bar fitted in the front wing drain channel each side is ideal for this purpose, but care must be taken not to damage the wings or their paintwork. If this type of tool is not available (or cannot be fabricated), the engine can be supported by blocks or a second jack from underneath.

2 Disconnect the battery negative (earth) lead (refer to Chapter 5A, Section 1).

3 Refer to Chapter 4A and remove the air cleaner and air inlet components as necessary for access to the transmission. Disconnect the clutch cable from the clutch release lever as described in Chapter 6.

4 Undo the retaining nut, and detach the speedometer drive cable from the transmission. Position the cable out of the way.

5 Unbolt and disconnect the radio earth strap from the transmission.

6 Extract the transmission breather tube from the aperture in the chassis side member.

7 Engage 4th gear – this will ease realignment and adjustment of the gearchange linkage during the refitting procedures.

8 Unscrew and remove the three upper transmission-to-engine flange bolts. Note that one bolt secures the main earth strap to the battery, and one bolt retains the coolant hose locating strap **(see illustration)**.

9 Unscrew and remove the two nuts securing the left-hand rear engine/transmission mounting bracket to the transmission **(see illustration)**.

10 Apply the handbrake, then raise the vehicle at the front. Support it on axle stands at a sufficient height to allow the transmission to be withdrawn from under the front end (see *Jacking and vehicle support*).

11 Fit the engine support bar, or failing this, position a jack under the engine. Whichever is used, raise the engine so that its weight is taken from the mountings.

12 Undo the two retaining bolts, and detach the rear left-hand engine/transmission mounting bracket from the engine/transmission **(see illustration)**.

13 Similarly, undo the two retaining bolts and detach the front left-hand engine/transmission mounting bracket from the engine/transmission **(see illustration)**.

14 Disconnect the lead connector from the reversing light switch.

15 Detach the wiring, and then unbolt and withdraw the starter motor. See Chapter 5A for full details.

16 Before disconnecting the gearshift rod, mark the relative fitted positions of the gearshift rod and the selector shaft, as a guide for refitting and adjustment.

17 Undo the gearshift rod stabiliser-to-transmission retaining bolt. Separate the stabiliser from the transmission (noting the washer fitted between the stabiliser and the transmission). Tie the gearshift rod and stabiliser up out of the way.

18 Referring to Chapter 10 for details, detach the track rod end balljoint from the steering arm on the left-hand side, and the suspension arm-to-spindle carrier balljoint on the left and right-hand sides.

19 Insert a suitable lever between the driveshaft inner CV joint and the transmission, and carefully lever the driveshaft free from the transmission. Lever against the reinforcement rib to avoid damaging the transmission housing, and have an assistant pull the suspension strut outwards on the side being detached, to assist in the driveshaft withdrawal from the transmission. As the driveshaft is withdrawn, be prepared for escaping oil.

20 When the driveshaft is detached from the transmission, tie it up out of the way. Do not allow the inner CV joint to be angled more than 17 degrees, and do not force the outer CV joint past its stop, or the joints may be damaged.

21 Repeat the above procedure and detach the driveshaft on the opposite side. After removal of both driveshafts, plug the apertures in the differential (or preferably and if available, insert old CV joints) to prevent further oil leakage, and to immobilise the differential gears.

22 Partially lower the engine and transmission, then unscrew the retaining nut and remove the engine/transmission mounting bracket from the transmission.

23 Unscrew and remove the remaining engine-to-transmission retaining bolts. Note that two bolts on the bulkhead side also secure the mounting bracket stay. Make a final check to ensure that all of the

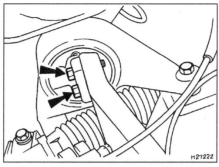
7.12 Unscrew the rear left-hand mounting bolts (arrowed)

transmission connections have been detached and are positioned out of the way.

24 Check that the engine remains securely supported. The method of supporting the transmission during its removal is largely a matter of personal choice and/or the facilities available. It can be supported from above, and lowered (using a conventional hoist) onto a trolley for withdrawal from under the vehicle **(see illustration)**. Failing this, it can be supported underneath with a suitable trolley jack, and withdrawn from under the front end. Whichever method is employed, engage the aid of an assistant to help guide the transmission down and clear of the surrounding components in the engine compartment.

25 Withdraw the transmission from the engine, taking care not to allow the weight of the transmission to rest on the input shaft at any time. Once the input shaft is clear of the clutch unit, the transmission can be lowered and manoeuvred down through the engine compartment, and then withdrawn from underneath the vehicle.

Refitting

26 Refitting is a reversal of removal, but note the following additional points:
a) Make sure that all mating faces are clean.
b) Apply a smear of high-melting-point grease to the splines of the transmission input shaft. Do not apply too much, otherwise there is the possibility of the grease contaminating the clutch friction disc.

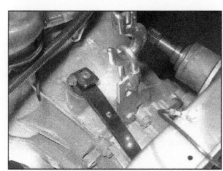
7.24 Supporting the weight of the transmission from above during its removal using a fabricated bracket

7.13 Unscrew the front left-hand mounting bolts (arrowed)

c) Where applicable, ensure that the engine adapter plate is correctly seated on the locating dowels on the engine.
d) Fit new snap-rings to the grooves in the inner end of each driveshaft CV joint, and ensure that they are felt to snap fully into engagement as they are fitted into position in the transmission.
e) Locate the left-hand engine/transmission mounting bracket over the three studs, and fit the retaining nut from underneath.
f) Temporarily lower the vehicle, then raise the engine/transmission to align the mounting brackets on the left-hand side with the threaded holes in the rubber mountings. Refit the two bolts securing the front left engine/transmission mounting bracket, then repeat this procedure and secure the rear left-hand bracket. The vehicle can then be raised and supported on axle stands at the front end again, to allow the remaining refitting operations to be carried out.
g) Refer to Chapters 8 and 10 for details on reconnecting the driveshafts to the transmission and the suspension arm/steering balljoint and track rod end balljoint.
h) Reconnect and adjust the gearchange linkage as described in Section 2.
i) Tighten all nuts and bolts to the specified torque settings.
j) Replenish the transmission oil, and check the level with reference to Chapter 1.
k) On models with a self-adjusting clutch, operate the clutch and check it for satisfactory operation. On models with a manually-adjusted clutch, check and if necessary adjust the clutch pedal free play as described in Chapter 1.

8 Manual transmission overhaul – general

No work can be carried out to the transmission until the engine/transmission has been removed from the car and cleaned externally.

Overhauling a manual transmission is a difficult and involved job for the DIY home mechanic. In addition to dismantling and reassembling many small parts, clearances must be precisely measured and, if necessary, changed by selecting shims and spacers. Internal transmission components are also often difficult to obtain, and in many instances, are extremely expensive. Because of this, if the transmission develops a fault or becomes noisy, the best course of action is to have the unit overhauled by a specialist repairer, or to obtain an exchange reconditioned unit.

Nevertheless, it is not impossible for the more experienced mechanic to overhaul the transmission, provided the special tools are available, and that the job is done in a deliberate step-by-step manner so that nothing is overlooked.

The tools necessary for an overhaul may include internal and external circlip pliers, bearing pullers, a slide hammer, a set of pin punches, a dial test indicator, and possibly a hydraulic press. In addition, a large, sturdy workbench and a vice will be required.

During dismantling of the transmission, make careful notes of how each component is fitted, to make reassembly easier and accurate.

Before dismantling the transmission, it will help if you have some idea which area is malfunctioning. Certain problems can be closely related to specific areas in the transmission, which can make component examination and replacement easier.

Chapter 8
Driveshafts

Contents

Degrees of difficulty

Easy, suitable for novice with little experience		**Fairly easy,** suitable for beginner with some experience		**Fairly difficult,** suitable for competent DIY mechanic		**Difficult,** suitable for experienced DIY mechanic		**Very difficult,** suitable for expert DIY or professional	

Specifications

Type
All diesel models . . . . 25-spline driveshaft
1.3 and 1.4 litre petrol models, except automatic transmission or ABS . 23-spline driveshaft

Lubrication
Driveshaft joint grease type . . . . Supplied with repair kit
Outer joint grease quantity . . . . 40 grams
Inner joint grease quantity . . . . 95 grams

Torque wrench settings

	Nm	lbf ft
Hub/driveshaft retaining nut	270	199
Intermediate shaft bearing flange nuts	26	19
Roadwheel nuts	85	63

1 General information

Drive is transmitted from the differential to the front wheels by means of two unequal-length steel driveshafts. On certain models, one or both of the driveshafts incorporate a vibration/harmonic damper, which is either bolted or pressed in position on the shaft. Some models with the later TC (non-intercooled turbo) engine featured an intermediate driveshaft on the right-hand side.

Each driveshaft consists of three main components – the sliding tripod type inner CV joint, the main driveshaft (which is splined at each end) and a fixed type outer CV joint **(see illustration)**. The inner end section of the tripod type joint is secured in the differential by the engagement of a snap-ring, whilst the outer (ball and cage type) CV joint is secured in the front hub by the stub axle nut. The nut has a shouldered outer section which is peened over to lock it in position.

On most models the only repairs possible are the renewal of the rubber gaiters and the renewal of the inner joint spiders. When sourcing used parts from a breakers, note that smaller-engined petrol Escorts have driveshafts with a different number of hub splines. Wear or damage to the outer constant velocity joints or the driveshaft splines can only be rectified by fitting a complete new driveshaft assembly. On certain later models, the outer CV joint may be available separately; seek the advice of a Ford dealer if component renewal is anticipated.

2 Driveshafts – removal and refitting

Removal

1 Remove the wheel trim from the front roadwheel on the side concerned, then using a small pin punch, peen back the locking portion of the front hub/driveshaft nut. Loosen off the nut about half-a-turn.
2 Loosen off the front roadwheel retaining nuts on the side concerned.
3 Chock the rear wheels then jack up the front of the car and support it on axle stands (see *Jacking and vehicle support*). Remove the appropriate roadwheel, and unscrew and remove the hub/driveshaft retaining nut and washer **(see illustration)**.

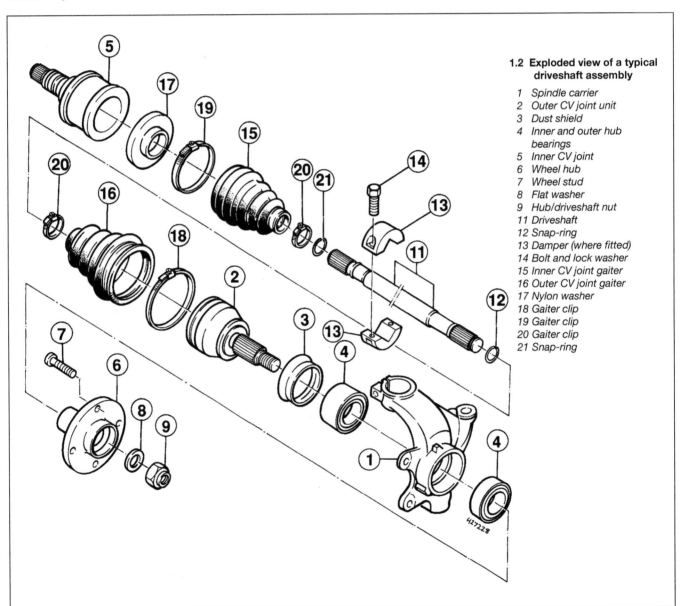

1.2 Exploded view of a typical driveshaft assembly

1 Spindle carrier
2 Outer CV joint unit
3 Dust shield
4 Inner and outer hub bearings
5 Inner CV joint
6 Wheel hub
7 Wheel stud
8 Flat washer
9 Hub/driveshaft nut
11 Driveshaft
12 Snap-ring
13 Damper (where fitted)
14 Bolt and lock washer
15 Inner CV joint gaiter
16 Outer CV joint gaiter
17 Nylon washer
18 Gaiter clip
19 Gaiter clip
20 Gaiter clip
21 Snap-ring

2.3 Remove the hub/driveshaft retaining nut and washer

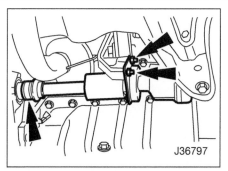

J36797

2.7 Driveshaft intermediate bearing flange nuts (arrowed) – TC engines

2.8 Driveshaft separation from the front wheel hub using a conventional puller – note the spacer (arrowed)

4 Undo the two bolts, and remove the brake caliper from the spindle carrier. Support the caliper from above, to prevent the hydraulic hose from being strained or distorted.
5 Detach the relevant track rod end balljoint from the steering arm (see Chapter 10).
6 Remove the Torx-head pinch-bolt and nut securing the lower suspension arm balljoint to the spindle carrier. As it is withdrawn, note the fitted direction of the bolt (to ensure correct refitting). Lever the suspension arm downwards to detach it from the spindle carrier unit. Refer to Chapter 10 for the full procedure.
7 On models with the TC (non-intercooled turbo) engine, undo the two intermediate shaft bearing flange nuts **(see illustration)**. The intermediate shaft was discontinued after January 1997.
8 Release the driveshaft from its location in the hub by pulling the spindle carrier outwards, away from the centre of the vehicle. Do not fully withdraw the shaft from the hub at this stage, but ensure that it is free to be withdrawn when required. If it is tight in the hub, lightly tap its outer end with a soft-faced hammer, or use a conventional puller and spacer as shown **(see illustration)**.
9 Insert a suitable lever between the inner driveshaft joint and the transmission case, adjacent to a reinforcing rib, then prise free the inner joint from the differential **(see illustration)**. If it proves reluctant to move, strike the lever firmly with the palm of the hand. Be careful not to damage the adjacent components, and be prepared for oil spillage from the transmission case through the vacated driveshaft aperture. If possible, plug

the aperture (or preferably, and if available, insert an old CV joint) to prevent leakage and to immobilise the differential gears. Do not allow the inner tripod joint to bend more than 17 degrees, or it may be damaged. The outer joint must not be bent past its stop (more than 45 degrees).
10 Withdraw the driveshaft from the hub, and remove it as a unit from the vehicle. If the driveshaft on the opposing side is to be removed also, the differential must be immobilised by the insertion of an old CV joint or a suitable shaft before the other shaft is removed.
11 Remove the snap-ring from the groove in the splines of the inner joint tripod housing **(see illustration)**. *This snap-ring must be renewed each time the driveshaft is withdrawn from the differential. The hub/driveshaft retaining nut and the track rod end balljoint split pin must also be renewed when refitting the driveshaft.*

Refitting

12 Fit a new snap-ring to the groove in the splines of the inner joint tripod housing.
13 On models with the TC (non-intercooled turbo) engine, offer up the intermediate shaft, and tighten the bearing flange nuts to the specified torque.
14 Smear the splines at the wheel hub end of the shaft with grease, then insert it into the spindle carrier. Use the old nut and retaining washer to assist in drawing the shaft into position, and as it is fitted, rotate the brake disc to assist in centralising the wheel bearings.

15 Remove the temporarily-fitted plug (or the old CV joint) from the differential housing. Lightly smear the oil seal lips in the differential housing with grease, then insert the inner driveshaft joint. Align the splines, and push it into position so that the snap-ring is clearly felt to engage in the groove of the differential side gear **(see illustration)**.
16 Reconnect the suspension lower arm balljoint to the spindle carrier. Insert the pinch-bolt (in its original direction of fitting), ensure that the bolt is fully engaged in the groove of the ball-stud, then fit and tighten the retaining nut to the specified torque wrench setting (Chapter 10).
17 Reconnect the track rod end balljoint to the steering arm as described in Chapter 10.
18 Refit the brake caliper unit to the spindle carrier, and tighten the retaining bolts to the specified torque (see Chapter 9).
19 Refit the roadwheel, and lightly tighten its retaining nuts.
20 Fit a new hub nut and washer, and tighten the nut as much possible at this stage. As the nut is being tightened, rotate the roadwheel to ensure that the wheel bearings seat correctly.
21 Lower the vehicle to the ground, then tighten the hub nut to the specified torque wrench setting. Using a pin punch, stake-lock the nut in the groove in the end of the axle stub.
22 Tighten the roadwheel nuts to the specified torque setting.
23 Check the level of the transmission oil, and top-up if necessary with the recommended lubricant (see Chapter 1).

2.9 Levering the driveshaft free from the transmission

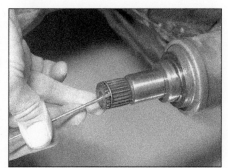

2.11 Prising free the snap-ring from the groove in the inner end of the driveshaft

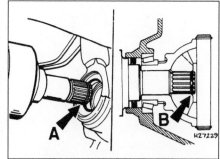

H27229

2.15 Snap-ring (A) must be renewed and fully engage in groove (B)

3.6 Release and withdraw the gaiter from the inner CV joint housing

3 Driveshaft inner CV joint gaiter – renewal

1 The inner CV joint gaiter can only be renewed once the inner CV joint has been detached at the transmission end. This can be done with the driveshaft fully removed (as described in Section 2), or by leaving it in situ in the wheel hub. The latter method is described below. If it is wished to fully remove the driveshaft, refer to Section 2 for details, then proceed as described in paragraphs 6 to 14 inclusive in this Section to renew the gaiter.
2 Loosen off the front roadwheel nuts on the side concerned.
3 Chock the rear wheels then jack up the front of the car and support it on axle stands (see *Jacking and vehicle support*). Remove the appropriate roadwheel.

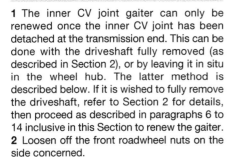

3.11a Fit the new gaiter over the inboard end of the driveshaft . . .

3.12 Tripod refitted onto the driveshaft with the match-marks aligned (arrowed)

3.9 Remove the snap-ring from the tripod end of the driveshaft

4 Detach the track rod end balljoint from the steering arm as described in Chapter 10.
5 Remove the Torx-head pinch-bolt and nut securing the lower suspension arm balljoint to the spindle carrier. As it is withdrawn, note the fitted direction of the bolt (to ensure correct refitting). Lever the suspension arm downwards to detach it from the spindle carrier.
6 Note the direction of fitting of the inner joint gaiter retaining clips, then release the clips from the gaiter, and slide the gaiter back along the driveshaft (away from the transmission) together with the large nylon washer. **(see illustration)**.
7 Get an assistant to help pull the suspension strut outwards, and separate the driveshaft and tripod from the tripod housing. With the driveshaft disconnected at the inner end, do not allow the outer CV joint to be angled past its stop (see paragraph 9 in the previous Section).

3.11b . . . and locate the nylon washer (note its orientation)

3.14 Special pliers are required to securely clamp the inner gaiter clip on the driveshaft

8 Wipe the grease from the tripod joint assembly.
9 Prise free the snap-ring retaining the tripod on the inner end of the driveshaft **(see illustration)**. Check if the inner end face of the driveshaft and the tripod are 'match-marked' for position, then remove the tripod from the shaft, followed by the large nylon washer and the old gaiter.
10 Clean the driveshaft. Note that the joint retaining snap-ring, the track rod end balljoint split pin and the gaiter retaining clips must be renewed on reassembly.
11 Slide the new gaiter into position on the shaft to allow sufficient access for reassembly of the tripod joint. Locate the large nylon washer over the shaft and into the gaiter **(see illustrations)**.
12 Refit the tripod on the driveshaft. It must be fitted with the chamfered edge leading (towards the driveshaft), and with the match-marks aligned **(see illustration)**. Secure it in position using a new snap-ring. Ensure that the snap-ring is fully engaged in its groove.
13 Refit the driveshaft and tripod to the tripod housing, then pack the housing with the specified type and quantity of grease.
14 Move the gaiter along the driveshaft, and locate it over the joint and onto its inner and outer seatings. Ensure that it is correctly seated and not twisted or distorted, then fit the new retaining clips. The fitted direction of the clips must be as noted during removal. The inner clip is a pinch-clamp type, secured using special pliers as shown **(see illustration)**. In the event of such pliers not being available, the gaiter can be secured at this point by a suitable nylon cable-tie.
15 Reconnect the suspension lower arm balljoint to the spindle carrier. Insert the pinch-bolt (in its original direction of fitting), ensure that the bolt is fully engaged in the groove of the ball-stud, then fit and tighten the retaining nut to the specified torque setting (Chapter 10).
16 Reconnect the track rod end balljoint to the steering arm as described in Chapter 10.
17 Refit the roadwheel and its retaining nuts, then lower the vehicle to the ground. Tighten the roadwheel nuts to the specified torque.

4 Driveshaft outer CV joint gaiter – renewal

1 The outer CV joint gaiter can be renewed with the driveshaft fully removed or with it in situ in the wheel hub, but with the outer CV joint disconnected. If the driveshaft has already been removed, proceed as described in paragraphs 6 to 14 inclusive to renew the outer CV joint gaiter.
2 Loosen off the front roadwheel nuts on the side concerned.
3 Check that the handbrake is fully applied, then jack up the front of the vehicle and support it on axle stands. Remove the roadwheel.

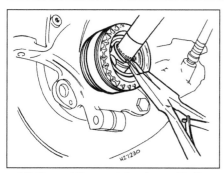

4.7 Expand the snap-ring to enable the driveshaft to be withdrawn from the outer CV joint

4.11a Locate the new snap-ring (arrowed) in the outer CV joint . . .

4.11b . . . partially lubricate the joint . . .

4 Detach the track rod end balljoint from the steering arm as described in Chapter 10.
5 Remove the Torx-head pinch-bolt and nut securing the lower suspension arm balljoint to the spindle carrier. As it is withdrawn, note the fitted direction of the bolt (to ensure correct refitting). Lever the suspension arm downwards to detach it from the spindle carrier.
6 Note the direction of fitting of the outer CV joint gaiter retaining clips, then release the clips from the gaiter, and slide the gaiter back along the driveshaft (towards the transmission end).
7 To disconnect the driveshaft from the outer CV joint, first wipe away the grease from the joint. Using suitable circlip pliers, expand the snap-ring, and have an assistant simultaneously pull the CV joint outwards (or when in situ, pull the suspension strut outwards) to separate the driveshaft from the CV joint **(see illustration)**. Whilst the driveshaft is detached at the outer end, do not allow the inner (tripod) joint to be angled beyond 17 degrees, or the joint may be damaged.
8 Withdraw the gaiter from the driveshaft.
9 Clean the driveshaft. **Note:** *The CV joint retaining snap-ring, the track rod end balljoint split pin and the gaiter retaining clips must be renewed.*
10 Slide the new gaiter along on the shaft to allow access for reassembly of the outer CV joint.
11 Locate a new snap-ring into position in the outer CV joint, then lubricate the joint with some of the specified grease **(see illustrations)**.
12 Engage the driveshaft with the CV joint, and push them together so that the circlip engages in the groove of the driveshaft **(see illustration)**. If the task is being carried out with the spindle carrier attached, pull the suspension strut outwards, and guide the driveshaft into the CV joint. Progressively release the suspension until the shaft is fully engaged with the joint, and the snap-ring engages in the groove in the driveshaft.

13 Pack the joint with the remainder of the specified grease.
14 Move the gaiter along the driveshaft, and locate it over the joint and onto its inner and outer seatings. Check that it is correctly seated and not twisted or distorted, then fit new retaining clips. The fitted direction of the clips must be as noted during removal.
15 Reconnect the suspension lower arm balljoint to the spindle carrier. Insert the pinch-bolt (in its original direction of fitting), ensure that the bolt is fully engaged in the groove of the ball-stud, then fit and tighten the retaining nut to the specified torque wrench setting (Chapter 10).
16 Reconnect the track rod end balljoint to the steering arm as described in Chapter 10.
17 Refit the roadwheel and tighten its nuts, then lower the vehicle to the ground. Tighten the roadwheel nuts to the specified torque wrench setting.

**5 Driveshafts –
inspection and overhaul**

1 Remove the driveshaft as described in Section 2.
2 Clean away all external dirt and grease from the driveshaft and gaiters.
3 Note the direction of fitting of the inner and outer CV joint gaiter retaining clips, then release the clips from the gaiters, and slide the gaiters along the driveshaft towards the centre.
4 Wipe the grease from the inner and outer CV joints.
5 Withdraw the inner joint tripod housing from the driveshaft, then prise free the snap-ring retaining the tripod on the inboard end of the driveshaft. Check if the inner end face of the driveshaft and the tripod are 'match-marked' for position, then remove the tripod from the shaft, followed by the large nylon washer and the gaiter.

6 Using suitable circlip pliers, expand the snap-ring and have an assistant simultaneously pull the outboard joint outwards to separate the shaft from the joint.
7 If removing the vibration damper from the right-hand driveshaft, mark its relative position on the shaft before unbolting it.
8 Thoroughly clean the joint components, and examine them for wear or damage. A repair kit may resolve a minor problem, but extensive wear or damage will necessitate renewal of the component concerned or the complete driveshaft.
9 Where the joints and possibly even the gaiters, are found to be in a serviceable condition, it will still be necessary to renew the CV joint retaining snap-rings, the gaiter retaining clips, and also to obtain the recommended type and quantity of CV joint grease.
10 Reassembly of the joints is as described in Section 3 (paragraphs 10 to 14) for the inner CV joint, and Section 4 (paragraphs 9 to 14) for the outer CV joint. If the vibration damper unit was removed from the right-hand driveshaft, ensure that it is refitted in the same position as noted during removal.
11 Refit the driveshaft on completion as described in Section 2.

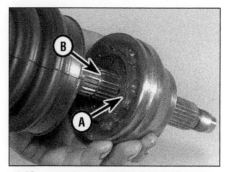

4.12 . . . and reassemble the shaft to the joint so that the circlip (A) engages in the groove in the shaft (B)

Chapter 9
Braking system

Contents

Degrees of difficulty

| **Easy,** suitable for novice with little experience | | **Fairly easy,** suitable for beginner with some experience | | **Fairly difficult,** suitable for competent DIY mechanic | | **Difficult,** suitable for experienced DIY mechanic | | **Very difficult,** suitable for expert DIY or professional | |

Specifications

Front brakes

Type	Ventilated disc, with single-piston sliding calipers
Disc diameter	240.0 mm
Disc thickness	20.0 mm
Minimum disc thickness	18.0 mm
Maximum disc run-out (disc fitted)	0.1 mm
Minimum brake pad lining thickness	1.5 mm
Maximum disc thickness variation	0.015 mm

Rear drum brakes

Type	Drum with leading and trailing shoes and automatic adjusters
Nominal drum diameter	203.0 mm
Maximum drum diameter	1.0 mm above nominal diameter
Minimum brake lining thickness	1.0 mm

Torque wrench settings

	Nm	lbf ft
ABS hydraulic unit to bracket:		
Pre-1996 models	23	17
1996-on models	10	7
ABS wheel speed sensor bolts	10	7
Brake hose bracket to suspension strut	18	13
Caliper anchor bracket to spindle carrier	58	43
Caliper piston housing to anchor bracket:		
Bendix caliper	50	37
Teves caliper	23	17
Drum/hub to rear axle flange	66	49
Master cylinder to servo	23	17
Rear wheel cylinder to backplate	15	11
Roadwheel nuts	85	63
Servo unit to bracket/bulkhead	25	18

2.2a Extract the R-clip from the cross-pin . . .

1 General information

The braking system is of the diagonally split, dual-circuit hydraulic type, with servo assistance to the front disc brakes and rear drum brakes. The dual-circuit hydraulic system is a safety feature – in the event of a malfunction somewhere in one of the hydraulic circuits, the other circuit continues to operate, providing at least some braking effort. Under normal circumstances, both brake circuits operate in unison, to provide efficient braking.

The master cylinder (and the vacuum servo unit to which it is bolted) is located on the left-hand side of the bulkhead in the engine compartment. On all right-hand drive variants, they are jointly operated via a transverse cross-link from the brake pedal. As there is no manifold vacuum supply for the servo unit, vacuum is supplied by an engine-driven pump, mounted on the cylinder head.

Brake pressure control valves are fitted in-line to each rear brake circuit, their function being to regulate the braking force available at each rear wheel, reducing the possibility of the rear wheels locking up under heavy braking. Van models also have a 'light-laden' valve incorporated into the rear braking circuits for the same reason.

The front brake discs are of the ventilated type on all models. The front brake calipers are of single sliding piston type, mounted on the front spindle carriers each side.

2.3 Undo the retaining nut (arrowed) and release the brake hose support bracket from the suspension strut

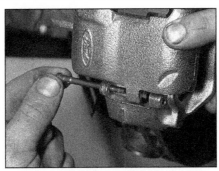

2.2b . . . and withdraw the pin from the base of the caliper

Each rear brake shoe assembly is operated by a twin-piston wheel cylinder. The leading brake shoe in each brake unit has a thicker lining than the trailing shoe, so that they wear proportionally. To take up the brake adjustment as the linings wear, each rear brake assembly incorporates an automatic adjuster mechanism.

The cable-operated handbrake acts on both rear brakes, to provide an independent means of brake operation.

An anti-lock braking system (ABS) is available on some models, and has many of the components in common with the conventional braking system. Further details on ABS can be found later in this Chapter.

Note: *When servicing any part of the system, work carefully and methodically; also observe scrupulous cleanliness when overhauling any part of the hydraulic system. Always renew components (in axle sets, where applicable) if in doubt about their condition, and use only genuine Ford replacement parts, or at least those of known good quality. Note the warnings given in 'Safety first!' and at relevant points in this Chapter concerning the dangers of asbestos dust and hydraulic fluid.*

2 Front brake pads – renewal

⚠️ *Warning: Disc brake pads MUST be renewed on both front wheels at the same time – NEVER renew*

2.5 Withdraw the inner and outer brake pads from the anchor bracket

the pads on only one wheel, as uneven braking may result. The front brake calipers will be of Bendix or Teves manufacture, and if they or their component parts require renewal, ensure that the correct type is fitted. Dust created by wear of the pads may contain asbestos, which is a health hazard. Never blow it out with compressed air, and do not inhale any of it. DO NOT use petroleum-based solvents to clean brake parts – use brake cleaner or methylated spirit only. DO NOT allow any brake fluid, oil or grease to contact the brake pads or disc. Also refer to the warning in Section 13 concerning the dangers of hydraulic fluid.

1 Chock the rear wheels, and loosen the front wheel nuts. Jack up the front of the car and support it on axle stands (see *Jacking and vehicle support*). Remove the front roadwheels.

Bendix caliper

2 Extract the R-clip from the cross-pin, and withdraw the pin from the base of the caliper **(see illustrations)**.

3 Undo the nut, and release the brake hose support bracket from the suspension strut **(see illustration)**.

4 Swing the caliper upwards to allow access to the brake pads, and if necessary, tie the caliper up in the raised position.

5 Withdraw the inner and outer brake pads from the anchor bracket **(see illustration)**. If the old pads are to be refitted, ensure that they are identified so that they can be returned to their original positions.

6 Brush the dust and dirt from the caliper and piston, but *do not inhale it, as it is a health hazard*. Inspect the dust cover around the piston for damage and for evidence of fluid leaks, which if found will necessitate caliper overhaul as described in Section 3. Inspect the anti-rattle plate for corrosion, and if necessary renew it.

7 If new brake pads are to be fitted, the caliper piston will need to be pushed back into its housing, to allow for the extra pad thickness – use a C-clamp to do this. Note that, as the piston is pressed back into the bore, it will displace the fluid in the system, causing the fluid level in the brake master cylinder reservoir to rise and possibly overflow. To avoid this possibility, a small quantity of fluid should be syphoned from the reservoir. If any brake fluid is spilt onto the bodywork, hoses or adjacent components in the engine compartment, wipe it clean without delay.

8 Prior to refitting, check that the pads and the disc are clean. Where new pads are to be installed, peel the protective backing paper from them. If the old pads are to be refitted, ensure that they are correctly located as noted during their removal.

9 Locate the inner and outer brake pads into position in the caliper anchor bracket.

10 Lower the caliper down, insert the cross-pin and fit the R-clip to secure.

2.16 Hold the caliper support spring with a pair of pliers, and prise the end out using a screwdriver

2.17a Prise free the blanking plugs from the caliper upper and lower mounting bolts

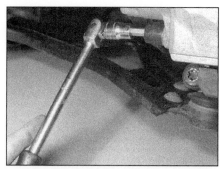

2.17b Using a suitable Allen key socket bit . . .

11 Reconnect the brake hose bracket to the suspension strut, ensuring the brake hose is not twisted, stretched or distorted in any way. Tighten the brake hose support bracket nut to the specified torque setting.

12 Repeat the procedure on the opposite front brake.

13 Before lowering the vehicle, check that the fluid level in the brake master cylinder reservoir is up to the Maximum mark, and top-up with the specified fluid if required (see *Weekly checks*). Depress the brake pedal a few times to position the pads against the disc, then recheck the fluid level in the reservoir and further top-up the fluid level if necessary.

14 Refit the roadwheels, then lower the vehicle to the ground. Tighten the roadwheel retaining nuts to the specified torque.

15 To allow the new brake pads to bed-in properly and reach full efficiency, a running-in period of approximately 100 miles or so should be observed before hard use and heavy braking.

Teves caliper

16 Hold the caliper support spring with a pair of pliers, and prise it out of its location in the caliper housing using a screwdriver **(see illustration)**.

17 Prise free the blanking plugs from the caliper upper and lower mounting bolts. Unscrew the bolts, then withdraw the caliper from the anchor bracket **(see illustrations)**. Suitably support the caliper to avoid straining the brake hose.

18 Withdraw the pads from the caliper piston housing or anchor bracket. The outer pad will normally remain in position in the anchor bracket, but the inner pad will stay attached to the piston in the caliper, and may need to be carefully prised free **(see illustrations)**. If the old pads are to be refitted, ensure that they are identified so that they can be returned to their original positions.

19 Brush the dust and dirt from the caliper and piston, but *do not inhale it, as it is a health hazard*. Inspect the dust cover around the piston for damage and for evidence of fluid leaks, which if found will necessitate caliper overhaul as described in Section 3.

20 If new brake pads are to be fitted, the caliper piston will need to be pushed back into

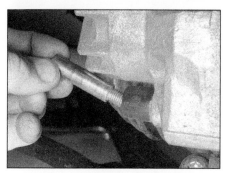

2.17c . . . unscrew and remove the bolts . . .

2.17d . . . then withdraw the caliper from the anchor bracket and disc

its housing, to allow for the extra pad thickness – use a C-clamp to do this. Note that, as the piston is pressed back into the bore, it will displace the fluid in the system, causing the fluid level in the brake master cylinder reservoir to rise and possibly overflow. To avoid this possibility, a small quantity of fluid should be syphoned from the reservoir. If any brake fluid is spilt onto the bodywork, hoses or adjacent components in the engine compartment, wipe it clean without delay.

21 Prior to refitting, check that the pads and the disc are clean. Where new pads are to be installed, peel the protective backing paper from them. If the old pads are to be refitted, ensure that they are correctly located as noted during their removal.

22 Locate the inner and outer brake pad into position in the caliper. Relocate the caliper into position on the anchor bracket, and insert the mounting bolts.

23 Tighten the mounting bolts to the specified torque, and refit the blanking plugs. Relocate the caliper support spring.

24 Repeat the procedure on the opposite front brake.

25 Before lowering the vehicle, check the that the fluid level in the brake master cylinder reservoir is up to the Max level mark, and top-up with the specified fluid type if required (see *Weekly checks*). Depress the brake pedal a few times to position the pads against the disc, then recheck the fluid level in the reservoir and further top-up the fluid level if necessary.

26 Refit the roadwheels, then lower the vehicle to the ground. Tighten the roadwheel retaining nuts to the specified torque.

27 To allow the new brake pads to bed-in and reach full efficiency, a running-in period of approximately 100 miles or so should be observed before hard use and heavy braking.

2.18a Withdraw the outer pad from the anchor bracket . . .

2.18b . . . and the inner pad from the piston in the caliper

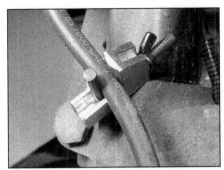

3.2 Brake hose clamp fitted to the front flexible brake hose

3.3 Unscrew the brake hose-to-caliper banjo union bolt (arrowed) and recover the copper sealing washers

3.8 Brake caliper anchor bracket securing bolts (arrowed)

3 Front brake caliper –
removal, overhaul and refitting

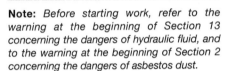

Note: *Before starting work, refer to the warning at the beginning of Section 13 concerning the dangers of hydraulic fluid, and to the warning at the beginning of Section 2 concerning the dangers of asbestos dust.*

Removal

1 Chock the rear wheels, and loosen the front wheel nuts. Jack up the front of the car and support it on axle stands (see *Jacking and vehicle support*). Remove the front roadwheels.
2 Fit a brake hose clamp to the flexible brake hose leading to the front brake caliper. This will minimise brake fluid loss during subsequent operations **(see illustration)**.

Bendix caliper

3 Unscrew the brake hose-to-caliper banjo union bolt, and recover the copper sealing washers **(see illustration)**. Cover or plug the open hydraulic unions to keep them clean.
4 Extract the R-clip from the cross-pin at the base of the caliper, and withdraw the cross-pin.
5 Prise free the blanking plug from the caliper-to-anchor bracket pivot bolt at the top, then support the caliper and unscrew the bolt.
6 Withdraw the caliper from anchor bracket and brake pads, and remove it from the car.
7 To remove the caliper anchor bracket, first withdraw the brake pads. If they are likely to

be re-used, mark them for identification (inner and outer, right- or left-hand as applicable) to ensure that they are installed in their original locations when refitting.
8 Unscrew the two retaining bolts, and withdraw the anchor bracket from the spindle carrier **(see illustration)**.

Teves caliper

9 Loosen (but do not completely unscrew) the union on the caliper end of the flexible brake hose **(see illustration)**.
10 Remove the front brake pads as described in Section 2.
11 Support the caliper in one hand, and prevent the brake hose from turning with the other hand. Unscrew the caliper from the hose, making sure that the hose is not twisted unduly or strained. Once the caliper is detached, cover or plug the open hydraulic unions to keep them clean.
12 If required, the caliper anchor bracket can be unbolted and removed from the spindle carrier.

Overhaul

13 With the caliper on the bench, wipe away all traces of dust and dirt, but *avoid inhaling the dust, as it is a health hazard.*
14 Remove the piston from its bore by applying low air pressure (from a foot pump, for example) into the caliper hydraulic fluid hose port. In the event of a high-pressure air hose being used, keep the pressure as low as possible, to enable the piston to be extracted, but to avoid the piston being ejected too quickly and being damaged. Position a

suitable piece of wood between the caliper frame and the piston to prevent this possibility. Any fluid remaining in the caliper will probably be ejected with the piston.
15 Using a suitable hooked tool, carefully extract the dust cover from its groove in the piston and the seal from its groove in the caliper bore, but take care not to scratch or damage the piston and/or the bore in the caliper.
16 Clean all the parts in methylated spirit or clean brake fluid, and wipe dry using a clean lint-free cloth **(see illustration)**. Inspect the piston and caliper bore for signs of damage, scuffing or corrosion. If these conditions are evident, renew the caliper body assembly.
17 If the components are in satisfactory condition, a repair kit which includes a new seal and dust cover must be obtained.
18 Lubricate the piston bore in the caliper and the seal with clean brake fluid. Carefully fit the seal in the caliper bore, using fingers only (no tools) to manipulate it into position in its groove. When in position, check that it is not distorted or twisted.
19 Locate the dust cover over the piston so that its inner diameter is engaged in the piston groove. Smear the area behind the piston groove with the special lubricating grease supplied in the repair kit, then insert the piston into the caliper. Push the piston into position in the bore, and simultaneously press the dust cover into the piston housing so that it is seated correctly **(see illustration)**. Take particular care not to distort or damage the seal or cover as they are fitted.

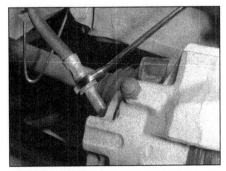

3.9 Loosening the flexible brake hose at the caliper

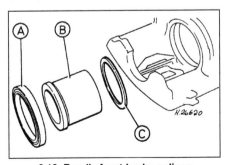

3.16 Bendix front brake caliper components showing the dust cover (A), piston (B) and piston seal (C)

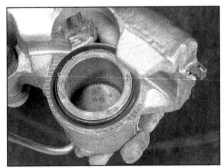

3.19 Piston and dust seal in position in the caliper

Refitting

Bendix caliper

20 If the anchor bracket was removed, fit it into position on the spindle carrier, and tighten the retaining bolts to the specified torque.

21 Locate the brake pads into the anchor bracket. Where new pads are to be installed, peel the protective backing paper from them. If the old pads are to be refitted, ensure that they are correctly located in their original positions as noted during their removal.

22 Refit the caliper to the anchor bracket, and loosely locate the caliper-to-anchor bracket pivot bolt. Swing the unit down, and insert the cross-pin and its R-clip. Tighten the caliper-to-anchor bracket bolt to the specified torque.

23 Unplug the hydraulic hose, and check that the unions are clean. Reconnect the hose to the caliper, using new copper washers if necessary. Tighten the brake hose union banjo bolt, then turn the steering from lock-to-lock to ensure that the hose does not foul on the wheel housing or suspension components.

24 Bleed the brake hydraulic system as described in Section 13. Providing suitable precautions were taken to minimise loss of fluid, it should only be necessary to bleed the relevant front brake.

25 Refit the roadwheel, lower the vehicle to the ground, and then tighten the wheel nuts to the specified torque.

Teves caliper

26 If the anchor bracket was removed, fit it into position on the spindle carrier, and tighten the retaining bolts to the specified torque.

27 Unplug the hydraulic hose, and check that the unions are clean. Reconnect the caliper to the hose so that the hose is not twisted or strained. The hose union connection can be fully tightened when the caliper is refitted.

28 Refit the brake pads as described in Section 2.

29 The brake hydraulic hose can now be fully tightened. When secured, turn the steering from lock-to-lock to ensure that the hose does not foul on the wheel housing or suspension components.

4.3 Checking the brake disc thickness using a micrometer

30 Bleed the brake hydraulic system as described in Section 13. Providing suitable precautions were taken to minimise loss of fluid, it should only be necessary to bleed the relevant front brake.

31 Refit the roadwheel, lower the vehicle to the ground, then tighten the wheel nuts to the specified torque.

4 Front brake disc – inspection, removal and refitting

Note: *Before starting work, refer to the warning at the beginning of Section 2 concerning the dangers of asbestos dust.*

Inspection

Note: *If a disc requires renewal, BOTH front discs should be renewed or reground at the same time to ensure even and consistent braking. New brake pads should also be fitted.*

1 Chock the rear wheels then jack up the front of the car and support it on axle stands (see *Jacking and vehicle support*). Remove the appropriate front roadwheel.

2 Temporarily refit two of the wheel nuts to diagonally-opposite studs, with the flat sides of the nuts against the disc. Tighten the nuts progressively, to hold the disc firmly.

3 Scrape any corrosion from the disc. Rotate the disc, and examine it for deep scoring, grooving or cracks. Using a micrometer, measure the thickness of the disc in several places **(see illustration)**. Light wear and scoring is normal, but if excessive, the disc should be removed, and either reground by a specialist, or renewed. If regrinding is undertaken, at least the minimum thickness must be maintained. Obviously, if the disc is cracked, it must be renewed.

4 Using a dial gauge, check that the disc run-out, measured at a point 10.0 mm from the outer edge of the disc, does not exceed the limit given in the *Specifications*. To do this, fix the measuring equipment, and rotate the disc, noting the variation in measurement as the disc is rotated **(see illustration)**. The difference between the minimum and maximum measurements recorded is the disc run-out.

> **HAYNES HINT** *If a dial gauge is not available, check the run-out by placing a fixed pointer near the outer edge, in contact with the disc face. Rotate the disc and measure the maximum displacement of the pointer with feeler blades.*

5 If the run-out is greater than the specified amount, check for variations of the disc thickness as follows. Mark the disc at eight positions 45° apart, then using a micrometer, measure the disc thickness at the eight positions, 15.0 mm in from the outer edge. If

the variation between the minimum and maximum readings is greater than the specified amount, the disc should be renewed.

Removal

6 Remove the caliper and its anchor bracket with reference to Section 3, but do not disconnect the hydraulic brake hose. Suspend the caliper assembly from the front suspension coil spring, taking care to avoid straining the brake hose.

7 Remove the wheel nuts which were temporarily refitted in paragraph 2.

8 Using a Torx-type socket bit or driver, unscrew the screw securing the disc to the hub, and withdraw the disc. If it is tight, lightly tap its rear face with a hide or plastic mallet.

Refitting

9 Refit the disc in a reversal of the removal sequence. If new discs are being fitted, first remove their protective coating. Ensure complete cleanliness of the hub and disc mating faces and tighten the screw securely.

10 Refit the caliper/anchor bracket with reference to Section 3.

11 Refit the roadwheel, lower the vehicle to the ground, and tighten the wheel nuts to the specified torque.

5 Rear brake drum – removal, inspection and refitting

Note: *Before starting work, refer to the warning at the beginning of Section 6 concerning the dangers of asbestos dust.*

Removal

1 Chock the front wheels, and loosen the rear wheel nuts on the side concerned. Jack up the rear of the car and support it on axle stands (see *Jacking and vehicle support*). Remove the appropriate rear roadwheel. On pre-1996 models, release the handbrake. On 1996-on models, unclip the handbrake lever gaiter to gain access to the adjuster nut on the side of the lever and slacken the cable right off.

2 On all except Van models, undo the four bolts securing the drum/hub to the rear axle

4.4 Checking the brake disc run-out using a dial gauge

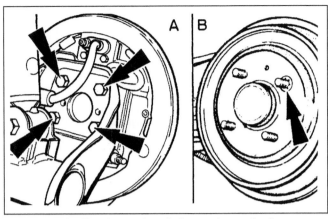
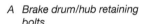

5.2a Rear brake drum/hub securing methods

A *Brake drum/hub retaining bolts*

B *Brake drum retaining clip on Van models*

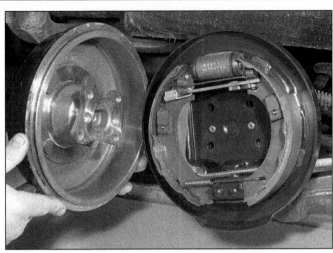

5.2b Removing the rear brake drum/hub

flange, then withdraw the drum/hub from the axle **(see illustrations)**. If the brake drum is stuck on the shoes, remove the rubber access plug from the inside face of the brake backplate, and release the automatic brake adjuster by levering the release catch on the adjuster pawl through the backplate.

3 On Van models, prise free the drum retaining clip from the wheel nut stud, then withdraw the drum over the studs and remove it. Note that the retaining clip must be renewed during reassembly.

4 With the brake drum removed, brush or wipe the dust from the drum, brake shoes, wheel cylinder and backplate. *Take great care*

6.3 Removing a shoe steady spring

6.4 Disengage the leading brake shoe from the bottom anchor . . .

not to inhale the dust, as it may contain asbestos.

5 If required, remove the hub from the drum – see Chapter 10.

Inspection

Note: *If a brake drum requires renewal, BOTH rear drums should be renewed at the same time to ensure even and consistent braking. New brake shoes should also be fitted.*

6 Clean the inside surfaces of the brake drum and hub, then examine the internal surface of the brake drum for signs of scoring or cracks. If any deterioration of the friction surface is evident, renewal of the drum is necessary. To detach the hub from the drum, refer to Chapter 10.

Refitting

7 Check that the automatic brake adjuster is fully retracted, then according to type, refit the drum/hub to the axle. Tighten the retaining bolts to the specified torque, or fit the drum over the wheel studs, and press a new retaining clip over one of the studs.

Pre-1996 models

8 With the brake drum refitted, refit the roadwheel. Fully depress the brake pedal several times, to actuate the rear brake adjuster and take up the adjustment. Check that the rear wheels spin freely when the

6.5a . . . then from the wheel cylinder at the top

brakes are released, then apply the handbrake, lower the vehicle and tighten the wheel nuts to the specified torque.

1996-on models

9 With the brake drum refitted, refit the roadwheel. Adjust the handbrake cable, as described in Chapter 1. Fully depress the brake pedal several times, to actuate the rear brake adjuster and take up the adjustment. Check that the rear wheels spin freely when the brakes are released, then apply the handbrake, lower the vehicle and tighten the wheel nuts to the specified torque.

6 Rear brake shoes – renewal

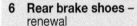

⚠️ *Warning: Drum brake shoes MUST be renewed on both rear wheels at the same time – NEVER renew the shoes on only one wheel, as uneven braking may result. Also, the dust created by wear of the shoes may contain asbestos, which is a health hazard. Never blow it out with compressed air, and don't inhale any of it. An approved filtering mask should be worn when working on the brakes. DO NOT use petroleum-based solvents to clean brake parts – use brake cleaner or methylated spirit only.*

1 Remove the rear brake drum with reference to Section 5.

2 Note the fitted positions of the springs and the adjuster strut.

3 Remove the shoe steady springs by depressing and turning them through 90° **(see illustration)**. Remove the springs and pins.

4 Pull the leading brake shoe from the bottom anchor, and disconnect the lower return spring **(see illustration)**.

5 Move the bottom ends of the brake shoes towards each other, then disconnect the tops of the shoes from the wheel cylinder. Be careful not to damage the wheel cylinder

6.5b Elastic band fitted round the wheel cylinder to prevent piston ejection

6.7a Disconnecting the handbrake cable from the trailing brake shoe

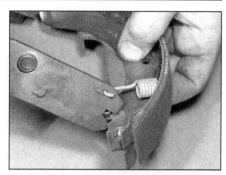

6.7b Disconnecting the support spring from the strut

rubber boots. To prevent the wheel cylinder pistons from being accidentally ejected, fit a suitable elastic band (or wire) lengthways over the cylinder/pistons **(see illustrations)**.
6 Disconnect the upper return (pull-off) spring from the brake shoes.
7 Unhook the handbrake cable from the handbrake operating lever on the trailing shoe. Disconnect the support spring from the strut, twist the trailing shoe through 90°, and detach it from the strut **(see illustrations)**.
8 Disconnect the strut from the leading shoe. As the strut is pulled from the shoe, the automatic adjuster will operate and release the pawl from the shoe **(see illustration)**.
9 Clean the adjuster strut and its associated components.
10 Clean the backplate, then apply a little high-melting-point grease to the shoe contact points on the backplate and the lower anchor plate **(see illustration)**.

11 Transfer the strut and the upper return spring onto the new leading shoe **(see illustration)**.
12 Locate the other end of the upper return spring into the new trailing shoe, then twisting the shoe, engage the strut support spring and strut. When reconnected, check that the cam and pawl of the automatic adjuster have engaged **(see illustrations)**.
13 Remove the elastic band (or wire retainer) from the wheel cylinder. Reconnect the handbrake cable to the operating lever on the trailing shoe, and refit the trailing shoe assembly into position on the backplate. As the shoe is engaged over the wheel cylinder, be careful not to damage the rubber dust cover.
14 Reconnect the lower return spring to the trailing shoe and, checking that the handbrake operating lever is resting on the lever stop head (not wedged against the side), locate the shoe in the bottom anchor plate. Refit the

steady pin, spring and cup to secure the shoe in position.
15 Offer the leading shoe onto the backplate and insert its steady pin, spring and cup to hold it in place.
16 Reconnect the lower return spring to the leading shoe, using a screwdriver to stretch the spring end into the location hole.
17 Refit the upper return spring, using a screwdriver to stretch the spring end into the location hole.
18 Check that the brake shoes and their associated components are correctly refitted, then refit the brake drum with reference to Section 5.
19 Repeat the procedure on the remaining rear brake.

7 Rear wheel cylinder – removal, overhaul and refitting

Note: *Before starting work, refer to the warning at the beginning of Section 13 concerning the dangers of hydraulic fluid.*

Removal

1 Remove the brake drum as described in Section 5.
2 Pull the brake shoes apart at the top end, so that they are just clear of the wheel cylinder. The automatic adjuster will hold the shoes in this position so that the cylinder can be withdrawn.
3 Using a brake hose clamp or self-locking wrench with protected jaws, clamp the flexible

6.8 Disconnecting the strut from the leading brake shoe

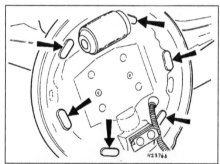

6.10 Brake shoe contact points (arrowed) to be lubricated on the backplate

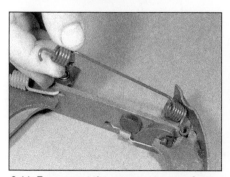

6.11 Reconnect the upper return spring to the leading . . .

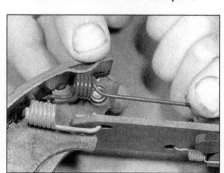

6.12a . . . and trailing shoe

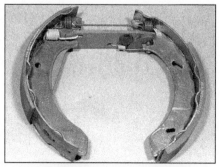

6.12b Brake shoes, strut and upper springs reconnected

brake hose forward of the shock absorber (midway between the hose protective sleeve and the hose rigid connection bracket on the underside of the body). This will minimise brake fluid loss during subsequent operations.
4 Wipe away all traces of dirt around the brake hose union at the rear of the wheel cylinder, then loosen off the hose-to-wheel cylinder union nut **(see illustration)**.
5 Unscrew the two bolts securing the wheel cylinder to the backplate.
6 Withdraw the wheel cylinder from the backplate so that it is clear of the brake shoes, then holding the brake hose steady to prevent it twisting, unscrew and detach the wheel cylinder from the hose. Plug the hose, to prevent the possible ingress of dirt and to minimise further fluid loss whilst the cylinder is detached from it.

Overhaul

7 Clean the external surfaces of the cylinder, then pull free the dust cover from each end of the cylinder.
8 The pistons and seals will probably shake out; if not, use a foot pump to apply air pressure through the hydraulic union and eject them.
9 Clean the pistons and the cylinder by washing in fresh hydraulic fluid or methylated spirits (not petrol, paraffin or any other mineral-based fluid). Examine the surfaces of the pistons and the cylinder bores. Look for any signs of rust, scoring or metal-to-metal rubbing, which if evident, will necessitate renewal of the wheel cylinder **(see illustration)**.
10 Begin reassembly by lubricating the first piston in clean hydraulic fluid. Manipulate its new seal into position so that its raised lip faces away from the brake shoe bearing face of the piston.
11 Insert the piston into the cylinder from the opposite end of the cylinder body, and push it through to its normal location in the bore.
12 Insert the spring into the cylinder, then fit the second new seal into position on the

second piston (as described for the first) and fit the second piston into the wheel cylinder. Take care not to damage the lip of the seal as the piston is inserted into the cylinder – additional lubrication and a slight twisting action may help. Only use fingers (no tools) to manipulate the piston and seal into position.
13 Fit the new dust covers to each end of the piston.

Refitting

14 Wipe clean the backplate, and remove the plug from the end of the hydraulic hose. Carefully screw the cylinder onto the hose connector, and then fit the cylinder onto the backplate. Tighten the retaining bolts to securely, then fully tighten the hydraulic hose union.
15 Retract the automatic brake adjuster mechanism so that the brake shoes engage with the pistons of the wheel cylinder.
16 Remove the clamp from the flexible brake hose. Ensure that the protective sleeve on the hose is adjacent to the shock absorber **(see illustration 7.4)**.
17 Refit the brake drum with reference to Section 5.
18 Bleed the brake hydraulic system as described in Section 13. Providing suitable precautions were taken to minimise loss of fluid, it should only be necessary to bleed the relevant rear brake.

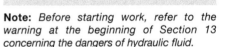

8 Rear brake backplate – removal and refitting

Removal

1 On Hatchback/Saloon/Estate models, remove the brake drum/hub assembly as described in Section 5. On Van models, remove the brake drum as described in Section 5, then remove the rear hub assembly as described in Chapter 10.

2 Remove the rear brake shoes as described in Section 6.
3 Remove the wheel cylinder from the backplate as described in Section 7.
4 Compress the three retaining lugs, and release the handbrake cable from the back-plate by pushing it back through the plate.
5 Drill out the pop-rivets securing the back-plate to the rear axle, and remove the backplate.

Refitting

6 Refit in the reverse order of removal. Check that the plate is correctly located (with the wheel cylinder aperture at the top) before riveting it into position.
7 Refit the handbrake cable, and ensure that the retaining lugs are secure.
8 Refit the wheel cylinder as described in Section 7.
9 Refit the rear brake shoes as described in Section 6.
10 Refit the brake drum/hub as described in Section 5, or the rear hub assembly as described in Chapter 10, according to model.
11 On completion, bleed the brake hydraulic system as described in Section 13.

9 Master cylinder – removal, overhaul and refitting

Note: *Before starting work, refer to the warning at the beginning of Section 13 concerning the dangers of hydraulic fluid.*

Removal

1 Disconnect the wiring multi-plug from the fluid level warning indicator in the reservoir filler cap, then remove the filler cap from the reservoir. Note that the filler cap must not be inverted. The reservoir should now be emptied by siphoning or drawing out the fluid with a pipette.
2 Identify each brake pipe and its connection

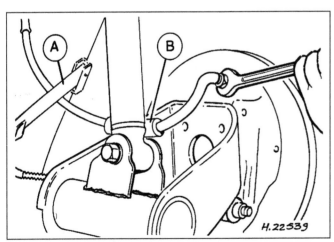

7.4 Disconnecting the hydraulic hose from the rear wheel cylinder. Note the hose clamp (A) and the protective sleeve on the hose (B)

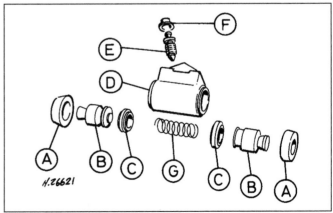

7.9 Rear wheel cylinder components

A Dust cover	D Cylinder	F Dust cap
B Piston	body	G Spring
C Piston seal	E Bleed nipple	

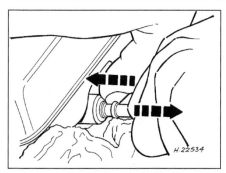

9.2 Disconnecting the brake fluid return pipes from the reservoir on ABS models

to the master cylinder. Unscrew the fluid line to master cylinder union nuts and disconnect the fluid lines. On models equipped with ABS, when disconnecting the fluid return pipes from the reservoir, press the retaining boss into the reservoir and pull free the fluid line **(see illustration)**. Plug the connections and tape over the pipe ends, to prevent the entry of dust and dirt.

3 Unscrew the mounting nuts and withdraw the master cylinder from the servo unit.

Overhaul

4 With the master cylinder removed, empty any remaining fluid from it, and clean it externally.

5 Secure the master cylinder in a vice fitted with soft-faced jaws to avoid damaging the cylinder.

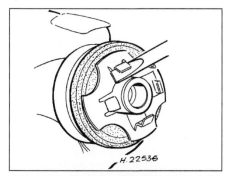

9.11a Release the seal retainer tabs on the primary piston

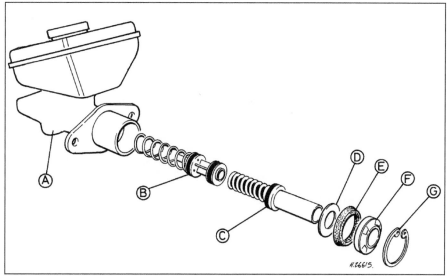

9.10 Exploded view of the master cylinder

A Master cylinder body	C Primary piston	E Seal
		F Plastic spacer
B Secondary piston	D Steel washer	G Circlip

6 Withdraw the hydraulic fluid reservoir from the top of the master cylinder by pulling and rocking it free from its retaining seals.

7 Extract the reservoir seals from the top face of the master cylinder.

8 Extract the circlip from its groove in the inner port at the rear of the master cylinder.

9 Pull free the primary piston from the rear end of the master cylinder bore, together with the spacer, seal and steel washer.

10 Extract the secondary piston assembly by shaking or lightly tapping it free from the cylinder **(see illustration)**.

11 To dismantle the primary piston and to remove its seal, undo the retaining screw and detach the spring from the piston. Lever the seal retainer tabs free using a suitable screwdriver and remove the seal. As it is removed, note the fitted direction of the seal on the piston **(see illustrations)**.

12 To dismantle the secondary piston, pull free the spring (note its orientation), remove the seal retainer using the same method as

that for the primary piston seal, and remove the seal (noting its direction of fitting). Prise free the seal from the other end of the secondary piston, again noting its direction of fitting **(see illustration)**.

13 Wash all components of the cylinder in methylated spirit or clean hydraulic brake fluid of the specified type. Do not use any other type of cleaning fluid.

14 Inspect the master cylinder and piston assemblies for any signs of excessive wear or damage. Deep scoring in the cylinder bore and/or on the piston surfaces will necessitate a new master cylinder being fitted.

15 If the cylinder is in a serviceable condition, obtain a cylinder seals/repair kit. Once removed, the seals must always be renewed.

16 Check that all components are perfectly clean before they refitted. Smear them in new brake fluid of the specified type as they are assembled. *Do not allow grease, old fluid or any other lubricant to contact the components during reassembly.*

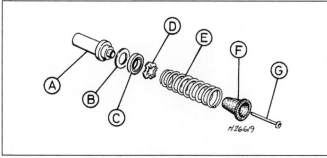

9.11b Primary piston components

A Piston	D Seal	F Boot
B Shim	retainer	G Retaining
C Seal	E Spring	screw

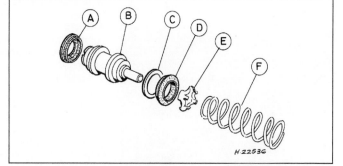

9.12 Secondary piston components

A Seal	C Shim	E Seal retainer
B Piston	D Seal	F Spring

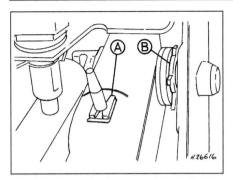

10.4 Brake pedal-to-cross-link circlip (A) and the brake pedal cross-link retaining clip (B)

17 Reassemble each piston in the reverse order of dismantling. Ensure that the seals are correctly orientated, and that the retainers are securely fitted.
18 Lubricate the pistons before refitting them to the cylinder and as they are inserted, use a twisting action to assist in pushing them into position.
19 With the secondary and primary pistons in position, fit the steel washer, a new seal, and the spacer; secure them with the circlip. Ensure that the circlip is fully engaged into its retaining groove in the rear end of the cylinder.

Refitting

20 Before refitting the master cylinder, clean the mounting faces.
21 Refitting is a reversal of removal. Ensure that the vacuum servo unit seal is in position, and tighten the master cylinder retaining nuts to the specified torque. Finally bleed the hydraulic system as described in Section 13.

10 Brake pedal –
removal and refitting

Removal

1 Disconnect the battery negative (earth) lead (refer to Chapter 5A, Section 1).
2 Working inside the car, move the driver's seat fully to the rear, to allow maximum working area.
3 Disconnect the wiring connector from the

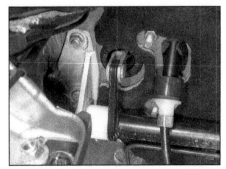

11.5 Brake system cross-link mounting to the bulkhead

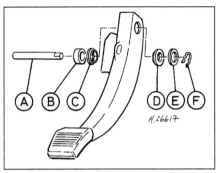

10.7 Brake pedal components

A Pivot shaft	D Bush
B Spacer	E Washer
C Bush	F Clip

stop-light switch, then twist the switch and release it from the mounting bracket.
4 Using a suitable hooked tool, extract the circlip from the pedal cross-link **(see illustration)**.
5 Prise free and remove the retaining clip securing the pedal-to-cross-link rod.
6 Press the brake pedal pivot shaft through the mounting box just far enough then release and remove the pedal and spacers.
7 Prise the bushes out from each side of the brake pedal, and renew them if necessary **(see illustration)**.

Refitting

8 Prior to refitting, apply a small amount of molybdenum disulphide grease to the brake pedal pivot shaft.
9 Refit in the reverse order to removal. Ensure that the pedal bushes are correctly located, and that the pedal shaft D section locates in the pedal box right-hand support.
10 On completion, refit the stop-light switch, and adjust it as described in Chapter 12.

11 Brake pedal-to-servo cross-link –
removal and refitting

Removal

1 Disconnect the battery negative (earth) lead (refer to Chapter 5A, Section 1).
2 Remove the vacuum servo unit (Section 14).
3 Where necessary, remove the air cleaner components as described Chapter 4A to allow increased access to the cross-link assembly.
4 Working inside the vehicle, prise free and remove the retaining clip from the brake pedal-to-cross-link pushrod.
5 Arrange for an assistant to support the weight of the cross-link assembly on the engine compartment side of the bulkhead. Fold down the bulkhead trim covering in the footwell on each side, to allow access to the cross-link support bracket securing nuts on the bulkhead. Unscrew the nuts on each side of the bulkhead, and remove the cross-link

assembly from the bulkhead in the engine compartment **(see illustration)**.
6 Clean the linkage components, and examine the bushes for excessive wear. Renew the bushes if necessary.

Refitting

7 Refitting of the cross-link assembly is a reversal of the removal procedure. Refer to Section 14 to refit the vacuum servo unit.
8 On completion, bleed the brake hydraulic system as described in Section 13.

12 Hydraulic pipes and hoses –
renewal

Note: *Before starting work, refer to the warning at the beginning of Section 13 concerning the dangers of hydraulic fluid.*
1 If any pipe or hose is to be renewed, minimise hydraulic fluid loss by removing the master cylinder reservoir cap, placing a piece of plastic film over the reservoir and sealing it with an elastic band. Flexible hoses can be sealed, if required, using a proprietary brake hose clamp **(see illustration)**; metal brake pipe unions can be plugged (if care is taken not to allow dirt into the system) or capped immediately they are disconnected. Place a wad of rag under any union that is to be disconnected, to catch any spilt fluid.
2 If a flexible hose is to be disconnected, unscrew the brake pipe union nut before removing the spring clip which secures the hose to its mounting. Depending upon the make of the particular caliper, the other end of the hose may be connected simply by screwing it into its tapped hole or by using a hollow bolt with banjo end fitting. Use a new copper sealing washer on each side of the banjo union.
3 To unscrew the union nuts, it is preferable to obtain a brake pipe spanner of the correct size; these are available from most large motor accessory shops. Failing this, a close-fitting open-ended spanner will be required, though if the nuts are tight or corroded, their flats may be rounded-off if the spanner slips. In such a case, a self-locking wrench is often the only way to unscrew a stubborn union, but it follows that the pipe and the damaged nuts

12.1 Brake hose clamp fitted to minimise fluid loss

must be renewed on reassembly. Always clean a union and surrounding area before disconnecting it. If disconnecting a component with more than one union, make a careful note of the connections before disturbing any of them.

4 If a brake pipe is to be renewed, it can be obtained, cut to length and with the union nuts and end flares in place, from Ford dealers. All that is then necessary is to bend it to shape, following the line of the original, before fitting it to the car. Alternatively, most motor accessory shops can make up brake pipes from kits, but this requires very careful measurement of the original, to ensure that the replacement is of the correct length. The safest answer is usually to take the original to the shop as a pattern.

5 Before refitting, blow through the new pipe or hose with dry compressed air. Do not overtighten the union nuts. It is not necessary to exercise brute force to obtain a sound joint.

6 If flexible rubber hoses are renewed, ensure that the pipes and hoses are correctly routed, with no kinks or twists, and that they are secured in the clips or brackets provided.

7 After fitting, bleed the hydraulic system as described in Section 13, wash off any spilt fluid, and check carefully for fluid leaks.

13 Hydraulic system – bleeding

Warning: Brake fluid is poisonous; wash off immediately and thoroughly in the case of skin contact, and seek immediate medical advice if any fluid is swallowed or gets into the eyes. Certain types of hydraulic fluid are inflammable, and may ignite when allowed into contact with hot components; when servicing any hydraulic system, it is safest to assume that the fluid IS inflammable, and to take precautions against the risk of fire as though it is petrol that is being handled. Hydraulic fluid is also an effective paint stripper, and will attack plastics; if any is spilt, it should be washed off immediately, using copious quantities of clean water. Finally, it is hygroscopic (it absorbs moisture from the air). The more moisture is absorbed by the fluid, the lower its boiling point becomes, leading to a dangerous loss of braking under hard use. Old fluid may be contaminated and unfit for further use. When topping-up or renewing the fluid, always use the recommended type, and ensure that it comes from a freshly-opened sealed container.

1 The correct operation of any hydraulic system is only possible after removing all air from the components and circuit; and this is achieved by bleeding the system.

2 During the bleeding procedure, add only clean, unused hydraulic fluid of the recommended type; never re-use fluid that has already been bled from the system. Ensure that sufficient fluid is available before starting work.

3 If there is any possibility of incorrect fluid being already in the system, the brake components and circuit must be flushed completely with uncontaminated, correct fluid, and new seals should be fitted throughout the system.

4 If hydraulic fluid has been lost from the system, or air has entered because of a leak, ensure that the fault is cured before proceeding further.

5 Park the vehicle on level ground, and apply the handbrake. Switch off the engine, then (where applicable) depress the brake pedal several times to dissipate the vacuum from the servo unit.

6 Check that all pipes and hoses are secure, unions tight and bleed screws closed. Remove the dust caps (where applicable), and clean any dirt from around the bleed screws.

7 Unscrew the master cylinder reservoir cap, and top-up the master cylinder reservoir with the specified fluid to the Maximum level (see *Weekly checks*). *Remember to maintain the fluid level at least above the Minimum level line throughout the procedure, otherwise there is a risk of further air entering the system.*

8 There are a number of one-man, do-it-yourself brake bleeding kits currently available from motor accessory shops. It is recommended that one of these kits is used whenever possible, as they greatly simplify the bleeding operation, and also reduce the risk of expelled air and fluid being drawn back into the system. If such a kit is not available, the basic (two-man) method must be used, which is described in detail below.

9 If a kit is to be used, prepare the vehicle as described previously, and follow the kit manufacturer's instructions, as the procedure may vary slightly according to the type being used; generally, they are as outlined below in the relevant sub-section.

10 Whichever method is used, the same sequence must be followed (paragraphs 11 and 12) to ensure the removal of all air from the system.

Bleeding

11 If the system has been only partially disconnected, and suitable precautions were taken to minimise fluid loss, it should be necessary to bleed only that part of the system (ie the primary or secondary circuit).

12 If the complete system is to be bled, then it is suggested that you work in the following sequence:
a) *Left-hand front wheel.*
b) *Right-hand rear wheel.*
c) *Right-hand front wheel.*
d) *Left-hand rear wheel.*

Basic (two-man) method

13 Collect a clean glass jar, a suitable length of plastic or rubber tubing which is a tight fit over the bleed screw, and a ring spanner to fit the screw. The help of an assistant will also be required.

14 Remove the dust cap from the first screw in the sequence (if not already done). Fit a suitable spanner and tube to the screw, place the other end of the tube in the jar, and pour in sufficient fluid to cover the end of the tube.

15 Ensure that the master cylinder reservoir fluid level is maintained at least above the Minimum level throughout the procedure.

16 Have the assistant fully depress the brake pedal several times to build up pressure, then maintain it down on the final downstroke.

17 While pedal pressure is maintained, unscrew the bleed screw (approximately one turn) and allow the compressed fluid and air to flow into the jar. The assistant should maintain pedal pressure, following the pedal down to the floor if necessary, and should not release the pedal until instructed to do so. When the flow stops, tighten the bleed screw again. Have the assistant release the pedal slowly, and recheck the reservoir fluid level.

18 Repeat the steps given in paragraphs 16 and 17 until the fluid emerging from the bleed screw is free from air bubbles. If the master cylinder has been drained and refilled, and air is being bled from the first screw in the sequence, allow at least five seconds between cycles for the master cylinder passages to refill.

19 When no more air bubbles appear, tighten the bleed screw securely, remove the tube and spanner, and refit the dust cap (where applicable). Do not overtighten the bleed screw.

20 Repeat the procedure on the remaining screws in the sequence, until all air is removed from the system and the brake pedal feels firm again.

Using a one-way valve kit

21 As their name implies, these kits consist of a length of tubing with a one-way valve fitted, to prevent expelled air and fluid being drawn back into the system; some kits include a translucent container, which can be positioned so that the air bubbles can be more easily seen flowing from the end of the tube.

22 The kit is connected to the bleed screw, which is then opened **(see illustration)**. The

13.22 Bleeding a front brake using a one-way valve kit

15.2 Detaching the vacuum hose from the servo unit

user returns to the driver's seat, depresses the brake pedal with a smooth, steady stroke, and slowly releases it; this is repeated until the expelled fluid is clear of air bubbles.

23 Note that these kits simplify work so much that it is easy to forget the master cylinder reservoir fluid level; ensure that this is maintained at least above the Minimum level at all times.

Using a pressure-bleeding kit

24 These kits are usually operated by the reservoir of pressurised air contained in the spare tyre. However, note that it will probably be necessary to reduce the pressure to a lower level than normal; refer to the instructions supplied with the kit.

25 By connecting a pressurised, fluid-filled container to the master cylinder reservoir, bleeding can be carried out simply by opening each screw in turn (in the specified sequence), and allowing the fluid to flow out until no more air bubbles can be seen in the expelled fluid.

26 This method has the advantage that the large reservoir of fluid provides an additional safeguard against air being drawn into the system during bleeding.

27 Pressure-bleeding is particularly effective when bleeding 'difficult' systems, or when bleeding the complete system at the time of routine fluid renewal.

All methods

28 When bleeding is complete, and firm pedal feel is restored, wash off any spilt fluid, tighten the bleed screws securely, and refit their dust caps.

16.3 Vacuum pump pushrod (1) must be retracted fully – resting on lowest point of cam lobe (2)

29 Check the hydraulic fluid level in the master cylinder reservoir, and top-up if necessary.

30 Discard any hydraulic fluid that has been bled from the system; it will not be fit for re-use.

31 Check the feel of the brake pedal. If it feels at all spongy, air must still be present in the system, and further bleeding is required. Failure to bleed satisfactorily after a reasonable repetition of the bleeding procedure may be due to worn master cylinder seals.

14 Vacuum servo unit – testing, removal and refitting

Testing

1 To test the operation of the servo, depress the footbrake four or five times to exhaust the vacuum, then start the engine while keeping the footbrake depressed. As the engine starts, there should be a noticeable 'give' in the brake pedal as vacuum builds up. Allow the engine to run for at least two minutes, and then switch it off. If the brake pedal is depressed again, it should be possible to detect a hiss from the servo when the pedal is depressed. After about four or five applications, no further hissing will be heard, and the pedal will feel considerably firmer.

2 Before assuming that a problem exists in the servo itself, check the non-return valve as described in the next Section. The problem may also be due to a faulty vacuum pump (see Section 24).

Removal

3 Refer to Section 9 and remove the master cylinder.

4 Disconnect the vacuum hose at the servo non-return valve by pulling it free. If it is reluctant to move, assist it by prising it free using a screwdriver with its blade inserted under the elbow flange.

5 Working inside the vehicle, move the front passenger seat fully rearwards, then peel back the footwell trim from the inner bulkhead on that side, to gain access to the two servo bracket retaining nuts. Unscrew and remove the nuts.

16.4 Disconnecting the vacuum hose union from the pump

6 Unscrew and remove the four nuts securing the servo unit to the mounting bracket.

7 Withdraw the servo unit so that its studs are clear of the bracket and pivot the inner bracket to one side. Extract the clevis pin to release the actuating rod from its shaft, then remove the servo unit.

8 Note that the servo unit cannot be dismantled for repair or overhaul and, if faulty, must be renewed.

Refitting

9 Refitting is a reversal of removal. Refer to Section 9 for details of refitting the master cylinder.

15 Vacuum servo unit vacuum hose and non-return valve – removal, testing and refitting

Removal

1 Depress the brake pedal three or four times to exhaust any remaining vacuum from the servo unit.

2 Carefully pull free and detach the servo vacuum hose from the servo unit **(see illustration)**. If the hose is reluctant to move, prise it free with the aid of a screwdriver, inserting its blade under the flange of the elbow.

3 Detach the vacuum hose at the connector in the line from the vacuum pump.

4 If the hose or the fixings are damaged or in poor condition, they must be renewed.

Non-return valve testing

5 Examine the non-return valve for damage and signs of deterioration, and renew it if necessary. The valve may be tested by blowing through its connecting hoses in both directions. It should only be possible to blow from the servo end to the manifold end.

Refitting

6 Refitting is a reversal of removal. If fitting a new non-return valve, ensure that it is fitted the correct way round.

16 Vacuum pump – removal and refitting

Removal

1 Disconnect the battery negative lead (see Chapter 5A, Section 1).

2 Remove the cylinder head cover as described in Chapter 2A.

3 Using a suitable socket or spanner on the crankshaft pulley bolt, turn the crankshaft until the vacuum pump pushrod (operated by the lobe on the end of the camshaft) is fully retracted into the cylinder head **(see illustration)**.

4 Unscrew the union nut and disconnect the vacuum hose from the top of the pump **(see illustration)**.

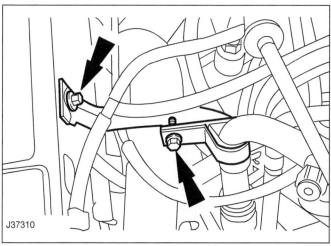

16.5 Air conditioning pipe support bracket bolts (arrowed)

16.9 Injector pulse sensor wiring plug (arrowed)

5 On models with air conditioning, remove the two bolts securing the pipe support bracket, and move the pipes to one side (see illustration).

6 Using the information in Chapter 4A, remove the air inlet ducts from the air cleaner and the body front panel.

7 Remove the fuel heater as described in Chapter 4A.

8 Referring to Chapter 1 if necessary, remove the fuel filter and its mounting bracket.

9 Disconnect the wiring plug from the oil pressure switch, and the glow plug main feed wire. On later models, also disconnect the plugs for the radiator fan switch and injector pulse sensor (see illustration).

10 Release the retaining clip and disconnect the oil return hose from the base of the pump. Be prepared for some oil spillage as the hose is disconnected and mop up any spilt oil.

11 Evenly and progressively slacken the bolts securing the pump to the front of the cylinder head. Note that there is no need to completely remove the lower bolt, as the lower end of the pump is slotted (see illustration).

12 Remove the pump from the engine compartment, along with its sealing ring. Discard the sealing ring, a new one should be used on refitting (see illustration).

Refitting

13 Ensure the pump and cylinder head mating surfaces are clean and dry, and fit the new sealing ring to the pump recess.

14 Manoeuvre the pump into position, ensuring the sealing ring remains correctly seated, and tighten the pump mounting bolts securely.

15 Reconnect the oil return hose to the base of the pump and secure it in position with the retaining clip.

16 Reconnect all wiring, and refit any components removed for access, referring to the relevant Chapters as necessary.

17 Reconnect the vacuum hose to the pump, tightening its union nut securely.

18 On completion, run the engine and check for correct servo operation as described in Section 14 before taking the vehicle out on the road.

17 Vacuum pump – testing and overhaul

Note: A vacuum gauge will be required for this check.

1 The operation of the braking system vacuum pump can be checked using a vacuum gauge.

2 Disconnect the vacuum pipe from the pump, and connect the gauge to the pump union using a suitable length of hose.

3 Start the engine and allow it to idle, then measure the vacuum created by the pump. As a guide, after one minute, a minimum of approximately 500 mm Hg should be recorded. If the vacuum registered is significantly less than this, it is likely that the pump is faulty. However, seek the advice of a Ford dealer before condemning the pump.

4 Overhaul of the vacuum pump is not possible, since no components are available separately for it. If faulty, the complete pump assembly must be renewed.

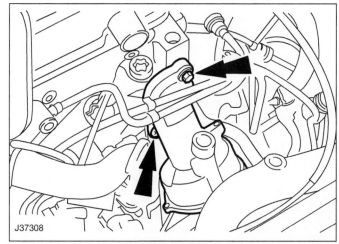

16.11 Vacuum pump mounting bolts (arrowed) – remove the top one, just loosen the bottom one

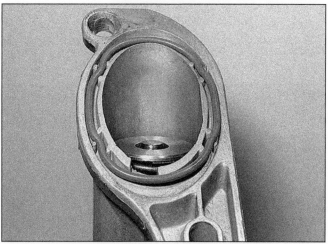

16.12 Vacuum pump flange with O-ring

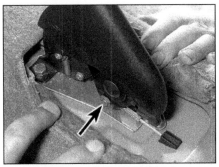

18.6 Handbrake primary cable-to-lever pin and retaining clip (arrowed)

18 Handbrake lever – removal and refitting

Removal

1 Chock the roadwheels to secure the vehicle.
2 Remove the front seats as described in Chapter 11.
3 Where applicable, remove the centre console as described in Chapter 11.
4 Peel back the carpet from the area around the handbrake lever to provide suitable access the lever and fittings. Release the handbrake.
5 Detach the handbrake warning light lead from the switch.
6 Prise free the retaining clip and remove the primary cable pin **(see illustration)**.

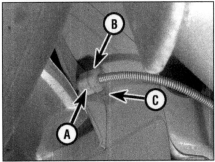

20.4 Handbrake cable adjuster nut (A) locknut (B) and lockpin (C)

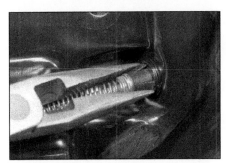

20.6a Compress the handbrake cable retaining lugs to release the cable from the brake backplate

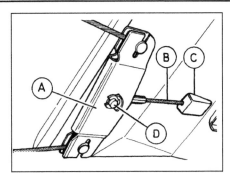

19.4 Handbrake cable equaliser components

A Equaliser
B Primary cable
C Cable guide
D Equaliser pin and spring clip

7 Undo the two retaining bolts, and remove the handbrake lever and spreader plate.

Refitting

8 Refit in the reverse order of removal. Ensure that the retaining bolts are securely tightened. Check the handbrake adjustment as described in Chapter 1 to complete.

19 Handbrake primary cable – removal and refitting

Removal

1 Release the primary cable from the handbrake lever, as described in the previous Section.
2 Chock the front wheels then jack up the rear of the car and support it on axle stands (see *Jacking and vehicle support*).
3 Where necessary, detach the exhaust system and remove the heat shields from the underside floorpan to allow access to the primary cable connections underneath the vehicle.
4 Release the spring clip securing the pin, and extract the equaliser/cable pin. Detach the equaliser from the primary cable **(see illustration)**.
5 Detach the cable guide from the floorpan, then withdraw the cable rearwards from the vehicle.

20.6b Release the handbrake cable from its locating clips

Refitting

6 Refit in the reverse order of removal. Ensure that the cable guide is secured in the floorpan, and lubricate the pivot pin with a liberal amount of high-melting-point grease.
7 Refit the exhaust system and heat shields.
8 Refer to Chapter 1 for details, and adjust the handbrake as required before lowering the vehicle to the ground.

20 Handbrake cable – removal and refitting

Removal

1 Chock the front wheels, and loosen the rear wheel nuts. Jack up the rear of the car and support it on axle stands (see *Jacking and vehicle support*). Fully release the handbrake lever and remove the rear roadwheels.
2 Refer to the previous Section for details, and disconnect the handbrake primary cable from the equaliser.
3 Disengage the right/left-hand cable(s) from the equaliser (as required).
4 Remove the lockpin from the adjuster, and the spring clip from the cable guides on the side concerned, then detach them from the underbody **(see illustration)**.
5 Remove the rear brake drum(s) and shoes as described in Sections 5 and 6 respectively.
6 Compress the handbrake cable retainer lugs and release the cable from the backplate, then pull the cable through. Release the cable from the underbody fixings, and remove it from the vehicle **(see illustrations)**.

Refitting

7 Refitting is a reversal of the removal procedure – see Sections 5 and 6 for refitting the brake shoes and drums.
8 When the cable is fully refitted (but before lowering the vehicle rear wheels to the ground) check and adjust the handbrake as described in Chapter 1.

21 Brake pressure control valves – removal and refitting

Note: *Before starting work, refer to the warning at the beginning of Section 13 concerning the dangers of hydraulic fluid.*

Removal

1 The pressure control valves are located in the engine compartment, fixed to the left-hand inner wing panel or screwed directly into the master cylinder fluid outlet ports **(see illustration)**.
2 Minimise hydraulic fluid loss by removing the master cylinder reservoir cap, placing a piece of plastic film over the reservoir and sealing it with an elastic band. Detach the rigid brake pipes from the valves. As the pipes

21.1 Inner wing-mounted brake pressure control valves

are disconnected, tape over the exposed ends, or fit plugs, to prevent the ingress of dirt and excessive fluid loss.

3 To remove the inner wing panel mounted assembly, unscrew and remove the valve support bracket retaining nut (under the wheel arch), and remove the valve assembly from the vehicle. To remove the valves from the bracket, slide free the retaining clips and detach the valve(s).

4 To remove the master cylinder mounted valves, unscrew them from the master cylinder body.

Refitting

5 Refitting is a reversal of the removal procedure.

6 On completion, bleed the complete hydraulic system as described in Section 13.

22 Light-laden valve (Van models) – removal and refitting

Note: *Before starting work, refer to the warning at the beginning of Section 13 concerning the dangers of hydraulic fluid.*

Removal

1 For this operation, the vehicle must be raised for access underneath at the rear, but must still be resting on its wheels. Suitable ramps (or an inspection pit) will therefore be required. If positioning the vehicle on a pair of ramps, chock the front roadwheels.

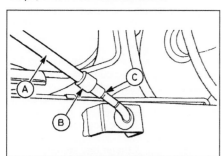

23.2a Light-laden valve linkage adjustment

A Spacer tube   C Setting
B Rubber seal   groove

2 Detach the brake pipes from the valve **(see illustration)**, and drain the fluid into a suitable container for disposal. Due to its location, care will be needed not to spill the fluid onto the hands – wear suitable protective gloves.

3 Detach the spring clip from the link rod at the axle end. Withdraw the washer and the valve link rod from the bracket on the axle, but take care not to dismantle the spacer tube from the link rod.

4 The axle bracket bush must be removed for renewal if it is worn or damaged.

5 Unscrew and remove the two retaining bolts, then withdraw the valve and the link rod from the mounting bracket.

Refitting

6 Where applicable, fit the new bush into the axle bracket.

7 Relocate the valve on the mounting bracket, and fit the retaining bolts.

8 Check that the brake pipe connections are clean, then reconnect the pipes.

9 Smear the axle bush end of the link rod with a small amount of general-purpose grease. Fit the link rod into the bush, refit the washer, and secure with the spring clip.

10 Bleed the brake hydraulic system as described in Section 13. If the original valve has been refitted, ensure that the valve is held fully open whilst bleeding. If a new valve has been fitted, the bleed clip must be left in position whilst the system is completely bled, then removed. The valve will need to be adjusted as described in the following Section.

23 Light-laden valve (Van models) – adjustment

1 For this operation, the vehicle must be raised for access underneath at the rear, but must be standing on its wheels. Suitable ramps (or an inspection pit) will therefore be required. If positioning the vehicle on a pair of ramps, chock the front roadwheels. The vehicle must be empty, and the fuel tank no more than half-full.

2 To adjust an original light-laden valve

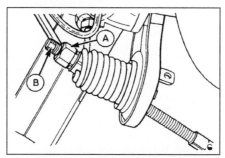

23.2b Light-laden valve linkage adjustment on a used valve, showing adjuster nut (A) and flats on the end of the rod (B)

22.2 Brake pipe connections to the light-laden valve

linkage, grip the flats on the end of the rod to prevent it from rotating, and turn the adjuster nut to position the end face of the rubber seal within the setting groove width **(see illustrations)**.

3 To adjust a new light-laden valve, rotate the spacer tube to position the end face of the rubber seal within the setting groove width, then crimp over the end of the spacer tube against the threaded rod flats (next to the knurled section) **(see illustration)**.

24 Anti-lock braking system (ABS) – general information

Pre-1996 models

A Teves Mk. IV anti-lock braking system is available on certain models in the range. The system operates in conjunction with the conventional braking system but additionally comprises a hydraulic unit, an ABS module, a wheel speed sensor on each front wheel hub, and a combined pedal position sensor and brake stop-light switch assembly.

The hydraulic unit consists of a twin-circuit electric pump and a twin-channel valve block containing one inlet and one outlet solenoid valve for each hydraulic channel.

The ABS module is located in the engine compartment, and has four main functions: to control the ABS system; to monitor the rotational speed of the front wheels; to monitor the electric components in the system; and to

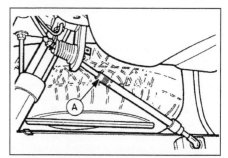

23.3 Light-laden valve adjustment on a new valve showing the crimping point (A)

provide 'on-board' system fault diagnosis. The electrical functions of the ABS module are continuously monitored by two micro-processors, and these also periodically check the solenoid-operated valves by means of a test pulse during the operation of the system. The module checks the signals sent by the system sensors to provide a means of fault diagnosis. In the event of a fault occurring in the ABS system, a warning light on the instrument panel will come on and remain on until the ignition is switched off. A particular fault is represented by a two-digit code stored within the module memory. A fault code reader or similar system tester is required to read the codes, so in the event of a fault being indicated, the vehicle must be taken to a Ford garage for analysis.

The ABS system functions as follows. During normal braking, pressure from the brake pedal is applied to the master cylinder by the servo unit pushrod. The servo unit pushrod acts directly on the pressure piston in the master cylinder. The resulting increase in hydraulic pressure moves the intermediate piston in the cylinder, and the pressure which increases in front of the intermediate piston flows through the open inlet solenoid valves in the hydraulic unit valve block, to the brake calipers and wheel cylinders. The outlet solenoid valves in the valve block remain shut.

The wheel speed sensors continually monitor the speed of the front wheels by generating an electrical signal as the wheel is rotated. This information is passed to the ABS module which is then able to determine wheel speed, wheel acceleration and wheel deceleration. The module compares the signals received from each front wheel and if the onset of lock at either wheel is detected, a signal is sent to the hydraulic unit which regulates the brake pressure in the hydraulic circuit for the relevant wheel.

ABS hydraulic pressure regulation is carried out in three phases; pressure holding, pressure reduction and pressure build-up.

In the pressure holding phase, to prevent any further build-up of hydraulic pressure in the circuit being controlled, the inlet solenoid valve in the hydraulic unit is shut and the outlet solenoid valve remains shut. The pressure cannot now be increased in the controlled circuit by any further application of the brake pedal.

If the wheel speed sensor signals indicate that wheel rotation has now stabilised, the ABS module will instigate the pressure build-up phase, allowing braking to continue. If wheel lock is still detected after the pressure holding phase, the module instigates the pressure reduction phase.

A controlled braking operation can be instigated with a pressure reduction phase or it can follow a pressure holding phase. The inlet solenoid valve is, or remains shut and the outlet solenoid valve is opened. As long as the outlet solenoid valve is open, the brake fluid discharges back into the master cylinder reservoir.

If the brake pedal begins to creep down during a pressure reduction phase, a signal is sent to the ABS module from the combined pedal position sensor and brake stop light switch assembly mounted on the brake pedal bracket. When this signal is detected, the ABS module activates the electric pump on the hydraulic unit. Hydraulic fluid is pumped from the master cylinder reservoir back into the brake hydraulic circuit, forcing back the master cylinder piston (and the brake pedal). When the module detects that the pedal has returned to its initial position, the pump is switched off.

The pressure build-up phase is instigated after the wheel rotation has stabilised. The outlet solenoid valve is shut and the inlet solenoid valve is opened. The brake pressure from the master cylinder flows through the inlet solenoid valve to the relevant brake caliper/wheel cylinder allowing braking to continue.

The whole ABS control cycle takes place four to ten times per second for each affected wheel and this ensures maximum braking effect and control during ABS operation.

The rear wheels are not fitted with wheel speed sensors, but are prevented from locking up (under all braking conditions) by means of a load-apportioning valve incorporated in each rear circuit. These valves are housed in a common casting, and are actuated by an arm connected to the rear axle. The load-apportioning valve is checked for adjustment and set during the vehicle pre-delivery inspection using a special tool. Any further checks or adjustments required must therefore be entrusted to a Ford dealer.

1996-on models

The Teves 20-I anti-lock braking system fitted to later models is a totally revised version of the original system, with a number of significant differences to the hydraulic unit and ABS module software. From 1998 onwards, the system may also optionally incorporate traction control.

As with the earlier system, Teves 20-I operates in conjunction with the conventional braking system but additionally comprises a hydraulic unit, an ABS module, and a wheel speed sensor on each wheel hub (four in total). The function of the ABS module is essentially the same as on the earlier system however, to reduce external electrical connections to a minimum and improve reliability, the module is now integral with the hydraulic unit.

The hydraulic unit consists of an electric motor operating a return pump with eccentric drive and twin radial pistons, inlet and outlet solenoid valves, pressure accumulators and pulsation dampers. The unit controls the hydraulic pressure applied to the brake for each individual front wheel and each individual rear wheel. The return pump is switched on when the ABS is activated and returns hydraulic fluid, drained off during the

pressure reduction phase, back into the brake circuit.

The ABS system functions as follows. During normal braking, pressure from the brake pedal is applied to the master cylinder by the vacuum servo unit pushrod. The servo unit pushrod acts directly on the pressure piston in the master cylinder which pressurises the hydraulic fluid in the brake pipes to the hydraulic control unit. The inlet solenoid valve and outlet solenoid valve both remain in the 'at rest' position (inlet solenoid valve open and outlet solenoid valve closed). Hydraulic pressure is transmitted to each brake caliper or wheel cylinder, thus operating the brakes. When the brake pedal is released, a one-way valve opens allowing the hydraulic pressure in the circuit to rapidly decrease.

The ABS module continually monitors wheel speed from the signals provided by the wheel speed sensors. If the module detects the incidence of wheel lock on one or more wheels, ABS is automatically initiated in three phases: pressure holding, pressure reduction and pressure build-up. As the system operates individually on each wheel, any or all of the wheels could be in any one of the following phases at any particular moment.

In the pressure holding phase, to prevent any further build-up of hydraulic pressure in the circuit being controlled, the ABS module closes the inlet solenoid valve and allows the outlet solenoid valve to remain closed. The hydraulic fluid line from the master cylinder to the brake caliper or wheel cylinder is closed, and the hydraulic fluid in the controlled circuit is maintained at a constant pressure. The pressure cannot now be increased in that circuit by any further application of the brake pedal.

If the wheel speed sensor signals indicate that wheel rotation has now stabilised, the ABS module will instigate the pressure build-up phase, allowing braking to continue. If wheel lock is still detected after the pressure holding phase, the module instigates the pressure reduction phase.

In the pressure reduction phase, the inlet solenoid valve remains closed and the outlet solenoid valve is opened by means of a series of short activation pulses. The pressure in the controlled circuit decreases rapidly as the fluid flows from the brake caliper or wheel cylinder into the pressure accumulator. At the same time, the ABS module actuates the electric motor to operate the return pump. The hydraulic fluid is then pumped back into the pressure side of the master cylinder. This process creates a pulsation which can be felt in the brake pedal action, but which is softened by the pulsation damper.

The pressure build-up phase is instigated after the wheel rotation has stabilised. The inlet and outlet solenoid valves are returned to the at rest position (inlet solenoid valve open and exhaust solenoid valve closed) which re-opens the hydraulic fluid line from the master cylinder to the brake caliper or wheel cylinder.

Hydraulic pressure is reinstated, thus re-introducing operation of the brake. After a brief period, a short pressure holding phase is re-introduced and the ABS module continually shifts between pressure build-up and pressure holding until the wheel has decelerated to a sufficient degree where pressure reduction is once more required.

The whole ABS control cycle takes place 4 to 10 times per second for each affected wheel and this ensures maximum braking effect and control during ABS operation.

Where the system incorporates traction control, essentially the reverse principle is applied. When the ABS module detects that one or more front wheels are rotating faster than the reference value, the brake is actually applied on the relevant wheel(s) to reduce the rotational speed.

To prevent rear wheel lock-up, the ABS module contains additional software for rear brake hydraulic fluid pressure regulation during normal (non-ABS regulated) braking. As the rear brake hydraulic pressure is controlled by the ABS module and hydraulic unit, the mechanical load-apportioning valves used in the earlier system are not required.

25 Anti-lock braking system (ABS) components – removal and refitting

Hydraulic unit

Pre-1996 models

1 Disconnect the battery negative (earth) lead (refer to Chapter 5A, Section 1).
2 Remove the filler cap from the master cylinder reservoir (noting that the filler cap must not be inverted). The reservoir should now be emptied by siphoning or drawing out the fluid with a pipette.
3 Identify each brake pipe and its connection to the master cylinder, then unscrew the union nuts and disconnect them **(see illustration)**. When disconnecting the fluid return pipes from the reservoir, press the retaining boss into the reservoir, and pull free the fluid line. Plug the connections, and tape over the pipe ends, to prevent the entry of dust and dirt.
4 Disconnect the wiring multi-plug adjacent to the hydraulic unit.
5 Unscrew the union nuts, and disconnect the fluid pipes from the hydraulic unit at the rear. Plug the connections.
6 Unscrew the retaining nut securing the multi-plug connector bracket, and the nut and bolt securing the hydraulic unit to the bracket **(see illustration)**. Withdraw the hydraulic unit from the bracket, and remove it from the vehicle.
7 Prise free and detach the fluid return lines from the hydraulic unit **(see illustration)**. Plug the connections, and tape over the pipe ends, to prevent the entry of dust and dirt.
8 Remove the plugs from the connections as

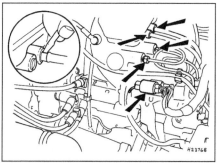

25.3 Detach the hydraulic lines and the wiring multi-plug from the points indicated

the pipes and fluid return lines are refitted. Refit in the reverse order of removal, noting the torque settings for the unit-to-bracket nut and bolt. Ensure that all connections are clean and secure.
9 On completion, bleed the system as described in Section 13. Inspect the hydraulic line connections at the master cylinder/hydraulic unit for any sign of leaks.

1996-on models

10 Disconnect the battery negative (earth) lead (refer to Chapter 5A, Section 1).
11 Remove the filler cap from the master cylinder reservoir (noting that the filler cap must not be inverted). The reservoir should now be emptied by siphoning or drawing out the fluid with a pipette.
12 Identify each brake pipe and its connection to the hydraulic unit, then unscrew the union nuts and disconnect them. Plug the connections, and tape over the pipe ends, to prevent the entry of dust and dirt.
13 Disconnect the wiring multi-plug from the ABS module located on the side of the hydraulic unit.
14 Undo the three bolts and remove the hydraulic unit from the engine compartment.
15 Refit in the reverse order of removal, ensuring that all connections are clean and secure.

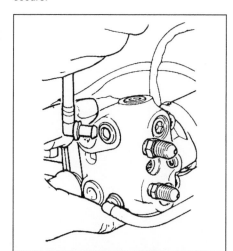

25.7 Disconnect the fluid return lines from the ABS hydraulic unit

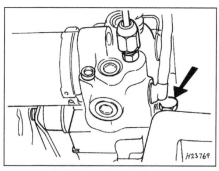

25.6 ABS hydraulic unit-to-bracket retaining bolt location

16 On completion, bleed the system as described in Section 13. Inspect the hydraulic line connections at the hydraulic unit for any sign of leaks.

ABS module

Pre-1996 models

17 Disconnect the battery negative (earth) lead (refer to Chapter 5A, Section 1).
18 The module is situated opposite the battery, at the rear of the engine compartment. Swing the retaining clip out of the way, and disconnect the wiring multi-plug from the module.
19 Unscrew and remove the three retaining bolts, and withdraw the module from the vehicle **(see illustration)**.
20 Refit in the reverse order of removal, but take particular care when reconnecting the multi-plug.

1996-on models

21 The ABS module on later models is an integral part of the hydraulic unit and cannot be separated.

Front speed sensor

22 An ABS wheel speed sensor is fitted in the front spindle carrier on each side. To remove a sensor, apply the handbrake, then raise and support the front of the vehicle on axle stands so the front wheels are clear of the ground.
23 Unclip and detach the sensor cable from the wiring loom. Unscrew the retaining bolt, and withdraw the sensor from its location in the spindle carrier. Remove the sensor and lead from the vehicle.

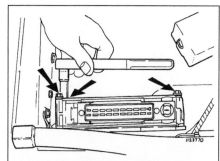

25.19 Location of the ABS module retaining bolts

24 If renewing the sensor, the replacement must have the correct lead length (on models fitted with an anti-roll bar, the lead is longer).

25 Refit in the reverse order of removal. When inserting the sensor into position, ensure that the mating surfaces are clean, free from oil and grease. Feed the cable through the wheel arch, and ensure that it is clipped in position. Secure the cable with any ties provided. When the sensor is refitted, turn the steering from lock to lock, to ensure that the sensor lead does not foul on any steering or suspension components before lowering the vehicle to the ground.

Rear speed sensor

26 Rear wheel speed sensors are only fitted to 1996-on models, equipped with the Teves 20-I anti-lock braking system.

27 The removal and refitting procedure is essentially the same as for the front wheel speed sensor except that the rear sensor is bolted to the brake backplate rather than the front spindle carrier.

Front speed sensor ring

28 Referring to Chapter 10 for details, remove the spindle carrier, then remove the wheel hub from the spindle carrier.

29 Where applicable, unscrew and remove the sensor ring-to-hub retaining bolts, then detach the sensor ring from the hub. In some instances, the sensor ring will be press-fitted on the hub, and will require a suitable withdrawal tool to remove it.

30 Refitting is a reversal of the removal procedure. Ensure that the sensor and hub mating faces are clean. Refer to the appropriate Sections in Chapter 10 for details on refitting the hub and spindle carrier.

Rear speed sensor ring

31 Remove the rear brake drum/hub assembly as described in Chapter 10, Section 10.

32 Extract the sensor ring from the drum/hub assembly. The sensor ring is a press-fit on the hub, and will require a suitable withdrawal tool to remove it.

33 Press the new sensor ring onto the hub, then refit the hub/drum assembly as described in Chapter 10.

Load-apportioning valve

34 The removal of the load-apportioning valve on pre-1996 ABS-equipped models is not recommended, since a special resetting tool is required to adjust the valve when it is refitted. The removal and refitting of the load-apportioning valve is therefore a task to be entrusted to a suitably-equipped Ford dealer.

Chapter 10
Suspension and steering

Contents

Degrees of difficulty

Easy, suitable for novice with little experience	Fairly easy, suitable for beginner with some experience	Fairly difficult, suitable for competent DIY mechanic	Difficult, suitable for experienced DIY mechanic	Very difficult, suitable for expert DIY or professional 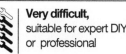

Specifications

Wheel alignment and steering angles
Front wheel toe setting (all models):
Tolerance allowed before resetting required	0.5 mm toe-out to 4.5 mm toe-in (0°05' toe-out to 0°45' toe-in)
Adjustment setting (if required)	2.0 mm toe-in ± 1.0 mm (0°20' toe-in ± 0°10')

Roadwheels
Wheel types and sizes (dependent on model):
Steel	13 x 5 (Heavy Duty Van) or 14 x 6
Alloy	13 x 5, 14 x 6, or 15 x 6

Tyres
Tyre sizes (dependent on model)	165R 13-C, 165R 13-T, 165R13-REINF, 175/70R 13 82T, 175/70R 13 82H, 185/50R 14H/V, 185/60R 14 82H, 185/60R 14 V, 195/50R 15 V
Tyre pressures	See Weekly checks

Torque wrench settings

	Nm	lbf ft
Front suspension		
Anti-roll bar link to suspension strut	50	37
Anti-roll bar link to anti-roll bar	50	37
Anti-roll bar-to-subframe clamp bolts	24	18
Hub/driveshaft retaining nut	270	199
Lower arm balljoint-to-spindle carrier clamp bolt	54	40
Lower arm to subframe bolts (using torque-to-yield method with vehicle standing on its wheels):		
Stage 1	50	37
Stage 2	Slacken completely	
Stage 3	50	37
Stage 4	Tighten through a further 90°	
Subframe retaining bolts	85	63
Suspension strut top mounting nuts:		
Two-nut mounting (early models)	46	34
Three-nut mounting (models built January 1995-on)	34	25
Suspension strut piston rod nut	58	43
Suspension strut-to-spindle carrier clamp bolt	85	63
Rear suspension (Hatchback, Saloon and Estate)		
Axle front mounting bracket bolts	50	37
Axle front bush/bracket pivot nuts/bolts*	120	88
Rear hub bearing nut	260	192
Shock absorber lower mounting (Estate)	69	51
Shock absorber upper mounting (Estate)	50	37
Strut lower mounting (Hatchback and Saloon)	120	88
Strut upper mounting nuts (Hatchback and Saloon)	35	25
Strut upper through-bolt (Hatchback and Saloon)	50	37
Torque to be measured from the bolt head (not the nut)		
Rear suspension (Van)		
Axle/spring U-bolt nuts	41	30
Front spring mounting bolt	84	62
Rear hub bearing nut	260	192
Rear shackle lower mounting bolt	84	62
Rear shackle upper stud/nut	50	37
Shock absorber lower mounting	68	50
Shock absorber mounting bracket to body	35	25
Shock absorber upper mounting	50	37
Steering (manual)		
Adjustable steering through-bolt	7	5
Steering column mounting nuts	25	18
Steering column-to-pinion shaft clamp bolt	25	18
Steering gear-to-subframe bolts	84	62
Steering wheel-to-column shaft bolt	50	37
Track rod end balljoint-to-spindle carrier arm	28	20
Track rod end balljoint-to-track rod locknut	63	46
Track rod to steering rack	79	58
Steering (power-assisted)		
Adjustable steering through-bolt	7	5
Pressure hose union to pump	17	13
Steering column mounting nuts	25	18
Steering column-to-pinion shaft clamp bolt	25	18
Steering gear-to-subframe bolts:		
Stage 1	15	11
Stage 2	Tighten through a further 90°	
Steering pump bolts	25	18
Steering pump pulley bolts	25	18
Steering wheel-to-column shaft bolt	50	37
Track rod end balljoint-to-spindle carrier arm	28	20
Track rod end balljoint-to-track rod locknut	63	46
Track rod to steering rack	79	58
Roadwheel nuts	See Chapter 1	

1 General information

The independent front suspension is of the MacPherson strut type, incorporating coil springs and integral telescopic shock absorbers. The struts are attached to spindle carriers at their lower ends, and the carriers are in turn attached to the lower suspension arm by balljoints. High-series models are fitted with an anti-roll bar, and this is attached to the subframe and lower suspension arms by link rods with rubber bushes.

On all except Van models, the semi-independent rear suspension is of trailing arm type, incorporating a twist type axle beam. This inverted V-section beam allows a limited torsional flexibility, giving each rear wheel a certain amount of independent movement whilst at the same time maintaining the track and wheel camber control for the rear axle. The axle is attached to the body by rubber void bushes, via brackets mounted on the underside of the body. Each bracket has a conical seating peg to ensure accurate alignment of the axle. It is important to note that the vehicle must never be jacked up at the rear under the axle beam. The axle beam itself is maintenance-free but where required, the pivot bushes of the trailing arm can be renewed.

The rear suspension struts on Hatchback and Saloon models are similar to those used for the front suspension, the combined coil spring and shock absorber being mounted between the suspension turret in the luggage area at the top and the trailing arm, inboard of the stub axle at the bottom. The Estate model differs in that the coil spring is separate from the shock absorber, and is enclosed between the underbody and the trailing suspension arm.

On Van models, the rear suspension comprises a transverse beam axle which is supported by a single leaf spring each side. Telescopic shock absorbers are used to control vertical movement.

A variable-ratio type rack-and-pinion steering gear is fitted, together with a conventional column and two-section shaft. The steering gear is bolted to the front subframe. A steering column height adjustment mechanism is fitted to some models, and power-assisted steering is also available.

2 Front spindle carrier – removal and refitting

Removal

1 Remove the wheel trim on the relevant side for access to the driveshaft/hub nut. Using a suitable pin punch, peen back the locking tab securing the driveshaft/hub nut, then loosen off the nut.

2.3 Disconnect the brake hose from the front suspension strut

2.6b Prise open the joint . . .

2.9a Remove the suspension strut-to-spindle carrier clamp bolt . . .

2.6a Removing the lower arm-to-spindle clamp bolt and nut

2.6c . . . and detach the lower arm balljoint from the spindle

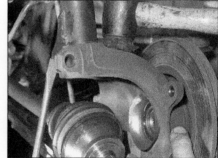
2.9b . . . and separate the spindle carrier from the strut

2 Chock the rear wheels, and loosen the relevant front roadwheel nuts. Jack up the front of the car and support it on axle stands (see *Jacking and vehicle support*). Remove the front roadwheel.
3 Unscrew the retaining nut, and detach the brake hose and its locating bracket from the suspension strut **(see illustration)**.
4 Unscrew the brake caliper-to-carrier retaining bolts, then withdraw the caliper and suspend it from a suitable fixing in the inner wing to avoid straining the brake hose. Where applicable, detach the ABS sensor and its lead clip from the spindle carrier.
5 Extract the split pin from the track rod end balljoint, then unscrew the nut and detach the rod from the spindle carrier using a conventional balljoint removal tool, but take care not to damage the balljoint seal.
6 Note the direction of fitting, then unscrew and remove the lower arm balljoint-to-spindle carrier clamp bolt. Prise the joint open carefully using a large flat-bladed tool, and detach the balljoint from the spindle carrier **(see illustrations)**. Take care not to damage the balljoint seal during the separation procedures.
7 Unscrew the brake disc retaining screw, and remove the brake disc from the hub.
8 Unscrew and remove the driveshaft/hub nut and washer. Note that a new nut will be required for refitting.
9 Note the direction of fitting, then unscrew and remove the suspension strut-to-spindle retaining bolt. Prise open the clamping slot using a suitable wedged tool, and release the spindle from the strut. If necessary, tap the spindle carrier downwards to separate the two components **(see illustrations)**.
10 Connect up a universal puller to the spindle carrier, and withdraw it from the driveshaft. When the driveshaft is free of the

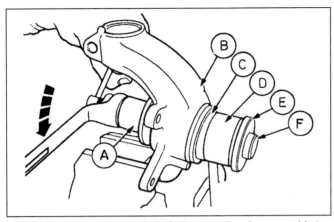

3.6 Using home-made tools to fit the outer bearing assembly to the spindle carrier

A Steel tube
B Spindle carrier
C Bearing
D Steel tube
E Flat washer
F Threaded bolt

4.2a Strut top mounting (early type), showing protective cap (A) over piston rod nut and strut top mounting nuts (B)

spindle, suspend it from a suitable fixing point under the wheel arch. This will prevent it from hanging down and its joint being pivoted excessively.

Refitting

11 Refitting is a reversal of removal, but observe the following points:

a) Ensure that all mating faces, particularly those of the disc and hub flange, are clean before refitting.

b) Lubricate the hub splines with molybdenum disulphide grease, and take care not to dislodge the hub bearings as the driveshaft is refitted through the hub.

c) Tighten all nuts and bolts to the specified torque. Fit a new split pin to the track rod end balljoint nut to secure it. When reconnecting the suspension lower arm balljoint to the spindle carrier, ensure that the clamp bolt is fully engaged in the locating groove, and prevent the bolt from turning as the nut is tightened.

d) With the (new) hub nut tightened to its specified torque setting, stake the nut flange into the groove in the end of the driveshaft.

3 Front hub bearings – renewal

Note: The front hub bearings should only be removed from the spindle carrier if they are to be renewed. The removal procedure renders the bearings unserviceable, and they must not be re-used. Prior to dismantling, it should be noted that a hub/bearing puller and an assortment of metal tubes of various diameters (and preferably, a press) will be required. Unless these tools are available, the renewal of the spindle carrier/hub bearings will have to be entrusted to a Ford garage. Under no circumstances attempt to tap the hub bearings into position, as this will render them

unserviceable. On ABS-equipped models, care must be taken during the bearing removal and refitting procedures not to damage the ABS wheel sensor ring.

Removal

1 Remove the spindle carrier from the vehicle as described in Section 2.

2 The hub must now be removed from the bearing inner races. It is preferable to use a press to do this, but it is possible to drive out the hub using a length of metal tube of suitable diameter.

3 Part of the inner race will remain on the hub, and this should be removed using a puller.

4 Extract the bearing retaining circlip using circlip pliers, then drive the bearing outer race from the spindle carrier. Do not allow the bearing to tilt during its withdrawal from the housing, or it will jam and possibly damage the surface of the bore. Any burrs left in a bearing bore will prevent the new bearing from seating correctly. If necessary, insert the old inner race to facilitate removal of the bearing.

5 Thoroughly clean the bearing bore and hub before reassembly begins.

Refitting

6 Press the new outer bearing assembly into the spindle carrier, using a length of metal

4.2b When slackening piston rod nut, prevent piston rod from rotating by counter-holding it with an Allen key

tube of diameter slightly less than the outer race. Do not apply any pressure to the inner race. Alternatively, a long threaded rod or bolt, a nut and large flat washers may be used to draw the bearing into position **(see illustration)**.

7 Secure the bearing in the spindle carrier using the circlip.

8 Support the inner race on a length of metal tube, then press the hub fully into the bearing.

9 Check that the hub spins freely in the bearings, then refit the spindle carrier as described in Section 2.

4 Front suspension strut – removal and refitting

Removal

1 Chock the rear wheels, and loosen the relevant front roadwheel nuts. Jack up the front of the car and support it on axle stands (see *Jacking and vehicle support*). Remove the front roadwheel.

2 Open and support the bonnet. If the strut is to be dismantled, prise off its protective cap and slacken by one or two turns only - **do not fully unscrew** - the piston rod nut. As the nut slackens, prevent the piston rod from rotating by counter-holding it with an Allen key **(see illustrations)**.

3 Detach the front brake hose from the support bracket on the strut.

4 Where applicable, unbolt and detach the anti-roll bar link rod from the suspension strut.

5 Unscrew and remove the strut-to-spindle carrier clamp bolt.

6 Note the direction of fitting, then unscrew and remove the lower arm balljoint-to-spindle carrier clamp bolt. Prise the joint open using a large flat-bladed tool, and detach the balljoint from the spindle carrier. Take care not to damage the balljoint seal during the separation procedures.

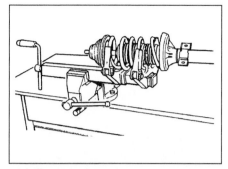

5.2 Ford special tool in use to compress the front suspension strut coil spring

7 Prise open the spindle carrier-to-strut joint, and separate the carrier from the strut. Tap the carrier downwards using a soft-faced hammer to release it from the strut if necessary.

8 Support the weight of the strut underneath, and unscrew the two nuts securing it to the turret at the top. Lower the strut and remove it from the vehicle.

Refitting

9 Refitting is a reversal of removal. Tighten all the retaining bolts to the specified torque. When reconnecting the suspension lower arm balljoint to the spindle carrier, ensure that the clamp bolt is fully engaged in the locating groove, and prevent the bolt from turning as the nut is tightened.

5 Front suspension strut – dismantling, examination and reassembly

⚠️ **Warning: Before attempting to dismantle the suspension strut, a suitable tool to hold the coil spring in compression must be obtained. Adjustable coil spring compressors which can be positively secured to the spring coils are readily available, and are recommended for this operation. Any attempt to dismantle the strut without such a tool is likely to result in damage or personal injury.**

Dismantling

1 With the strut removed from the vehicle, clean away all external dirt, then mount it upright in a vice.

2 Fit the spring compressor tool (ensuring that it is fully engaged) and compress the coil spring until all tension is relieved from the upper mounting **(see illustration)**.

3 Hold the strut piston with an Allen key, and unscrew the nut with a ring spanner.

4 Withdraw the cup, retainer (top mounting), the bearing and upper spring seat, followed by the gaiter and the bump stop **(see illustration)**.

5 The suspension strut and coil spring can now be separated. If a new coil spring or strut is to be fitted, the original coil spring must be

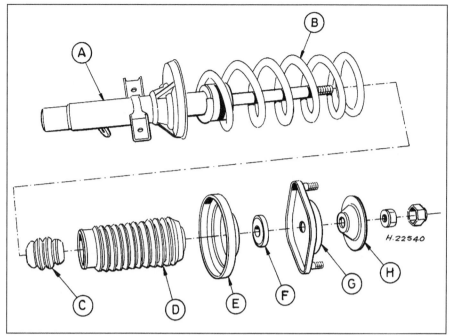

5.4 Front suspension strut components - early type (two-nut) top mounting shown

A Strut	D Gaiter	F Bearing
B Spring	E Upper spring	G Top mounting
C Bump stop	seat	H Top mounting cup

released from the compressor. If it is to be re-used, the coil spring can be left in compression.

Examination

6 With the strut assembly now completely dismantled, examine all the components for wear, damage or deformation, and check the bearing for smoothness of operation. Renew any of the components as necessary.

7 Examine the strut for signs of fluid leakage. Check the strut piston for pitting along its length, and check the strut body for signs of damage or elongation of the mounting bolt holes. Test the operation of the strut, holding it in an upright position, by moving the piston through a full stroke, and then through short strokes of 50 to 100 mm. In both cases, the resistance felt should be smooth and continuous. If the resistance is jerky, or uneven, or if there is any visible sign of wear or damage to the strut, renewal is necessary.

Reassembly

8 Reassembly is a reversal of dismantling, but make sure that the spring ends are correctly located in the upper and lower seats **(see illustrations)**. Check that the bearing is correctly fitted to the piston rod seat. Tighten the upper nut to the specified torque.

6 Front suspension anti-roll bar – removal and refitting

Removal

1 Remove the front subframe as described in Section 9. If only the anti-roll bar bushes are to be renewed, this can be done without removing the subframe or anti-roll bar (see paragraph 3).

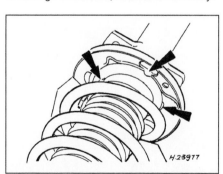

5.8a Spring location in the lower seat

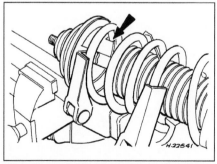

5.8b Spring end location in the upper seat

6.3 Anti-roll bar-to-subframe mounting

2 Unscrew the retaining nuts or bolts, and remove the anti-roll bar mounting brackets from the subframe each side, then withdraw the anti-roll bar from the subframe.

3 Check the bar for damage, and the rubber bushes for wear and deterioration. Renewing the bushes can be achieved without removing the bar – the bushes are split. If the bar-to-subframe mountings are disconnected, the bushes can be opened up and prised off the bar, and new ones fitted **(see illustration)**. Lubricate the new bushes with rubber grease, prior to fitting. If the link rod bushes need renewal, new link rods must be fitted.

Refitting

4 Refitting is a reversal of the removal procedure. Tighten the retaining nuts/bolts to the specified torque setting.

7 Front suspension lower arm – removal and refitting

Removal

1 Chock the rear wheels, and loosen the relevant front roadwheel nuts. Jack up the front of the car and support it on axle stands (see *Jacking and vehicle support*). Remove the front roadwheel.

2 Note the direction of fitting, then unscrew and remove the lower arm balljoint-to-spindle carrier clamp bolt. Prise the joint open using a large flat-bladed tool, and detach the balljoint from the spindle carrier. Take care not to

damage the balljoint seal during the separation procedures.

3 Unscrew and remove the inboard retaining bolts on the subframe, and withdraw the suspension arm from it **(see illustration)**.

4 If the balljoint and/or the inboard mounting bushes are found to be in poor condition, the complete suspension arm must be renewed. The suspension arm must also be renewed if it has suffered structural damage.

Refitting

5 Refitting is a reversal of the removal procedure, but note the following special points:

a) *When reconnecting the arm to the subframe, the bolts must be fitted from underneath, and hand-tightened until the vehicle is resting on its wheels.*

b) *When reconnecting the suspension lower arm balljoint to the spindle carrier, ensure that the clamp bolt is fully engaged in the locating groove, and prevent the bolt from turning as the nut is tightened.*

c) *Fully tighten the suspension arm-to-subframe bolts when the vehicle is lowered and is standing on its wheels. These bolts must then be tightened in the sequence specified.*

8 Subframe – removal and refitting

Removal

1 Chock the rear wheels, and loosen the front roadwheel nuts. Jack up the front of the car and support it on axle stands (see *Jacking and vehicle support*). Remove the front roadwheels.

2 Disconnect the battery negative (earth) lead (refer to Chapter 5A, Section 1).

3 Fit an engine support bar (or a sling and hoist) to support the combined weights of the engine and transmission when the subframe is detached (as during engine/transmission removal and refitting).

4 Centralise the steering so that it is in the straight-ahead position, then working within the vehicle, unscrew and remove the steering column-to-pinion shaft clamp bolt.

7.3 Suspension arm-to-subframe retaining bolts (arrowed)

5 Undo the engine/transmission mounting bracket bolts at the subframe connection **(see illustration)**.

6 Where necessary, undo the retaining nuts and detach the exhaust downpipe. Remove the exhaust heat shields as necessary for access to the gear linkage.

7 Disconnect the gear linkage at the transmission (see Chapter 7).

8 Extract the split pin and unscrew the track rod end balljoint nut on each side, then using a conventional separator tool, detach each joint from its spindle carrier connection.

9 Note the direction of fitting, then unscrew and remove the lower arm balljoint-to-spindle carrier clamp bolt. Prise the joint open using a large flat-bladed tool, and detach the balljoint from the spindle carrier. Take care not to damage the balljoint seal during the separation procedure.

10 Unscrew the retaining bolt, and detach the right-hand engine support bar from the subframe.

11 Unscrew and remove the second engine/transmission mounting bolt.

12 Where applicable, unscrew the retaining nuts and detach the anti-roll bar link rods from the suspension strut and anti-roll bar, each side **(see illustrations)**.

13 Where applicable, detach the power-assisted steering hydraulic lines from the steering gear (refer to Section 23 for details).

14 Locate suitable support jacks or blocks under the subframe to support it, then unscrew and remove the eight subframe fixing bolts from the positions shown **(see illustration)**. Lower the support jacks or

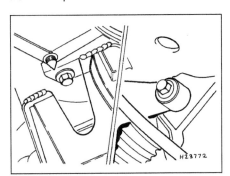

8.5 Engine/transmission mounting bracket securing bolt locations on the subframe

8.12a Link rod-to-strut connection

8.12b Link rod-to-bar connection

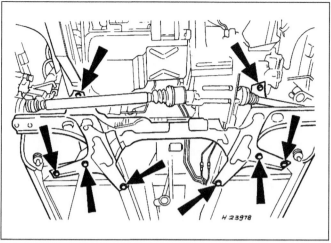
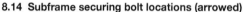

8.14 Subframe securing bolt locations (arrowed)

9.4 Remove the outer grease cap from the centre of the rear hub . . .

blocks and withdraw the subframe. As it is lowered, disengage the steering pinion shaft from the column.

15 When the subframe is lowered from the vehicle, the steering gear, the suspension arms and the anti-roll bar (where applicable) can be unbolted and removed from it as necessary.

16 If the subframe and/or its associated components have suffered damage or are in poor condition, they must be renewed.

Refitting

17 Refitting is a reversal of removal, but observe the following points:

a) *Ensure that all mating faces are clean before refitting.*

b) *When raising the subframe into position, ensure that the location dowels engage in the guide bores in the floorpan, and carefully engage the steering pinion shaft with the column shaft. Check that the various fixing bolt holes are in alignment, then loosely insert all of the retaining bolts before tightening them to the specified torque setting.*

c) *When reconnecting the suspension lower arm balljoint to the spindle carrier, ensure that the clamp bolt is fully engaged in the locating groove, and prevent the bolt from turning as the nut is tightened.*

d) *Tighten all nuts and bolts to the specified torque. Fit a new split pin to the track rod end balljoint nut to secure it.*

e) *On completion, have the front wheel toe setting checked (see Section 27).*

9 Rear hub bearings – renewal

1 Chock the front wheels, and loosen the relevant rear roadwheel nuts. Jack up the rear of the car and support it on axle stands (see *Jacking and vehicle support*). Remove the appropriate rear roadwheel.

2 On pre-1996 models, release the handbrake. On 1996-on models, unclip the handbrake lever gaiter to gain access to the adjuster nut on the side of the lever and slacken the cable right off. If the drum is stuck on the shoes, remove the rubber blanking plug from the inside face of the brake backplate, reach through with a suitable screwdriver, and release the automatic brake adjuster by levering the catch from the pawl.

3 On certain models, the brake drum may be removed independently of the hub if desired. Remove the drum retaining screw (if fitted), and withdraw the drum off the wheel hub.

4 Prise free the outer grease cap from the centre of the hub **(see illustration)**. The cap will be deformed during its removal, and will need to be renewed when the hub is refitted.

5 Unscrew and remove the hub nut, but note that the hub nut threads on pre-1996 models are 'handed' according to side – right-hand to right, left-hand to left **(see illustration)**. *A left-hand thread unscrews in a **clockwise** direction.* The hub nuts fitted to models from 1996 onwards are both right-hand thread.

6 Withdraw the brake drum/hub from the spindle of the rear stub axle **(see illustration)**.

7 Use a screwdriver or suitable lever to prise free the grease retainer (seal) from the hub bore, but take care not to damage the bore surface.

8 Remove the inner and outer bearing cones from the bore of the hub.

9 To remove the bearing cups from the hub, drive them out using a suitable punch. Drive each cup from its respective end by tapping it alternately at diametrically-opposed points **(see illustration)**. Do not allow the cups to tilt in the bore, or the surfaces may become burred and prevent the new bearings from seating correctly as they are fitted.

10 Clean the bore and spindle thoroughly before reassembly.

11 To reassemble, tap the new bearing cups into position in the hub, using a piece of

9.5 . . . unscrew the hub nut . . .

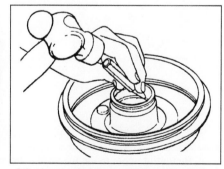

9.6 . . . and remove the brake drum

9.9 Use a suitable punch to drive out the bearing cups from the rear hub

10.3 Rear strut lower mounting on Hatchback and Saloon models

tubing slightly smaller in its outside diameter than that of the bearing cup. Ensure that the cups are squarely inserted and abut their respective shoulders in the hub.

12 Pack the inner bearing cone with grease, and insert it into its cup in the hub.

13 To fit the grease retainer (seal), first lubricate its inner lip to ease installation, then lightly tap the seal into position using a block of wood. Ensure that the seal is correctly orientated.

14 Pack the outer bearing cone with grease, and fit it into position in its cup.

15 The brake drum/hub or separate wheel hub (according to model) can now be refitted to the axle spindle. Before fitting into position, first check that the brake surface area in the drum is free of grease and oil. Locate the drum/hub into position, then fit a new retaining nut. Tighten it to the specified torque wrench setting whilst simultaneously rotating the assembly to ensure that the bearings are correctly seated.

16 Carefully tap the new hub grease cap into position in a progressive manner around its outer edge until it is fully fitted.

Pre-1996 models

17 Refit the rubber blanking plug to the brake backplate, and firmly apply the footbrake a few times to take up the brake adjustment. Check that the rear brakes do not bind when the brakes are released. Refit the roadwheel, lower the vehicle and then tighten the retaining nuts to the specified torque setting.

1996-on models

18 Refit the rubber blanking plug to the brake backplate. Adjust the handbrake cable, as described in Chapter 1, and firmly apply the footbrake a few times to take up the brake adjustment. Check that the rear brakes do not bind when the brakes are released. Refit the roadwheel, lower the vehicle and then tighten the retaining nuts to the specified torque setting.

10 Rear strut (Hatchback and Saloon models) – removal and refitting

Removal

1 Chock the front wheels, then jack up the rear of the car and support it on axle stands (see *Jacking and vehicle support*). Remove the inner wheel arch trim.

2 On ABS-equipped models, unscrew the retaining nut and detach the load-apportioning valve connecting link (where fitted) from the axle beam.

3 Unscrew and remove the securing bolt from the strut-to-axle mounting **(see illustration)**.

4 Prise free the protective cap from the top of the shock absorber mounting, located in the luggage compartment **(see illustration)**.

5 Unscrew and remove the two retaining nuts to detach the strut from its upper mounting. **Do not** unscrew the central (horizontal) upper mounting through-bolt and nut, or the spring could be uncontrollably released.

6 Withdraw the suspension strut from the vehicle.

Refitting

7 Refitting is a reversal of the removal procedure, but note the following points:
a) With the suspension strut located to its upper mounting, tighten the retaining nuts to the specified torque wrench setting.
b) When reconnecting the suspension strut to the lower mounting, hand-tighten the retaining bolt, then lower the vehicle so that it is standing on its wheels before fully tightening the bolt to its specified torque.

11 Rear strut (Hatchback and Saloon models) – dismantling, examination and reassembly

⚠ *Warning: Before attempting to dismantle the suspension strut, a suitable tool to hold the coil spring in compression must be obtained. Adjustable coil spring compressors which can be positively secured to the spring coils are readily available, and are recommended for this operation. Any attempt to dismantle the strut without such a tool is likely to result in damage or personal injury.*

Dismantling

1 With the strut removed from the vehicle, clean away all external dirt, then secure it in a vice.

2 Fit the spring compressor tool (ensuring that it is fully engaged) and compress the coil spring until all tension is relieved from the upper mounting.

3 Unscrew and remove the upper mounting through-bolt and nut **(see illustration)**.

4 Withdraw the upper mounting cup and the spring seat.

5 The suspension strut and coil spring can now be separated. If the coil spring or strut is

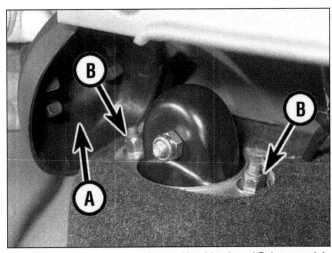

10.4 Rear strut upper mounting on Hatchback and Saloon models showing the protective cap (A) and the mounting nuts (B)

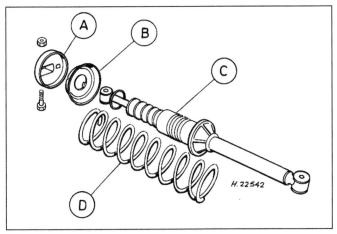

11.3 Rear strut components as fitted to Hatchback and Saloon models

A Upper mounting cup   C Suspension strut
B Spring seat   D Spring

to be renewed, the original coil spring must be released from the compressor. If it is to be re-used, the coil spring can be left in compression.

Examination

6 With the strut assembly now completely dismantled, examine all components for wear, damage or deformation. Renew any of the components as necessary.
7 Examine the strut for signs of fluid leakage. Check the strut piston for signs of pitting along its entire length, and check the strut body for signs of damage or elongation of the mounting bolt holes. Test the operation of the strut, holding it in an upright position, by moving the piston through a full stroke, and then through short strokes of 50 to 100 mm. In both cases, the resistance felt should be smooth and continuous. If the resistance is jerky, or uneven, or if there is any visible sign of wear or damage to the strut, renewal is necessary.

Reassembly

8 Reassembly is a reversal of the dismantling procedure but note the following points:
 a) When the spring is located over the suspension strut, the spring seat, cup and through-bolt fitted, tighten the retaining bolt to the specified torque setting.
 b) When reassembled, check that the upper and lower spring tails are correctly engaged with their spring seats before removing the spring compressor.

12 Rear axle (Hatchback, Saloon and Estate models) – removal and refitting

Removal

1 Chock the front wheels, and loosen the rear roadwheel nuts. Jack up the rear of the car and support it on axle stands (see *Jacking and vehicle support*). Remove the rear roadwheels.
2 Refer to Chapter 9 for details, and disconnect the handbrake cable equaliser from the primary cable. Detach the non-adjustable cable circlip and the cable from the underbody fastenings.
3 Disconnect the rear brake flexible hydraulic brake hoses from their rigid line connections. Clamp the hoses before disconnecting them, to minimise the fluid loss and air entry into the hydraulic system.
4 On ABS-equipped models, undo the retaining nut and detach the ABS load-apportioning valve (where fitted) from the axle beam. Do not remove the load-apportioning valve (see Chapter 9, Section 25).

Hatchback and Saloon models

5 Locate suitable jacks or axle stands under the axle beam to support its weight (not to lift it), then unscrew the mounting bracket bolts each side **(see illustration)**.

6 Unscrew and remove the strut-to-axle mounting bolt each side.
7 Check that all associated fittings are clear, then lower the axle and remove it from under the vehicle.
8 If the twist beam axle has been damaged, it must be renewed. Refer to Chapter 9 for details on removing the rear brakes from the axle. To remove the front mounting/pivot brackets from the axle, unscrew the pivot bolt.

Estate models

9 Position a jack under the coil spring area of the suspension arm (not under the axle beam) each side, and raise them so that they just take the weight of the trailing arms.
10 Unscrew and remove the shock absorber retaining bolt from the lower attachment point to the rear axle each side.
11 Slowly lower the jack under the suspension arm each side, and allow the trailing arms to drop and the compression in the coil springs to be released.
12 With the coil springs fully relaxed, withdraw them from their mounting locations between the body and the suspension arms. As they are removed, mark each for its direction of fitting and side so that they are refitted to their original locations.
13 Reposition the jacks, or place axle stands under the axle beam to support its weight (not to lift it), then unscrew the mounting bracket bolts each side.
14 Check that all associated fittings are clear, then lower the axle and remove it from under the vehicle.
15 If the twist beam axle has been damaged, it must be renewed. Refer to Chapter 9 for details on removing the rear brakes from the axle. To remove the front mounting/pivot brackets from the axle, unscrew the pivot bolt.

Refitting

16 Refitting is a reversal of the removal procedure, but note the following:
 a) Reconnect the axle at the front floor mountings first, and tighten the retaining bolts to the specified torque setting.
 b) On Hatchback and Saloon models, reconnect the axle to the suspension struts, but do not fully retighten the securing bolts until after the vehicle is lowered to the ground and is standing on its wheels.
 c) On Estate models, when relocating the coil springs between the body and the suspension arm each side, ensure that they are correctly orientated, and that their tails abut against the stops. When the coil springs are correctly located, raise the jacks under the suspension arms, and reconnect the shock absorber each side.
 d) Ensure that all brake fluid line connections are clean before reconnecting them. Refer to the appropriate Sections in Chapter 9 for specific details on reconnecting the brake lines, bleeding the brake hydraulic

system, and for reconnecting the handbrake cable and its adjustment.
 e) When the vehicle is lowered and is standing on its wheels, tighten the suspension fastenings to the specified torque wrench settings.

13 Rear axle pivot bushes (Hatchback, Saloon and Estate models) – renewal

1 Chock the front wheels, then jack up the rear of the car and support it on axle stands (see *Jacking and vehicle support*).
2 Position a suitable support (preferably adjustable) under the axle twist beam so that it is capable of carrying the weight of the axle (not the weight of the vehicle).
3 Unscrew the nuts and pivot bolts, then lower the rear axle so that the bushes are clear of their mounting brackets. Take care not to allow the brake pipes to become distorted and stretched – if necessary, disconnect the hydraulic lines (see Chapter 9 for details).
4 Using a steel tube of suitable diameter, various flat washers and a long bolt and nut, draw the bush out of its location in the axle arm.
5 Clean the bush eye in the axle arm; lubricate it, and the new bush, with a soapy solution (washing-up liquid, for example) prior to installation.
6 Locate the new bush in position, together with the steel tube, washers, bolt and nut as used for removal. Ensure that the bush flange is positioned on the outside, then draw the bush fully into position so that its lip is engaged.
7 Raise the axle to reposition the bush pin bores in line with the bolt holes in the mounting brackets, then insert the pivot bolts. Screw the retaining nuts into position on the pivot bolts, but do not fully tighten them at this stage.
8 If necessary, reconnect the brake lines, then bleed the braking system as described in Chapter 9.
9 Lower the vehicle to the ground, then tighten the rear axle pivot bolts nuts to the specified torque wrench setting.

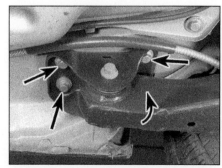

12.5 Rear axle forward mounting bolts (arrowed)

14.3 Rear shock absorber-to-axle mounting (Estate models)

14 Rear shock absorber (Estate and Van models) – removal, testing and refitting

Removal

1 Chock the front wheels, and loosen the relevant rear roadwheel nuts. Jack up the rear of the car and support it on axle stands (see *Jacking and vehicle support*). Remove the appropriate rear roadwheel.

2 On Estate models, position a jack under the coil spring area of the suspension arm (not under the axle beam), and raise it to just take the weight of the suspension.

3 Unscrew and remove the shock absorber retaining bolt from the lower mounting **(see illustration)**.

4 On Estate models, unscrew the retaining nuts securing the shock absorber top mounting on the underside of the body (from underneath) and withdraw the shock absorber **(see illustration)**.

5 On Van models, unscrew and remove the four shock absorber upper mounting bracket-to-body retaining bolts **(see illustration)**. Remove the shock absorber and its upper mounting bracket from the vehicle. To disconnect the shock absorber from the mounting bracket, unscrew the retaining nut, withdraw the through-bolt and remove the shock absorber from the bracket.

Testing

6 Mount the shock absorber in a vice, gripping it by the lower mounting. Check the

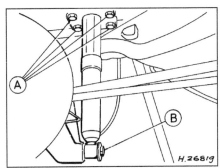

14.5 Shock absorber upper (A) and lower (B) mountings on Van models

14.4 Rear shock absorber upper mounting (Estate models)

mounting rubbers for damage and deterioration. Examine the shock absorber for signs of fluid leakage. Extend the shock absorber, then check the piston for signs of pitting along its entire length. Check the body for signs of damage or elongation of the mounting bolt holes. Test the operation of the shock absorber, by moving the piston through a full stroke, and then through short strokes of 50 to 100 mm. In both cases, the resistance felt should be smooth and continuous. If the resistance is jerky, or uneven, or if there is any visible sign of wear or damage to the strut, renewal of the complete is necessary.

Refitting

7 Refitting is a reversal of removal procedure. Tighten the retaining nuts and bolts to the specified torque wrench settings (where given), then lower the vehicle to the ground.

15 Rear coil springs (Estate models) – removal and refitting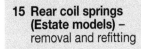

Removal

1 Chock the front wheels, and loosen the rear roadwheel nuts. Jack up the rear of the car and support it on axle stands (see *Jacking and vehicle support*). Remove the rear roadwheels.

2 Position a jack under the coil spring area of the suspension arm (not under the axle beam) each side, and raise them so that they just take the weight of the trailing arms.

3 Unscrew and remove the shock absorber

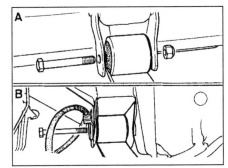

16.5 Leaf spring rear (A) and front (B) locations and securing bolts

retaining bolt from the lower attachment point to the rear axle each side.

4 Slowly lower the jack under the suspension arm each side, and allow the trailing arms to drop and the compression in the coil springs to be released. Check that no excessive strain is imposed on the handbrake cables and/or the hydraulic hoses to the rear brakes. Disconnect them as described in Chapter 9 if necessary.

5 With the coil springs fully relaxed, withdraw them from their mounting locations between the body and the suspension arms. As they are removed, mark each for its direction of fitting and side, so that they are refitted to their original locations (where applicable).

Refitting

6 Refitting is a reversal of the removal procedure but note the following points:
a) *When relocating the coil springs between the body and the suspension arm each side, ensure that they are correctly orientated, and that their tails abut against the stops.*
b) *When the coil springs are correctly located, raise the jacks under the suspension arms, and reconnect the shock absorber each side.*
c) *Tighten the retaining bolts to the specified torque setting.*
d) *If the brake cables and/or the hydraulic hoses were detached, refer to Chapter 9 for the reconnecting details, and to bleed the hydraulic system.*

16 Rear leaf spring, shackle and bushes (Van models) – removal, inspection and refitting

Removal

1 Chock the front wheels, and loosen the relevant rear roadwheel nuts. Jack up the rear of the vehicle and support it on axle stands (see *Jacking and vehicle support*). Remove the appropriate rear roadwheel.

2 Position a jack under the rear axle, then raise the jack to support the weight of the axle, and to take the loading from the front and rear spring mountings.

3 Unscrew and remove the shock absorber lower mounting bolt, and detach the shock absorber from its mounting bracket.

4 Unscrew and remove the spring-to-axle U-bolt retaining nuts, and remove the U-bolts. Remove the counterplate and the bump stop from the top of the spring.

5 Unscrew and remove the mounting bolt and nut from the rear spring shackle **(see illustration)**.

6 Unscrew and remove the retaining nut or bolt (as applicable) from the front mounting. Withdraw the mounting bolt (noting the flat washer fitted under the bolt head), then lower the jack under the axle just enough to allow the spring to be removed. Carefully withdraw the spring from the vehicle.

Inspection

7 If the spring mounting (shackle) bolts are noticeably worn, they must be renewed. If the spring eye bushes are worn and in need of replacement, they can be withdrawn using a suitable drawbolt and spacer. New bushes can be pressed into position in the spring eye using a vice (or press).

8 If required, the rear spring shackle can be removed by unscrewing the retaining nut, removing the inboard shackle plate and withdrawing the outboard shackle plate complete with the upper shackle stud. The upper split type bushes must be renewed if they are worn.

Refitting

9 Refit the rear shackle, and initially hand-tighten the shackle bolt and nut.

10 Relocate the spring over the axle, align the front spring eye with the mounting, and insert the bolt. Loosely secure the bolt (and where applicable, the nut) at this stage.

11 Align the rear spring eye with the shackle at the rear, and loosely fit the mounting bolt and nut.

12 Locate the counterplate and bump stop on the top of the spring over the axle, then refit the U-bolts and fit the retaining nuts. The jack under the axle may need to be raised to enable the U-bolt assemblies to be relocated.

13 Reconnect the shock absorber to the rear axle, then tighten the various fixings to their specified torque wrench settings.

14 Refit the roadwheel, and lower the vehicle to the ground.

17 Rear axle (Van models) – removal and refitting
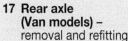

Removal

1 Chock the front wheels, and loosen the rear roadwheel nuts. Jack up the rear of the vehicle and support it on axle stands (see *Jacking and vehicle support*). Remove the rear roadwheels.

2 Position a single jack centrally (or preferably, two jacks each side of centre) under the axle beam, and raise to just take the weight of the axle – do not lift the vehicle.

18.3 Remove the outer horn pad from the centre of the steering wheel

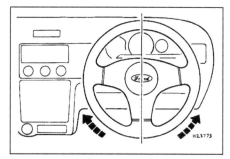

18.2 Steering wheel alignment – centralised within a tolerance of 30° each side of vertical

3 Clamp the hydraulic hoses of the light-laden valve, to prevent excessive fluid loss and the ingress of air and dirt into the hydraulic system, then disconnect the hydraulic lines to the light-laden valve and remove the clips.

4 Refer to Chapter 9 for details, and remove the brake drum/hubs and then the backplate from the rear axle on each side. The backplates may be left attached to the axle, but it will still be necessary to detach the wheel cylinder brake line, and also to disconnect and withdraw the handbrake cable from each rear brake backplate. As each assembly is removed, keep them separated, and mark them to identify the right- and left-hand assemblies. Note that they are 'handed', and must not be confused or they could be incorrectly refitted later.

5 Unscrew and remove the shock absorber lower fixing bolts, and detach them from the rear axle.

6 Unscrew and remove the axle-to-leaf spring U-bolt retaining nuts, remove the U-bolts, then carefully lower the axle and remove it from under the vehicle.

Refitting

7 Refitting is a reversal of the removal procedure, but note the following:
a) *Reconnect the axle to the spring, reconnect the U-bolts and the shock absorbers to the axle on each side, and then tighten the retaining bolts to the specified torque wrench settings.*
b) *Refer to the appropriate Sections in*

18.4 Prise free the inner horn pad and detach the wires

Chapter 9 to refit the brake backplate and brake assemblies, and ensure that they are correctly located according to side.
c) *Ensure that all brake fluid line connections are clean before reconnecting them. Refer to the appropriate Sections in Chapter 9 for specific details on reconnecting the brake lines, bleeding the brake hydraulic system, and reconnecting the handbrake cable. Details of handbrake adjustment will be found in Chapter 1.*

18 Steering wheel – removal and refitting

Removal

Models without air bag

1 Disconnect the battery negative (earth) lead (refer to Chapter 5A, Section 1).

2 Turn the ignition key to release the steering lock, then set the front roadwheels in the straight-ahead position. With the steering centralised, the steering wheel should be positioned as shown **(see illustration)**. Move the ignition key to the OFF position.

3 Prise free the outer pad from the centre of the steering wheel **(see illustration)**.

4 Prise free the inner horn pad **(see illustration)**, then note the connections and detach the horn wiring at the spade connectors (these differ in size to ensure correct refitting). Once the wiring is free, withdraw the inner horn pad. As it is withdrawn, note that it has a directional arrow mark which points up when the steering wheel is in the straight-ahead position.

5 Unscrew the retaining bolt from the centre of the steering wheel, then gripping the wheel each side, pull and withdraw it from the column shaft **(see illustrations)**.

 HAYNES HiNT *If the wheel is tight, tap it up near the centre, using the palm of your hand, or twist it from side to side, whilst pulling upwards to release it from the shaft splines.*

18.5a . . . unscrew the retaining bolt . . .

18.5b . . . and withdraw the steering wheel

Models with air bag

⚠ *Warning: Handle the air bag with extreme care as a precaution against personal injury, and always hold it with the cover facing away from your body. If in doubt concerning any proposed work involving the air bag or its control circuitry, consult a Ford dealer or other qualified specialist.*

6 Disconnect the battery negative (earth) lead (refer to Chapter 5A, Section 1).

⚠ *Warning: Before proceeding, wait a minimum of 15 minutes, as a precaution against accidental firing of the air bag. This period ensures that any stored energy in the back-up capacitor is dissipated.*

7 Undo the two screws, and remove the steering column upper shroud.

8 Turn the steering wheel as necessary so that one of the air bag retaining bolts becomes accessible from the rear of the steering wheel. Undo the bolt, then turn the steering wheel again until the second bolt is accessible. Undo this bolt also.

9 Withdraw the air bag from the steering wheel far enough to access the wiring multi-plug. Some force may be needed to free the

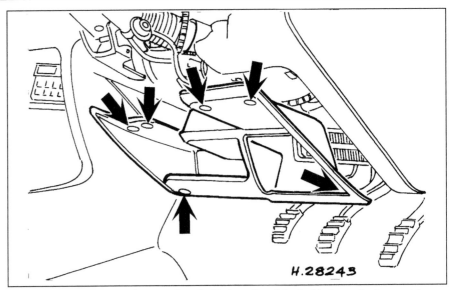

18.12 Undo the screws (arrowed) and withdraw the detachable lower facia panel from beneath the steering column

air bag from the additional steering wheel spoke retainers.

10 Disconnect the multi-plug from the rear of the air bag, and remove the air bag from the vehicle.

⚠ *Warning: Position the air bag module in a safe place, with the mechanism facing downwards as a precaution against accidental operation.*

11 Undo the four screws, and remove the steering column lower shroud.

12 Undo the screws and withdraw the detachable lower facia panel from beneath the steering column **(see illustration)**.

13 Where applicable, undo the single screw and withdraw the Passive Anti-Theft System (PATS) transceiver from the ignition switch/steering lock barrel **(see illustration)**.

14 Release the steering column wiring harness from the retaining clips, and

disconnect the air bag control module wiring harness multi-plug **(see illustration)**.

15 Turn the steering wheel so the roadwheels are in the straight-ahead position, then remove the ignition key to lock the steering.

16 Unscrew the retaining bolt from the centre of the steering wheel, then insert the ignition key and turn it to position I. Grip the steering wheel each side, then pull and withdraw it from the column shaft.

Refitting

17 Refit in the reverse order of removal. Ensure that the indicator stalk is set in its central (off) position, to avoid damaging it with the tag of the wheel as it is pushed down the shaft. Make sure the wheel is centralised, as noted on removal. Turn the ignition key to position I (steering unlocked). Tighten the retaining bolt to the specified torque.

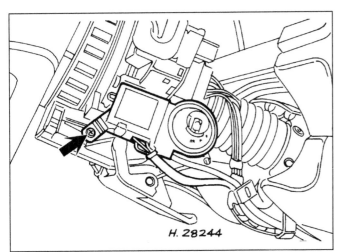

18.13 Undo the screw (arrowed) and withdraw the Passive Anti-Theft System (PATS) transceiver from the ignition switch/steering lock barrel

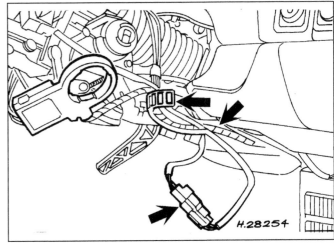

18.14 Release the steering column wiring harness and multi-plug as indicated

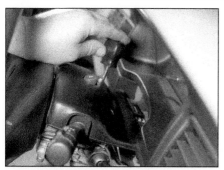

19.3a Remove the upper . . .

19.3b . . . and lower column shrouds

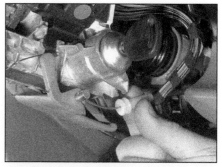

19.6 Detach the bonnet release cable from the lever

19 Steering column –
removal and refitting

Removal

1 Disconnect the battery negative (earth) lead (refer to Chapter 5A, Section 1).
2 Remove the steering wheel as described in the previous Section.
3 Remove the screws and withdraw the steering column upper and lower shrouds **(see illustrations)**.
4 Remove the multi-function switch assembly from the column, referring to Chapter 12.
5 Disconnect the ignition switch multi-plug, and release the wiring from the wiring loom guide.
6 Detach the bonnet release cable from the lever, then remove the lever from the column **(see illustration)**.
7 Unscrew and remove the clamp bolt securing the steering column to the pinion shaft.
8 Loosen off the column lower retaining nuts, then unscrew and remove the upper retaining nuts. Remove the steering column from the vehicle.

Refitting

9 Refitting is a reversal of the removal procedure, but note the following:
a) Tighten the respective retaining bolts to their specified torque settings.
b) Check that the steering is centralised with the wheels in the straight-ahead position

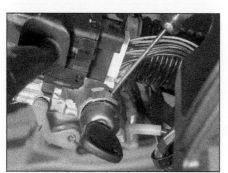

20.3 Releasing the steering lock

before refitting the steering wheel as described in Section 18.
c) Refit the steering wheel before securing the steering column coupling to the pinion shaft with the clamp bolt.
d) Ensure that the wiring connections are securely made. On completion, check for satisfactory operation of the steering, the column switches and the horn.

20 Steering column –
dismantling and reassembly

Dismantling

1 Remove the steering column as described in the previous Section, then securely locate it in a vice fitted with protective jaws.
2 Remove the upper thrust bearing tolerance ring from the column, then withdraw the column shaft from the column tube.
3 Insert the ignition key into the lock/switch, and turn it to the I position. Now use a small screwdriver or a suitable rod to depress the plunger in the side of the barrel, and simultaneously pull on the key to withdraw the lock/switch from the column **(see illustration)**.
4 Withdraw the spring from the column shaft.
5 Prise free the lower and upper thrust bearings from the column tube and the lock/switch body.
6 To remove the steering column height adjuster (where fitted) unscrew the through-bolt and locknut, remove the handle and lockplates, then remove the adjuster from the column.
7 If any part of the steering column (and in particular, the universal joints) is found to be excessively worn, or if any part of the column assembly has been damaged, it must be renewed; no repairs are possible.

Reassembly

8 Reassembly is a reversal of the dismantling procedure, but note the following points:
a) When refitting the height adjuster, coat the threads of the through-bolt with Loctite, and locate the handle in the locked position. Tighten the retaining bolt and nut to the specified torque setting.

b) Take care when fitting the lower thrust bearing into the column tube and the upper bearing to the steering lock/ignition switch body.
c) When fitting the steering column lock/ignition switch, ensure that the key is in the I position. As the switch/lock is fitted into its barrel, it may be necessary to move the key clockwise and anti-clockwise slightly, to enable the housing drive to align with the barrel and fully engage.
d) When assembling the column shaft to the tube, ensure that the upper thrust bearing tolerance ring is fitted with its tapered face towards the bearing.

21 Steering gear rubber gaiters
– renewal

1 Remove the track rod end balljoint and its locknut from the track rod (see Section 26).
2 Release the clip(s), and slide the gaiter off the rack-and-pinion housing and track rod **(see illustration)**.
3 Scrape off all grease from the old gaiter, and apply to the track rod inner joint. Wipe clean the seating areas on the rack-and-pinion housing and track rod.
4 Slide the new gaiter onto the housing and track rod, and tighten the clip(s).
5 Refit the track rod end balljoint as described in Section 26.

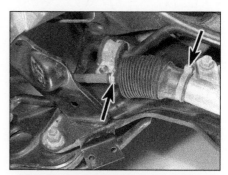

21.2 Steering gear gaiter and retaining clips (arrowed)

22 Steering gear (manual steering) – removal and refitting

Removal

1 Disconnect the battery negative (earth) lead (refer to Chapter 5A, Section 1).
2 Refer to Section 8 for details, and remove the subframe from the vehicle as described. Note that complete removal of the subframe may not be necessary if it is carefully lowered to allow access to the steering gear for its separation and withdrawal.
3 Unscrew and remove the two steering gear-to-subframe retaining bolts, then withdraw the assembly from the vehicle (see illustrations).

Refitting

4 Refit the steering gear to the subframe in the reverse order of removal, and tighten the retaining bolts to the specified torque setting.
5 Refer to Section 8 for the relevant details on refitting the subframe assembly to the vehicle.

23 Steering gear (power-assisted steering) – removal and refitting

Removal

1 Disconnect the battery negative (earth) lead (refer to Chapter 5A, Section 1).
2 Refer to Section 8 and proceed as described in paragraphs 1 to 12 inclusive, then proceed as follows.
3 Undo the retaining screws, and detach the clips securing the power steering hydraulic pressure pipes to the steering gear.
4 Position a suitable container under the hydraulic pipe connections to the steering gear. Unscrew the bolt securing the hydraulic valve clamp plate to the valve body on the steering rack, then detach the pipes from the valve body. Withdraw the pipes from the steering gear, and drain the hydraulic fluid into the container (see illustration).
5 Plug the exposed ends of the hydraulic line

22.3a Steering gear bolt (arrowed) to the subframe on the right-hand side

connections, to prevent the ingress of dirt and further fluid loss. Note that new O-ring seals will be needed for the pressure and return hose connections when reconnecting.
6 Locate suitable jacks or blocks under the subframe to support it, then unscrew and remove the eight subframe fixing bolts (see illustration 8.14). Lower the support jacks or blocks, and withdraw the subframe. As it is lowered, disengage the steering gear shaft from the column. Note that complete removal of the subframe from the vehicle may not be necessary if it is carefully lowered to allow access to the steering gear for its separation and withdrawal.
7 Unscrew and remove the two steering gear-to-subframe retaining bolts, then withdraw the from the vehicle.

Refitting

8 Refit the steering gear to the subframe in the reverse order of removal, and tighten the retaining bolts to the specified torque setting.
9 Refer to Section 8 for the relevant details, and refit the subframe assembly to the vehicle. When the subframe is loosely in position, remove the temporary plugs from the hydraulic fluid lines, and check that the connections are clean. Fit new O-ring seals to the pressure and return hoses, then reconnect the hydraulic lines to the steering gear. Check that the hydraulic lines and fixings are secure, then continue refitting the steering gear and subframe as described in Section 8.
10 On completion, top-up the power steering fluid reservoir and bleed the system as

22.3b Steering gear bolt (arrowed) to the subframe on the left-hand side

described in Section 25. Check for any signs of fluid leakage from the system hoses and connections. Finally, have the front wheel toe setting checked (see Section 27).

24 Power-assisted steering pump – removal and refitting

Removal

1 Gain access to the power steering pump auxiliary drivebelt, using the information in Chapter 1. Loosen the three pump pulley securing bolts (the pulley can be held stationary using a 9 mm Allen key in the pulley hub), then remove the drivebelt and take off the pulley.
2 Position a suitable container beneath the power steering pump, then release the hose clip securing the low-pressure fluid hose, and disconnect the hose from the pump (see illustration). Allow the fluid to drain from the hoses (and the pump) into the container.
3 Unscrew the high-pressure fluid union, again taking precautions against fluid spillage, and separate the pipe from the pump (see illustration). Plug the exposed ends of the hydraulic hoses and the pump connections, to prevent the ingress of dirt and excessive fluid loss.
4 Support the pump, then unscrew the four mounting bolts (three in front, one behind) and remove the pump from the vehicle (see illustration).

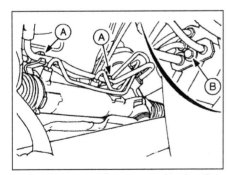

23.4 Power steering gear and hydraulic pipe connections

A Hydraulic pipe locating clips
B Valve clamp plate bolt

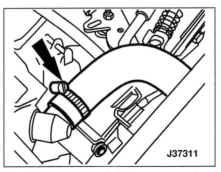

24.2 Low-pressure fluid hose connection (arrowed) – later-type pump

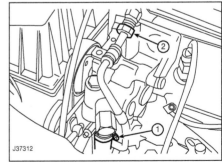

24.3 Low-pressure (1) and high-pressure (2) fluid pipe connections – early-type pump

Refitting

5 Refitting is a reversal of removal, noting the following points:
  a) *Fit the three pump front mounting bolts before the single rear one.*
  b) *Remove the plugs from the pipes, and ensure that the pipes are located correctly so that they do not foul any surrounding components.*
  c) *Tighten all nuts and bolts, and the high-pressure union, to the specified torque.*
  d) *Refit the pump pulley, using the Allen key to hold the pulley as the bolts are tightened, then refit and tension the drivebelt as described in Chapter 1.*
  e) *On completion, fill the power steering system with the specified fluid up to the maximum level mark, and bleed the system as described in Section 25. Check for any signs of fluid leakage from the system hoses and connections.*

25 Power-assisted steering system – bleeding

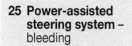

1 This will normally only be required if any part of the hydraulic system has been disconnected.
2 Referring to *Weekly checks*, remove the fluid reservoir filler cap, and top-up with the specified fluid to the maximum level mark.
3 Start the engine and allow it to idle, slowly moving the steering from lock-to-lock four times to purge out the air, then top-up the level in the fluid reservoir. Add the fluid slowly, to prevent the possibility of aeration of the fluid in the circuit.
4 Switch the engine off, then recheck the fluid level in the reservoir, and further top-up if necessary. Finally check the system hoses and connections for any signs of fluid leaks, which if found, must be rectified.

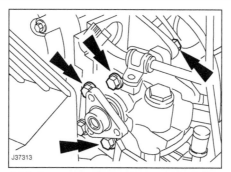

24.4 Power steering pump mounting bolts (arrowed)

26 Track rod end balljoint – removal and refitting

Removal

1 Apply the handbrake, then jack up the front of the vehicle and support it on axle stands. Remove the appropriate front roadwheel.
2 Using a suitable spanner, slacken the track rod end balljoint locknut on the track rod by a quarter of a turn **(see illustration)**. Hold the balljoint stationary with another spanner engaged with the flats at its inner end to prevent it from turning.
3 Extract the split pin, then loosen off the retaining nut. If the balljoint is to be renewed, the nut can be fully removed. If the existing balljoint is to be reconnected, the nut should be slackened off a couple of turns only at first, and left in position to protect the joint threads as the joint is separated from the spindle carrier. To release the tapered shank of the joint from the spindle carrier, use a balljoint separator tool as shown **(see illustration)**. If the joint is to be re-used, take care not to damage the rubber dust cover when using a separator tool.

4 Count the number of exposed threads visible on the inner section of the track rod, and record this figure.
5 Unscrew the balljoint from the track rod, counting the number of turns necessary to remove it.

Refitting

6 Screw the balljoint into the track rod the number of turns noted during removal until the balljoint just contacts the locknut. Now tighten the locknut while holding the balljoint.
7 Engage the shank of the balljoint with the spindle carrier arm, and refit the locknut. Tighten the locknut to the specified torque.

HAYNES HiNT *If the balljoint shank turns while the locknut is being tightened, lever down on the top of the balljoint with a stout bar. The tapered fit of the shank will lock it and prevent rotation as the nut is tightened.*

8 Refit the roadwheel, and lower the vehicle to the ground.
9 Finally, have the front wheel toe setting checked (see Section 28).

27 Wheel alignment and steering angles – general information

General

1 A car's steering and suspension geometry is defined in four basic settings – all angles are expressed in degrees (toe settings are also expressed as a measurement); the relevant settings are camber, castor, steering axis inclination, and toe-setting. With the exception of front wheel toe-setting, none of these settings are adjustable.

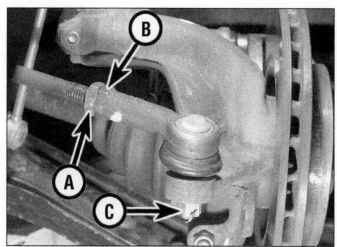

26.2 Track rod end balljoint showing the locknut (A) retaining flats (B) and the balljoint-to-spindle carrier arm retaining nut and split pin (C)

26.3 Balljoint separator tool in position. Note that the nut should be left loosely in position when the thread of the joint is to be protected for re-use

Front wheel toe setting

2 Due to the special measuring equipment necessary to accurately check the wheel alignment, and the skill required to use it properly, checking and adjustment is best left to a Ford dealer or similar expert. Note that most tyre-fitting shops now possess sophisticated checking equipment. The following is provided as a guide, should the owner decide to carry out a DIY check.

3 The front wheel toe setting is checked by measuring the distance between the front and rear inside edges of the roadwheel rims. Proprietary toe measurement gauges are available from motor accessory shops. Adjustment is made by screwing the track rods in or out of their track rod end balljoints, to alter the effective length of the track rod assemblies.

4 For **accurate** checking, the vehicle **must** be at the kerb weight, ie unladen and with a full tank of fuel.

5 Before starting work, check the tyre pressures and tread wear, the condition of the hub bearings, the steering wheel free play, and the condition of the front suspension components (see Chapter 1). Correct any faults found.

6 Park the vehicle on level ground, check that the front roadwheels are in the straight-ahead position, then rock the rear and front ends to settle the suspension. Release the handbrake, and roll the vehicle backwards 1 metre, then forwards again, to relieve any stresses in the steering and suspension components.

7 Measure the distance between the front edges of the wheel rims and the rear edges of the rims. Subtract the smallest measurement from the largest, and check that the result is within the specified range.

8 If adjustment is necessary, apply the handbrake, then jack up the front of the vehicle and support it securely on axle stands (see *Jacking and vehicle support*). Turn the steering wheel onto full-left lock, and record the number of exposed threads on the right-hand track rod. Now turn the steering onto full-right lock, and record the number of threads on the left-hand side. If there are the same number of threads visible on both sides, then subsequent adjustment should be made equally on both sides. If there are more threads visible on one side than the other, it will be necessary to compensate for this during adjustment. **Note:** *It is most important that after adjustment, the same number of threads are visible on each track rod end.*

9 First clean the track rod end threads; if they are corroded, apply penetrating fluid before starting adjustment. Release the rubber gaiter outboard clips (where necessary), and peel back the gaiter; apply a smear of grease to the inside of the gaiter, so that both are free, and will not be twisted or strained as their respective track rods are rotated.

10 Use a straight-edge and a scriber or similar to mark the relationship of each track rod to its track rod end balljoint, then, holding each track rod in turn, unscrew its locknut fully.

11 Alter the length of the track rods, bearing in mind the note made in paragraph 8. Screw them into or out of the track rod end balljoints, rotating the track rods using a self-grip wrench. Shortening the track rods (screwing them into their track rod end balljoints) will reduce toe-in/increase toe-out.

12 When the setting is correct, hold the track rods and securely tighten the track rod end balljoint locknuts. Count the exposed threads to check the length of both track rods. If they are not the same, then the adjustment has not been made equally, and problems will be encountered with tyre scrubbing in turns; also, the steering wheel spokes will no longer be horizontal when the wheels are in the straight-ahead position.

13 If the track rod lengths are the same, lower the vehicle to the ground and re-check the toe setting; re-adjust if necessary. When the setting is correct, tighten the track rod end balljoint locknuts to the specified torque setting. Ensure that the rubber gaiters are seated correctly, and are not twisted or strained, and secure them in position with new retaining clips (where necessary).

Chapter 11
Bodywork and fittings

Contents

Degrees of difficulty

Easy, suitable for novice with little experience	Fairly easy, suitable for beginner with some experience	Fairly difficult, suitable for competent DIY mechanic	Difficult, suitable for experienced DIY mechanic	Very difficult, suitable for expert DIY or professional

Specifications

Torque wrench settings	Nm	lbf ft
Bonnet hinge bolts	10	7
Bonnet latch bolts	10	7
Boot lid hinge bolts	24	18
Boot lid latch screws	10	7
Boot lid striker screws	10	7
Front seat belt height adjuster bolt	35	26
Front seat slide to floor	25	18
Front seat slide to frame nuts	25	18
Seat belt anchor bolts	38	28
Seat belt lower anchorage rail securing bolt	38	28
Tailgate hinge bolts	24	18
Tailgate lock screws	10	7
Tailgate striker screws	10	7

1 General information

The bodyshell and underframe on all models is of all-steel welded construction, incorporating progressive crumple zones at the front and rear, and a rigid centre safety cell. The body style range is comprehensive, and includes the 3- and 5-door Hatchback, the 4-door Saloon, the 5-door Estate, and the Van.

A multi-stage anti-corrosion process is applied to all new vehicles. This includes zinc phosphating on some panels, the injection of wax into boxed sections, and a wax and PVC coating applied to the underbody for its protection.

Inertia reel seat belts are fitted to all models, and from the 1994 model year onwards, the front seat belt stalks are mounted on automatic mechanical tensioners (also known as 'grabbers'). In the event of a serious front impact, a spring mass sensor releases a coil spring which pulls the stalk buckle downwards and tensions the seat belt. It is not possible to reset the tensioner once fired, and it must therefore be renewed. Later models may alternatively be fitted with pyrotechnic front seat belt tensioners. These units are activated by the air bag control module and tension the front seat belts by means of a contained explosive charge which operates within the seat belt mechanism.

Central locking is a standard or optional fitment on all models. Where double-locking is also fitted, the lock mechanism is disconnected (when the system is in use) from the interior door handles, making it impossible to open any of the doors or the tailgate/boot lid from inside the vehicle. This means that, even if a thief should break a side window, it will not be possible to open the door using the interior handle.

2 Maintenance – bodywork and underframe

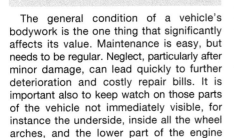

The general condition of a vehicle's bodywork is the one thing that significantly affects its value. Maintenance is easy, but needs to be regular. Neglect, particularly after minor damage, can lead quickly to further deterioration and costly repair bills. It is important also to keep watch on those parts of the vehicle not immediately visible, for instance the underside, inside all the wheel arches, and the lower part of the engine compartment.

The basic maintenance routine for the bodywork is washing – preferably with a lot of water, from a hose. This will remove all the loose solids which may have stuck to the vehicle. It is important to flush these off in such a way as to prevent grit from scratching the finish. The wheel arches and underframe need washing in the same way, to remove any accumulated mud, which will retain moisture and tend to encourage rust. Oddly enough, the best time to clean the underframe and wheel arches is in wet weather, when the mud is thoroughly wet and soft. In very wet weather, the underframe is usually cleaned of large accumulations automatically, and this is a good time for inspection.

Periodically, except on vehicles with a wax-based underbody protective coating, it is a good idea to have the whole of the underframe of the vehicle steam-cleaned, engine compartment included, so that a thorough inspection can be carried out to see what minor repairs and renovations are necessary. Steam-cleaning is available at many garages, and is necessary for the removal of the accumulation of oily grime, which sometimes is allowed to become thick in certain areas. If steam-cleaning facilities are not available, there are some excellent grease solvents available which can be brush-applied; the dirt can then be simply hosed off. Note that these methods should not be used on vehicles with wax-based underbody protective coating, or the coating will be removed. Such vehicles should be inspected annually, preferably just prior to Winter, when the underbody should be washed down, and any damage to the wax coating repaired. Ideally, a completely fresh coat should be applied. It would also be worth considering the use of such wax-based protection for injection into door panels, sills, box sections, etc, as an additional safeguard against rust damage, where such protection is not provided by the vehicle manufacturer.

After washing paintwork, wipe off with a chamois leather to give an unspotted clear finish. A coat of clear protective wax polish will give added protection against chemical pollutants in the air. If the paintwork sheen has dulled or oxidised, use a cleaner/polisher combination to restore the brilliance of the shine. This requires a little effort, but such dulling is usually caused because regular washing has been neglected. Care needs to be taken with metallic paintwork, as special non-abrasive cleaner/polisher is required to avoid damage to the finish. Always check that the door and ventilator opening drain holes and pipes are completely clear, so that water can be drained out. Brightwork should be treated in the same way as paintwork. Windscreens and windows can be kept clear of the smeary film which often appears, by the use of proprietary glass cleaner. Never use any form of wax or other body or chromium polish on glass.

3 Maintenance – upholstery and carpets

Mats and carpets should be brushed or vacuum-cleaned regularly, to keep them free of grit. If they are badly stained, remove them from the vehicle for scrubbing or sponging, and make quite sure they are dry before refitting. Seats and interior trim panels can be kept clean by wiping with a damp cloth. If they do become stained (which can be more apparent on light-coloured upholstery), use a little liquid detergent and a soft nail brush to scour the grime out of the grain of the material. Do not forget to keep the headlining clean in the same way as the upholstery. When using liquid cleaners inside the vehicle, do not over-wet the surfaces being cleaned. Excessive damp could get into the seams and padded interior, causing stains, offensive odours or even rot.

Note: *If the inside of the vehicle gets wet accidentally, it is worthwhile taking some trouble to dry it out properly, particularly where carpets are involved.*

⚠ **Warning: Do not leave oil or electric heaters inside the vehicle.**

4 Minor body damage – repair

Repairs of minor scratches in bodywork

If the scratch is very superficial, and does not penetrate to the metal of the bodywork, repair is very simple. Lightly rub the area of the scratch with a paintwork renovator, or a very fine cutting paste, to remove loose paint from the scratch, and to clear the surrounding bodywork of wax polish. Rinse the area with clean water.

Apply touch-up paint to the scratch using a fine paint brush; continue to apply fine layers of paint until the surface of the paint in the scratch is level with the surrounding paintwork. Allow the new paint at least two weeks to harden, then blend it into the surrounding paintwork by rubbing the scratch area with a paintwork renovator or a very fine cutting paste. Finally, apply wax polish.

Where the scratch has penetrated right through to the metal of the bodywork, causing the metal to rust, a different repair technique is required. Remove any loose rust from the bottom of the scratch with a penknife, then apply rust-inhibiting paint to prevent the formation of rust in the future. Using a rubber or nylon applicator, fill the scratch with bodystopper paste. If required, this paste can be mixed with cellulose thinners to provide a very thin paste which is ideal for filling narrow scratches. Before the stopper-paste in the scratch hardens, wrap a piece of smooth cotton rag around the top of a finger. Dip the finger in cellulose thinners, and quickly sweep it across the surface of the stopper-paste in the scratch; this will ensure that the surface of the stopper-paste is slightly hollowed. The scratch can now be painted over as described earlier in this Section.

Repairs of dents in bodywork

When deep denting of the vehicle's bodywork has taken place, the first task is to pull the dent out, until the affected bodywork almost attains its original shape. There is little point in trying to restore the original shape completely, as the metal in the damaged area will have stretched on impact, and cannot be reshaped fully to its original contour. It is better to bring the level of the dent up to a point which is about 3 mm below the level of the surrounding bodywork. In cases where the dent is very shallow anyway, it is not worth trying to pull it out at all. If the underside of the dent is accessible, it can be hammered out gently from behind, using a mallet with a wooden or plastic head. Whilst doing this, hold a suitable block of wood firmly against the outside of the panel, to absorb the impact from the hammer blows and thus prevent a large area of the bodywork from being 'belled-out'.

Should the dent be in a section of the bodywork which has a double skin, or some other factor making it inaccessible from behind, a different technique is called for. Drill several small holes through the metal inside the area – particularly in the deeper section. Then screw long self-tapping screws into the holes, just sufficiently for them to gain a good purchase in the metal. Now the dent can be pulled out by pulling on the protruding heads of the screws with a pair of pliers.

The next stage of the repair is the removal of the paint from the damaged area, and from an inch or so of the surrounding 'sound' bodywork. This is accomplished most easily by using a wire brush or abrasive pad on a power drill, although it can be done just as effectively by hand, using sheets of abrasive paper. To complete the preparation for filling, score the surface of the bare metal with a screwdriver or the tang of a file, or alternatively, drill small holes in the affected area. This will provide a really good 'key' for the filler paste.

To complete the repair, see the Section on filling and respraying.

Repairs of rust holes or gashes in bodywork

Remove all paint from the affected area, and from an inch or so of the surrounding 'sound' bodywork, using an abrasive pad or a wire brush on a power drill. If these are not available, a few sheets of abrasive paper will do the job most effectively. With the paint removed, you will be able to judge the severity of the corrosion, and therefore decide whether to renew the whole panel (if this is possible) or to repair the affected area. New body panels are not as expensive as most people think, and it is often quicker and more satisfactory to fit a new panel than to attempt to repair large areas of corrosion.

Remove all fittings from the affected area, except those which will act as a guide to the original shape of the damaged bodywork (eg headlight shells etc). Then, using tin snips or a hacksaw blade, remove all loose metal and any other metal badly affected by corrosion. Hammer the edges of the hole inwards, in order to create a slight depression for the filler paste.

Wire-brush the affected area to remove the powdery rust from the surface of the remaining metal. Paint the affected area with rust-inhibiting paint, if the back of the rusted area is accessible, treat this also.

Before filling can take place, it will be necessary to block the hole in some way. This can be achieved by the use of aluminium or plastic mesh, or aluminium tape.

Aluminium or plastic mesh, or glass-fibre matting, is probably the best material to use for a large hole. Cut a piece to the approximate size and shape of the hole to be filled, then position it in the hole so that its edges are below the level of the surrounding bodywork. It can be retained in position by several blobs of filler paste around its periphery.

Aluminium tape should be used for small or very narrow holes. Pull a piece off the roll, trim it to the approximate size and shape required, then pull off the backing paper (if used) and stick the tape over the hole; it can be overlapped if the thickness of one piece is insufficient. Burnish down the edges of the tape with the handle of a screwdriver or similar, to ensure that the tape is securely attached to the metal underneath.

Bodywork repairs – filling and respraying

Before using this Section, see the Sections on dent, deep scratch, rust holes and gash repairs.

Many types of bodyfiller are available, but generally speaking, those proprietary kits which contain a tin of filler paste and a tube of resin hardener are best for this type of repair. A wide, flexible plastic or nylon applicator will be found invaluable for imparting a smooth and well-contoured finish to the surface of the filler.

Mix up a little filler on a clean piece of card or board – measure the hardener carefully (follow the maker's instructions on the pack), otherwise the filler will set too rapidly or too slowly. Using the applicator, apply the filler paste to the prepared area; draw the applicator across the surface of the filler to achieve the correct contour and to level the surface. As soon as a contour that approximates to the correct one is achieved, stop working the paste – if you carry on too long, the paste will become sticky and begin to 'pick-up' on the applicator. Continue to add thin layers of filler paste at 20-minute intervals, until the level of the filler is just proud of the surrounding bodywork.

Once the filler has hardened, the excess can be removed using a metal plane or file. From then on, progressively-finer grades of abrasive paper should be used, starting with a 40-grade production paper, and finishing with a 400-grade wet-and-dry paper. Always wrap the abrasive paper around a flat rubber, cork, or wooden block – otherwise the surface of the filler will not be completely flat. During the smoothing of the filler surface, the wet-and-dry paper should be periodically rinsed in water. This will ensure that a very smooth finish is imparted to the filler at the final stage.

At this stage, the 'dent' should be surrounded by a ring of bare metal, which in turn should be encircled by the finely 'feathered' edge of the good paintwork. Rinse the repair area with clean water, until all of the dust produced by the rubbing-down operation has gone.

Spray the whole area with a light coat of primer – this will show up any imperfections in the surface of the filler. Repair these imperfections with fresh filler paste or bodystopper, and once more smooth the surface with abrasive paper. Repeat this spray-and-repair procedure until you are satisfied that the surface of the filler, and the feathered edge of the paintwork, are perfect. Clean the repair area with clean water, and allow to dry fully.

The repair area is now ready for final spraying. Paint spraying must be carried out in a warm, dry, windless and dust-free atmosphere. This condition can be created artificially if you have access to a large indoor working area, but if you are forced to work in the open, you will have to pick your day very carefully. If you are working indoors, dousing the floor in the work area with water will help to settle the dust which would otherwise be in the atmosphere. If the repair area is confined to one body panel, mask off the surrounding panels; this will help to minimise the effects of

a slight mis-match in paint colours. Bodywork fittings (eg chrome strips, door handles etc) will also need to be masked off. Use genuine masking tape, and several thicknesses of newspaper, for the masking operations.

Before commencing to spray, agitate the aerosol can thoroughly, then spray a test area (an old tin, or similar) until the technique is mastered. Cover the repair area with a thick coat of primer; the thickness should be built up using several thin layers of paint, rather than one thick one. Using 400-grade wet-and-dry paper, rub down the surface of the primer until it is really smooth. While doing this, the work area should be thoroughly doused with water, and the wet-and-dry paper periodically rinsed in water. Allow to dry before spraying on more paint.

Spray on the top coat, again building up the thickness by using several thin layers of paint. Start spraying at one edge of the repair area, and then, using a side-to-side motion, work until the whole repair area and about 2 inches of the surrounding original paintwork is covered. Remove all masking material 10 to 15 minutes after spraying on the final coat of paint.

Allow the new paint at least two weeks to harden, then, using a paintwork renovator, or a very fine cutting paste, blend the edges of the paint into the existing paintwork. Finally, apply wax polish.

Plastic components

With the use of more and more plastic body components by the vehicle manufacturers (eg bumpers, spoilers, and in some cases major body panels), rectification of more serious damage to such items has become a matter of either entrusting repair work to a specialist in this field, or renewing complete components. Repair of such damage by the DIY owner is not really feasible, owing to the cost of the equipment and materials required for effecting such repairs. The basic technique involves making a groove along the line of the crack in the plastic, using a rotary burr in a power drill. The damaged part is then welded back together, using a hot-air gun to heat up and fuse a plastic filler rod into the groove. Any excess plastic is then removed, and the area rubbed down to a smooth finish. It is important that a filler rod of the correct plastic is used, as body components can be made of a variety of different types (eg polycarbonate, ABS, polypropylene).

Damage of a less serious nature (abrasions, minor cracks etc) can be repaired by the DIY owner using a two-part epoxy filler repair material. Once mixed in equal proportions, this is used in similar fashion to the bodywork filler used on metal panels. The filler is usually cured in twenty to thirty minutes, ready for sanding and painting.

If the owner is renewing a complete component himself, or if he has repaired it with epoxy filler, he will be left with the problem of finding a suitable paint for finishing

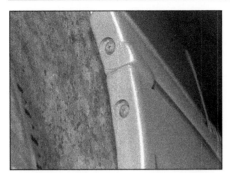

6.4 Front bumper retaining screws

6.5 Front bumper retaining nuts

which is compatible with the type of plastic used. At one time, the use of a universal paint was not possible, owing to the complex range of plastics encountered in body component applications. Standard paints, generally speaking, will not bond to plastic or rubber satisfactorily. However, it is now possible to obtain a plastic body parts finishing kit which consists of a pre-primer treatment, a primer and coloured top coat. Full instructions are normally supplied with a kit, but basically, the method of use is to first apply the pre-primer to the component concerned, and allow it to dry for up to 30 minutes. Then the primer is applied, and left to dry for about an hour before finally applying the special-coloured top coat. The result is a correctly-coloured component, where the paint will flex with the plastic or rubber, a property that standard paint does not normally possess.

5 Major body damage – repair

Where serious damage has occurred, or large areas need renewal due to neglect, it means that complete new panels will need welding-in, and this is best left to professionals. If the damage is due to impact, it will also be necessary to check completely the alignment of the bodyshell, and this can only be carried out accurately by a Ford dealer, using special jigs. If the body is left misaligned, it is primarily dangerous, as the car will not handle properly; secondly, uneven stresses will be imposed on the steering, suspension and possibly transmission, causing abnormal wear, or complete failure, particularly to such items as the tyres.

6 Bumpers – removal and refitting

Removal

Front bumper (pre-1996 models)

1 Remove the radiator grille as described in Section 36.

2 Chock the rear wheels then jack up the front of the car and support it on axle stands (see *Jacking and vehicle support*).

3 Release the six fasteners and two clips, and remove the splash shield from the underside of the vehicle at the front. The six fasteners will either be clip types or plastic screws, in which case they can be prised free or unscrewed, or pop-rivets, which will need to be drilled through.

4 Undo the two bumper-to-wing retaining screws at the rear edge of the bumper each side **(see illustration)**.

5 Unscrew and remove the four bumper retaining nuts (two each side) securing the bumper to the front end of the vehicle **(see illustration)**.

6 Disconnect the wiring from the bumper-mounted lights or indicators, where fitted.

7 Enlist the aid of an assistant, and carefully withdraw the bumper forwards from the vehicle.

Front bumper (1996-on models)

8 Remove the radiator grille as described in Section 36.

9 Tie the radiator to the front body panel to secure it in place during subsequent operations.

10 Chock the rear wheels, then jack up the front of the car and support it on axle stands (see *Jacking and vehicle support*).

11 Undo the five screws each side and remove the left-hand and right-hand wheel arch liner extensions.

12 Release the hose from the right-hand radiator support.

13 Undo the two bolts each side and remove the left-hand and right-hand radiator support.

14 Undo the two screws each side securing the edge of the bumper to the wheel arch.

15 Where applicable, disconnect the wiring multi-plugs to the bumper-mounted light assemblies.

16 Undo the four bumper retaining nuts (two each side) securing the bumper to the front end of the vehicle.

17 Enlist the aid of an assistant, and carefully withdraw the bumper forwards from the vehicle.

Rear (single-piece) bumper

18 Prise free the number plate light from the bumper, then detach the wiring connectors and remove the light.

19 Undo the two retaining screws securing the forward ends of the bumper to the trailing end of the wheel arch each side **(see illustration)**.

6.19 Rear bumper retaining screws

6.21a Rear bumper retaining nuts (Hatchback and Saloon models)

6.21b Rear (upper) bumper retaining nut (Estate models)

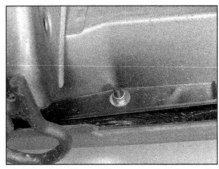

6.21c Rear (lower) bumper retaining nut (Estate models)

20 Where applicable, remove the rear trim panel in the rear luggage compartment to gain access to the bumper securing nuts.
21 Unscrew and remove the bumper retaining nuts from the rear panel each side **(see illustrations)**. On some models, access to the nuts is from underneath the vehicle; on others, it is from within the luggage compartment after removal of the appropriate rear trim panel. Enlist the aid of an assistant, to help in pulling the bumper outwards to clear the body each side, and withdraw it rearwards from the vehicle.

Rear quarter bumper

22 Reach behind the bumper, compress the rear number plate light retaining clips, and extract the light from the bumper. Disconnect the wiring connectors and remove the light.
23 Working from above, between the bumper and the vehicle rear panel, undo the two Torx-type retaining screws and then remove the quarter bumper **(see illustration)**.

Refitting

24 Refitting is a reversal of the removal procedure. Check the bumper for alignment before fully tightening the retaining nuts/screws. On rear bumpers, check the operation of the rear number plate light on completion.

7 Bonnet – removal, refitting and adjustment

Removal

1 Open the bonnet, and support it in the open position using the stay.
2 Release the fasteners and remove the insulation panel from the underside of the bonnet.
3 Disconnect the windscreen washer hose from its connection to the washer jet, and from the locating clips on the bonnet and hinge.
4 Undo the retaining screw, and detach the

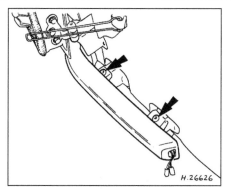

6.23 Rear quarter bumper retaining screw locations (arrowed)

earth lead from the bonnet near the left-hand hinge. Also, where applicable, disconnect the heated washer multi-plug and wiring from the bonnet.
5 To assist in correctly realigning the bonnet when refitting it, mark the outline of the hinges with a soft pencil, then loosen the two hinge retaining bolts each side.
6 With the help of an assistant, remove the stay, unscrew the four bolts and lift the bonnet from the vehicle.

Refitting and adjustment

7 Refitting is a reversal of removal. Position the bonnet hinges within the outline marks made during removal, but alter its position as necessary to provide a uniform gap all round. Adjust the rear height of the bonnet by repositioning it on the hinges. Tighten the hinge retaining bolts to the specified torque. Adjust the front height by repositioning the lock with reference to Section 9, and turn the rubber buffers on the engine compartment front crosspanel up or down to support the bonnet.
8 Ensure that the washer, wiring and earth lead connections are cleanly and securely made. Check the windscreen washer for satisfactory operation on completion.

8 Bonnet release cable – removal and refitting

Removal

1 With the bonnet open, disconnect the cable from the locating slot in the lock frame, then release the inner cable nipple from the lock **(see illustration)**.
2 Working inside the vehicle, undo the four retaining screws, and lower the bottom shroud from the steering column.
3 Detach the inner cable nipple from the release lever, then withdraw the cable through the bulkhead (noting its routing) and remove it from the engine compartment side **(see illustration)**.

Refitting

4 Refitting is a reversal of removal. On completion, check that the bonnet catch and release operate in a satisfactory manner.

9 Bonnet lock – removal and refitting

Removal

1 With the bonnet open, disconnect the cable from the locating slot in the lock frame, then release the inner cable nipple from the lock.
2 Unscrew the three retaining screws, and remove the lock from the vehicle.

Refitting

3 Refitting is a reversal of removal, but adjust the lock height so that the bonnet line is flush with the front wings, and so that it shuts securely without force. If necessary, adjust the lock laterally so that the striker enters the lock recess correctly; it may also be necessary to reposition the striker. Tighten the bonnet lock retaining screws to the specified torque.

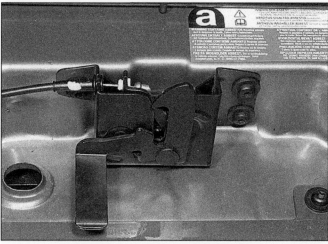

8.1 Bonnet release cable and lock

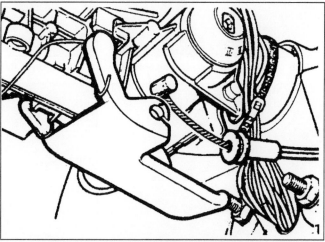

8.3 Detach the cable from the bonnet release lever on the steering column

10.1a Release the regulator retaining clip as shown . . .

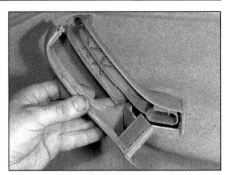

10.1b . . . and withdraw the manual window regulator handle

10 Door inner trim panel – removal and refitting

Removal

Pre-1996 models

1 On models fitted with manual window regulators, fully shut the window, note the position of the regulator handle, then release the spring clip and withdraw the handle. The clip can be released by inserting a clean cloth between the handle and the door trim, and pulling the cloth back against the open ends of the clip to release its tension whilst simultaneously pulling the handle from the regulator shaft splines **(see illustrations)**.

2 Prise free the trim capping from the door handle, taking care not to break the single retaining clip, then undo the retaining screws and remove the handle **(see illustrations)**.

3 Undo the retaining screw from the inner door handle bezel, then slide free and remove the bezel **(see illustrations)**.

4 Unscrew and remove the door trim panel retaining screws **(see illustration)**, lift the panel to disengage it from the top edge clips (along the window edge), then remove the panel.

5 If required (and where fitted), the door pocket can be detached from the trim panel by unscrewing the three retaining screws, one of which is fitted from the inside-out. If an ashtray is fitted to the trim, it can be removed by carefully prising it free. If the door lock inner release or other internal components of the door are to be inspected or removed, first withdraw the bezel from the inner door release, then remove the insulation sheet from the door as follows.

6 Access to the inner door can be made by carefully extracting the insulator from the inner release, then peeling back the insulation sheet.

10.2a Remove the door handle trim capping . . .

In order not to damage and distort the insulation sheet, use a suitable knife to cut through the peripheral adhesive strip whilst the sheet is progressively peeled back and away from the door. Avoid touching the strip with the hands, as skin oils will adversely affect its adhesive properties **(see illustrations)**.

1996-on models

7 Prise free the trim capping from the recess in the door pull, then undo the retaining screw behind.

8 On models fitted with manual window regulators, fully shut the window, note the position of the regulator handle, then release the spring clip and withdraw the handle. The clip can be released by inserting a clean cloth between the handle and the door trim, and pulling the cloth back against the open ends of the clip to release its tension whilst simultaneously pulling the handle from the regulator shaft splines.

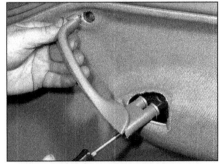

10.2b . . . and undo the retaining screws

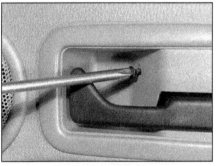

10.3a Undo the retaining screw . . .

10.3b . . . and remove the bezel

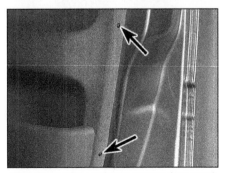

10.4 Door trim retaining screws (arrowed)

10.6a Remove the insulation surrounding the inner release handle

10.6b Cut through the adhesive to remove the door insulation sheet

9 Prise free the trim capping from the inner door handle bezel, undo the retaining screw then slide free and remove the bezel.

10 Prise free the trim cappings, where applicable and undo the eight screws securing the trim panel to the door.

11 Lift the panel to disengage it from the top edge, then remove the panel.

12 Access to the inner door can be made by carefully extracting the insulator from the inner release, then peeling back the insulation sheet. In order not to damage and distort the insulation sheet, use a suitable knife to cut through the peripheral adhesive strip whilst the sheet is progressively peeled back and away from the door. Avoid touching the strip with the hands, as skin oils will adversely affect its adhesive properties.

Refitting

13 Refitting is a reversal of removal, but where necessary, apply suitable mastic to the door panel before fitting the insulation sheet. When the door trim panel is refitted, check the operation of the door catch release and the window regulator (where applicable).

11 Door window glass –
removal and refitting

Removal

Front door window glass

1 Remove the inner trim panel and the insulation sheet from the door (Section 10).

2 Prise free the inner and outer weatherstrips from the bottom of the window aperture in the door.

3 Wind the window up to close it, then have an assistant hold the window firmly in this position whilst you unscrew the window-to-regulator retaining screws through the aperture in the inner door **(see illustration)**.

4 Lower the window regulator, then tilting the window as required, withdraw it outwards from the door **(see illustration)**.

Rear door window glass

5 Remove the inner trim panel and insulation sheet (see Section 10).

6 Remove the window aperture exterior trim.

7 Wind down the window and remove the inner and outer weatherstrips from the bottom of the window aperture.

8 Move the window winder mechanism so that the pivot between the slider at the bottom of the window and the mechanism is accessible through the opening in the bottom of the door panel. Detach the window winder mechanism from the slider at the bottom of the window.

9 Remove the three upper retaining screws from the window slider.

10 Remove the lower retaining screw from the window slider.

11 Tip the glass to disengage it and remove the glass from outside the door.

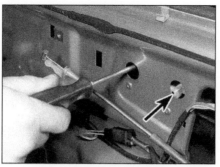
11.3 Undo the glass-to-regulator screws through apertures shown

Refitting

12 Refitting is a reversal of removal, but note then following:
  a) Where applicable, ensure that the wiring looms in the door are clear of the window and its regulating mechanism, and that the connections are secure.
  b) On refitting the window glass, check that it operates fully and freely before refitting the insulation sheet and the door trim panel.

12 Door window regulator –
removal and refitting

Removal

1 Remove the door trim and the insulation sheet as described in Section 10.

2 Locate the glass in the door so that the guide channel can be detached from the regulator. Disconnect the ball and socket(s) (two per front door, one per rear door), then lower the glass to the base of the door.

3 The regulator is secured by seven pop-rivets (front door) or four pop-rivets (rear door). Drill through the centre of each rivet, detach the regulator from the door, and withdraw it from the lower aperture **(see illustration)**.

Refitting

4 Refitting is a reversal of removal. Obtain the correct number of rivets to fit the regulator to the door. Check that the operation of the

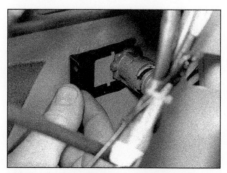
13.2a Remove the inner retaining clip . . .

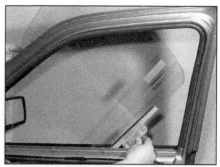
11.4 Removing the window

12.3 Drilling out the door window regulator rivets

window regulator is satisfactory before refitting the door trim.

13 Door lock, lock cylinder and handles –
removal and refitting

Removal

1 Remove the door inner trim panel and the insulation sheet as described in Section 10. Proceed as described below in the appropriate sub-Section.

Door lock barrel

2 Where fitted, undo the two screws and remove the door lock barrel shield. Slide free the barrel retaining clip, detach the connecting rod and remove the lock barrel **(see illustrations)**.

13.2b . . . and withdraw the lock barrel from the door

13.6 Door lock retaining screws

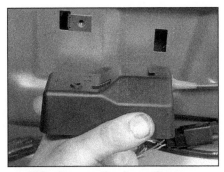

13.8a Remove the door release . . .

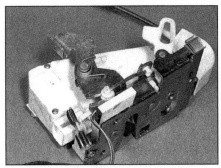

13.8b . . . and the door lock with cable

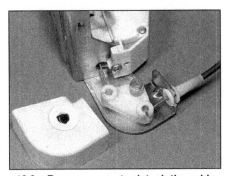

13.8c Remove cover to detach the cable from the lock

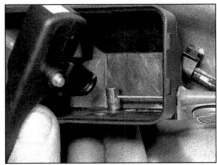

13.10a Detach the inner release handle . . .

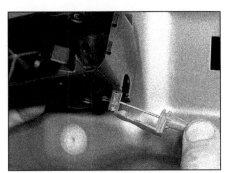

13.10b . . . and disconnect the cable from the casing

Door lock

3 Remove the lock barrel as described above.

4 On models with central locking, detach the wiring multi-plugs from the lock motor (attached to and removed with the lock).

5 Unscrew and remove the inner door release retaining screw.

6 Unscrew and remove the three door lock retaining screws **(see illustration)**.

7 Remove the window rear guide (rear doors only).

8 Slide free the inner release from the door, then withdraw the lock together with the remote control inner release and cable. If required, the connecting cable to the inner release handle can be detached from the lock by removing the cover, sliding the outer cable from its locating slot in the lock, and then

withdrawing the inner cable from the actuating pivot on the lock **(see illustrations)**.

9 On models with central locking, undo the two retaining screws to detach the lock from the actuating motor.

Inner release handle

10 Slide free the inner release and detach it from the door, then disconnect the release operating cable from the release handle case **(see illustrations)**.

Exterior release handle

11 Undo the two retaining screws, detach the link rod from the release arm of the exterior handle, and remove the handle from the door **(see illustration)**. Note that on the rear doors it will be necessary to remove the blanking plug in the edge of the door to gain access to one of the handle securing screws **(see illustration)**.

Refitting

12 Refitting is a reversal of removal. Check for satisfactory operation of the lock and its associated components before refitting the door trim. Check that the striker enters the lock centrally when the door is closed. If necessary, loosen it with a Torx key, re-position and re-tighten it.

14 Door – removal and refitting

Removal

1 Fully open the door, then untwist and detach the wiring multi-plug connector **(see illustration)**.

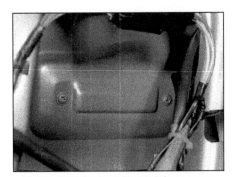

13.11a Exterior handle retaining screws

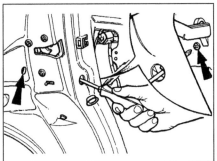

13.11b Exterior handle retaining screw access point in rear door

14.1 Disconnect the wiring multi-plug connector

2 Disconnect the door check strap by unscrewing the Torx screw on the door pillar **(see illustration)**.
3 Support the door on blocks of wood.
4 Unscrew the door hinge pin retaining bolt from each hinge **(see illustration)**, then lift the door clear of the hinges.

Refitting

5 Refitting is a reversal of removal. Check that the striker enters the lock centrally when the door is closed. If necessary, loosen it with a Torx key, re-position and re-tighten it.

15 Exterior mirror and glass –
removal and refitting

Removal

1 If the mirror glass is to be removed, insert a thin flat-bladed tool between the glass and the housing, and carefully prise it free. Where applicable, disconnect the wiring from the connectors on the rear face of the mirror **(see illustrations)**.
2 To remove the mirror, first remove the door trim as described in Section 10.
3 Undo the door mirror trim retaining screw, and remove the trim **(see illustration)**.
4 Carefully prise free the control unit from the trim, and where applicable, detach the wiring connector from the adjuster.
5 Support the mirror, undo the three retaining screws, and remove the mirror from the door.
6 The motor can be removed if required by undoing the three retaining screws **(see illustration)**.

Refitting

7 Refit in the reverse order of removal. Check that the operation of the mirror adjuster is satisfactory.

16 Interior mirror –
removal and refitting

Removal

1 Using a length of strong thin cord or fishing line, break the adhesive bond between the base of the mirror and the glass. Have an assistant support and remove the mirror as it is released.
2 If the original mirror is to be refitted, thoroughly clean its base with methylated spirit and a lint-free cloth. Allow a period of one minute for the spirit to evaporate. Clean the windscreen black patch in a similar manner.

Refitting

3 During the installation of the mirror, it is important that the mirror base, windscreen black patch and the adhesive patch are not

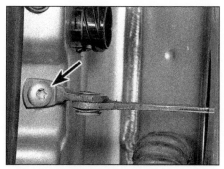

14.2 Door check strap screw (arrowed)

touched or contaminated in any way – poor adhesion will result.
4 Prior to fitting the mirror, the temperature inside the vehicle should ideally be around 20°C. While this isn't critical, it's worth ensuring that the inside of the vehicle is as warm and dry as possible.
5 With the contact surfaces thoroughly cleaned, remove the protective tape from one side of the adhesive patch, and press it firmly into contact with the mirror base.
6 If fitting the mirror to a new windscreen, the protective tape must first be removed from the windscreen black patch.
7 Warm the mirror base and the adhesive patch for about 30 seconds to a temperature of 50 to 70°C. Peel back the protective tape from the other side of the adhesive patch on the mirror base, then align the mirror base and the windscreen patch, and press the mirror firmly into position. Hold the base of the mirror

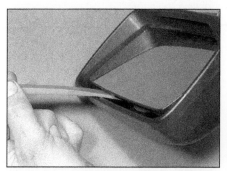

15.1a Prise free the door mirror glass . . .

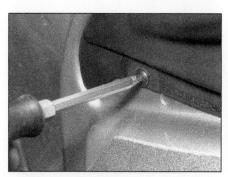

15.3 Undo the screw and remove the mirror trim

14.4 Door hinge pin bolt (arrowed)

firmly against the windscreen for a minimum period of two minutes to ensure full adhesion.
8 Wait at least thirty minutes before adjusting the mirror position.

17 Boot lid –
removal, refitting and adjustment

Removal

1 Open the boot lid, and mark the position of the hinges with a pencil.
2 Where applicable, disconnect the wiring multi-plug and the earth lead for the central locking motor from the boot lid **(see illustration)**. Attach a suitable length of strong cord to the end of the wire, then withdraw the lead from the boot lid. Detach the cord and leave it in position in the boot. This will then

15.1b . . . and detach the wiring connectors, where applicable

15.6 Mirror motor and retaining screws (arrowed)

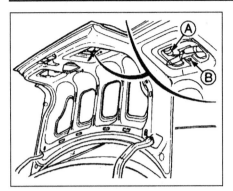

17.2 Multi-plug (A) and earth lead (B) connection points in the boot lid

act as an aid to guiding the wiring through the lid when it is refitted.

3 Place cloth rags beneath each corner of the boot lid to prevent damage to the paintwork.

4 With the help of an assistant, unscrew the mounting bolts and lift the boot lid from the car.

Refitting and adjustment

5 Refitting is a reversal of removal. Check that the boot lid is correctly aligned with the surrounding bodywork, with an equal clearance around its edge. Adjustment is made by loosening the hinge bolts and moving the boot lid within the elongated mounting holes. Tighten the hinge bolts to the specified torque setting. Check that the lock enters the striker centrally when the boot lid is closed, and if necessary adjust the striker's position within the elongated holes.

18 Boot lid lock components – removal and refitting

Removal

Lock barrel

1 Open the boot and undo the screw securing the barrel retaining clip, then remove the clip.

2 Detach the barrel from the link rod, and withdraw the lock from the boot lid.

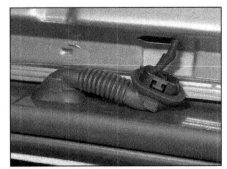

19.4 Detach the wiring connector from the tailgate

Lock

3 Open the boot lid and remove the lock barrel (see above for details).

4 Undo the three retaining screws, then withdraw the lock from the boot lid.

Lock striker and remote release

5 Open the boot, undo the two retaining screws, and remove the trim from the rear face of the luggage compartment.

6 Using a soft pencil, mark an outline around the striker and the release unit, to act as a guide for repositioning on refitting. Undo the two Torx-type screws, and remove the lock striker and the release unit. Detach the operating cable from the release unit to remove it.

Release cable

7 Remove the striker and release unit as described above, then detach the release cable from it.

8 Detach and remove the kick panel trim beneath the front and rear doors on the driver's side. Fold back the carpet from around the boot lid lock release handle.

9 Withdraw the outer cable from the slot in the lever mounting plate, then detach the inner cable from the lever.

10 Remove the appropriate side trim panels from the rear of the vehicle on the side concerned, to expose the cable routing.

 HAYNES HiNT *Where the cable has to pass through cavities in the body, tie a suitable length of cord to the cable end before pulling the cable through and removing it. The cord can be untied from the cable, and left in situ in the vehicle. It will then act as a 'puller-guide' when the cable is being refitted.*

Refitting

11 Refitting is a reversal of removal. When refitting the lock, check that the striker enters the lock centrally when the boot lid is closed, and if necessary re-position the striker by loosening the mounting screws. Tighten the lock and striker mounting screws to the specified torque setting.

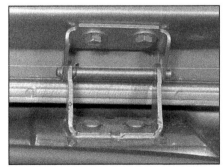

19.6 Tailgate hinge and retaining bolts

19 Tailgate – removal, refitting and adjustment

Removal

1 Open the tailgate, then undo the seven retaining screws and remove the trim panel from the tailgate.

2 Using a soft pencil, mark the fitted position outline around the tailgate hinges to act as a guide for repositioning when refitting.

3 Prise free and remove the plug for access to the washer jet, then detach the hose from the jet. Attach a suitable length of strong cord to the end of the hose to assist in guiding the hose back through the aperture of the tailgate when it is being refitted. Now prise free the flexible grommet on the left-hand side, and withdraw the washer jet hose from the tailgate. Undo the cord from the hose, and leave it in position in the tailgate.

4 Where applicable, detach the central locking lead multi-connector and earth lead from the tailgate **(see illustration)**. Attach a suitable length of strong cord to the end of the wire, to assist in guiding the wiring back through the aperture of the tailgate when it is being refitted. Now prise free the flexible grommet on the right-hand side, and withdraw the central locking wires from the tailgate. Undo the cord from the wire, and leave it in position in the tailgate.

5 Have an assistant support the tailgate in the open position, then prise open the support strut balljoint securing clip, and detach the strut each side from the tailgate.

6 Unscrew and remove the hinge bolts, then lift the tailgate clear of the vehicle **(see illustration)**.

Refitting and adjustment

7 Refitting is a reversal of removal, but check that the tailgate is correctly aligned with the surrounding bodywork, with an equal clearance around its edge. Adjustment is made by loosening the hinge bolts and moving the tailgate within the elongated mounting holes. Tighten the hinge bolts to the specified torque setting. Adjust the rear height by turning the rubber bump stop each side in the desired direction. Check that the striker enters the lock centrally when the tailgate is closed, and if necessary adjust the position of the striker within the elongated holes.

20 Tailgate support strut – removal and refitting

Removal

1 Support the tailgate in its open position. If both struts are to be removed, the tailgate will need to be supported by an alternative means.

2 Disconnect each end of the support strut

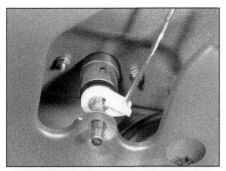

21.2 Tailgate lock barrel, operating rod and retaining nuts

21.5 Undo the three tailgate lock retaining screws

21.6 Tailgate lock striker and release unit retaining screws

by prising out the spring clip retainers with a small screwdriver and pulling the strut from the ball mountings.

Refitting

3 Refitting is a reversal of removal, but note that the piston end of the strut faces downwards.

21 Tailgate lock components – removal and refitting

Removal

Lock barrel

1 Open the tailgate, then remove the seven screws and remove the inner trim panel from the rear of the luggage area.
2 Depending on type, unscrew and remove the lock barrel clip retaining screw, then remove the clip or undo the two retaining nuts **(see illustration)**.
3 Disengage the operating rod and remove the barrel.

Lock

4 Open the tailgate and remove the lock barrel as described above.
5 Undo the three Torx-type retaining screws and remove the lock. Where applicable, detach the wiring in-line connector from the lock **(see illustration)**.

Striker and release unit

6 Using a soft pencil, mark an outline around the striker and the release unit to act as a guide for repositioning on refitting. Undo the two Torx-type screws (and where applicable, the earth lead screw), then remove the lock striker and release unit. Detach the operating cable from the release unit to remove it **(see illustration)**.

Release cable

7 Remove the striker and release unit as described above, then detach the release cable from it.
8 Detach and remove the kick panel trim beneath the front and rear doors on the driver's side. Fold back the carpet from around the tailgate release handle.

9 Withdraw the outer cable from the slot in the lever mounting plate, then detach the inner cable from the lever.
10 Remove the appropriate side trim panels from the rear of the vehicle on the side concerned, to expose the cable routing.

> **HAYNES HINT** *Where the cable has to pass through cavities in the body, tie a suitable length of cord to the cable end before pulling the cable through and removing it. The cord can be untied from the cable, and left in situ in the vehicle. It will then act as a 'puller-guide' when the cable is being refitted.*

Refitting

11 Refitting is a reversal of removal. When refitting the lock, check that the striker enters the lock centrally when the tailgate is closed, and if necessary re-position the striker by loosening the mounting screws. Tighten the lock and striker mounting screws to the specified torque setting.

22 Central locking system control module – removal and refitting

Removal

1 Disconnect the battery negative (earth) lead (refer to Chapter 5A, Section 1).
2 Remove the front footwell side cowl trim

22.3 Central locking system control module location

panel from the driver's side, as described in Section 34.
3 Withdraw the central locking module from its location bracket, and detach the multi-plug wiring connections from it **(see illustration)**.

Refitting

4 Refit in the reverse order of removal. Check the operation of the system to complete.

23 Windscreen and fixed windows – removal and refitting

Removal

Windscreen, rear quarter and rear window/tailgate glass

1 The windscreen, rear quarter and rear window/tailgate glass are bonded in place with special mastic. Special tools are required to cut free the old glass and fit replacements, together with cleaning solutions and primers. It is therefore recommended that this work is entrusted to a Ford dealer or windscreen replacement specialist.

Rear Van window(s)

2 Working from the inner face of the door concerned, use a blunt-ended instrument to push the inner lip of the weatherseal beneath the window frame, starting at the top. Get an assistant to support the window on the outside during this operation.
3 With the weatherseal free, withdraw the window from the door.

Refitting

4 Clean the window and aperture in the body/frame. Petrol or spirit-based solvents must not be used for this purpose, as they are harmful to the weatherstrip.
5 Fit the weatherseal on the window, then insert a cord in the weatherseal groove so that the ends project from the bottom of the window and are overlapped by approximately 150 mm.
6 Locate the window on its location aperture, and pass the ends of the cord inside the vehicle. Have an assistant hold the window in position.

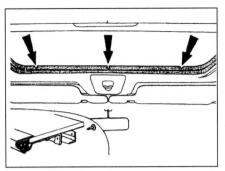

27.2 Sunroof lower frame-to-glass panel retaining screws (arrowed)

7 Slowly pull one end of the cord (at right-angles to the window frame, towards the centre of the glass) so that the lip of the weatherseal goes over the aperture. At the same time, have the assistant press firmly on the outside of the window. When the cord reaches the middle top of the window, pull the remaining length of cord to position the other half of the weatherseal.

24 Door and tailgate weatherstrips – removal and refitting

Removal

1 To remove a weatherstrip seal from its aperture flange, grip the strip at its joint end, and progressively pull it free, working around the aperture to the other end of the strip.

Refitting

2 First check that the contact surfaces of the weatherstrip and the aperture flange are clean. Check around the aperture flange for any signs of distortion, and rectify as necessary.
3 To refit the weatherstrip, start by roughly locating its ends midway along the base of the aperture concerned, but do not press them into position over the flange at this stage. Proceed as follows, according to type.

Door weatherstrip

4 In the case of a door weatherstrip, press the strip into position at the corners to initially

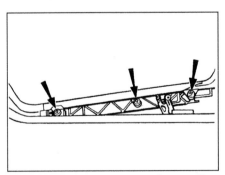

27.3 Loosen off these screws (arrowed) to adjust the sunroof glass panel

locate it. Check that the distances between each contact point are such that the strip will fit smoothly around the aperture (without distortion), then firmly press the strip fully into position, starting at the top edge and working down each side to finish at the bottom joint. Check that the seal is correctly located, then apply a suitable sealant to the joint, to prevent the possibility of water leakage through it caused by capillary action.
5 Shut the door, and check it for fit. Adjust if required by resetting the position of the striker plate to suit.

Tailgate weatherstrip

6 Position the ends of the weatherstrip so that they are centralised within 300 mm of the tailgate striker plate. A new weatherstrip will need to be measured and cut to length. Progressively fit the weatherstrip around the aperture flange, squeezing it closed over the flange by hand to secure. When fitted, check that it is not distorted, then close the tailgate and check it for fit. Adjustment of the striker plate and the tailgate bump stops may be necessary to obtain a satisfactory fit and seal.

25 Body side-trim mouldings and adhesive emblems – removal and refitting

Removal

1 Insert a length of strong cord (fishing line is ideal), between the moulding or emblem concerned, and break the adhesive bond between the moulding (or emblem) and the panel.
2 Thoroughly clean all traces of adhesive from the panel using methylated spirit, and allow the moulding/emblem location to dry.

Refitting

3 Peel back the protective paper from the rear face of the new moulding/emblem, and then fit it into position on the panel concerned, taking care not to touch the adhesive. When in position, apply a hand pressure to the moulding/emblem for a short period to ensure maximum adhesion to the panel.

26 Roof moulding (Van models) – removal and refitting

Removal

1 Prise free and lift the moulding up from the roof at the front end, then pull the moulding from its location channel in the roof.
2 Clean the contact faces of the moulding and the roof channel before refitting.

Refitting

3 Locate the moulding into position over the channel, check that it is correctly realigned,

then progressively press it into place using the palm of the hand.

27 Sunroof – checking and adjustment

1 The sunroof should operate freely, without sticking or binding, as it is opened and closed. When in the closed position, check that the panel is flush with the surrounding roof panel, the maximum allowable gap at the front edge being 1.0 mm.
2 If adjustment is required, open the sun blind, then undo and remove the three lower frame-to-glass panel retaining screws **(see illustration)**. Slide the lower frame back into the roof.
3 Loosen off the central and front securing screws, adjust the glass roof panel so that it is flush at its front edge with the roof panel, then retighten the securing screws **(see illustration)**.
4 Pull the lower frame forwards, insert and tighten its retaining screws to complete.

28 Sunroof panel – removal and refitting

Removal

1 Open the sun blind, unscrew and remove the three screws securing the lower frame, and slide the frame back into the roof.
2 Undo the three roof panel-to-sliding gear screws, then push the panel up and out to remove it from the vehicle. Have an assistant lift the panel free from above as it is raised, to avoid the possibility of the panel and/or the surrounding roof from being damaged.

Refitting

3 Refit in the reverse order of removal. When the panel is in position, adjust it as described in the previous Section.

29 Sunroof weatherstrip – removal and refitting

Removal

1 Wind the sunroof panel into the tilted open position, then grip the ends of the weatherstrip and pull it free from the flanged periphery of the roof panel.
2 Clean the contact faces of the panel and the weatherstrip (where the original strip is to be used) before refitting.

Refitting

3 Refit in the reverse order of removal. Ensure that the weatherstrip joint is located in the middle of the rear face of the panel.

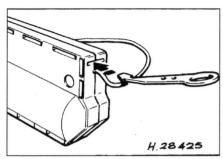

30.2 Inserting the seat belt 'transit clip' (early type shown) to immobilise the mechanical seat belt pre-tensioner

30.3a Front seat/runner rear outboard retaining bolt

30.3b Front seat/runner rear inboard retaining bolts

30.4 Front seat/runner forward mounting bolt

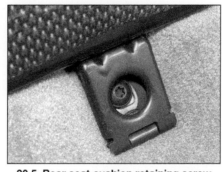

30.5 Rear seat cushion retaining screw (Saloon)

30.6 Rear seat backrest-to-cushion hinge screws

30 Seats –
removal and refitting

Removal

Front seat

⚠ **Warning: On vehicles fitted with mechanical seat belt pre-tensioning stalks, be careful when handling the seat, as the tensioning device ('grabber') contains a powerful spring, which could cause injury if released in an uncontrolled fashion. The tensioning mechanism should be immobilised by inserting a safety 'transit clip' available from Ford parts stockists (see illustration 30.2). You are strongly advised to seek the advice of a Ford dealer as to the correct use of the 'transit clip' and the safety implications before proceeding.**

⚠ **Warning: On vehicles fitted with pyrotechnic seat belt pre-tensioners, disconnect the battery negative (earth) lead (refer to Chapter 5A, Section 1), then wait a minimum of two minutes before proceeding.**

1 On later models, pull off the trim cover from the base of the seat, adjacent to the door aperture.

2 On vehicles fitted with mechanical seat belt pre-tensioning stalks, fit the safety 'transit clip' **(see illustration)**. On vehicles fitted with pyrotechnic seat belt pre-tensioners, disconnect the wiring multi-plug located behind the previously removed trim cover.

3 Slide the seat forwards to the full extent of its travel, then unscrew and remove the rear mounting bolts (one on the outer slide and two on the inner) **(see illustrations)**. On some models it will be necessary to prise open and remove the trim cover for access to the mounting bolts

4 Now slide the seat fully to the rear, then unscrew the front securing bolt each side **(see illustration)**. Lift the seat and remove it from the vehicle.

Rear seat cushion

5 Prise free the blanking plugs, then unscrew and remove the cushion hinge retaining screw each side **(see illustration)**. Remove the cushion from the vehicle.

Rear seat backrest

6 Pivot the rear seat cushion forwards, then fold the backrest down. Undo the two screws retaining the hinge to the backrest each side,

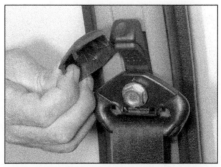

31.5 Remove the cover for access to the seat belt upper anchor bolt

and remove the backrest from the vehicle **(see illustration)**.

Refitting

7 Refitting is a reversal of the removal procedure. Where applicable, tighten the seat belt anchor bolts to the specified torque.

31 Seat belts –
removal and refitting

Removal

Note: *Seat belts and associated components which have been subject to impact loads must be renewed.*

Front seat belt (3-door Hatchback)

1 Prise free the upper cover, then unscrew and remove the front seat belt upper anchor plate retaining bolt. Remove the plate and spacer.

2 Undo the lower anchor rail retaining bolt, pivot the rail towards the centre of the vehicle, pull it free from its mounting and then slide the belt from the rail.

3 Remove the rear quarter trim panel as described in Section 32.

4 Unscrew the bolt retaining the inertia reel unit, then remove the reel and the belt.

Front seat belt (all other models)

5 Prise free the cover, then unscrew and remove the front seat belt upper anchor plate retaining bolt. Remove the plate and spacer **(see illustration)**.

31.9 Inertia reel unit and retaining bolt

6 Unscrew and remove the lower anchor plate retaining bolt.

7 Remove the trim from the centre B-pillar by pulling free the weatherstrip, unscrewing the two retaining screws, withdrawing the trim from the panel and detaching the securing pegs (where applicable).

8 Undo the six screws retaining the scuff plate in position, extract the belt from the slotted hole, and remove the scuff plate.

9 Undo the retaining bolt, and detach the inertia reel unit from the central pillar **(see illustration)**.

Front seat belt height adjuster

10 Prise free the upper cover, then unscrew and remove the front seat belt upper anchor plate retaining bolt. Remove the plate and spacer.

11 Remove the trim from the centre B-pillar by pulling free the weatherstrip, unscrewing the two retaining screws, withdrawing the trim from the panel and detaching the securing pegs (where applicable).

12 Unscrew the retaining bolts and remove the height adjuster **(see illustration)**.

Front seat belt stalk

> ⚠ *Warning: On vehicles fitted with mechanical or pyrotechnic seat belt pre-tensioners, any work on the seat belt stalk should be entrusted to a Ford dealer. The following procedure is therefore only applicable to models with conventional seat belt stalks which DO NOT incorporate any form of pre-tensioning device.*

31.28 Rear seat belt upper anchor bolt

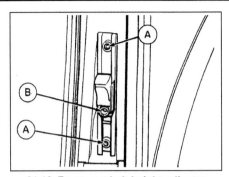

31.12 Front seat belt height adjuster retaining bolts (A) and anchor plate bolt (B)

13 Remove the relevant front seat as described in Section 30.

14 Undo the single retaining bolt and remove the stalk from the side of the seat.

Rear seat belts (3-door Hatchback)

15 Prise free the upper cover, then unscrew and remove the front seat belt upper anchor plate retaining bolt. Remove the plate and spacer.

16 Undo the lower anchor rail retaining bolt, pivot the rail towards the centre of the vehicle, pull it free from its mounting and then slide the belt from the rail.

17 Lift the rear seat cushion for access, then unscrew the bolt and remove the centre buckle/belt anchor plate **(see illustration)**.

18 Unscrew the lower reel belt anchor plate bolt.

19 Unscrew and remove the upper anchor plate bolt, and detach the plate and spacer from the rear C-pillar.

20 Pivot the rear seat backrest down, and undo the two Torx screws securing the backrest.

21 Remove the trim from the centre B-pillar by pulling free the weatherstrip, unscrewing the two retaining screws, withdrawing the trim from the panel and detaching the securing pegs (where applicable).

22 Remove the rear quarter trim panel (Section 32).

23 Remove the trim panel from the C-pillar as described in Section 32.

24 Undo the three Torx bolts, and detach the rear seat backrest catch bracket.

25 Unscrew the inertia reel retaining bolt, and withdraw the inertia reel unit and belt.

Rear seat belts (5-door Hatchback)

26 Lift the rear seat cushion for access, then unscrew the retaining bolt and remove the centre buckle/belt anchor plate.

27 Unscrew the lower reel belt anchor plate bolt.

28 Detach the cover for access, then unscrew and remove the anchor plate and spacer from the C-pillar **(see illustration)**.

29 Pivot the rear seat backrest down, and undo the two Torx screws securing the backrest catch.

30 Remove the trim panel from the C-pillar as described in Section 32.

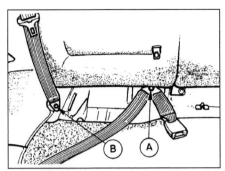

31.17 Rear seat belt anchor plates for the central buckle/belt (A) and the reel belt (B)

31 Undo the three Torx bolts, and detach the rear seat backrest catch bracket.

32 Unscrew the inertia reel retaining bolt, and withdraw the inertia reel unit and belt.

Rear seat belts (Saloon)

33 Lift the rear seat cushion for access, then unscrew the retaining bolt and remove the centre buckle/belt anchor plate.

34 Unscrew the lower reel belt anchor plate bolt.

35 Detach the cover for access, then unscrew and remove the anchor plate and spacer from the C-pillar.

36 Pivot the rear seat backrest down, and remove the trim panel from the C-pillar as described in Section 32.

37 Unscrew the retaining nut, and remove the rear seat backrest catch pull knob from its bracket in the boot. Pull the cable from the clip on the underside of the boot.

38 Undo the two Torx screws, and release the seat back catch from the mounting bracket.

39 Undo the three Torx bolts, and detach the rear seat backrest catch bracket.

40 Unscrew the inertia reel retaining bolt, and withdraw the inertia reel unit and belt.

Rear seat belts (Estate)

41 Lift the rear seat cushion for access, unscrew the retaining bolt and remove the centre buckle/belt anchor plate.

42 Unscrew the lower reel belt anchor plate bolt.

43 Detach the cover for access, then unscrew and remove the anchor plate and spacer from the C-pillar.

31.46 Rear seat backrest catch mounting (Estate models)

44 Pivot the rear seat backrest down, undo the two Torx screws and remove the backrest catch.

45 Detach and remove the C and D-pillar trim panels, followed by the rear luggage area trim panel, as described in Section 32.

46 Undo the three Torx screws, and detach the backrest catch mounting **(see illustration)**.

47 Unscrew the retaining bolt, and remove the inertia reel/belt unit **(see illustration)**.

Refitting

48 On all models, refitting of the front and rear seat belts is a reversal of the removal procedure. Tighten all fastenings to the specified torque, and check for satisfactory operation.

32 Interior trim panels – removal and refitting

Removal

Windscreen A-pillar trim

1 Pull free the weatherstrip from the flange on the A-pillar. Undo the retaining screw, release the retaining clips and withdraw the trim from the pillar.

Centre B-pillar

2 Pull free the weatherstrip from the pillar flange. Prise free the cover, then unscrew and remove the front seat belt upper anchor plate retaining bolt. Remove the plate and spacer.

3 On 5-door models, undo the two screws securing the centre pillar trim.

4 Carefully prise free and detach the trim from the central pillar (to which it is attached by plastic pegs).

Rear C-pillar trim (Hatchback)

5 Hinge the rear seat cushion forwards, and lower the seat backrest.

6 Where fitted, undo the three screws to withdraw the speaker, and detach the speaker wire. Do not remove the speaker itself.

7 Undo the two Torx-type retaining screws, and remove the backrest catch. Also prise free and remove the rear suspension top mounting cover (just to the rear of the catch).

8 Unscrew and remove the rear seat belt lower anchor plate bolt.

9 Prise free the seat belt upper anchor plate cover, then unscrew the retaining bolt and detach the upper anchor plate and spacer.

10 Prise free the door weatherstrip from the pillar flange.

11 On 3-door models, remove the rear quarter trim as described later in this Section.

12 Undo the retaining screws and withdraw the trim panel from the pillar, feeding the seat belt and anchor through the trim. Note that it is necessary to remove a cover for access to the rear retaining screw.

Rear C-pillar trim (Saloon)

13 Hinge the rear seat cushion forwards, and lower the seat backrest.

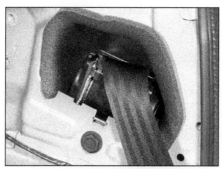

31.47 Rear seat inertia reel unit (Estate models)

14 Detach and remove the rear parcel shelf (see paragraphs 22 to 24).

15 Unscrew and remove the rear seat belt lower anchor plate bolt.

16 Prise free the seat belt upper anchor plate cover, then unscrew the retaining bolt and detach the upper anchor plate and spacer.

17 Undo the two C-pillar retaining screws. Prise free the door weatherstrip from the C-pillar flange, then carefully prise free the trim panel from the pillar, feeding the seat belt through it as it is withdrawn.

C-pillar trim (Estate)

18 Hinge the rear seat cushion forwards, and lower the seat backrest.

19 Prise free the seat belt upper anchor plate cover, then unscrew the retaining bolt and detach the upper anchor plate and spacer.

20 Carefully prise free and remove the trim panel from the C-pillar.

D-pillar trim (Estate)

21 Prise free the trim panel from the D-pillar to release it from the retaining clips, and remove the trim.

Rear parcel shelf (Saloon)

22 Hinge down the rear seat backrest. Where fitted, detach and remove the rear speakers from the parcel shelf.

23 Undo the retaining screw, and remove the seat belt guide trim panel each side.

24 Unscrew and remove the three parcel shelf retaining screws, then lift the panel at the front edge to detach it from the four plastic retaining clips, and withdraw the panel from the car.

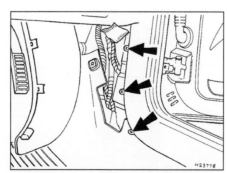

32.30 Location of front footwell side cowl trim panel retaining tabs (arrowed)

Rear quarter trim panel

25 Detach the front seat belt at its upper and lower anchor points, as described in Section 31.

26 Detach and remove the centre B-pillar trim as described previously in this Section.

27 Undo the two scuff plate retaining screws, and ease the plate away from the quarter panel.

28 Hinge forward the rear seat cushion and backrest, then detach the belt trim guide bezel from the quarter panel.

29 Unscrew and remove the retaining screws at the rear of the panel. Prise free the quarter panel from the B-pillar, and withdraw the panel. As it is withdrawn, disengage the seat belt and anchors through the panel slots.

Front footwell side cowl trim panel

30 Rotate the plastic retaining clip at the front of the panel through 90° to release the panel at the forward fixing, then ease the panel away from the three tab fasteners at the rear edge **(see illustration)**.

Scuff plate

31 Remove the front footwell side cowl trim panel as described above.

32 Prise free the door weatherstrip from the door sill flange.

33 On 5-door Hatchback, Saloon, Estate and Van models, unscrew and remove the screw at the lower end of the B-pillar trim (just above the seat belt slot in the scuff plate).

34 Unscrew and remove the six scuff plate retaining screws, then feeding the seat belt through it (where applicable), withdraw the scuff plate.

Luggage area trim (Hatchback and Saloon)

35 Hinge down the rear seat backrest(s), and on Hatchback models, prise free and remove the trim cap from the rear suspension top mounting.

36 Prise free the trim panel clips using a suitable flat-bladed tool **(see illustrations)**.

37 Unscrew and remove the two trim retaining screws together with their large washers, then withdraw the trim panel.

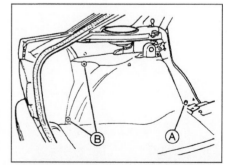

32.36a Luggage area trim retaining clip (A) and screws (B) – Hatchback models

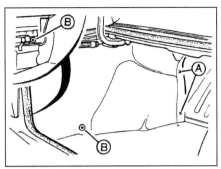

32.36b Luggage area trim retaining clips (A) and screws (B) – Saloon models

Luggage area trim (Estate)

38 Lift the rear seat cushion and unscrew the scuff plate screw at the rear, then unscrew and remove the two luggage area trim screws **(see illustration)**.

39 Hinge down the rear seat backrest, then prise free the upper cover and remove the rear seat belt upper anchor plate retaining bolt. Remove the plate and spacer.

40 Undo the two Torx screws, and remove the rear seat backrest catch.

41 Prise the trim panel from the C-pillar, and remove it.

42 Similarly, prise the trim panel from the D-pillar, and remove it.

43 Undo the screw attaching the trim panel to the C-pillar, then the screws securing the luggage area trim panel to the D-pillar **(see illustration)**.

44 Undo the three luggage area trim panel-to-floor screws, and the single screw securing the panel to the rear crossmember.

45 Lift the trim panel to release it from the inner side panel, then withdraw it.

Partition panel (Van)

46 Working from the front of the panel, unscrew and remove the three panel-to-crossmember bolts on its lower edge.

47 Working from the rear of the panel, unscrew and remove the two bolts securing the panel to the rear face of the B-pillar each side, then withdraw the partition panel.

Sun visor

48 Release the visor from the retaining clip, undo the two retaining screws at its hinge

33.5 Side vent panel removal on the driver's side

mounting, and remove the visor. To remove the retaining clip, prise open the cover flap to expose the retaining screw, then undo the screw and remove the clip.

Passenger grab handle

49 Prise back the trim flaps at each end of the grab handle to expose the screws. Undo the screws and remove the handle.

Refitting

50 Refitting is a reversal of the removal procedure. Ensure any wiring connections are securely made. Tighten the seat belt fixings to the specified torque and check the seat belt(s) for satisfactory operation on completion.

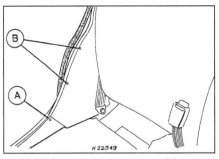

32.38 Rear scuff plate screw (A) and luggage area trim forward screws (B) (Estate models)

---

33 Facia – removal and refitting

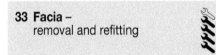

⚠ Warning: On vehicles fitted with a passenger's air bag, seek the advice of a Ford dealer concerning safety implications when removing the facia assembly.

Removal

Pre-1996 models

1 Disconnect the battery negative (earth) lead.

2 Refer to Chapter 10 for details, and remove the steering wheel.

3 Undo the two upper and four lower retaining screws, and remove the upper and lower steering column shrouds.

33.8a Pull free the weatherstrip for access to the outboard facia screws

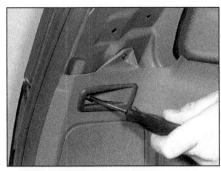

32.43 Luggage area side trim retaining screws removal (Estate)

4 Refer to the appropriate Chapters concerned for details, and remove the following facia-associated items:
  a) *Steering column multi-function switch (Chapter 12).*
  b) *Instrument panel (Chapter 12).*
  c) *Heating/ventilation controls and control panel (Chapter 3).*
  d) *Cigar lighter and ashtray (Chapter 12).*
  e) *Radio/cassette player (Chapter 12).*
  f) *Clock (Chapter 12).*

5 Undo the two retaining screws, and remove the side vent panel from the facia on the driver's side. As it is withdrawn, disconnect any wiring connections from the panel-mounted switches **(see illustration)**.

6 Undo the two hinge/retaining screws securing the glovebox lid, and remove it. Undo the two catch screws, and remove the lock/catch. As the catch is withdrawn, disconnect the bulbholder/switch wiring connector.

7 Where fitted, detach and remove the footwell lights from the driver's and passenger's side lower facia.

8 Pull free the weatherstrip from the leading edge of the door aperture each side to gain access to the outboard mounting screws. Unscrew and remove the retaining screws from the points indicated **(see illustrations)**.

9 With the help of an assistant, withdraw the facia from its mounting. As it is withdrawn, note the routing of the cables attached to the facia, then detach the cable-ties and remove the facia from the vehicle.

10 The associated components of the facia can (if required) be detached by undoing the appropriate retaining screws.

1996-on models

11 Disconnect the battery negative (earth) lead (refer to Chapter 5A, Section 1).

12 Refer to Chapter 10 for details, and remove the steering wheel.

13 Undo the single retaining screw, and withdraw the steering column multi-function switch upwards from the column. Detach the wiring connector and cable-tie clips from the switch.

14 Detach the three multi-plugs located at the rear of the detachable lower facia panel then disconnect them.

15 Detach and remove the footwell lights from the driver and passenger side lower facia.

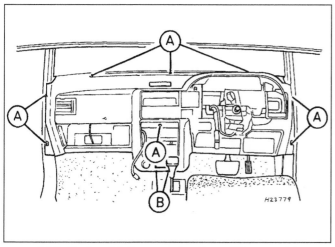

33.8b Facia retaining screw locations A (screw only)
and B (screw and washers)

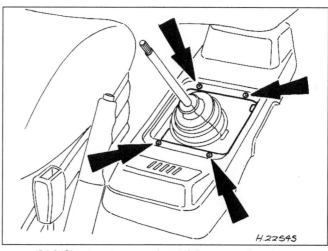

34.2 Short centre console retaining screw locations
(arrowed)

16 Refer to Chapter 12 and remove the radio/
cassette player.
17 Remove the footwell side cowl trim panel
on the driver's side by rotating the retaining
clip at the front of the panel through 90°, then
ease the panel away from the three tab
fasteners at the rear edge.
18 Pull free the weatherstrip from the leading
edge of the door aperture each side. Undo
the two screws and release the upper portion
of the scuff plate from the area below the
facia. Undo the retaining screw and remove
the A-pillar trim on each side.
19 Undo the lower bolt and detach the earth
lead from the cowl panel beneath the facia on
the driver's side.
20 Unclip and withdraw the fusebox from its
location below the facia. Disconnect the three
multi-plugs from the relay panel on top of the
fusebox.
21 Disconnect the two multi-plugs adjacent
to the driver's side cowl panel.
22 Detach the right-hand and left-hand
heater control cables from the heater
assembly.
23 Remove the centre console as described
in Section 34.
24 Carefully prise up the trim covers over the
three retaining screws along the upper edge
of the facia, adjacent to the windscreen. Undo
and remove the three screws now exposed.
25 Carefully prise out the blanking plug from
the upper edge of the radio aperture below
the heater controls. Undo and remove the
retaining screw now exposed.
26 Undo the remaining retaining screws at
each side of the facia and at the base below
the ashtray housing.
27 Detach the speedometer cable from the
retaining clip on the bulkhead in the engine
compartment.
28 Move the gear lever to the rear and ease
the facia from its location. When sufficient
clearance exists, disconnect the speedometer
cable from the instrument panel and the multi-
plug from the air bag control module.

29 With the aid of an assistant, manoeuvre
the facia clear of the steering column and out
from the driver's side of the car.

Refitting

30 Refitting is a reversal of the removal
procedure. Ensure that all wiring and cables
are correctly routed and securely
reconnected. Refer to the appropriate
Chapters for details on refitting the associated
fittings to the facia panel.
31 When the facia panel is completely
refitted, reconnect the battery then test the
various facia and steering column switches to
ensure that they operate in a satisfactory
manner.

34 Centre console –
removal and refitting

Removal

Short console – pre-1996 models

1 Unscrew and remove the knob from the
gear lever, then prise free the lever gaiter and
bezel. Slide the gaiter and bezel up the lever,
and lift them off.

2 Unscrew the four retaining screws, and
remove the console (see illustration).

Long console – pre-1996 models

3 Disconnect the battery negative (earth) lead
(refer to Chapter 5A, Section 1).
4 Remove the knob from the gear lever, then
prise free the lever gaiter and bezel. Slide the
gaiter and bezel up the lever, and lift them off.
5 On vehicles with electric windows or an
electrically-operated luggage compartment
lock, carefully prise out the switch panel or
switch, and disconnect the wiring connectors.
6 Undo the four console retaining nuts and
two screws (see illustration).
7 Pull up the handbrake lever as far as
possible, and manipulate the console over the
handbrake lever and gear lever. If insufficient
clearance exists, slacken the handbrake
adjuster as described in Chapter 1.

Long console – 1996-on models

8 Disconnect the battery negative (earth) lead
(refer to Chapter 5A, Section 1).
9 Remove the knob from the gear lever, then
prise free the lever gaiter and bezel. Slide the
gaiter and bezel up the lever, and lift them off.
10 Push the switch assembly (where fitted)
out from the underside of the console,
disconnect the multi-plugs and remove the
assembly.

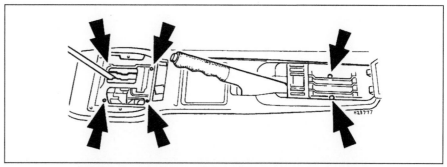

34.6 Long centre console retaining nut and screw locations
(arrowed)

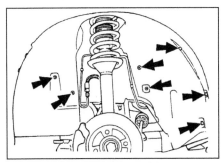

35.2 Wheel arch liner retaining screw locations (arrowed)

11 Release the handbrake lever surround from the console and slide the surround and gaiter off the lever.

12 Undo the four nuts and remove the gear lever floor gaiter and retaining plate. Recover the O-ring.

13 Open the stowage box lid at the rear of the console and undo the screw in the stowage box floor. On models without a stowage box, prise off the trim cap and undo the screw now exposed.

14 Pull up the handbrake lever as far as possible, lift the console up at the rear and slide it rearwards to release it from the facia at the front. If insufficient clearance exists between the console and handbrake lever, slacken the handbrake adjuster as described in Chapter 1.

15 Lift the console over the handbrake and gear lever and remove it from the car.

Refitting

16 Refitting is a reversal of removal. Where it was necessary to slacken the handbrake adjustment for removal of the console, re-check the adjustment as described in Chapter 1.

35 Wheel arch liners – removal and refitting

Removal

1 Apply the handbrake, then loosen off the front roadwheel nuts on the side concerned. Raise the vehicle at the front end, and support it on axle stands (see *Jacking and vehicle support*). Remove the roadwheel.

2 Unscrew and remove the seven Torx-type retaining screws **(see illustration)**.

3 Press the liner inwards at the top to disengage it from the locating tang, then withdraw it from the vehicle.

Refitting

4 Refit in the reverse order of the removal procedure. Tighten the roadwheel nuts to the specified torque wrench setting.

36 Radiator grille – removal and refitting

Removal

Pre-1993 models

1 Raise and support the bonnet. Unscrew and remove the four retaining screws along the top edge of the grille, then carefully lift the grille free, and disengage it from the locating socket each side at the bottom **(see illustration)**.

1993 to 1996 models

2 Raise and support the bonnet. Undo the three nuts securing the grille to the inside of the bonnet, and lift off the grille.

1996-on models

3 Raise and support the bonnet. Unscrew and remove the screws on the top face, release the upper and edge retaining studs and remove the air deflector **(see illustration)**.

4 Undo the two screws (one each side) and remove the grille **(see illustration)**.

Refitting

5 Refit in the reverse order of removal.

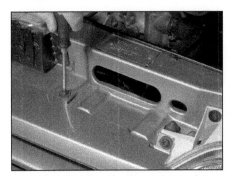

36.1 Radiator (front) grille panel retaining screw removal – pre-1993 models

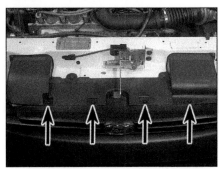

36.3 Air deflector top edge retaining screws (arrowed) – 1996-on models

36.4 Radiator grille side retaining screw (arrowed) – 1996-on models

Chapter 12
Body electrical systems

Contents

Degrees of difficulty

Easy, suitable for novice with little experience		Fairly easy, suitable for beginner with some experience		Fairly difficult, suitable for competent DIY mechanic		Difficult, suitable for experienced DIY mechanic		Very difficult, suitable for expert DIY or professional	

Specifications

Fuses
Refer to wiring diagrams

Relays (pre-1996 models)

No	Colour	Circuit
R1	Grey	Heated windscreen
R2	Red	Windscreen wiper intermittent control
R3	Grey	Heated rear windscreen
R4	Dark green	Anti-lock braking (system)
R5	Violet	Anti-lock braking (pump)
R6	White/Yellow	Main beam
R7	Orange	Rear wiper intermittent control
R8	Green/Red/Yellow	Engine management supply relay
R9	-	
R10	Brown	Magnetic clutch (air conditioning system)
R11	Green	Air conditioning system
R12	Brown	Engine running
R13	-	
R14	-	
R15	-	
R16	-	
R17	Yellow	Interior light delay
R18	Green	Electric windows
R19	Grey	Rear foglight (module)
R20	Spare	
R21	- / White	Busbar/front foglights (module)
R22	Blue	Headlight washer system
R23	White	Dip beam
R24	- / Red or Yellow	Busbar/alarm
R25	White	Front foglights
R26	Black	Steering lock/ignition switch
R27	-	

Relays (1996 and 1997 models)

No	Colour	Circuit
R1	Black	Ignition lock
R2	Brown	Engine management
R3	-	
R4	Brown	Magnetic clutch (air conditioning system)
R5	Grey	Heated mirrors/rear window timer
R6	Red	Windscreen wiper intermittent control
R7	Orange	Rear wiper intermittent control
R8	Brown	Dip beam
R9	Brown	Main beam
R10	Brown	Main beam (right-hand drive only)
R11	Yellow	Interior light delay
R12	Grey	Rear foglights
R13	Yellow	Starter inhibitor
R14	White	Front foglight control
R15	Brown	Front foglight supply
R16	Blue	Headlight washer system
R17	Blue	Air conditioning system
R18	-	
R19	-	
R20	-	
R21	Violet	Anti-lock braking system
R22	Dark green	Anti-lock braking system

Relays (1998-on models)

No	Colour	Circuit
R1	Black	Ignition lock
R2	Brown	Engine management
R3	-	
R4	Brown	Magnetic clutch (air conditioning system)
R5	Grey	Heated mirrors/rear window timer
R6	Red	Windscreen wiper intermittent control
R7	Orange	Rear wiper intermittent control
R8	Brown	Dip beam
R9	Brown	Main beam
R10	-	
R11	Yellow	Interior light delay
R12	-	
R13	Green	Starter inhibitor
R14	White	'Lights-on' audible warning
R15	Brown	Front foglights
R16	Blue	Headlight washer system
R17	Blue/brown	Air conditioning system
R18	-	
R19	Brown	Rear foglights
R20	-	
R21	-	
R22	White	Anti-theft alarm system

Bulbs

	Wattage
Brake stop/tail lights (Estate/Van)	21/5
Brake stop-lights (Hatchback/Saloon)	21
Cigar lighter illumination bulb	1.4
Clock illumination bulb	1.2
Courtesy light	10
Front indicator lights	21
Glovebox illumination light bulb	10
Hazard warning light switch bulb	1.3
Headlights (halogen H4)	60/55
High-level stop-light	5
Instrument panel illumination bulb	2.6
Instrument panel warning lights	1.3
Luggage area illumination bulb	10
Rear direction indicators	21
Rear foglights	21
Rear number plate light (Hatchback/Saloon/Estate)	10

Bulbs (continued)

	Wattage
Rear number plate light (Van)	5
Reversing lights	21
Side indicator repeater lights	5
Sidelights	5
Tail lights (Hatchback/Saloon)	5

Torque wrench settings

	Nm	lbf ft
Horn-to-body retaining nuts	30	22
Wiper arm nut	20	15
Wiper motor (new) to mounting bracket	12	9
Wiper motor (original) to mounting bracket	10	7
Wiper motor arm-to-spindle nut	24	18
Wiper motor bracket to bulkhead (or tailgate)	7	5

1 General information and precautions

General information

The electrical system is of 12-volt negative earth type. Power for the lights and all electrical accessories is supplied by a lead/acid battery, which is charged by the engine-driven alternator.

This Chapter covers repair and service procedures for the various electrical components not associated with the engine. Information on the battery, alternator, and starter motor can be found in Chapter 5A.

It should be noted that, prior to working on any component in the electrical system, the battery negative lead should first be disconnected, to prevent the possibility of electrical short-circuits and/or fires. If a radio/cassette player with anti-theft security code is fitted, refer to the information given in the reference sections of this manual before disconnecting the battery.

Precautions

⚠️ **Warning: Before carrying out any work on the electrical system, read through the precautions given in 'Safety first!' at the beginning of this manual and in Chapter 5A, Section 1.**

⚠️ **Warning: Later models are equipped with an air bag system. When working on the electrical system, refer to the precautions given in Section 29, to avoid the possibility of personal injury.**

2 Electrical fault finding – general information

Note: *Refer to the precautions given in 'Safety first!' and in Section 1 of this Chapter before starting work. The following tests relate to testing of the main electrical circuits, and should not be used to test delicate electronic circuits (such as engine management systems, anti-lock braking systems, etc), particularly where an electronic control unit is used.*

General

1 A typical electrical circuit consists of an electrical component, any switches, relays, motors, fuses, fusible links or circuit breakers related to that component, and the wiring and connectors which link the component to both the battery and the chassis. To help to pinpoint a problem in an electrical circuit, wiring diagrams are included at the end of this manual.

2 Before attempting to diagnose an electrical fault, first study the appropriate wiring diagram, to obtain a more complete understanding of the components included in the particular circuit concerned. The possible sources of a fault can be narrowed down by noting whether other components related to the circuit are operating properly. If several components or circuits fail at one time, the problem is likely to be related to a shared fuse or earth connection.

3 Electrical problems usually stem from simple causes, such as loose or corroded connections, a faulty earth connection, a blown fuse, a melted fusible link, or a faulty relay. Visually inspect the condition of all fuses, wires and connections in a problem circuit before testing the components. Use the wiring diagrams to determine which terminal connections will need to be checked, in order to pinpoint the trouble-spot.

4 The basic tools required for electrical fault-finding include a circuit tester or voltmeter (a 12-volt bulb with a set of test leads can also be used for certain tests); a self-powered test light (sometimes known as a continuity tester); an ohmmeter (to measure resistance); a battery and set of test leads; and a jumper wire, preferably with a circuit breaker or fuse incorporated, which can be used to bypass suspect wires or electrical components. Before attempting to locate a problem with test instruments, use the wiring diagram to determine where to make the connections.

5 To find the source of an intermittent wiring fault (usually due to a poor or dirty connection, or damaged wiring insulation), a 'wiggle' test can be performed on the wiring. This involves wiggling the wiring by hand, to see if the fault occurs as the wiring is moved. It should be possible to narrow down the source of the fault to a particular section of

wiring. This method of testing can be used in conjunction with any of the tests described in the following sub-Sections.

6 Apart from problems due to poor connections, two basic types of fault can occur in an electrical circuit – open-circuit, or short-circuit.

7 Open-circuit faults are caused by a break somewhere in the circuit, which prevents current from flowing. An open-circuit fault will prevent a component from working, but will not cause the relevant circuit fuse to blow.

8 Short-circuit faults are normally caused by a breakdown in wiring insulation, which allows a feed wire to touch either another wire, or an earthed component such as the bodyshell. This allows the current flowing in the circuit to 'escape' along an alternative route, usually to earth. As the circuit does not now follow its original complete path, it is known as a 'short' circuit. A short-circuit fault will normally cause the relevant circuit fuse to blow.

Finding an open-circuit

9 To check for an open-circuit, connect one lead of a circuit tester or voltmeter to either the negative battery terminal or a known good earth.

10 Connect the other lead to a connector in the circuit being tested, preferably nearest to the battery or fuse.

11 Switch on the circuit, bearing in mind that some circuits are live only when the ignition switch is moved to a particular position.

12 If voltage is present (indicated either by the tester bulb lighting or a voltmeter reading, as applicable), this means that the section of the circuit between the relevant connector and the battery is problem-free.

13 Continue to check the remainder of the circuit in the same fashion.

14 When a point is reached at which no voltage is present, the problem must lie between that point and the previous test point with voltage. Most problems can be traced to a broken, corroded or loose connection.

Finding a short-circuit

15 To check for a short-circuit, first disconnect the load(s) from the circuit (loads are the components which draw current from a circuit, such as bulbs, motors, heating elements, etc).

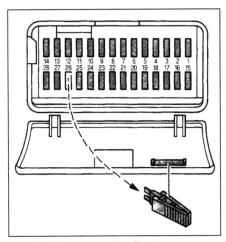

3.1 Fuse removal using tweezers

16 Remove the relevant fuse from the circuit, and connect a circuit tester or voltmeter to the fuse connections.

17 Switch on the circuit, bearing in mind that some circuits are live only when the ignition switch is moved to a particular position.

18 If voltage is present (indicated either by the tester bulb lighting or a voltmeter reading, as applicable), this means that there is a short-circuit.

19 If no voltage is present, but the fuse still blows with the load(s) connected, this indicates an internal fault in the load(s).

Finding an earth fault

20 The battery negative terminal is connected to 'earth' – the metal of the engine/transmission and the car body – and most systems are wired so that they only receive a positive feed, the current returning via the metal of the car body. This means that the component mounting and the body form part of that circuit. Loose or corroded mountings can therefore cause a range of electrical faults, ranging from total failure of a circuit, to a puzzling partial fault. In particular, lights may shine dimly (especially when another circuit sharing the same earth point is in operation), motors (eg wiper motors or the radiator cooling fan motor) may run slowly, and the operation of one circuit may have an

apparently-unrelated effect on another. Note that earth straps are used between certain components, such as the engine/transmission and the body, usually where there is no metal-to-metal contact between components, due to flexible rubber mountings, etc.

21 To check whether a component is properly earthed, disconnect the battery, and connect one lead of an ohmmeter to a known good earth point. Connect the other lead to the wire or earth connection being tested. The resistance reading should be zero; if not, check the connection as follows.

22 If an earth connection is thought to be faulty, dismantle the connection, and clean back to bare metal both the bodyshell and the wire terminal or the component earth connection mating surface. Be careful to remove all traces of dirt and corrosion, then use a knife to trim away any paint, so that a clean metal-to-metal joint is made. On reassembly, tighten the joint fasteners securely; if a wire terminal is being refitted, use serrated washers between the terminal and the bodyshell, to ensure a clean and secure connection. When the connection is remade, prevent the onset of corrosion in the future by applying a coat of petroleum jelly or silicone-based grease, or by spraying on (at regular intervals) a proprietary water-dispersant lubricant.

3 Fuses and relays – general information

Note: *It is important to note that the ignition switch and the appropriate electrical circuit must always be switched off before any of the fuses (or relays) are removed and renewed. In the event of the fuse/relay having to be removed, the vehicle anti-theft system must be de-activated and the battery earth lead detached. When disconnecting the battery, refer to Chapter 5A, Section 1.*

1 The main fuse and relay block is located below the facia panel on the driver's side within the vehicle. The fuses can be inspected and if necessary renewed, by unclipping and removing the access cover. Each fuse location is numbered – refer to the fuse chart in the wiring diagrams to check which circuits

are protected by each fuse. Plastic tweezers are attached to the inside face of the cover to remove and fit the fuses **(see illustration)**.

2 To remove a fuse, use the tweezers provided to pull it out of the holder. Slide the fuse sideways from the tweezers. The wire within the fuse is clearly visible, and it will be broken if the fuse is blown.

3 Always renew a fuse with one of an identical rating. Never renew a fuse more than once without tracing the source of the trouble. The fuse rating is stamped on top of the fuse.

4 Additional 'main' fuses are located separately in a box positioned in front of the battery and these are accessible for inspection by first raising and supporting the bonnet, then unclipping and hinging back the cover from the fusebox **(see illustration)**. Each of these fuses is lettered for identification – refer to the wiring diagrams to check which circuits they protect. To remove fuses A, B and C, it is first necessary to remove the fusebox. Fuses D and E can be removed from their locations by carefully pulling them free from the location socket in the box. In the event of one of these fuses blowing, it is essential that the circuits concerned are checked and any faults rectified before renewing the faulty fuse. If necessary, entrust this task to a Ford dealer or a competent automotive electrician.

5 With the exception of the indicator flasher relay, the remainder of the relays are fitted to the reverse side of the 'in-vehicle' fuse board. To inspect a relay mounted on the main fuse board, disconnect the battery, remove the fusebox cover and unclip the fusebox. Unscrew the six securing screws to detach and remove the lower facia panel on the driver's side. Carefully withdraw the fuse/relay block.

6 The various relays can be removed from their respective locations on the fuse board by carefully pulling them from the sockets **(see illustration)**.

7 The direction indicator flasher relay is attached to the base of the multi-function switch unit. Access to the relay is made by undoing the retaining screws and removing the steering column lower shroud. The relay can then be withdrawn from the base of the switch **(see illustration)**.

3.4 Additional 'main' fuses at the front of the battery

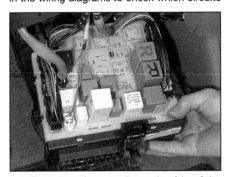

3.6 Relay locations on the underside of the fuse board

3.7 Direction indicator flasher relay removal

8 If a system controlled by a relay becomes inoperative and the relay is suspect, listen to the relay as the circuit is operated. If the relay is functioning, it should be possible to hear it click as it is energised. If the relay proves satisfactory, the fault lies with the components or wiring of the system. If the relay is not being energised, then it is not receiving a main supply voltage or a switching voltage, or the relay is faulty.

4 Switches – removal and refitting

Ignition switch

1 Disconnect the battery negative (earth) lead (refer to Chapter 5A, Section 1).
2 Undo the two upper and four lower retaining screws, and remove the upper and lower shrouds from the steering column.
3 Where applicable, undo the single screw and withdraw the Passive Anti-Theft System (PATS) transceiver from the ignition switch/steering lock barrel.
4 Insert the key and turn the ignition switch to position I. Depress the two ignition switch-to-lock securing tabs, and withdraw the switch from the lock **(see illustrations)**.
5 Undo the six retaining screws, and remove the lower facia panel on the driver's side. Unclip the fusebox panel, then detach the ignition switch wiring multi-plug connector from the fusebox. Release the switch wire from the tie clips and remove the switch.
6 Refitting is a reversal of the removal procedure. When relocating the switch to the steering lock, the barrel driveshaft must align with the switch shaft as it is pushed into position. Check the switch for satisfactory operation on completion.

Steering column switch

7 Remove the steering wheel as described in Chapter 10.
8 Undo the two upper and four lower retaining screws, and remove the upper and lower steering column shrouds.
9 Undo the single retaining screw, and withdraw the switch upwards from the steering column. Detach the wiring connector and cable-tie clips from the switch **(see illustrations)**.
10 Separate the indicator/hazard warning relay and switch from the indicator switch unit.
11 Refit in the reverse order of removal. Refer to Chapter 10 for information required when refitting the steering wheel.

Facia switches

12 Disconnect the battery negative (earth) lead (refer to Chapter 5A, Section 1).
13 The facia and associated panel-mounted switches are secured in position by integral plastic or metal retaining clips. In some

4.4a Depress the lock tabs . . .

4.4b . . . and remove the ignition switch

instances, it is possible to release the switch from the panel using a suitable small screwdriver inserted between the switch and the facia to lever the switch from its aperture, but take care not to apply too much force when trying this method.

> **HAYNES HiNT**
> Where a switch is reluctant to be released, remove the section of the facia panel or the adjoining panel or component to allow access to the rear side of the switch and compress the retaining clips to enable the switch to be withdrawn.

14 Once the switch is released and partially withdrawn from the panel, detach the wiring connector and remove the switch **(see illustration)**.
15 Refitting is a reversal of removal.

Courtesy light switches

16 Disconnect the battery negative (earth) lead (refer to Chapter 5A, Section 1).
17 With the door open, undo the retaining screw and withdraw the switch from the door pillar. Pull out the wiring slightly, and tie a piece of string to it, so that it can be retrieved if it drops down into the door pillar.
18 Disconnect the wiring from the switch.
19 Refitting is a reversal of removal.

Luggage area contact plate

20 Disconnect the battery negative (earth) lead (refer to Chapter 5A, Section 1).
21 Open the tailgate, undo the two securing screws and remove the rear trim panel to gain access to the rear side of the plate.
22 Release the side retaining clips using a thin-bladed screwdriver, and push the contact plate from its location in the body **(see illustration)**.

4.9a Undo the retaining screw . . .

4.9b . . . lift the switch clear and detach the wiring connector

4.14 Facia switch removal

4.22 Luggage area contact plate removal from the rear panel

4.27 Contact switch unit in the tailgate

4.32 Handbrake warning light switch

23 Disconnect the wiring connectors and remove the plate.
24 Refit in the reverse order of removal.

Luggage area contact switch

25 Disconnect the battery negative (earth) lead (refer to Chapter 5A, Section 1).
26 Open the tailgate and remove its inner trim panel.
27 Working through the access aperture in the tailgate, use a thin-bladed screwdriver to depress the switch retaining clips and extract the switch from the panel (see illustration).
28 Disconnect the wiring connectors and remove the switch.
29 Refit in the reverse order of removal. Make sure that the pins and their contacts are clean. On completion, check the operation of the rear wipers, courtesy light, heated rear window and the tailgate release/central locking system.

Handbrake warning light switch

Pre-1996 models

30 Disconnect the battery negative (earth) lead (refer to Chapter 5A, Section 1).
31 Refer to Chapter 11 for details, and remove the front passenger (left-hand) seat and the centre console.
32 Detach the wiring connector from the handbrake warning light switch, then undo the two retaining screws and remove the switch (see illustration).
33 Refit in the reverse order of removal. Check that the switch operates in a satisfactory manner before refitting the console and seat.

1996-on models

34 Disconnect the battery negative (earth) lead (refer to Chapter 5A, Section 1).
35 Carefully prise up the gaiter and trim surround from the handbrake lever.
36 Disconnect the multi-plug, undo the screw and remove the switch from the lever.
37 Refit in the reverse order of removal.

Brake stop-light switch

38 Disconnect the battery negative (earth) lead (refer to Chapter 5A, Section 1).
39 The brake stop-light switch is attached to the brake pedal mounting bracket (see illustration).
40 Detach the wiring connector from the switch, then twist the switch through a quarter of a turn (90°) and withdraw it from the bracket (see illustration).
41 Insert the switch into its locating slot in the pedal bracket.
42 Support the brake pedal in the 'at rest' position and push the switch down until the switch plunger is fully in.
43 Turn the switch through 40° to back it off 1.0 mm and lock it in position.
44 Reconnect the wiring and the battery and test the switch operation.

Heater/blower motor switch

Pre-1996 models

45 Disconnect the battery negative (earth) lead (refer to Chapter 5A, Section 1).
46 Carefully prise free the three heater/fresh air and blower/air conditioning switch control knobs.

47 Unscrew and remove the two instrument bezel retaining screws, and remove the bezel.
48 Undo the four screws, and remove the heater panel facia. Detach the wiring connector to the heater panel illumination bulb.
49 Compress the switch tabs to pull free the switch, then detach the wiring multi-plug from the switch (see illustration).
50 Refit in the reverse order of removal.

1996-on models

51 Disconnect the battery negative (earth) lead (refer to Chapter 5A, Section 1).
52 Undo the two retaining screws, and remove the upper steering column shroud.
53 Similarly, undo the four screws and remove the lower steering column shroud.
54 Refer to Chapter 10 and remove the steering wheel.
55 Carefully prise free the three heater/fresh air and blower/air conditioning switch control knobs.
56 Undo the two retaining screws from the underside top edge of the instrument panel bezel and withdraw the bezel. Disconnect the wiring multi-plugs and remove the bezel.
57 Compress the switch tabs to pull free the switch, then detach the wiring multi-plug from the switch.
58 Refit in the reverse order of removal.

Electric window switches

59 Disconnect the battery negative (earth) lead (refer to Chapter 5A, Section 1).
60 On pre-1996 models, insert a thin-bladed screwdriver between the switch and the console, then carefully prise free the switch from its location. If the switch is reluctant to release, do not apply excessive force; remove the centre console (see Chapter 11 for details) and release the switch from the underside.
61 On 1996 models, carefully prise up the gaiter and trim surround from the base of the gear lever.
62 Detach the wire connector from the switch, and remove it.
63 Refit in the reverse order of removal, then check the switch for satisfactory operation.

Electric door mirror switch

64 Disconnect the battery negative (earth) lead (refer to Chapter 5A, Section 1).

4.39 Brake stop-light switch location

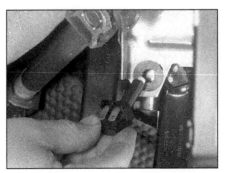

4.40 Brake stop-light switch removal

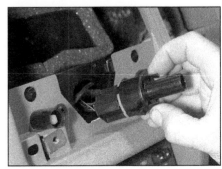

4.49 Heater blower motor switch removal – pre-1996 models

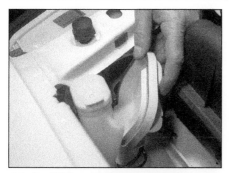

5.1 On 1996-on models, remove the cover from the rear of the headlight

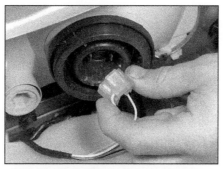

5.2a Headlight bulb wiring connector on pre-1996 models . . .

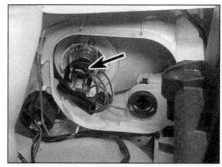

5.2b . . . and on 1996-on models (arrowed)

65 Carefully prise free the switch using a thin-bladed screwdriver as a lever, but insert a suitable protective pad between the screwdriver and the housing to avoid damage.
66 Detach the wiring multi-plug connector and remove the switch.
67 Refit in the reverse order of removal, then adjust the mirror and check that the operation of the switch is satisfactory.

Headlight beam adjuster switch
68 Refer to Section 9.

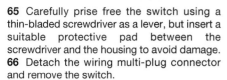

5 Bulbs (exterior lights) – renewal

Note: *Ensure all exterior lights are switched off before disconnecting the wiring connectors to any exterior light bulbs. The headlight and front sidelight bulbs are removable from within the engine compartment with the bonnet raised. Note that if a bulb fails, and has just been in use, it will still be extremely hot, particularly in the case of a headlight bulb.*

Headlight
1 On 1996-on models, release the spring clip and remove the cover from the rear of the headlight unit **(see illustration)**.
2 Pull free the wiring connector from the rear of the headlight on the side concerned. On pre-1996 models, prise free the protector cap from the rear of the headlight unit **(see illustrations)**.

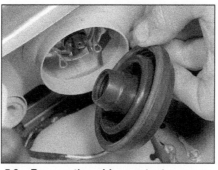

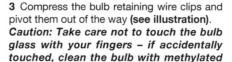

5.2c Remove the rubber protector cap on pre-1996 models

3 Compress the bulb retaining wire clips and pivot them out of the way **(see illustration)**.
Caution: Take care not to touch the bulb glass with your fingers – if accidentally touched, clean the bulb with methylated spirit.
4 Withdraw the bulb from its location in the headlight **(see illustration)**.
5 Fit the new bulb using a reversal of the removal procedure. Make sure that the tabs on the bulb support are correctly located in the lens assembly.
6 Check the headlight beam alignment as described in Section 8.

Front sidelight
7 On 1996-on models, release the spring clip and remove the cover from the rear of the headlight unit.
8 On pre-1996 models, compress the wire retaining clip, and detach the wiring

5.3 . . . compress the clips . . .

connector from the sidelight **(see illustration)**.
9 Pull free the sidelight bulbholder from its location in the rear of the headlight **(see illustration)**.
10 Remove the bulb from the bulbholder.
11 Fit the new bulb using a reversal of the removal procedure. Check for satisfactory operation on completion.

Front direction indicator
Pre-1996 models
12 Unhook the retaining spring from the rear of the direction indicator, and move the direction indicator forwards in order to release it **(see illustration)**.
13 Turn the direction indicator bulbholder and pull it free from the indicator (do not pull on the wire).
14 Depress and twist the bulb to remove it from the bulbholder **(see illustration)**.

5.4 . . . and withdraw the headlight bulb

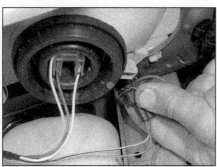

5.8 Detach the wiring connector from the sidelight bulb on pre-1996 models

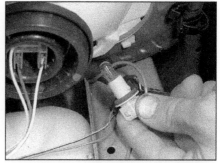

5.9 Removing the sidelight bulbholder

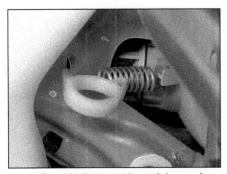

5.12 Front indicator unit retaining spring

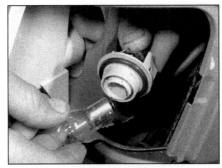

5.14 Front indicator bulb renewal on pre-1996 models

5.15 Engage the tags in their locating slots when refitting the front indicator unit

15 Fit the new bulb using a reversal of the removal procedure. As the light is fitted into position, engage its tags in the slots of the headlight **(see illustration)**. Check for satisfactory operation on completion.

1996-on models

16 Turn the direction indicator bulbholder anti-clockwise and withdraw it from the rear of the headlight unit.
17 Depress and twist the bulb to remove it from the bulbholder.
18 Fit the new bulb and bulbholder using a reversal of the removal procedure. Check for satisfactory operation on completion.

Front indicator side repeater

19 On early models with a square light unit, turn the light in a clockwise direction to release it from the front wing. On later models with an oval light unit, push the unit sideways

(depending how the unit was last fitted, this will either be forwards or backwards, but no great force should be needed), then unhook it from the wing **(see illustration)**.
20 Pull out the bulbholder and wiring, then remove the bulb **(see illustration)**.
21 Fit the new bulb using a reversal of the removal procedure, and check for satisfactory operation.

Front foglight

1996-on models

22 Working under the front bumper, remove the protective cap from the rear of the foglight unit.
23 Push the retaining clip outward and remove the bulb assembly.
24 Disconnect the wiring at the in-line connector and remove the bulb.
25 Fit the new bulb using a reversal of the

removal procedure, and check for satisfactory operation.

Rear light cluster

Hatchback and Saloon models

26 On pre-1993 model year vehicles, working in the luggage area, press the lock tabs (recessed in the rear face of the bulbholder on the side concerned) in towards the centre, and pull free the bulbholder. On 1993 to 1995 models, release the two clips and remove the light cluster trim. Disconnect the wiring multi-plug, press the bulbholder retainer upwards, and pull free the bulbholder **(see illustrations)**. On 1996-on models, press the lock tabs in the rear face of the bulbholder in towards the centre, and pull free the bulbholder.
27 Depress and twist the bulb concerned to remove it from the holder **(see illustration)**.
28 Fit the new bulb using a reversal of the removal procedure. Relocate the holder by pressing it in until the retainers engage. Refit the multi-plug, where applicable. Check the operation of the rear lights on completion.

Estate models

29 Prise back the rear trim cover on the side concerned to gain access to the light from within the luggage area. Press the lock tab down, lift the holder a fraction and withdraw it **(see illustration)**.
30 Depress and twist free the bulb concerned from the holder.
31 Fit the new bulb using a reversal of the removal procedure. Relocate the holder by sliding the lower end into position first, then

5.19 Removing a later-type oval side repeater light

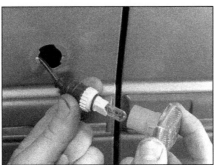

5.20 Side repeater light assembly

5.26a Rear bulbholder removal on pre-1993 Saloon and Hatchback models

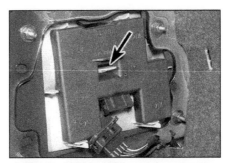

5.26b On 1993 to 1995 models, press the bulbholder retainer (arrowed) upwards and pull free the bulbholder

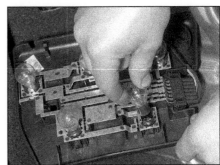

5.27 Removing a bulb from the bulbholder

press the upper end into position so that it clicks into place. Check the operation of the rear lights on completion.

Van models

32 Working from within the rear of the vehicle on the side concerned, turn the appropriate bulbholder in an anti-clockwise direction and withdraw the holder.
33 Depress and untwist the bulb to release it from its holder.
34 Fit the new bulb using a reversal of the removal procedure. Check the rear lights for satisfactory operation on completion.

Number plate lights

35 Prise the number plate light from the rear bumper using a screwdriver **(see illustration)**.
36 Disconnect the wiring plug and earth lead from the light.
37 On Hatchback, Saloon and Estate models, prise open the plastic retaining clip to withdraw the bulbholder from the light unit, then depress and untwist the bulb to remove it from the holder **(see illustrations)**.
38 To remove the bulb on Van models, twist the bulbholder anti-clockwise and withdraw it, then pull free the bulb.
39 Fit the new bulb using a reversal of the removal procedure. Check the operation of the lights on completion.

Rear foglight (1993-on models)

40 With the tailgate open, release the cover from the inner trim panel to access the bulbholder.
41 Twist the bulbholder anti-clockwise and withdraw it, then pull free the bulb.
42 Fit the new bulb using a reversal of the removal procedure. Check the operation of the light on completion.

High-level stop-light

43 Open the tailgate on Hatchback and Estate models, or enter the rear passenger compartment on Saloon models.
44 Undo the two retaining screws and withdraw the light unit from its location.
45 Spread the edges of the light unit outward to release the bulbholder and reflector. Release the four locating tags and separate the reflector from the bulbholder.

5.29 Rear light cluster removal on Estate models

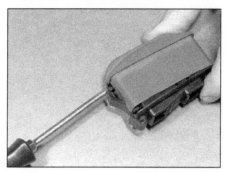

5.37a Prise open the clip . . .

46 Pull free the relevant bulb(s) from the bulbholder.
47 Fit the new bulb(s) and the light unit using a reversal of the removal procedure. Check the operation of the light on completion.

6 Bulbs (interior lights) – renewal

Courtesy lights

1 Prise out the light using a small flat-bladed screwdriver **(see illustration)**.
2 Release the festoon-type bulb from the spring contacts.
3 Fit the new bulb using a reversal of the removal procedure. Check the tension of the spring contacts, and if necessary bend them so that they firmly contact the bulb end caps.

5.35 Number plate light removal from the bumper on Estate models

5.37b . . . and separate the number plate light unit and bulbholder

Luggage area light

4 Prise free and withdraw the light **(see illustration)**. On later models, turn the bulbholder anti-clockwise and remove it from the light unit.
5 Pull free the bulb from its holder and remove it.
6 Fit the new bulb and refit the light using a reversal of the removal procedure.

Instrument panel and warning lights

7 Remove the instrument panel as described in Section 10.
8 Turn the bulbholder a quarter-turn to align the shoulders with the slots, then remove it and pull the capless bulb from the bulbholder **(see illustration)**.
9 Fit the new bulb in reverse order.

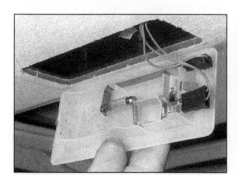

6.1 Roof-mounted courtesy light removal

6.4 Luggage area light removed for bulb replacement

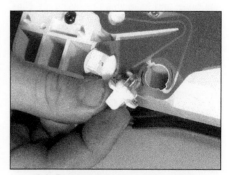

6.8 Bulbholder removal from the instrument panel

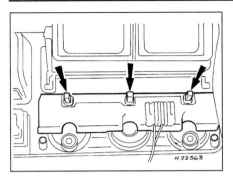

6.11 Heater control panel illumination bulb locations (arrowed)

6.23 Glovebox light switch/bulbholder removal

6.27 Bulbholder attachment at the rear of the clock

Heater control illumination

Pre-1996 models

10 Undo the two retaining screws from its upper edge, and withdraw the instrument panel surround.
11 Carefully prise free the three heater/fresh air and blower/air conditioning switch control knobs, then undo the heater control panel retaining screws. Withdraw the panel from the facia just enough to gain access to the bulbs on its rear face **(see illustration)**.
12 Twist the bulbs anti-clockwise to remove them.
13 Refit in the reverse order of removal, and check for satisfactory operation on completion.

1996-on models

14 Disconnect the battery negative (earth) lead (refer to Chapter 5A, Section 1).
15 Undo the two retaining screws, and remove the upper steering column shroud.
16 Similarly, undo the four retaining screws and remove the lower steering column shroud.
17 Refer to Chapter 10 and remove the steering wheel.
18 Carefully prise free the three heater/fresh air and blower/air conditioning switch control knobs.
19 Undo the two retaining screws from the underside top edge of the instrument panel bezel. Release the bezel from the retaining clips (two at the top, four along the bottom, and one at the side furthest away from the steering wheel). Use a screwdriver with protective pad or cloth to prevent damage to the bezel and facia when releasing the clips. Withdraw the bezel and disconnect the wiring multi-plugs.
20 Twist the bulbs anti-clockwise to remove them.
21 Refit in the reverse order of removal, and check for satisfactory operation on completion.

Glovebox light

22 Open the glovebox, then undo the two retaining screws and withdraw the light/switch unit.
23 Prise free the switch/bulbholder, then untwist and remove the bulb from the holder **(see illustration)**.

24 Fit the new bulb using a reversal of the removal procedure.

Hazard warning light tell-tale

25 Pull free the cover from the switch, then pull free the bulb from the switch/holder.
26 Refit in the reverse order of removal, and check for satisfactory operation.

Clock illumination

Pre-1996 models

27 Engage the hooked ends of a pair of circlip pliers in the two holes in the underside of the clock bezel as shown, and carefully pull free the clock from its aperture in the facia. The bulbholder can then be untwisted and withdrawn from the rear face of the clock and the bulb renewed **(see illustration)**.
28 Refit in the reverse order of removal.

1996-on models

29 Remove the instrument panel bezel as described in paragraphs 14 to 19 above.
30 Twist the relevant bulbholder anti-clockwise to remove, then remove the bulb from the holder.
31 Refit in the reverse order of removal, and check for satisfactory operation on completion.

Cigar lighter illumination

32 Remove the lighter as described in Section 13.
33 On pre-1996 models, withdraw the illumination ring from the facia. Remove the bulb from the illumination ring.
34 On 1996-on models, remove the

7.5 Headlight unit retaining screws (arrowed)

bulbholder from the lighter housing and remove the bulb from the holder.
35 Refit in the reverse order of removal. Check for satisfactory operation on completion.

7 Exterior light units – removal and refitting

1 Disconnect the battery negative (earth) lead (refer to Chapter 5A, Section 1), before removing any of the light units.

Headlight

Pre-1996 models

2 Open and support the bonnet, then on pre-1993 models, undo the four screws along the top edge of the grille panel, and lift the panel clear.
3 Remove the front direction indicator as described later in this Section.
4 Detach the wiring connections from the headlight and sidelight in the rear of the appropriate headlight unit.
5 Working through the cut-out of the direction indicator, unscrew the headlight lower retaining screw, then undo the two upper securing screws from the points indicated **(see illustration)**. On later models, there is an additional upper retaining screw. Withdraw the headlight forwards from the vehicle.
6 If a new headlight is to be fitted, remove the headlight and sidelight bulbs/holders, and transfer them to the new light unit as described in Section 5. The individual parts of the headlight are not otherwise renewable.
7 Refitting is a reversal of the removal procedure. When fitting the headlight into position, ensure that the location pin sits in its recess, and note the arrangement of the insulating washers on the retaining screws **(see illustrations)**. Loosely locate the headlight, and temporarily fit the indicator to check that the gap between the headlight and the indicator is even. Fully tighten the upper retaining screws, then remove the indicator to tighten the lower headlight screw.
8 When the headlight and indicator units are fitted and their wiring connectors attached, check the lights for satisfactory operation before fitting the front grille panel.

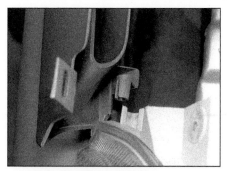

7.7a Headlight engagement pin

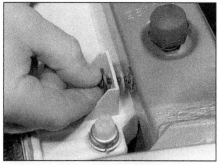

7.7b Headlight retaining screw showing washer arrangement

7.25 Rear light lens showing the retaining nuts

9 Finally, check the headlight beam alignment as described in Section 8.

1996-on models

10 Remove the radiator grille and the front bumper as described in Chapter 11.
11 Undo the three screws securing the headlight unit to the body panel.
12 Pull the locating spigots out of the retaining plate.
13 Disconnect the wiring connectors at the rear and remove the headlight unit.
14 Refitting is a reversal of the removal procedure. Check the lights for operation and check the headlight beam alignment as described in Section 8 on completion.

Front direction indicator

Pre-1996 models

15 Unhook the retaining spring from the rear of the direction indicator (see illustration 5.12).
16 Move the direction indicator forwards in order to release it.
17 Turn the bulbholder and release it from the rear of the direction indicator.
18 Remove the direction indicator from the vehicle.
19 Refitting is a reversal of removal. Check that the operation of the indicator is satisfactory on completion.

1996-on models

20 On 1996-on models, the direction indicator is an integral part of the headlight unit. Refer to paragraphs 10 to 14.

Indicator side repeater

21 Raise and support the bonnet. Detach the indicator wiring multi-plug at the bulkhead, and attach a length of string to the connector end of the wire going to the side repeater. This will act as a guide to feed the wire back through the body channels when refitting the repeater unit.
22 On early models with a square light unit, turn the light in a clockwise direction to release it from the front wing. On later models with an oval light unit, push the unit sideways, then unhook it from the wing (see Section 5). When the wiring connector and string are drawn through, they can be separated and the string left in position.

23 Refitting is a reversal of removal. Attach the wire to the string and draw it through the body panels, then disconnect the string and reconnect the light multi-plug at the bulkhead. When the light is refitted, check for satisfactory operation.

Rear light cluster

24 Working in the luggage area, release the rear bulbholder (according to type) from the side concerned as described in Section 5.
25 Unscrew the mounting nuts and withdraw the rear light lens from the rear of the vehicle (see illustration).
26 Renew the seal gasket if it is in poor condition. Refit in the reverse order to removal, and check for satisfactory operation of the rear lights on completion.

Number plate lights

27 Prise the number plate light from the rear bumper using a small screwdriver, then disconnect the wiring plug.
28 Refitting is a reversal of removal.

Rear foglight (1993-on)

29 With the tailgate open, undo the ten retaining screws and withdraw the tailgate inner trim panel.
30 Disconnect the bulbholder multi-plug, then undo the retaining nut and remove the foglight.
31 Refitting is a reversal of removal.

High-level stop-light

32 Removal and refitting is described as part of the bulb renewal procedure in Section 5.

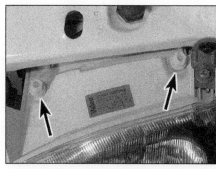

8.2 Headlight beam adjustment screws (arrowed)

8 Headlight beam alignment – general information

1 Accurate adjustment of the headlight beam is only possible using optical beam-setting equipment, and this work should therefore be carried out by a Ford dealer or service station with the necessary facilities.
2 For reference, the headlight adjustment screws are located on the top of the headlight unit. The outer adjuster alters the horizontal height of the beam and the inner adjuster alters the vertical beam height (see illustration).
3 Later models may be equipped with a variable-position electrical beam adjuster unit – this can be used to adjust the vertical position of the headlight beam, to compensate for the relevant load which the vehicle is carrying. An adjuster switch is provided on the facia. The adjuster switch should be positioned as follows, according to the load being carried in the vehicle. Note that higher switch positions may be necessary if the vehicle is towing a trailer.

Hatchback, Saloon and Estate

Position 0   Front seat(s) occupied, luggage compartment empty
Position 1.5 Front seat(s) occupied, luggage compartment loaded up to 100 kg
Position 1.5 Front and rear seat(s) occupied, luggage compartment loaded up to 30 kg
Position 2.5 Front and rear seats fully occupied, luggage compartment fully loaded
Position 3.5 Driver's seat only occupied, luggage compartment fully loaded

Van models

Position 0   Front seat(s) occupied, luggage compartment empty or loaded up to 100 kg
Position 3.5 Driver's seat only occupied, luggage compartment fully loaded

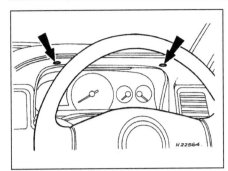

10.3 Instrument panel bezel retaining screw locations (arrowed)

10.4a Instrument cluster retaining screws on pre-1996 models

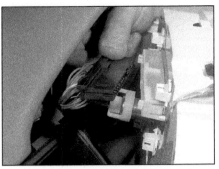

10.4b Detach the wiring multi-plugs from the instrument panel

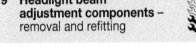

9 Headlight beam adjustment components – removal and refitting

General

1 Refer to Section 8.

Adjuster switch

Removal

2 Remove the instrument panel bezel as described in Section 10.
3 Depress the retaining tabs on the side of the switch body and push the switch out from its location.

Refitting

4 Refitting is a reversal of removal.

Adjuster motor

Removal

5 Remove the relevant headlight unit as described in Section 7.
6 Disconnect the wiring connector from the adjuster motor.
7 Rotate the adjuster motor body to release it from the headlight unit. Withdraw the motor and detach the motor balljoint from the adjuster lever. Take care, as the adjuster lever is easily broken.
8 Remove the motor.

Refitting

9 Engage the motor balljoint with the headlight adjuster lever until it is heard to click into place. Refit the motor body to the headlight unit, and rotate the motor to lock it in position.
10 Refit the headlight as described in Section 7.

10 Instrument panel – removal and refitting

Removal

Pre-1996 models

1 Disconnect the battery negative (earth) lead (refer to Chapter 5A, Section 1).
2 Although not strictly necessary, in order to withdraw the instrument panel, the removal of the steering wheel will provide much improved access, particularly when detaching (and subsequently reconnecting) the speedometer cable and wiring multi-plugs from the rear of the unit. Refer to Chapter 10 for steering wheel removal and refitting procedures.
3 Undo the two retaining screws from the underside top edge of the instrument panel bezel and withdraw the bezel, releasing it from the location clips each side and underneath (see illustration).
4 Unscrew and remove the four instrument

panel screws, and carefully withdraw the panel to the point where the wiring multi-plugs and the speedometer cable can be detached from the rear (see illustrations). Note that it may be necessary to push the speedometer cable through the from the engine compartment side to allow the instrument panel to be sufficiently withdrawn. Take care when handling the instrument panel whilst it is removed, and position it in a safe place where it will not get knocked or damaged. If a tachometer is fitted, do not lay the panel on its face for extended periods, as the silicone fluid in the tachometer may well be released.

1996-on models

5 Disconnect the battery negative (earth) lead (refer to Chapter 5A, Section 1).
6 Undo the two retaining screws, and remove the upper steering column shroud.
7 Similarly, undo the four retaining screws and remove the lower steering column shroud.
8 Refer to Chapter 10 and remove the steering wheel.
9 Carefully prise free the three heater/fresh air and blower/air conditioning switch control knobs.
10 Undo the two retaining screws from the underside top edge of the instrument panel bezel. Release the bezel from the retaining clips using a screwdriver with protective pad or cloth to prevent damage to the bezel and facia (see illustrations). Withdraw the bezel and disconnect the wiring multi-plugs.

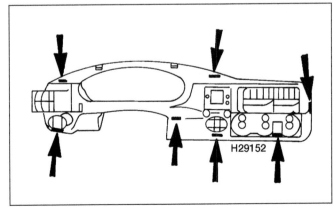

10.10a On 1996-on models, release the instrument panel bezel retaining clips (arrowed) . . .

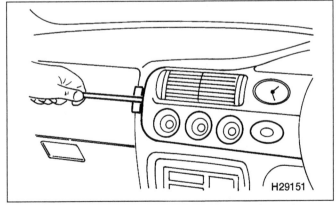

10.10b . . . using a screwdriver and protective pad

11 Unscrew and remove the four instrument panel retaining screws, and carefully withdraw the panel to the point where the wiring multi-plugs and the speedometer cable (where fitted) can be detached from the rear. Note that it may be necessary to push the speedometer cable through from the engine compartment side to allow the instrument panel to be sufficiently withdrawn. Take care when handling the instrument panel whilst it is removed, and position it in a safe place where it will not get knocked or damaged. If a tachometer is fitted, do not lay the panel on its face for extended periods, as the silicone fluid in the tachometer may well be released.

Refitting

12 Refitting is a reversal of removal. On completion check the function of all electrical components.

---

11 Instrument panel components –
removed and refitting

(corrected: removal and refitting)

Removal (pre-1996 models)

1 Remove the instrument panel as described in Section 10. As mentioned, take particular care when handling the panel.

Printed circuit

2 Untwist and remove all of the illumination light bulbs/holders from the rear of the instrument panel **(see illustration)**.
3 Carefully release and remove the wiring multi-plug connector from the rear face of the panel. Pull free the printed circuit, releasing it from the securing pins and the air-cored gauge terminals on the rear face of the panel.

Speedometer

4 Remove the odometer reset knob, then release the four securing clips and remove the two bulbs and the panel surround from the panel. Withdraw the speedometer **(see illustration)**.

Tachometer

5 Remove the odometer reset knob, release

the securing clips, remove the two bulbs and the panel surround from the panel.
6 Applying great care, detach the printed circuit from the air-cored gauge terminals, and remove the tachometer from the panel. Do not lay the gauge on its face for extended periods, as the silicone fluid in the tachometer may well be released.

Fuel/temperature gauge

7 Remove the odometer reset knob, release the securing clips, remove the two bulbs and the panel surround from the panel.
8 Applying great care, detach the printed circuit from the air-cored gauge terminals. Undo the two retaining screws, and remove the fuel/temperature gauge from the panel **(see illustration)**.

Removal (1996-on models)

Note: *It would appear that some late (1998-onwards) models were fitted with electronic instruments. In the absence of any information from the manufacturer, these instruments are NOT covered in this manual.*

9 Remove the instrument panel as described in Section 10. As mentioned, take particular care when handling the panel.
10 Untwist and remove the two illumination light bulbs/holders from the top of the instrument panel.
11 Release the four retaining lugs and remove the instrument panel glass.

Tachometer

12 Undo the two retaining screws and carefully lift out the tachometer.

Fuel/temperature gauge

13 Undo the two screws and carefully lift out the combined fuel/temperature gauge.

Speedometer

14 Release the retainers and withdraw the speedometer from the panel.

Printed circuit

15 Untwist and remove all of the illumination/warning light bulbs/holders from the rear of the instrument panel.
16 Carefully release and remove the two

11.2 Rear face of the instrument panel

wiring multi-plug connectors from the rear face of the panel. Release all the pin contacts from the instrument panel body then carefully pull free the printed circuit. If necessary, the pin contacts can be removed from the printed circuit after the circuit is removed.

Refitting

17 Refitting is a reversal of removal.

---

12 Speedometer cable –
removal and refitting

Note: *Does not apply to later models fitted with electronic instruments.*

Removal

1 Remove the instrument panel (Section 10).
2 Unscrew the speedometer cable from the pinion/speed sensor on the transmission.
3 Release the cable-ties and retaining clips in the engine compartment, and withdraw the cable grommet from the bulkhead.
4 Note the cable routing for use when refitting. Pull the speedometer cable through into the engine compartment, and remove it from the car.

Refitting

5 Refitting is the reversal of removal. Ensure that the cable is routed as noted before removal, secured with the relevant clips and cable-ties, and that the grommet is properly located in the bulkhead.

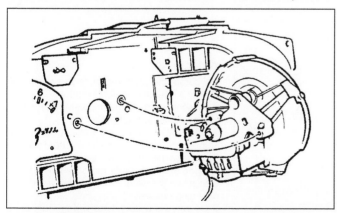

11.4 Speedometer removal from the instrument cluster

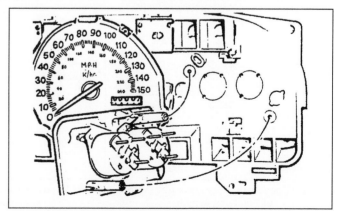

11.8 Air-cored fuel/temperature gauge removal from the instrument cluster

16.2 Windscreen wiper arm retaining nut

13 Cigar lighter –
removed and refitting

Removal (pre-1996 models)

1 Disconnect the battery negative (earth) lead (refer to Chapter 5A, Section 1).
2 Undo the two screws and remove the stowage compartment above the cigar lighter.
3 Reaching through the stowage compartment aperture, disconnect the wiring from the cigar lighter.
4 Extract the lighter element, then reach through with a thin-bladed screwdriver and remove the bulbholder housing from the lighter body.

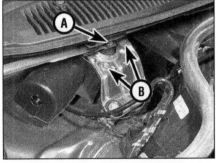

17.3 Windscreen wiper motor showing link arm-to-spindle connection (A) and two of the wiper motor-to-mounting bolts (B)

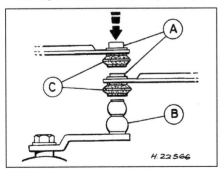

17.7a Windscreen wiper linkage to motor balljoint connection

A Pivot bush   C Rubber seal
B Wiper motor arm

5 Push the lighter body from the rear to free it from the illumination ring.
6 If required, the lighter illumination ring can be pulled free and withdrawn from the facia.

Removal (1996-on models)

7 Disconnect the battery negative (earth) lead (refer to Chapter 5A, Section 1).
8 Remove the stowage compartment above the cigar lighter by simply pulling it out of the aperture in the facia.
9 Reaching through the stowage compartment aperture, disconnect the wiring from the cigar lighter.
10 Extract the lighter element, press the ashtray in at the sides to release the retaining lugs and remove the ashtray and cigar lighter assembly from the facia.
11 Remove the bulbholder housing from the lighter body then push the lighter body from the rear to free it from the ashtray.
12 Release the catches at the side and withdraw the lighter body from the illumination ring.

Refitting

13 Refitting is a reversal of removal. On pre-1996 models, engage the bulbholder housing with the illumination ring before fitting the ring.

14 Clock –
removal and refitting

Removal

1 Disconnect the battery negative (earth) lead (refer to Chapter 5A, Section 1).
2 On pre-1996 models, proceed as described in Section 6, paragraph 29, and carefully prise the clock from the facia. Disconnect the wiring plug from the rear face of the clock.
3 On 1996-on models, remove the instrument panel bezel as described in Section 6, paragraphs 14 to 19. Undo the three screws and remove the clock from the instrument panel bezel.

Refitting

4 Refitting is a reversal of removal. Reset the clock on completion.

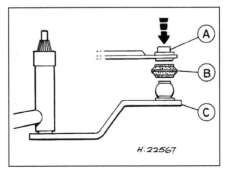

17.7b Windscreen wiper linkage-to-pivot shaft connection

A Pivot bush   C Pivot shaft
B Rubber seal

15 Horn –
removal and refitting

Removal

1 The horn(s) are located on the body front valance, behind the front bumper. To remove a horn, first apply the handbrake, then jack up the front of the vehicle and support it on axle stands (see *Jacking and vehicle support*).
2 Disconnect the horn wiring plug(s).
3 Unscrew the nut securing the horn(s) to the mounting bracket, and remove the horn(s) from the vehicle.

Refitting

4 Refitting is a reversal of removal. Tighten the retaining nut to the specified torque.

16 Wiper arms –
removal and refitting

Removal

1 With the wiper(s) 'parked' (ie in the normal at-rest position), mark the positions of the blade(s) on the screen, using a wax crayon or strips of masking tape.
2 Lift up the plastic cap from the bottom of the wiper arm, and loosen the nut one or two turns **(see illustration)**.
3 Lift the wiper arm, and release it from the taper on the spindle by moving it from side to side.
4 Completely remove the nut and washer, then withdraw the wiper arm from the spindle.

Refitting

5 Refitting is a reversal of the removal procedure. Make sure that the arm is fitted in the previously-noted position. Tighten the wiper arm nut to the specified torque.

17 Windscreen wiper
motor and linkage –
removal and refitting

Removal

Wiper motor

1 Operate the wiper motor, then switch it off so that it returns to its rest position.
2 Disconnect the battery negative (earth) lead (refer to Chapter 5A, Section 1).
3 Unscrew and remove the link arm-to-motor spindle retaining nut **(see illustration)**. Disengage the arm from the spindle.
4 Undo the three wiper motor retaining bolts, then move the wiper motor sideways from its mounting bracket.
5 Detach the wiper motor wiring multi-plug, withdraw the wiper motor and remove its insulating cover.

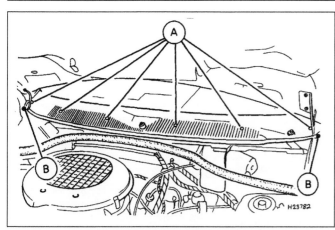

18.4 Remove the plastic screws (A) and the cross-head screws (B) to remove the cowl grille

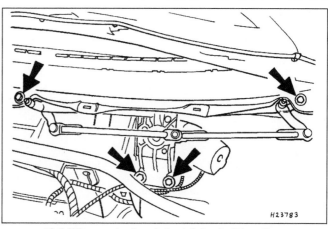

18.5 Wiper motor bracket retaining bolt locations

Linkage

6 Remove the windscreen wiper arms (and blades) from the pivots as described in Section 16.

7 Disconnect the battery negative (earth) lead (refer to Chapter 5A, Section 1). Move the wiper linkage to the required position for access to the linkage balljoints, then carefully prise free the linkages from their ball pins using a suitable open-ended spanner as a lever **(see illustrations)**.

8 Remove the rubber seal from the pivot bushes. Where the surfaces of the ball pins are damaged, the pivot shaft and/or motor must be renewed. The rubber seals which are located over the edge of the pivot bushes must be renewed during refitting.

Refitting

9 Refitting is a reversal of removal. Lubricate the pivot bushes and the rubber seals during reassembly. When reconnecting the link arm on the motor spindle, ensure that the arm lug engages in the slot in the taper of the motor spindle. Tighten all fastenings to the specified torque settings (where given). Check for satisfactory operation on completion.

18 Windscreen wiper pivot shaft – removal and refitting

Removal

1 Operate the wiper motor, then switch it off so that it returns to its rest position.

2 Disconnect the battery negative (earth) lead (refer to Chapter 5A, Section 1).

3 Remove the windscreen wiper arms as described in Section 16.

4 Detach and remove the cowl grille. This is secured by six plastic screws and two cross-head screws located under plastic caps **(see illustration)**.

5 Unscrew and remove the four wiper motor bracket retaining bolts, then remove the wiper motor bracket assembly **(see illustration)**. Disconnect the wiring multi-plug as the motor bracket assembly is withdrawn.

6 Prise free the wiper linkage from the pivot shaft using a suitable open-ended spanner.

7 On pre-1996 models, pull free the pivot shaft cap from the housing, release the circlip, withdraw the two special washers and remove

the pivot shaft. The special washer and spring washer can then be removed from the shaft **(see illustration)**.

8 On 1996-on models, release the circlip, withdraw the special washer and sealing ring, followed by a further two special washers and remove the pivot shaft. The spring washer can then be removed from the shaft **(see illustration)**.

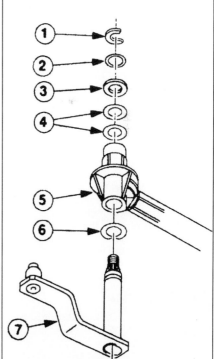

18.8 Wiper pivot shaft components (1996-on models)

1 Circlip	4 Special washers
2 Special washer	(0.15 mm)
(1.8 mm)	5 Bush
3 Sealing	6 Spring washer
ring	7 Pivot shaft

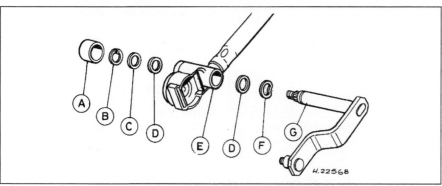

18.7 Wiper pivot shaft components (pre-1996 models)

A Cap
B Circlip
C Special washer (1.8 mm)
D Special washer (0.15 mm)
E Bush
F Spring washer
G Pivot shaft

19.7a Tailgate wiper motor and mounting bolts (arrowed) on Hatchback models

19.7b Tailgate wiper motor and mounting bolts (arrowed) on Estate models

Refitting

8 Refitting is a reversal of removal. Lubricate the pivot shaft, bushes and rubber seals during reassembly. When reconnecting the link arm on the motor spindle, ensure that the arm lug engages in the slot in the taper of the motor spindle. Tighten all fastenings to the specified torque settings (where given).Check for satisfactory operation on completion.

19 Tailgate wiper motor assembly – removal and refitting

Removal

1 Operate the wiper, then switch it off so that it returns to its rest position. Note that the wiper motor will only operate with the tailgate shut, as the spring-tensioned connector pins must be in contact with the contact plates.
2 Disconnect the battery negative (earth) lead (refer to Chapter 5A, Section 1).
3 Remove the wiper arm (see Section 16).
4 Unscrew the nut from the spindle housing protruding through the tailgate.
5 Undo the eight plastic screws (early models), ten screws (later models) and remove the trim panel from inside the tailgate.
6 Disconnect the earth lead and the wiring multi-plug to the wiper motor.
7 Unbolt and remove the wiper assembly from inside the tailgate **(see illustrations)**.
8 If necessary, the wiper motor can be

detached from its mounting bracket by unscrewing the three retaining bolts. As they are detached, note the location of the washers and insulators.

Refitting

9 Refitting is a reversal of removal. When the wiper arm is refitted, its park position should be set correctly. On Hatchback models, the distance from the point where the arm meets the centre of the wiper blade should be 90 ± 5 mm from the bottom of the rear window. On Estate models, this distance should be 75 ± 5 mm.

20 Washer system components – removal and refitting

Removal

Washer pump

1 To remove the pump from the reservoir, first syphon out any remaining fluid from the reservoir, then detach the washer hoses and the wiring multi-plug to the washer pump. The pump can now be pulled (or if required), levered free from the reservoir.

Reservoir and pump

2 To remove the washer reservoir and pump, first unscrew and remove the reservoir retaining bolt in the engine compartment.
3 Refer to Chapter 11 for details, and remove

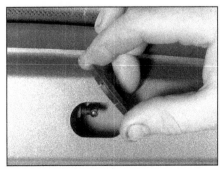

20.9 Remove trim for access to the tailgate washer nozzle

20.10 Washer nozzle removal

the wheel arch liner trim on the left-hand side.
4 Detach the pump multi-plug, the washer low fluid level switch multi-plug (where fitted) and the pump hoses, and disconnect them from the reservoir. Drain any fluid remaining in the reservoir/pump into a suitable container.
5 Unscrew and remove the two reservoir retaining bolts from under the wheel arch, then remove the reservoir and pump from the vehicle.
6 If required, pull or prise free the pump to remove it from the reservoir.

Hoses

7 The hose system to the windscreen washers is in sections, with nylon connector pieces where required. This means that any section of hose can be renewed individually when required. Access to the hoses in the engine compartment is good, but it will be necessary to detach and remove the insulation panel from the underside of the bonnet to allow access to the hoses and connections to the washer nozzles.
8 The front washer reservoir also supplies the rear tailgate washer by means of a tube running along the left-hand side within the body apertures.

Windscreen/tailgate washer nozzles

9 These are secured to the body panels by retaining tabs which are an integral part of the washer nozzle stem. To remove a washer nozzle, first detach and remove the insulation from the underside of the bonnet, or the appropriate trim piece (according to type) for the tailgate washer **(see illustration)**.
10 Using suitable needle-nosed pliers, squeeze together the nozzle retaining tabs, twist the nozzle a quarter of a turn, and withdraw it from its aperture in the body **(see illustration)**. Once withdrawn, the hose can be detached and the nozzle removed. Do not allow the hose to fall into the body whilst the nozzle is detached – tape the hose to the body to prevent this.

Headlight washer nozzles

11 Unclip the cover from the nozzle assembly below the headlight.
12 Withdraw the nozzle together with its mounting bracket out from under the front bumper and detach the washer hose.

Refitting

13 Refitting is a reversal of removal. Always renew the pump-to-reservoir seal washer, and ensure that all connections are securely made. When reconnecting the pump hoses, ensure that the hose marked with white tape is connected to the corresponding white connection on the pump.
14 On completion, top-up the washer reservoir (see *Weekly checks*) and check that the operation of the washers is satisfactory. If necessary, adjust the washer jets by inserting a pin into the centre of the jet and directing the flow at the top part of the windscreen/rear window.

21.2 Radio/cassette removal

24.1 Door-mounted speaker removal

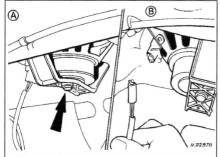

24.2 Bolt (A) and wiring plug (B) of the shelf-mounted speaker on Saloon models

21 Radio/cassette player – removal and refitting

Removal

1 Disconnect the battery negative (earth) lead (refer to Chapter 5A, Section 1).
2 In order to release the radio retaining clips, two U-shaped rods must be inserted into the special holes on each side of the radio **(see illustration)**. If possible, it is preferable to obtain purpose-made rods from an audio specialist, as these have cut-outs which snap firmly into the clips so that the radio can be pulled out. Pull the unit squarely from its aperture, or it may jam. If the unit proves difficult to withdraw, remove the cassette tray (or where applicable, the CD player) from beneath the unit, then reach through the aperture and ease it out from behind. From 1993 model year onwards, on some audio units it will first be necessary to remove the two side bezels using a Ford tool, to gain access to the removal tool holes.
3 With the radio/cassette sufficiently withdrawn, disconnect the feed, earth, aerial and speaker leads. Where applicable, also detach and remove the plastic support bracket from the rear of the unit.

Refitting

4 Refitting is a reversal of removal. When the leads are reconnected to the rear of the unit, press it into position to the point where the retaining clips are felt to engage. Reactivate the unit in accordance with the code and the instructions given in the Ford Audio Operating Manual supplied with the vehicle.

22 Compact disc player – removal and refitting

The removal and refitting procedures for this (where fitted) are similar to those described for the radio/cassette player in the previous Section, but do not remove the bezel securing screws above the CD player.

23 Compact disc autochanger – removal and refitting

Removal

1 Remove the front passenger seat as described in Chapter 11.
2 Undo the three screws each side securing the autochanger to the mounting brackets.
3 Disconnect the wiring connector and remove the autochanger.

Refitting

4 Refitting is a reversal of removal.

24 Speakers – removal and refitting

Removal

Door-mounted speaker

1 Remove the trim panel from the door concerned as described in Chapter 11. Undo the speaker retaining screws, then withdraw the speaker from the door and disconnect the wiring **(see illustration)**. Note that the speaker must not be detached from its moulding.

Parcel shelf-mounted speaker (Saloon)

2 Detach the wiring connector from the

24.3 Rear parcel shelf-mounted speaker (Hatchback models)

speaker, then loosen off the speaker retaining bolt sufficiently to allow the speaker to be withdrawn, leaving the bracket and bolt in position in the speaker recess **(see illustration)**.

Parcel tray-mounted speaker (Hatchback)

3 Unscrew the three retaining screws, lower the speaker from the parcel tray, then detach the wiring connections **(see illustration)**. Note that the speaker and its moulding must not be separated.

Luggage area speaker (Estate)

4 Remove the appropriate luggage area side trim panel as described in Chapter 11 for access to the speaker.
5 Unscrew the three retaining screws, withdraw the speaker and detach the wiring connections **(see illustration)**. Note that the speaker and its moulding must not be separated.

Refitting

6 Refitting is a reversal of removal.

25 Radio aerial – removal and refitting

Removal

1 Disconnect the battery negative (earth) lead (refer to Chapter 5A, Section 1).
2 Remove the trim cover from the access aperture in the headlining beneath the aerial

24.5 Luggage area-mounted speaker (Estate models)

by carefully prising it free. On models with a sunroof, remove the operating handle (manual type) then release the trim caps over the two roof console retaining screws. Undo the screws and slide the console rearwards to release the retaining clips. Remove the roof console after disconnecting the wiring connectors (where applicable).

3 Working through the aperture in the headlining, undo the single retaining screw, withdraw the aerial and detach the cable base from the roof.

Refitting

4 Refitting is a reversal of removal. Ensure that the contact surfaces of both the body panel and the aerial are clean before fitting the aerial into position.

26 Power amplifier – removal and refitting

Removal

1 This is fitted to models equipped with the Premium Sound System, and is located in the area between the glovebox and the bulkhead.
2 To remove the amplifier, undo the retaining screw, lower the unit complete with its support bracket, and detach the wiring multi-plug connectors. If required, the bracket and the amplifier can be separated by unscrewing the four Torx screws.

Refitting

3 Refit in the reverse order of removal.

27 Anti-theft systems – general information

Anti-theft alarm system

1 This system provides an added form of vehicle security **(see illustration)**. When the system is activated, the alarm will sound if the vehicle is broken into through any one of the doors, the bonnet, boot (or tailgate). The alarm will also be triggered if the ignition system is turned on or the radio/cassette disconnected whilst the system is activated.
2 This system is activated/de-activated whenever one of the front doors is locked/unlocked by the key. The system operates on all doors, the bonnet and boot lid (or tailgate)

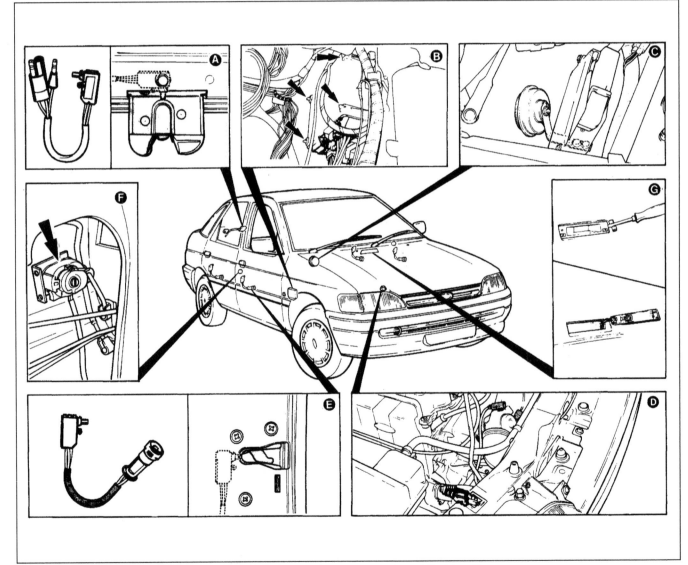

27.1 Anti-theft alarm system components and their locations

A Trip switch (luggage
   compartment)
B System module
C Alarm horn
D Alarm switch (bonnet)
E Alarm switch (doors)
F Activation switches
G Clock

whenever each door is individually locked (or, in the case of central locking, when the central locking is engaged). In addition, the starting system is also immobilised when the system is activated.

3 A further security feature included is that even though the battery may be disconnected whilst the system is activated, the alarm activation continues as soon as the battery is reconnected. Because of this feature, it is important to ensure that the system is de-activated before disconnecting the battery at any time, such as when working on the vehicle.

4 The system incorporates a diagnostic mode to enable Ford technicians to quickly identify any faults in the system.

Passive Anti-Theft System

5 From the 1994 model year onwards, a Passive Anti-Theft System (PATS) is fitted. This system, (which works independently of the standard alarm system) is a vehicle immobiliser which prevents the engine from being started unless a specific code, programmed into the ignition key, is recognised by the PATS transceiver.

6 The PATS transceiver, fitted around the ignition switch, decodes a signal from the ignition key as the key is turned from position O to position II. If the coded signal matches that stored in the memory of the PATS module, the engine will start. If the signal is not recognised, the engine will crank on the starter but will not fire.

28 Anti-theft system components – removal and refitting

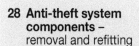

Removal

1 Before disconnecting any components of the anti-theft alarm system, first check that the system is de-activated, then disconnect the battery negative (earth) lead (refer to Chapter 5A, Section 1).

Door lock switch

2 Remove the trim panel and the insulation sheet from the door, as described in Chapter 11. On later models, undo the two screws and remove the door lock assembly shield.
3 Detach the wiring multi-plug connector from the alarm switch in the door (see illustration).
4 Release the snap-lock catch, withdraw the switch from the door lock cylinder, and remove it from the door.

Door lock ajar switch

5 Remove the trim panel and the insulation sheet from the door – see Chapter 11.
6 Detach the wiring multi-plug from the door lock ajar switch.
7 Remove the door lock as described in Chapter 11.
8 Release the retaining clip, and detach the

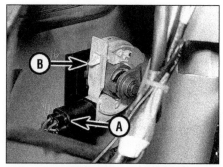

28.3 Door lock switch wiring connector (A) and retaining catch (B)

door ajar switch from the door lock. It is probable that the retaining clip will break when releasing the switch, in which case it will need to be renewed.

Boot lid/tailgate ajar switch

9 Undo the retaining screws, and remove the trim panel from the boot lid or tailgate (as applicable).
10 Detach the wiring loom multi-plug, then referring to Chapter 11 for details, remove the lock from the boot lid/tailgate.
11 Release the retaining clip and detach the ajar switch from the lock unit. It is probable that the retaining clip will break when releasing the switch, in which case it will need to be renewed.

Bonnet alarm switch

12 Grip the switch flange, and pull the switch up and clear of its aperture in the front cross-panel (see illustration).
13 Disconnect the wiring connector and remove the switch.

Alarm horn (pre-1994 models)

14 Where the vehicle is fitted with ABS, detach and remove the ABS module as described in Chapter 9.
15 Detach the wiring from the horn, undo the horn bracket retaining bolts, and remove the horn together with its retaining bracket.

Alarm horn (1994-on models)

16 Remove the C-pillar interior trim and the luggage area trim on the left-hand side.
17 Undo the horn retaining bolt and lift the unit off the two retaining hooks.
18 Disconnect the wiring and remove the horn.

Alarm system module

19 Detach and remove the cowl side trim kick panel from the driver's side front footwell.
20 Detach the wiring multi-plug from the module, then release the module from the four retaining clips and remove it.

PATS transceiver

21 Undo the two upper and four lower retaining screws, and remove the steering column upper and lower shrouds.
22 Undo the five screws and withdraw the detachable lower facia panel from beneath the steering column.

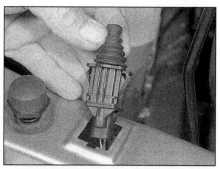

28.12 Bonnet alarm switch removal (anti-theft alarm system)

23 Undo the single screw, and withdraw the PATS transceiver from the ignition switch/steering lock barrel (see illustration).
24 Release the wiring harness from the clips on the steering column, trace the harness under the facia, and disconnect the wiring multi-plug. Remove the transceiver from the car.

PATS module

25 Refer to Chapter 11 and remove the facia.
26 Disconnect the wiring multi-plug from the PATS module, located on the bulkhead on the passenger's side.
27 Pull the module downwards to remove it from the mounting bracket.

Refitting

28 The refitting of the respective components is a reversal of the removal procedure. Ensure that all component retaining clips are secure, that the wiring looms are correctly routed, and that the wiring connections are secure. Check for satisfactory operation of the systems to complete.

29 Air bag system – general information, precautions and system de-activation

General information

All models from 1994 onwards are fitted with a driver's air bag, which is designed to prevent serious chest and head injuries to the

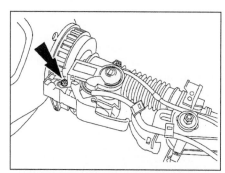

28.23 Undo the screw (arrowed) and withdraw the PATS transceiver from the ignition switch/steering lock barrel

driver during an accident. A similar bag for the front seat passenger is also available. The combined sensor and electronics for the air bag(s) is located next to the steering column inside the vehicle, and contains a back-up capacitor, crash sensor, decelerometer, safety sensor, integrated circuit and microprocessor. The air bags are inflated by gas generators, which force the bags out from their locations in the centre of the steering wheel, and the passenger's side facia, where applicable. A 'clock spring' ensures that a good electrical connection is maintained with the driver's air bag at all times – as the steering wheel is turned in each direction, the spring winds and unwinds.

Precautions

 Warning: The following precautions must be observed when working on vehicles equipped with an air bag system, to prevent the possibility of personal injury.

General precautions

The following precautions **must** be observed when carrying out work on a vehicle equipped with an air bag:
a) *Do not disconnect the battery with the engine running.*
b) *Before carrying out any work in the vicinity of the air bag, removal of any of the air bag components, or any welding work on the vehicle, de-activate the system as described in the following sub-Section.*
c) *Do not attempt to test any of the air bag system circuits using test meters or any other test equipment.*
d) *If the air bag warning light comes on, or any fault in the system is suspected, consult a Ford dealer without delay. Do not attempt to carry out fault diagnosis, or any dismantling of the components.*

Precautions to be taken when handling an air bag

a) *Transport the air bag by itself, bag upward.*
b) *Do not put your arms around the air bag.*
c) *Carry the air bag close to the body, bag outward.*
d) *Do not drop the air bag or expose it to impacts.*
e) *Do not attempt to dismantle the air bag unit.*
f) *Do not connect any form of electrical equipment to any part of the air bag circuit.*

Precautions to be taken when storing an air bag unit

a) *Store the unit in a cupboard with the air bag upward.*
b) *Do not expose the air bag to temperatures above 80ºC.*
c) *Do not expose the air bag to flames.*
d) *Do not attempt to dispose of the air bag – consult a Ford dealer.*
e) *Never refit an air bag which is known to be faulty or damaged.*

De-activation of air bag system

The system must be de-activated as follows, before carrying out any work on the air bag components or surrounding area:
a) *Switch off the ignition.*
b) *Remove the ignition key.*
c) *Switch off all electrical equipment.*
d) *Disconnect the battery negative lead.*
e) *Insulate the end of the battery negative lead and the battery negative terminal to prevent any possibility of contact.*
f) *Wait for at least fifteen minutes before carrying out any further work.*

30 Air bag system components – removal and refitting

 Warning: Refer to the precautions given in Section 29 before attempting to carry out work on the air bag components.

Driver's air bag unit

Removal

1 De-activate the air bag system as described in Section 29.
2 Undo the two screws, and remove the steering column upper shroud.
3 Turn the steering wheel as necessary so that one of the air bag retaining bolts becomes accessible from the rear of the steering wheel. Undo the bolt, then turn steering wheel again until the second bolt is accessible. Undo this bolt also.
4 Withdraw the air bag from the steering wheel far enough to access the wiring multi-plug **(see illustration)**. Some force may be needed to free the unit from the additional steering wheel spoke retainers.
5 Disconnect the multi-plug from the rear of the unit, and remove it from the vehicle.

Refitting

6 Refitting is a reversal of the removal procedure.

Passenger's air bag unit

Removal (pre-1996 models)

7 De-activate the air bag system as described in Section 29.

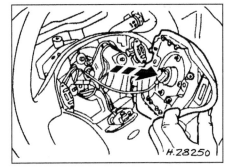

30.4 Withdrawing the air bag from the steering wheel

8 Open the glovebox and undo the three screws at the top of the glovebox aperture.
9 Remove the centre and left-hand (passenger's side) face level air vents as described in Chapter 3.
10 Working through the air vent apertures, undo the air bag surround retaining nuts, and withdraw the surround and air bag unit from the facia.
11 Disconnect the two wiring connectors from the rear of the air bag unit, and unclip the wiring harness from the mounting bracket.
12 Undo the two bolts each side and the two bolts in the centre and remove the mounting brackets from the air bag surround.
13 Withdraw the air bag unit from the surround.

Refitting

14 Refitting is a reversal of the removal procedure, ensuring that the wiring is correctly routed.

Removal (1996-on models)

15 De-activate the air bag system as described in Section 29.
16 Remove the facia as described in Chapter 11.
17 Open the glovebox and undo the two air bag surround retaining screws at the top of the glovebox aperture.
18 Undo the four nuts securing the air bag mounting brackets to the facia.
19 Undo the two retaining screws and carefully withdraw the air bag surround and air bag unit from the facia. Disconnect the two wiring connectors from the rear of the air bag unit and remove the assembly from the facia. Note that on later models there is only one air bag wiring connector.
20 Undo the two screws and remove the face level air vent from the air bag surround.
21 Undo the two screws each side and remove the left-hand and right-hand mounting brackets from the air bag unit and the surround.
22 Undo the remaining two retaining screws and slide the air bag unit out of the surround.

Refitting

23 Refitting is a reversal of the removal procedure, ensuring that the wiring is correctly routed.

Air bag control module

Removal

24 De-activate the air bag system as described in Section 29.
25 Undo the six screws and withdraw the detachable lower facia panel from beneath the steering column.
26 Remove the instrument panel as described in Section 9.
27 Support the module and undo the mounting bolts.
28 Disconnect the multi-plug from the module, by pressing the locking tab upwards and swivelling the retaining strap. Remove the module from the car.

30.33 Removing the air bag clock spring assembly from the steering wheel

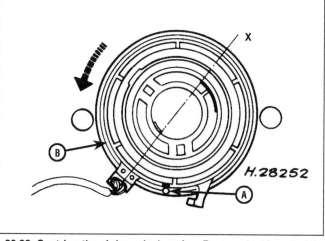

30.38 Centring the air bag clock spring. Depress locking pin (A) and rotate outer rotor (B) anti-clockwise (X is the relative position of the direction indicator cancelling cam to the cable connector – see text)

Refitting

29 Refitting is a reversal of the removal procedure.

Air bag clock spring

Removal

30 De-activate the air bag system as described in Section 29.
31 Remove the steering wheel as described in Chapter 10.
32 Disconnect the wires at the two horn terminals in the centre of the steering wheel.
33 Undo the three retaining screws, and remove the clock spring/horn slip ring from the steering wheel **(see illustration)**. As the unit is withdrawn, note which aperture in the steering wheel the air bag wiring passes through, as an aid to reassembly.

Refitting

34 Apply a smear of molybdenum disulphide grease to the horn slip rings.
35 Position the clock spring/horn slip ring on the steering wheel, and secure with the retaining screws.
36 Reconnect the two horn wires to their terminals.
37 The clock spring must now be centred as follows.
38 Depress the locking pin, and rotate the clock spring outer rotor fully anti-clockwise until it is tight **(see illustration)**.
39 Now turn the outer rotor approximately 3.75 turns clockwise, then release the locking pin. Ensure that the locking pin engages when it is released.
40 Check that the relative position of the direction indicator cancelling cam to the cable connector on the clock spring assembly is as shown **(see illustration 30.38)**.
41 Refit the steering wheel as described in Chapter 10.

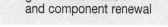

31 Auxiliary warning system – general information and component renewal

General information

1 An auxiliary warning system is available as an option on certain models. On pre-1996 models, the system has three functions – low fuel warning, low washer fluid level warning, and an 'ignition off, lights on, driver's door open' warning. On 1996-on models the system has only two functions – 'ignition off, lights on, driver's door open' warning, and door ajar warning (when an anti-theft alarm system is fitted).
2 The low fuel and washer fluid level warnings are provided by warning lights in the instrument panel and the 'ignition off, lights on, driver's door open' warning is provided by an audible alarm tone.
3 The warning lights are activated by floats which monitor the fuel and fluid levels. The float for the low fuel level is an integral part of the fuel gauge sender, and activates the warning light when the fuel level in the tank drops to below 10 litres (2.2 gallons). The float for the washer fluid level is contained in the fluid reservoir, and consists of a magnet which operates a reed switch inserted in the side of the reservoir. When the fluid level falls to the level of the reed switch, the magnet on the float activates the switch to illuminate the warning light.
4 The alarm tone for the 'ignition off, lights on, driver's door open' warning is activated by the driver's door courtesy light switch if the door is opened with the ignition switched off and the lights left on. On pre-1996 models, the operation of the system is controlled by a control module assembly located under the facia above the fusebox. This module also emits the alarm tone for the 'ignition off, lights

on, driver's door open' warning. On 1996-on models, the alarm tone is emitted by a relay buzzer located under the facia either above the fusebox or mounted on the main fuse board. The door ajar warning light is operated by the anti-theft alarm system module.

Component renewal

Warning lights

5 The procedure for warning light bulb renewal is contained in Section 6.

Low fuel level float (pre-1996 models)

6 The low fuel level float is part of the fuel gauge sender – removal and refitting procedures are contained in Chapter 4A.

Low washer fluid level reed switch (pre-1996 models)

7 Remove the windscreen washer reservoir as described in Section 20.
8 Withdraw the switch from the side of the reservoir by levering against the switch body.
9 Ensure that the sealing grommet is correctly fitted in the reservoir, then push the switch fully into the grommet to refit.
10 Refit the washer reservoir (see Section 20).

Control module assembly/relay buzzer

11 Disconnect the battery negative (earth) lead (refer to Chapter 5A, Section 1).
12 Undo the six screws and withdraw the detachable lower facia panel from beneath the steering column. On later models, detach the courtesy light assembly and any additional wiring clipped to the panel.
13 On pre-1998 models, unclip the control module, and disconnect the multi-plug. On 1998-on models, remove the relay buzzer from the relay board (refer to the *Specifications*, and Section 3 for additional information).
14 Refitting is a reversal of removal.

32 Wiring diagrams –
general information

General

1 The diagrams included in this manual represent a typical selection of the most relevant diagrams for most Escorts, and for most DIY users – space limitations prevent us from including every diagram issued by the manufacturers.

1994 models

2 Some Escorts produced immediately prior to the last facelift (January 1995) had an anomaly in their wiring harnesses. It seems that, during the period from roughly January 1994 to January 1995, some Escorts had earth wiring which was black in colour, instead of the conventional brown. Since this appears to be the only difference, a complete set of new diagrams for just one year's worth of production has not been included. The potential for black earth wiring should be borne in mind, however, when working on a model of this age (late L-reg or early M-reg).

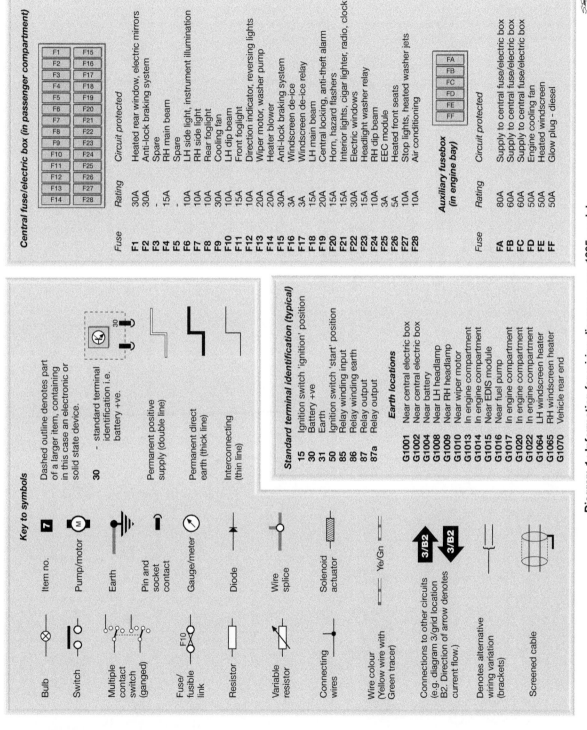

Central fuse/electric box (in passenger compartment)

Fuse	Rating	Circuit protected
F1	30A	Heated rear window, electric mirrors
F2	30A	Anti-lock braking system
F3	-	Spare
F4	15A	RH main beam
F5	-	Spare
F6	10A	LH side light, instrument illumination
F7	10A	RH side light
F8	10A	Rear foglight
F9	30A	Cooling fan
F10	10A	LH dip beam
F11	15A	Front foglight
F12	10A	Direction indicator, reversing lights
F13	20A	Wiper motor, washer pump
F14	20A	Heater blower
F15	30A	Anti-lock braking system
F16	3A	Windscreen de-ice
F17	15A	Windscreen de-ice relay
F18	15A	LH main beam
F19	20A	Central locking, anti-theft alarm
F20	15A	Horn, hazard flashers
F21	15A	Interior lights, cigar lighter, radio, clock
F22	30A	Electric windows
F23	15A	Headlight washer relay
F24	10A	RH dip beam
F25	3A	EEC module
F26	5A	Heated front seats
F27	10A	Stop lights, heated washer jets
F28	10A	Air conditioning

Auxiliary fusebox (in engine bay)

Fuse	Rating	Circuit protected
FA	80A	Supply to central fuse/electric box
FB	60A	Supply to central fuse/electric box
FC	60A	Supply to central fuse/electric box
FD	50A	Engine cooling fan
FE	50A	Heated windscreen
FF	50A	Glow plug - diesel

Key to symbols

Bulb; Switch; Multiple contact switch (ganged); Fuse/fusible link; Resistor; Variable resistor; Connecting wires; Wire colour (Yellow wire with Green tracer) Ye/Gn; Connections to other circuits (e.g. diagram 3/grid location B2. Direction of arrow denotes current flow.); Denotes alternative wiring variation (brackets); Screened cable

Item no.; Pump/motor; Earth; Pin and socket contact; Gauge/meter; Diode; Wire splice; Solenoid actuator

Dashed outline denotes part of a larger item, containing in this case an electronic or solid state device.

30 - standard terminal identification i.e. battery +ve.

Permanent positive supply (double line); Permanent direct earth (thick line); Interconnecting (thin line)

Standard terminal identification (typical)

15 Ignition switch 'ignition' position
30 Battery +ve
31 Earth
50 Ignition switch 'start' position
85 Relay winding input
86 Relay winding earth
87 Relay output
87a Relay output

Earth locations

G1001 Near central electric box
G1002 Near central electric box
G1004 Near battery
G1008 Near LH headlamp
G1009 Near RH headlamp
G1010 Near wiper motor
G1013 In engine compartment
G1014 In engine compartment
G1015 Near EDIS module
G1016 Near fuel pump
G1017 In engine compartment
G1020 In engine compartment
G1022 In engine compartment
G1064 LH windscreen heater
G1065 RH windscreen heater
G1070 Vehicle rear end

Diagram 1: Information for wiring diagrams, pre-1995 models

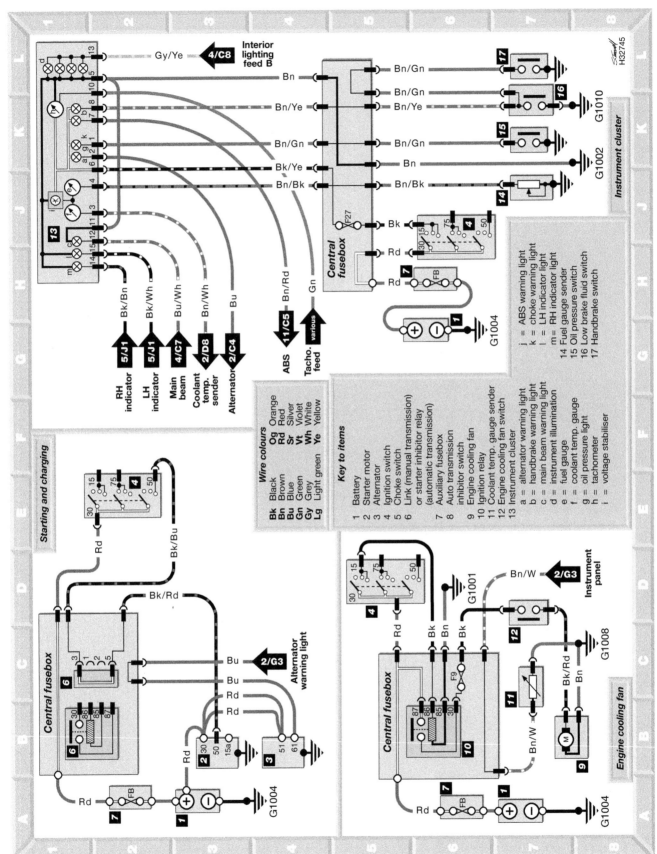

Diagram 2 : Typical starting, charging, engine cooling fan and instrument cluster, pre-1995 models

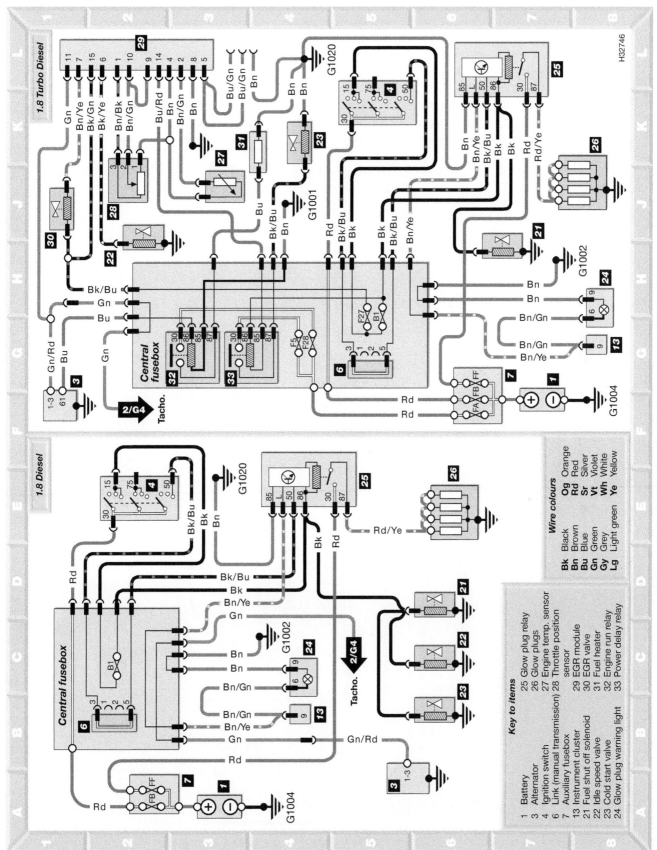

Diagram 3 : Typical engine electrical systems, pre-1995 models

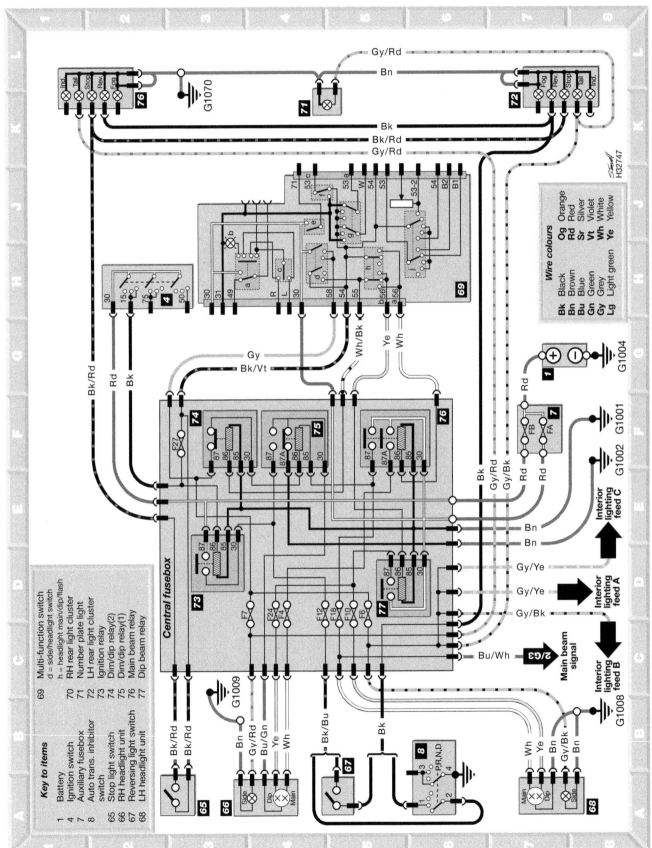

Key to items

1	Battery
4	Ignition switch
7	Auxiliary fusebox
8	Auto trans. inhibitor switch
65	Stop light switch
66	RH headlight unit
67	Reversing light switch
68	LH headlight unit
69	Multi-function switch
	d = side/headlight switch
	h = headlight main/dip/flash
70	RH rear light cluster
71	Number plate light
72	LH rear light cluster
73	Ignition relay
74	Dim/dip relay(2)
75	Dim/dip relay(1)
76	Main beam relay
77	Dip beam relay

Wire colours

Bk	Black	**Og**	Orange
Bn	Brown	**Rd**	Red
Bu	Blue	**Sr**	Silver
Gn	Green	**Vt**	Violet
Gy	Grey	**Wh**	White
Lg	Light green	**Ye**	Yellow

Diagram 4 : Typical exterior lighting - headlight/sidelight, stop and reversing lights - pre 1995 models

H32747

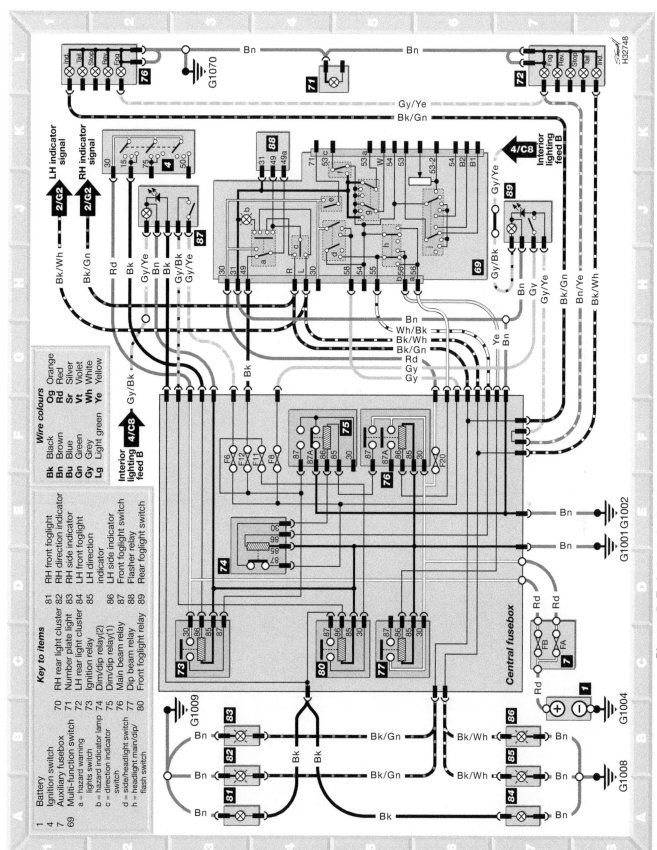

Diagram 5 : Typical exterior lighting - fog and direction indicator lights - pre 1995 models

Key to items

1	Battery	81	RH front foglight
4	Ignition switch	82	RH direction indicator
7	Auxiliary fusebox	83	RH side indicator
69	Multi-function switch	84	LH front foglight
70	RH rear light cluster	85	LH direction indicator
71	Number plate light	86	LH side indicator
72	LH rear light cluster	87	Front foglight switch
73	Ignition relay	88	Flasher relay
74	Dim/dip relay(2)	89	Rear foglight switch
75	Dim/dip relay(1)		
76	Main beam relay		
77	Dip relay		
80	Front foglight relay		

a = hazard warning lights switch
b = hazard indicator lamp
c = direction indicator switch
d = side/headlight switch
h = headlight main/dip/flash switch

Wire colours

Bk	Black	Og	Orange
Bn	Brown	Rd	Red
Bu	Blue	Sr	Silver
Gn	Green	Vt	Violet
Gy	Grey	Wh	White
Lg	Light green	Ye	Yellow

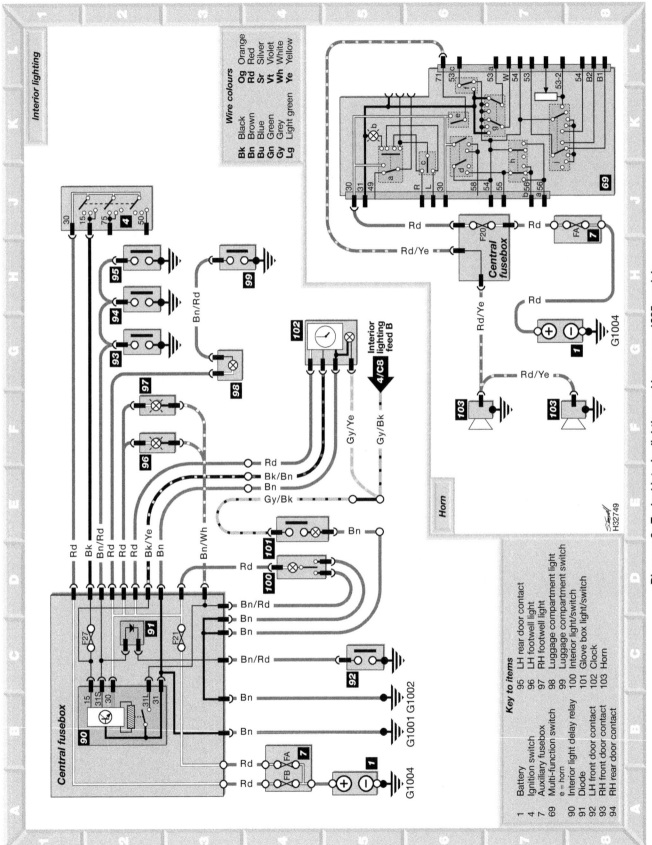

Diagram 6 : Typical interior lighting and horn - pre 1995 models

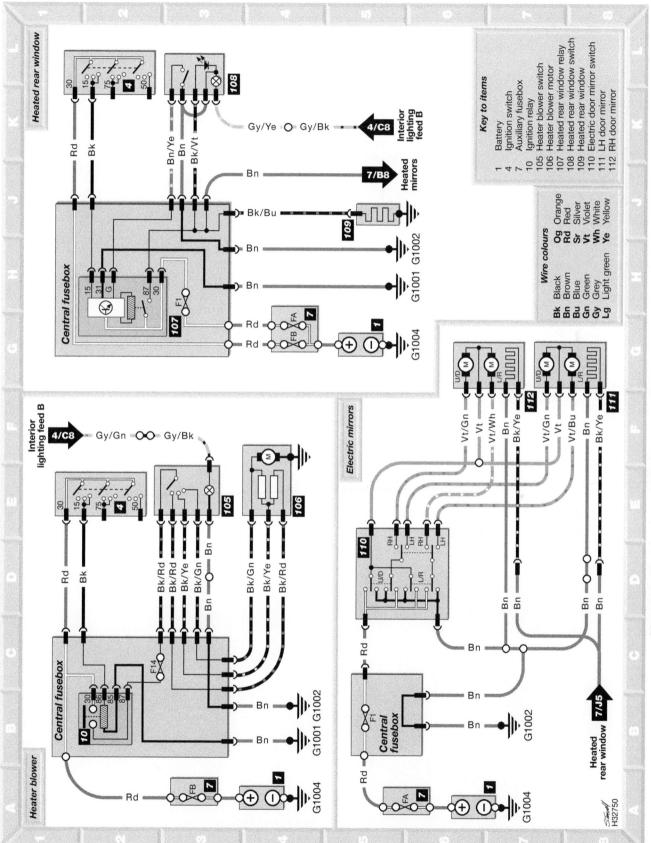

Diagram 7 : Electric mirrors, heated rear screen, heater blower – pre 1995 models

H32750

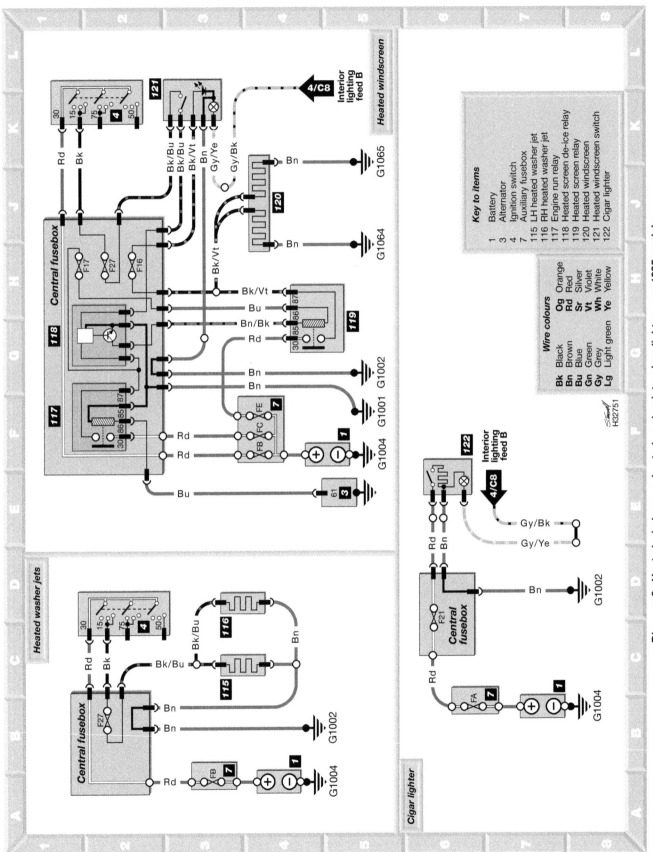

Key to items

1 Battery
3 Alternator
4 Ignition switch
7 Auxiliary fusebox
115 LH heated washer jet
116 RH heated washer jet
117 Engine run relay
118 Heated screen de-ice relay
119 Heated screen relay
120 Heated windscreen
121 Heated windscreen switch
122 Cigar lighter

Wire colours

Bk	Black	**Og**	Orange
Bn	Brown	**Rd**	Red
Bu	Blue	**Sr**	Silver
Gn	Green	**Vt**	Violet
Gy	Grey	**Wh**	White
Lg	Light green	**Ye**	Yellow

H32751

Diagram 8 : Heated windscreen, heated washer jets, cigar lighter - pre 1995 models

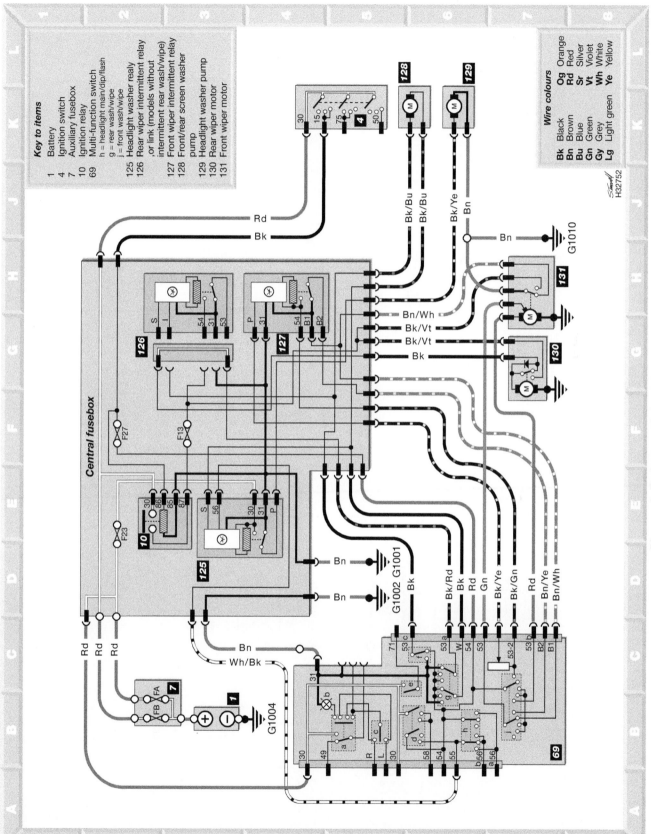

Diagram 9 : Typical wash/wipe - pre 1995 models

Key to items

1	Battery
4	Ignition switch
7	Auxiliary fusebox
10	Ignition relay
69	Multi-function switch
	h = headlight main/dip/flash
	g = rear wash/wipe
	j = front wash/wipe
125	Headlight washer realy
126	Rear wiper intermittent relay
	or link (models without
	intermittent rear wash/wipe)
127	Front wiper intermittent relay
128	Front/rear screen washer
	pump
129	Headlight washer pump
130	Rear wiper motor
131	Front wiper motor

Wire colours

Bk	Black	Og	Orange
Bn	Brown	Rd	Red
Bu	Blue	Sr	Silver
Gn	Green	Vt	Violet
Gy	Grey	Wh	White
Lg	Light green	Ye	Yellow

H32752

Central fusebox

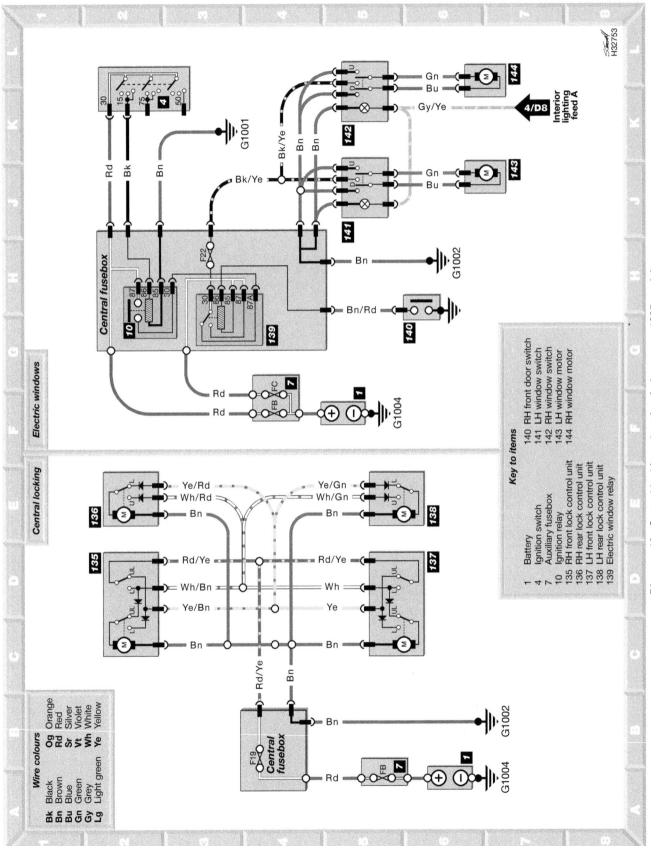

Diagram 10 : Central locking, electric windows - pre 1995 models

Key to items

1	Battery
4	Ignition switch
7	Auxiliary fusebox
10	Ignition relay
135	RH front lock control unit
136	RH rear lock control unit
137	LH front lock control unit
138	LH rear lock control unit
139	Electric window relay
140	RH front door switch
141	LH window switch
142	RH window switch
143	LH window motor
144	RH window motor

Wire colours

Bk	Black	Og	Orange
Bn	Brown	Rd	Red
Bu	Blue	Sr	Silver
Gn	Green	Vt	Violet
Gy	Grey	Wh	White
Lg	Light green	Ye	Yellow

Electric windows

Central locking

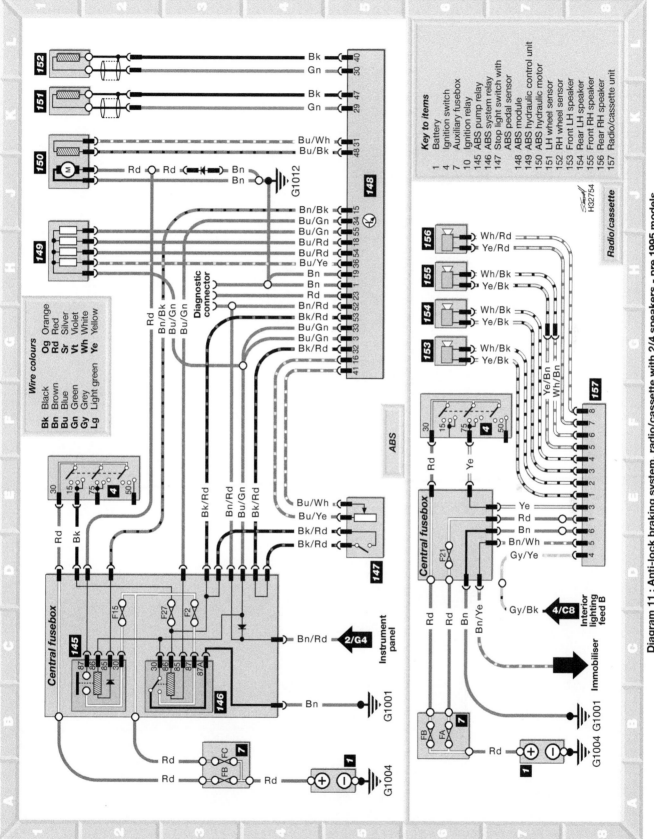

Key to items

1   Battery
4   Ignition switch
7   Auxiliary fusebox
10 Ignition relay
145 ABS pump relay
146 ABS system relay
147 Stop light switch with
     ABS pedal sensor
148 ABS module
149 ABS hydraulic control unit
150 ABS hydraulic motor
151 LH wheel sensor
152 RH wheel sensor
153 Front LH speaker
154 Rear LH speaker
155 Front RH speaker
156 Rear RH speaker
157 Radio/cassette unit

Wire colours

Bk Black	**Og** Orange
Bn Brown	**Rd** Red
Bu Blue	**Sr** Silver
Gn Green	**Vt** Violet
Gy Grey	**Wh** White
Lg Light green	**Ye** Yellow

H32754

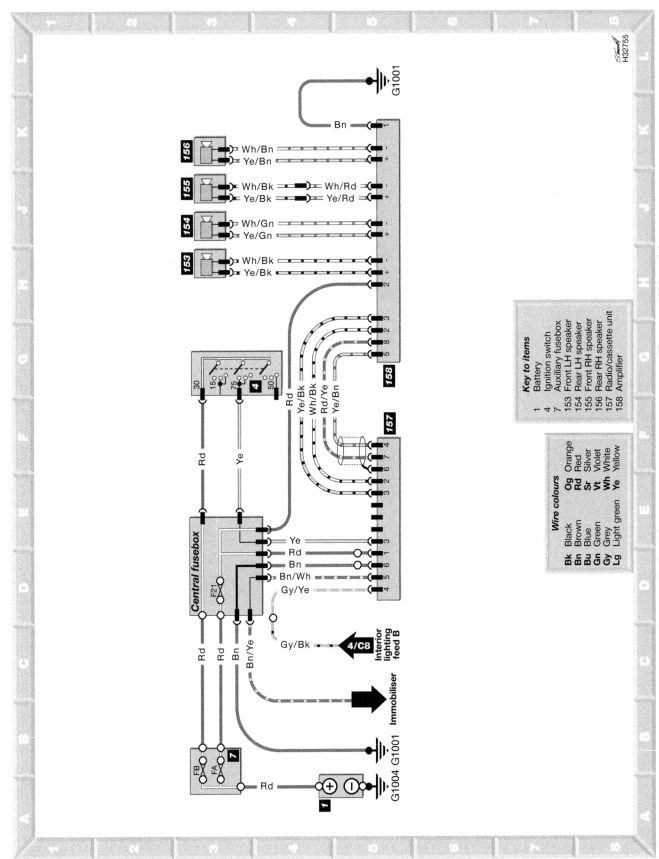

Diagram 12 : Radio/cassette with 4 speakers and amplifier - pre 1995 models

Key to items

1 Battery
4 Ignition switch
7 Auxiliary fusebox
153 Front LH speaker
154 Rear LH speaker
155 Front RH speaker
156 Rear RH speaker
157 Radio/cassette unit
158 Amplifier

Wire colours

Bk	Black	**Og**	Orange
Bn	Brown	**Rd**	Red
Bu	Blue	**Sr**	Silver
Gn	Green	**Vt**	Violet
Gy	Grey	**Wh**	White
Lg	Light green	**Ye**	Yellow

H32755

H32756
T.M.Marke

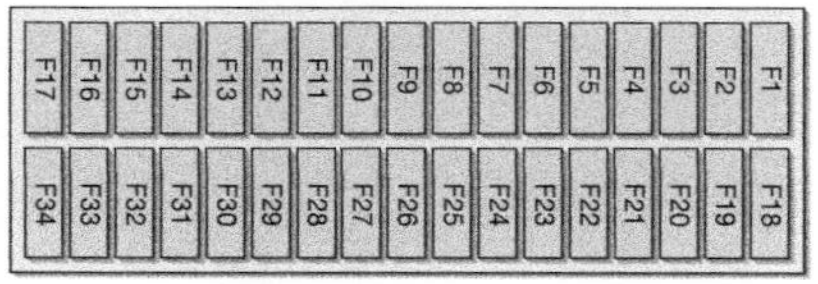

Auxiliary fusebox (in engine bay)

FA	
FB	
FC	
FD	
FE	
FF	

Auxiliary fusebox

Fuse	Rating	Circuit protected
FA	80A	Supply to central fusebox
FB	60A	Supply to central fusebox
FC	60A	Supply to central fusebox
FD	40/50A	Engine cooling fan
FE	50A	Heated windscreen
FF	50A	Glow plug – diesel

Earth locations

G1001	RH 'A' pillar
G1002	RH 'A' pillar
G1004	On engine bulkhead left hand side
G1008	Engine compartment front left hand side
G1009	Engine compartment front right hand side
G1010	On engine bulkhead
G1012	Engine compartment right hand side
G1017	On engine
G1019	Engine compartment front right hand side
G1020	Engine compartment front left hand side
G1022	LH 'A' pillar
G1024	In luggage compartment left hand side
G1025	Behind dash panel
G1028	Behind dash panel (cabriolet)
G1046	Under right hand tail light
G1047	Under centre console
G1050	On tailgate (estate)
G1063	Right hand 'C' pillar (cabriolet, 4 door saloon) or in tailgate (estate)
G1070	Vehicle rear end
G1072	Right hand 'C' pillar (van)
G1076	Right hand 'A' pillar
G1078	Right hand side of dash
G1100	Passenger 'A' pillar

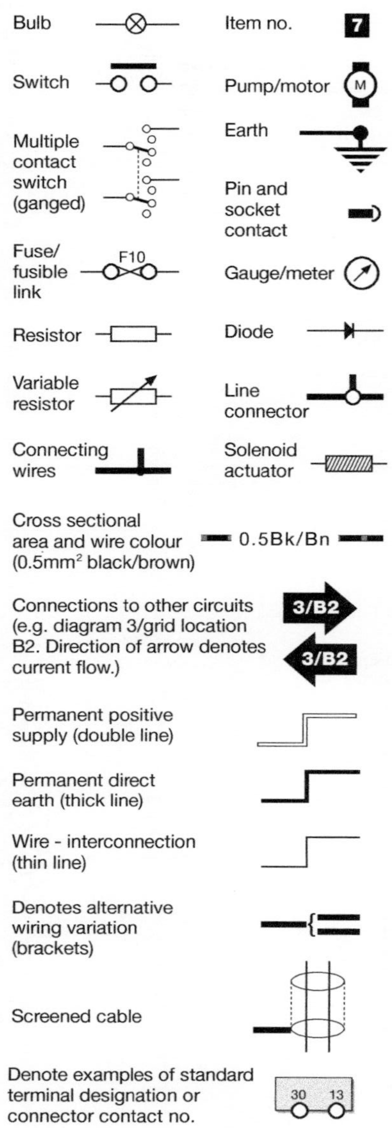

Central fusebox (in passenger compartment)

F1	F18
F2	F19
F3	F20
F4	F21
F5	F22
F6	F23
F7	F24
F8	F25
F9	F26
F10	F27
F11	F28
F12	F29
F13	F30
F14	F31
F15	F32
F16	F33
F17	F34

Central fusebox

Fuse	Rating	Circuit protected
F1	10A	Rear fog lights
-	-	-
F3	10A	RH sidelights
-	-	-
F5	15A	LH main beam
F6	15A	RH main beam, auxiliary driving light
F7	3A	Fuel injection module
F8	10A	LH sidelight
F9	10A	Anti-lock brakes
F10	30A	Headlight washer system
F11	10A	Control lights
F12	7.5A	Airbag
F13	20A	Cold start valve, engine management system, fuel shut off
F14	10A	Oxygen sensor
F15	10A	LH dipped beam
F16	20A	Ignition coil
F17	10A	RH dipped beam
F18	30A	Electric windows and sunroof
-	-	-
F20	25A	Heater blower
F21	3A	Anti-lock brake module
F22	30A	Cooling fan
F23	15A	Heated seats
F24	20A	Wiper motor, washer pump
F25	30A	Anti-lock braking system
F26	10A	Direction indicators and reversing lights
F27	25A	Heated rear window and heated mirrors
F28	15A	Horn, hazard flasher
F29	15A	Interior lights, cigar lighter, clock, radio
F30	20A	Central door locking, power seats
F31	15A	Front foglights
F32	15A	Air cond. magnetic clutch
F33	20A	Fuel pump
F34	15A	Heated washer jets, brake lights

Key to symbols

- Bulb
- Switch
- Multiple contact switch (ganged)
- Fuse/fusible link
- Resistor
- Variable resistor
- Connecting wires
- Cross sectional area and wire colour (0.5mm² black/brown) — 0.5Bk/Bn
- Connections to other circuits (e.g. diagram 3/grid location B2. Direction of arrow denotes current flow.)
- Permanent positive supply (double line)
- Permanent direct earth (thick line)
- Wire - interconnection (thin line)
- Denotes alternative wiring variation (brackets)
- Screened cable
- Denote examples of standard terminal designation or connector contact no.
- Item no.
- Pump/motor
- Earth
- Pin and socket contact
- Gauge/meter
- Diode
- Line connector
- Solenoid actuator

Diagram 13 : Information for wiring diagrams - post 1995 models

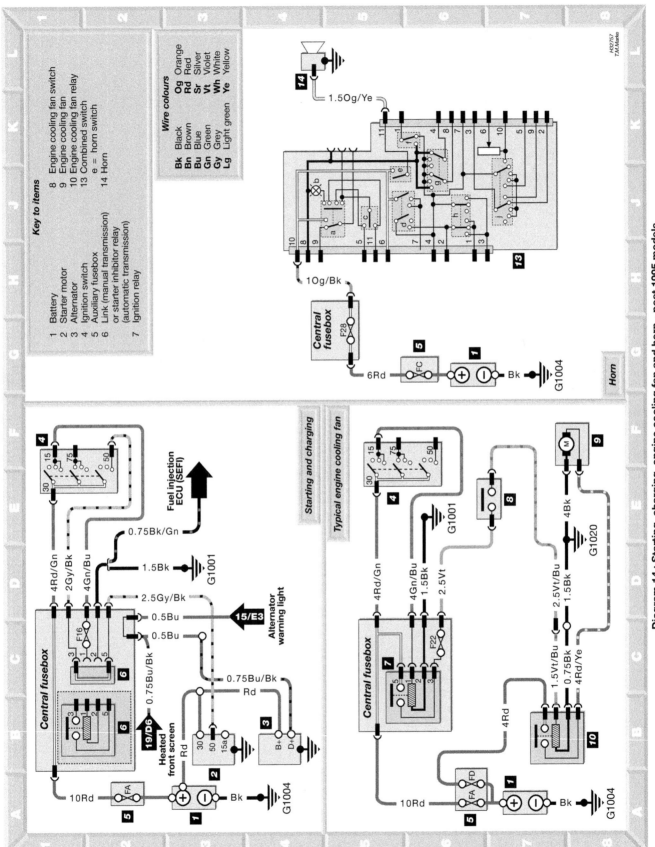

H32757
T.M.Marke

Key to items

1 Battery
2 Starter motor
3 Alternator
4 Ignition switch
5 Auxiliary fusebox
6 Link (manual transmission)
  or starter inhibitor relay
  (automatic transmission)
7 Ignition relay

8 Engine cooling fan switch
9 Engine cooling fan
10 Engine cooling fan relay
13 Combined switch
  e = horn switch
14 Horn

Wire colours

Bk	Black	**Og**	Orange
Bn	Brown	**Rd**	Red
Bu	Blue	**Sr**	Silver
Gn	Green	**Vt**	Violet
Gy	Grey	**Wh**	White
Lg	Light green	**Ye**	Yellow

Horn

Starting and charging

Typical engine cooling fan

Diagram 14 : Starting, charging, engine cooling fan and horn - post 1995 models

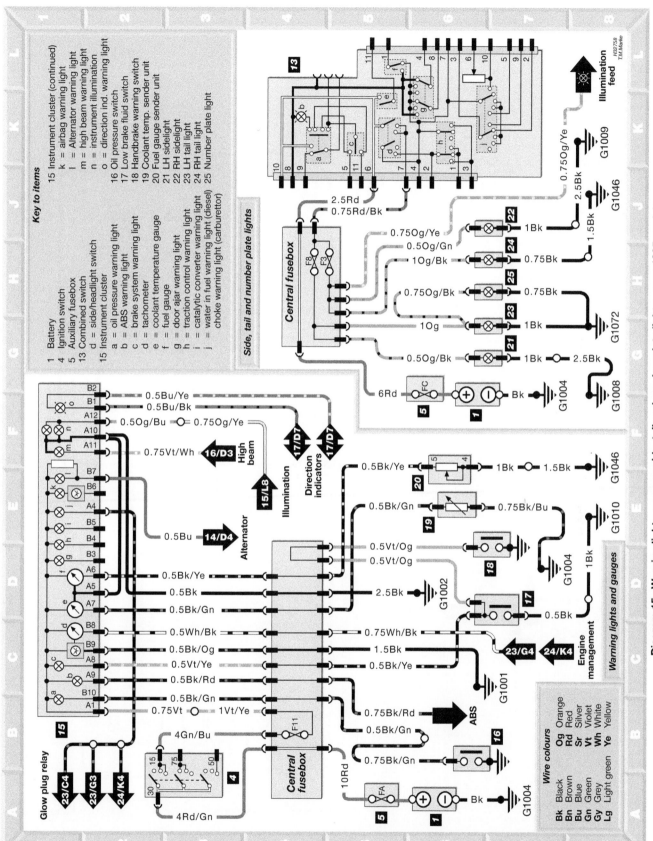

Key to items

15 Instrument cluster (continued)
k = airbag warning light
l = Alternator warning light
m = high beam warning light
n = instrument illumination
o = direction ind. warning light
16 Oil pressure switch
17 Low brake fluid switch
18 Handbrake warning switch
19 Coolant temp. sender unit
20 Fuel gauge sender unit
21 LH sidelight
22 RH sidelight
23 LH tail light
24 RH tail light
25 Number plate light

1 Battery
4 Ignition switch
5 Auxiliary fusebox
13 Combined switch
d = side/headlight switch
15 Instrument cluster
a = oil pressure warning light
b = ABS warning light
c = brake system warning light
d = tachometer
e = coolant temperature gauge
f = fuel gauge
g = door ajar warning light
h = traction control warning light
i = catalytic converter warning light
j = water in fuel warning light (diesel)
choke warning light (carburettor)

Side, tail and number plate lights

Warning lights and gauges

Wire colours

Bk	Black	Og	Orange
Bn	Brown	Rd	Red
Bu	Blue	Sr	Silver
Gn	Green	Vt	Violet
Gy	Grey	Wh	White
Lg	Light green	Ye	Yellow

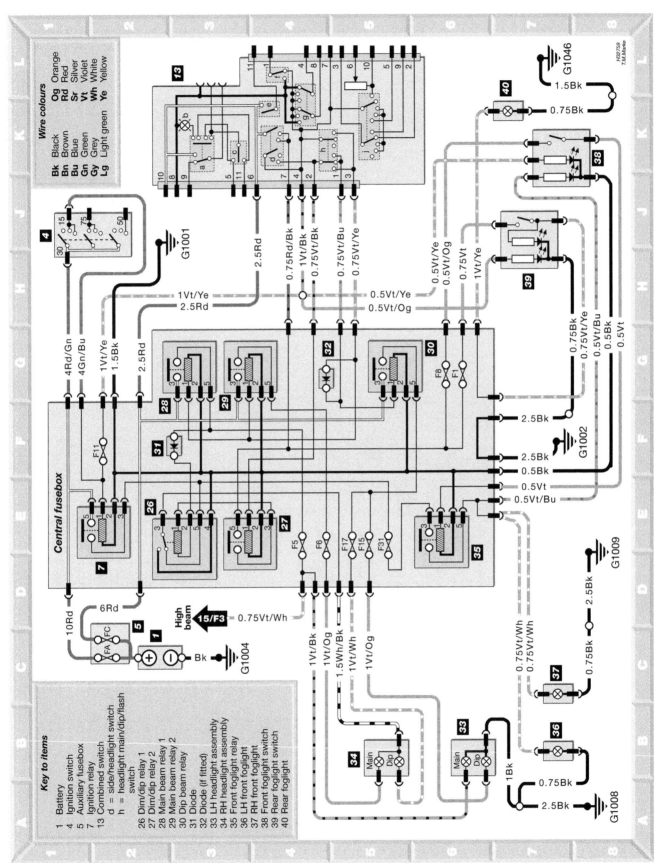

Diagram 16 : Headlights (dim/dip), front and rear foglights - post 1995 models

Wire colours

Bk	Black
Bn	Brown
Bu	Blue
Gn	Green
Gy	Grey
Lg	Light green
Og	Orange
Rd	Red
Sr	Silver
Vt	Violet
Wh	White
Ye	Yellow

Key to items

1 Battery
4 Ignition switch
5 Auxiliary fusebox
7 Ignition relay
13 Combined switch
   d = side/headlight switch
   h = headlight main/dip/flash
   switch
26 Dim/dip relay 1
27 Dim/dip relay 2
28 Main beam relay 1
29 Main beam relay 2
30 Dip beam relay
31 Diode
32 Diode (if fitted)
33 LH headlight assembly
34 RH headlight assembly
35 Front foglight relay
36 LH front foglight
37 RH front foglight
38 Front foglight switch
39 Rear foglight switch
40 Rear foglight

Central fusebox

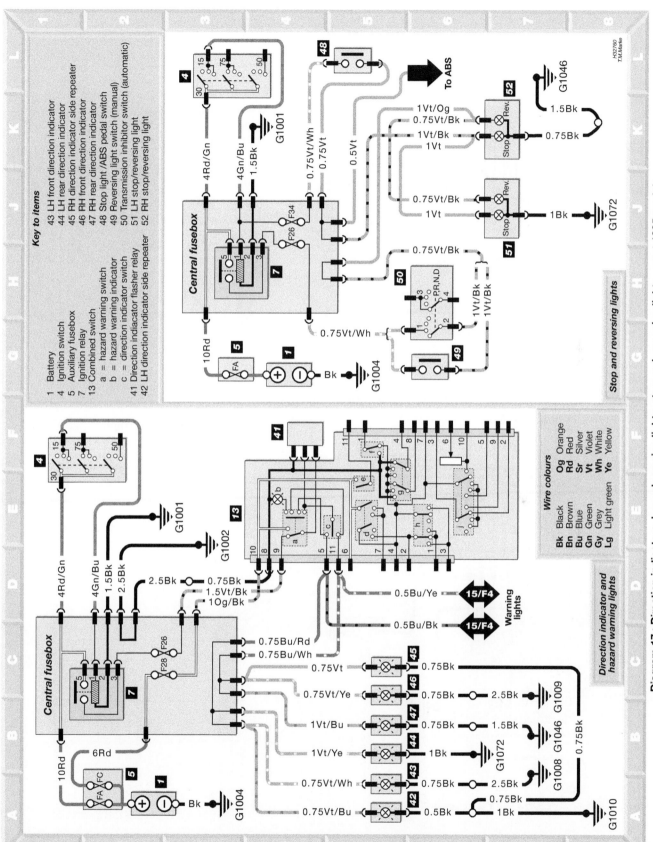

Key to items

1   Battery
4   Ignition switch
5   Auxiliary fusebox
7   Ignition relay
13 Combined switch
  a = hazard warning switch
  b = hazard warning indicator
  c = direction indicator switch
41 Direction indicator flasher relay
42 LH direction indicator side repeater

43 LH front direction indicator
44 LH rear direction indicator
45 RH direction indicator side repeater
46 RH front direction indicator
47 RH rear direction indicator
48 Stop light / ABS pedal switch
49 Reversing light switch (manual)
50 Transmission inhibitor switch (automatic)
51 LH stop/reversing light
52 RH stop/reversing light

Wire colours

Bk Black	**Og** Orange	
Bn Brown	**Rd** Red	
Bu Blue	**Sr** Silver	
Gn Green	**Vt** Violet	
Gy Grey	**Wh** White	
Lg Light green	**Ye** Yellow	

Stop and reversing lights

Direction indicator and hazard warning lights

Diagram 17 : Direction indicators, hazard warning lights, stop and reversing lights - post 1995 models

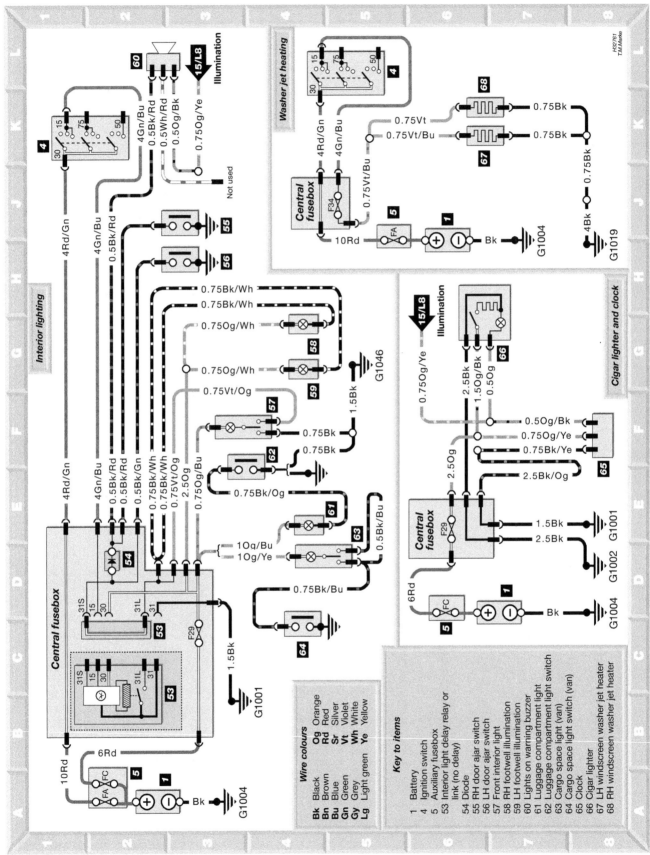

Diagram 18 : Interior lighting, cigar lighter, clock and heated washer jets - post 1995 models

Wire colours

Bk	Black
Bn	Brown
Bu	Blue
Gn	Green
Gy	Grey
Lg	Light green
Og	Orange
Rd	Red
Sr	Silver
Vt	Violet
Wh	White
Ye	Yellow

Key to items

1 Battery
4 Ignition switch
5 Auxiliary fusebox
53 Interior light delay relay or link (no delay)
54 Diode
55 RH door ajar switch
56 LH door ajar switch
57 Front interior light
58 RH footwell illumination
59 LH footwell illumination
60 Lights on warning buzzer
61 Luggage compartment light
62 Luggage compartment light switch
63 Cargo space light (van)
64 Cargo space light switch (van)
65 Clock
66 Cigar lighter
67 LH windscreen washer jet heater
68 RH windscreen washer jet heater

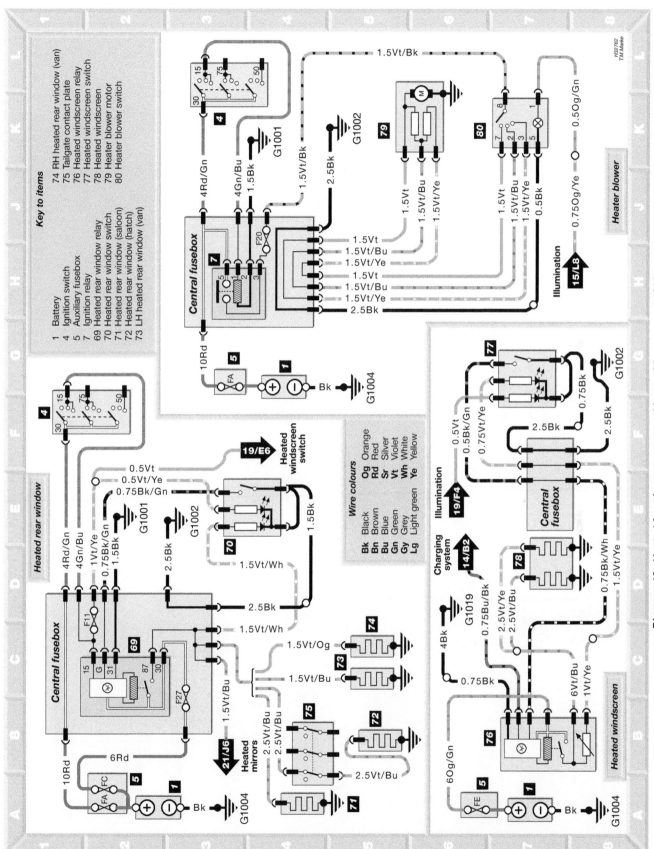

Key to items

1 Battery
4 Ignition switch
5 Auxiliary fusebox
7 Ignition relay
69 Heated rear window relay
70 Heated rear window switch (saloon)
71 Heated rear window (hatch)
72 Heated rear window (van)
73 LH heated rear window (van)
74 RH heated rear window (van)
75 Tailgate contact plate
76 Heated windscreen relay
77 Heated windscreen switch
78 Heated windscreen
79 Heater blower motor
80 Heater blower switch

Wire colours

Bk	Black	Og	Orange
Bn	Brown	Rd	Red
Bu	Blue	Sr	Silver
Gn	Green	Vt	Violet
Gy	Grey	Wh	White
Lg	Light green	Ye	Yellow

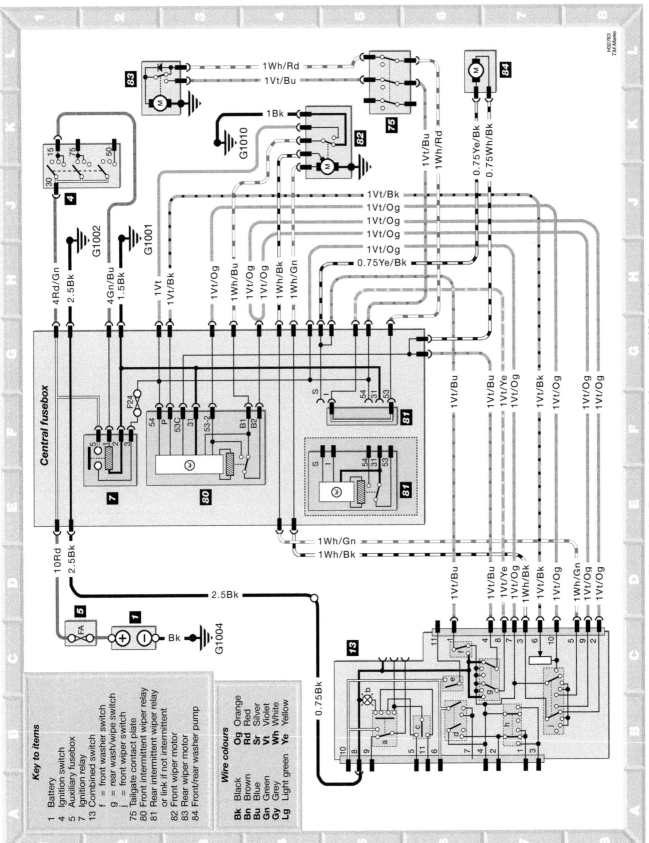

Diagram 20 : Front and rear wash/wipe - post 1995 models

Key to items

1 Battery
4 Ignition switch
5 Auxiliary fusebox
7 Ignition relay
13 Combined switch
  f = front washer switch
  g = rear wash/wipe switch
  j = front wiper switch
75 Tailgate contact plate
80 Front intermittent wiper relay
81 Rear intermittent wiper relay
  or link if not intermittent
82 Front wiper motor
83 Rear wiper motor
84 Front/rear washer pump

Wire colours

Bk Black
Bn Brown
Bu Blue
Gn Green
Gy Grey
Lg Light green
Og Orange
Rd Red
Sr Silver
Vt Violet
Wh White
Ye Yellow

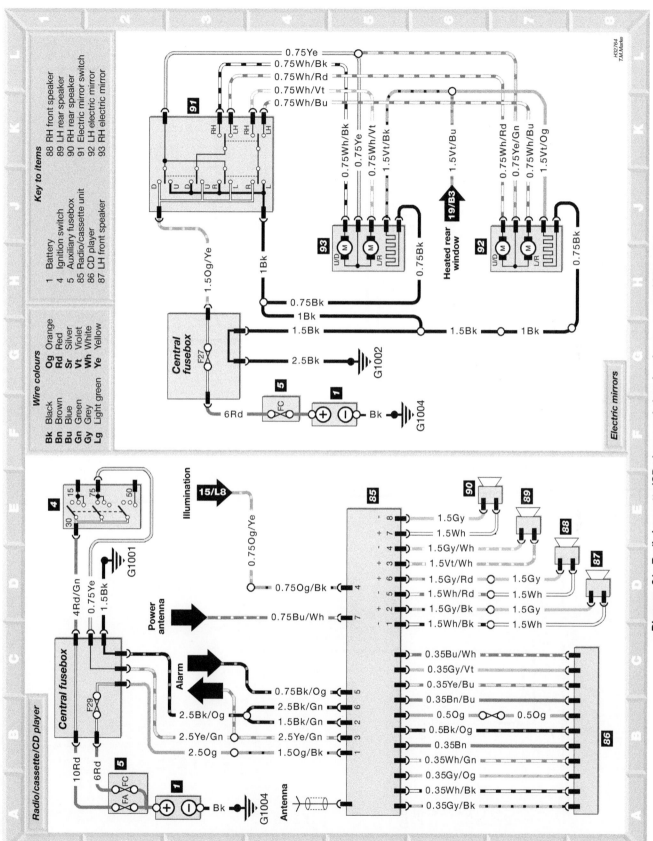

Key to items

1	Battery
4	Ignition switch
5	Auxiliary fusebox
85	Radio/cassette unit
86	CD player
87	LH front speaker
88	RH front speaker
89	LH rear speaker
90	RH rear speaker
91	Electric mirror switch
92	LH electric mirror
93	RH electric mirror

Wire colours

Bk	Black	Og	Orange
Bn	Brown	Rd	Red
Bu	Blue	Sr	Silver
Gn	Green	Vt	Violet
Gy	Grey	Wh	White
Lg	Light green	Ye	Yellow

Electric mirrors

Radio/cassette/CD player

Diagram 21 : Radio/cassette/CD player and electric mirrors - post 1995 models

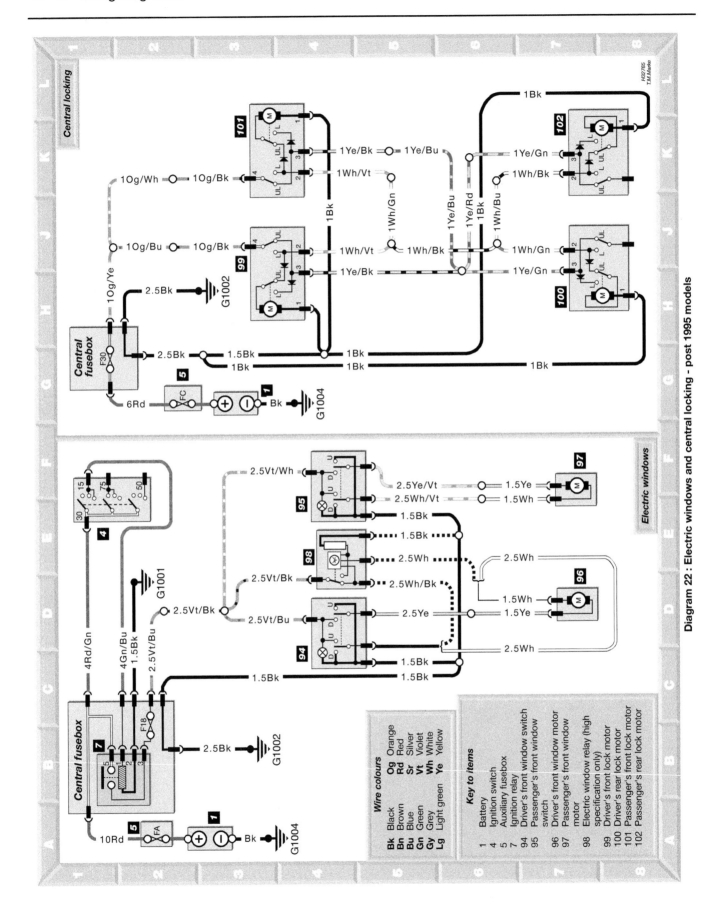

Diagram 22 : Electric windows and central locking - post 1995 models

Wire colours

Bk	Black	**Og**	Orange
Bn	Brown	**Rd**	Red
Bu	Blue	**Sr**	Silver
Gn	Green	**Vt**	Violet
Gy	Grey	**Wh**	White
Lg	Light green	**Ye**	Yellow

Key to items

1 Battery
4 Ignition switch
5 Auxiliary fusebox
7 Ignition relay
94 Driver's front window switch
95 Passenger's front window switch
96 Driver's front window motor
97 Passenger's front window motor
98 Electric window relay (high specification only)
99 Driver's front lock motor
100 Driver's rear lock motor
101 Passenger's front lock motor
102 Passenger's rear lock motor

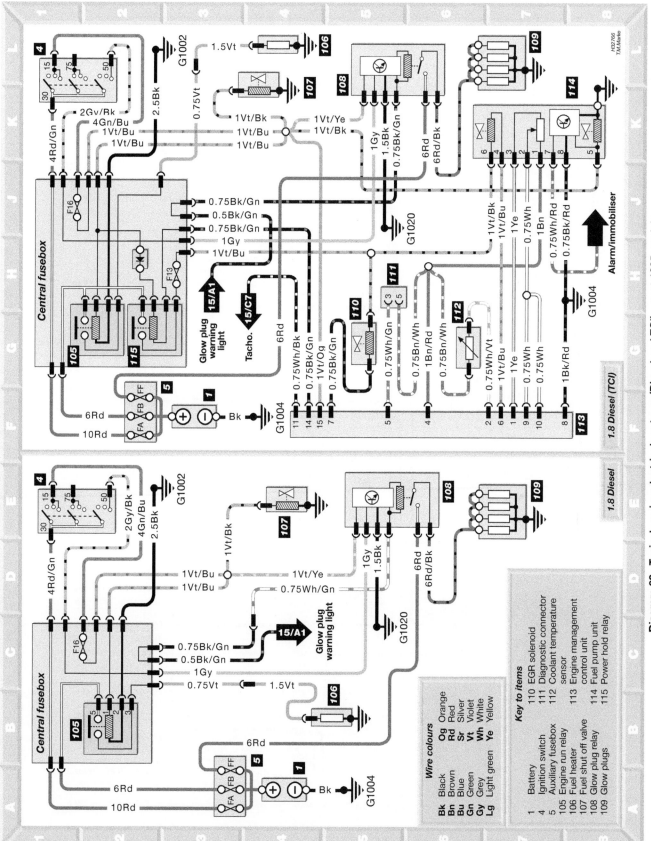

Diagram 23 : Typical engine electrical systems (Diesel and TCI) - post 1995 models

Wire colours

Bk	Black	**Og**	Orange
Bn	Brown	**Rd**	Red
Bu	Blue	**Sr**	Silver
Gn	Green	**Vt**	Violet
Gy	Grey	**Wh**	White
Lg	Light green	**Ye**	Yellow

Key to items

1	Battery	110	EGR solenoid
4	Ignition switch	111	Diagnostic connector
5	Auxiliary fusebox	112	Coolant temperature
105	Engine run relay		sensor
106	Fuel heater	113	Engine management
107	Fuel shut off valve		control unit
108	Glow plug relay	114	Fuel pump unit
109	Glow plugs	115	Power hold relay

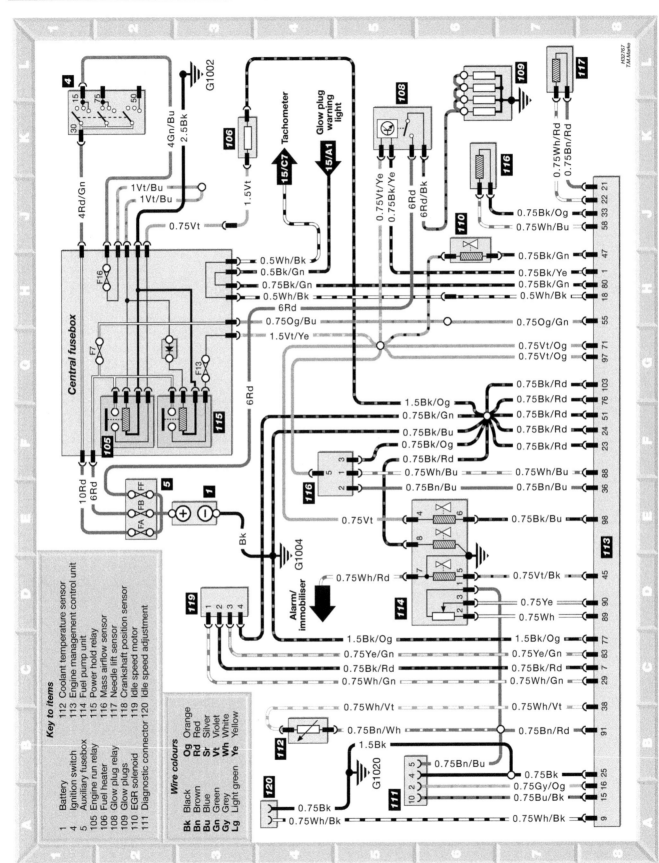

Diagram 24 : Typical engine electrical system (TC) - post 1995 models

Key to items
1 Battery
4 Ignition switch
5 Auxiliary fusebox
105 Engine run relay
106 Fuel heater
108 Glow plug relay
109 Glow plugs
110 EGR solenoid
111 Diagnostic connector
112 Coolant temperature sensor
113 Engine management control unit
114 Fuel pump unit
115 Power hold relay
116 Mass airflow sensor
117 Needle lift sensor
118 Crankshaft position sensor
119 Idle speed motor
120 Idle speed adjustment

Wire colours
Bk Black
Bn Brown
Bu Blue
Gn Green
Gy Grey
Lg Light green
Og Orange
Rd Red
Sr Silver
Vt Violet
Wh White
Ye Yellow

Dimensions and weights

Note: *All figures are approximate, and may vary according to model. Refer to manufacturer's data for exact figures.*

Dimensions

Overall length:
Escort Hatchback	4036 mm
Escort Estate	4268 mm
Escort Van	4256 mm
Escort/Orion Saloon	4229 mm

Overall width – including mirrors . . . . 1875 mm

Overall height (unladen):
Escort Hatchback	1395 mm
Escort Estate	1409 mm
Escort Van	1625 mm
Escort/Orion Saloon	1395 mm

Wheelbase:
All models except Escort Van	2525 mm
Escort Van	2598 mm

Front track . . . . 1440 mm

Rear track:
All models except Escort Van	1439 to 1462 mm*
Escort Van	1436 mm

Dependent on rear brake type/specification.

Weights

Kerb weight*:
Escort 3-door Hatchback	901 to 1006 kg
Escort 5-door Hatchback	921 to 1026 kg
Escort Estate	976 to 1041 kg
Escort/Orion 4-door Saloon	1006 to 1021 kg
Escort Van	975 to 1010 kg

Maximum gross vehicle weight:
Escort 3-door Hatchback	1350 to 1450 kg
Escort 5-door Hatchback	1375 to 1475 kg
Escort Estate	1425 to 1525 kg
Escort/Orion 4-door Saloon	1425 to 1500 kg
Escort Van	575 to 1800 kg

Maximum roof rack load . . . . 75 kg

Maximum towing weight . . . . Refer to your Ford dealer for weights and legal requirements concerning anticipated gradients and altitudes.

Exact kerb weight varies depending on model – refer to VIN plate.

Length (distance)

Inches (in)	x 25.4	= Millimetres (mm)	x 0.0394	= Inches (in)
Feet (ft)	x 0.305	= Metres (m)	x 3.281	= Feet (ft)
Miles	x 1.609	= Kilometres (km)	x 0.621	= Miles

Volume (capacity)

Cubic inches (cu in; in³)	x 16.387	= Cubic centimetres (cc; cm³)	x 0.061	= Cubic inches (cu in; in³)
Imperial pints (Imp pt)	x 0.568	= Litres (l)	x 1.76	= Imperial pints (Imp pt)
Imperial quarts (Imp qt)	x 1.137	= Litres (l)	x 0.88	= Imperial quarts (Imp qt)
Imperial quarts (Imp qt)	x 1.201	= US quarts (US qt)	x 0.833	= Imperial quarts (Imp qt)
US quarts (US qt)	x 0.946	= Litres (l)	x 1.057	= US quarts (US qt)
Imperial gallons (Imp gal)	x 4.546	= Litres (l)	x 0.22	= Imperial gallons (Imp gal)
Imperial gallons (Imp gal)	x 1.201	= US gallons (US gal)	x 0.833	= Imperial gallons (Imp gal)
US gallons (US gal)	x 3.785	= Litres (l)	x 0.264	= US gallons (US gal)

Mass (weight)

Ounces (oz)	x 28.35	= Grams (g)	x 0.035	= Ounces (oz)
Pounds (lb)	x 0.454	= Kilograms (kg)	x 2.205	= Pounds (lb)

Force

Ounces-force (ozf; oz)	x 0.278	= Newtons (N)	x 3.6	= Ounces-force (ozf; oz)
Pounds-force (lbf; lb)	x 4.448	= Newtons (N)	x 0.225	= Pounds-force (lbf; lb)
Newtons (N)	x 0.1	= Kilograms-force (kgf; kg)	x 9.81	= Newtons (N)

Pressure

Pounds-force per square inch (psi; lbf/in²; lb/in²)	x 0.070	= Kilograms-force per square centimetre (kgf/cm²; kg/cm²)	x 14.223	= Pounds-force per square inch (psi; lbf/in²; lb/in²)
Pounds-force per square inch (psi; lbf/in²; lb/in²)	x 0.068	= Atmospheres (atm)	x 14.696	= Pounds-force per square inch (psi; lbf/in²; lb/in²)
Pounds-force per square inch (psi; lbf/in²; lb/in²)	x 0.069	= Bars	x 14.5	= Pounds-force per square inch (psi; lbf/in²; lb/in²)
Pounds-force per square inch (psi; lbf/in²; lb/in²)	x 6.895	= Kilopascals (kPa)	x 0.145	= Pounds-force per square inch (psi; lbf/in²; lb/in²)
Kilopascals (kPa)	x 0.01	= Kilograms-force per square centimetre (kgf/cm²; kg/cm²)	x 98.1	= Kilopascals (kPa)
Millibar (mbar)	x 100	= Pascals (Pa)	x 0.01	= Millibar (mbar)
Millibar (mbar)	x 0.0145	= Pounds-force per square inch (psi; lbf/in²; lb/in²)	x 68.947	= Millibar (mbar)
Millibar (mbar)	x 0.75	= Millimetres of mercury (mmHg)	x 1.333	= Millibar (mbar)
Millibar (mbar)	x 0.401	= Inches of water (inH₂O)	x 2.491	= Millibar (mbar)
Millimetres of mercury (mmHg)	x 0.535	= Inches of water (inH₂O)	x 1.868	= Millimetres of mercury (mmHg)
Inches of water (inH₂O)	x 0.036	= Pounds-force per square inch (psi; lbf/in²; lb/in²)	x 27.68	= Inches of water (inH₂O)

Torque (moment of force)

Pounds-force inches (lbf in; lb in)	x 1.152	= Kilograms-force centimetre (kgf cm; kg cm)	x 0.868	= Pounds-force inches (lbf in; lb in)
Pounds-force inches (lbf in; lb in)	x 0.113	= Newton metres (Nm)	x 8.85	= Pounds-force inches (lbf in; lb in)
Pounds-force inches (lbf in; lb in)	x 0.083	= Pounds-force feet (lbf ft; lb ft)	x 12	= Pounds-force inches (lbf in; lb in)
Pounds-force feet (lbf ft; lb ft)	x 0.138	= Kilograms-force metres (kgf m; kg m)	x 7.233	= Pounds-force feet (lbf ft; lb ft)
Pounds-force feet (lbf ft; lb ft)	x 1.356	= Newton metres (Nm)	x 0.738	= Pounds-force feet (lbf ft; lb ft)
Newton metres (Nm)	x 0.102	= Kilograms-force metres (kgf m; kg m)	x 9.804	= Newton metres (Nm)

Power

Horsepower (hp)	x 745.7	= Watts (W)	x 0.0013	= Horsepower (hp)

Velocity (speed)

Miles per hour (miles/hr; mph)	x 1.609	= Kilometres per hour (km/hr; kph)	x 0.621	= Miles per hour (miles/hr; mph)

Fuel consumption*

Miles per gallon, Imperial (mpg)	x 0.354	= Kilometres per litre (km/l)	x 2.825	= Miles per gallon, Imperial (mpg)
Miles per gallon, US (mpg)	x 0.425	= Kilometres per litre (km/l)	x 2.352	= Miles per gallon, US (mpg)

Temperature

Degrees Fahrenheit = ($°C$ x 1.8) + 32

Degrees Celsius (Degrees Centigrade; $°C$) = ($°F$ - 32) x 0.56

It is common practice to convert from miles per gallon (mpg) to litres/100 kilometres (l/100km), where mpg x l/100 km = 282

Spare parts are available from many sources, including maker's appointed garages, accessory shops, and motor factors. To be sure of obtaining the correct parts, it will sometimes be necessary to quote the vehicle identification number (see *Vehicle identification*). If possible, it can also be useful to take the old parts along for positive identification. Items such as starter motors and alternators may be available under a service exchange scheme – any parts returned should always be clean.

Our advice regarding spare part sources is as follows.

Officially-appointed garages

This is the best source of parts which are peculiar to your car, and which are not otherwise generally available (eg badges, interior trim, certain body panels, etc). It is also the only place at which you should buy parts if the vehicle is still under warranty.

Accessory shops

These are very good places to buy materials and components needed for the maintenance of your car (oil, air and fuel filters, spark plugs, light bulbs, drivebelts, oils and greases, brake pads, touch-up paint, etc). Components of this nature sold by a reputable shop are of the same standard as those used by the car manufacturer.

Besides components, these shops also sell tools and general accessories, usually have convenient opening hours, charge lower prices, and can often be found not far from home. Some accessory shops have parts counters where the components needed for almost any repair job can be purchased or ordered.

Motor factors

Good factors will stock all the more important components which wear out comparatively quickly, and can sometimes supply individual components needed for the overhaul of a larger assembly (eg brake seals and hydraulic parts, bearing shells, pistons, valves, alternator brushes). They may also handle work such as cylinder block reboring, crankshaft regrinding and balancing, etc.

Tyre and exhaust specialists

These outlets may be independent, or members of a local or national chain. They frequently offer competitive prices when compared with a main dealer or local garage, but it will pay to obtain several quotes before making a decision. When researching prices, also ask what 'extras' may be added – for instance, fitting a new valve and balancing the wheel are both commonly charged on top of the price of a new tyre.

Other sources

Beware of parts or materials obtained from market stalls, car boot sales or similar outlets. Such items are not invariably sub-standard, but there is little chance of compensation if they do prove unsatisfactory. In the case of safety-critical components such as brake pads, there is the risk not only of financial loss but also of an accident causing injury or death.

Second-hand components or assemblies obtained from a car breaker can be a good buy in some circumstances, but this sort of purchase is best made by the experienced DIY mechanic.

Modifications are a continuing and unpublicised process in vehicle manufacture, quite apart from major model changes. Spare parts manuals and lists are compiled upon a numerical basis, the individual vehicle identification numbers being essential to correct identification of the component concerned.

When ordering spare parts, always give as much information as possible. Quote the vehicle model, year of manufacture, body and engine numbers as appropriate.

Jacking and vehicle support

The jack supplied with the vehicle tool kit should only be used for changing the roadwheels – see *Wheel changing* at the front of this manual. When jacking up the vehicle to carry out repair or maintenance tasks, a pillar or trolley type jack of suitable lifting capacity must be used, supplemented with axle stands positioned only beneath the appropriate points under the vehicle **(see illustrations)**. Note that the vehicle must never be jacked up at the rear under the axle beam.

*The maximum kerb weight of the vehicle must not be exceeded when jacking and supporting the vehicle. Do not under any circumstances jack up the rear of the vehicle under the rear axle. **Never** work under, around or near a raised vehicle unless it is supported in at least two places with axle stands.*

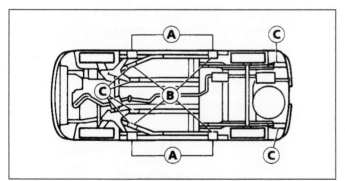

Jacking point locations on vehicle underbody – all models except Van

A *Jacking points for emergency jack supplied with vehicle*
B *Jacking points for workshop jack*
C *Support points for axle stands or workshop jack – jack to be used under points B and C only*

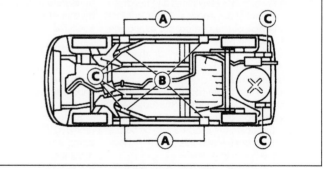

Jacking point locations on vehicle underbody – Van models

A *Jacking points for emergency jack supplied with vehicle*
B *Jacking points for workshop jack*
C *Support points for axle stands or workshop jack – jack to be used under points B and C only*

Whenever servicing, repair or overhaul work is carried out on the car or its components, observe the following procedures and instructions. This will assist in carrying out the operation efficiently and to a professional standard of workmanship.

Joint mating faces and gaskets

When separating components at their mating faces, never insert screwdrivers or similar implements into the joint between the faces in order to prise them apart. This can cause severe damage which results in oil leaks, coolant leaks, etc upon reassembly. Separation is usually achieved by tapping along the joint with a soft-faced hammer in order to break the seal. However, note that this method may not be suitable where dowels are used for component location.

Where a gasket is used between the mating faces of two components, a new one must be fitted on reassembly; fit it dry unless otherwise stated in the repair procedure. Make sure that the mating faces are clean and dry, with all traces of old gasket removed. When cleaning a joint face, use a tool which is unlikely to score or damage the face, and remove any burrs or nicks with an oilstone or fine file.

Make sure that tapped holes are cleaned with a pipe cleaner, and keep them free of jointing compound, if this is being used, unless specifically instructed otherwise.

Ensure that all orifices, channels or pipes are clear, and blow through them, preferably using compressed air.

Oil seals

Oil seals can be removed by levering them out with a wide flat-bladed screwdriver or similar implement. Alternatively, a number of self-tapping screws may be screwed into the seal, and these used as a purchase for pliers or some similar device in order to pull the seal free.

Whenever an oil seal is removed from its working location, either individually or as part of an assembly, it should be renewed.

The very fine sealing lip of the seal is easily damaged, and will not seal if the surface it contacts is not completely clean and free from scratches, nicks or grooves. If the original sealing surface of the component cannot be restored, and the manufacturer has not made provision for slight relocation of the seal relative to the sealing surface, the component should be renewed.

Protect the lips of the seal from any surface which may damage them in the course of fitting. Use tape or a conical sleeve where possible. Lubricate the seal lips with oil before fitting and, on dual-lipped seals, fill the space between the lips with grease.

Unless otherwise stated, oil seals must be fitted with their sealing lips toward the lubricant to be sealed.

Use a tubular drift or block of wood of the appropriate size to install the seal and, if the seal housing is shouldered, drive the seal down to the shoulder. If the seal housing is unshouldered, the seal should be fitted with its face flush with the housing top face (unless otherwise instructed).

Screw threads and fastenings

Seized nuts, bolts and screws are quite a common occurrence where corrosion has set in, and the use of penetrating oil or releasing fluid will often overcome this problem if the offending item is soaked for a while before attempting to release it. The use of an impact driver may also provide a means of releasing such stubborn fastening devices, when used in conjunction with the appropriate screwdriver bit or socket. If none of these methods works, it may be necessary to resort to the careful application of heat, or the use of a hacksaw or nut splitter device.

Studs are usually removed by locking two nuts together on the threaded part, and then using a spanner on the lower nut to unscrew the stud. Studs or bolts which have broken off below the surface of the component in which they are mounted can sometimes be removed using a stud extractor. Always ensure that a blind tapped hole is completely free from oil, grease, water or other fluid before installing the bolt or stud. Failure to do this could cause the housing to crack due to the hydraulic action of the bolt or stud as it is screwed in.

When tightening a castellated nut to accept a split pin, tighten the nut to the specified torque, where applicable, and then tighten further to the next split pin hole. Never slacken the nut to align the split pin hole, unless stated in the repair procedure.

When checking or retightening a nut or bolt to a specified torque setting, slacken the nut or bolt by a quarter of a turn, and then retighten to the specified setting. However, this should not be attempted where angular tightening has been used.

For some screw fastenings, notably cylinder head bolts or nuts, torque wrench settings are no longer specified for the latter stages of tightening, "angle-tightening" being called up instead. Typically, a fairly low torque wrench setting will be applied to the bolts/nuts in the correct sequence, followed by one or more stages of tightening through specified angles.

Locknuts, locktabs and washers

Any fastening which will rotate against a component or housing during tightening should always have a washer between it and the relevant component or housing.

Spring or split washers should always be renewed when they are used to lock a critical component such as a big-end bearing retaining bolt or nut. Locktabs which are folded over to retain a nut or bolt should always be renewed.

Self-locking nuts can be re-used in non-critical areas, providing resistance can be felt when the locking portion passes over the bolt or stud thread. However, it should be noted that self-locking stiffnuts tend to lose their effectiveness after long periods of use, and should then be renewed as a matter of course.

Split pins must always be replaced with new ones of the correct size for the hole.

When thread-locking compound is found on the threads of a fastener which is to be re-used, it should be cleaned off with a wire brush and solvent, and fresh compound applied on reassembly.

Special tools

Some repair procedures in this manual entail the use of special tools such as a press, two or three-legged pullers, spring compressors, etc. Wherever possible, suitable readily-available alternatives to the manufacturer's special tools are described, and are shown in use. In some instances, where no alternative is possible, it has been necessary to resort to the use of a manufacturer's tool, and this has been done for reasons of safety as well as the efficient completion of the repair operation. Unless you are highly-skilled and have a thorough understanding of the procedures described, never attempt to bypass the use of any special tool when the procedure described specifies its use. Not only is there a very great risk of personal injury, but expensive damage could be caused to the components involved.

Environmental considerations

When disposing of used engine oil, brake fluid, antifreeze, etc, give due consideration to any detrimental environmental effects. Do not, for instance, pour any of the above liquids down drains into the general sewage system, or onto the ground to soak away. Many local council refuse tips provide a facility for waste oil disposal, as do some garages. If none of these facilities are available, consult your local Environmental Health Department, or the National Rivers Authority, for further advice.

With the universal tightening-up of legislation regarding the emission of environmentally-harmful substances from motor vehicles, most vehicles have tamperproof devices fitted to the main adjustment points of the fuel system. These devices are primarily designed to prevent unqualified persons from adjusting the fuel/air mixture, with the chance of a consequent increase in toxic emissions. If such devices are found during servicing or overhaul, they should, wherever possible, be renewed or refitted in accordance with the manufacturer's requirements or current legislation.

Note: It is antisocial and illegal to dump oil down the drain. To find the location of your local oil recycling bank, call this number free.

The vehicle identification plate is located on the top of the front crossmember in the engine compartment (see illustration). In addition to many other details, it carries the Vehicle Identification Number (VIN), maximum vehicle weight information, and codes for interior trim and body colours.

The *Vehicle Identification Number (VIN)* is given on the vehicle identification plate. It is also located in a recess in the floor to the right-hand side of the driver's seat, access being gained after lifting the aperture cover (see illustration). On later models, the number is also stamped on a metal tag fixed to the right-hand side of the facia, which can be read through the windscreen.

The *body number and paint code numbers* are located on the vehicle identification plate.

The *engine number and code* are located on the left-hand end of the cylinder block, below and in front of the fuel filter housing (see illustration).

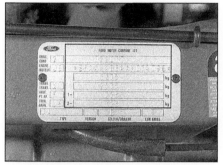

Vehicle identification plate

Chassis number stamped into the floor to the right of the driver's seat

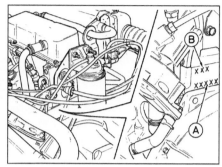

Engine number (A) and engine code (B)

Disconnecting the battery

Several systems fitted to the vehicle require battery power to be available at all times, either to ensure that their continued operation (such as the clock) or to maintain control unit memories (such as that in the engine management system's ECU) which would be wiped if the battery were to be disconnected. Whenever the battery is to be disconnected therefore, first note the following, to ensure that there are no unforeseen consequences of this action:

a) First, on any vehicle with central locking, it is a wise precaution to remove the key from the ignition, and to keep it with you, so that it does not get locked in, if the central locking should engage accidentally when the battery is reconnected.

b) On cars equipped with an engine management system, the system's ECU will lose the information stored in its memory – referred to by Ford as the 'KAM' (Keep-Alive Memory) – when the battery is disconnected. This includes idling and operating values, and any fault codes detected – in the case of the fault codes, if it is thought likely that the system has developed a fault for which the corresponding code has been logged, the vehicle must be taken to a Ford dealer for the codes to be read, using the special diagnostic equipment necessary for this. Whenever the battery is disconnected, the information relating to idle speed control and other operating values will have to be re-programmed into the unit's memory. The ECU does this by itself, but until then, there may be surging, hesitation, erratic idle and a generally inferior level of performance. To allow the ECU to relearn these values, start the engine and run it as close to idle speed as possible until it reaches its normal operating temperature, then run it for approximately two minutes at 1200 rpm. Next, drive the vehicle as far as necessary – approximately 5 miles of varied driving conditions is usually sufficient – to complete the relearning process.

c) If the battery is disconnected while the alarm system is armed or activated, the alarm will remain in the same state when the battery is reconnected. The same applies to the engine immobiliser system (where fitted).

d) If a Ford 'Keycode' audio unit is fitted, and the unit and/or the battery is disconnected, the unit will not function again on reconnection until the correct security code is entered. Details of this procedure, which varies according to the unit and model year, are given in the 'Ford Audio Systems Operating Guide' supplied with the vehicle when new, with the code itself being given in a 'Radio Passport' and/or a 'Keycode Label' at the same time. Ensure you have the correct code before you disconnect the battery. For obvious security reasons, the procedure is not given in this manual. If you do not have the code or details of the correct procedure, but can supply proof of ownership and a legitimate reason for wanting this information, the vehicle's selling dealer may be able to help.

Devices known as 'memory-savers' (or 'code-savers') can be used to avoid some of the above problems. Precise details vary according to the device used. Typically, it is plugged into the cigarette lighter, and is connected by its own wires to a spare battery; the vehicle's own battery is then disconnected from the electrical system, leaving the 'memory-saver' to pass sufficient current to maintain audio unit security codes and ECU memory values, and also to run permanently-live circuits such as the clock, all the while isolating the battery in the event of a short-circuit occurring while work is carried out.

⚠ *Warning: Some of these devices allow a considerable amount of current to pass, which can mean that many of the vehicle's systems are still operational when the main battery is disconnected. If a 'memory-saver' is used, ensure that the circuit concerned is actually 'dead' before carrying out any work on it.*

Introduction

A selection of good tools is a fundamental requirement for anyone contemplating the maintenance and repair of a motor vehicle. For the owner who does not possess any, their purchase will prove a considerable expense, offsetting some of the savings made by doing-it-yourself. However, provided that the tools purchased meet the relevant national safety standards and are of good quality, they will last for many years and prove an extremely worthwhile investment.

To help the average owner to decide which tools are needed to carry out the various tasks detailed in this manual, we have compiled three lists of tools under the following headings: *Maintenance and minor repair, Repair and overhaul*, and *Special*. Newcomers to practical mechanics should start off with the *Maintenance and minor repair* tool kit, and confine themselves to the simpler jobs around the vehicle. Then, as confidence and experience grow, more difficult tasks can be undertaken, with extra tools being purchased as, and when, they are needed. In this way, a *Maintenance and minor repair* tool kit can be built up into a *Repair and overhaul* tool kit over a considerable period of time, without any major cash outlays. The experienced do-it-yourselfer will have a tool kit good enough for most repair and overhaul procedures, and will add tools from the *Special* category when it is felt that the expense is justified by the amount of use to which these tools will be put.

Maintenance and minor repair tool kit

The tools given in this list should be considered as a minimum requirement if routine maintenance, servicing and minor repair operations are to be undertaken. We recommend the purchase of combination spanners (ring one end, open-ended the other); although more expensive than open-ended ones, they do give the advantages of both types of spanner.

☐ *Combination spanners:*
  Metric - 8 to 19 mm inclusive
☐ *Adjustable spanner - 35 mm jaw (approx.)*
☐ *Spark plug spanner (with rubber insert) - petrol models*
☐ *Spark plug gap adjustment tool - petrol models*
☐ *Set of feeler gauges*
☐ *Brake bleed nipple spanner*
☐ *Screwdrivers:*
  Flat blade - 100 mm long x 6 mm dia
  Cross blade - 100 mm long x 6 mm dia
  Torx - various sizes (not all vehicles)
☐ *Combination pliers*
☐ *Hacksaw (junior)*
☐ *Tyre pump*
☐ *Tyre pressure gauge*
☐ *Oil can*
☐ *Oil filter removal tool*
☐ *Fine emery cloth*
☐ *Wire brush (small)*
☐ *Funnel (medium size)*
☐ *Sump drain plug key (not all vehicles)*

Repair and overhaul tool kit

These tools are virtually essential for anyone undertaking any major repairs to a motor vehicle, and are additional to those given in the *Maintenance and minor repair* list. Included in this list is a comprehensive set of sockets. Although these are expensive, they will be found invaluable as they are so versatile - particularly if various drives are included in the set. We recommend the half-inch square-drive type, as this can be used with most proprietary torque wrenches.

The tools in this list will sometimes need to be supplemented by tools from the *Special* list:

☐ *Sockets (or box spanners) to cover range in previous list (including Torx sockets)*
☐ *Reversible ratchet drive (for use with sockets)*
☐ *Extension piece, 250 mm (for use with sockets)*
☐ *Universal joint (for use with sockets)*
☐ *Flexible handle or sliding T "breaker bar" (for use with sockets)*
☐ *Torque wrench (for use with sockets)*
☐ *Self-locking grips*
☐ *Ball pein hammer*
☐ *Soft-faced mallet (plastic or rubber)*
☐ *Screwdrivers:*
  Flat blade - long & sturdy, short (chubby), and narrow (electrician's) types
  Cross blade – long & sturdy, and short (chubby) types
☐ *Pliers:*
  Long-nosed
  Side cutters (electrician's)
  Circlip (internal and external)
☐ *Cold chisel - 25 mm*
☐ *Scriber*
☐ *Scraper*
☐ *Centre-punch*
☐ *Pin punch*
☐ *Hacksaw*
☐ *Brake hose clamp*
☐ *Brake/clutch bleeding kit*
☐ *Selection of twist drills*
☐ *Steel rule/straight-edge*
☐ *Allen keys (inc. splined/Torx type)*
☐ *Selection of files*
☐ *Wire brush*
☐ *Axle stands*
☐ *Jack (strong trolley or hydraulic type)*
☐ *Light with extension lead*
☐ *Universal electrical multi-meter*

![Sockets and reversible ratchet drive]

Sockets and reversible ratchet drive

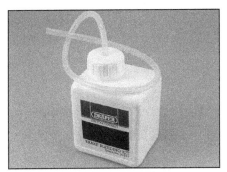

Brake bleeding kit

Torx key, socket and bit

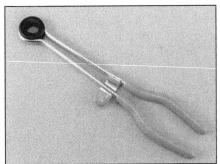

Hose clamp

Angular-tightening gauge

Special tools

The tools in this list are those which are not used regularly, are expensive to buy, or which need to be used in accordance with their manufacturers' instructions. Unless relatively difficult mechanical jobs are undertaken frequently, it will not be economic to buy many of these tools. Where this is the case, you could consider clubbing together with friends (or joining a motorists' club) to make a joint purchase, or borrowing the tools against a deposit from a local garage or tool hire specialist. It is worth noting that many of the larger DIY superstores now carry a large range of special tools for hire at modest rates.

The following list contains only those tools and instruments freely available to the public, and not those special tools produced by the vehicle manufacturer specifically for its dealer network. You will find occasional references to these manufacturers' special tools in the text of this manual. Generally, an alternative method of doing the job without the vehicle manufacturers' special tool is given. However, sometimes there is no alternative to using them. Where this is the case and the relevant tool cannot be bought or borrowed, you will have to entrust the work to a dealer.

- [ ] *Angular-tightening gauge*
- [ ] *Valve spring compressor*
- [ ] *Valve grinding tool*
- [ ] *Piston ring compressor*
- [ ] *Piston ring removal/installation tool*
- [ ] *Cylinder bore hone*
- [ ] *Balljoint separator*
- [ ] *Coil spring compressors (where applicable)*
- [ ] *Two/three-legged hub and bearing puller*
- [ ] *Impact screwdriver*
- [ ] *Micrometer and/or vernier calipers*
- [ ] *Dial gauge*
- [ ] *Stroboscopic timing light*
- [ ] *Dwell angle meter/tachometer*
- [ ] *Fault code reader*
- [ ] *Cylinder compression gauge*
- [ ] *Hand-operated vacuum pump and gauge*
- [ ] *Clutch plate alignment set*
- [ ] *Brake shoe steady spring cup removal tool*
- [ ] *Bush and bearing removal/installation set*
- [ ] *Stud extractors*
- [ ] *Tap and die set*
- [ ] *Lifting tackle*
- [ ] *Trolley jack*

Buying tools

Reputable motor accessory shops and superstores often offer excellent quality tools at discount prices, so it pays to shop around.

Remember, you don't have to buy the most expensive items on the shelf, but it is always advisable to steer clear of the very cheap tools. Beware of 'bargains' offered on market stalls or at car boot sales. There are plenty of good tools around at reasonable prices, but always aim to purchase items which meet the relevant national safety standards. If in doubt, ask the proprietor or manager of the shop for advice before making a purchase.

Care and maintenance of tools

Having purchased a reasonable tool kit, it is necessary to keep the tools in a clean and serviceable condition. After use, always wipe off any dirt, grease and metal particles using a clean, dry cloth, before putting the tools away. Never leave them lying around after they have been used. A simple tool rack on the garage or workshop wall for items such as screwdrivers and pliers is a good idea. Store all normal spanners and sockets in a metal box. Any measuring instruments, gauges, meters, etc, must be carefully stored where they cannot be damaged or become rusty.

Take a little care when tools are used. Hammer heads inevitably become marked, and screwdrivers lose the keen edge on their blades from time to time. A little timely attention with emery cloth or a file will soon restore items like this to a good finish.

Working facilities

Not to be forgotten when discussing tools is the workshop itself. If anything more than routine maintenance is to be carried out, a suitable working area becomes essential.

It is appreciated that many an owner-mechanic is forced by circumstances to remove an engine or similar item without the benefit of a garage or workshop. Having done this, any repairs should always be done under the cover of a roof.

Wherever possible, any dismantling should be done on a clean, flat workbench or table at a suitable working height.

Any workbench needs a vice; one with a jaw opening of 100 mm is suitable for most jobs. As mentioned previously, some clean dry storage space is also required for tools, as well as for any lubricants, cleaning fluids, touch-up paints etc, which become necessary.

Another item which may be required, and which has a much more general usage, is an electric drill with a chuck capacity of at least 8 mm. This, together with a good range of twist drills, is virtually essential for fitting accessories.

Last, but not least, always keep a supply of old newspapers and clean, lint-free rags available, and try to keep any working area as clean as possible.

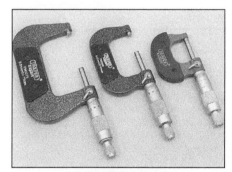

Micrometers

Dial test indicator ("dial gauge")

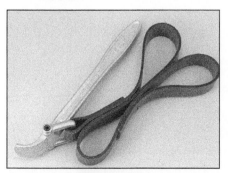

Strap wrench

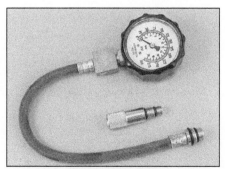

Compression tester

Fault code reader

This is a guide to getting your vehicle through the MOT test. Obviously it will not be possible to examine the vehicle to the same standard as the professional MOT tester. However, working through the following checks will enable you to identify any problem areas before submitting the vehicle for the test.

Where a testable component is in borderline condition, the tester has discretion in deciding whether to pass or fail it. The basis of such discretion is whether the tester would be happy for a close relative or friend to use the vehicle with the component in that condition. If the vehicle presented is clean and evidently well cared for, the tester may be more inclined to pass a borderline component than if the vehicle is scruffy and apparently neglected.

It has only been possible to summarise the test requirements here, based on the regulations in force at the time of printing. Test standards are becoming increasingly stringent, although there are some exemptions for older vehicles.

An assistant will be needed to help carry out some of these checks.

The checks have been sub-divided into four categories, as follows:

1 Checks carried out **FROM THE DRIVER'S SEAT**

2 Checks carried out **WITH THE VEHICLE ON THE GROUND**

3 Checks carried out **WITH THE VEHICLE RAISED AND THE WHEELS FREE TO TURN**

4 Checks carried out on **YOUR VEHICLE'S EXHAUST EMISSION SYSTEM**

---

1 Checks carried out **FROM THE DRIVER'S SEAT**

Handbrake

☐ Test the operation of the handbrake. Excessive travel (too many clicks) indicates incorrect brake or cable adjustment.

☐ Check that the handbrake cannot be released by tapping the lever sideways. Check the security of the lever mountings.

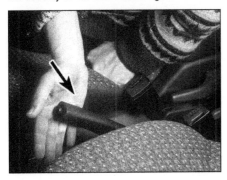

Footbrake

☐ Depress the brake pedal and check that it does not creep down to the floor, indicating a master cylinder fault. Release the pedal, wait a few seconds, then depress it again. If the pedal travels nearly to the floor before firm resistance is felt, brake adjustment or repair is necessary. If the pedal feels spongy, there is air in the hydraulic system which must be removed by bleeding.

☐ Check that the brake pedal is secure and in good condition. Check also for signs of fluid leaks on the pedal, floor or carpets, which would indicate failed seals in the brake master cylinder.

☐ Check the servo unit (when applicable) by operating the brake pedal several times, then keeping the pedal depressed and starting the engine. As the engine starts, the pedal will move down slightly. If not, the vacuum hose or the servo itself may be faulty.

Steering wheel and column

☐ Examine the steering wheel for fractures or looseness of the hub, spokes or rim.

☐ Move the steering wheel from side to side and then up and down. Check that the steering wheel is not loose on the column, indicating wear or a loose retaining nut. Continue moving the steering wheel as before, but also turn it slightly from left to right.

☐ Check that the steering wheel is not loose on the column, and that there is no abnormal

movement of the steering wheel, indicating wear in the column support bearings or couplings.

Windscreen, mirrors and sunvisor

☐ The windscreen must be free of cracks or other significant damage within the driver's field of view. (Small stone chips are acceptable.) Rear view mirrors must be secure, intact, and capable of being adjusted.

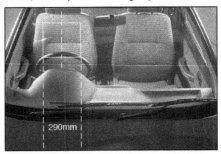

☐ The driver's sunvisor must be capable of being stored in the "up" position.

Seat belts and seats

Note: *The following checks are applicable to all seat belts, front and rear.*

☐ Examine the webbing of all the belts (including rear belts if fitted) for cuts, serious fraying or deterioration. Fasten and unfasten each belt to check the buckles. If applicable, check the retracting mechanism. Check the security of all seat belt mountings accessible from inside the vehicle.

☐ Seat belts with pre-tensioners, once activated, have a "flag" or similar showing on the seat belt stalk. This, in itself, is not a reason for test failure.

☐ The front seats themselves must be securely attached and the backrests must lock in the upright position.

Doors

☐ Both front doors must be able to be opened and closed from outside and inside, and must latch securely when closed.

2 Checks carried out **WITH THE VEHICLE ON THE GROUND**

Vehicle identification

☐ Number plates must be in good condition, secure and legible, with letters and numbers correctly spaced – spacing at (**A**) should be at least twice that at (**B**).

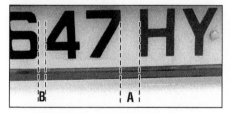

☐ The VIN plate and/or homologation plate must be legible.

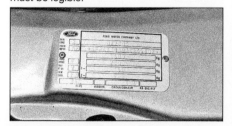

Electrical equipment

☐ Switch on the ignition and check the operation of the horn.

☐ Check the windscreen washers and wipers, examining the wiper blades; renew damaged or perished blades. Also check the operation of the stop-lights.

☐ Check the operation of the sidelights and number plate lights. The lenses and reflectors must be secure, clean and undamaged.

☐ Check the operation and alignment of the headlights. The headlight reflectors must not be tarnished and the lenses must be undamaged.

☐ Switch on the ignition and check the operation of the direction indicators (including the instrument panel tell-tale) and the hazard warning lights. Operation of the sidelights and stop-lights must not affect the indicators - if it does, the cause is usually a bad earth at the rear light cluster.

☐ Check the operation of the rear foglight(s), including the warning light on the instrument panel or in the switch.

☐ The ABS warning light must illuminate in accordance with the manufacturers' design. For most vehicles, the ABS warning light should illuminate when the ignition is switched on, and (if the system is operating properly) extinguish after a few seconds. Refer to the owner's handbook.

Footbrake

☐ Examine the master cylinder, brake pipes and servo unit for leaks, loose mountings, corrosion or other damage.

☐ The fluid reservoir must be secure and the fluid level must be between the upper (**A**) and lower (**B**) markings.

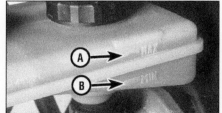

☐ Inspect both front brake flexible hoses for cracks or deterioration of the rubber. Turn the steering from lock to lock, and ensure that the hoses do not contact the wheel, tyre, or any part of the steering or suspension mechanism. With the brake pedal firmly depressed, check the hoses for bulges or leaks under pressure.

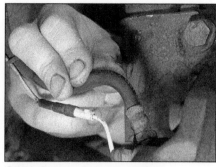

Steering and suspension

☐ Have your assistant turn the steering wheel from side to side slightly, up to the point where the steering gear just begins to transmit this movement to the roadwheels. Check for excessive free play between the steering wheel and the steering gear, indicating wear or insecurity of the steering column joints, the column-to-steering gear coupling, or the steering gear itself.

☐ Have your assistant turn the steering wheel more vigorously in each direction, so that the roadwheels just begin to turn. As this is done, examine all the steering joints, linkages, fittings and attachments. Renew any component that shows signs of wear or damage. On vehicles with power steering, check the security and condition of the steering pump, drivebelt and hoses.

☐ Check that the vehicle is standing level, and at approximately the correct ride height.

Shock absorbers

☐ Depress each corner of the vehicle in turn, then release it. The vehicle should rise and then settle in its normal position. If the vehicle continues to rise and fall, the shock absorber is defective. A shock absorber which has seized will also cause the vehicle to fail.

Exhaust system

☐ Start the engine. With your assistant holding a rag over the tailpipe, check the entire system for leaks. Repair or renew leaking sections.

3 Checks carried out
WITH THE VEHICLE RAISED AND THE WHEELS FREE TO TURN

Jack up the front and rear of the vehicle, and securely support it on axle stands. Position the stands clear of the suspension assemblies. Ensure that the wheels are clear of the ground and that the steering can be turned from lock to lock.

Steering mechanism

☐ Have your assistant turn the steering from lock to lock. Check that the steering turns smoothly, and that no part of the steering mechanism, including a wheel or tyre, fouls any brake hose or pipe or any part of the body structure.
☐ Examine the steering rack rubber gaiters for damage or insecurity of the retaining clips. If power steering is fitted, check for signs of damage or leakage of the fluid hoses, pipes or connections. Also check for excessive stiffness or binding of the steering, a missing split pin or locking device, or severe corrosion of the body structure within 30 cm of any steering component attachment point.

Front and rear suspension and wheel bearings

☐ Starting at the front right-hand side, grasp the roadwheel at the 3 o'clock and 9 o'clock positions and rock gently but firmly. Check for free play or insecurity at the wheel bearings, suspension balljoints, or suspension mountings, pivots and attachments.
☐ Now grasp the wheel at the 12 o'clock and 6 o'clock positions and repeat the previous inspection. Spin the wheel, and check for roughness or tightness of the front wheel bearing.

☐ If excess free play is suspected at a component pivot point, this can be confirmed by using a large screwdriver or similar tool and levering between the mounting and the component attachment. This will confirm whether the wear is in the pivot bush, its retaining bolt, or in the mounting itself (the bolt holes can often become elongated).

☐ Carry out all the above checks at the other front wheel, and then at both rear wheels.

Springs and shock absorbers

☐ Examine the suspension struts (when applicable) for serious fluid leakage, corrosion, or damage to the casing. Also check the security of the mounting points.
☐ If coil springs are fitted, check that the spring ends locate in their seats, and that the spring is not corroded, cracked or broken.
☐ If leaf springs are fitted, check that all leaves are intact, that the axle is securely attached to each spring, and that there is no deterioration of the spring eye mountings, bushes, and shackles.

☐ The same general checks apply to vehicles fitted with other suspension types, such as torsion bars, hydraulic displacer units, etc. Ensure that all mountings and attachments are secure, that there are no signs of excessive wear, corrosion or damage, and (on hydraulic types) that there are no fluid leaks or damaged pipes.
☐ Inspect the shock absorbers for signs of serious fluid leakage. Check for wear of the mounting bushes or attachments, or damage to the body of the unit.

Driveshafts (fwd vehicles only)

☐ Rotate each front wheel in turn and inspect the constant velocity joint gaiters for splits or damage. Also check that each driveshaft is straight and undamaged.

Braking system

☐ If possible without dismantling, check brake pad wear and disc condition. Ensure that the friction lining material has not worn excessively, (A) and that the discs are not fractured, pitted, scored or badly worn (B).

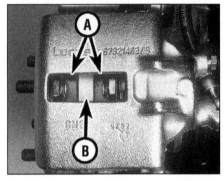

☐ Examine all the rigid brake pipes underneath the vehicle, and the flexible hose(s) at the rear. Look for corrosion, chafing or insecurity of the pipes, and for signs of bulging under pressure, chafing, splits or deterioration of the flexible hoses.
☐ Look for signs of fluid leaks at the brake calipers or on the brake backplates. Repair or renew leaking components.
☐ Slowly spin each wheel, while your assistant depresses and releases the footbrake. Ensure that each brake is operating and does not bind when the pedal is released.

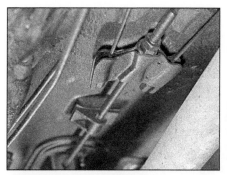

□ Examine the handbrake mechanism, checking for frayed or broken cables, excessive corrosion, or wear or insecurity of the linkage. Check that the mechanism works on each relevant wheel, and releases fully, without binding.

□ It is not possible to test brake efficiency without special equipment, but a road test can be carried out later to check that the vehicle pulls up in a straight line.

Fuel and exhaust systems

□ Inspect the fuel tank (including the filler cap), fuel pipes, hoses and unions. All components must be secure and free from leaks.

□ Examine the exhaust system over its entire length, checking for any damaged, broken or missing mountings, security of the retaining clamps and rust or corrosion.

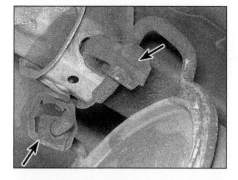

Wheels and tyres

□ Examine the sidewalls and tread area of each tyre in turn. Check for cuts, tears, lumps, bulges, separation of the tread, and exposure of the ply or cord due to wear or damage. Check that the tyre bead is correctly seated on the wheel rim, that the valve is sound and properly seated, and that the wheel is not distorted or damaged.

□ Check that the tyres are of the correct size for the vehicle, that they are of the same size and type on each axle, and that the pressures are correct.

□ Check the tyre tread depth. The legal minimum at the time of writing is 1.6 mm over at least three-quarters of the tread width. Abnormal tread wear may indicate incorrect front wheel alignment.

Body corrosion

□ Check the condition of the entire vehicle structure for signs of corrosion in load-bearing areas. (These include chassis box sections, side sills, cross-members, pillars, and all suspension, steering, braking system and seat belt mountings and anchorages.) Any corrosion which has seriously reduced the thickness of a load-bearing area is likely to cause the vehicle to fail. In this case professional repairs are likely to be needed.

□ Damage or corrosion which causes sharp or otherwise dangerous edges to be exposed will also cause the vehicle to fail.

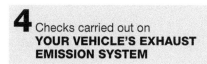

4 Checks carried out on **YOUR VEHICLE'S EXHAUST EMISSION SYSTEM**

Petrol models

□ Have the engine at normal operating temperature, and make sure that it is in good tune (ignition system in good order, air filter element clean, etc).

□ Before any measurements are carried out, raise the engine speed to around 2500 rpm, and hold it at this speed for 20 seconds. Allow the engine speed to return to idle, and watch for smoke emissions from the exhaust tailpipe. If the idle speed is obviously much too high, or if dense blue or clearly-visible black smoke comes from the tailpipe for more than 5 seconds, the vehicle will fail. As a rule of thumb, blue smoke signifies oil being burnt (engine wear) while black smoke signifies unburnt fuel (dirty air cleaner element, or other carburettor or fuel system fault).

□ An exhaust gas analyser capable of measuring carbon monoxide (CO) and hydrocarbons (HC) is now needed. If such an instrument cannot be hired or borrowed, a local garage may agree to perform the check for a small fee.

CO emissions (mixture)

□ At the time of writing, for vehicles first used between 1st August 1975 and 31st July 1986 (P to C registration), the CO level must not exceed 4.5% by volume. For vehicles first used between 1st August 1986 and 31st July 1992 (D to J registration), the CO level must not exceed 3.5% by volume. Vehicles first

used after 1st August 1992 (K registration) must conform to the manufacturer's specification. The MOT tester has access to a DOT database or emissions handbook, which lists the CO and HC limits for each make and model of vehicle. The CO level is measured with the engine at idle speed, and at "fast idle". The following limits are given as a general guide:

At idle speed -
    CO level no more than 0.5%
At "fast idle" (2500 to 3000 rpm) -
    CO level no more than 0.3%
    (Minimum oil temperature 60°C)

□ If the CO level cannot be reduced far enough to pass the test (and the fuel and ignition systems are otherwise in good condition) then the carburettor is badly worn, or there is some problem in the fuel injection system or catalytic converter (as applicable).

HC emissions

□ With the CO within limits, HC emissions for vehicles first used between 1st August 1975 and 31st July 1992 (P to J registration) must not exceed 1200 ppm. Vehicles first used after 1st August 1992 (K registration) must conform to the manufacturer's specification. The MOT tester has access to a DOT database or emissions handbook, which lists the CO and HC limits for each make and model of vehicle. The HC level is measured with the engine at "fast idle". The following is given as a general guide:

At "fast idle" (2500 to 3000 rpm) -
    HC level no more than 200 ppm
    (Minimum oil temperature 60°C)

□ Excessive HC emissions are caused by incomplete combustion, the causes of which can include oil being burnt, mechanical wear and ignition/fuel system malfunction.

Diesel models

□ The only emission test applicable to Diesel engines is the measuring of exhaust smoke density. The test involves accelerating the engine several times to its maximum unloaded speed.

Note: *It is of the utmost importance that the engine timing belt is in good condition before the test is carried out.*

□ The limits for Diesel engine exhaust smoke, introduced in September 1995 are:
Vehicles first used before 1st August 1979:
    Exempt from metered smoke testing, but must not emit "dense blue or clearly visible black smoke for a period of more than 5 seconds at idle" or "dense blue or clearly visible black smoke during acceleration which would obscure the view of other road users".
Non-turbocharged vehicles first used after 1st August 1979: 2.5m-1
Turbocharged vehicles first used after 1st August 1979: 3.0m-1
□ Excessive smoke can be caused by a dirty air cleaner element. Otherwise, professional advice may be needed to find the cause.

Engine

- ☐ Engine fails to rotate when attempting to start
- ☐ Engine rotates, but will not start
- ☐ Engine starts, but stops again
- ☐ Engine will not stop when switched off
- ☐ Misfiring/rough idle
- ☐ Lack of power
- ☐ Fuel consumption excessive
- ☐ Engine knocking or rattling
- ☐ Oil consumption excessive
- ☐ Starter motor noisy or excessively-rough in engagement
- ☐ Oil pressure warning light illuminated with engine running

Cooling system

- ☐ Overheating
- ☐ Overcooling
- ☐ External coolant leakage
- ☐ Internal coolant leakage
- ☐ Corrosion

Fuel and exhaust systems

- ☐ Fuel leakage and/or fuel odour
- ☐ Black smoke in exhaust
- ☐ Blue or white smoke in exhaust
- ☐ Excessive noise or fumes from exhaust system
- ☐ Injector pipe(s) break or split repeatedly

Clutch

- ☐ Pedal travels to floor – no pressure or very little resistance
- ☐ Clutch fails to disengage (unable to select gears)
- ☐ Clutch slips (engine speed increases, with no increase in vehicle speed)
- ☐ Judder as clutch is engaged
- ☐ Noise when depressing or releasing clutch pedal

Manual transmission

- ☐ Noisy in neutral with engine running
- ☐ Noisy in one particular gear
- ☐ Difficulty engaging gears
- ☐ Jumps out of gear
- ☐ Vibration
- ☐ Lubricant leaks

Driveshafts

- ☐ Clicking or knocking noise on turns (at slow speed on full-lock)
- ☐ Vibration when accelerating or decelerating

Braking system

- ☐ Vehicle pulls to one side under braking
- ☐ Noise (grinding or high-pitched squeal) when brakes applied
- ☐ Excessive brake pedal travel
- ☐ Brake pedal feels spongy when depressed
- ☐ Excessive brake pedal effort required to stop vehicle
- ☐ Judder felt through brake pedal or steering wheel when braking
- ☐ Brakes binding
- ☐ Rear wheels locking under normal braking

Suspension and steering systems

- ☐ Vehicle pulls to one side
- ☐ Wheel wobble and vibration
- ☐ Excessive pitching and/or rolling around corners, or during braking
- ☐ Wandering or general instability
- ☐ Excessively-stiff steering
- ☐ Excessive play in steering
- ☐ Lack of power assistance
- ☐ Tyre wear excessive

Electrical system

- ☐ Battery will only hold a charge for a few days
- ☐ Ignition (no-charge) warning light remains illuminated with engine running
- ☐ Ignition (no-charge) warning light fails to come on
- ☐ Lights inoperative
- ☐ Instrument readings inaccurate or erratic
- ☐ Horn inoperative, or unsatisfactory in operation
- ☐ Windscreen/tailgate wipers
- ☐ Windscreen/tailgate washers
- ☐ Electric windows
- ☐ Central locking system

Introduction

The vehicle owner who does his or her own maintenance according to the recommended service schedules should not have to use this section of the manual very often. Modern component reliability is such that, provided those items subject to wear or deterioration are inspected or renewed at the specified intervals, sudden failure is comparatively rare. Faults do not usually just happen as a result of sudden failure, but develop over a period of time. Major mechanical failures in particular are usually preceded by characteristic symptoms over hundreds or even thousands of miles. Those components which do occasionally fail without warning are often small and easily carried in the vehicle.

With any fault-finding, the first step is to decide where to begin investigations. Sometimes this is obvious, but on other occasions, a little detective work will be necessary. The owner who makes half a dozen haphazard adjustments or replacements may be successful in curing a fault (or its symptoms), but will be none the wiser if the fault recurs, and ultimately may have spent more time and money than was necessary. A calm and logical approach will be found to be more satisfactory in the long run. Always take into account any warning signs or abnormalities that may have been noticed in the period preceding the fault – power loss, high or low gauge readings, unusual smells, etc – and remember that failure of components such as fuses may only be pointers to some underlying fault.

The pages which follow provide an easy reference guide to the more common problems which may occur during the operation of the vehicle. These problems and their possible causes are grouped under headings denoting various components or systems, such as Engine, Cooling system, etc. The Chapter and/or Section which deals with the problem is also shown in brackets. Whatever the fault, certain basic principles apply. These are as follows:

Verify the fault. This is simply a matter of being sure that you know what the symptoms are before starting work. This is particularly important if you are investigating a fault for someone else, who may not have described it very accurately.

Don't overlook the obvious. For example, if the vehicle won't start, is there fuel in the tank? (Don't take anyone else's word on this particular point, and don't trust the fuel gauge either!) If an electrical fault is indicated, look for loose or broken wires before using the test gear.

Cure the disease, not the symptom. Substituting a flat battery with a fully-charged one will get you off the hard shoulder, but if the underlying cause is not attended to, the new battery will go the same way.

Don't take anything for granted. Particularly, don't forget that a 'new' component may itself be defective (especially if it's been rattling around in the boot for months), and don't leave components out of a fault diagnosis sequence just because they are new or recently fitted. When you do finally diagnose a difficult fault, you'll probably realise that all the evidence was there from the start.

Diesel fault diagnosis

The majority of starting problems on small diesel engines are electrical in origin. The mechanic who is familiar with petrol engines but less so with diesel may be inclined to view the diesel's injectors and pump in the same light as the spark plugs and distributor, but this is generally a mistake.

When investigating complaints of difficult starting for someone else, make sure that the correct starting procedure is understood and is being followed. Some drivers are unaware of the significance of the preheating warning light - many modern engines are sufficiently forgiving for this not to matter in mild weather, but with the onset of winter problems begin.

As a rule of thumb, if the engine is difficult to start but runs well when it has finally got going, the problem is electrical (battery, starter motor or preheating system). If poor performance is combined with difficult starting, the problem is likely to be in the fuel system. The low pressure (supply) side of the fuel system should be checked before suspecting the injectors and injection pump. The most common fuel supply problem is air getting into the system, and any pipe from the fuel tank forwards must be scrutinised if air leakage is suspected. Normally the pump is the last item to suspect, since unless it has been tampered with there is no reason for it to be at fault.

Engine

Engine fails to rotate when attempting to start

- ☐ Battery terminal connections loose or corroded (*Weekly checks*).
- ☐ Battery discharged or faulty (Chapter 5A).
- ☐ Broken, loose or disconnected wiring in the starting circuit (Chapter 5A).
- ☐ Defective starter solenoid or switch (Chapter 5A).
- ☐ Defective starter motor (Chapter 5A).
- ☐ Flywheel ring gear or starter pinion teeth loose or broken (Chapter 2A or 5A).
- ☐ Engine earth strap broken or disconnected (Chapter 5A).

Engine rotates, but will not start

- ☐ Fuel tank empty.
- ☐ Battery discharged or inadequate capacity (engine rotates slowly) (Chapter 5A).
- ☐ Battery terminal connections loose or corroded (*Weekly checks*).
- ☐ Incorrect use of preheating system, or preheating system fault (Chapter 5B).
- ☐ Immobiliser or anti-theft alarm faulty or incorrectly used (Chapter 12).
- ☐ Fuel waxing (in very cold weather).
- ☐ Overfuelling or cold start advance mechanism defective (Chapter 4A).
- ☐ Air filter element dirty or clogged (Chapter 1).
- ☐ Blockage in exhaust system (Chapter 4B).
- ☐ Poor compressions (Chapter 2A).
- ☐ Air in fuel system (Chapter 4A).
- ☐ Restriction in fuel feed or return (Chapter 1).
- ☐ Stop solenoid defective (Chapter 4A).
- ☐ Injector(s) faulty (Chapter 4A).
- ☐ Injection pump timing incorrect, or pump internal fault (Chapter 4A).
- ☐ Valve timing incorrect, possibly through a poorly-fitted timing belt (Chapter 2A).
- ☐ Major mechanical failure (eg camshaft drive) (Chapter 2A or 2B).

Engine starts but stops again

- ☐ Fuel very low in tank.
- ☐ Air in fuel system (Chapter 4A).
- ☐ Idle adjustment incorrect (Chapter 4A).
- ☐ Restriction in fuel feed or return (Chapter 1).
- ☐ Air cleaner dirty or blockage in air intake system (Chapter 1 or 4A).
- ☐ Blockage in exhaust system (Chapter 4B).
- ☐ Injector(s) faulty (Chapter 4A).

Engine will not stop when switched off

- ☐ Stop solenoid defective (Chapter 4A).

Misfiring/rough idle

- ☐ Air cleaner dirty or blockage in air intake system (Chapter 1 or 4A).
- ☐ Air in fuel system (Chapter 4A).
- ☐ Restriction in fuel feed or return (Chapter 1).
- ☐ Valve clearances incorrect (Chapter 2A).
- ☐ Valve(s) sticking, valve spring(s) weak or broken, or poor compressions (Chapter 2A or 2B).
- ☐ Overheating (Chapter 3).
- ☐ Injector pipe(s) wrongly connected or wrong type (Chapter 4A).
- ☐ Valve timing incorrect, possibly through a poorly-fitted timing belt (Chapter 2A).
- ☐ Injector(s) faulty (Chapter 4A).
- ☐ Injection pump timing incorrect, or pump internal fault (Chapter 4A).
- ☐ Cylinder head gasket blown (Chapter 2A).

Lack of power

- ☐ Accelerator linkage not moving through full travel (cable slack or pedal obstructed) (Chapter 4A).
- ☐ Injection pump control linkages sticking or maladjusted (Chapter 4A).
- ☐ Air in fuel system (Chapter 4A).
- ☐ Restriction in fuel feed or return (Chapter 1).
- ☐ Valve timing incorrect, possibly through a poorly-fitted timing belt (Chapter 2A).
- ☐ Injection pump timing incorrect, or pump internal fault (Chapter 4A).
- ☐ Blockage in exhaust system (Chapter 4B).
- ☐ Brakes binding (Chapter 1 or 9).
- ☐ Clutch slipping (Chapter 6).
- ☐ Turbo boost pressure inadequate, when applicable (Chapter 4A).
- ☐ Valve clearances incorrect (Chapter 2A).
- ☐ Injector(s) faulty (Chapter 4A).
- ☐ Injection pump timing incorrect, or pump internal fault (Chapter 4A).

Fuel consumption excessive

- ☐ External leakage, or fuel passing into sump (worn rings/bores, or pump overfuelling).
- ☐ Air cleaner dirty or blockage in air intake system (Chapter 1 or 4A).
- ☐ Valve clearances incorrect (Chapter 2A).
- ☐ Valve timing incorrect, possibly through a poorly-fitted timing belt (Chapter 2A).
- ☐ Injection pump timing incorrect, or pump internal fault (Chapter 4A).
- ☐ Injector(s) faulty (Chapter 4A).
- ☐ Unsympathetic driving style, or adverse conditions.
- ☐ Tyres under-inflated (*Weekly checks*).

Engine (continued)

Engine knocking or rattling

- ☐ Air in fuel system (Chapter 4A).
- ☐ Fuel grade incorrect or quality poor (engine will also knock if petrol is used accidentally).
- ☐ Valve clearances incorrect (Chapter 2A).
- ☐ Injector(s) faulty (Chapter 4A).
- ☐ Worn timing belt tensioner or idler pulleys (Chapter 2A).
- ☐ Ancillary component fault (water pump, alternator, etc) (Chapter 3 or 5A).
- ☐ Valve timing incorrect, possibly through a poorly-fitted timing belt (Chapter 2A).
- ☐ Injection pump timing incorrect, or pump internal fault (Chapter 4A).
- ☐ Piston protrusion excessive/head gasket thickness inadequate (after repair) (Chapter 2A or 2B).
- ☐ Valve recess incorrect (after repair) (Chapter 2B).
- ☐ Piston rings broken or worn (Chapter 2B).
- ☐ General engine wear - pistons and/or bores, crankshaft bearings, camshaft, etc (Chapter 2A or 2B).

Oil consumption excessive

- ☐ External leakage (standing or running).
- ☐ New engine not yet run-in.
- ☐ Engine oil incorrect grade/poor quality, or oil level too high (*Weekly checks*).
- ☐ Crankcase ventilation system obstructed (Chapter 1).
- ☐ General engine wear - pistons and/or bores, valve stem oil seals, etc (Chapter 2B).

Starter motor noisy or excessively-rough in engagement

- ☐ Flywheel ring gear or starter pinion teeth loose or broken (Chapter 2A or 5A).
- ☐ Starter motor mounting bolts loose or missing (Chapter 5A).
- ☐ Starter motor internal components worn or damaged (Chapter 5A).

Oil pressure warning light illuminated with engine running

- ☐ Low oil level or incorrect oil grade (*Weekly checks*).
- ☐ Faulty oil pressure warning light switch (Chapter 2A).
- ☐ Worn engine bearings and/or oil pump (Chapter 2B).
- ☐ High engine operating temperature (Chapter 3).
- ☐ Oil pick-up strainer clogged (Chapter 2B).

Cooling system

Overheating

- ☐ Insufficient coolant in system (*Weekly checks*).
- ☐ Thermostat faulty (Chapter 3).
- ☐ Radiator core blocked or grille restricted (Chapter 3).
- ☐ Radiator electric cooling fan(s) or coolant temperature sensor faulty (Chapter 3).
- ☐ Pressure cap faulty (Chapter 3).
- ☐ Inaccurate coolant temperature gauge sender (Chapter 3).
- ☐ Airlock in cooling system (Chapter 1).
- ☐ Blockage in exhaust system (Chapter 4B).
- ☐ Cylinder head gasket blown (Chapter 2A).

Overcooling

- ☐ Thermostat faulty (Chapter 3).
- ☐ Inaccurate coolant temperature gauge sender (Chapter 3).

External coolant leakage

- ☐ Deteriorated or damaged hoses or hose clips (Chapter 1).
- ☐ Radiator core or heater matrix leaking (Chapter 3).
- ☐ Pressure cap faulty (Chapter 3).
- ☐ Water pump leaking (Chapter 3).
- ☐ Boiling due to overheating (Chapter 3).
- ☐ Core plug leaking (Chapter 2B).

Internal coolant leakage

- ☐ Leaking cylinder head gasket (Chapter 2A).
- ☐ Cracked cylinder head or cylinder bore (Chapter 2B).

Corrosion

- ☐ Infrequent draining and flushing (Chapter 1).
- ☐ Incorrect antifreeze mixture, or inappropriate antifreeze type (*Weekly checks* and Chapter 1).

Fuel and exhaust systems

Fuel leakage and/or fuel odour

- ☐ Damaged or corroded fuel tank, pipes or connections (Chapter 1).

Black smoke in exhaust

- ☐ Air cleaner dirty or blockage in air intake system (Chapter 1 or 4A).
- ☐ Valve clearances incorrect (Chapter 2A).
- ☐ Turbo boost pressure inadequate, when applicable (Chapter 4A).
- ☐ Valve timing incorrect, possibly through a poorly-fitted timing belt (Chapter 2A).
- ☐ Injection pump timing incorrect, or pump internal fault (Chapter 4A).

Blue or white smoke in exhaust

- ☐ Engine oil incorrect grade or poor quality, or fuel passing into sump (worn rings/bores, or pump overfuelling).
- ☐ Glow plug(s) defective, or controller faulty (smoke at start-up only) (Chapter 5B).
- ☐ Air cleaner dirty or blockage in air intake system (Chapter 1 or 4A).
- ☐ Valve timing incorrect, possibly through a poorly-fitted timing belt (Chapter 2A).

- ☐ Injection pump timing incorrect, or pump internal fault (Chapter 4A).
- ☐ Injector(s) faulty (Chapter 4A).
- ☐ General engine wear - pistons and/or bores, valve stem oil seals, etc (Chapter 2B).

Excessive noise or fumes from exhaust system

- ☐ Leaking exhaust system or manifold joints (Chapter 1 or 4B).
- ☐ Leaking, corroded or damaged silencers or pipe (Chapter 1 or 4B).
- ☐ Broken mountings, causing body or suspension contact (Chapter 1 or 4B).

Injector pipe(s) break or split repeatedly

- ☐ Missing or wrongly located clamps (Chapter 4A).
- ☐ Wrong type or length of pipe (Chapter 4A).
- ☐ Faulty injector (Chapter 4A).

Clutch

Pedal travels to floor – no pressure or very little resistance

- [ ] Broken clutch cable (Chapter 6).
- [ ] Faulty clutch adjuster (Chapter 1 or 6).
- [ ] Incorrect clutch pedal free play adjustment (Chapter 1).
- [ ] Broken clutch release bearing or fork (Chapter 6).
- [ ] Broken diaphragm spring in clutch pressure plate (Chapter 6).

Clutch fails to disengage (unable to select gears)

- [ ] Faulty clutch adjuster (Chapter 1 or 6).
- [ ] Incorrect clutch pedal free play adjustment (Chapter 1).
- [ ] Clutch disc sticking on transmission input shaft splines (Chapter 6).
- [ ] Clutch disc sticking to flywheel or pressure plate (Chapter 6).
- [ ] Faulty pressure plate assembly (Chapter 6).
- [ ] Clutch release mechanism worn or incorrectly assembled (Chapter 6).

Clutch slips (engine speed increases, with no increase in vehicle speed)

- [ ] Faulty clutch adjuster (Chapter 1 or 6).
- [ ] Incorrect clutch pedal free play adjustment (Chapter 1).
- [ ] Clutch disc linings excessively worn (Chapter 6).
- [ ] Clutch disc linings contaminated with oil or grease (Chapter 6).
- [ ] Faulty pressure plate or weak diaphragm spring (Chapter 6).

Judder as clutch is engaged

- [ ] Clutch disc linings contaminated with oil or grease (Chapter 6).
- [ ] Clutch disc linings excessively worn (Chapter 6).
- [ ] Clutch cable sticking or frayed (Chapter 6).
- [ ] Faulty or distorted pressure plate or diaphragm spring (Chapter 6).
- [ ] Worn or loose engine/transmission mountings (Chapter 2A).
- [ ] Clutch disc hub or transmission input shaft splines worn (Chapter 6 or 7).

Noise when depressing or releasing clutch pedal

- [ ] Worn clutch release bearing (Chapter 6).
- [ ] Worn or dry clutch pedal bushes (Chapter 6).
- [ ] Faulty pressure plate assembly (Chapter 6).
- [ ] Pressure plate diaphragm spring broken (Chapter 6).
- [ ] Broken clutch disc cushioning springs (Chapter 6).

Manual transmission

Noisy in neutral with engine running

- [ ] Input shaft bearings worn (noise apparent with clutch pedal released, but not when depressed) (Chapter 7).
- [ ] Clutch release bearing worn (noise apparent with clutch pedal depressed, possibly less when released) (Chapter 6).

Noisy in one particular gear

- [ ] Worn, damaged or chipped gear teeth (Chapter 7).*

Difficulty engaging gears

- [ ] Clutch fault (Chapter 6).
- [ ] Worn or damaged gear linkage (Chapter 7).
- [ ] Incorrectly-adjusted gear linkage (Chapter 7).
- [ ] Worn synchroniser assemblies (Chapter 7).*

Jumps out of gear

- [ ] Worn or damaged gear linkage (Chapter 7).
- [ ] Incorrectly-adjusted gear linkage (Chapter 7).

- [ ] Worn synchroniser assemblies (Chapter 7).*
- [ ] Worn selector forks (Chapter 7).*

Vibration

- [ ] Lack of oil (Chapter 1).
- [ ] Worn bearings (Chapter 7).*

Lubricant leaks

- [ ] Leaking differential side gear oil seal (Chapter 7).
- [ ] Leaking housing joint (Chapter 7).*
- [ ] Leaking input shaft oil seal (Chapter 7).*
- [ ] Leaking selector shaft oil seal (Chapter 7).
- [ ] Leaking speedometer drive pinion O-ring (Chapter 7).

* Although the corrective action necessary to remedy the symptoms described is beyond the scope of the home mechanic, the above information should be helpful in isolating the cause of the condition, so that the owner can communicate clearly with a professional mechanic.

Driveshafts

Clicking or knocking noise on turns (at slow speed on full-lock)

- [ ] Lack of constant velocity joint lubricant (Chapter 8).
- [ ] Worn outer constant velocity joint (Chapter 8).

Vibration when accelerating or decelerating

- [ ] Worn inner constant velocity joint (Chapter 8).
- [ ] Bent or distorted driveshaft (Chapter 8).

Braking system

Note: *Before assuming that a brake problem exists, make sure that the tyres are in good condition and correctly inflated, that the front wheel alignment is correct, and that the vehicle is not loaded with weight in an unequal manner. Apart from checking the condition of all pipe and hose connections, any faults occurring on the Anti-lock Braking System (ABS) should be referred to a Ford dealer for diagnosis.*

Vehicle pulls to one side under braking

☐ Worn, defective, damaged or contaminated front or rear brake shoes on one side (Chapter 1).
☐ Seized or partially-seized front or rear brake caliper/wheel cylinder piston (Chapter 9).
☐ A mixture of brake pad/shoe lining materials fitted between sides (Chapter 1).
☐ Brake caliper mounting bolts loose (Chapter 9).
☐ Rear brake backplate mounting bolts loose (Chapter 9).
☐ Worn or damaged steering or suspension components (Chapter 10).

Noise (grinding or high-pitched squeal) when brakes applied

☐ Brake pad or shoe friction lining material worn down to metal backing Chapter 1).
☐ Excessive corrosion of brake disc or drum (may be apparent after the vehicle has been standing for some time) (Chapter 1).

Excessive brake pedal travel

☐ Inoperative rear brake self-adjust mechanism (Chapter 9).
☐ Rear wheel cylinders leaking (Chapter 9).
☐ Faulty master cylinder (Chapter 9).
☐ Air in hydraulic system (Chapter 9).

Brake pedal feels spongy when depressed

☐ Air in hydraulic system (Chapter 9).
☐ Rear wheel cylinders leaking (Chapter 9).

☐ Deteriorated flexible rubber brake hoses (Chapter 9).
☐ Master cylinder mounting nuts loose (Chapter 9).
☐ Faulty master cylinder (Chapter 9).

Excessive brake pedal effort required to stop vehicle

☐ Faulty vacuum servo unit (Chapter 9).
☐ Disconnected, damaged or insecure brake servo vacuum hoses (Chapter 9).
☐ Brake vacuum pump leaking or faulty (Chapter 9).
☐ Primary or secondary hydraulic circuit failure (Chapter 9).
☐ Seized brake caliper or wheel cylinder piston(s) (Chapter 9).
☐ Brake pads or brake shoes incorrectly fitted (Chapter 9).
☐ Incorrect grade of brake pads or brake shoes fitted (Chapter 1).
☐ Brake pads or brake shoe linings contaminated (Chapter 1).

Judder felt through brake pedal or steering wheel when braking

☐ Excessive run-out or distortion of front discs or rear discs/drums (Chapter 9).
☐ Brake pad or brake shoe linings worn (Chapter 1).
☐ Brake caliper or rear brake backplate mounting bolts loose (Chapter 9).
☐ Wear in suspension or steering components or mountings (Chapter 10).

Brakes binding

☐ Seized brake caliper or wheel cylinder piston(s) (Chapter 9).
☐ Faulty handbrake mechanism (Chapter 9).
☐ Faulty master cylinder (Chapter 9).

Rear wheels locking under normal braking

☐ Rear brake pad/shoe linings contaminated (Chapter 1).
☐ Faulty brake pressure regulator (Chapter 9).

Suspension and steering systems

Note: *Before diagnosing suspension or steering faults, be sure that the trouble is not due to incorrect tyre pressures, mixtures of tyre types, or binding brakes.*

Vehicle pulls to one side

☐ Defective tyre (Chapter 1).
☐ Excessive wear in suspension or steering components (Chapter 10).
☐ Incorrect front wheel alignment (Chapter 10).
☐ Accident damage to steering or suspension components (Chapter 10).

Wheel wobble and vibration

☐ Front roadwheels out of balance (vibration felt mainly through the steering wheel) (Chapter 1).
☐ Rear roadwheels out of balance (vibration felt throughout the vehicle) Chapter 1).
☐ Roadwheels damaged or distorted (Chapter 1).
☐ Faulty or damaged tyre (*Weekly checks*).
☐ Worn steering or suspension joints, bushes or components (Chapter 10).
☐ Roadwheel nuts loose (Chapter 1).
☐ Wear in driveshaft joint, or loose driveshaft nut (vibration worst when under load) (Chapter 8).

Excessive pitching and/or rolling around corners, or during braking

☐ Defective shock absorbers (Chapter 10).

☐ Broken or weak coil/leaf spring and/or suspension component (Chapter 10).
☐ Worn or damaged anti-roll bar or mountings (Chapter 10).

Wandering or general instability

☐ Incorrect front wheel alignment (Chapter 10).
☐ Worn steering or suspension joints, bushes or components (Chapter 10).
☐ Tyres out of balance (*Weekly checks*).
☐ Faulty or damaged tyre (*Weekly checks*).
☐ Roadwheel nuts loose (Chapter 1).
☐ Defective shock absorbers (Chapter 10).

Excessively-stiff steering

☐ Lack of steering gear lubricant (Chapter 10).
☐ Seized track-rod end balljoint or suspension balljoint (Chapter 10).
☐ Broken or slipping auxiliary drivebelt (Chapter 1).
☐ Incorrect front wheel alignment (Chapter 10).
☐ Steering rack or column bent or damaged (Chapter 10).

Excessive play in steering

☐ Worn steering column universal joint(s) or flexible coupling (Chapter 10).
☐ Worn steering track-rod end balljoints (Chapter 10).
☐ Worn rack-and-pinion steering gear (Chapter 10).
☐ Worn steering or suspension joints, bushes or components (Chapter 10).

Suspension and steering systems (continued)

Lack of power assistance

- [ ] Broken or slipping auxiliary drivebelt (Chapter 1).
- [ ] Incorrect power steering fluid level (Chapter 1).
- [ ] Restriction in power steering fluid hoses (Chapter 10).
- [ ] Faulty power steering pump (Chapter 10).
- [ ] Faulty rack-and-pinion steering gear (Chapter 10).

Tyre wear excessive

Tyres worn on inside or outside edges

- [ ] Tyres under-inflated (wear on both edges) (*Weekly checks*).
- [ ] Incorrect camber or castor angles (wear on one edge only) (Chapter 10).
- [ ] Worn steering or suspension joints, bushes or components (Chapter 10).
- [ ] Excessively-hard cornering.
- [ ] Accident damage.

Tyre treads exhibit feathered edges

- [ ] Incorrect toe setting (Chapter 10).

Tyres worn in centre of tread

- [ ] Tyres over-inflated (*Weekly checks*).

Tyres worn on inside and outside edges

- [ ] Tyres under-inflated (*Weekly checks*).

Tyres worn unevenly

- [ ] Tyres out of balance (*Weekly checks*).
- [ ] Excessive wheel or tyre run-out (Chapter 1).
- [ ] Worn shock absorbers (Chapter 10).
- [ ] Faulty tyre (*Weekly checks*).

Electrical system

Note: *For problems associated with the starting system, refer to the faults listed under 'Engine' earlier in this Section.*

Battery will only hold a charge for a few days

- [ ] Battery defective internally (Chapter 5A).
- [ ] Battery electrolyte level low (Chapter 1).
- [ ] Battery terminal connections loose or corroded (*Weekly checks*).
- [ ] Auxiliary drivebelt worn or incorrectly-adjusted (Chapter 1).
- [ ] Alternator not charging at correct output (Chapter 5A).
- [ ] Alternator or voltage regulator faulty (Chapter 5A).
- [ ] Short-circuit causing continual battery drain (Chapters 5A and 12).

Ignition (no-charge) warning light remains illuminated with engine running

- [ ] Auxiliary drivebelt broken, worn, or incorrectly-adjusted (Chapter 1).
- [ ] Alternator brushes worn, sticking, or dirty (Chapter 5A).
- [ ] Alternator brush springs weak or broken (Chapter 5A).
- [ ] Internal fault in alternator or voltage regulator (Chapter 5A).
- [ ] Disconnected or loose wiring in charging circuit (Chapter 5A).

Ignition (no-charge) warning light fails to come on

- [ ] Warning light bulb blown (Chapter 12).
- [ ] Broken, disconnected, or loose wiring in warning light circuit (Chapters 5A and 12).
- [ ] Alternator faulty (Chapter 5A).

Lights inoperative

- [ ] Bulb blown (Chapter 12).
- [ ] Corrosion of bulb or bulbholder contacts (Chapter 12).
- [ ] Blown fuse (Chapter 12).
- [ ] Faulty relay (Chapter 12).
- [ ] Broken, loose, or disconnected wiring (Chapter 12).
- [ ] Faulty switch (Chapter 12).

Instrument readings inaccurate or erratic

Instrument readings increase with engine speed

- [ ] Faulty voltage regulator (Chapter 12).

Gauges give no reading

- [ ] Faulty gauge sender unit (Chapter 3 or 4A).
- [ ] Wiring open-circuit (Chapter 12).
- [ ] Faulty gauge (Chapter 12).

Gauges give continuous maximum reading

- [ ] Faulty gauge sender unit (Chapter 3 or 4A).
- [ ] Wiring short-circuit (Chapter 12).
- [ ] Faulty gauge (Chapter 12).

Horn inoperative, or unsatisfactory in operation

Horn fails to operate

- [ ] Blown fuse (Chapter 12).
- [ ] Cable or cable connections loose or disconnected (Chapter 12).
- [ ] Faulty horn (Chapter 12).

Horn emits intermittent or unsatisfactory sound

- [ ] Cable connections loose (Chapter 12).
- [ ] Horn mountings loose (Chapter 12).
- [ ] Faulty horn (Chapter 12).

Horn operates all the time

- [ ] Horn push either earthed or stuck down (Chapter 12).
- [ ] Horn cable to horn push earthed (Chapter 12).

Windscreen/tailgate wipers

Wipers fail to operate, or operate very slowly

- [ ] Wiper blades stuck to screen, or linkage seized (Chapter 12).
- [ ] Blown fuse (Chapter 12).
- [ ] Cable or cable connections loose or disconnected (Chapter 12).
- [ ] Faulty relay (Chapter 12).
- [ ] Faulty wiper motor (Chapter 12).

Wiper blades sweep over the wrong area of glass

- [ ] Wiper arms incorrectly-positioned on spindles (Chapter 1).
- [ ] Excessive wear of wiper linkage (Chapter 1).
- [ ] Wiper motor or linkage mountings loose or insecure (Chapter 12).

Wiper blades fail to clean the glass effectively

- [ ] Wiper blade rubbers worn or perished (*Weekly checks*).
- [ ] Wiper arm tension springs broken, or arm pivots seized (Chapter 1).
- [ ] Insufficient windscreen washer additive to adequately remove road film (*Weekly checks*).

Windscreen/tailgate washers

One or more washer jets inoperative

- [ ] Blocked washer jet (*Weekly checks* or Chapter 1).
- [ ] Disconnected, kinked or restricted fluid hose (Chapter 1).
- [ ] Insufficient fluid in washer reservoir (*Weekly checks*).

Electrical system (continued)

Washer pump fails to operate

☐ Broken or disconnected wiring or connections (Chapter 12).
☐ Blown fuse (Chapter 12).
☐ Faulty washer switch (Chapter 12).
☐ Faulty washer pump (Chapter 12).

Washer pump runs for some time before fluid is emitted from jets

☐ Faulty one-way valve in fluid supply hose (Chapter 12).

Electric windows

Window glass will only move in one direction

☐ Faulty switch (Chapter 12).

Window glass slow to move

☐ Incorrectly-adjusted door glass guide channels (Chapter 11).
☐ Regulator seized or damaged, or lack of lubrication (Chapter 11).
☐ Door internal components or trim fouling regulator (Chapter 11).
☐ Faulty motor (Chapter 12).

Window glass fails to move

☐ Incorrectly-adjusted door glass guide channels (Chapter 11).
☐ Blown fuse (Chapter 12).

☐ Faulty relay (Chapter 12).
☐ Broken or disconnected wiring or connections (Chapter 12).
☐ Faulty motor (Chapter 12).

Central locking system

Complete system failure

☐ Blown fuse (Chapter 12).
☐ Faulty relay (Chapter 12).
☐ Broken or disconnected wiring or connections (Chapter 12).

Latch locks but will not unlock, or unlocks but will not lock

☐ Faulty master switch (Chapter 11).
☐ Broken or disconnected latch operating rods or levers (Chapter 11).
☐ Faulty relay (Chapter 12).

One lock motor fails to operate

☐ Broken or disconnected wiring or connections (Chapter 12).
☐ Faulty lock motor (Chapter 11).
☐ Broken, binding or disconnected latch operating rods or levers (Chapter 11).
☐ Fault in door latch (Chapter 11).

A

ABS (Anti-lock brake system) A system, usually electronically controlled, that senses incipient wheel lockup during braking and relieves hydraulic pressure at wheels that are about to skid.

Air bag An inflatable bag hidden in the steering wheel (driver's side) or the dash or glovebox (passenger side). In a head-on collision, the bags inflate, preventing the driver and front passenger from being thrown forward into the steering wheel or windscreen.

Air cleaner A metal or plastic housing, containing a filter element, which removes dust and dirt from the air being drawn into the engine.

Air filter element The actual filter in an air cleaner system, usually manufactured from pleated paper and requiring renewal at regular intervals.

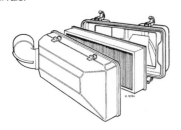

Air filter

Allen key A hexagonal wrench which fits into a recessed hexagonal hole.

Alligator clip A long-nosed spring-loaded metal clip with meshing teeth. Used to make temporary electrical connections.

Alternator A component in the electrical system which converts mechanical energy from a drivebelt into electrical energy to charge the battery and to operate the starting system, ignition system and electrical accessories.

Ampere (amp) A unit of measurement for the flow of electric current. One amp is the amount of current produced by one volt acting through a resistance of one ohm.

Anaerobic sealer A substance used to prevent bolts and screws from loosening. Anaerobic means that it does not require oxygen for activation. The Loctite brand is widely used.

Antifreeze A substance (usually ethylene glycol) mixed with water, and added to a vehicle's cooling system, to prevent freezing of the coolant in winter. Antifreeze also contains chemicals to inhibit corrosion and the formation of rust and other deposits that would tend to clog the radiator and coolant passages and reduce cooling efficiency.

Anti-seize compound A coating that reduces the risk of seizing on fasteners that are subjected to high temperatures, such as exhaust manifold bolts and nuts.

Asbestos A natural fibrous mineral with great heat resistance, commonly used in the composition of brake friction materials.

Asbestos is a health hazard and the dust created by brake systems should never be inhaled or ingested.

Axle A shaft on which a wheel revolves, or which revolves with a wheel. Also, a solid beam that connects the two wheels at one end of the vehicle. An axle which also transmits power to the wheels is known as a live axle.

Axleshaft A single rotating shaft, on either side of the differential, which delivers power from the final drive assembly to the drive wheels. Also called a driveshaft or a halfshaft.

B

Ball bearing An anti-friction bearing consisting of a hardened inner and outer race with hardened steel balls between two races.

Bearing The curved surface on a shaft or in a bore, or the part assembled into either, that permits relative motion between them with minimum wear and friction.

Bearing

Big-end bearing The bearing in the end of the connecting rod that's attached to the crankshaft.

Bleed nipple A valve on a brake wheel cylinder, caliper or other hydraulic component that is opened to purge the hydraulic system of air. Also called a bleed screw.

Brake bleeding Procedure for removing air from lines of a hydraulic brake system.

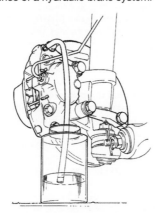

Brake bleeding

Brake disc The component of a disc brake that rotates with the wheels.

Brake drum The component of a drum brake that rotates with the wheels.

Brake linings The friction material which contacts the brake disc or drum to retard the vehicle's speed. The linings are bonded or riveted to the brake pads or shoes.

Brake pads The replaceable friction pads that pinch the brake disc when the brakes are applied. Brake pads consist of a friction material bonded or riveted to a rigid backing plate.

Brake shoe The crescent-shaped carrier to which the brake linings are mounted and which forces the lining against the rotating drum during braking.

Braking systems For more information on braking systems, consult the *Haynes Automotive Brake Manual*.

Breaker bar A long socket wrench handle providing greater leverage.

Bulkhead The insulated partition between the engine and the passenger compartment.

C

Caliper The non-rotating part of a disc-brake assembly that straddles the disc and carries the brake pads. The caliper also contains the hydraulic components that cause the pads to pinch the disc when the brakes are applied. A caliper is also a measuring tool that can be set to measure inside or outside dimensions of an object.

Camshaft A rotating shaft on which a series of cam lobes operate the valve mechanisms. The camshaft may be driven by gears, by sprockets and chain or by sprockets and a belt.

Canister A container in an evaporative emission control system; contains activated charcoal granules to trap vapours from the fuel system.

Canister

Carburettor A device which mixes fuel with air in the proper proportions to provide a desired power output from a spark ignition internal combustion engine.

Castellated Resembling the parapets along the top of a castle wall. For example, a castellated balljoint stud nut.

Castor In wheel alignment, the backward or forward tilt of the steering axis. Castor is positive when the steering axis is inclined rearward at the top.

Catalytic converter A silencer-like device in the exhaust system which converts certain pollutants in the exhaust gases into less harmful substances.

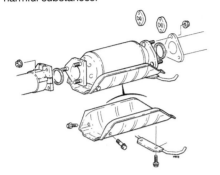

Catalytic converter

Circlip A ring-shaped clip used to prevent endwise movement of cylindrical parts and shafts. An internal circlip is installed in a groove in a housing; an external circlip fits into a groove on the outside of a cylindrical piece such as a shaft.

Clearance The amount of space between two parts. For example, between a piston and a cylinder, between a bearing and a journal, etc.

Coil spring A spiral of elastic steel found in various sizes throughout a vehicle, for example as a springing medium in the suspension and in the valve train.

Compression Reduction in volume, and increase in pressure and temperature, of a gas, caused by squeezing it into a smaller space.

Compression ratio The relationship between cylinder volume when the piston is at top dead centre and cylinder volume when the piston is at bottom dead centre.

Constant velocity (CV) joint A type of universal joint that cancels out vibrations caused by driving power being transmitted through an angle.

Core plug A disc or cup-shaped metal device inserted in a hole in a casting through which core was removed when the casting was formed. Also known as a freeze plug or expansion plug.

Crankcase The lower part of the engine block in which the crankshaft rotates.

Crankshaft The main rotating member, or shaft, running the length of the crankcase, with offset "throws" to which the connecting rods are attached.

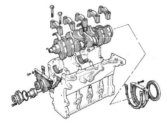

Crankshaft assembly

Crocodile clip See Alligator clip

D

Diagnostic code Code numbers obtained by accessing the diagnostic mode of an engine management computer. This code can be used to determine the area in the system where a malfunction may be located.

Disc brake A brake design incorporating a rotating disc onto which brake pads are squeezed. The resulting friction converts the energy of a moving vehicle into heat.

Double-overhead cam (DOHC) An engine that uses two overhead camshafts, usually one for the intake valves and one for the exhaust valves.

Drivebelt(s) The belt(s) used to drive accessories such as the alternator, water pump, power steering pump, air conditioning compressor, etc. off the crankshaft pulley.

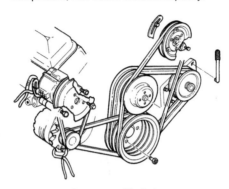

Accessory drivebelts

Driveshaft Any shaft used to transmit motion. Commonly used when referring to the axleshafts on a front wheel drive vehicle.

Drum brake A type of brake using a drum-shaped metal cylinder attached to the inner surface of the wheel. When the brake pedal is pressed, curved brake shoes with friction linings press against the inside of the drum to slow or stop the vehicle.

E

EGR valve A valve used to introduce exhaust gases into the intake air stream.

Electronic control unit (ECU) A computer which controls (for instance) ignition and fuel injection systems, or an anti-lock braking system. For more information refer to the *Haynes Automotive Electrical and Electronic Systems Manual.*

Electronic Fuel Injection (EFI) A computer controlled fuel system that distributes fuel through an injector located in each intake port of the engine.

Emergency brake A braking system, independent of the main hydraulic system, that can be used to slow or stop the vehicle if the primary brakes fail, or to hold the vehicle stationary even though the brake pedal isn't depressed. It usually consists of a hand lever that actuates either front or rear brakes mechanically through a series of cables and linkages. Also known as a handbrake or parking brake.

Endfloat The amount of lengthwise movement between two parts. As applied to a crankshaft, the distance that the crankshaft can move forward and back in the cylinder block.

Engine management system (EMS) A computer controlled system which manages the fuel injection and the ignition systems in an integrated fashion.

Exhaust manifold A part with several passages through which exhaust gases leave the engine combustion chambers and enter the exhaust pipe.

F

Fan clutch A viscous (fluid) drive coupling device which permits variable engine fan speeds in relation to engine speeds.

Feeler blade A thin strip or blade of hardened steel, ground to an exact thickness, used to check or measure clearances between parts.

Feeler blade

Firing order The order in which the engine cylinders fire, or deliver their power strokes, beginning with the number one cylinder.

Flywheel A heavy spinning wheel in which energy is absorbed and stored by means of momentum. On cars, the flywheel is attached to the crankshaft to smooth out firing impulses.

Free play The amount of travel before any action takes place. The "looseness" in a linkage, or an assembly of parts, between the initial application of force and actual movement. For example, the distance the brake pedal moves before the pistons in the master cylinder are actuated.

Fuse An electrical device which protects a circuit against accidental overload. The typical fuse contains a soft piece of metal which is calibrated to melt at a predetermined current flow (expressed as amps) and break the circuit.

Fusible link A circuit protection device consisting of a conductor surrounded by heat-resistant insulation. The conductor is smaller than the wire it protects, so it acts as the weakest link in the circuit. Unlike a blown fuse, a failed fusible link must frequently be cut from the wire for replacement.

G

Gap The distance the spark must travel in jumping from the centre electrode to the side electrode in a spark plug. Also refers to the spacing between the points in a contact breaker assembly in a conventional points-type ignition, or to the distance between the reluctor or rotor and the pickup coil in an electronic ignition.

Adjusting spark plug gap

Gasket Any thin, soft material - usually cork, cardboard, asbestos or soft metal - installed between two metal surfaces to ensure a good seal. For instance, the cylinder head gasket seals the joint between the block and the cylinder head.

Gasket

Gauge An instrument panel display used to monitor engine conditions. A gauge with a movable pointer on a dial or a fixed scale is an analogue gauge. A gauge with a numerical readout is called a digital gauge.

H

Halfshaft A rotating shaft that transmits power from the final drive unit to a drive wheel, usually when referring to a live rear axle.

Harmonic balancer A device designed to reduce torsion or twisting vibration in the crankshaft. May be incorporated in the crankshaft pulley. Also known as a vibration damper.

Hone An abrasive tool for correcting small irregularities or differences in diameter in an engine cylinder, brake cylinder, etc.

Hydraulic tappet A tappet that utilises hydraulic pressure from the engine's lubrication system to maintain zero clearance (constant contact with both camshaft and valve stem). Automatically adjusts to variation in valve stem length. Hydraulic tappets also reduce valve noise.

I

Ignition timing The moment at which the spark plug fires, usually expressed in the number of crankshaft degrees before the piston reaches the top of its stroke.

Inlet manifold A tube or housing with passages through which flows the air-fuel mixture (carburettor vehicles and vehicles with throttle body injection) or air only (port fuel-injected vehicles) to the port openings in the cylinder head.

J

Jump start Starting the engine of a vehicle with a discharged or weak battery by attaching jump leads from the weak battery to a charged or helper battery.

L

Load Sensing Proportioning Valve (LSPV) A brake hydraulic system control valve that works like a proportioning valve, but also takes into consideration the amount of weight carried by the rear axle.

Locknut A nut used to lock an adjustment nut, or other threaded component, in place. For example, a locknut is employed to keep the adjusting nut on the rocker arm in position.

Lockwasher A form of washer designed to prevent an attaching nut from working loose.

M

MacPherson strut A type of front suspension system devised by Earle MacPherson at Ford of England. In its original form, a simple lateral link with the anti-roll bar creates the lower control arm. A long strut - an integral coil spring and shock absorber - is mounted between the body and the steering knuckle. Many modern so-called MacPherson strut systems use a conventional lower A-arm and don't rely on the anti-roll bar for location.

Multimeter An electrical test instrument with the capability to measure voltage, current and resistance.

N

NOx Oxides of Nitrogen. A common toxic pollutant emitted by petrol and diesel engines at higher temperatures.

O

Ohm The unit of electrical resistance. One volt applied to a resistance of one ohm will produce a current of one amp.

Ohmmeter An instrument for measuring electrical resistance.

O-ring A type of sealing ring made of a special rubber-like material; in use, the O-ring is compressed into a groove to provide the sealing action.

Overhead cam (ohc) engine An engine with the camshaft(s) located on top of the cylinder head(s).

Overhead valve (ohv) engine An engine with the valves located in the cylinder head, but with the camshaft located in the engine block.

Oxygen sensor A device installed in the engine exhaust manifold, which senses the oxygen content in the exhaust and converts this information into an electric current. Also called a Lambda sensor.

P

Phillips screw A type of screw head having a cross instead of a slot for a corresponding type of screwdriver.

Plastigage A thin strip of plastic thread, available in different sizes, used for measuring clearances. For example, a strip of Plastigage is laid across a bearing journal. The parts are assembled and dismantled; the width of the crushed strip indicates the clearance between journal and bearing.

Plastigage

Propeller shaft The long hollow tube with universal joints at both ends that carries power from the transmission to the differential on front-engined rear wheel drive vehicles.

Proportioning valve A hydraulic control valve which limits the amount of pressure to the rear brakes during panic stops to prevent wheel lock-up.

R

Rack-and-pinion steering A steering system with a pinion gear on the end of the steering shaft that mates with a rack (think of a geared wheel opened up and laid flat). When the steering wheel is turned, the pinion turns, moving the rack to the left or right. This movement is transmitted through the track rods to the steering arms at the wheels.

Radiator A liquid-to-air heat transfer device designed to reduce the temperature of the coolant in an internal combustion engine cooling system.

Refrigerant Any substance used as a heat transfer agent in an air-conditioning system. R-12 has been the principle refrigerant for many years; recently, however, manufacturers have begun using R-134a, a non-CFC substance that is considered less harmful to the ozone in the upper atmosphere.

Rocker arm A lever arm that rocks on a shaft or pivots on a stud. In an overhead valve engine, the rocker arm converts the upward movement of the pushrod into a downward movement to open a valve.

Rotor In a distributor, the rotating device inside the cap that connects the centre electrode and the outer terminals as it turns, distributing the high voltage from the coil secondary winding to the proper spark plug. Also, that part of an alternator which rotates inside the stator. Also, the rotating assembly of a turbocharger, including the compressor wheel, shaft and turbine wheel.

Runout The amount of wobble (in-and-out movement) of a gear or wheel as it's rotated. The amount a shaft rotates "out-of-true." The out-of-round condition of a rotating part.

S

Sealant A liquid or paste used to prevent leakage at a joint. Sometimes used in conjunction with a gasket.

Sealed beam lamp An older headlight design which integrates the reflector, lens and filaments into a hermetically-sealed one-piece unit. When a filament burns out or the lens cracks, the entire unit is simply replaced.

Serpentine drivebelt A single, long, wide accessory drivebelt that's used on some newer vehicles to drive all the accessories, instead of a series of smaller, shorter belts. Serpentine drivebelts are usually tensioned by an automatic tensioner.

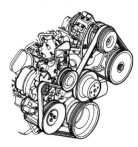

Serpentine drivebelt

Shim Thin spacer, commonly used to adjust the clearance or relative positions between two parts. For example, shims inserted into or under bucket tappets control valve clearances. Clearance is adjusted by changing the thickness of the shim.

Slide hammer A special puller that screws into or hooks onto a component such as a shaft or bearing; a heavy sliding handle on the shaft bottoms against the end of the shaft to knock the component free.

Sprocket A tooth or projection on the periphery of a wheel, shaped to engage with a chain or drivebelt. Commonly used to refer to the sprocket wheel itself.

Starter inhibitor switch On vehicles with an automatic transmission, a switch that prevents starting if the vehicle is not in Neutral or Park.

Strut See MacPherson strut.

T

Tappet A cylindrical component which transmits motion from the cam to the valve stem, either directly or via a pushrod and rocker arm. Also called a cam follower.

Thermostat A heat-controlled valve that regulates the flow of coolant between the cylinder block and the radiator, so maintaining optimum engine operating temperature. A thermostat is also used in some air cleaners in which the temperature is regulated.

Thrust bearing The bearing in the clutch assembly that is moved in to the release levers by clutch pedal action to disengage the clutch. Also referred to as a release bearing.

Timing belt A toothed belt which drives the camshaft. Serious engine damage may result if it breaks in service.

Timing chain A chain which drives the camshaft.

Toe-in The amount the front wheels are closer together at the front than at the rear. On rear wheel drive vehicles, a slight amount of toe-in is usually specified to keep the front wheels running parallel on the road by offsetting other forces that tend to spread the wheels apart.

Toe-out The amount the front wheels are closer together at the rear than at the front. On front wheel drive vehicles, a slight amount of toe-out is usually specified.

Tools For full information on choosing and using tools, refer to the *Haynes Automotive Tools Manual*.

Tracer A stripe of a second colour applied to a wire insulator to distinguish that wire from another one with the same colour insulator.

Tune-up A process of accurate and careful adjustments and parts replacement to obtain the best possible engine performance.

Turbocharger A centrifugal device, driven by exhaust gases, that pressurises the intake air. Normally used to increase the power output from a given engine displacement, but can also be used primarily to reduce exhaust emissions (as on VW's "Umwelt" Diesel engine).

U

Universal joint or U-joint A double-pivoted connection for transmitting power from a driving to a driven shaft through an angle. A U-joint consists of two Y-shaped yokes and a cross-shaped member called the spider.

V

Valve A device through which the flow of liquid, gas, vacuum, or loose material in bulk may be started, stopped, or regulated by a movable part that opens, shuts, or partially obstructs one or more ports or passageways. A valve is also the movable part of such a device.

Valve clearance The clearance between the valve tip (the end of the valve stem) and the rocker arm or tappet. The valve clearance is measured when the valve is closed.

Vernier caliper A precision measuring instrument that measures inside and outside dimensions. Not quite as accurate as a micrometer, but more convenient.

Viscosity The thickness of a liquid or its resistance to flow.

Volt A unit for expressing electrical "pressure" in a circuit. One volt that will produce a current of one ampere through a resistance of one ohm.

W

Welding Various processes used to join metal items by heating the areas to be joined to a molten state and fusing them together. For more information refer to the *Haynes Automotive Welding Manual*.

Wiring diagram A drawing portraying the components and wires in a vehicle's electrical system, using standardised symbols. For more information refer to the *Haynes Automotive Electrical and Electronic Systems Manual*.

Note: *References throughout this index are in the form "**Chapter Number**" • "**Page Number**"*

Preserving Our Motoring Heritage

< The Model J Duesenberg Derham Tourster. Only eight of these magnificent cars were ever built – this is the only example to be found outside the United States of America

Almost every car you've ever loved, loathed or desired is gathered under one roof at the Haynes Motor Museum. Over 300 immaculately presented cars and motorbikes represent every aspect of our motoring heritage, from elegant reminders of bygone days, such as the superb Model J Duesenberg to curiosities like the bug-eyed BMW Isetta. There are also many old friends and flames. Perhaps you remember the 1959 Ford Popular that you did your courting in? The magnificent 'Red Collection' is a spectacle of classic sports cars including AC, Alfa Romeo, Austin Healey, Ferrari, Lamborghini, Maserati, MG, Riley, Porsche and Triumph.

A Perfect Day Out

Each and every vehicle at the Haynes Motor Museum has played its part in the history and culture of Motoring. Today, they make a wonderful spectacle and a great day out for all the family. Bring the kids, bring Mum and Dad, but above all bring your camera to capture those golden memories for ever. You will also find an impressive array of motoring memorabilia, a comfortable 70 seat video cinema and one of the most extensive transport book shops in Britain. The Pit Stop Cafe serves everything from a cup of tea to wholesome, home-made meals or, if you prefer, you can enjoy the large picnic area nestled in the beautiful rural surroundings of Somerset.

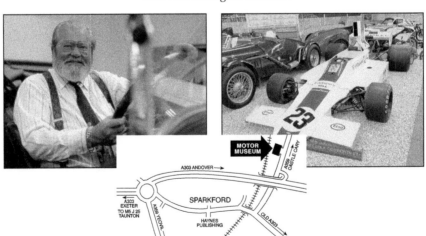

> John Haynes O.B.E., Founder and Chairman of the museum at the wheel of a Haynes Light 12.

< Graham Hill's Lola Cosworth Formula 1 car next to a 1934 Riley Sports.

The Museum is situated on the A359 Yeovil to Frome road at Sparkford, just off the A303 in Somerset. It is about 40 miles south of Bristol, and 25 minutes drive from the M5 intersection at Taunton.
Open 9.30am - 5.30pm (10.00am - 4.00pm Winter) 7 days a week, *except Christmas Day, Boxing Day and New Years Day*
Special rates available for schools, coach parties and outings Charitable Trust No. 292048